Anneli Aejmelaeus
The Traditional Prayer in the Psalms

―――――

Ludwig Schmidt
Literarische Studien zur Josephsgeschichte

Anneli Aejmelaeus

The Traditional Prayer in the Psalms

Ludwig Schmidt

Literarische Studien zur Josephsgeschichte

Walter de Gruyter · Berlin · New York
1986

Beiheft zur Zeitschrift für die alttestamentliche Wissenschaft
Herausgegeben von Otto Kaiser
167

Library of Congress Cataloging-in-Publication Data

Aejmelaeus, Anneli.
  The traditional prayer in the Psalms.
  (Beiheft zur Zeitschrift für die alttestamentliche Wissenschaft ; 167)
  Bibliography: p.
  Includes index.
  1. Bible. O.T. Psalms–Criticism, interpretation, etc.
2. Prayer–Biblical teaching. 3. Bible. O.T. Genesis XXXVII-L–Criticism, interpretation, etc. 4. Joseph (Son of Jacob) I. Schmidt, Ludwig, 1940– . Literarische Studien zur Josephsgeschichte. 1986. II. Title. III. Title: Literarische Studien zur Josephsgeschichte. IV. Series.
BS1430.2.A27 1986   223'.206   86-24293
ISBN 0-89925-279-6 (U.S.)

CIP-Kurztitelaufnahme der Deutschen Bibliothek

Aejmelaeus, Anneli:
The traditional prayer in the Psalms / Anneli Aejmelaeus. Literarische Studien zur Josephsgeschichte / Ludwig Schmidt. – Berlin ; New York : de Gruyter, 1986.
  (Beiheft zur Zeitschrift für die alttestamentliche Wissenschaft ; 167)
  ISBN 3-11-010480-6
NE: Schmidt, Ludwig: Literarische Studien zur Josephsgeschichte; Schmidt, Ludwig: [Sammlung]; Zeitschrift für die alttestamentliche Wissenschaft / Beiheft

© Copyright 1986 by Walter de Gruyter & Co., Berlin 30.
Printed in Germany – Alle Rechte des Nachdrucks, einschließlich des Rechts der Herstellung von Photokopien – auch auszugsweise – vorbehalten.
Satz und Druck: Hubert & Co., Göttingen
Bindearbeiten: Lüderitz & Bauer, Berlin 61

Inhaltsverzeichnis

Anneli Aejmelaeus: The Traditional Prayer in the Psalms   1
Ludwig Schmidt: Literarische Studien zur Josephsgeschichte . . . 121

Anneli Aejmelaeus

The Traditional Prayer
in the Psalms

To Lars

Acknowledgements

The piece of research which is here published was carried out for the most part in Göttingen, where I had the opportunity to spend an enriching and inspiring working period of 16 months, a time which in spite of the theme of my study leaves no room for complaint. For this opportunity I owe thanks to the generosity of the Alexander von Humboldt Foundation.

I wish to express warm thanks to my host in Göttingen, Prof. Robert Hanhart for his kindly care and encouragement as well as to Prof. Rudolf Smend and Dr. Hermann Spieckermann for reading and discussing with me an early version of the study. I would also like to thank my colleagues at home, Prof. Ilmari Soisalon-Soininen and Prof. Timo Veijola for their encouragement and advice. Further thanks are due to the Academy of Finland for supporting my work.

I should like to thank Mr. Peter Jones, B.A., for revising my English.

I also owe a debt of gratitude to Prof. Otto Kaiser for recommending my study for inclusion in the series BZAW and to the Alexander von Humboldt Foundation for financial support of the publication.

I dedicate this study to my husband, Dr. Lars Aejmelaeus, who has shared with me all the pleasures and hardships of academic life.

Helsinki, February 5, 1985   Anneli Aejmelaeus

Contents

Introduction		9
1.	Formal Analysis of the Imperative Petition	15
1.1	"Save", "deliver", "help"	16
1.2	"Have mercy"	21
1.3	Petitions Connected with the Priestly Blessing	24
1.4	"Hear", "see"	26
1.5	"Answer"	29
1.6	"Arise", "awake"	31
1.7	"Return"	34
1.8	"Judge", "vindicate"	37
1.9	"Hasten to my aid", "turn to me"	39
1.10	"Teach", "lead"	40
1.11	"Remember"	42
1.12	Petitions against the Enemy	42
1.13	Petitions with Negation	45
1.14	A Few General Remarks on the Imperative Petitions	47
1.15	Clusters of Imperative Petitions	50
2.	Formal Analysis of Elements Connected with the Petition	54
2.1	Address of the Petition	54
2.2	Expressions in the Immediate Context of the Petition	59
2.2.1	The Question of "Motivations for Divine Intervention"	59
2.2.2	Prepositional Phrases	60
2.2.3	Clauses in the Immediate Context of the Petition	64
2.2.3.1	Coordinate Clauses Introduced by ו	64
2.2.3.2	Relative Clauses	66
2.2.3.3	Final Clauses Introduced by פן	67
2.2.3.4	Clauses Introduced by כי	68
2.2.3.5	Other Types of Clauses	79
2.2.4	Conclusions	83
3.	The Form of the Traditional Prayer	85
3.1	The Pattern of Traditional Prayer as a Compositional Factor	86
3.2	The Simple Form of Individual Prayer	88

3.3	The Origin and Relative Dating of the Traditional Prayer	99
3.4	The Developed Form of the Traditional Prayer	103
3.5	Prayer Literature in the Psalter	106
4.	Conclusions and Methodological Considerations	109
Abbreviations		112
Bibliography		113
Index of Biblical Passages		301

Introduction

>»Das bedeutendste Stück der Klagelieder ist die Bitte.«
> Hermann Gunkel

It has long been customary to refer to certain psalms in the Old Testament Psalter as psalms of complaint. Gunkel's (and Begrich's) *Einleitung in die Psalmen,* the foundation of all modern research on the psalms, distinguishes between complaint psalms of the individual and those of the congregation and provides an analysis of the formal characteristics of these genres which – with little variation – has been reproduced in a number of studies and standard works.[1] As regards the psalms of individual complaint – to the interpretation of which the present study would like to contribute – their treatment in the scholarly literature after Gunkel reveals no greater interest in continuing the formal research towards the refinement of Gunkel's results, but concentrates on the contents and the background situations of the various psalms of the genre and particularly on the sociological aspects of their »Sitz-im-Leben«.[2] It might seem that the formal analysis had already exhausted its possibilities.[3] Nevertheless, the scheme concerned with the structure of the individual complaint psalms – a list of elements which may or may not occur, in one order or another, in these psalms – leaves plenty of room for further research. In the absence of a clear scheme, scholars often refer to the great variety of forms within the genre.[4] But, a new approach on the basis of Gunkel's pioneer work on the one hand, and of the advances made in the study of the OT and the psalms after him on the other, will, I believe, enable the texts themselves

---

[1] As regards the individual complaint psalms, see e.g. Kraus' commentary on the psalms, which up to and including the fourth edition shows little that diverges from Gunkel (pp. xlv–li) and after the changes of the fifth edition still mainly follows the old scheme (pp. 49–60). See also Westermann 1977, 48–52; Gerstenberger 1977, 200–201, and 1980, 118–134.

[2] See e.g. Delekat *Asylie und Schutzorakel am Zionheiligtum,* 1967, Beyerlin *Die Rettung der Bedrängten in den Feindpsalmen der Einzelnen auf institutionelle Zusammenhänge untersucht,* 1970, Seybold *Das Gebet des Kranken im Alten Testament,* 1973, Gerstenberger *Der bittende Mensch: Bittritual und Klagelied des Einzelnen im Alten Testament,* 1980.

[3] Gerstenberger, for instance, regards the more detailed formal analysis of the complaint psalms as unnecessary; see 1980, 4–6, 119, 165–166.

[4] See e.g. Gerstenberger 1980, 11, 19, 63.

to reveal something more of their character and origin. The present work is an attempt in this direction.

The purpose of the present study is to inquire into the most central element of the individual complaint psalms, that part of the psalm which may be called *prayer* in the strict sense of the word. Although the genre was named according to complaint and although the element of complaint often constitutes the greater part of a psalm, the individual complaint psalms are characteristically prayer psalms.[5] The OT Psalter does not contain complaints as distinct from prayer. In his history of the complaint, Westermann finds the most characteristic feature of the stage of development represented by the Book of Psalms precisely in this combination of complaint and prayer.[6] What ist then actually the function of prayer here? Complaint as such may appear as a description of misery and suffering with its standard expressions and metaphors, without necessarily even mentioning God. Prayer, on the other hand, is of its very essence speech to God and in particular appeal to God. It implies address to God in the vocative sense, as well as the use of pronouns and verbal forms in the second person singular, particularly the imperative.[7] In the presence of an unquestionable prayer even elements that in themselves do not address God appear as parts of the prayer. The fact that the Psalter does not know complaint without prayer, although such complaint, even curses, to God, surely existed, may perhaps be taken as an indication of the theological thinking which guided the selection of material and the fixation of the collection of the OT psalms. The psalms were obviously seen as models of prayer, a norm for what could be said to God in a prayer.[8] Another central element which has attracted the attention of scholars by its frequent appearance in connection with prayer and complaint is the affirmation of confi-

---

[5] Gunkel-Begrich 1933, 218: »Das bedeutendste Stück der Klagelieder ist die Bitte. Sie ist das Herzstück der Gattung ...« See also Gerstenberger 1980, 119–127. The new division of the genres in the fifth edition of Kraus' commentary (1978, 36–68) includes psalms of prayer (»Gebetslieder«) which, however, is a larger group combining psalms of complaint and psalms of thanksgiving, both individual and congregational. At least with regard to Gunkel's definition of genre, which stresses the three aspects of unity between the psalms that belong to one genre, the unity of form and language, the unity of ideas, and the unity of »Sitz-im-Leben«, it seems most problematic to regard such an enormous group of very different psalms as one genre.

[6] Westermann 1977, 125–164.

[7] For the function of the imperative in ordinary requests as well as prayers, see Gerstenberger 1980, 28–29.

[8] The normativity of the psalm prayers is particularly stressed by Fuchs 1982, 300. Gerstenberger 1980, 18–19, speaks of »Ritualisierung des Bittvorganges«, the fixing of the forms which are recognized and accepted as petition, both in profane everyday petitions and in prayers.

dence in God.⁹ Appeal to God in a prayer and confidence in him seem to form the framework in which complaint was regarded as acceptable.

Against a background of its central importance, even theologically, the element of prayer in the psalms may justifiably be regarded as suitable for more detailed formal analysis. The present study does not aim at a full description of the group of psalms concerned, but merely at a more precise characterization of the form of one element and of its function in its context. Several questions of importance, e.g. the various themes and situations of the complaint, remain peripheral and are dealt with only when necessary for the discussion and interpretation of the prayer element. I have chosen as my point of departure the imperative prayer, i.e. the kind of petition that addresses itself directly to God in the second person imperative or the corresponding negation with אל and the subjunctive.¹⁰ The occurrences of petitions in this form will be traced through the whole Psalter, in order not to impose unnecessary limitations on the material and to be able to compare the petitions of the various genres. A closer analysis of the context of the imperative petitions, however, is carried out in the group of psalms generally recognized as individual complaints, although excluded from the main discussion are the acrostic psalms which clearly represent a later development in the psalmodic tradition.¹¹ Finally, an attempt will be made to follow the historical development discernible in the formal variation of the element studied.

That the formally distinguished group of imperative prayers is taken here as the sole point of departure requires a few words of explanation. Gerstenberger has argued that even other forms, the third person subjunctive in particular, may assume the function of a petition.¹² In his discussion of the prayer element, he thus regards both imperatives in the second person singular and subjunctives in the third person as equally important in his analysis. This, however, poses certain problems, not the least of which is the difficulty involved in recognizing a subjunctive. It is often difficult to distinguish between e.g. a clause that expresses belief in the punishment coming to an enemy from God and

---

⁹ Particularly, Begrich, »Die Vertrauensäußerungen im israelitischen Klagelied des Einzelnen und in seinem babylonischen Gegenstück«, in *ZAW* 46 (1928), 221–260 (= *Gesammelte Studien,* ThB 21, 168–216).

¹⁰ In a few cases the immediate context of the imperative (or the corresponding negation) includes a petition expressed in the subjunctive, particularly in the second person singular, or in the cohortative. These cases are naturally taken into consideration in our discussion of the »imperative prayer«.

¹¹ The acrostic psalms containing imperative petitions are Ps 9–10, 25, and 119. Such psalms as 19 and 139 also contain individual petitions, but are excluded from our discussion, since they are not considered individual complaint proper.

¹² Gerstenberger 1980, 121.

one that desires it.¹³ In this respect, negated cases are, of course, unambiguous. Another and more serious difficulty is concerned with the question of the nature of the wish expressed in the third person subjunctive form. Is it primarily a prayer or perhaps, when it is directed against the enemy, a curse rather than anything else? It is true that a few subjunctive forms and cohortatives occur in close connection with the imperative petitions, but without this immediate connection the repeated use of the subjunctive, particularly in the third person, most probably implies an original setting other than prayer. To circumvent these difficulties and to avoid far too wide an approach, I shall concentrate on the imperative prayer and its particular function in the complaint psalms of the individual. The significance of this decision will be seen as the study proceeds.

The task of the present study includes testing a few of the details of Gunkel's description of the build-up of individual complaint psalms. The *Einleitung* divides the prayer elements into two groups, initial pleas in the introduction of the psalm and actual petitions for help in the main part of the psalm.¹⁴ One may assume that an analysis of the imperative prayer will either validify or refute this conception of two kinds of petition, repeated by various scholars after Gunkel, but never questioned. Furthermore, Gunkel's description includes an element of »motivation for divine intervention«, which occurs particularly in close connection with the prayer element.¹⁵ In my analysis of the context of the petitions I shall look for expressions of this type. If elements are found that may justifiably be called »motivations for divine intervention«, their form and connection with the petition should be defined more precisely.

In more recent research, it is above all Gerstenberger whose studies have provided us with deeper insights concerning the reality behind the psalms of individual complaint.¹⁶ In a most impressive way he postulates – on the basis of Babylonian parallels – the existence of smaller forms of ritual life practised, with the assistance of a cultic expert, by the members of a primary group for the sole purpose of acquiring help for one of their suffering fellow members.¹⁷ As far as the rites

---

[13] Gerstenberger seems to support an interpretation favouring the subjunctive in several ambiguous cases; see 1980, 126, where e.g. Ps 11:6 and 63:10 are presented as wishes against the enemy, Ps 73:18,27 even as typical cases of such wishes, and Ps 73:24 as »eine echte Bitte«. As I see it, it is more appropriate to interpret these cases as statements in the indicative.

[14] Gunkel-Begrich 1933, 221, 240.

[15] Gunkel-Begrich 1933, 130–132, 231–239.

[16] Gerstenberger, *Der bittende Mensch: Bittritual und Klagelied des Einzelnen im Alten Testament*, WMANT 51, Neukirchen-Vluyn 1980.

[17] Gerstenberger 1980, 134–160.

are concerned, we do not possess any detailed information concerning such procedures in ancient Israel. Nevertheless, Gerstenberger's thesis furnishes us with a highly credible description of the function of the psalms of individual complaint as prayer, appeal to God, and of their »Sitz-im-Leben« as conditioned by situations of human misery and the need for help. How this is reflected in the actual petitions used is one of the questions I hope to answer in the present study.

A remarkable discovery in the psalms exegesis of the last few decades, represented particularly by Becker, is what may be called »rereading« or »reinterpretation«, i.e. the recognition of several layers in the psalms, layers created by their use in new situations and the attachment of new verses and sections accordingly.[18] From this standpoint it is possible to find resolution of several of the controversial questions that have bedevilled research into the psalms. For instance, the »I« of the individual complaint psalms was originally an individual petitioner, but could obviously be reinterpreted as referring to a collective.[19] Even to the most difficult question of dating the psalms a more fruitful approach may be made from the angle of »reinterpretation«. As is well known, scholarly opinion has differed widely in dating the psalms on either side of the Exile: some have regarded all or most of the psalms as pre-exilic, others wish to see all or most of them as post-exilic.[20] But, if the psalms are not regarded as literary manifestations of a certain author at a certain time, but are understood as the results of a process of growth throughout the centuries, then it is possible to find within one psalm both ancient and late elements. Accordingly, the elements of which a psalm consists may be found to be older than the psalm in its final form.

Although the present work concentrates on the study of certain smaller units within the individual complaints and not of the complaints in their final entirety, it is not possible to avoid the issue of dating the findings at least in broad outline, with the Exile as the dividing line. In the absence of absolute criteria, one must often content oneself with relative datings and proceed by way of probabilities. Certain changes brought about by the Exile are often clearly detectable in the

---

[18] Becker, *Israel deutet seine Psalmen*, SBS 18, Stuttgart 1966, and *Wege der Psalmenexegese*, SBS 78, Stuttgart 1975. See also Veijola 1982, 22–46, and Beyerlin *ZThK* 73 (1976), 446–460.

[19] See Becker 1966, 22–24, and 1975, 85–98.

[20] As a result of this confusion, the statements about the date – if there are any – in the newer literature are often extremely vague. E.g. Gerstenberger dates the rites where individual complaints were used to the time before the Deuteronomistic reform (1980, 153), but concerning the psalms in question, only pronounces the shorter ones as containing more old material (1980, 123 note 43).

psalms: despair caused by the experience of being forsaken by Yahweh in congregational complaints, mention of destruction, deportation and captivity, prayer for return etc. Another indication of lateness is influence from the wisdom literature. Against this background, it seems to be a reasonable hypothesis to regard individual prayers which reveal a narrow perspective of personal experience as probably pre-exilic.[21] There would have been no reason to discard old traditions of individual prayer and to develop entirely new ones of this type. On the contrary, it is obvious that the »songs of Zion« were cherished and handed down to succeeding generations. On the other hand, individual complaint psalms could provide excellent material for the exilic »reinterpretation«.

An approach that differs widely from that of the traditional exegesis of the psalms can be found in Culley's *Oral Formulaic Language in the Biblical Psalms*,[22] a study that deserves more attention than it has received hitherto. Although its perspective is rather narrow, it nevertheless achieves results relevant to the theories of the composition and transmission of the psalms, or at least one part of them. Culley looks for characteristics of oral composition in the psalms and finds them – the recurring formulaic phrases and the »adding style«, i.e. the type of composition in which the lines follow each other without a clear overall plan – particularly in individual complaints. Although the psalms of the OT Psalter obviously have a long literary history, some consideration at least should be given to the oral tradition behind it.

As for the Babylonian parallels which have been found to share many features with the individual complaint psalms of the OT, the present writer does not consider it necessary to go into the primary sources, but relies here on the work of others, particularly on W. Mayer's *Untersuchungen zur Formensprache der babylonischen »Gebetsbeschwörungen«*.[23] The similarities between the Babylonian and the Israelite psalms have often been underlined by scholars. Nevertheless, there are also clear differences between them. Since prayer always correlates with the theology – with the conception of God – a closer picture of the psalm prayers may also be expected to reveal particular Israelite characteristics and differences in comparison with the Babylonian parallels. This comparison is, however, regarded as subordinate to the main theme of the present study.

---

[21] In this connection, »individual« and »personal« must be understood as the opposite of collective.

[22] Near and Middle East Series 4, Toronto 1967.

[23] Studia Pohl: Series Maior 5, Rome 1976. Comparison between the Babylonian and OT parallels is found in Widengren's *The Accadian and Hebrew Psalms of Lamentation as Religious Documents: A Comparative Study*. Uppsala 1937.

1. Formal Analysis of the Imperative Petition

The imperative prayer is a highly frequent phenomenon in the OT Book of Psalms. Indeed, nothing else could be expected of texts characterized as Israel's response to Yahweh. When each and every case of the imperative as well as its negation with אל and the subjunctive, used in this function, is counted, we arrive at a total of 450 occurrences – 58 of them representing the negated form – divided among 77 psalms of various genres. A single occurrence is found in each of 15 psalms, the highest number of occurrences 62 being found in Ps 119. These extremes apart, the remaining psalms in question reveal an average of 6 occurrences for each psalm. Furthermore, in the immediate context of these imperatives we find 20 cases of the subjunctive in the second person singular, 13 cases in the third person, and 6 cases of the cohortative with אל, all of which may be understood as part of the petition.

The large number of psalms containing imperative petitions immediately demonstrates that the mere appearance of prayers in this form does not function as a distinguishing feature by which the genre of a psalm may be determined. They also clearly appear outside the group of complaint psalms. If attention is paid only to the individual complaint psalms, we find 254 occurrences – of which 41 are negated – in 42 psalms. Petitions in the subjunctive occur in these psalms 16 times in the second person, 13 in the third person, the cohortative being found 6 times. On the other hand, not all psalms of the Psalter contain imperative petitions. As for the psalms generally regarded as individual complaint psalms, most of them reveal several occurrences of imperative petitions, which to this genre seem to be more or less indispensable. The ones with no occurrence hardly justify their inclusion in the genre of individual complaint.

It has been observed by Gunkel and others that the petitions contained in the psalms are often stereotyped in character, recurring in a number of psalms, and semantically unspecific in relation to the possible situations in which they were intended to be used.[24] It has also been pointed out that parallels to the OT stereotyped petitions are found in ritual texts and psalms of other ancient peoples of the Middle East.[25] In

---

[24] See Gunkel-Begrich 1933, 218–220; Gerstenberger 1980, 119–121.
[25] Gunkel-Begrich *ibid.* Listings of parallel prayers are found in Widengren 1937, 258–274; a more detailed discussion of the Babylonian prayer language can be found in Mayer 1976, 210–306.

fact, the occurrences of certain recurring prayer imperatives may be found to be responsible for a large number of the total 450 occurrences. By counting only the most common imperative petitions »save« (הושיע, הציל, and a few other verbs), »have mercy« (חנן), »listen« (שמע, הקשיב, האזין, etc.), »look« (ראה, הביט), and »answer« (ענה) we cover as much as one third of the whole material. Moreover, if only petitions in the individual complaint psalms are considered and of these the ones in the affirmative, the cases mentioned account for almost one half.

The following analysis will give statistical information on the occurrence of imperative petitions together with a discussion of the semantic aspect of the prayers. The material is arranged in groups according to frequency and content. The more frequent types of petitions are naturally discussed in greater detail. In anticipation of the further discussion of the context of the petition in the genre of individual complaint, occurrences in all other genres, the acrostic psalms included, are given in parentheses. This will also facilitate comparison between the genres.

1.1 »Save«, »deliver«, »help«

The largest group of imperative petitions related to each other in meaning consists of expressions with verbs denoting »to save«, »to redeem«, »to deliver«, »to help«, in most cases connected with the object suffix of the first person singular »save me«, »redeem me« etc.

הושיעני	3:8, 6:5, 7:2, 22:22, 31:17, 54:3, 59:3, 69:2, 71:2, 109:26, (119:94), (119:146)		
הושיענו	(106:47)		
הושיעה	12:2, (20:10), 28:9, (60:7), 86:16, (108:7), (118:25)		
הושע	86:2		
הצילני	7:2, (25:20), 31:3, 31:16, 39:9, 51:16, 59:2, 59:3, 69:15, 109:21, (119:170), 142:7, 143:9, (144:7), (144:11)		
הצילנו	(79:9)		
הצילה	22:21, 120:2		
פדני	26:11, 69:19, (119:134)	פדנו	(44:27)
פדה	(25:22)		
פלטני	31:2, 71:4		
פלטה	17:13		
חלצני	(119:153), 140:2		
חלצה	6:5		

The semantic field even includes the following less frequent cases:

מלטה	(116:4)		
גאלני	(119:154)	גאלה	69:19
פצני	(144:7), (144:11)		
רצה להצילני	40:14		
הוציאני	(25:17)	הוציאה	142:8
עזרני	109:26, (119:86)	עזרנו	(79:9)
הבה עזרת מצר	(60:13), (108:13)		
היה־עזר לי	30:11		

The subjunctive in the second person singular has been used of the above-mentioned verbs to express a petition in the immediate context of an imperative in four cases: Ps 43:1 תפלטני, 71:2 תצילני ותפלטני, 143:11 תוציא מצרה נפשי. In such cases the subjunctive normally appears after the imperative. The two cases of subjunctive in Ps 71:2, however, precede the imperative, but follow a cohortative אל־אבושה.

The total number of cases in this group of prayer imperatives is 64, and they are divided among 34 psalms. If only individual complaint psalms are considered, we find 38 cases in 22 psalms. It may be observed that some of the above cases occur parallel with each other, e.g.

Ps 7:2   הושיעני מכל־רדפי והצילני
Save me from all my pursuers and deliver me.

Ps 22:21–22   הצילה מחרב נפשי   מיד־כלב יחידתי
                 הושיעני מפי אריה   ומקרני רמים עניתני(?)
Deliver my soul from the sword, my precious life from the power of the dog. Save me from the mouth of the lion, my poor soul(?) from the horns of the wild oxen.

Ps 59:3   הצילני מפעלי און   ומאנשי דמים הושיעני
Deliver me from those who work evil and save me from bloodthirsty men.

Ps 109:26   עזרני יהוה אלהי   הושיעני כחסדך
Help me, O Yahweh my God. Save me according to your steadfast love.

See also Ps 31:2–3, (144:7, 11).
    That these imperative petitions are often concerned with situations of physical danger is shown by the attachment of a prepositional phrase with מן, e.g. הצילני מאיבי »deliver me from my enemies« Ps 59:2, 143:9; הצילני מטיט »rescue me from the mire« Ps 69:15; פלמה נפשי מרשע חרבך »deliver my life from the wicked by your sword« Ps 17:13; הצילני מיד־אויבי ומרדפי »deliver me from the hand of my enemies and my persecutors« Ps 31:16; see also Ps (25:17,22), 71:4, (119:134), 120:2, 140:2, 142:7,8, (144:7,11), and the above examples Ps 7:2, 22:21–22, 59:3. Even in Ps 39:9 and 51:16 the petition הצילני most probably concerns a dangerous situation. In Ps 39:9 מכל־פשעי should be vocal-

ized as a participle: »from all those who transgress against me" (cf. e. g. Ps 51:15).²⁶ In Ps 51:16 the difficult expression הצילני מדמים more probably refers to deliverance from imminent death as a victim of »bloodshed« rather than from being »bloodguilty«.²⁷ Even most of the other cases without a prepositional phrase reveal in their wider context a connection with enemies or other dangers. No clear picture of the possible situation is given in Ps (60:7) (and its parallel 108:7), 86:2, 16, (118:25), and in most of the frequent cases in Ps (119), in psalms from a presumably late date.²⁸

The object of the saving act in most of the above cases – as might be expected in individual complaints is expressed by the object suffix of the first person singular, whereas the corresponding plural only appears four times. A noun object appears in the following cases: נפשי »my soul«/»my life« Ps 6:5, 17:13, (116:4), 120:2 (of which Ps 6:5 and 116:4 clearly refer to the threat of death); עבדך »your servant« Ps 86:2, לבן־אמתך »the son of your handmaid« Ps 86:16, המלך »the king« Ps (20:10), ישראל Ps (25:22), עמך »your people« Ps 28:9. Whether ימינך in Ps (60:7) (and the parallel 108:7) should be understood »by your right hand«,²⁹ or as an object perhaps referring to the king (cf. Ps 80:18),³⁰ or rather as contamination from cases where ימין appears with the perfect (Ps 98:1), is problematic.

The verbal root ישע (hi. »to save«, »to deliver«) is frequently used in the OT, particularly in Judg, Sam, and Kings, to denote not only deliverance from personal dangers but especially the action of Yahweh or a person sent by him in overcoming dangerous situations threatening the very existence of Israel.³¹ Of the total of 354 occurences of the verb and its cognate nouns, however, as many as 136 are found in the Book of Psalms. The number of verbal forms in the psalms is 56. The verbal root נצל (hi. »to deliver«, »to rescue«) occurs frequently in similar connections as ישע and in the psalms often parallel to it.³² The two roots have an approximately equal frequency in verbal forms (ישע hi. 184, נצל

---

²⁶ The main argument is the parallelism with the latter part of the verse (נבל); see Gunkel 1926, 167, and Kraus 1978, 452. The non-existence of parallels to the reading of the MT could be seen as a further argument.

²⁷ Of the two alternatives Gunkel 1926, 227, prefers the former, but resorts to a conjecture: מִדָּמָם »from the land of silence«; see also Kraus 1978, 547.

²⁸ See e.g. the datings of Kraus 1978, 587, 762, 979, 1000.

²⁹ Both Weiser 1963, 296, and Kraus 1978, 585, give the rendering »mit deiner Rechten«.

³⁰ For Ps 80:18 איש ימינך, see Gunkel 1926, 353, according to whom it refers to the people, and Kraus 1978, 724, according to whom to the king. In Ps 60:7 Gunkel 1926, 259, regards ימינך as an object, but corrects the verb to הושיעה.

³¹ For ישע, see Sawyer TWAT III, 1035–1059. For its significance in the Deuteronomistic history, see Veijola 1977, 76–82.

³² For נצל, see Bergmann THAT II, 96–99.

hi. 188), but נצל has no cognate nouns. The psalms include 45 occurrences of נצל.

The preference for either one of the two verbs ישע hi. and נצל hi. seems to vary to a great extent throughout the OT. In the Pentateuch, נצל is found three times as frequently as ישע,[33] whereas the Deuteronomistic history and DtIs prefer ישע, particularly when Yahweh is the subject.[34] It seems that the root נצל was the more common in an earlier phase, whereas ישע and the various cognate nouns grew in favour and acquired more of a theological colouring denoting in particular Yahweh's saving action.[35] It should also be noted that ישע hi. appears more often than נצל hi. without a prepositional phrase stating the danger. In a few late psalms הושיע/הושעא seems to have developed into a prayer word (Ps 60:7/108:7, 86:2,16, 119:94,146) or even a praising word (Ps 118:25) without connection with a clear situation where help is needed.[36] As for the relative dating of the use of ישע hi. in the psalm prayers and its more theological use in the Deuteronomistic history and DtIs, it seems that the latter presupposes the former rather than the reverse. Particularly, the use of ישע hi. parallel to other verbs of the semantic field and in prayers concerning personal matters in the individual complaint psalms speaks for a greater age in relation to the more specialized use in exilic writings.[37] Support for this judgment may be found in Jer 2:27 where Jeremiah reproaches his listeners for forgetting Yahweh but in moments of danger praying קומה והושיענו »arise and save us«. In the time of Jeremia הושיענו/הושיעני must have been a common petition.

Of the other verbs listed above, גאל (qal »to ransom«), פדה (qal »to redeem«), מלט (pi. »to deliver«), and עזר (qal »to help«) are found more frequently outside the Book of Psalms (גאל 11 occurrences in the psalms/96 in the OT, פדה 14/70, מלט 5/28, עזר 16/76), whereas פלט

---

[33] Verbal forms of ישע appear in Ex twice, in Num once, and in Deut four times.
[34] DtIs reveals 56 cases of ישע, 6 of נצל.
[35] See Sawyer TWAT III, 1038–1039. N.B. II Kings 18:19–35 where the speech of Rabshakeh, obviously on purpose, only includes נצל.
[36] For Ps 118:25, see Kraus 1978, 984. The frequent use of the petition in complaint psalms seems to suffice as the background for the development.
[37] The use of ישע hi. in the complaint psalms is very much in keeping with the theophora names from this root, which were favoured in Hebrew as well as in other Semitic languages and which we encounter long before the appearance of the verb in normal usage. The oldest datable evidence for the use of the verb and the only one outside the OT is the stele of Mesha, although with Chemosh as the saving god. The verb had possibly poetic and solemn connotations in the earlier phase. On the other hand, it soon became archaic again in the post-exilic writings. For ישע, see Sawyer TWAT III, 1035–1059, and Stolz THAT I, 785–790. For the theophora names, see Noth 1928.

(pi. »to deliver«) and חלץ (pi. »to deliver«) are more common in the psalms (חלץ 10/14, פלט 19/25) and פצה (qal »to rescue«) in this sense only appears in Ps (144).³⁸ The concrete background of most of these verbs and their usage in the psalms in contexts referring to specific dangers is in keeping with the character of individual complaint psalms as prayers arising from situations in everyday life and from the need for help. It is typical of all of the verbs discussed in this section, except for עזר, that they imply a momentary act of saving. This is obviously the actual difference between עזר »to help« and ישע hi. which is also often rendered by »to help« and perhaps even the reason for the conspicuously low frequency of the former in the petitions.³⁹

Since some of the above verbs were also employed in certain juridical contexts – גאל and פדה in cases where possessions or persons were returned to the lawful owner or to his family or were set free by a payment⁴⁰ and ישע hi. in cases where a person pleaded for his rights in cases of injustice⁴¹ – it has been suggested that Hebrew juridical and religious vocabularies would be closely connected with each other and that prayer in particular would have been understood as a juridical speech before Yahweh.⁴² In this connection it is hardly possible to argue for or against this assumption. In the case of ישע nothing speaks for a primarily juridical origin, whereas גאל and פדה are less characteristic of the petitions studied. The dominant tone of the present group of petitions seems to be the appeal for help in an emergency situation. The petitions »save« and »deliver« obviously form a constituent part of the prayer of the Israelite, no matter which period is surveyed. This prayer, the most normal and spontaneous reaction of a human being in trouble, is naturally found also among other peoples.⁴³

Outside the Psalter, similar petitions are found in various parts of the OT. Gen 32:12 contains Jacob's petition when he is about to meet Esau: הצילני נא מיד אחי מיד עשו כי־ירא אנכי אתו פן־יבוא והכני אם על־ בנים – »Deliver me from the hand of my brother, from the hand of Esau, for I fear him, lest he come and destroy me, the mothers with the children« – attributable either to J or to the Deuteronomistic redaction.⁴⁴ In Jer 17:14 we may read one of Jeremiah's personal prayers:

---

³⁸ See Ringgren גאל, TWAT I, 884–890; Stamm פדה, THAT II, 389–406; Barth חלץ, TWAT I, 1003–1008. – The statistics above only concern the stems mentioned.
³⁹ See Bergmann THAT II, 256–259.
⁴⁰ See Ringgren TWAT I, 886–887; Stamm THAT II, 391–398.
⁴¹ See Sawyer TWAT III, 1047–1049.
⁴² Seeligmann *VT Suppl* XVI (1967), 274–278. See also Ringgren TWAT I, 887; Stamm THAT II, 396; Stolz THAT I, 787; Sawyer TWAT III, 1056.
⁴³ For the corresponding Babylonian prayers, see Mayer 1976, 225–227.
⁴⁴ Both v. Rad 1952–53, 258, and Westermann 1981, 614–623, regard the passage as be-

רפאני יהוה וארפא הושיעני ואושעה כי תהלתי אתה – »Heal me, O Yahweh, and I shall be healed; save me, and I shall be saved; for you are my praise«. Jer 2:27 quotes a prayer: קומה והושיענו – »Arise and save us«. So does Is 44:17, a prayer to an idol: הצילני כי אלי אתה – »Deliver me, for you are my god«. In the Deuteronomistic history we find II Kings 19:19 (parallel Is 37:20) Hezekiah's prayer: ועתה יהוה אלהינו הושיענו – נא מידו – »So now, O Yahweh our God, save us from his hand«;[45] in Judg 10:15 the prayer of the people of Israel: חטאנו ··· אך הצילנו נא היום הזה – »We have sinned ... only deliver us this day«; in I Sam 12: 10 a similar prayer is quoted in Samuel's speech: חטאנו ··· ועתה הצילנו מיד איבינו – »We have sinned ... but now deliver us out of the hand of our enemies«.[46] In II Chr 14:10 we read the Chronistic prayer of Asa: עזרנו יהוה אלהינו כי־עליך נשענו – »Help us, O Yahweh our God, for we rely on you« – where – typical of the Chronicler – עזר has taken the place of ישׁע hi.[47] That the type of petition most common in the psalms does not occur more often in other texts is rather astonishing. But, as already remarked by Wendel, prayers with actual petitions are extremely rare in the narrative texts of the OT.[48]

1.2 »Have mercy«

One of the most frequently occurring imperative petitions is »have mercy«, the imperative form of the verb חנן always appearing with the object suffix of the first person:

חנני	4:2, 6:3, (9:14 חנני), (25:16), 26:11, 27:7, 30:11, 31:10, 41:5, 41:11, 51:3, 56:2, 57:2 *bis*, 86:3, 86:16, (119:29), (119:58), (119:132)
חננו	(123:3 *bis*)

These 21 occurrences are divided among 15 psalms (14 of them among 11 individual complaints). Seven of these psalms also contain imperative petitions of the first group above, but only three times do they occur in closer connection with each other (Ps 26:11, 86:2–3,16), al-

---

longing to J. Smend 1981, 65, however, hints at the Deuteronomistic redaction as its origin. See the discussion below pp. 89–90.

[45] For the Deuteronomistic character of this passage, see Gray 1970, 667.
[46] For the Deuteronomistic character of these passages, see Soggin 1981, 201–203; Smend 1981, 116.
[47] For the Chronistic origin of this passage, see Ackroyd 1973, 137. The Deuteronomistic favourite ישׁע hi. is not used independently by the Chronicler; see Bergmann THAT II, 259.
[48] Wendel 1931, 9.

though still hardly constituting a parallelism. Thus, no actual dependence exists between these two kinds of imperative petition. No recurring formula includes the two.

On the other hand, the contexts of the petition חנני also seem to imply concrete troubles experienced by the petitioner more often than, for instance, guilt. In Ps 41 the context does mention the sins of the petitioner, but also mentions his enemies. In Ps 27 the prayer concerns the state of being deserted by people and by God, but also mentions evil people causing affliction. The clearest connection with prayer for forgiveness of sins naturally occurs in Ps 51.

> Ps 51:3   חנני אלהים כחסדך   כרב רחמיך מחה פשעי
> Have mercy on me, O God, according to your steadfast love;
> according to your abundant mercy blot out my transgressions.

The instances in Ps (119) also tend to ask for spiritual assistance – rather than concrete help – but the attitude is quite the opposite to that of Ps 51:3.

> Ps 119:132   פנה־אלי וחנני   כמשפט לאהבי שמך
> Turn to me and be gracious to me, as is right for those who love your name.

This prayer seeks God's »favour« in return for the supplicant's own efforts to be pious. Against this background, it is obvious that the petition חנני did not primarily ask for forgiveness of sins, but for »mercy« in the sense of »pity«, »sympathy« for a person in distress, or »favour«. In practice »favour« could also mean the removal of the misfortunes which trouble the petitioner. It is possible that the petition »have mercy« was used particularly in situations where the cause of the trouble was not evident and where »disfavour« before Yahweh perhaps could be suspected.[49] This could be the case e.g. in Ps 6:

> Ps 6:2–3   יהוה אל־באפך תוכיחני ואל־בחמתך תיסרני
>   חנני יהוה כי אמלל אני רפאני יהוה כי נבהלו עצמי
> O Yahweh, do not rebuke me in your anger, nor punish me in your wrath.
> Have mercy on me, O Yahweh, for I am weak; heal me, O Yahweh,
> for my bones are troubled.

This kind of a prayer was probably used and intended to be used in case of illness.[50] In the context of Yahweh's »disfavour« it is natural that the question of sin also arises, as in the case of Ps 41:

---

[49] For חנן, see Freedman-Lundbom TWAT III, 23–40, according to whom the verb implies a situation of earlier »disfavour«.

[50] Seybold 1973, 169, regards Ps 6 as one of the psalms which with some probability were connected with illness, whereas Ps 38, 41, and 88 are such with certainty.

Ps 41:5   יהוה חנני רפאה נפשי כי־חטאתי לך
O Yahweh, be gracious to me; heal me, for I have sinned agains you.

Sin is seen as the cause of »disfavour« and suffering.[51]

The verb חנן may, nevertheless, be considered to belong mainly to religious vocabulary in the OT. Its subject is nearly always God, and more than half of its occurrences in qal are found in the psalms (28/54). On the other hand, the root originally had a more general application.[52] The cognate noun חן, occurring particularly in the phrase מצא חן בעיני »find favour in the eyes of«, is in turn favoured in books other than the Psalter (only two occurrences here) and often used of human relationships.

Outside the psalms, the imperative form of חנן is found only once, viz.

Is 33:2   יהוה חננו לך קוינו
                 היה זרעם לבקרים אף־ישועתנו בעת צרה
O Yahweh, be gracious to us; we wait for you.
Be our(?) arm every morning, our salvation in the time of trouble.

In the wish form it appears in the priestly blessing Num 6:24—26:

Num 6:25   יאר יהוה פניו אליך ויחנך
Yahweh make his face shine upon you and be gracious to you.

However, on the basis of its frequency in the psalms and its appearance even in the two citations of prayer in Ps 30:11 and 40:5—11, the imperative חנני may be regarded as one of the most basic petitions of individual complaint prayers.[53]

Imperative prayers which unambiguously ask for *forgiveness of sins* are not very common in the psalms. Several such petitions occur in Ps 51: מחה פשעי »blot out my transgressions« Ps 51:3, וכל־עונתי מחה »blot out all my iniquities« Ps 51:11, הרבה כבסני מעוני ומחטאתי טהרני »wash me thoroughly from my iniquity and cleanse me from my sin« Ps 51:4, הסתר פניך מחטאי »hide your face from my sins« Ps 51:11.[54] In other psalms we find the following cases: מנסתרות נקני »clear me from hidden faults« Ps (19:13)), וכפר על־חטאתינו »forgive our sins« Ps (79:9), ושא לכל־חטאותי »forgive all my sins« Ps (25:18). On the other hand, Yahweh is praised for bestowing forgiveness (Ps 65:4, 103:8—12).

---

[51] For the thinking concerning sin and its consequences in the OT, see v. Rad 1966, I 278—281.
[52] The nonreligious origin is stressed by Zimmerli ThWNT IX, 366—372.
[53] For corresponding cases in the Babylonian prayers, see Mayer 1976, 225—226.
[54] Cf. the two verbal forms in Ps 51:9 תחמאני and תכבסני which are usually considered to be subjunctives of the second person singular. This is, however, not necessary, particularly since no imperative form precedes.

1.3 *Petitions Connected with the Priestly Blessing*

Encouraged by the frequent appearance of one of the clauses of the priestly blessing Num 6:24–26 in the imperative form חנני, we shall proceed by asking whether other such connections exist.

The first blessing in Num 6:24 יברכך יהוה »Yahweh bless you« is found several times in the psalms in the third person wish form (Ps 29: 11, 67:2,7,8, 115:12 *bis*, 13, 128:5, 134:3),[55] but only once converted into the imperative prayer in Ps 28.

Ps 28:9[56]　　　　　　　הושיעה את־עמך וברך את־נחלתך
Save your people and bless your heritage.

The only other imperative petitions using ברך pi. occur in Deut 26:15 where blessing is asked for Israel in connection with the tithes, Deut 33:11 in Moses' blessing to Levi, and II Sam 7:29 where David asks blessing for his family. The imperative ברך pi. never occurs in an individual prayer requesting blessing directly for the supplicant himself.[57]

The second blessing וישמרך »and keep you« is paralleled by a few more occurrences of the imperative petition form (»keep«):

שמרני　　　16:1, 17:8, 140:5, 141:9
שמרה　　　(25:20), 86:2

The cases without the object suffix include נפשי as the object. In three cases the prayer mentions a specific danger in a prepositional phrase with מן: מפני רשעים »from the wicked« Ps 17:9, מידי רשע »from the hands of the wicked« Ps 140:5, מידי פח »from the trap« Ps 141:9. The two cases of שמרה נפשי »watch over my soul/me« are not connected with any clearly expressed situation and can perhaps be seen as spiritualized prayers.

What is special about these prayers, however, is that except for Num 6:24 שמר hardly appears in this connection – Yahweh as the subject and a human object – outside the Psalter (see Gen 28:15,20, Ps 12:8, 41:3, 91:11, 121:3–5,7,8). Of the only other cases where שמר appears in a prayer, I Kings 8:25 asks Yahweh to keep a promise, I Chr 29:18 to keep the hearts of Israel. It does not seem probable that the imperative petition שמרני in the psalms should be interpreted as the characteristic petition of a person seeking asylum in the temple, as sug-

---

[55] For the interpretation of the verbal forms concerned as subjunctives, see Kraus 1978, 377–383, 620–622, 960–966, 1040, 1069. Ps (67) reveals clear dependence on Num 6: 24–26; for its interpretation as a »Segenspsalm«, see Crüsemann 1969, 199–201.

[56] Verse Ps 28:9 is obviously a later addition to the individual complaint psalm; see Gunkel 1929, 120.

[57] For ברך, see Scharbert TWAT I, 808–841.

gested for Ps 16:1.⁵⁸ The occurrences are too rare to justify such a definite conclusion. The contexts rather point towards a general meaning »keep from dangers«. Moreover, it may be observed that the verb שמר is used extremely frequently – particularly in Deut and the literature dependent on it – of the human activity of keeping the law (cf. Ps 119: 17,44,88,134,146).⁵⁹ Curiously enough, even ברך more often appears with a human subject in expressions of gratitude towards Yahweh.

The semantic field of »keeping«, »watching« is represented in a few other petitions which use other verbs and other verbal forms. Ps 19:14 contains the imperative form of חשך in a petition: גם מזדים חשך עבדך. The second person singular of the subjunctive appears in connection with the imperative in the following cases: Ps 17:8 תסתירני, 59:2 תשגבני, 64:2–3 תצר, תסתירני, 140:2,5 תנצרני (N.B. שמרני in the same verse). The third person subjunctive is found once: Ps 69:30 ישועתך אלהים תשגבני.

Another imperative petition corresponding to one of the clauses of the priestly blessing in Num 6:24–26 is »let your face shine«

האר פניך   31:17 (האירה), (80:4), (80:8), (80:20), (119:135).

Five occurrences, but only three psalms and of these only one an individual complaint psalm. The only other occurrences of the idiom are Ps 67:2 and Dan 9:17, of which the former reveals a direct dependence on Num 6:24–26.

For an explanation of the scarcity of correspondences between the priestly blessing and the imperative petitions of the psalms, one could with good reason refer to the difference in the »Sitz-im-Leben« of the two parts concerned. The imperative petitions in the psalms arise from emergency situations where Yahweh's help and pity for a suffering supplicant is needed. They do not aim at securing continuous blessings in life.⁶⁰ Even the petition שמרני in the psalms mainly attaches itself to dangerous situations and not to constant »keeping and watching« by Yahweh (cf. Gen 28:15,20 and Ps 121), which, however, was probably the purport of the priestly blessing. On the other hand, one cannot dismiss the problem without asking whether the difference in the »Sitz-im-Leben« infallibly implies a different language when the help and blessing of Yahweh is sought in different situations and for different groups of people. The only actual link is the use of the verb חנן. As for the remaining expressions, the scarcity of this particular use of ברך and שמר outside Num 6:24–26 and the absence in Num 6:24–26 of one of the main expressions for Yahweh's help and protection in the psalms

---

⁵⁸ See Kraus 1978, 263.
⁵⁹ For the various usages of שמר, see Sauer THAT II, 982–987.
⁶⁰ For the characterization of complaint psalms as prayers pleading for help in concrete situations of peril and suffering, see Gerstenberger 1980, 114, 116, 157–158; and 1971, 68–69, 72. Cf. also Fuchs 1982, 294–299.

and in large parts of the OT, viz. ישע hi., seem to speak for a greater difference – in time or space – between the background milieus of the two types of approaching Yahweh. Whether the priestly blessing should be considered ancient or originating with P,[61] its coming into contact with other traditions rather late could be responsible for the difference in language, and the psalms that manifest direct contact with it may well have used it as their source text.[62]

1.4 »Hear«, »see«

The semantic field of »hearing« is richly exemplified in the imperative petitions of the psalms. If we add to these prayer imperatives those pleading for visual attention, we arrive at a group with a total of 54 imperatives divided among 27 psalms, i. e. a group of petitions comparable in size with our first group in Section 1.1 (»save«, »deliver« etc.).

שמע	4:2, 17:6, 27:7, 28:2, 30:11, 54:4, 64:2, 143:1
שמעה	17:1, 39:13, 61:2, (84:9), 102:2, (119:149), 130:2
האזינה	5:2, 17:1, 39:13, 54:4, 55:2, (80:2), (84:9), 86:6, 140:7, 141:1, 143:1
הקשיבה	5:3, 17:1, 55:3, 61:2, 86:6, 142:7
הטה אזנך	17:6 (הט), 31:3, 71:2, 86:1, 88:3, 102:3
ראה	(9:14), (25:18), (25:19), 59:5, (80:15), (84:10), (119:153), (119:159), (139:24), 142:5
הביטה	13:4
הבט	(74:20), (80:15), (84:10), 142:5
בינה	5:2

A remarkable number of these petitions is found in individual complaint psalms (39 cases in 19 psalms), however, with a clear emphasis on the petitions for hearing, whereas most of those for visual attention appear outside this group, in congregational complaints and acrostic psalms. Parallelism between two or more of these imperatives occurs rather frequently, e. g.

---

[61] According to Noth 1966, 53, Num 6:24–26 is embedded in P, but – impossible to date – could be of much older origin. Scharbert TWAT I, 822, however, dates the priestly blessing »in der mittleren Königszeit«.

[62] This would, of course, imply a late dating for e. g. Ps 67, which, however, has generally been considered to be possibly pre-exilic (see e. g. Kraus 1978, 622). For the interpretation of literary dependence as a characteristic of post-exilic writings, see Holm-Nielsen *StTh* XIV (1960), 22–23. – The scarcity of the verbs ברך and שמר with Yahweh as the subject and the rarity and late appearance of theophora names from these roots seem to speak for the late dating of Num 6:24–26.

Ps 5:2–3   אמרי האזינה יהוה   בינה הגיגי
           הקשיבה לקול שועי   מלכי ואלהי

Give ear to my words, O Yahweh; give heed to my groaning.
Hearken to the sound of my cry, my King and my God.

Ps 84:9–10   יהוה אלהים צבאות שמעה תפלתי
             האזינה אלהי יעקב סלה[63]
             מגננו ראה אלהים   והבט פני משיחך

O Yahweh, God Sabaoth, hear my prayer;
give ear, O God of Jacob. Selah.
Behold our shield, O God, and look upon the face of your anointed.

See also Ps 17:1,6, 39:13, 54:4, 61:2 (80:15), 143:1.

It is amazing how many different verbs and expressions were used in the above petitions for »hearing«. The normal word for »to hear«, שמע, is of course the one most frequently used, but the denominative (from אזן) and often poetic האזין (hi.) »to give ear« is not far behind. The third verb קשב hi. »to hearken«, »to heed« appears five times in parallelism with either one of the two mentioned, only once independently (Ps 142:7). The expression המה אזנך »incline your ear« again is more independent, appearing even in parallelism with שמע as the first member (Ps 17:6). That the petitions for hearing so often appear in parallelism with each other indicates a certain emphasis on petitions of this type.

In three cases one of the above imperatives is paralleled with a further petition in the third person subjunctive, likewise asking for the acceptance of the prayer: Ps 88:3 תבוא לפניך תפלתי המה־אזנך לרנתי – »Let my prayer come before you, incline your ear to my cry«; Ps 102:2 יהוה שמעה תפלתי ושועתי אליך תבוא – »Hear my prayer, O Yahweh; let my cry come to you«; Ps 130:2 אדני שמעה קולי תהיינה אזניך קשבות לקול תחנוני – »O Lord, hear my voice; let your ears be attentive to the voice of my supplications«.

As objects of the petitions for hearing we find in the great majority of cases words referring to the prayer, such as תפלתי »my prayer« Ps 4:2, 39:13, 54:4, 55:2, 61:2, (84:9), 86:6, 102:2, 143:1; רנתי »my cry« Ps 17:1, 61:2, 88:3, 142:7; (קול) תחנוני »(the voice of) my supplications« Ps 28:2, 140:7, 143,1; 86:6 (תחנונותי); to the voice of the petitioner, קולי »my voice« Ps 64:2, (119:149), 141:1; or directly to the petitioner himself, לי/אלי »(incline your ear) to me« Ps 31:2, 71:2, 102:3; 17:6, 55:3. The suffix of the first person singular appears almost without exception in all cases.[64] Only three cases do not contain an object at all: Ps 30:11, (80:2), 86:1. The petitions for visual attention – ראה »see«, נבט hi. »look« – a few times refer to the misery or the enemies of

---

[63] For the restoration of the original form of the verse, see Kraus 1978, 747.
[64] The only object without the first person suffix is Ps 17:1 צדק, for which, however, BHS offers conjectures: אל צדק/צדקי (part of the address) or צעקתי.

the petitioner, עניי (9:14), (25:18), (119:153); אויבי (25:19), but appear in similar contexts also without an explicit object, Ps 13:4, 59:5, (80:15).⁶⁵ An extreme and unique case is found in Ps (119:159) ראה כי־פקודיך אהבתי »see that I love your precepts«.

These petitions seldom appear alone without other petitions within the same psalm. For this reason and for the often initial position of these imperatives, Gunkel saw in them merely the first opening plea which prepared the way for the actual petitions coming later after the complaint.⁶⁶ However, it is hardly correct to consider them as merely preparatory. It may be observed that such psalms as Ps 88 and Ps 130 (cf. also Ps 84) contain no other explicit petition than the petition for hearing. On the other hand, these petitions also occur in the middle of the psalm (Ps 86:6, 140:7, 142:7) and at the end (Ps 39:13). And, even in the opening verses of a psalm they are often interwoven with other types of petition (see e.g. Ps 4:2, 28:2, 54:3–4, 55:2–3, 64:2–3, 102:2–3). The plea for hearing should rather be understood as a humble prayer for contact with Yahweh (N.B. Ps 130). Since Yahweh is never asked to hear a thanksgiving,⁶⁷ this particular plea – although it in no way alludes to the situation – seems to imply a desperate need for this contact and for help. The kind of help needed may be inferred from the complaint that follows. To judge from its frequency and its appearance also in one of the few citations of a prayer Ps 30:11, the petition for hearing constitutes one of the main petitions in the individual complaint psalms. Its importance is emphasized by expressions which bring out the conviction of being heard and in thanksgiving the experience that Yahweh has heard the supplicant's prayer (e.g. Ps 4:4, 5:4, 6:9–10, 10:17, 18:7, 22:25, 28:6, 31:23, 34:7, 34:18, 40:2, 55:18, 65:3, 66:19, 69:34, 94:9, 116:1, 145:19). This conviction is the very basis on which a prayer may be pronounced and it also comprises the content of the thanksgiving. On the other hand, the thanksgiving seldom mentions that Yahweh has seen the misery of the supplicant (Ps 31:8, 138:6).

Parallels to the present group of petitions in the psalms are found elsewhere in the OT as follows.⁶⁸ In Deut 33:7 Moses' blessing to Judah begins: שמע יהוה קול יהודה. – »Hear, O Yahweh, the voice of Judah«. Jer 18:19 contains one of Jeremiah's personal petitions: הקשיבה

---

⁶⁵ In Ps 139:24 ראה is more or less equivalent to הנה, i.e. is most likely an interjection.
⁶⁶ Gunkel-Begrich 1933, 218–219. Several other frequently occurring prayer imperatives were included by Gunkel in the category of the »initial plea«. The repeated occurrence of the prayer word and its initial position in the psalm does not, however, imply that the prayer is less meaningful in comparison with the other petitions. See below pp. 87–88.
⁶⁷ This detail is stressed by Schult THAT II, 979.
⁶⁸ For corresponding Babylonian petitions, see Mayer 1976, 214–217.

יהוה אלי ושמע לקול יריבי – »Give heed to me, O Yahweh, and hear the voice of my adversaries«. The prayer of Hezekiah in II Kings 19:16 (and the parallel Is 37:17) combines both of the above types of petition: המה יהוה אזנך ושמע פקח יהוה עיניך וראה ושמע את דברי סנחריב – »Incline your ear, O Yahweh, and hear; open your eyes, O Yahweh, and see; and hear the words of Sennacherib«. Neh 3:36 contains a petition within the narration: שמע אלהינו כי־היינו בוזה – »Hear, O our God, for we are despised«. Daniel's prayer contains several occurrences of the petitions in question in Dan 9:17–19 ועתה שמע אלהינו אל־תפלת עבדך ואל־תחנוניו ··· המה אלהי אזנך ושמע פקחה עיניך וראה ··· אדני שמעה אדני סלחה אדני הקשיבה ועשה ··· – »And now, O our God, hear the prayer of your servant and his supplications ... O my God, incline your ear and hear; open your eyes and see ... O Lord, hear; O Lord, forgive; O Lord, give heed and act ...« The imperative ראה is found several times in Lam, in verses 1:9 and 20 and together with הביטה in verses 1:11, 2:20, and 5:1. Is 63:15 includes the petitions הבט משמים וראה (cf. Ps 80:15). The petitions for visual attention seem to become more frequent in later texts.

1.5 *»Answer«*

Closely related to the last-mentioned prayer imperatives is the petition »answer« – always with the first person object suffix – which occurs as often as 15 times in 12 psalms (11 times in 8 individual complaints):

עניני	4:2, 13:4, 27:7, 55:3, (60:7 Q), 69:14, 69:17, 69:18, 86:1, 102:3, (108:7), (119:145), 143:1, 143:7
עננו	(20:10*, cf. BHS), (60:7 K)

In about half of the cases עניני »answer me« occurs in the close context of a petition for hearing (Ps 4:2, 13:4, 27:7, 55:3, 86:1, 102:3, 143:1).

In his discussion of the characteristic petitions of the individual complaint psalms, Gunkel lists several rather infrequent petitions, but pays no attention to עניני.[69] Even after Gunkel this petition has hardly been recognized by scholars as »typical«.[70] Just as in the case of שמע, it may be observed here that the psalms even contain expressions of the conviction that Yahweh does answer (Ps 3:5, 17:6, 38:16, 86:7, 119:26, 120:1) and of thanksgiving for the answer (Ps 34:5, 65:6, 118:5,21,

---

[69] See Gunkel-Begrich 1933, 218–221. This petition does not seem to be frequent in the Babylonian parallel texts.

[70] See e.g. Kraus 1978, 243, where הביטה in Ps 13:4 is mentioned as »typical«, but not עניני.

138:3). This emphasizes more fully this particular item in complaint prayers.

That the above petitions have often been overlooked may at least partly depend on their translation. In the Septuagint they were rendered by using the verbs ἐπακούειν and εἰσακούειν. As a matter of fact, the verb ענה was rendered by these two verbs in all of its occurrences but one (Ps 119:42) in the Book of Psalms. Moreover, the Septuagint of the Psalter does not differentiate between שמע and ענה, since the former is also frequently rendered by εἰσακούειν.[71] This translation tradition was obviously followed by German translators in the employment of the German verb »erhören« by Luther and by several others after him.[72] Neither ἐπ-/εἰσακούειν nor »erhören«, however, adequately corresponds to ענה, which, in contrast to שמע, denotes the reaction to and not only the »favourable« hearing of a person's speech.[73] This becomes particularly clear in those few cases which add to the petition the adverbial מהר »hastily«, e.g. Ps 102:3 מהר ענני.[74] The petition ענני pleads for more than hearing only, for something that follows after the hearing of the prayer.

What kind of a reaction then is expected from Yahweh in the above petitions? Whether they specifically aim at receiving an oracle through the priest in the temple[75] is impossible to infer on the basis of the contents of the psalms in question. Most of them describe dangerous situations threatening the supplicant. In a thanksgiving psalm, in Ps 34:5 the verb ענה is connected with דרש »to seek«, »to ask«, possibly a term for the invocation of oracles: דרשתי את־יהוה וענני – »I sought

---

[71] The normal rendering for ענה, viz. ἀποκρίνεσθαι, was used in the psalms only once in Ps 119:42 where the petitioner is the subject (and twice for ענה pi.). The Greek Psalter is unique in its consistent employment of εἰσακούειν and ἐπακούειν to render ענה. The former equivalent – being otherwise a rendering of שמע – appears only in Job with some frequency, whereas the latter also occurs elsewhere, particularly in cases where Yahweh is the subject. The reason for this usage – in the psalms as well as elsewhere – is probably theological.

[72] See Luther's translation and the various commentaries l.c. Gunkel uses both »erhören« and »antworten«, Weiser »antworten« only in Ps 27:7, Kraus »antworten« only in Ps 143:1. Moreover, »erhören« is employed by Luther also for שמע (see Ps 4:2, 54:4, 143:1, 17:1).

[73] For ענה, see Labuschagne THAT II, 335–341. The German verb »erhören« is used only in connection with prayer, obviously under the influence of Bible translations (see Duden 1976, 731–732). For εἰσακούειν and ἐπακούειν, see LSJ 493, 605.

[74] The renderings ταχὺ εἰσακουσόν μου and »erhöre mich eilends« do not bring out the emergent need for a reaction, for an answer.

[75] Begrich ZAW 52 (1934), 81–92 (= Gesammelte Studien 217–231). Referring to Begrich – although Begrich himself does not make this connection – Kraus suggests this interpretation for Ps 13:4, 102:3, 143:1 (1978, 243, 866, 1117).

Yahweh and he answered me«.⁷⁶ But, since the psalm is acrostic, the verb דרש is probably conditioned by the acrostic scheme and the psalm hardly dates back to the time when the invoking and receiving of oracles was still practised.⁷⁷ The second half of the verse ומכל־מגורותי הצילני »and delivered me from all my fears« does not necessarily imply an oracle, either, but perhaps a more concrete »answer«. Furthermore, another thanksgiving psalm refers to an »answer« by deeds, Ps 65:6 נוראות בצדק תעננו »by dread deeds thou dost answer us with deliverance" (RSV). And finally, it may be worth noting that the prayer cited as Elijah's prayer at the most dramatic moment at Mount Carmel was precisely: ענני יהוה ענני »answer me, O Yahweh, answer me« (I Kings 18:37). The same petition עננו »answer us« was addressed to Baal (I Kings 18:26), and both of the opposed parts looked forward to »an answer by fire« (I Kings 18:24). This passage, the only one including the petition ענני outside the psalms, surely has nothing to do with the invoking of oracles.

Hence, we may conclude that ענני is a petition, fairly typical of individual complaint psalms and one which pleads for something more than hearing only, not necessarily for an answer by words, but for a reaction by deeds. Even if the verb ענה appears in connection with explicit oracles (e.g. I Sam 23:2–4, 11–12), it is too ordinary a word to be interpreted automatically as a special term for this particular practice.⁷⁸ In a complaint psalm, intended for use in various situations, the petition ענני had the advantage of an extremely wide applicability.

1.6 »Arise«, »awake«

In our search for frequently recurring prayer imperatives in the psalms, we now consider petitions which ask Yahweh to »arise« to help. Gunkel regarded even these petitions as examples of the »initial plea«.⁷⁹

קומה	3:8, 7:7, (9:20), (10:12), 17:13, 35:2, (44:27), (74:22), (82:8), (132:8)
רומה	(21:14), 57:6, 57:12, (108:6)
הנשא	7:7, (94:2)
עורה	7:7, (44:24), 59:5
העירה	35:23 (cf. עוררה (80:3))
הקיצה	35:23, (44:24), 59:6
הופיעה	(80:2), (94:1 ע-)

---

⁷⁶ For דרש, see Wagner TWAT I, 313–329.
⁷⁷ For the dating, see Kraus 1978, 418.
⁷⁸ Against Veijola 1982, 204.
⁷⁹ Gunkel-Begrich 1933, 219.

This, not exactly homogeneous, group of petitions is divided among 16 psalms. It may, however, be observed that a good half of these psalms are obviously not individual complaint psalms.

The context of most of these petitions clearly mentions or implies enemies, whom Yahweh is expected to either destroy or judge. This reference contains an astonishing resemblance to the words which according to Num 10 were recited whenever the Ark of the Covenant was moved.

Num 10:35 קומה יהוה ויפצו איביך וינסו משנאיך מפניך
Arise, O Yahweh, and let your enemies be scattered; and let them that hate you flee before you.

In קומה we are probably dealing with an ancient petition which was used first in connection with the Ark and the holy war, then also in other connections.[80] Ps 132:8 – although having nothing to do with the holy war – explicitly connects the petition קומה with the Ark, viz. with the bringing of the Ark to Jerusalem.[81] The notion of the holy war and direct dependence on Num 10:35 can, on the other hand, be detected in Ps 68:2, in a hymn praising Yahweh for his great deeds.[82]

What then is the exact meaning of the petition קומה? The verb קום is one of the most common in OT Hebrew and has a large variety of usages.[83] To begin with, it is hardly probable that Yahweh's sitting on the Ark as on a throne or sitting as a judge plays any role here.[84] In narrative texts קום is often used to denote »setting forth« in connection with another verb denoting the main action (e.g. Gen 24:10, 32:23, 43:15). In the psalms again we often find it connected with the enemy who »rises against« the supplicant (e.g. Ps 3:2, 54:5, 86:14). Along these lines we could perhaps understand the petition קומה: it was used to ask Yahweh to set forth with the Ark to aid Israel in her war and to stand up against the enemies of Israel – and of Yahweh as well. As with

---

[80] See Noth 1966, 71–72. Noth considers the prayer Num 10:35–36 to have come from an earlier source and to have been embedded in J. According to Smend 1966, 58, it may have been used as early as the time of the judges and the early kingdom. See also Jeremias, *Festschrift v. Rad* 1971, 187–188, particularly note 17.

[81] N.B. the close connection with II Sam 6–7. See also Kraus 1978, 1063, and Veijola 1982, 75.

[82] See Kraus 1978, 629–632. Cf. however, Crüsemann 1969, 306 note 1, who does not consider Ps 68 a hymn.

[83] See Gesenius-Buhl 707; Koehler-Baumgartner³ 1015–1016; Amsler THAT II, 635–641.

[84] Against v. Rad *Gesammelte Studien* 116, and Noth 1966, 71–72, on the one hand, Beyerlin 1970, 131, on the other. On the Ark as a throne in connection with Num 10:35, see Smend 1966, 58 note 10: »nur eine der Vorstellungen, die man erwarten könnte, und nicht die wahrscheinlichste«.

Num 10:35, most of the cases in the psalms primarily connote an encounter with the enemy rather than a desperate need for help in danger.⁸⁵ Interestingly enough, Jer 2:27 and Ps 3:8 combine קומה with the petition הושיעני/הושיענו. Nevertheless, it is hardly correct to regard the verb קום merely as an auxiliary emphasizing the following verb, but as a verb denoting an independent action. On the other hand, it is plausible that a verb as unspecific as קום could appear with a different nuance in different contexts. Particularly in the case of individual complaints, the petition קומה was removed from the contexts of the Ark and the holy war and could be combined with an adverb like בעזרתי »for my help« Ps 35:2. In Ps 132:8 the connotation is, however, entirely cultic: קומה appears in connection with the Ark, it is true, but combined with a local adverb למנוחתך »to your resting place« to express merely movement from one place to another.⁸⁶ Thus, the occurrences in the psalms must be understood, on the one hand, against the background of Num 10:35, but on the other, represent adaptations of the original context.

In Ps 7:7 we find קומה connected with the imperative הנשא nif. »raise yourself«, which also occurs in Ps (94:2) in a similar context, used obviously in both cases for the sake of parallelism. On the other hand, רומה »be exalted« seems to have an entirely different context and function: it expresses no petition, but is obviously to be understood as praise (cf. Ps 18:47, 99:2, 113:4, 138:6).⁸⁷ In עורה »wake up« and the related imperatives we are probably dealing with petitions which have a quite different, possibly Canaanitic, origin.⁸⁸ Three psalms, Ps 7, 35, and (44), however, combine them with קומה in the context of Yahweh's intervention. The same connotations occur with הופיעה, which is used in two congregational psalms to call forth Yahweh's glorious appearance in the judgement and destruction of enemies.⁸⁹

---

[85] For the warlike connotations, see Amsler THAT II, 639. Schnutenhaus ZAW 76 (1964), 6–8, shares this view, but considers קום to be a verb expressing Yahweh's epiphany.
[86] According to Veijola 1982, 74–75, the writer of Ps 132 was a contemporary of »DtrN« and deliberately tried to archaize. קומה could be taken as one of his archaisms. That he employed קומה in a different meaning, however, would mean for the proper use of this petition a much earlier, pre-deuteronomistic dating.
[87] Dahood 1966 I, 134–135, translates רומה by »rejoice«. Weiser 1963, 25–26, connects this as well as the other petitions in the present section to theophany. The verb does not, however, necessarily imply movement; see Stähli THAT II, 760.
[88] Kraus 1978, 196. See also Dahood 1966 I, 268, who sees עורה as a poetic image without theological content.
[89] For the connection with theophany, see Weiser 1963, 25–26; Kraus 1978, 722, 823; Jeremias 1965, 147.

1.7 »Return«

The nearest context of קומה יהוה in Num 10:35 reveals another prayer which was used in connection with the Ark, viz. when it was set down in the camp. Even this prayer may help us in our interpretation of a few parallel petitions in the psalms.

Num 10:36   שובה יהוה רבבות אלפי ישראל
    Return, O Yahweh, to (?) the ten thousand thousands of Israel.

The imperative שובה, the exact meaning of which has puzzled many scholars, appears in one of the psalms mentioned in the previous section, Ps 7, in a similar way to the close context of קומה.

Ps 7:7–8
קומה יהוה באפך
הנשא בעברות צוררי
ועורה אלי משפט צוית
ועדת לאמים תסובבך
ועליה למרום שובה

Arise, O Yahweh, in your anger,
lift yourself up against the fury of my enemies;
and awake, O my God, you have ordered that justice be done.
Let the assembly of the peoples be gathered about you;
and over it return up to the heights.

For both of these instances of שובה a correction to שֵׁבָה »sit« (< ישׁב) has been suggested, although with no text-critical support and with no parallel texts in the OT.⁹⁰ That both texts have been considered together as parallels is obviously correct, but on the other hand the double occurrence of the petition שובה here should encourage one to look for a feasible interpretation rather than to resort to conjecture. In this connection one should also consider another puzzling instance of the verb שוב in Ps 7:13.

Ps 7:12–13   אלהים שפט צדיק ואל זעם בכל־יום
             אם־לא ישוב חרבו ילטש

The problem concerns not only the meaning of the verb but also its subject. On the basis of the preceding line, the most logical subject – although seldom accepted as such – is God, the Divine Judge. After the mention of the punishing action and anger of God, here as well as in Ps 7:7–8 (קומה יהוה באפך) and in Num 10:35–36, the expected »return«

---

⁹⁰ See the apparatus of BHS for Num 10:36 and Ps 7:8. As far as Num 10:36 is concerned, v. Rad *Gesammelte Studien*, 116, is for the conjecture; Noth 1966, 62, and Smend 1966, 58 note 10, do not consider it well enough grounded. Gunkel 1926, 26, and Kraus 1978, 191, are for the conjecture in Ps 7:8. Beyerlin 1970, 98 note 91, regards שובה as meaningless and both cases as a result of the same confusion.

of Yahweh can only mean »return from anger«, »return from battle« after execution of the punishment.[91] Concrete »return from battle« may very well have been the original purport of the latter part of the ancient prayer formula in Num 10:36, which obviously very early became obscure to the readers.[92] Even to the Septuagint translators it was far from clear. They rendered the imperative שובה literally by ἐπίστρεφε in Num 10:36 and ἐπίστρεψον in Ps 7:8, but did not understand ישוב in Ps 7:13 as referring to God – just like most translators after them – and rendered here ἐὰν μὴ ἐπιστραφῆτε.[93] However, to interpret שוב – one of the most common verbs in OT Hebrew – in the close context of expressions of Yahweh's anger as »to return from anger« not only solves the problem connected with the disposition of Ps 7, with which Kraus keeps fumbling in the dark,[94] but also provides a probable solution to most of the remaining cases of the petition שובה in the complaint psalms.

The crucial verses Ps 7:12–13 should thus be rendered: »Yahweh[95] vindicates the righteous, and God bursts out in wrath every day.[96] If he does not return (from his wrath), he sharpens his sword and draws his bow and shoots.« The following verse describes the weapons that the wrathful Judge will use against the enemy (לו). In connection with the holy war – or a fight against private enemies – it is not uncommon to hear of Yahweh using weapons; cf. e.g. a similar context in Ps 35:2–3, the thanksgiving in Ps 18:15, or Deut 32:40–42.

In verse 15 we again hear of the arrogance of the enemy: הנה יחבל־און והרה עמל וילד שקר. – »Behold, he conceives evil, and is pregnant with mischief, and brings forth lies«. The typical wording contrasts the dishonourable methods of the enemy with Yahweh's righteous fight. When Yahweh is fighting in his wrath, the enemy shall fall into his own trap (16–17). Of this the petitioner may be sure on the basis of what was said in verses 13–14, and there is no need to postulate a missing link of an oracle or the like. A correct understanding of אם־לא ישוב suffices to restore logic and meaning to the psalm.

The imperative form of the verb שוב occurs not only in Ps 7 but also in Ps 6:5 (שובה), (80:15) (שוב־נא), (85:5) (שובנו[97]), (90:13) (שובה), and

---

[91] Cf. Ps 18:38: a warrior does not return before destroying the enemy. Smend 1966, 58 note 10, points out that שוב may denote return from war.
[92] Noth 1966, 72, considers it probable that something is missing from Num 10:36. Could it possibly have been as in Ps 7:8 למרום על־ (cf. also Ps 68:19)? A good reason to omit this from Num 10:36 would have been the thought of Yahweh staying with the camp of the Israelites.
[93] We do not possess any evidence of a possible Hebrew variant reading.
[94] Kraus 1978, 199–200.
[95] For the Divine Name in Ps 7:12, see Gunkel 1926, 26; Kraus 1978, 190.
[96] Gunkel 1926, 23, translates here: »›Jahve‹ richtet den Gerechten ›und vergilt dem‹, der jeden Tag flucht«, which results from reading ישוב as ישיב already in verse 12 (see ibid. 26).
[97] In Ps 85:5 the suffix in שובנו is possibly a misspelling for נא (cf. BHS as well as Ps 80:15).

(126:4) (K. שבותנו את־יהוה שובה). All of these psalms – except Ps 126 – speak of the wrath of Yahweh, not against enemies, however, but against Israel or the supplicant himself. The difference in situation explains the appearance of שובה without connection with קומה, although the general idea expressed by the verb שוב is closely related. Ps 6, the only individual complaint psalm in this group, asks Yahweh »not to punish in wrath« (verse 2). The petitioner's distress is clearly seen as caused by Yahweh's anger which should now be averted: שובה יהוה חלצה נפשי »return (from your wrath), Yahweh, save my life« (verse 5). The congregational complaints in question also lament over Yahweh's wrath and wish to see it averted. In the context of Ps 80:15, verse 5 asks: עד־מתי עשנת »how long will you, i.e. will your anger smoke?«[98] Ps 85:5–6 clearly speaks of Yahweh's return from his anger as the aim of the prayer:

שובנו [99] אלהי ישענו והפר כעסך עמנו
הלעולם תאנף־בנו תמשך אפך לדר ודר

Return again, O God of our salvation, and put away your indignation toward us.
Will you be angry with us for ever? Will you prolong your anger to all generations?

Ps 90:7–9,11 lament over the heavy burden of Yahweh's wrath, whereas verse 13 pleads: שובה יהוה ... והנחם »return (from your wrath), Yahweh ... and have pity«.[100] Even if the imperative petition שובה without closer specification is not very frequent – in addition to the cases mentioned only Is 63:17 offers a comparable instance – the above interpretation may be considered justified by its recurrence in similar contexts and also plausible in the light of other usages of שוב.[101] In prose texts the verb שוב is also found with the closer specification מחרון אף »from the glow of anger« in Ex 32:12 (here even a petition), Deut 13:18, Josh 7:26, II Kings 23:26, and Jon 3:9.[102] Consequently,

---

[98] Gunkel 1926, 354, unnecessarily resorts to a conjecture: עד־מתי ענשת »wie lange läßt du büßen«.
[99] See note 97 above.
[100] Cf. also Ex 32:12 where the context allows הנחם in connection with שובה to be rendered »repent«.
[101] For the various usages of שוב, see Holladay 1958, who discusses the complete material without, however, offering any solution to our problematic cases (e.g. Ps 7:8,13 and 80:15 *ibid.* 82–83). The above interpretation (»return from anger«) is shared in the case of Ps 6:5 by Gunkel 1926, 23; in the case of Ps 90:13 by Gunkel 1926, 399, and Weiser 1963, 410 (»laß dich gereuen«).
[102] See Holladay 1958, 76–77, where, however, the cases with the specification are presented as a separate group from Ps 6:5 and 90:13. These two cases as well as Is 63:17 denote according to Holladay »to change the total direction of his (*sc.* God's) activity«.

emendations of שוב in the cases under discussion, either to another verb (ישב) or to another form (hif'il),¹⁰³ are unnecessary.

In Ps 126:4, however, we are concerned with another idiom, the problematic שוב שבות, a late idiom expressing return from the Exile.¹⁰⁴ This expression quite obviously has nothing to do with the cases of שוב discussed above, just as Ps 126 makes not a single mention of Yahweh's anger. A common word like שוב has the capacity to create several different idioms, which could perhaps even be used as a play on words. Also the hif'il of שוב occurs in two kinds of petitions: »bring us back« Ps (80:4,8,20), and »revenge« Ps 28:4, (79:12), (94:2). On the other hand, distance in time and detachment from the situation soon obscures such idioms.

1.8 »Judge«, »vindicate«

The prayers which include the petition קומה discussed above appealed to Yahweh as the Divine Judge and asked him to fight the enemies of the petitioner. The attitude of these prayers is rather bold and they imply – at least in the case of an individual complaint – emphasis on the innocence of the petitioner. This is explicitly expressed in Ps 7: 4–6, 17:1,3–5, and 35:11–14. From this background of unjust oppression or innocent suffering also arise the imperative petitions which ask for justice:

שפטני	7:9, 26:1, 35:24, 43:1
שפטה	(82:8)
ריבה	35:1, 43:1, (74:22), (119:154)

Two individual complaints Ps 7 and 35 connect these prayers with קומה – and as a matter of fact the individual cause with the holy war.¹⁰⁵ At least in the case of Ps 7, one asks whether the petitioner should be regarded as a private person or perhaps rather as a representative of the

---

¹⁰³ See page 34 note 90. As for Ps 85:5, the correction to the hif'il (Gunkel 1926, 375; Weiser 1963, 388; Kraus 1978, 753) is unnecessary, since also the second half of the verse asks Yahweh to put away his wrath. The hif'il occurs in Ps 80:4, 8, 20, but clearly in a different idiom.

¹⁰⁴ Whether שבות or שבית, from שבה or שוב, it does not change the purport of the idiom or the fact that the idiom is not older than the Exile. The scope of this study does not allow a longer discussion of this idiom, but it obviously has nothing to do with the hif'il of שוב in Ps 80:4,8,20 (against Kraus 1978, 757). Cf. the different interpretations of the idiom in question in the various lexica as well as Soggin THAT II, 884–891, and Holladay 1958, 110–115.

¹⁰⁵ For the difficulties involved in this combination of the individual and the universal, see Weiser 1963, 92–93, who sees the solution in the theophany; Kraus 1978, 195–198.

people, as a king or a military commander.¹⁰⁶ Ps 26 and 43 more clearly give the impression of an individual petitioner appealing for justice. The two congregational psalms in the present group, Ps 74 and 82, which also employ קומה, appeal to Yahweh in his own cause – not the petitioners': ריבה ריבך »maintain your own cause« Ps 74:22, שפטה הארץ כי־אתה תנחל בכל־הגוים »judge the earth, for to you belong all nations« Ps 82:8.

Several scholars have regarded the prayers where the petitioner appeals for justice in his own case – שפטני »vindicate me« and ריבה את־יריבי/ריבי »fight my cause« – as indication of an actual practice of lawsuits and trials in the temple.¹⁰⁷ The thesis, first introduced by Schmidt, has been opposed by Gemser who suggests a metaphorical interpretation.¹⁰⁸ One of Gemser's arguments is the combination of the judicial metaphors with other quite different metaphors, e.g. in Ps 35 images of battle, wild animals and hunting. Seeligmann, on the other hand, points out that at least in the case of Ps 43 there is no necessity to interpret the situation of the petitioner as that of one unjustly accused.¹⁰⁹ Appeal to God as a judge and a helper – also a human judge was seen as the helper of the oppressed and those in need – was possible in every kind of distress.¹¹⁰ Whether or not prayer was primarily understood as juridical speech before God,¹¹¹ judicial metaphors in fact have a firm place in religious speech, in the OT as well as its parallel texts.¹¹²

> The second person of the subjunctive of a verb belonging to the semantic field under discussion, viz. תדינני, appears in Ps 54:3 in the immediate context of the imperative petition הושיעני.

One of the individual complaints mentioned above, Ps 26, not only pleads for justice, but assures the innocence of the supplicant by further petitions for a trial by Yahweh: »try me«, »test me«. Similar petitions occur in no other psalm except Ps 139.

---

¹⁰⁶ According to Kraus 1978, 196, it is possible to hear in Ps 7 »die Gebetsformel eines Königs nachklingen«. This interpretation should not, however, be confused with the idea of »corporate personality« (for which, e.g. Mowinckel 1962, II 134; Becker 1975, 88–89). N.B. that also I Kings 8:44–45 connects Yahweh's judgement with battle; see Gamper 1966, 230.
¹⁰⁷ See particularly Schmidt 1928, Delekat 1967, Beyerlin 1970.
¹⁰⁸ Gemser *VT Suppl* III (1960), 120–137 (particularly 128). See also Gamper 1966, 234–236.
¹⁰⁹ Seeligmann *VT Suppl.* XVI (1967), 277.
¹¹⁰ *Ibid.* 276–278. Cf. Babylonian parallels to the petitions in question, which often refer to illness; Mayer 1976, 221–225.
¹¹¹ See p. 20 note 42.
¹¹² See particularly Gamper 1966; Gemser *VT Suppl* III (1960), 120–137.

בחנני	26:2, (139:23)	
נסני	26:2	
צרופה K.[113]	26:2	
חקרני	(139:23)	
דע	(139:23 bis)	

In the case of Ps 26, one of the verbs used צרף is primarily connected with the work of a goldsmith, so that the metaphor is not purely judicial here, either. The wider context in Ps 139, on the other hand, is characterized by devotion and confidence in Yahweh rather than judicial images.

1.9 »Hasten to my aid«, »turn to me«

One of the recurring imperative petitions which Gunkel lists among the most typical is חושה »hasten«,[114] one of the few petitions asking Yahweh to draw nearer for the benefit of the supplicant.

חושה   22:20, 38:23, 40:14, 70:2, 70:6, 71:12 Q, 141:1

The imperative חושה is always completed with a prepositional phrase, with לעזרתי »to my aid« in all cases, except Ps 70:6 and 141:1 which read לי »to me«.[115] All of the six psalms concerned are individual complaints. A further characteristic of the petition חושה is its concurrence with negated petitions, e. g. אל־תרחק »be not far« and אל־תאחר »do not tarry« (cf. Section 1.13 below), seldom with the more common types of petition discussed above (cf. however, Ps 22:20–22). It is remarkable that a parallel for this petition has been found in the texts of Ugarit.[116] As for the use of the verb חוש in the OT in general, the above-mentioned cases constitute about one half of the occurrences in qal (7/17; hi. 5).[117] Representing a group of their own, the petitions closely resemble each other in form and thought, but are not paralleled by other cases.

Within the psalms petitions studied in the present work we come across a semantically related expression מהרה/מהר in Ps 31:3, 69:18, 102:3, 143:7. This form should not, however, be mistaken for the imperative, although the outward appearance is indistinguishable,[118] but

---

[113] Bauer-Leander, 306, understand the K. צרופה as a dialect form of the imperative.
[114] Gunkel-Begrich 1933, 219–220.
[115] BHS gives in the apparatus a conjecture for יחשב לי in Ps 40:18 according to Ps 70:6: »melius חושה־לי«. The conjecture makes the two verses almost equal. On the other hand, it is possible that the difference in Ps 40:18 is intentional.
[116] See Beyse TWAT II, 821–822. For Babylonian parallels, see Mayer 1976, 213.
[117] The total figures include all cases of חוש without differentiation of חוש II.
[118] Gerstenberger 1980, 121, regards מהר as a prayer imperative. See, however, Gesenius-Buhl 403; Beyse TWAT II, 821.

must be understood as an adverb. Except with the imperative form in the cases mentioned above, this adverb מהר/מהרה »hastily« occurs in connection with a subjunctive in Ps 79:8 and even other forms (see e.g. Deut 9:12, Ps 37:2).

Another imperative petition which asks Yahweh to move towards the petitioner is

    פנה   (25:16), 69:17, 86:16, (119:132)

All four cases include the prepositional phrase אלי »to me«.[119] All of them also refer to the mercy of Yahweh turning to help the person praying, three cases by employment of a further petition חנני »have mercy on me«, one in a prepositional phrase כרב רחמיך »according to your abundant mercy« (Ps 69:17). To the above-mentioned cases we could add the imperative petition קרבה אל־נפשי »draw near to my soul« in Ps 69:19, in the close context of פנה (verse 17). The petition לכה לישעתה לנו »come to save us« in Ps (80:3), in a congregational complaint, is quite unique.[120]

1.10 »Teach«, »lead«

Blessings and guidance more intellectual in character are asked for, particularly in petitions of the late acrostic psalms.

למדני	(25:4), (25:5), (119:12), (119:26), (119:64), (119:66), (119:68), (119:108), (119:124), (119:135), 143:10
הבינני	(119:27), (119:34), (119:73), (119:125), (119:169)
הורני	27:11, 86:11, (119:33)
הודיעני	(25:4), 39:5, (90:12ע־), 143:8
נחני	5:9, 27:11, (139:24)
הדריכני	(25:5), (119:35)

All of these cases – except for four: Ps (25:5) למדני (repetition of verse 4) and (119:34,73,125) הבינני – include an object or another closer specification, as to what kind of guidance is asked for. Most cases concern the way of life according to Yahweh's will and refer to it as his »way« or his »commandments«. The latter – with varying vocabulary – is the characteristic expression in Ps 119: למדני חקיך »teach me your statutes« in verses 12, 26, 64, 68, and 135, למדני משפטיך »teach me your

---

[119] Although the same equivalents are often used for both, פנה and שוב, discussed in Section 1.7, are not synonyms, the former denoting particularly »turning *to* something«, the latter »returning *back* to the initial point of departure«. See Holladay 1958, 53–54.

[120] Petitions of the type discussed in this section are obviously more frequent in Babylonian prayers; see Mayer 1976, 211–213.

ordinances« in verses 108 and 124, but also combined expressions occur: הורני יהוה דרך חקיך »teach me, O Yahweh, the way of your statutes« verse 33, דרך־פקודיך הבינני »make me understand the way of your precepts« verse 27, הדריכני בנתיב מצותיך »lead me in the path of your commandments« verse 35. Ps 25 again uses the metaphor of the »way«, but the aim of the petitions in

Ps 25:4–5   דרכיך יהוה הודיעני ארחותיך למדני
            הדריכני באמתך ולמדני כי־אתה אלהי ישעי

Make me to know your ways, O Yahweh; teach me your paths.
Lead me in your truth and teach me, for you are the God of my salvation.

is obviously the same, guidance in the correct way of life.[121] But, these petitions do not spring from an emergency situation. This could perhaps be the case in Ps 5:9 and 27:11 (2 instances) only, since these petitions include a mention of the enemy (למען שררי) and appear in the context of other expressions for distress. In the case of Ps 86:11 and 143:8 the picture is not clear. Two further petitions, Ps 39:5 and 90:12, concern the consciousness of the shortness of life.

The vocabulary used in the above petitions for a more intellectual or spiritual guidance is to a great extent that of Deut, or more precisely, of the Deuteronomistic frame of Deut.[122] The religious atmosphere, at least behind the acrostic psalms, is obviously the post-exilic zeal for an ever closer observance of the Torah. It is remarkable that petitions of this type are not characteristic of individual complaint proper.

The petition for guidance appears in two cases in the form of subjunctive, once in the second person in Ps 61:3 בצור־ירום ממני תנחני,[123] once in the third person in Ps 143:10 רוחך טובה תנחני (parallel to למדני).

In connection with the present group of petitions it may be appropriate to mention another speciality of Ps 119, the imperative petition חיני »give me life« which appears in verses 25, 37, 40, 88, 107, 149, 154, 156, 159. The only parallel to these petitions is the second person subjunctive תחיני Ps 143:11.[124] All of these petitions include a prepositional phrase referring to Yahweh's »word«, »righteousness«, or the like. There is no reason to list this petition among the petitions typical of individual complaints, as Gunkel-Begrich do.[125] Its vagueness rather characterizes a late phase in psalmodic prayers where no concrete background situation is discernible.

---

[121] See e.g. the interpretation of Gunkel 1926, 107, or of Kraus 1978, 352–353.
[122] N.B. the various words for »commandment« as well as the use of the words דרך (see Kraus 1978, 353; e.g. Deut 9:12,16) and למד (see Jenni THAT I, 874). For the composition of Deut, see Smend 1981, 71–73.
[123] For the interpretation as a petition, see Gunkel 1926, 260; Kraus 1978, 591.
[124] See also Ps 71:20 תחיינו K., תחיני Q. and Ps 80:19 תחינו, which are probably not to be understood as subjunctives.
[125] Gunkel-Begrich 1933, 220.

1.11 »Remember«

A recurring petition which does not appear in the ordinary individual complaint psalms, but only in acrostic psalms, in psalms of the congregation, and in those for the king, is »remember«.

זכר   (25:6), (25:7), (74:2), (74:18), (74:22), (89:48), (89:51), (106:4 -נִי), (119:49), (132:1), (137:7)

These petitions, like the petitions »hear« and »see« (שמע, ראה, etc.; see Section 1.4), appeal for Yahweh's attention, but do not imply an immediate emergency as particularly »hear« does. They often refer to things in the past, whether grace or disgrace, to rouse Yahweh into action. Several parallels for these petitions are found in other books of the OT. Parallels for the cases referring to Yahweh's mercy in the past in Ps 25:6, 74:2, 106:4, 119:49 are found in Ex 32:13, Deut 9:27, Jer 14:21, Neh 1:8, for the cases referring to distress and shame Ps 74:18,22, 89:51, 137:7 in Jer 15:15, Lam 3:19, 5:1, for the case referring to all the trouble taken by David Ps 132:1 in II Kings 20:3 (and the parallel Is 38:3), Jer 18:20, Neh 5:19, 13:14,22,29,31, and for the case referring to the shortness of life Ps 89:48 in Job 7:7, 10:9. Ps 25:7 as well as Judg 16:28 seem to employ the petition זכר simply as a plea for help.[126] Some of the parallel passages can without doubt be attributed to the Deuteronomistic school (Ex 32:13, Deut 9:27, II Kings 20:3 // Is 38:3),[127] of the others several occur in exilic or post-exilic writings (Lam, Neh). Even Samson's prayer Judg 16:28 obviously has a redactional origin.[128] Everything speaks for the conclusion that the petition זכר was not commonly used until the time of the Exile – if not only shortly prior to it (Jer) – and may be regarded as a criterion for a relatively late dating, at least when other criteria speak for the same. That it is consistently absent from the individual complaint proper is a fact which deserves consideration in connection with the dating of these psalms or the materials used in them.[129]

1.12 Petitions against the Enemy

Although the enemy who acts against the supplicant is often designated as the cause of the petition, most of the imperative petitions discussed above have been petitions for the benefit of the supplicant. The clearest cases directed against the enemy were found in Sections 1.6

---

[126] Cf. also Neh 6:14 and 13:29 where the petition זכר is directed against evil people.
[127] See Veijola 1982, 74–75 note 12, 89 note 8.
[128] See Wendel 1931, 68; Gunkel 1913, 46.
[129] For the frequent parallels in the apocrypha and pseudepigrapha, see Johnson 1948, 46–47.

(קוּמָה) and 1.8 above. In addition to these, there are in the psalms some forty imperative petitions which pray for the destruction of or injury to the enemy. But the list of these petitions contains few repeated occurrences of a verb. In other words, the petitions against the enemy do not reveal stereotyped petitions comparable to the groups discussed above.

Petitions for revenge occur on three occasions: Ps 28:4 הָשֵׁב גְּמוּלָם לָהֶם »requite them for their work«, which is preceded by two occurrences of תֵּן לָהֶם »give them« used in the sense of הָשֵׁב »requite«;[130] Ps (79:12), (94:2) הָשֵׁב.[131]

The following imperative petitions aim at the violent end of the enemy: Ps 5:11 הַדִּיחֵמוֹ »cast them out«, Ps 17:13 הַכְרִיעֵהוּ »bring him down«, Ps 54:7 הַצְמִיתֵם »destroy them«, Ps 56:8 הוֹרֵד עַמִּים »cast down the peoples«, Ps 59:12 הוֹרִידֵמוֹ »bring them down«, Ps 59:14 כַּלֵּה *bis* »consume (them)«.[132] The wrath of Yahweh is invoked twice: Ps 69:25 שְׁפָךְ־עֲלֵיהֶם זַעְמֶךָ »pour out your indignation upon them«, Ps (79:6) שְׁפֹךְ חֲמָתְךָ אֶל־הַגּוֹיִם »pour out your wrath over the nations«. Two of the above contexts include an imperative concerning condemnation of the enemy: Ps 5:11 הַאֲשִׁימֵם »make them bear their guilt«, Ps 69:28 תְּנָה־עָוֹן עַל־עֲוֹנָם »add to them guilt upon guilt«.

A number of various imperatives aim at injury to the enemy: Ps 35:1 לְחַם אֶת־לֹחֲמָי »fight against those who fight me« (N.B. the following verses which contain verbs denoting the handling of weapons), Ps (10:15) שְׁבֹר זְרוֹעַ רָשָׁע »break the arm of the wicked«, Ps (58:7) הֲרָס־שִׁנֵּימוֹ בְּפִימוֹ »break the teeth in their mouths« and מַלְתְּעוֹת כְּפִירִים נְתֹץ »tear out the fangs of the young lions«, Ps 59:12 הֲנִיעֵמוֹ »make them totter«, Ps 109:6 הַפְקֵד עָלָיו רָשָׁע »appoint a wicked man against him«. In the problematic case of Ps 55:10 בַּלַּע אֲדֹנָי פַּלַּג לְשׁוֹנָם which in the MT as well as in the Septuagint contains two imperative forms many scholars resort to a conjecture resulting in a text without any petition.[133] Even if the words used are uncommon – in this group of petitions there are no stereotypes – one ought not to exclude the possibility of at least בַּלַּע having originally been meant as a petition, not, however, in the sense of »confuse« but of »destroy«.[134] For further examples of

---

[130] For the second תֵּן לָהֶם the apparatus of BHS suggests: »frt dl«.
[131] Cf. p. 37 above.
[132] For the second כַּלֵּה, see the apparatus of BHS: »l frt כֻּלָּם«.
[133] Gunkel 1926, 236, translates the corrected passage as follows: »vor dem ›verderblichen Sturm‹ ›ihrer Kehle‹, ›dem Sturzbach‹ ihrer Lippen«. Gunkel's judgement over the MT is (*ibid.* 240): »eine solche Bitte ist in diesem Zusammenhange ganz unmöglich«. In the light of all the other violent petitions in the present section, it is difficult to see why. The corrections and rendering of Gunkel are shared by Kissane 1953, I 237, and Kraus 1978, 559–560.
[134] The traditional rendering of the MT, »Confound, O Lord, divide their tongue«, is represented in the commentaries of Oesterley 1939, 284, and Weiser 1963, 282, both

petitions against the enemy, see Ps (9:21), (83:10), (83:12), (83:14), (83:17), 59:6, 140:9 *bis* (the last three cases contain a negated form).

In the close context of imperative petitions, in most cases petitions mentioned above, we can find a few cases of petitions against the enemy in the subjunctive form. In the second person of the subjunctive, we find the following: Ps (10:15) תדרוש »seek out«, Ps (83:16) תרדפם »pursue them« and תבהלם »terrify them«, Ps 143:12 תצמית »destroy« (N.B. the perfect consecutive that follows). Subjunctives of the third person are found in alternation with imperative forms in Ps 69:23,24,25,26 *bis,*28,29 *bis,* 5:11, 7:8–10, 59:12–14, immediately after imperative forms in Ps (58:8–9), 109:6–15. A separate section of curses against the enemy often begins with יבשו »let them be put to shame«: Ps 31:18–19, 35:4–6,26, 40:15–16, 70:3–4, 71:13, (83:18–19). These curse sections frequently reveal even other similarities with each other, subjunctives such as יחפרו »let them be put to disgrace« Ps 35:4,26, 40:15, 70:3, (83:18), יכלמו »let them be put to dishonour« Ps 35:4, 40:15, 70:3, יסגו אחור »let them be turned back« Ps 35:4, 40:15, 70:3, and an opposite wish that the righteous may rejoice Ps 35:27, 40:17, 70:5 (cf. also Ps 5:12). In addition to the passages mentioned, there are cases where it is difficult to decide whether to interpret the verbal forms as subjunctives or indicatives, e.g. Ps 54:7, 140:10–11, 141:10. Negated formulations in the third person occur in Ps (9:20), (19:14), 35:19,24–25, (36:12 *bis*), 69:26,28,29, 109:12,14, (119:122), the cases in Ps 69 and 109 and Ps 35:19, however, without immediate connection with the imperative.

It is obvious on the basis of the discussion so far that the petitions against the enemy in certain respects clearly diverge from the petitions for the benefit of the supplicant. The imperative petitions that directly aim at violent action against the enemy include few petitions that would recur in several psalms. Indeed, most of them seem rather to have been created for each context independently. On the other hand, there are stereotyped wishes against the enemy, i.e. curses in the third person, which form sections of their own separate from the imperative petitions. All in all, wishes in the third person are most frequent precisely in this field of meaning.[135] Gunkel saw the origin of the third person

---

of whom connect this petition with the confusion of tongues in Babel (Gen 11), a hardly appropriate connection. It is not at all probable that the occurrences of בלע should be understood as derived from two or three different roots (Gesenius-Buhl, I בלע »verschlingen«, II בלע »verwirren«; Koehler-Baumgartner[3], I בלע »verschlingen«, II בלע »mitteilen«, III בלע »verwirren«); see Schüpphaus TWAT I, 658–661. With a partial alteration of the vocalization in Ps 55:10 we come to the following suggestion: »destroy, O Lord, the stream (פֶּלַג) of their tongue«, i.e. »their plots«. Dahood 1966–70, II 28, renders the line: »destroy, O Lord, their forked tongue«. Parallels for this usage of בלע may be found e.g. in Ps 21:10 and Lam 2:8.

[135] According to Gunkel-Begrich 1933, 224–225, all the various themes of petitions appear in the third person subjunctive form as well. It should, however, be noted that the wishes against the enemy are far more frequent than other types of wishes and that the latter usually occur singly and in subordination to imperative petitions. On the other hand, the difficulty of distinguishing the subjunctive form causes a great deal of variation in the interpretations of the various scholars. – For the third person curse forms and their oriental parallels, see Schottroff 1969, 156–162.

curses in primitive magical thinking.¹³⁶ It may be that in an earlier phase this was the principal manner of expressing the desire to see the enemy injured and that only later on were direct petitions in the imperative employed for the same purpose as well as being connected with the earlier wishes. It is, first of all, the existence of stereotyped wishes against the enemy without connection with the second person imperative and, secondly, the alternation in a few contexts of imperative petitions and third person curses which are not stereotyped in character which suggest that petitions and wishes against the enemy are not only residual of old thinking habits, but were produced up to the youngest phases found in the Book of Psalms.¹³⁷ Circumstances in the exilic and post-exilic times were naturally a favourable environment for the development of petitions of this kind. It may be added, although this hardly constitutes evidence for or against a particular dating, that petitions against the enemy in most cases occur at the end of longer psalms, seldom in the opening verses, and often give the impression of being loosely connected with the beginning of the psalm.¹³⁸

1.13 *Petitions with Negation*

The second person imperative is negated by אל with the subjunctive. These negated »imperative« petitions cover about 13% of our material and a few of them also recur in several psalms, just like the normal imperatives.

The negated imperative petitions have been treated by scholars separately as *averting petitions*¹³⁹ or as petitions that actually represent *accusation* against God.¹⁴⁰ Neither of the explanations is, however, satisfactory for the whole body of negated petitions in the second person.

---

¹³⁶ Gunkel-Begrich 1933, 228; see also Gunkel 1926, 477.
¹³⁷ As for the alternation between the imperative and the third person subjunctive forms, it does not occur in other types of prayer. As a matter of fact, a passage like Ps 69: 23–29 which contains both imperatives and subjunctives differs only slightly from a passage of third person curses like that in Ps 109:6–15. The former looks like a late and only partially successful attempt to adapt a curse for a prayer. Curiously enough, several of the examples of the imperative petitions in the text above contain the longer and presumably older form of the third person plural suffix, viz. ־מו. According to Gesenius-Kautzsch, 268, however, this form of suffix was used almost exclusively by younger poets and obviously as a deliberate archaism. And finally, it may be noted that the cruel petitions and curses against the enemy did not die out with the close of the canon (cf. e.g. PsSal 12:4).
¹³⁸ Only Ps 35 and (94) begin with the violent petitions.
¹³⁹ See Gerstenberger 1980, 120.
¹⁴⁰ See Westermann 1977, 142.

As examples in which the characterization *averting petition* is appropriate we could include the following:

- אל־תוכיחני and אל־תיסרני both of which occur in Ps 6:2 and 38:2 and aim at avoiding punishment,
- אל־תעלני בחצי ימי Ps 28:3, אל־תמשכני Ps 26:9, אל־תאסף נפשי Ps 102:25 which aim at avoiding untimely death;
- אל־תבישני Ps (119:31), (119:116) (cf. also אל־אבושה in the cohortative in Ps (25:2), (25:20), 31:2, 31:18, 71:1), חרפת נבל אל־תשימני Ps 39:9 which aim at avoiding shame,
- ואל־תבוא במשפט Ps 143:2 which aims at avoiding judgement,
- בל־תניחני לעשקי Ps (119:121) which aims at avoiding oppression.

This not particularly numerous group of petitions consists mainly of cases which occur only once.[141]

The following group of negated petitions may be interpreted as *accusation* against God. Each of these cases could possibly be replaced by a למה question with the verb concerned in the affirmative.[142]

אל־תרחק	»be not far« Ps 22:12,20, 35:22, 38:22, 71:12
אל־תסתר פניך	»do not hide your face« Ps 27:9, 69:18, 102:3, 143:7
אל־תחרש	»be not quiet« Ps 28:1, 35:22, 39:13, (83:2), 109:1
אל־תתעלם	»do not hide yourself« Ps 55:2
אל־תשקט	»be not still« Ps (83:2)
אל־תשכח	»do not forget« Ps (74:19,23)
אל־תעזבני	»do not forsake me« Ps 27:9, 38:2, 71:9,18, (119:8)
אל־תשליכני	»do not cast me off« Ps 51:13, 71:9
אל־תטשני	»do not cast me off« Ps 27:9
אל־תזנח	»do not cast off« Ps (44:24)
אל־תער נפשי	»do not leave me unprotected« Ps 141:8
אל־תאחר	»do not tarry« Ps 40:18, 70:6

Parallel למה questions are actually found for several of these petitions in the psalms: (1) אל־תרחק »be not far« – למה תעמד ברחוק »why do you stand afar off?« Ps (10:1), (2) אל־תסתר פניך »do not hide your

---

[141] Gerstenberger 1980, 120, lists under the title »abwehrende Bitte« various kinds of negated petitions, including the group discussed below in the text. To be precise, all negated petitions do not aim at averting something. The negated form may contain a petition that actually asks for Yahweh's attention or saving action. On the other hand, there are some negated subjunctives of the third person which constitute averting wishes (Ps 9:20, 19:14, 35:24–25, 36:12, 69:16, 119:122). Some of these are also included in Gerstenberger's list.

[142] Cf. Westermann 1977, 152.

face« – למה פניך תסתיר »why do you hide your face?« Ps (44:25), (3) אל־תעזבני »do not forsake me« – למה עזבתני »why have you forsaken me?« Ps 22:2, (4) אל־תזנח »do not cast off« – למה זנחתני »why have you cast me off?« Ps 43:2, cf. Ps (74:1), 88:15, (5) אל־תשכח »do not forget« – למה שכחתני »why have you forgotten me?« Ps (42:10).

On the other hand, these negated petitions could be regarded as variants of some of the more common positive prayer imperatives. אל־תרחק »be not far« and אל־תאחר »do not tarry« correspond to חושה »hasten«, which occurs in the same psalms (except for Ps 35). אל־תסתר פניך »do not hide your face« corresponds to האר פניך »let your face shine«, אל־תחרש »be not quiet« perhaps to ענני »answer to me«. The various cases of »do not forsake« could be thought of as corresponding to »save« in its different formulations. That is, the negated form of a petition need not as such contain any special notion that would class it as a special type of petition. It could perhaps rather be felt as stylistically more effective. In any case, these negated petitions are by no means averting in character.

In addition to the above groups of negated petitions, a few more examples may be given of single occurrences which permit no grouping: אל־תחן »do not spare (the evil-doers)« Ps 59:6, אל־תהרגם »do not slay them« Ps 59:12, אל־תצל מפי דבר־אמת »do not take the word of truth out of my mouth« Ps (119:43), מעשי ידיך אל־תרף »do not forsake the work of your hands« Ps (138:8), אל־תתן מאויי רשע »do not grant the desires of the wicked« Ps 140:9.

1.14 *A Few General Remarks on the Imperative Petitions*

We have now discussed the great majority of occurrences of the imperative petition and its negation in the psalms. The remaining cases not mentioned above – approximately 10% of the whole material and less than 7% of the cases in the individual complaint psalms – occur only once or a few times and are intended for the benefit of the petitioner or his group.

What strikes us in the material discussed is the very general nature of the imperative petitions and the wide distribution of certain basic prayer words. It may be observed that the prayers do not usually ask for any specific gifts or favours.[143] The imperatives »give« and »do« are almost absent. Indeed, »give« תן/תנה occurs six times, but three instances, Ps 28:4 *bis* and 69:28, request punishment for the enemy (cf. p. 43 above), one prays for the king Ps (72:1), and one desires to give glory

---

[143] This observation was also made by Gerstenberger 1980, 120.

to the name of Yahweh Ps (115:1). The only remaining תנה Ps 86:16
asks for strength: תנה־עזך לעבדך. Strange to say, this is a rare prayer in
the OT psalms.

»Do« עשה occurs four times, of which one occurrence Ps (83:10)
requests the destruction of the enemy, Ps 86:17 a sign, and Ps 109:21
and (119:124) something specified as למען שמך »for your name's sake«
and כחסדך »according to your grace«. Of the four occurrences of »set«
שיתה in petitions, three are directed against the enemy Ps (9:21),
(83:12), (83:14), one Ps 141:3 is a more specific petition asking for
שמרה לפי »a guard over my mouth«.

In complaint psalms which often deal with illness one would expect to find frequent occurrences of the petition »heal«. Even this petition is one of the rare ones, with only three instances: רפאני Ps 6:3,
רפאה נפשי Ps 41:5, and רפה שבריה »repair its breaches« Ps (60:4) in an
entirely different context.

As observed in the above discussion of the imperative prayers, petitions corresponding to the various clauses of the priestly blessing could have been expected to appear in the psalms, but only חנני »have mercy upon me« represents this vocabulary with any frequency. We could perhaps continue a little further with this negative definition of the contents of the imperative prayers. There are several situations in life for which one could expect to find a prayer in a collection of prayers representative of OT religion. For instance, in narrative texts we often read about women praying to have a child. Hardly any psalm is appropriate to this situation. Furthermore, famines and natural catastrophes surely occurred in Palestine in OT times. No prayer in the psalms clearly corresponds to these situations. No prayer asks for rain or the growth of crops, although these are seen as gifts of Yahweh.[144] No prayer asks Yahweh to »go with« or to »be with« the petitioner, although these expressions are used to describe communion with Yahweh in other texts (see e.g. Gen 28:15,20, Num 14:9, Gen 26:24, Ps 23:4).

The reasons for the absence of a certain kind of petition may be various. In some cases it may depend on the penetration of the theology of a certain period in other textes, but not in the traditional prayers of the psalms. It may also have to do with the »Sitz-im-Leben« of the prayer psalms or with their transmission. It is obvious that the material we possess in the Book of Psalms is a very limited sample which has survived from the rich traditions of psalms and prayers available to the Israelites during the various periods of their history.[145] It is particularly

---

[144] The Babylonian counterparts, on the other hand, contain prayers which pertain to quite specific situations in life and accurately described states of the body. See Mayer 1976, 210–306.

[145] Cf. Weiser 1963, 68; Culley 1967, 99.

the stereotyped character of the majority of the petitions which seems to suggest that the psalmodic prayer rests on a long tradition from which – whether in the form of established prayer words and a general outline or in the form of already fixed longer units of prayer – it draws its main contents.

As for the form of the petitions, it is interesting to note that more than one third of the cases include the suffix of the first person singular. Of the cases without any object suffix, the ones with the ending ה־ are clearly more frequent than the ordinary forms of the second person masculine of the imperative, whereas the particle נא is quite rare in this connection. One of the petitions frequently occurs in both the longer and the shorter form, viz. שמעה/שמע (see Section 1.4 above), but without any discernible difference in the usage. It is possible that the ending ה־ gives a certain emphasis to the imperative,[146] but it is also possible that it was used for the sake of poetic rhythm, which for the most part is no longer within our reach.

It was observed that the subjunctive of the second person appeared in a few cases in the immediate context of the imperative.[147] This is perhaps a relatively late feature which aims at softening the usually straightforward employment of the imperative. Actual forms of politeness were not found, except for one single occurrence of רצה להצילני »be pleased to deliver me« Ps 40:14.[148] Petitions are not addressed to Yahweh in the third person, and even if the petitioner calls himself עבדך »your servant«, the petition is formulated in the imperative (Ps (19:14), 27:9, 31:17, 86:2, (119:17), (119:122), (119:124), (119:125), (119:176), 143:2).[149] The occasional use of the negated cohortative of the first person (Ps (25:2), (25:20), 31:2, 31:18, 71:1, 69:15) hardly expresses anything other than fearfulness. The use of the third person subjunctive in a few cases forms a natural parallel to the imperative (Ps 88:3, 102:2, 130:2), but in the wishes against the enemy most probably originates in curses (see Section 1.12 above). Thus, it may be concluded

---

[146] Gesenius-Kautzsch 138–139.

[147] In most of the cases there is no distinction between the imperfect and the subjunctive. That the latter term is used here depends on the obvious function of these forms in connection with the imperative. The same applies to the third person of the subjunctive, except that in this case even the context is not always helpful.

[148] The utmost simplicity of most of the petitions is also seen in the fact that the infinitives are found in them most rarely (see Ps 31:3, 71:3 with ל; Ps 4:2, 28:2, 64:2 with ב). My attention was called to this detail by Prof. I. Soisalon-Soininen.

[149] To judge from the examples mentioned, this partial circumlocution also seems to be a late feature. It should also be noted that psalms which use the third person as a blessing form (Ps 20 and 121) address the person who is blessed in the second person singular.

that the imperative is the most characteristic and unambiguous form of petition in the psalms and other forms only appear as petition in subordination to it.[150]

1.15 *Clusters of Imperative Petitions*

So far our analysis of the prayer element in the psalms has been a listing of instances of different prayer imperatives. The material has been collected from the whole Book of Psalms, although with a distinction made between the individual complaint proper and other genres of psalms by parenthesizing the instances in the latter. On the one hand, it was clearly seen that the occurrence of imperative petitions or even certain types of imperative petition is not a determining characteristic of individual complaints. Most of the prayer imperatives with higher frequencies were found to occur in different types of psalms. On the other hand, the prayers that occur outside the group of individual complaints provide material for comparison, which helps in the evaluation of the prayers within this group. Some prayer words were from the beginning obviously equally at home in individual and congregational prayers, but shifting from individual to congregational or from congregational to individual prayers was also possible. Of the latter type of shifting we have a probable example in the imperative petition קומה, originally used in connection with undertakings of the whole people, as Num 10:35 suggests. On the other hand, it was observed that a few frequently recurring petitions, למדני »teach me« and זכר »remember« for instance, do not occur in individual complaints proper, but speak for a relatively late dating. It also seems that the prayer imperatives with single occurrences, i. e. those outside the stereotyped groups, are somewhat more likely to appear in other psalms than the individual complaints.

However, among the psalms commonly regarded as individual complaints a few contain no imperative petition at all, viz. Ps 11, 52, 62, and 63.[151] Since Ps 11, 52, and 62 are for the most part addressed to the enemy – only the last verses Ps 52:11 and 62:13 address God – the genre of these psalms should probably be reconsidered.[152] They are hardly prayer psalms. Ps 63 again is comparable to Ps 23, a psalm of confidence with an address to God but with no explicit petition.[153]

---

[150] Against Gerstenberger 1980, 119–121, who emphasizes the equality in function of all possible grammatical forms as petitions. See also p. 12 note 13 above.

[151] For the interpretation as complaint psalms, see Kraus 1978, 57, and Gerstenberger 1980, 118 note 27. Cf. also Gunkel 1926, 228, 262–263, 266–267.

[152] For Ps 11 and 52, a similar comment is found in Gunkel-Begrich 1933, 212.

[153] There is no reason to follow Gerstenberger 1980, 118 note 27, in including Ps 73, 75, 77, and 121 in the genre of individual complaint. These psalms contain no actual peti-

The next step involves an examination of the contexts of the prayer imperatives, first of all the clustering of several petitions together into one »act« of praying. There are petitions which occur singly, even cases with only one prayer imperative in the whole psalm (Ps 12, 16, 64, 88, 120, 130[154]). On the other hand, clusters of four imperatives are quite common within two or three successive verses (e. g. Ps 6:2–3, 22:20–22, 26:1–2, 51:3–5, 55:2–3). Even successions of 8–9 prayer imperatives are found without any larger element intruding (e. g. Ps 69:17–19, 86:1–6, 119:33–40). As was observed in the above discussion of the various prayer imperatives, certain types of petition repeatedly occur together, as corresponding parts in a pair of parallel lines or half-lines. The clusters of prayer imperatives, however, reveal a great variety of different combinations, so that no fixed rules can be discovered here. But, one may ask whether there are incompatible pairs among the more frequent lexical items. Our observations here are limited to the individual complaint psalms.

The largest group of prayer imperatives, those in the semantic field of »save«, »deliver«, may be found to occur in connection with all other types of petition. In eight cases the cluster includes two or more imperatives of the same group. Connected with the petition »save«, we find the petition for hearing five times, »answer« four times, »have mercy« three times. Although the context of the petition »save«, »deliver« often implies enemies, petitions directed against the enemy usually do not appear in the immediate context (except for Ps 17:13). The petition for hearing again clusters with »answer« on six occasions. The petition »arise« was found to retain something of its original connection with the holy war (cf. Num 10:35) even in individual prayers, in that it clusters with petitions for justice (Ps 7:7–9, 35:1–3, 22–24) and with the specific petitions directed against the enemy (Ps 17:13, 35:1–3, 59: 5–6). On the other hand the immediate context of these petitions does not include the petitions »have mercy« or »answer« and only seldom

---

tion (cf. p. 12 note 13 above), and Ps 73, 75, and 77 are only partly addressed to God, Ps 121 not at all. Kraus 1978, 56–57 (with reference to Seybold and Beyerlin), includes in his genre of individual prayer psalms Ps 23 and 103 which do not contain petitions, but are rather expressions of confidence and thankfulness. This leaves us with the following group of psalms which contain individual prayers in the imperative form: Ps 3–7, 12, 13, 16, 17, 22, 26–28, 30 with a quoted petition, 31, 35, 38–40, 41 with a quoted prayer, 43, 51, 54–57, 59, 61, 64, 69–71, 86, 88, 102, 109, 120, 130, 140–143. These psalms which have the appearance of individual prayer (or include quotation of such) are considered the main object of interest in the present study. The acrostic psalms which contain similar features, viz. Ps 9–10, 25, and 119, are regarded as a separate group.

[154] N.B. the petitions in the third person subjunctive in Ps 88:3 and 130:2 and in the second person subjunctive in Ps 64:2–3.

the petition for hearing. The petition »hasten« again in most of its appearances clusters with negated petitions. All in all, so much variety exists that model prayers for different situations can hardly be built on the basis of these clusters of petitions. If nothing more, the clusterings perhaps reveal something about the connotations of the various prayer words. The two groups of petitions that do not occur in immediate clusters represent, on the one hand, the prayers of a humble and suffering petitioner seeking communion with God, his acceptance and help, and on the other, prayers that invoke direct and powerful action on the part of God against the injustice experienced by the petitioner. Since suffering was generally connected with sin or disfavour before God, the former type of prayer often implies a certain anxiety expressed in repeated pleas for hearing and for mercy and in a few psalms in petitions for forgiveness of sins. The latter type again often includes asseverations of innocence on the part of the supplicant.

Against this background of great variety in the clusterings of various petitions in the psalms, it is rather astonishing to find larger similarities between as many as three psalms, similarities that include the petitions and words closely connected with them. The clustering of prayer phrases into »runs« of several formulas was noted particularly by Culley in his study *Oral Formulaic Language in the Biblical Psalms*.[155] Looking for formulas and formulaic phrases which would speak for an origin in oral composition for the OT psalms, he found that the greatest number of formulas occur exactly in the prayers of individual complaint psalms.[156] His listings naturally give no complete picture of all prayers in the psalms, not even of all the recurring prayer imperatives, since only cases with several words in common are of interest to him. His results, however, provide a framework which we may use in the evaluation of our findings.

The »runs« of imperative prayers which Culley mentions in his work are two:

(1) Ps 38:22–23 אל־תרחק ממני חושה לעזרתי »be not far from me; hasten to my aid«
Ps 22:20 and 71:12 repeat these words with little variation.

(2) Ps 69:18 אל־תסתר פניך (מעבדך כי צר לי) מהר ענני »do not hide your face (from your servant, for I am in distress), make haste to answer me«
Ps 102:3–4 and 143:7 repeat the words outside the brackets within two lines, Ps 102:3 even reads ביום צר־לי »in the day of my distress«.

---

[155] Near and Middle East Series 4, Toronto 1967.
[156] Culley 1967, 102–111. See also Culley's presentation of the techniques of oral poetry among several other peoples (*ibid.* 1–20), which is most elucidating.

In addition to these two »runs«, close resemblance is found between Ps 31:2–4 and 71:1–3 [157] and between Ps 6:2 and 38:2.

A certain amount of formulaic language is also found in the wishes and curses expressed in the third person subjunctive. A remarkable resemblance is found between Ps 40:14–18, 70:2–6, and 35:4, 26–27.[158] Between the former two the similarities include two imperative petitions which frame the subjunctive section, viz. לעזרתי חושה »hasten to my aid« Ps 40:14, 70:2, אל־תאחר »do not tarry« Ps 40:18, 70:6. However, there is no connection between the formulaic language of the imperative prayers and of the third person subjunctive wishes and curses. As far as the verb is concerned, they both use their own vocabulary. Also from this viewpoint the imperative prayers may thus be considered to constitute a whole, a discussion of which does not suffer excessively from the exclusion of the third person material.

After listing the formulas and the »runs« of several formulas which appear in the various parts of the psalms, Culley proceeds by examining the ratio of formulaic language in the psalms. Some individual complaints reach a high score: Ps 142 65%, Ps 143 60%, Ps 54 53%, Ps 40:13–18 50%, Ps 86 49%, Ps 6 48%, Ps 31 40%, Ps 27:7–14 40%, Ps 71 36%.[159] Thus, according to Culley the probability of a background of oral composition most of all pertains to psalms of individual complaint.

To conclude, our discussion of the imperative prayers in the psalms, particularly in the individual complaint psalms, has revealed a large number of stereotyped expressions and conventional language common to most of them. On the other hand, clear recurring clusters or »runs« of prayer imperatives were not found to be very frequent. In a way this is understandable, since it would not have been reasonable to include in the Psalter texts that resemble each other more than the psalms now do.[160] Nevertheless, the conventional vocabulary of prayer – and its limitations – should be given serious consideration as regards its implications for the origin of the genre and the original »Sitz-im-Leben«. There is much to support Culley's thesis of the origin in oral composition where a stock of traditional language could be used rather freely in different combinations according to the needs of the situation. When due recognition is also given to the possibility of literary dependence between various psalms, a better understanding of the genre may perhaps be reached.

---

[157] Culley's interpretation of the similarities between Ps 31:2–4 and 71:1–3 is that they form a »run« of several phrases (*ibid.* 93). However, one could perhaps consider here also the possibility of literary dependence or dependence on an already fixed oral psalm.

[158] Cf. also Ps 71:12–13.

[159] Culley 1967, 103. Of the thanksgivings and hymns only Ps 9:2–15 (42%), Ps 96 (65%), Ps 98 (50%), and Ps 97 (42%) reach the same level.

[160] Thus, the economy of the collection of psalms may be thought to have worked towards a decrease in the material Culley is dealing with. Cf. Culley 1967, 99.

2. Formal Analysis of Elements Connected with the Petition

Having discussed the verbal part of the petition, the various prayer imperatives and their distribution in the psalms, we now continue by analyzing the elements which appear in connection with this essential constituent. It is the aim of this analysis to elucidate the structure of individual complaint psalms, in particular the role the imperative prayer plays in it. The discussion concerns all expressions in the immediate context of the prayer imperatives or clusters of such, in order to define which elements along with the petitions are most constitutive for the composition of the prayer sections and to discover possible patterns behind the individual cases. At this stage we regard the cluster of prayer imperatives as the unit we must focus on, although single imperatives have to be taken into consideration in some cases. The discussion concerns the 42 psalms which were found to contain individual complaint prayers – or more precisely the 84 clusters of individual prayer in them – although psalms outside this group occasionally appear in the discussion for the sake of comparison.

2.1 *Address of the Petition*

The vast majority of prayer imperatives or clusters of such are immediately connected with the address to God. The usual address is the Divine Name in one form or another, but epithets are also used. As regards the variation between יהוה and אלהים, it has been pointed out that one part of the Psalter, the so-called »Elohistic Psalter« (Ps 42–83) tends to employ the latter. For our purposes, it suffices simply to note this fact.

The most frequently occuring address connected with the imperative prayer is יהוה with 57 occurrences in prayers of individual complaint psalms.[161] It is even found several times within one cluster of prayer imperatives (e.g. Ps 6:2–3, 40:14). The address is introduced by ואתה at Ps 22:20, 41:11, 59:6, 109:21, and other appellatives or epithets are added as follows: יהוה אלהי »Yahweh, my God« Ps 7:2, 13:4, 35:24, 109:26; ואתה יהוה אדני »but you, Yahweh my Lord« Ps 109:21;

---

[161] In other genres we find 9 additional cases connected with prayers.

יהוה אלהי ישועתי »Yahweh, God of my salvation« Ps 88:2; ואתה יהוה (-אלהים) צבאות (אלהי ישראל) »and you, Yahweh (God) Sabaoth (God of Israel)« Ps 59:6.¹⁶² Of the longer addresses Ps 7:2 and 88:2 are separated from the first imperative by a few words.

The address אלהים appears 20 times in connection with imperative prayers, all occurrences but one – as could be expected – in the Elohistic Psalter.¹⁶³ Gunkel, as well as some other commentators, changes all of these cases of אלהים back to יהוה.¹⁶⁴ Combinations with אלהי occur as follows: אלהי צדקי »God of my right« Ps 4:2, אלהי ישעי »God of my salvation« Ps 27:9, אלהי תהלתי »God of my praise« Ps 109:1, אלהי תשועתי »God of my salvation« Ps 51:16. Most scholars, however, omit the last-mentioned *metri causa*.¹⁶⁵ »My God« אלהי is found – in addition to the above-mentioned cases of יהוה אלהי – at Ps 3:8, 5:3 (מלכי ואלהי »my King and my God«), 35:23 אלהי ואדני »my God and my Lord«),¹⁶⁶ 38:22, 40:18, 59:2, 71:4,12. Unlike the single »Elohistic« אלהים, the combined forms do not usually replace יהוה, but appear parallel to it or otherwise in close context to it.

»My Lord« אדני is connected with the imperative prayer in the MT at Ps 35:17,22,23 (see above), 55:10, 130:2, 86:3, of which, however, all but the first and the last are uncertain.¹⁶⁷

The short form אל occurs at Ps 16:1 and 17:6, and אלי »my God« should perhaps be read at Ps 7:7 (cf. LXX κύριε ὁ θεός μου)¹⁶⁸ and 102:25.¹⁶⁹

Other epithets are not very frequently used in connection with the imperative prayers in individual complaint psalms. We find once in the MT מגננו אדני »O Lord, our shield« at Ps 59:12, which, however, does

---

¹⁶² In Ps 59:6 only ואתה יהוה צבאות should be considered original; see Gunkel 1926, 254; Kraus 1978, 580. In Ps 35:24 Gunkel (1926, 150) omits אלהי *metri causa;* in Ps 109:21 he (*ibid.* 480) suggests one should read the imperative ראני instead of אדני.

¹⁶³ The extraordinary combination אלהים צבאות which occurs in the MT at Ps 59:6 (cf. above note 162), 80:5,8,15,20, and 84:9 must be seen as a result of the Elohistic redaction; see e.g. Gunkel 1926, 254. For the Elohistic Psalter, see Kraus 1978, 10–11. Cf. Delekat 1967, 343–380, according to whose curious explanation the older tradition often contained בעל or בעלי in place of the present אלהים as well as יהוה.

¹⁶⁴ Gunkel 1926, see e.g. Ps 43:1, 51:3,12,16, 54:3,4, 56:2,8, but also 5:11, the only case outside the Elohistic Psalter. See also Kraus 1978 *l. c.*

¹⁶⁵ See Gunkel 1926, 227; Kraus 1978, 540. In addition to the cases mentioned above, we find in other genres יהוה אלהינו Ps 106:47; אלהי ישענו Ps 79:9, 85:5; אלהי יעקב Ps 84:9.

¹⁶⁶ Gunkel (1926, 150) omits ואדני.

¹⁶⁷ Gunkel (following some other scholars) omits אדני at Ps 35:22 and 23 (1926, 150) and reads Ps 55:10 in a completely different way (*ibid.* 240).

¹⁶⁸ Gunkel 1926, 26, and Weiser 1963, 90, are for the vocalization of אלי as »my God« rather than as a preposition. Kraus 1978, 191, is against it.

¹⁶⁹ Gunkel 1926, 440, however, reads a preposition here.

not fit the verse particularly well.¹⁷⁰ At Ps 18:1 the Divine Name is replaced by צורי »my rock«, at Ps 22:20 by אילותי, a *hapax,* perhaps interpretable as »my help« or »my strength«,¹⁷¹ at Ps 38:23 by אדני תשועתי »my Lord, my salvation«. The only participial epithet in individual complaint prayers is found at Ps 17:7 מושיע חוסים »saviour of those who seek refuge«.¹⁷²

The address to God in connection with imperative prayers – in most cases following the imperative – is found to appear with great regularity. Of the 82 clusters of prayer imperatives in the 42 psalms containing prayers of the individual petitioner, only seven do not contain any address in their immediate context (Ps 22:12, 26:9–11,¹⁷³ 28:9, 39:9–11, 69:25, 71:9, 109:6).

The address in connection with the prayer imperatives has a most important function. In general, the address – along with the use of the second person verbal forms and suffixes – is an essential part of the prayer. The petitioner has to utter the name of the God he is expecting to acquire help from. This is obviously the reason for the great consistency with which the address, and particularly the name יהוה, is used.¹⁷⁴ Since the name יהוה also appears in the close context of most of the epithets mentioned above and since the use of אלהים in the MT obviously depends on the work of a redactor, it seems that the address יהוה was an indispensable part of every prayer included in individual complaint psalms, particularly in the pre-exilic situation. Even more important this was in a polytheistic environment, with other gods threatening the position of Yahweh. The use of the name of Yahweh in the petition was in a way a confession of faith and a guarantee of the help to come.¹⁷⁵

Furthermore, it seems to be a remarkable characteristic of the petitions in the OT psalms that the address to God is by means of the single Divine Name יהוה. As few as the cases with a longer address or an epithet are in the MT, the omissions *metri causa* suggested by commentators make them even fewer. There seems to be no reason to speak

---

¹⁷⁰ Gunkel 1926, 255, suggests מנעמו, an imperative form, instead of מגננו. See also Kraus 1978, 580.

¹⁷¹ See Gesenius-Buhl 29–30 (connected with איל Ps 88:5; »Hilfe«); Koehler-Baumgartner³ 39 (»Kraft [al. Hilfe]«); Gunkel 1926, 89, »Hilfe«; Weiser 1963, 147, and Kraus 1978, 322, both »Stärke«.

¹⁷² See, however, Gunkel's conjecture (1926, 57): הושע חסה־בך, which also appears in BHS. A few more epithets in connection with imperative prayers are found in congregational psalms Ps 80:2, 84:10 (cf. Gunkel 1926, 372), 94:1, 2.

¹⁷³ Gunkel 1926, 112, adds יהוה here.

¹⁷⁴ Gerstenberger 1980, 37–38, observed a difference between ordinary everyday requests and prayers: the former rarely include the address. See also Wevers *VT* VI (1956), 80–87.

¹⁷⁵ See Wevers *VT* VI (1956), 84–87.

of hymnic elements in this connection.¹⁷⁶ It is worth noticing that nothing comparable to e.g. such epithets as »Creator« or »maker of heaven and earth« occurs in this connection. Gerstenberger seems to regard all the addresses connected with prayers which exceed the single יהוה or אלהים – be it with a suffix or a noun – and the metaphorical addresses as hymnic elements in the complaint psalms.¹⁷⁷ However, I find it difficult to see anything hymnic – not even »in weitestem Sinn« – in the few short epithets used in the prayers in question. Even for מושיע חוסים 17:7 – if it should be considered original – it seems to be exaggerated.¹⁷⁸

Accordingly, Begrich seems to be right in emphasizing in this connection the great discrepancy between Babylonian and Israelite prayers.¹⁷⁹ It is most typical of the former that they line up a long list of epithets as well as laudatory attributes and relative clauses before expressing the plea to the deity. Begrich interprets such an introduction in a prayer as flattery, the sole purpose of which is to persuade the deity to grant what is prayed for. The fact that this type of *captatio benevolentiae* is totally absent in the individual complaint psalms of the OT is significant from the theological point of view. Begrich sees a connection between this absence and the expressions of confidence in Yahweh, frequently found in the OT psalms, but hardly paralleled in the Babylonian counterparts: the Israelite had no need to persuade his God through flattery, but could trust in him that he cared.¹⁸⁰

Begrich's interpretation of the theology behind the two different ways of addressing the deity should not be taken as a desperate attempt to save something unique in the OT psalms.¹⁸¹ Indeed, it seems characteristic of the OT religion in its earliest form that the experience of Yahweh – or the God of the fathers – was as a merciful God and very close to those who worshiped him.¹⁸² The lack of epithets in prayers to Yahweh should be seen in this context. For further support, one may perhaps refer to the explanation of the name of Yahweh in Ex 3:14. Whether or not it is possible to derive יהוה from the root היה,¹⁸³ this un-

---

¹⁷⁶ Against Gerstenberger 1980, 128. The above view is also held by Gunkel-Begrich 1933, 213.
¹⁷⁷ Gerstenberger *ibid.*
¹⁷⁸ Crüsemann 1969, 125, even denies the hymnic character of larger epithets containing participles when they occur outside the pattern of the participial hymn.
¹⁷⁹ Begrich *ZAW* 46 (1928), 221–260 (= *Gesammelte Studien,* ThB 21, 168–216).
¹⁸⁰ Begrich *ZAW* 46 (1928), particularly 235, 250–251.
¹⁸¹ For this kind of criticism, see Gerstenberger 1980, 5 note 6.
¹⁸² See Alt 1929, 67–71; Müller 1980, 114–126.
¹⁸³ For this discussion, see e.g. v. Rad 1966, I 20–21; Rose 1978, 30–34; Bartelmus 1982, 226–235; Freedman-O'Connor TWAT III, 533–554. Only the last-mentioned article is for the derivation of יהוה from היה.

doubtedly early source[184] does not offer a description of Yahweh through epithets or other names, but rather seems to exclude any such description by the enigmatic words אהיה אשר אהיה.[185] If the absence or scarcity of epithets may be held to be an original feature of Yahweh worship, this means that the prayers of individual complaint in the OT had their own development in isolation from the Babylonian counterparts, although they certainly originate in a common background.

In contrast to the individual complaint psalms, certain other prayer texts are found to contain rich epithets and hymnic introductions: congregational complaints Ps 80, 89, 90; Jer 17:12–18; the prose prayers II Chr 20:6–12, Neh 1:5–11, 9:5–37, Dan 9:4–19; in the Greek OT the prayer of Mordecai Esth C 2–10, the prayer of Azariah Ode 7 (Dan 3: 26–45), the prayer of Manasseh Ode 12, III Macc 6:2–15. Since the longer type of address obviously becomes more frequent in later texts, it seems more likely that the use of the simple form of address – without epithets or with only a short one expressing a confession of faith rather than praise – was characteristic of early Israelite prayers.[186] It does not make sense to postulate (1) early and direct influence on Israelite complaint psalms by the Babylonian prayers, (2) omission of the large hymnic address, and (3) introduction of the same later. Crüsemann's hypothesis of the king's complaint as a combination of hymn and complaint – a kind of missing link – does not convince, either,[187] since it leaves us with the difficult question of why then only the king and not other petitioners would have used the hymnic introduction.[188]

---

[184] Most scholars consider Ex 3:14 to belong to the Elohistic source; see Eissfeldt 1922, l.c. Rose 1978, 34–39, however, connects it with the time of Josiah and with Deuteronomistic theology, a hardly tenable thesis. Compared with e.g. Ex 34, which Perlitt 1969, 203–216, has shown to be Deuteronomistic, Ex 3:14 clearly reveals no characteristics of Deuteronomistic theology. Bartelmus 1982, 235, is also against the late dating.

[185] For a non-etymological explanation of these words, see Bartelmus 1982, 226–235, particularly 228–229. v. Rad 1966, I 186–187, also stresses the existence of only one name for the God of Israel. That Yahweh in the surrounding verses is identified as the God of the fathers should not be taken as another name or as an actual epithet: it results from the attachment of the patriarch traditions by E to the Exodus and Moses traditions; see Alt 1929, 10–14.

[186] According to Westermann 1977, 157, praise in the introduction of a petition is definitely a late feature. As for the long introduction in Jacob's prayer Gen 32:10–13, Westermann 1981, 614–623, regards it as a later expansion to the originally short petition found in J. A few other scholars wish to attribute the whole prayer to the Deuteronomistic redaction of the Pentateuch; see Smend 1981, 65. Cf. the discussion below pp. 89–90.

[187] Crüsemann 1969, 291–292.

[188] Begrich ZAW 46 (1928), 247–248, observed quite the opposite within the Babylonian

On the other hand, the need to appeal to Yahweh's mercy and to remind him of his earlier great deeds before expressing a petition to him could possibly spring from the catastrophe of the Exile, from the experience of being totally forsaken by Yahweh. Although the Babylonian prayers are much older, it is possible that direct influence from them was felt only in this later situation.

2.2 Expressions in the Immediate Context of the Petition

2.2.1 The Question of »Motivations for Divine Intervention«

One of the most puzzling terms inherited from Gunkel is »Beweggründe des göttlichen Einschreitens« – »motivations for divine intervention«. It appears obviously for the first time as a set term[189] in Gunkel's commentary and then in the *Einleitung,* in the discussion of congregational complaints which dates from Gunkel himself as well as in that of individual complaints, mainly written by Begrich.[190] Ever since, it has been repeated wherever formal analysis of the psalms is conducted, although hardly anyone knows exactly what expressions are meant and what their actual significance is.[191] Admittedly, there is a certain amount of vagueness and inconsistency already in the *Einleitung* in that the »motivations« presented in the discussion of the individual complaint psalms hardly correspond to those found in the congregational complaints. It is particularly in the case of the individual psalms that the term becomes problematic.

The »motivations for divine intervention« appear according to Gunkel and Begrich in close connection with the petition of a complaint psalm and aim at emphasizing the plea by thoughts which particularly appeal to Yahweh. In congregational complaints Gunkel found reference to Yahweh's honour before the nations, his mercy in the past, the covenant, and to confidence in Yahweh as the only one able to help and also to confession of sins on the part of the people.[192] As for indi-

---

prayers: in the king's prayers he found shorter introductions and clearer expressions of confidence in the deity.

[189] In his *Ausgewählte Psalmen* Gunkel uses the same words but in a freer formulation when commenting on Ps 79:9–10 (1917, 107). On the other hand, he uses quite a different description of the same »motivations« in RGG² IV, 1625. The word »Beweggrund«, however, was used in the same context e.g. by de Wette 1856, 432 (Ps 79:10).

[190] Gunkel 1926, e.g. 22 (Ps 6:6); Gunkel-Begrich 1933, 130–132, 231–239. Both of these works employ quotation marks: »Beweggründe göttlichen Einschreitens«.

[191] Gerstenberger 1977, 201, advises abandoning the whole category. Kraus 1978, 51, however, lists it among the elements of the prayer psalms.

[192] Gunkel-Begrich 1933, 130–132.

vidual complaints, Begrich's »motivations« are prepositional phrases, which refer to Yahweh's mercy or righteousness, and clauses – often introduced by כי – which contain expressions of confidence, asseveration of innocence, or confession of sins.[193] Begrich gives particular emphasis to the expressions of confidence – which is quite understandable[194] – but on the other hand he seems to be very generous in including different expressions under the title »motivations for divine intervention«. In fact, an interpretation too broad may render the employment of a special term meaningless. This is obviously the cause of difficulty in the case of the »motivations for divine intervention«.

The following analysis is among other things a search for »motivations for divine intervention« in Gunkel's sense. For this not particularly simple task we need criteria as to which expressions may be characterized as such. The fact is that it is the deepest purpose of a prayer to bring about a »divine intervention«. Its background – as far as the complaint psalms are concerned – is an emergency situation and its aim to obtain help.[195] From this point of view the whole prayer psalm may be considered to be »motivation for divine intervention«, even the petition and certainly also the description of the misery of the petitioner. As for the expressions of confidence, it could indeed be maintained that the whole act of praying is based on confidence in God, being a manifestation of it. Why should one particular clause which contains such an expression be singled out as a special »motivation«? Thus, we must not accept just any expression of the semantic fields concerned as such a »motivation«. Firstly, we concentrate on expressions in the immediate context of the petition. Secondly, the »motivations« may be expected to give emphasis to the petition. And thirdly, to be indisputable the »motivations« should be syntactically connected with the petition. These criteria must be borne in mind in the following evaluation of the various expressions in the immediate context of the petition. As for expressions which do not justify the title »motivation for divine intervention«, it is our task to analyze, if possible, their function within the prayer as well.

2.2.2 Prepositional Phrases

The first group of expressions that draws our attention in the immediate context of petitions in individual complaint psalms consists of prepositional phrases which include divine attributes, such as חסד, צדקה, אמת, and a few others. They appear almost without exception in connection with petitions and obviously therefore have been characterized

---

[193] *Ibid.* 231–239.
[194] Cf. Begrich *ZAW* 46 (1928), 221–260.
[195] This is emphasized by Gerstenberger 1980, 60, 157–158; Fuchs 1982, 296.

as »motivations for divine intervention« by some scholars.¹⁹⁶ The expressions in question and their occurrences are as follows:¹⁹⁷

בצדקתך	5:9, 31:2, 71:2, 143:1, 143:11 (cf. also 119:40)
כצדקך	35:24 (cf. כצדקי 7:9)
בחסדך	31:17, 143:12
כחסדך	51:3, 109:26 (cf. also 25:7, 119:88, 119:124, 119:149, 119:159)
למען חסדך	6:5 (cf. also 44:27)
ברב־חסדך	69:14
כרב־רחמיך	51:3, 69:17
באמתך	54:7 (cf. also 25:5)
באמנתך	143:1
באמת ישעך	69:14
בשמך	54:3 (cf. על־דבר כבוד־שמך 79:9)
למען שמך	109:21, 143:11 (cf. also 25:11, 79:9)
בגבורתך	54:3
ברצונך	51:20 (cf. also 106:4)

Compared with the great consistency in the use of traditional prayer language, as described above, the frequency of several of the imperatives, and the regular use of the Divine Name, the above collection of prepositional phrases is not particularly impressive: some twenty cases distributed among ten psalms. Obviously, these expressions are not as frequent as is generally thought. Even with the indicative they show no greater frequency: ברב־חסדך Ps 5:8, למען שמו 23:3, 106:8, למען שמך 31:4, ברצונך 30:8, 89:18. On the other hand, the nouns in question occur far more frequently as objects and subjects, or with the preposition ב as objects of praise and trust. The fact that Ps 119 uses כחסדך has often as four times and בצדקתך once as well as introducing other expressions comparable to these – כדברך 119:25,28,107,169, כמשפטך 119:58,116,170, באמרתך 119:133, לאמרתך 119:154, כאמרתך 119:149,156 – may have wrongly led to the belief that expressions of this type would appear in other psalms equally frequently.¹⁹⁸

As for the interpretation of the above prepositional phrases, it is our task to test their function in the clause and in relation to the main verb: may they justifiably be regarded as »motivations« which

---

¹⁹⁶ Gunkel-Begrich 1933, 232; Kraus 1978, 51. Gunkel's commentary, however, does not use the term »Beweggründe göttlichen Einschreitens« of the phrases in question (Gunkel 1926 *l.c.*).
¹⁹⁷ Occurrences outside the actual genre of individual complaint psalms are given in parentheses. The verbal form of the petition is the second person subjunctive in Ps 143: 11 *bis*, 12, 54:3 2°, 71:2 (25:11 the perfect consecutive).
¹⁹⁸ All of the cases mentioned in Ps 119 occur in connection with prayer imperatives. In another type of connection we find כאמרתך at 119:41 and כדברך at 119:65.

strengthen the plea, or are at least some of them only adverbial phrases serving as modal or instrumental completion to the verb in the imperative? In this connection we need to pay attention to the meaning of the divine attribute in question as well as of the main verb.

Ps 35:24 שפטני כצדקך is the clearest example of a case where it is possible to understand the prepositional phrase as qualifying the action. Both words belong to juridical vocabulary and may be rendered together: »vindicate me according to your justice«.

Ps 5:9 נחני בצדקתך is paralleled by הושר לפני דרכך »make your way straight before me«, which suggests the interpretation »lead me in your righteous will«, i. e. »to live according to your justice«.¹⁹⁹ This rendering excludes the interpretation as a »motivation for divine intervention«.

In the two cases of Ps 51:3 חנני אלהים כחסדך כרב רחמיך מחה פשעי there seems to be a logical connection between the prepositional phrases and the prayer imperatives; what is prayed for is action in accordance with חסד and רחמים attributed to Yahweh: »Have mercy on me, O God, according to your steadfast love; according to your abundant mercy blot out my transgressions«. Whether this appeal to חסד and רחמים may be interpreted as a »motivation«, is difficult to decide.

In four cases the main verb is found to be הושיע: Ps 6:5 הושיעני, Ps 54:3 הושיעני כחסדך, Ps 109:26 הושיעני בחסדך, Ps 31:17 למען חסדך, אלהים בשמך הושיעני. The first three cases appeal to Yahweh's loving kindness as the source of his saving action, although the different prepositions create different shades of meaning: »save me for the sake of/by/according to your grace«.²⁰⁰ As for the fourth example, בשמך could possibly be understood as instrumental »by your name«, just as the parallel בגבורתך »by your strength«. In three further petitions with similar verbs, we find an appeal to Yahweh's צדקה: Ps 31:2 בצדקתך פלטני »in your righteousness deliver me«, Ps 71:2 בצדקתך תצילני ותפלטני »in your righteousness deliver me and rescue me«,²⁰¹ Ps 143:11 בצדקתך תוציא מצרה נפשי »in your righteousness bring me out of trouble«.²⁰¹

In two cases the petition ענני is surrounded by two prepositional phrases: Ps 69:14 אלהים ברב־חסדך ענני באמת ישעך »O God, in the abundance of your steadfast love answer me, with your faithful help«, Ps 143:1 באמנתך ענני בצדקתך »in your faithfulness answer me, in your

---

¹⁹⁹ For צדקה, see v. Rad 1966, I 382–390. Gunkel-Begrich 1933, 232, include the above case Ps 5:9 in »motivations for divine intervention«; on the other hand, Gunkel's commentary (1926, 19) as well as another paragraph of the *Einleitung* (Gunkel-Begrich 1933, 224 note 3) represent the interpretation given above. So does Weiser 1963, 86. Beyerlin 1970, 91–92, again, is opposed to it. Cf. also the elusive comments of Kraus 1978, 179.

²⁰⁰ For חסד, see v. Rad 1966, I 390–395; Zimmerli ThWNT IX, 372–377.

²⁰¹ N.B. the use of subjunctive instead of the imperative. See p. 49 above.

righteousness«. It is hardly possible to interpret any one of these four expressions as an object to ענה or as an instrumental adverb.[202] Neither is it possible to read any one of them as part of the preceding or the following clause.[203] The purpose of the double employment of prepositional phrases may have been to fill in the metre. In any case, the prepositional phrases seem to be flexible in use and vague enough to fit different contexts. In the most extreme cases we find an appeal to Yahweh's חסד and אמת in connection with petitions directed against the enemy: Ps 143:12 ובחסדך תצמית איבי »and in your steadfast love cut off my enemies«,[204] Ps 54:7 באמתך הצמיתם »in your faithfulness put an end to them«. Gunkel suggests as an emendation for both cases either בחמתך or בחרונך (»in your wrath«), because חסד and אמת seem impossible to him in connection with הצמית.[205] There are, however, few parallel cases to support the conjecture (cf. Ps 56:8 באף, 59:14 בחמה).

Of the remaining cases Ps 51:20 היטיבה ברצונך את־ציון appeals to Yahweh's favour, which merely adds emphasis to the plea »do good«. In Ps 69:17 כרב רחמיך פנה אלי again the plea »turn to me« is in itself neutral, but gains a definitely positive sense through the prepositional phrase. In two cases we find an appeal to the name of Yahweh: Ps 143:11 למען־שמך יהוה תחיני,[206] Ps 109:21 עשה־אתי למען שמך. Of all the prepositional phrases discussed above, למען שמך seems best to deserve the title of a »motivation for divine intervention«: it is a causal expression and appeals to Yahweh's honour, not to his qualities as a merciful God who can help the petitioner. As for the latter case Ps 109:21, the appearance of עשה without an object renders the interpretation of the verse difficult. In connection with verse 27 עשה could be understood as referring to the implementation of the curse in verses 6–20. The Septuagint reads ἔλεος here; on the other hand, however, it is difficult to explain why the object would have been omitted if it had belonged to the original text.

In most of the cases discussed above, it is impossible to define the exact function of the prepositional phrase in the clause. In a few examples it was possible to interpret it as an adverbial completion of the verb. In others we are obviously concerned with theological expressions which appeal to Yahweh's saving qualities and thus aim at strengthening the prayer. In so far as the adverbial interpretation is not possible, we may speak of »motivations for divine intervention«.

---

[202] Cf. Gunkel 1926, 294, who renders באמת ישעך in Ps 69:14 by »mit deiner treuen Hilfe«.
[203] Cf. LXX Ps 68:14, 142:1, where at least the editor connects the first prepositional phrase with the preceding clause.
[204] See note 201 above.
[205] Gunkel 1926, 236, 604.
[206] See note 201 above.

Having now discussed the prepositional phrases in their respective contexts, we return to their circulation in the psalms. More significant than their occurrence with this or that plea is obviously their accumulation in certain psalms. Many of these have generally been dated to a late period, particularly Ps 51, 69, and 143.[207] Bearing in mind that Ps 119 also contains numerous instances of the phrases in question, we may conclude that the prepositional phrases appealing to Yahweh's »grace«, »righteousness«, »name«, etc. were perhaps particularly favoured in post-exilic times and belong to the increasing theological reflection of that time.[208]

Even less frequent than the expressions discussed above are the prepositional phrases mentioning the enemy (»because of my enemies«):

למען שררי 5:9, 27:11
למען איבי 69:19

N. B. the similar context of the two cases in Ps 5:9 and 27:11.

When Gunkel-Begrich explicitly cite the two verses Ps 5:9 and 27:11 as examples of »motivations for divine intervention« with reference to the enemy,[209] the reader is tempted to believe that such expressions would be more frequent. The enemies do occur in the prayers frequently, but the prepositional phrases with מן after verbs denoting »to deliver« have no relevance here. As a »motivation for divine intervention«, »because of my enemies« expresses in short the thought contained in Ps 13:5: »lest my enemy say ›I have prevailed over him‹; lest my foes rejoice because I am shaken«.

To conclude, the above survey has shown that prepositional phrases used as »motivations for divine intervention« in the immediate context of petitions are fairly infrequent and thus cannot be regarded as an essential element of the imperative prayer.

2.2.3 Clauses in the Immediate Context of the Petitions

2.2.3.1 Coordinate Clauses Introduced by ו

On six occasions we find a coordinate clause immediately following the petition in individual complaint psalms. In connection with the imperative a coordinate clause may have various functions, the interpretation of which depends on the verbal forms of the clause on the one hand and on the contents of the two clauses on the other. In the usual

---

[207] For the datings, see e.g. Kraus 1978, 541, 642, 1116.
[208] Examples comparable to those in the psalms are found e.g. in Dan 9:16–19.
[209] Gunkel-Begrich 1933, 232.

case a coordinate clause following the imperative receives a final or a consecutive nuance.²¹⁰ In two cases, Ps 39:14 and 41:11, the final interpretation is clearly the most appropriate.²¹¹

Ps 39:14 השע ממני ואבליגה במרם אלך ואינני
Ps 41:11 ואתה יהוה חנני והקימני ואשלמה להם

The wish included in the coordinate clauses in these two cases is strengthened by the use of the cohortative verbal form.

In two further cases, Ps 86:17 and 109:26–27, both interpretations, the final as well as the consecutive, are possible.

Ps 86:17 עשה־עמי אות לטובה
ויראו שנאי ויבשו כי־אתה יהוה עזרתני ונחמתני
Ps 109:26–27 עזרני יהוה אלהי הושיעני כחסדך
וידעו כי־ידך זאת אתה יהוה עשיתה

The contents, however, seem to speak more for the consecutive interpretation: »so that those who hate me shall see«, »so that they shall know«. As for the forms ויראו and וידעו, the third person plural makes no distinction between the indicative and the subjunctive. The Septuagint, however, renders both cases by the Greek imperative.²¹²

On one occasion the coordinate clause in question takes the function of an object clause, the main verb being ראה.

Ps 142:5 הבים ימין וראה ואין־לי מכיר
אבד מנוס ממני אין דורש לנפשי

The object clause and what follows it may be characterized here as complaint.

Ps 143:7 אל־תסתר פניך ממני ונמשלתי עם־ירדי בור

The coordinate clause exceptionally opens with the perfect consecutive, which is sometimes used after a strong negation to express an undesired consequence (»lest«).²¹³ Here the connection with the negated petition, however, seems somewhat constrained. In Ps 28:1 the same clause appears in connection with פן and seems more appropriate there.

Ps 28:1 פן־תחשה ממני ונמשלתי עם־ירדי בור

The occurrence in Ps 143:7 may obviously be regarded as an imitation of an older psalm.²¹⁴ In fact, Ps 143 contains numerous examples of phrases and clauses which likewise appear in other psalms.²¹⁵

---

²¹⁰ For corresponding cases in the Pentateuch, see Aejmelaeus 1982, 15–19.
²¹¹ Cf. LXX Ps 38:14 ἵνα ἀναψύξω.
²¹² For similar renderings in the Pentateuch, see Aejmelaeus 1982, 20.
²¹³ See Aejmelaeus 1982, 17.   ²¹⁴ Gunkel 1926, 603.
²¹⁵ For the composition of this psalm, see pp. 104–105 below.

As regards »motivations for divine intervention«, coordination is usually not the proper form for such expressions. Only once, outside the individual complaint psalms, in Ps 60:13 (and its parallel 108:13) do we find a coordinate clause expressing a motivation after a petition: הבה־לנו עזרת מצר ושוא תשועת אדם.[216]

2.2.3.2 Relative Clauses

In a few cases the petition or cluster of petitions is followed by a relative clause introduced either by אשר or by זו. The contents of these relative clauses consist in all four cases of descriptions of the unjust.

Ps 64:2–4   שמע־אלהים קולי בשיחי   מפחד אויב תצר חיי
　　　　　　　תסתירני מסוד מרעים   מרגשת פעלי און
　　　　　　　אשר שננו כחרב לשונם   דרכו חצם דבר מר

The description of the treachery of the unjust continues for a further three verses (vv. 5–7), after which the psalm closes with an expression of the assuredness of Yahweh's punishment on them and of the joy of the righteous (vv. 8–11). The whole psalm thus discusses the problem caused by the enemy.

Ps 140:2–3,5   חלצני יהוה מאדם רע   מאיש חמסים תנצרני
　　　　　　　　אשר חשבו רעות בלב   כל־יום יגורו מלחמות
　　　　　　　　− − −
　　　　　　　　שמרני יהוה מידי רשע   מאיש חמסים תנצרני
　　　　　　　　אשר חשבו לדחות פעמי

In this case, the petitions and the description of the enemy introduced by אשר are repeated in two evenly formed strophes (also vv. 4 and 6 belong to the description), which fill the first half of the psalm. After the second section which consists of further petitions and curses even this psalm closes with expressions of confidence in Yahweh, resembling thus Ps 64 in the subject matter.

Ps 26:9–10   אל־תאסף עם־חטאים נפשי   ועם־אנשי דמים חיי
　　　　　　　 אשר־בידיהם זמה   וימינם מלאה שחד

These lines are part of the prayer of an innocent supplicant. Consequently, it is not so much a question of the enemy but of the unjust with whom the supplicant does not want to associate.

Ps 17:8–9   שמרני כאישון בת־עין   בצל כנפיך תסתירני
　　　　　　 מפני רשעים זו שדוני   איבי בנפש יקיפו עלי

---

[216] See Gunkel 1926, 258.

The description of the enemy continues in the next three verses (vv. 10–12), constituting together with the preceding petitions (vv. 6–8) the middle section in the prayer of one unjustly oppressed.

In all of the above cases, except Ps 26:9–10, the relative clause may be said to open up a larger section of the psalm which could be characterized as complaint. The relative pronoun thus functions as a link between the petitions and the complaint regarding the enemy.

2.2.3.3 Final Clauses Introduced by פן

Final subordination introduced by the negative conjunction פן appears in the immediate context of the petition in individual complaint psalms at Ps 7:3, 13:4–5 *bis*, 28:1, 59:12.[217] In this connection, the פן clause expresses the aim of the petition by stating the unwished-for consequences, if the prayer should not be heard. The three cases

Ps 7:2–3   הושיעני מכל־רדפי והצילני
           פן־יטרף כאריה נפשי פרק ואין מציל

Ps 13:4–5 הביטה ענני יהוה אלהי
           האירה עיני פן־אישן המות
           פן־יאמר איבי יכלתיו
           צרי יגילו כי אמוט

Ps 28:1   אליך יהוה אקרא צורי אל־תחרש ממני
           פן־תחשה ממני ונמשלתי עם־יורדי בור

clearly denote that the petitioner sees death before his eyes and prays to avert it. The extraordinary case

Ps 59:12   אל־תהרגם פן־ישכחו עמי

which is not in keeping with its context (cf. verse 14) obviously does not represent the conventional language of psalmodic prayers,[218] but rather shows resemblance to the theology in e.g. Judg 3:1,4.

None of the above פן clauses actually constitutes a »motivation for divine intervention«, although this thought may be close in Ps 13: 4–5 ... פן־יאמר איבי which is practically equal to למען איבי (see

---

[217] The positive למען occurs merely at Ps 60:7 and at the parallel 108:7 where it exceptionally precedes the main clause, i.e. the petition. In the individual complaint proper it has no occurrence. In the same function we find the final infinitive on three occasions, once in an individual complaint psalm Ps 142:8 and twice in a congregational one 106:5,47. The praise of Yahweh in the former case and the joy of the chosen in the latter are presented as valid goals for Yahweh's saving action.

[218] Cf. the free conjecture of the verse by Weiser 1963, 293: »Hab' kein Erbarmen mit ihnen«. Kraus 1978, 583, tries to iron out the contradiction.

p. 64).²¹⁹ The פֶן clauses do in a way strengthen the petition, but through a negative repetition rather than new thoughts which appeal to Yahweh.

2.2.3.4 Clauses Introduced by כִּי

Proceeding now to clauses introduced by כִּי, we find a richness of material, not found so far in our discussion of the expressions in the immediate context of the petitions. Since we are dealing here with the type of כִּי clause which is usually called causal or motivating – the rendering used for כִּי is mostly »for« –, the present section, in particular, may be expected to have relevance to the question of »motivations for divine intervention«.

In his study of profane petitions and prayers, Gerstenberger discovered that motivations are an essential element of the profane everyday petitions found in various OT texts.²²⁰ A great many of these motivations are expressed by a כִּי clause following the plea, which is found in 20% of the cases studied by Gerstenberger.²²¹ On the other hand, Gerstenberger wonders at the rarity of כִּי clauses in connection with prayers.²²² I cannot see why. As revealed by the discussion of our material below, one or more כִּי clauses are found in about half of the 84 clusters of petitions in the 42 psalms of individual complaint, i.e. in about 50% of the cases. The only reason why Gerstenberger does not see this must be his acceptance of wishes and curses in the third person form, along with the imperative petitions, as prayers of equal status. This methodological decision, which, however, does not contradict his analysis of the situation and function of complaint psalms, prevented him from seeing the special character of the imperative prayer.²²³

The numerous cases of כִּי clauses attached to imperative petitions are introduced below, arranged in groups according to their contents.

(a) In a great number of cases we find כִּי *introducing complaint*. These clauses may contain any one of the various aspects of complaint

---

²¹⁹ See Gunkel-Begrich 1933, 232.
²²⁰ Gerstenberger 1980, 40–42.
²²¹ *Ibid.* 40.
²²² *Ibid.* 127.
²²³ It is natural that a broad interpretation of prefixed verbal forms as subjunctives introduces numerous cases which do not include כִּי clauses. Accordingly, the percentage decreases. Cf. p. 12 note 13 above. Thus, Gerstenberger's view not only depends on the discussion of the imperatives and the subjunctives under one heading but on the inclusion of several uncertain cases as subjunctives. Furthermore, it is interesting to note that Gerstenberger several times warns of concentrating too much on the formal characteristics of the prayer element (*ibid.* e.g. 119).

found in the complaint psalms.²²⁴ They may contain a description of the petitioner's misery e.g.

Ps 6:2–4   יהוה אל־באפך תוכיחני   ואל־בחמתך תיסרני
חנני יהוה כי אמלל אני   רפאני יהוה כי נבהלו עצמי
ונפשי נבהלה מאד   ואת יהוה עד־מתי

Ps 31:10–11   חנני יהוה כי צר־לי   עששה בכעס עיני נפשי ובטני
כי כלו ביגון חיי ושנותי באנחה
כשל בעוני כחי   ועצמי עששו

Ps 86:1   הטה־יהוה אזנך ענני   כי־עני ואביון אני

Ps 102:2–4   יהוה שמעה תפלתי   ושועתי אליך תבוא
אל־תסתר פניך ממני   ביום צר לי
הטה־אלי אזנך   ביום אקרא מהר ענני
כי־כלו בעשן ימי   ועצמותי כמו־קד נחרו

In other cases the content of the כי clause consists of a complaint about the enemy, e.g.

Ps 27:11–12   הורני יהוה דרכך
ונחני בארח מישור למען שוררי
אל־תתנני בנפש צרי
כי קמו־בי עדי־שקר ויפח חמס

Ps 54:3–5   אלהים בשמך הושיעני   ובגבורתך תדינני
אלהים שמע תפלתי   האזינה לאמרי־פי
כי זרים קמו עלי   ועריצים בקשו נפשי   לא שמו אלהים לנגדם

Ps 59:2–4   הצילני מאיבי אלהי   ממתקוממי תשגבני
הצילני מפעלי און   ומאנשי דמים הושיעני
כי הנה ארבו לנפשי   יגורו עלי עזים

And some cases contain even a complaint against Yahweh, e.g.

Ps 38:2–4   יהוה אל־בקצפך תוכיחני   ובחמתך תיסרני
כי־חציך נחתו בי   ותנחת עלי ידך
אין־מתם בבשרי מפני זעמך

Moreover, it may be observed that in several psalms the function of כי is evidently not just to introduce one clause, single and separate, to motivate Yahweh's intervention. The complaining כי clauses may be observed to grow into a whole section of the psalm, the section contain-

---

²²⁴ Westermann 1977, 128–129, distinguishes between three kinds of complaint: complaint concerning oneself, complaint about the enemy, and complaint or accusation (»Anklage«) against God. For criticism of this »trinity«, see Gerstenberger 1977, 187.

ing the complaint (e.g. Ps 31:11–14, 102:4–12, 38:3–15; cf. above). Such cases may involve several instances of the conjunction כי, which do not seem to be used to introduce a chain of clauses motivating each other, but a cluster of motivations pointing towards the petition at the head of the series.

Cases with a petition or a cluster of petitions and a longer section of complaint introduced by כי may be found in the following psalms and parts of psalms:

(1) Ps 6:5–8 (כי v.6) In this psalm the imperative petitions and complaints alternate (cf. vv. 2–4 listed below). This second section of the psalm also refers to the ceasing of praise to Yahweh in death: at the same time a motivation for Yahweh's action and a complaint when confronted with the threat of death.

(2) Ps 31:10–14 (כי vv. 10, 11, 14) This section in the middle of Ps 31 constitutes an excellent example of the repeated use of כי within a longer section of complaint.

(3) Ps 38:2–15 (כי vv. 3, 5, 8) If we include vv. 16–21, which contain an expression of confidence in Yahweh, but then close in tones of complaint, we find four more cases of כי (vv. 16, 17, 18, 19). The final verses of the psalm (vv. 22–23) consist of a concluding prayer, which rounds off the whole.

(4) Ps 41:5–10 (כי v. 5) The prayer and complaint give the impression of being quoted (v. 5 אני־אמרתי), and not actually prayed in the context of vv. 2–4 and 12–14. V. 11 concludes the quotation with petitions in the imperative.

(5) Ps 51:3–8 (כי v. 5) The confession of sins in this psalm begins with a pattern similar to that of other complaint prayers: כי serves as a link between the petitions and the confession.

(6) Ps 55:10–15 (כי vv. 10, 13) In spite of the difficulties involved in its interpretation, this section of Ps 55 reveals a formal resemblance to the composition of the preceding instances. (Cf. p. 43.) The more conventional beginning of the psalm (vv. 2–9) again lacks כי at the crucial point.

(7) Ps 69:2–5 (כי v. 2) Here the petition and the complaint introduced by כי form the first section of a long psalm.

(8) Ps 88:2–19 (כי v.4) The description of misery and complaint against Yahweh actually makes up the whole psalm. The complaint is further emphasized by questions in vv. 11–13, 15–16, and a description of prayer appears in vv. 2, 10, 14. Here, too, כי has its place between the petition and the complaint.

(9) Ps 102:2–12 (כי vv. 4, 5, 10, 11) This first section of the psalm comprises a continuous description of the petitioner's misery, which differs from the latter part as regards both verse length and content.

The particle כי is used no less than four times to link the various parts of the complaint to the petitions.

(10) Ps 109:1–5 (כי v. 2) and

(11) Ps 109:21–25 (כי vv. 21, 22, the first one introducing another kind of motivation, the second one complaint) This psalm contains two prayer sections with imperative petitions and complaint, separated by a long curse against the enemy (vv. 6–20).[225]

(12) Ps 143:1–6 (כי vv. 2, 3) The two cases of כי one after the other can only be understood as parallel in their connection with the petitions, since the first one introduces a general truth, the second one a complaint.

(13) Ps 22:12–19 (כי v. 12 *bis*, 17) This middle section of Ps 22 resembles in its outward appearance the cases listed above. On the other hand, the psalm gives the impression of being arranged in two strophes of complaint with a section of petition (v. 12) between them and a longer one (vv. 20–22) closing the whole before going over to praise.[226] The character of v. 12 as a compositional item in the middle of the complaint sections is also supported by the fact that this petition includes no address (cf. p. 56 above).

The following list gives the remaining cases of petitions with כי introducing complaint, which, however, does not in these cases exceed two lines:

(14) Ps 5:9–10 (כי v. 10)

(15) Ps 6:2–4 (כי v. 3 *bis*) N.B. the alternation of petitions and כי clauses.

(16) Ps 12:2–3 (כי v. 2 *bis*)

(17) Ps 27:11–12 (כי v. 12)

(18) Ps 39:13 (כי v. 13) This final prayer section of the psalm includes in v. 14 a further imperative petition followed by a coordinate clause (cf. p. 65 above).

(19) Ps 54:3–5 (כי v. 5)

(20) Ps 56:2–3 (כי vv. 2, 3)

(21) Ps 59:2–4 (כי v. 4)

(22) Ps 69:18 (כי v. 18) The prayer section vv. 14–19 includes another כי clause in v. 17 (see below).

(23) Ps 71:9–11 (כי v. 10)

(24) Ps 86:1 (כי v. 1) Only this one of the numerous כי clauses in Ps 86:1–7 refers to the misery of the supplicant.

---

[225] I find it difficult to understand the curse section Ps 109:6–20 as a quotation of the words of the enemy (against Schmidt 1928, 41, and Kraus 1978, 920–923). The divergence between the singular (vv. 6–20) and the plural (vv. 25–31) does not suffice to justify this apologetic explanation.

[226] For discussion of the structure of Ps 22, see Westermann 1984, 64–65.

(25) Ps 142:7 (כי v. 7 *bis*) The various petitions in vv. 5–8 are connected once with a coordinate clause (cf. p. 65 above), twice with כי clauses, and once with a final infinitive (cf. p. 67 note 217).

(26) Ps 69:27 (כי v. 27) This motivating כי clause, which may be included here as a borderline case, appears in the middle of a section of petitions and curses against the enemy in Ps 69:23–29.

(b) In the following group of cases we find כי *introducing an expression of confidence in Yahweh* in connection with imperative petitions. These cases are not as numerous as the ones already discussed, and the passage of text attached to כי is usually shorter.

(1) Ps 16:1(–6) (כי v. 1) The petition, which is the only one in the psalm, and the motivation clause are as short as possible: שמרני אל כי־ חסיתי בך. The corruption of the following verses 3–4 a makes it difficult to interpret the psalm,[227] but it seems to contain only expressions of confidence in Yahweh and from v. 7 on thanksgiving, with no complaint at all.

(2) Ps 31:2–6 (כי vv. 4, 5) After various pleas for Yahweh to hear and save, the psalm continues with three verses of trust in Yahweh introduced by כי at v. 4 כי־סלעי ומצודתי אתה and again at 5 b כי־אתה מעוזי. The first part of the psalm (vv. 2–9) resembles Ps 16: both passages add to the petitions expressions of confidence and joy in Yahweh and faithfulness to him. However, Ps 31 continues as a complaint prayer (vv. 10–14; see a–2 above).

(3) Ps 71:1–8 (כי vv. 3, 5) The first verses bear a marked resemblance to those in Ps 31. In Ps 71 petitions and expressions of confidence alternate so that there are two כי clauses each attached to a petition or a cluster of petitions: v. 3 כי־סלעי ומצודתי אתה (= Ps 31:4) and v. 5 כי־אתה תקותי אדני יהוה מבטחי מנעורי. Vv. 6–7 continue with thoughts of trust and gratitude. Resembling the form of Ps 31 even here, the following section of Ps 71 contains a complaint prayer.

(4) Ps 43:1–2 (כי v. 2) The short motivation clause after the petitions כי־אתה אלהי מעוזי (cf. Ps 31:5) expresses confidence in Yahweh, but the next words introduce complaint.

(5) Ps 57:2–4 (כי v. 2) The first section of the psalm consists of the plea and expressions of confidence introduced by כי.

(6) Ps 61:2–6 (כי vv. 4, 6) Ps 61 resembles Ps 16 in that it contains no actual complaint, only the temporal infinitive construction בעטף לבי as part of a description of prayer in v. 3. After the petitions and expressions of confidence the psalm closes with a wish for the king (vv. 7–8) and a vow to praise Yahweh (v. 9).

---

[227] For the various conjectures, see Gunkel 1926, 52–53; Kraus 1978, 261.

(7) Ps 86:4–5 (כי vv. 4, 5)   One of the numerous petitions in Ps 86 is followed by two successive כי clauses which express confidence in and devotion to Yahweh:

שמח נפש עבדך כי אליך אדני נפשי אשא
כי־אתה אדני טוב וסלח ורב־חסד לכל־קראיך

N. B. the close similarity to the Deuteronomistic confession which occurs in Ps 86:15 as well as Ex 34:6, Joel 2:13, Jon 4:2, Ps 103:8.[228]

(8) Ps 143:8–10 (כי vv. 8 bis, 10)   After three petitions in close succession we find here motivations comparable to those in Ps 86 above:

השמיעני בבקר חסדך   כי־בך בטחתי
הודיעני דרך־זו אלך   כי־אליך נשאתי נפשי
הצילני מאיבי יהוה   אליך כסתי
למדני לעשות רצונך   כי־אתה אלוהי

כי should perhaps be read even before אליך כסתי, since ὅτι is found in the Septuagint rendering of this line, too.

(9) Ps 31:16–18 (כי v. 18)   A further section of petitions in Ps 31, already discussed twice (see a–2 and b–2 above), contains a short motivation clause which refers to the act of praying: כי קראתיך.

(10) Ps 5:2–3 (כי v. 3) כי־אליך אתפלל is comparable to the preceding case, but, in connection with the plea for hearing, it is pleonastic.

(11) Ps 86:3 (כי v. 3)   One of the numerous כי clauses in Ps 86 resembles the two last-mentioned cases: כי אליך אקרא כל־היום. (Cf. a–24 and b–7 above.)

(12) Ps 3:8–9 (כי v. 8)   This somewhat peculiar motivation expresses the petitioner's trust in Yahweh that he will destroy the enemy:

קומה יהוה   הושיעני אלהי
כי־הכית את־כל־איבי לחי שני רשעים שברת

(13) Ps 27:7–10 (כי v. 10)   After a series of mostly negated petitions we are here faced with a rather difficult case of כי:

אל־תטשני ואל־תעזבני אלהי ישעי
כי־אבי ואמי עזבוני ויהוה יאספני

The line that begins with כי is often rendered as a concessive sentence, because this interpretation seems to provide an acceptable meaning for the verse. On the other hand, comparison with the other cases of כי clauses following petitions suggests the interpretation as a motivation expressing confidence in Yahweh, in effective contrast with the disloy-

---

[228] For the Deuteronomistic character of these passages, see Smend 1981, 178.

alty of the parents: »... for my father and my mother have forsaken me, but Yahweh will take me up«. That this interpretation is actually found in the Septuagint – as well as in a few other translations and commentaries – shows that there is no urgent reason to use the concessive interpretation.²²⁹

(c) In the remaining cases of כי clauses attached to imperative petitions, it is not possible to discern any overall theme for all cases. Two of them resemble praise, four proclaim the petitioner's devoutness, two reproach the enemy, and one contains a theological sentence.
(1) Ps 69:17 and
(2) Ps 109:21 contain one and the same כי clause: כי־טוב חסדך.
(3) Ps 86:2 includes among numerous other motivation clauses: כי־חסיד אני. (See also a–24, b–7, and b–11 above.)
(4) Ps 26:1 כי־אני בתמי הלכתי and
(5) Ps 26:2–8 (כי v.3) כי־חסדך לנגד עיני והתהלכתי באמתך, two motivations in one psalm, each following a petition, assure the petitioner's innocence. In the latter case the assurance of innocence continues up to vv. 7–8 where it acquires tones of thankfulness.
(6) Ps 143:12 After a long series of petitions, several of which are followed by motivations, the whole Ps 143 closes with a כי clause: כי אני עבדך.
(7) Ps 5:11 A prayer against the enemy – the third prayer section in Ps 5 – is followed by כי־מרו בך, a motivation that brings out the enemies' guilt before Yahweh.
(8) Ps 28:5 In a similar context we find a motivation clause reproaching the enemies: כי לא יבינו אל־פעלת יהוה ואל־מעשה ידיו.
(9) Ps 51:18 The third section of prayer in Ps 51, viz. vv. 16–19, contains a theological sentence on the unacceptability of offerings – a borderline case of motivation introduced by כי: כי לא תחפץ זבח ואתנה עולה לא תרצה.

The extremely high frequency of כי introducing motivation clauses after imperative petitions may be illustrated by a few figures. Of the 42 psalms which contain prayers of individual complaint no less than 29 include at least one case of כי in this function, 10 of them three

---

²²⁹ This interpretation is shared by Gunkel 1926, 117, and Oesterley 1939, 195. As a further argument against the concessive interpretation one could consider the form of the supposed apodosis. This case would be an exception to the general rule observed in the great majority of apodoses: ו appears only in connection with a consecutive verbal form (see Aejmelaeus 1982, 126–127). For the concessive interpretation of כי, see Vriezen BZAW 77 (1958), 266–273, and Aejmelaeus, »Function and Interpretation of כי in Biblical Hebrew«, 1984.

or more cases. Of the 84 separate prayer sections in these psalms כי is found in 41. As many as 20 of these prayer sections stand at the beginning of the psalm, thus constituting a major compositional feature in this group of psalms.[230]

Indeed, the employment of imperative petitions and כי in the composition of organized prayer sections in the psalms in question may be analyzed a little further:

A. The most simple case involves one single occurrence of כי to link the petitions with expressions of complaint or confidence in Yahweh, which extend over a few lines (e.g. Ps 51:3–8, 69:2–5, 88:2–19, 109:1–5, 16:1–6).

B. In a few other cases, כי has been employed repeatedly within the passage attached to the petitions (e.g. Ps 31:2–6, 31:10–14, 38:2–15, 102:2–12).

C. The prayer section or even the whole psalm sometimes consists of repeated passages with petitions and shorter or longer כי periods (e.g. Ps 5:2–11, 6:2–8, 26:1–8, 27:7–12).

D. A few psalms reveal a skilful alternation of short petitions and short כי clauses of various kinds (e.g. Ps 86:1–5 four cases, 109:21–22 two cases, 142:7 two cases, 143:8–10 three cases, 69:14–19 two cases with כי, three with prepositional phrases).

Beyond doubt, the conjunction כי constitutes the most frequently employed syntactical medium in connection with imperative petitions. Although it is clear that not every single imperative petition or cluster of such in the individual complaint psalms follows the patterns outlined above – in 13 of our psalms we find no כי – but several petitions are rather scattered among all kinds of elements of the genre, no other particle, not even asyndesis, seems to be as significant for the composition of these psalms (cf. Section 2.2.3.5).

As regards the conventional language used in the psalmodic prayers, it is possible to find formulaic language even in the כי clauses or periods introduced by כי studied above.[231] We do not find very many identical motivation clauses, but some cases in the material show similarities to cases in other connections: e.g. כי־עני ואביון אני Ps 68:1, 109:22 (with variation Ps 25:16); כי־חסיתי בך Ps 16:1, 25:20 (with variation Ps 143:8); כי־היית מחסה לי Ps 61:4, whereas Ps 59:17 and 63:8 both in thanksgiving vary the noun; כי־טוב חסדך Ps 69:17, 109:21, and in another connection Ps 63:4. It is natural that shorter phrases

---

[230] Ps 43, which is usually interpreted together with Ps 42, has not been considered here. Of the 20 psalms which begin with a prayer section, three contain an introductory clause before the first petition (Ps 31, 71, 88).

[231] See Culley 1967, 111.

of conventional language which could be used in different connections are more frequently found than whole motivation clauses that recur.

To conclude, a few words must be said concerning *the function of* כי in connection with imperative petitions. In the above discussion, the clauses introduced by כי have been referred to as motivation clauses. Should we now regard them as equal to »motivations for divine intervention« in Gunkel's sense? Indeed, to call all the כי clauses »motivations for divine intervention« would hardly be appropriate. Some of them, particularly the shorter ones in the above groups (b) and (c), seem to justify this title, but in most of the cases כי only introduces the main content of the prayer section, whether complaint or confidence in Yahweh. Does this have any consequences for the interpretation of כי in these psalms? The answer is both yes and no. Should we perhaps grasp at another »meaning« for כי ? By no means. Instead, we must acquire a better understanding of the functions of כי.

As is well known, the conjunction כי is a multi-purpose conjunction which often causes difficulties for the interpreter because of the large variety of different logical connections in which it appears. Preceding its main clause a כי clause can mostly be interpreted as a conditional or a temporal subordinate clause. But which is it for sure? Or should it be understood as causal or concessive? Moreover, when the כי clause follows its main clause or does not seem to have one, the problems merely increase. A few of the functions of כי in this position, it is true, are not difficult to distinguish, viz. the function in connection with verbs which take a »that« clause as completion and the adversative function »but rather« after a negated main clause. But, even disregarding the problem of conditional or temporal interpretations in the case of a כי clause following its main clause, we are still left with a large number of כי clauses – in fact the largest group of all – which may be called, in the broadest sense of the term, causal. Even within this group a great variety of usage may be observed. The logical relationship of the causal כי clauses to the preceding clause ranges from a strictly causal and, for the main clause, necessary statement to a loose and indirect explanation. It is characteristic of the indirectly causal expressions that they do not state the cause for *what* is actually said in the main clause but rather the reason for *saying* it. A motivation, introduced by כי and following an imperative petition, is typically indirect in its causality, and this sometimes produces difficulties for the interpreter who aims at a logical rendering. Consequently, the emphatic interpretation of כי is sometimes suggested instead of the causal.[232] The more under-

---

[232] Dahood 1970, III 402–406, gives a list of cases in the psalms where he suggests the emphatic interpretation of כי. Several of the cases studied in the present work are included in this list (e.g. Ps 3:8, 56:2, 86:3).

standing, however, there is for the looseness and indirectness of the causal relation possible in connection with כי, so much the less is there room or need for the emphatic interpretation.[233]

In order to understand the use of כי and its function in connection with petitions, we must see it from the viewpoint of the Hebrew speaker or writer and in relation to the possibilities available in Hebrew. The principal methods used to join clauses were obviously parataxis through ו, אשר, כי, and asyndeton, which actually means disconnection. Parataxis was the normal method of connection for narration, and אשר was mainly used in relative clauses. To connect clauses in a more argumentative type of text, כי was most often resorted to, other conjunctions being far less frequently employed. The high frequency of כי and its wide applicability are obviously opposite sides of one and the same coin. As regards the more precise interpretation of a multi-purpose conjunction like כי, however, it is the context which plays a decisive role here. Consequently, cases which are analogous in respect of their context should receive an analogous interpretation. It is necessary for a meaningful communication that a multi-purpose conjunction cannot have *just any* »meaning« *anywhere*.[234] This means also that the interpreter is not free to choose any rendering he pleases of the renderings given in a dictionary. On the other hand, the interpreter must be alive to the fact that Hebrew does not make all the distinctions that other languages make concerning the logical relationships between clauses.

The type of context the present study is dealing with is characterized by the imperative form of a verb. Now, allowing a ו clause to follow an imperative produces in most cases a final or a consecutive clause (see p. 65 above). Or the whole may give the impression of a conditional sentence. On the other hand, the employment of a כי clause in this connection permits one to express a number of different thoughts in a causal, motivating, or explanatory relationship to the imperative. The intensity of the causal relationship apparently varies from case to case. Among the כי clauses found after petitions in the psalms a few wish to motivate Yahweh's action, others state the reason for appealing to Yahweh or for the need for help. Beyond doubt, כי is a connective in all of these cases, in broad terms a causal connective. The mechanics of a multi-purpose conjunction do not allow for its interpretation as an

---

[233] Cf. Aejmelaeus, »Function and Interpretation of כי in Biblical Hebrew«, 1984.
[234] As a matter of fact, a conjunction does not have any independent »meaning«. For the terminological distinction: *semantic value* designating the dependent semantic aspect of e.g. a particle, *meaning* reserved for the independent semantic aspect of a word, and *content* used of the independent semantic aspect of a phrase, a clause, or a sentence, see Dik 1968, 257–259.

emphatic particle in some cases and as a causal one in others which have a similar context. However, it seems to be characteristic of כי in this function that it connects not only clauses to one another, but sections of several clauses and not only with a main clause immediately preceding, but with a main clause that appeared a few lines earlier in the text.

. At this point I feel I should present a group of related cases of כי in the psalms and question the new interpretation of כי in imperative hymns introduced by Crüsemann in his *Studien zur Formgeschichte von Hymnus und Danklied in Israel*.[235] Crüsemann has no linguistic argument to offer for his interpretation that כי following an imperative inviting to praise should not introduce a motivation but instead the contents of the praise, even the words sung by the ones invited to praise. Crüsemann's decision is based on (1) כי having several »nuances of meaning«[236] and (2) the logic of the passage which according to him requires something other than a motivation. Hence, כי must be understood as an emphatic particle. From the viewpoint of normal Hebrew usage and in light of the above discussion, however, the possible functions for כי after the imperatives of verbs denoting »to praise«, »to sing«, »to declare«, and »to thank« would be to introduce either a motivation adhering to the imperative or possibly a completing „that" clause adhering to the meaning of the verbs mentioned. With these two alternatives one can hardly find any justification in adopting a third one.

As a matter of fact, the problem Crüsemann saw in the imperative hymns is very much the same as we have in the imperative prayers: a seemingly subordinate clause is used to express what appears to be the main content of the passage. The present writer prefers to regard the form of expression – כי following the imperative – in both cases as an idiosyncracy of the Hebrew language. It is conditioned by the need of a connective other than ו and the wide range of usage of כי from directly causal to motivating and loosely explanatory cases. That some cases seem to be more clearly causal than others should not automatically be regarded as an indication for later changes of the genre,[237] but rather as a phenomenon characteristic of the causal כי. But, in addition to these two, there is a third group of texts using the same linguistic form, viz. commands and prohibitions in the OT law collections, which also frequently appear with motivations introduced by כי. Indeed, the frequent occurrence of motivation clauses in connection with laws is

---

[235] WMANT 32, Neukirchen-Vluyn 1969. See particularly pp. 32–35.
[236] At this point, Crüsemann refers to Muilenburg *HUCA* XXXII (1961), 135–160, who does not construct his interpretation of כי on a sound linguistic basis.
[237] Crüsemann 1969, 34–35, 50, presumes such a change to have taken place in the imperative hymn: in a few late cases כי actually appears as a causal connective.

considered one of the major characteristics of OT law.²³⁸ In this light, the imperative accompanied by a motivating כי no longer appears as a special *form* characteristic of a certain genre in the OT, but simply as one of the basic modes of expression in a language with few syntactical resources. This background should be borne in mind when interpreting the various occurrences of the imperative followed by a motivating כי clause. If one wishes to hold the view that כי clauses express the contents of a prayer or of praise, one must conclude that Hebrew expresses these contents by means of a motivation clause.

Another great problem concerns the occurrence of כי clauses following one after the other without clear logical connections and apparently not as motivations of each other. On the basis of the above material from the complaint psalms, it would seem possible to understand such כי clauses as belonging to one main clause. This usage could perhaps more aptly be characterized as »paratactic«, since כי seems to be used here to line up statements in a more argumentative type of text, in a manner parallel to parataxis by ו in narration.²³⁹ The applicability of this explanation needs, however, to be confirmed by further research into the use of כי in poetic texts.

2.2.3.5 Other Types of Clauses

After the above description of clauses introduced by various connectives, what remains for us is to examine the occurrence of asyndetic clauses in the immediate context of imperative petitions. The evaluation of asyndesis, however, poses a problem due to its very nature: the lack of connective may indicate either asyndetic connection or disconnection. The judgement between these two possibilities is something which concerns the interpretation of the contents of the various statements in the individual cases. I shall first discuss instances where the clause or section introduced asyndetically after a petition reveals similarity in content to those introduced by the various connectives. At least in such cases one is justified in speaking of asyndetic connection.

Complaint which was frequently found to be introduced by כי appears in two psalms asyndetically connected with the petition: Ps 55: 2–6, 39:8–12. Particularly in the first-mentioned case a great resemblance to the cases with כי may be discerned in the form as well as in the content of the section.

---

²³⁸ Gemser *VT Suppl* I (1953), 50–66, describes the OT laws as unique in this respect. Even if it is not correct to regard this as a unique feature – see Sonsino 1980 – it is, nevertheless, remarkably characteristic.

²³⁹ König 1897, III:2,2 537, sees in the double use of כי in hymns (e.g. Ps 106:1, 107:1, 118:1, 136:1) »Neigung des Hebräischen zur Parataxe«.

Ps 55:2–4

האזינה אלהים תפלתי ואל־תתעלם מתחנתי
הקשיבה לי וענני אריד בשיחי
ואהימה מקול אויב מפני עקת רשע
כי־ימיטו עלי און ובאף ישטמוני

Expressions of confidence in Yahweh are introduced asyndetically after petitions in Ps 56:8–10 and 17:1–5. The latter case even includes an asseveration of the petitioner's innocence.

Ps 17:1–2

שמעה יהוה צדק הקשיבה רנתי
האזינה תפלתי בלא שפתי מרמה
מלפניך משפטי יצא עיניך תחזינה מישרים

Confidence in Yahweh's forgiveness may be found in Ps 130:2–4, although in a syntactically more complex form.[240]

Ps 130:2–4

אדני שמעה בקולי
תהיינה אזניך קשבות לקול תחנוני
אם־עונות תשמר־יה אדני מי יעמד
כי־עמך הסליחה למען תורא

In Ps 39:5 an asyndetic clause appears in a consecutive relationship to the petition, comparable to clauses introduced by ו.

Ps 39:5

הודיעני יהוה קצי ומדת ימי מה־היא
אדעה מה־חדל אני

(N.B. BHS nonn Mss ואדעה.) In four further instances similar verbal forms have been used to introduce clauses that follow the petitions: Ps 22:20–23 (אספרה »I will tell«), 35:17–18 (אודך »I will thank you«), 51:11–15 (אלמדה »I will teach«), 86:11–13 (אהלך »I shall walk«, אודך »I will thank you«, ואכבדה »and I will glorify«). E.g.

Ps 35:17–18

השיבה נפשי משאיהם מכפירים יחידתי
אודך בקהל רב בעם עצום אהללך

Whether one can also see in these instances a consecutive connection – i.e. a vow to give thanks – or perhaps disconnection and the beginning of a separate new section – i.e. a section of praise – is difficult to decide. The first-mentioned alternative gains support in Ps 86:11–13 by the presence of אהלך which is parallel to אודך: a common interpretation of the two verbs is possible only if it refers to the future, to the consequences of the petition being heard.[241] A similar interpretation

---

[240] Since אם does not express connection with the preceding context, this case may be considered comparable to those without any connective.

[241] The case is rendered problematic by the following line which contains motivation of praise introduced by כי. Nevertheless, verses 12–13 can hardly be regarded as an independent section of actual praise within the composition of Ps 86, since verses 14–17 once more take up complaint and petitions. See Gunkel-Begrich 1933, 247–248.

seems probable in Ps 35:17–18, since no actual content of praise follows.²⁴² In a similar way, Ps 51:15 reveals no connection with the following context and by the employment of the verb אלמדה more plausibly implies a vow of future activity.²⁴³ On the other hand, Ps 22 is distinguished by the inclusion of praise, actually a hymn, that follows immediately after the line אספרה שמך לאחי בתוך קהל אהללך (v. 23). Nevertheless, the change of person from the first person singular to the second person plural rather seems to suggest a break between verses 23 and 24.²⁴⁴ The vow in verse 23 may have brought about the addition of an independent section of praise at the end of the psalm. Thus, it is possible in each one of the above-mentioned cases to justify a consecutive relationship between the petitions and what is asyndetically attached to them.²⁴⁵ – In Ps 71:18 a similar thought is expressed in a temporal clause: עד אגיד זרועך לדור »till I proclaim your mighty arm to future generations«.

In a few cases, the lines following the petitions concern the enemy of the petitioner. In Ps 17:13–14 the enemy is described in a way comparable to a relative clause. In Ps 4:2–6 as well as Ps 120:1–4 the petitions are, surprisingly, followed by an address – not to Yahweh but to an enemy (לשון רמיה Ps 120:3) or enemies (בני איש Ps 4:3).²⁴⁶ The change of address actually implies interruption of the prayer, and the asyndeton in these cases must be interpreted as disconnection.

In five cases, closely resembling each other, Ps 35:1–6, 22–28, 40: 14–18, 70:2–5, 71:12–13, the sections asyndetically attached to the imperative petitions contain curses and wishes in the third person form against the enemy and in favour of the righteous. E. g.

Ps 70:2–5
    אלהים להצילני יהוה לעזרתי חושה
    יבשו ויחפרו מבקשי נפשי
    יסגו אחור ויכלמו חפצי רעתי
    ישובו על־עקב בשתם האמרים האח האח
    ישישו וישמחו בך כל־מבקשיך
    ויאמרו תמיד יגדל אלהים אהבי ישועתך

---

²⁴² For the interpretation as a vow, see e.g. Weiser 1963, 204; Kraus 1978, 429.
²⁴³ See Gunkel-Begrich 1933, 248.
²⁴⁴ For the interpretation of v. 23 as a vow, see Gunkel-Begrich 1933, 248. For the division of Ps 22 at this point, see Duhm 1922, 96; Schmidt 1934, 38.
²⁴⁵ Crüsemann 1969, 274–276, makes a distinction between 1) the Todah-formula (אודך) referring to Yahweh in the second person singular and expressing actual praise, and 2) the employment of the cohortative with reference to Yahweh in the third person to express a vow to give thanks to Yahweh. This distinction does not, however, apply in our cases: the cohortatives in our examples (Ps 22:23, 51:15, 86:11–12) are all combined with reference to Yahweh in the second person singular.
²⁴⁶ I prefer to read Ps 4:2 according to the MT as a prayer, against the conjectures of e.g. Gunkel 1926; 15–16, and with e.g. Schmidt 1934, 7–8, and Kraus 1978, 168–169.

It is typical that the lines containing curses do not address Yahweh. Curiously enough, the positive wishes, however, refer to Yahweh by means of the second person suffix in Ps 40:17 and 70:5, which are close parallels to each other. Another example of curses that follow petitions is found in Ps 140:7–11. In Ps 109:6–15 we find a unique section of heavy curses against the enemy introduced by one single imperative petition but with no reference to Yahweh.[247] It is obvious that curses and wishes in the third person originally had an existence of their own and were only later introduced into the context of prayer to Yahweh.[248] In the above-mentioned cases, the curses and wishes in the third person have simply been listed after the petitions.

In three cases, Ps 7:7–11, 102:25–28, 141:1–6, a section opening with imperative petitions further develops into more general thoughts, without, however, any syntactical links between the parts.

In the preceding discussion, the focus has been on the elements that follow the petitions. On the other hand, there are instances in which the petitions have no following context. In a number of cases a petition or a cluster of petitions is found at the end of a psalm with the function of a closing element: Ps 28:9, 38:22–23, 40:18, 51:20–21, 70:6.[249] Similarly, a cluster of petitions may close a section within a psalm: Ps 59:5–6. Sometimes the closing prayer may include a coordinate clause expressing the consequence wished-for: Ps 41:11, 86:16–17.[250] A few other petitions occur in isolation from other dependent elements: Ps 30:11, which is a quoted prayer, and Ps 57:6 and 12, which form a refrain independent from the context.[251]

Finally, we should discuss briefly a type of asyndetic clause which appears in connection with petitions in individual complaint psalms, gives emphasis to the petitions, but is apt to occur at the beginning of the prayer rather than at the end, viz. the expressions referring to the act of praying and/or to the petitioner's faith in Yahweh. Description

---

[247] Against Schmidt 1934, 199–202, and Kraus 1978, 921–923, who explain the section as a quotation of the enemy.

[248] Gunkel-Begrich 1933, 228–229.

[249] Ps 28:9 and 51:20–21 (which, in fact, includes a further asyndetic element in a consecutive function) are obviously later additions to the original individual complaints. In these two endings the narrow individual perspective of the psalm is widened to concern the whole of Israel. See Gunkel 1926, 120, 226, and for Ps 51 also Kraus 1978, 548.

[250] Cf. also Ps 71:12–13 where the petitions resemble e.g. Ps 38:22–23, but are completed by curses in the third person. This and many other instances of petitions may in an earlier phase have constituted a closing prayer, which, however, after the further growth of the psalm has come into the middle of it.

[251] The formal petition רומה in these two refrains actually constitutes praise rather than a plea. See Section 1.6 above.

of the act of praying or temporal reference to it appears as an introduction to the petitions in Ps 4:2, 17:6, 28:1, 69:14, 88:2, 120:1, 130:1, 141:1 (cf. Ps 28:2, 61:3 in the middle), an expression of »seeking refuge« (חסיתי) in Yahweh in Ps 7:2, 31:2, 71:1, confession of faith and trust in him in Ps 31:15, 39:8, 140:7, 35:22 (cf. Ps 27:8–9, 142:6 in the middle).[252] E. g.

Ps 28:1	אליך יהוה אקרא צורי אל־תחרש ממני
Ps 7:2	יהוה אלהי בך חסיתי הושיעני ...
Ps 140:7	אמרתי ליהוה אלי אתה האזינה ...

The frequency of these introductions to petitions should not be overemphasized: they occur in only 15 of the total 84 prayer sections in individual complaint psalms. In 9 psalms of the total of 42 psalms discussed here they function as the introduction of the whole psalm. On the other hand, as many as 23 of these 42 psalms begin immediately with the petitions.[253] Expressions describing the act of praying, »seeking refuge«, or confidence in Yahweh seem as such to be characteristic of prayer texts, but, being unspecific in relation to the theme of the prayer and expressive merely of the due attitude of the supplicant, they permit a flexible employment within all of the various elements of prayer psalms.

2.2.4 Conclusions

The above analysis of the immediate context of the imperative petitions in psalms of individual complaint started out as a search for »motivations for divine intervention«, in Gunkel's footsteps. The first group of expressions studied, prepositional phrases referring to Yahweh's divine attributes, used to strengthen and motivate the prayer, were found to be not at all frequent in the present material. It was also not clear whether all of the prepositional phrases found were to be interpreted unambiguously as »motivations for divine intervention« or rather as modal or instrumental completions to the main verb of the petition.

Among the various clauses which appear in connection with prayer imperatives, clauses introduced by כי were found to be frequent enough to be looked upon as a dominant feature of the type of text studied. It is true, the material revealed a certain degree of variety as to the contents of the כי clauses and to the extent of the text which could

---

[252] See Gunkel-Begrich 1933, 221–222. Cf. also similar thoughts introduced by כי in Section 2.2.3.4 above.

[253] Ps 43 was not considered here, since it is usually regarded as part of a larger whole beginning with Ps 42.

be included into the section governed by כי. But, in the first place, no other syntactical device was found to be employed with a frequency nearly as high as that of כי. One could have expected to find final clauses or relative clauses to have been used in this context more often than only a couple of times. What may be called asyndeton was found to appear more often than connectives other than כי, but in a closer scrutiny the instances of asyndeton after petitions were found to divide into smaller groups of cases, among which some actually represent disconnection, a few are comparable to the cases introduced by connectives, and others introduce into the context of prayer a vow to give thanks or some other new thought. No single syntactical pattern – except that with כי – was found to be repeated often enough to render it remarkable within the context of the whole genre.

In the second place, in spite of the variety within the usage it is possible to understand all the cases constructed with כי as examples and further developed forms of a commonly used language pattern in the Hebrew language, the employment of a motivation clause after the imperative. In this particular genre, the genre of individual complaint prayer, the common language pattern seems to have acquired – at least in the greater part of the instances – the pregnant function of carrying the very theme of the prayer.

It remains to pick up the threads of the analysis and to attempt an organized picture of the element of imperative prayer in the individual complaint, of its function in the composition of the psalms in question, as well as of its background and origin.

3. The Form of the Traditional Prayer

The formal analysis of the present study has been concerned with only one element – although an essential one – in the psalms of individual complaint in the OT Psalter, the imperative prayer together with its immediate context. Even if the focus was limited, the analysis revealed a great deal of regularity in the way complaint prayer to Yahweh was expressed and also pointed towards more far-reaching results concerning the structure of the psalms of this genre. The features which were found to recur, the imperative petitions, the address to Yahweh, and the introduction of expressions of complaint or confidence in Yahweh or the like by employment of the connective כי,[254] seem to constitute a basic pattern common to a great number of individual complaint psalms. This pattern may be understood as a kind of basic element or nucleus of which and around which further forms of prayer could in various ways develop or be developed. Since several characteristics of this basic prayer pattern point towards a longer tradition behind it, I suggest calling it the *traditional prayer.* Of these characteristics we have already discussed the employment of conventional prayer imperatives – a usage which hints at an oral background – and the address of the petitions by the single name of Yahweh which in all probability constitutes an early Israelite feature. Furthermore, the employment of the motivational connective כי in this connection obviously reflects one of the basic modes of expression, typical of Hebrew, particularly in connection with imperatives, and thus also the normal, traditional mode of expression in prayers, rather than a late poetic construction. In what follows, I shall try to demonstrate more closely the function of the pattern of traditional prayer in the psalms of individual complaint and, in spite of the general difficulties concerning the dating of psalms, to introduce further arguments in support of the thesis that the pattern represents a long tradition and an early origin rather than the opposite.

Even though one cannot expect to solve all the problems concerning the structure and origin of individual complaints through this one pattern of traditional prayer, I am convinced that it will bring more or-

---

[254] As far as אשר and asyndeton have been employed in the same context to introduce similar contents as כי, I regard them as exceptions which merely prove the rule. These exceptions add at the most 7 cases to the 41 cases with כי – many of these revealing double or triple employment – among the total 84 clusters of prayer.

der to the »variety of forms« which scholars claim to find in these psalms. The description of this genre has mostly come about by means of a list of elements which have been collected from the various psalms it includes and thus separated from their contexts. The artificiality of such a model structure is particularly evident in presentations which divide it into »introduction« and »main part«, with the result that the same elements »may« occur in both of them. Furthermore, it is the duty of the form critic – in order not to justify the accusation of practising »formula-criticism«[255] – to try to demonstrate how the formal findings fit in with the understanding of the whole and with the historical setting. Gunkel's idea of genre, the unity of forms, themes, and »Sitz-im-Leben«, already implies this.

3.1 The Pattern of Traditional Prayer as a Compositional Factor

A concurrence of imperative petitions with the two other frequently found parts of prayer, the address and the section introduced by כי, is attested at least once in two thirds of the psalms included in the present study. In 32 psalms of the total of 42, the imperative prayer stands right at the beginning of the psalm. Since כי has not been employed in 11 of these cases, the concurrence of the three parts even here can be seen in two thirds of the cases.[256]

Furthermore, prayers occurring at a later point in the psalms in question frequently follow the very same pattern. The relevant three parts are found in 17 prayer sections,[257] imperative petitions with כי but without the address – which later in a psalm obviously no longer constitutes an absolute necessity – in three sections.[258] The total number which these 20 cases should be compared to – after such imperative prayers which serve as a concluding element in a psalm[259] or as a refrain[260] as well as the one case (Ps 30:11) which contains but a frag-

---

[255] Noth, *Gesammelte Studien II*, 1969, 120, fears that »der ›Form-Geschichte‹ eine ›Formel-Geschichte‹ wird und --- die ›Formelgeschichte‹ sich zu einer ›Formel-Ungeschichte‹ entwickelt«.

[256] The pattern of traditional prayer is found at the beginning of Ps 5, 6, 12, 16, 26, 28, 31, 38, 51, 54, 56, 57, 59, 61, 69, 71, 86, 88, 102, 109, 143. Cf. also the use of אשר in Ps 64, 140, of פן Ps 7, and of asyndeton Ps 17, 55. The other psalms containing petitions at the beginning are Ps 4, 35, 70, 120, 130, 141.

[257] Ps 3:8, 5:9–10, 5:11, 6:5–8, 27:7–10, 27:11–12, 31:10–14, 31:16–18, 39:13–14, 41:5–10, 43:1–2, 51:16–19, 55:10–15, 69:14–19, 109:21–25, 142:5–8, 143:7–12. Cf. also the use of אשר/זו in Ps 17:7–12, 26:9, of asyndeton in Ps 39:9–12, 56:8–10.

[258] Ps 22:12, 69:25–27, 71:9–11.

[259] Ps 28:9, 38:22–23, 40:18d, 41:11, 51:20–21, 59:5b–6, 70:6, 86:16–17.

[260] Ps 57:6, 12.

ment of quoted prayer have been substracted – is 41. The pattern of traditional prayer is thus found in 21 of the 32 prayer sections in the initial position and in 20 of 41 cases in later positions, i.e. in 56% of all cases.

It seems that the prayer sections located further on in a psalm are less orderly in their arrangement of the various parts than the ones at the beginning of a psalm.[261] However, it is apparent in the great majority of cases that the imperative petitions are more closely connected with the following context than with the preceding context. The great number of prayers in the initial position certainly have no preceding context. Moreover, the close connection with the following context manifests itself in the frequent employment of connectives after the petitions, not only of כי but also אשר, פן, and ו. Asyndeton occurs after the petitions in 22 cases, which is 30% of the total of 73,[262] but even in formal asyndeton a connection with regard to the contents is discernible in several instances.

On the other hand, prayer sections are rarely introduced by connectives. In two cases ואתה is found to introduce the address, Ps 22:20, 109:21. In a further two cases ואני is found as part of an introductory clause, Ps 31:15–16, 69:14. Only once, in Ps 71:18, is actual connection with the preceding text effected by וגם, whereas in the four first-mentioned cases the connective may be understood as introductory to the whole prayer section. Thus, the various psalms most naturally seem to fall into sections which begin with the petitions. Curiously enough, a similar result could be obtained by an entirely different method, namely, by a survey of the poetic structure and the division into strophes of the psalms in question. In a list of words and expressions frequently marking the beginning of a strophe, recently offered by van der Lugt,[263] vocatives and imperatives seem to occupy a prominent place.

How, then, does this result compare with the description of the genre of individual complaint in general? In the usual listings of elements of this genre petitions appear at two points: (1) the initial plea in the so-called introductory part of the psalm and (2) the actual prayer for help after the complaint in the main part of the psalm.[264] Firstly,

---

[261] This statement concerns even the sections which reveal the three relevant parts.
[262] When discussing the following context, it is reasonable to use the total number of 73 which has been reached by subtracting the eight cases of concluding prayer, the two refrains, and the one fragmentary quoted prayer from the total of 84. Cf. p. 86 notes 259 and 260.
[263] van der Lugt 1980, 509–519. Interestingly enough, even ואתה and ואני discussed above are included in this list.
[264] Gunkel-Begrich 1933, 221, 240; Kraus 1978, 50–51; Gerstenberger 1977, 200; Westermann 1977, 48. This widely spread notion is even shared by Culley 1967, 110.

there are psalms which only contain one section of prayer at the beginning of the psalm (Ps 12, 16, 54, 61, 64, 88, 120, 130). In these cases at least, the so-called initial plea – whether one asking for hearing or for salvation – is nothing other than the actual prayer. Secondly, a petition can rarely be said to be a continuation of complaint.[265] On the contrary, complaint is often found to follow petitions and – what is even more – to be syntactically connected with them. Furthermore, in the case of a psalm containing two or more sections of prayer, all of them may be constructed according to the same pattern of traditional prayer. This need not, however, imply any hierarchy between the various prayers. The petitions occurring later in a psalm are in no way weightier than the ones at the beginning. Were this the case, then the petitions against the enemy would rate high, since they usually appear in the second or third section of a psalm (e.g. Ps 17, 55, 56, 69, 109). But, the petitions directed against the enemy are often inadequately formulated: e.g. they may lack the explicit address to Yahweh or they may combine imperatives and subjunctives. Prayers against the enemy even seem to deviate from the pattern of traditional prayer more often than prayers for the benefit of the petitioner. Even if these prayers have a prominent place in a few psalms, they can hardly be said to form their climax. As for the other types of petitions, they usually reveal no discernible increase in intensity as the psalm proceeds. However, the later a prayer section occurs in a psalm, the greater the ratio of petitions which only have one single or a few occurrences in the whole Psalter. One may, nevertheless, state that the stereotyped, conventional prayer imperatives – although many of them have been described as initial pleas, others as unspecific and inexpressive of the situation of the prayer – actually constitute the most significant petitions in the psalms in question. As regards the few cases where a petition occurs as a closing element, even here the first section of prayer and the closing prayer are of equal relevance, consisting often of the same or similar petitions.

3.2 *The Simple Form of Individual Prayer*

The pattern of traditional prayer, when employed in its most simple form – one imperative, one address, and one motivation clause – , was found to represent one of the most basic modes of speech in Hebrew (see above p.79). Among its various usages, this very same form is also the natural way of making an ordinary everyday request to another

---

[265] It is usual that the prayer is said to follow the complaint. See e.g. Gerstenberger 1980, 12; Westermann 1977, 164.

person, as shown by Gerstenberger.²⁶⁶ Several examples of such profane petitions may be found, for instance, in the most ancient sources of the Pentateuch.²⁶⁷

E.g. Gen 25:30	הלעיטני נא מן־האדם האדם הזה
	כי עיף אנכי
Gen 29:21	הבה את־אשתי כי מלאו ימי ...
Ex 32:1	קום עשה־לנו אלהים אשר ילכו
	לפנינו כי־זה משה ... לא ידענו
	מה־היה לו
Num 10:31	אל־נא תעזב אתנו כי על־כן
	ידעת חנתנו במדבר

Gerstenberger emphasizes the genetic affinity between profane petitions and petitions to God.²⁶⁸ Accordingly, one would except to find similar petitions in prose prayers. These are, however, seldom found to employ the same pattern and, indeed, seldom found to employ actual petitions.²⁶⁹ One example is, nevertheless, found in Gen.

E.g. Gen 32:12	הצילני נא מיד אחי מיד עשו
	כי־ירא אנכי אתו פן־יבוא והכני
	אם אל־בנים

According to Westermann, this verse belongs to J and – completed with the address from verse 10 – constitutes the oldest layer of the prayer of Jacob, whereas the surrounding verses represent theological expansion.²⁷⁰ On the other hand, the whole prayer Gen 32:10–13 is suspect, as being perhaps a result of a Deuteronomistic redaction.²⁷¹ It is obvious that the context would not suffer from the omission of the whole prayer. As is well known, prayers have also been used elsewhere as redactional insertions with a theological, didactic purpose.²⁷² But, as for the actual prayer in verse 12, it bears no mark of theological or didactic

---

²⁶⁶ Gerstenberger 1980, 40–42. However, it is characteristic of the profane petitions that they usually do not contain the address (*ibid.* 38) which is so essential in psalms prayers. One reason could be that the person addressed is in most cases mentioned in the immediate context before the quotation of the plea.
²⁶⁷ Eissfeldt 1922, *l.c.*, attributes three of the following examples to L, Ex 32:1 to E.
²⁶⁸ Gerstenberger 1980, 18.
²⁶⁹ See Wendel 1931, 9. Prayer imperatives are relatively seldom met outside the psalms.
²⁷⁰ Westermann 1981, 614–623. Appeal to Yahweh's earlier deeds before the petition, like Gen 32:10–11, is obviously a late feature; Westermann 1977, 157–158.
²⁷¹ Cf. Smend 1981, 65.
²⁷² See Plöger, *Festschrift Dehn* 1957, 35–49; Smend 1981, 63, 120.

reflection, nor does it contain typically Deuteronomistic vocabulary.²⁷³ Quite the opposite in fact: the prayer in verse 12 concerns only the concrete dangerous situation as such, with a link to the narrative in the mention of Jacob's fear (v. 8). From this viewpoint, it becomes difficult to challenge Westermann's analysis of the passage. The acceptance of verse 12 as part of an ancient source text (J) cannot be excluded.

As for the evaluation of the pattern of traditional prayer in psalms of individual complaint, the prayer of Jacob has relevance merely as a link between profane petitions, of which there are plenty in the various books of the OT, and the psalms petitions, also frequently found.²⁷⁴ What appears there in simple prose as the natural Hebrew form of a petition, either to another person or to Yahweh, is found in the psalms in poetic form, often with repetition and parallelism. Within prose, we find petitions referring to a specific need in a specific situation, whereas the poetic petitions in the psalms must be more universally applicable. Nevertheless, the common features seem to suggest that the basic and simple traditional Hebrew form of petition was used in the prayer psalms as a kind of nucleus to which other elements were attached. Here we probably have a link which connects the literary form of the psalms concerned far back to the time when no written models existed for prayers. The fact that this nucleus of the prayer psalms in particular contains conventional formulaic language – one of the conventional prayer words is also used in Gen 32:12 – which points towards a background of oral composition, further raises the necessity to reconsider the theories concerning the origin of these psalms. Even if we have in the individual complaint psalms models of prayer for cultic usage, these models were originally not an invention that the people had to adjust themselves to, but more probably an elaborated and at the same time canonized form of what was known to and practised by them even earlier.²⁷⁵ It is particularly the appearance of the pattern of traditional

---

²⁷³ The choice of הושיע instead of הציל could have been interpreted as Deuteronomistic, whereas הציל has less theological connotations; see Section 1.1 above. Another interesting lexical item here is the idiom אם על־בנים »mother with the children« which also appears in Hos 10:14.

²⁷⁴ Only few of the prose prayers in the OT reveal the same pattern: II Sam 24:10, I Kings 3:9, 19:4, Is 44:17, II Chr 14:10, Dan 9:19. See also Westermann 1984, 19–20 (»Die Psalmen im Zusammenhang der Geschichte des Gebetes«).

²⁷⁵ This view is shared by Fuchs 1982, 296, 311–313. Seybold 1973, 183–184, considers the origin of the complaints connected with illness rather private than cultic, but implies an origin in written form. Gerstenberger 1980, gives priority to the cultic use of the complaint prayers (see pp. 3–4, 168), but stresses also the existence of cultic prayer before the introduction of writing (p. 117, against Delekat) and the origin of complaint psalms among the people (pp. 118–119, against the theory of »democratizing«). Delekat 1967, 11, maintains that there were »private Klagegebete in poetischer Form

prayer which renders it more plausible that the cultic form grew out of living practice than the reverse.

The following examples from the psalms of individual complaint will illustrate the various possibilities in employing the simple traditional prayer and in combining it with other elements of these psalms.

Psalms which reveal in their entire composition the pattern of traditional prayer – address, petition, and complaint introduced by כי – are not common in the Psalter. The purest example of this type of psalm is perhaps Ps 88 which begins with an expanded form of address and description of prayer, but after the petition for hearing subsequently contains nothing but complaint.

Ps 88

2 יהוה אלהי ישועתי   יום־צעקתי בלילה נגדך
3 תבוא לפניך תפלתי   הטה־אזנך לרנתי
4 כי־שבעה ברעות נפשי   וחיי לשאול הגיעו
5 נחשבתי עם־יורדי בור   הייתי כגבר אין־איל
6 במתים חפשי   כמו חללים שכבי קבר
   אשר לא זכרתם עוד   והמה מידך נגזרו
7 שתני בבור תחתיות   במחשכים במצלות
8 עלי סמכה חמתך   וכל־משבריך ענית סלה

— — — — —

17 עלי עברו חרוניך   בעותיך צמתותני
18 סבוני כמים כל־היום   הקיפו עלי יחד
19 הרחקת ממני אהב ורע   מידעי מחשך

This most dreary and dejected complaint is characterized by frequent usage of second person forms and suffixes: i.e. it is composed in prayer form. It has been dated in widely different ways.[276] Whether or not completely archaic, it obviously reveals an archaic form and shows that prayer and complaint to Yahweh could also be expressed with this kind of simplicity.[277]

In a few other psalms this simple pattern is completed by a final petition which may be a repetition of the petition at the beginning. Interestingly enough, this is the case in Ps 41 in which verses 5–11 can only be understood as a quotation of a complaint prayer.[278]

... nie anders als rein literarisch«, a hardly tenable view. The features of oral *poetry*, discussed by Culley (1967), already speak against the origin in writing by private poets.

[276] E.g. Kissane 1954, II 84: post-exilic on the basis of subject matter. Oesterley 1939, 393: from the early Exile or the fourth century B.C., since the author knew Job! For other arguments and different datings, see Kraus 1978, 773.

[277] Seybold 1973, 169, regards Ps 88 as one of the few sure cases of prayer against illness. Duhm 1922, 333, points out that the psalm makes no mention of sins or enemies.

[278] Ps 41 has been considered a thanksgiving psalm with a quotation of complaint prayer by e.g. Schmidt 1934, 78; Crüsemann 1969, 242–243; Kraus 1978, 466. Kissane 1953, I 181, however, sees its line of thought as consistent.

```
Ps 41   5  אני־אמרתי יהוה חנני רפאה נפשי כי־חטאתי לך
        6  אויבי יאמרו רע לי   מתי ימות ואבד שמו
           - - - -
        9  דבר־בליעל יצוק בו  ואשר שכב לא־יוסיף לקום
       10  גם־איש שלומי אשר־בטחתי בו  אוכל לחמי הגדיל עלי עקב
       11  ואתה יהוה חנני והקימני  ואשלמה להם
```

This exceptionally long quotation, located within a thanksgiving psalm, may well have been a complaint psalm in its own right.[279]

A similar form is found in Ps 38, which along with the two examples above, Ps 88 and 41, implies, according to Seybold, a case of illness as its background situation.[280] Another common feature in these three psalms is mention of the estrangement of the friends and relations of the suffering supplicant.

```
Ps 38   2  יהוה אל־בקצפך תוכיחני  ובחמתך תיסרני
        3  כי־חציך נחתו בי  ותנחת עלי ידך
        4  אין־מתם בבשרי מפני זעמך  אין־שלום בעצמי מפני חטאתי
        5  כי עונתי עברו ראשי  כמשא כבד יכבדו ממני
           - - - -
       12  אהבי ורעי מנגד נגעי יעמדו  וקרובי מרחק עמדו
           - - - -
       19  כי־עוני אגיד  אדאג מחטאתי
       20  ואיבי חיים עצמו  ורבו שנאי שקר
       21  ומשלמי רעה תחת טובה  ישטנוני תחת רדופי־טוב
       22  אל־תעזבני יהוה  אלהי אל־תרחק ממני
       23  חושה לעזרתי  אדני תשועתי
```

Kraus wishes to date Ps 38 to a late time for the sake of similarities in thought to Job.[281] No evident dependence is, however, discernible. In fact, the unproblematic connection between suffering and guilt (vv. 4–5, 17–18) suggests quite the opposite. In this respect, Ps 38 resembles Ps 41 (v. 5), in respect of the experience of Yahweh's wrath Ps 88.[282]

It was discovered that an expression of confidence in Yahweh could also be attached to the imperative prayer by means of כי. Even

---

[279] This is actually implied when vv. 5–11 are regarded as a quotation. Crüsemann 1969, 243, regards the complaint prayer as »formgerecht«.

[280] Ps 38, 41, and 88 are the only OT psalms which Seybold 1973, 169, with certainty considers to be connected with illness. Against this background, it is interesting to note that the petitions used in these psalms are all different.

[281] Kraus 1978, 447. Oesterley 1939, 226, dates Ps 38 to the Greek period, in keeping with his general trend towards very definite and late datings.

[282] In addition to Ps 38 and 88, individual complaint over Yahweh's wrath is found only in Ps 6:2 (a close parallel to Ps 38:2) and 102:11.

with this theme it was obviously possible to let the basic pattern grow
into a whole psalm. As an example we may consider Ps 16.

Ps 16

    שמרני אל כי־חסיתי בך
2 אמרת ליהוה אדני אתה
    טובתי בל־עליך
    - - - -
7 אברך את־יהוה אשר יעצני אף־לילות יסרוני כליותי
8 שויתי יהוה לנגדי תמיד כי מימיני בל־אמוט
9 לכן שמח לבי ויגל כבודי אף־בשרי ישכן לבטח
10 כי לא־תעזב נפשי לשאול לא־תתן חסידך לראות שחת
11 תודיעני ארח חיים
    שבע שמחות את־פניך נעמות בימינך נצח

In spite of the difficulties caused by corruption in vv. 3–4, Ps 16 appears to be entirely characterized by confidence in Yahweh and thankfulness.[283] It begins as a prayer, but contains no complaint, no mention of guilt or suffering or Yahweh's wrath. The purpose of this kind of a prayer was perhaps to ensure Yahweh's favour. At least it does not imply an emergency situation.

Ps 61 and 57 reveal features similar to Ps 16: a petition at the beginning and expressions of confidence extending over several lines. But, other features also appear.

Ps 61

2 שמעה אלהים רנתי הקשיבה תפלתי
3 מקצה הארץ אליך אקרא בעטף לבי
    בצור־ירום ממני תנחני
4 כי־היית מחסה לי מגדל־עז מפני אויב
5 אגורה באהלך עולמים אחסה בסתר כנפיך סלה
6 כי־אתה אלהים שמעת לנדרי נתת ירשת יראי שמך

In v. 3 this prayer approaches complaint, and vv. 7–8 concern the king, but the tone of the prayer is confidence and the last word a vow of praise.[284]

With Ps 57 we are already proceeding to psalms in which the pattern of traditional prayer only constitutes one part in the whole composition.

---

[283] Several scholars have regarded Ps 16 as a psalm of confidence: Duhm 1922, 62; Gunkel-Begrich 1933, 255; Kissane 1953, I xv; even Kraus in the editions before the fifth (xlvii, 119). On the other hand, Wevers *VT* VI (1956), 95, regards Ps 16 as a prayer against illness.

[284] Ps 61 is normally regarded as an individual complaint; see e.g. Gunkel-Begrich 1933, 212; Kraus 1978, 592. On the other hand, Weiser 1963, 301–303, considers it to be a thanksgiving psalm.

Ps 57
2 חנני אלהים חנני כי בך חסיה נפשי
ובצל כנפיך אחסה עד יעבר הוות
3 אקרא לאלהים עליון לאל גמר עלי
4 ישלח משמים ויושיעני חרף שאפי סלה
ישלח אלהים חסדו ואמתו

The theme of confidence finally changes – through complaint (vv. 5,7) – into actual praise (vv. 8–11), framed by the refrain (vv. 6, 12)

רומה על־השמים אלהים על כל־הארץ כבודך

which is a kind of praising petition. The latter part of the psalm also appears as part of Ps 108.[285]

To call prayers like those in Ps 16, 61, and 57 »heard prayers« is hardly necessary as an explanation for the combination of petitions and expressions of confidence or thankfulness in them.[286] The cultic life probably offered opportunities also for less anxious prayers. The ones under discussion are more naturally explained as ordinary prayers of Yahweh's worshipers than as conditioned by oracles spoken by priests in the temple.[287] In the psalms under discussion the expressions of thankfulness directly develop from the confident attitude of the prayer.[288] Confidence in Yahweh should be seen as one of the main elements of the OT religion, rather than as a strange detail requiring a particular explanation. On the other hand, it must be admitted that the term »complaint psalm« does not characterize prayers of this type particularly well. It would perhaps be advisable to use the more general term »prayer psalm« of all psalms containing petitions to Yahweh, including »complaint psalms«.[289]

The examples have so far each revealed one instance of the pattern of traditional prayer. In a number of psalms this pattern is, however,

---

[285] Beyerlin 1970, 129–135, includes Ps 57 in his »Psalmen mit institutionsbezogenen Rettungsaussagen« and characterizes it as a prayer psalm, rather than a complaint psalm, and as such »gattungskomplex«.

[286] For the category of »heard prayers«, see Westermann 1977, 60.

[287] Cf. Begrich *ZAW* 52 (1934), 81–92 (= *Gesammelte Studien,* ThB 21, 217–231). See also Becker 1975, 62–65.

[288] I do not agree with Beyerlin 1970, 156, who considers the function of thanksgiving (or a vow of such) in prayer psalms to be to invoke Yahweh's help, i.e. to be a kind of *captatio benevolentiae*. See also Gunkel-Begrich 1933, 248. The more anxious individual complaints which imply an emergency situation do not contain thanksgiving.

[289] This distinction was suggested by Beyerlin 1970, 154–155, who could not include his »Psalmen mit institutionsbezogenen Rettungsaussagen« under the heading of complaint psalms. Although I do not quite see the difference between e.g. Ps 57 which is »institutionsbezogen« and Ps 56 and 59 which are not, the terminological distinction between prayer and complaint is welcome. Cf. also Kraus 1978, 49–60, who combines under the title »prayer psalms« both complaints and thanksgivings.

The Traditional Prayer in the Psalms

found to be employed repeatedly, e.g. Ps 31 and 71. These two psalms show a great deal of similarity in their first verses as well as in their overall composition. The first part of these psalms includes a prayer section containing expressions of confidence.

Ps 31
2 בְּךָ יהוה חָסִיתִי אַל־אֵבוֹשָׁה לְעוֹלָם בְּצִדְקָתְךָ פַלְּטֵנִי
3 הַטֵּה אֵלַי אָזְנְךָ מְהֵרָה הַצִּילֵנִי
   הֱיֵה לִי לְצוּר־מָעוֹז לְבֵית מְצוּדוֹת לְהוֹשִׁיעֵנִי
4 כִּי־סַלְעִי וּמְצוּדָתִי אָתָּה וּלְמַעַן שִׁמְךָ תַּנְחֵנִי וּתְנַהֲלֵנִי
5 תּוֹצִיאֵנִי מֵרֶשֶׁת זוּ טָמְנוּ לִי כִּי־אַתָּה מָעוּזִּי
6 בְּיָדְךָ אַפְקִיד רוּחִי פָּדִיתָה אוֹתִי יהוה אֵל אֱמֶת
7 שָׂנֵאתִי הַשֹּׁמְרִים הַבְלֵי־שָׁוְא וַאֲנִי אֶל־יהוה בָּטָחְתִּי
8 אָגִילָה וְאֶשְׂמְחָה בְּחַסְדֶּךָ
   אֲשֶׁר רָאִיתָ אֶת־עָנְיִי יָדַעְתָּ בְּצָרוֹת נַפְשִׁי
9 וְלֹא הִסְגַּרְתַּנִי בְּיַד־אוֹיֵב הֶעֱמַדְתָּ בַמֶּרְחָב רַגְלָי

Ps 71 begins with similar petitions, but continues for the most part with different expressions of confidence and thankfulness.

Ps 71
1 בְּךָ־יהוה חָסִיתִי אַל־אֵבוֹשָׁה לְעוֹלָם
2 בְּצִדְקָתְךָ תַּצִּילֵנִי וּתְפַלְּטֵנִי הַטֵּה־אֵלַי אָזְנְךָ וְהוֹשִׁיעֵנִי
3 הֱיֵה לִי לְצוּר מָעוֹן לָבוֹא תָּמִיד צִוִּיתָ לְהוֹשִׁיעֵנִי
   כִּי־סַלְעִי וּמְצוּדָתִי אָתָּה
4 אֱלֹהַי פַּלְּטֵנִי מִיַּד רָשָׁע מִכַּף מְעַוֵּל וְחוֹמֵץ
5 כִּי־אַתָּה תִקְוָתִי אֲדֹנָי יהוה מִבְטַחִי מִנְּעוּרָי
6 עָלֶיךָ נִסְמַכְתִּי מִבֶּטֶן מִמְּעֵי אִמִּי אַתָּה גוֹזִי בְּךָ תְהִלָּתִי תָמִיד
7 כְּמוֹפֵת הָיִיתִי לְרַבִּים וְאַתָּה מַחֲסִי־עֹז
8 יִמָּלֵא פִי תְּהִלָּתֶךָ כָּל־הַיּוֹם תִּפְאַרְתֶּךָ

After these tones of confidence and thanksfulness, both of these psalms entirely change their theme. A new imperative prayer introduces a section of complaint, which seems to have nothing in common with the first section.[290]

Ps 31
10 חָנֵּנִי יהוה כִּי צַר־לִי עָשְׁשָׁה בְכַעַס עֵינִי נַפְשִׁי וּבִטְנִי
11 כִּי כָלוּ בְיָגוֹן חַיַּי וּשְׁנוֹתַי בַּאֲנָחָה
    כָּשַׁל בַּעֲוֹנִי כֹחִי וַעֲצָמַי עָשֵׁשׁוּ
12 מִכָּל־צֹרְרַי הָיִיתִי חֶרְפָּה וְלִשְׁכֵנַי מְאֹד
    וּפַחַד לִמְיֻדָּעָי רֹאַי בַּחוּץ נָדְדוּ מִמֶּנִּי

---

[290] Kraus 1978, 394–395 and 652, calls both Ps 31 and 71 »Gebetsformular« and presupposes a process of tradition at least for Ps 31. It is characteristic of Kraus' exegesis that he attempts to elicit a »case history« behind the psalm, so also for Ps 71 (*ibid*. 653–654). E.g. Schmidt 1934, 56–58, divides Ps 31 in two, vv. 2–9 and 10–25, not however Ps 71 (cf. *ibid*. 134–135). Westermann 1984, 126, finds in Ps 31 several psalms: vv. 1–7 a psalm of confidence, vv. 10–19 a complaint, and vv. 8–9, 20–25 a thanksgiving.

13	נשכחתי כמת מלב הייתי ככלי אבד
14	כי שמעתי דבת רבים מגור מסביב
	בהוסדם יחד עלי לקחת נפשי זממו

Ps 71

9	אל־תשליכני לעת זקנה ככלות כחי אל־תעזבני
10	כי־אמרו אויבי לי ושמרי נפשי נועצו יחדו
11	לאמר אלהים עזבו רדפו ותפשוהו כי־אין מציל
12	אלהים אל־תרחק ממני אלהי לעזרתי חישה

Both of these extensive psalms contain about ten further verses and finally end on a note of praise. The various parts give the impression of being independent and of only being added one after the other.[291] There are several themes in both psalms, so that no clear picture can be obtained of the situation in which the psalms were used or meant to be used. The only recurring theme is the mention of old age in Ps 71:9 and 18. On the other hand, several links with other psalms, i.e. conventional phrases, even »runs« of several phrases, are found in both (e.g. Ps 31:2–4//71:1–3, 31:10//6:8, 31:21//27:5, 71:12–13//40:14–15//70:2–3).[292] The sections which follow the pattern of traditional prayer seem to be building blocks on which the whole composition rests. The use of one and the same block in both psalms makes this clear.[293] The term »adding style« which Culley uses to characterize oral poetry seems most appropriate in connection with these psalms.[294]

Furthermore, Ps 5 seems to be constructed in a similar way. The first section contains petitions to which כי links confident expressions describing the prayer and manifesting faith in Yahweh as the righteous God (vv. 2–8). The second section (vv. 9–10) contains petitions the cause of which are the petitioner's enemies. The petitions concern guidance and כי combines with them complaint against treacherous people. The third section (v. 11), the least extensive of all, consists of petitions directed against the enemies, followed by a כי clause. Vv. 12–13 finally conclude the psalm with expressions of joy and confidence. Towards the end the units seem to become less extensive and less independent. Interestingly enough, the prayer for guidance »because of my enemies« (vv. 9–10) has a close parallel in Ps 27:11–12.[295] In Ps 27 the preceding

---

[291] N.B. however, the absence of address in the second section of Ps 71 (v. 9).
[292] See above pp. 52–53.
[293] Culley 1967, 93, does not consider Ps 31:2–4 and 71:1–3 to be in a relationship of literary dependence on one another. What e.g. Kissane 1953, I 308, in the case of Ps 71 calls »a mosaic of passages from other psalms« should not be interpreted as quotations of written psalms but as utilization of the same oral tradition. Accordingly, parallel passages should not be textually forced in conformity with one another.
[294] For »adding style«, see Culley 1967, 97. Culley, however, concentrates on smaller units.
[295] N.B. the common vocabulary: נחני, דרכך, למען שוררי, and the root ישר (מישור/הושר).

verses (vv. 7–10) contain a prayer in affliction, by a person forsaken even by his parents (v. 10 כי). The two sections of prayer are, however, surrounded by passages, characterized by confidence in Yahweh, which are not addressed to Yahweh but refer to Yahweh in the third person form. In the final verse of the psalm (v. 14), the second person singular is used in an encouraging exhortation, which is possibly meant as an answer to the petitioner himself.²⁹⁶

As an example which more closely resembles the previous cases with actual complaint prayers we may consider Ps 6. The first prayer section combines the petitions which were found in Ps 38:2 and 41:5.

Ps 6 2 יהוה אל־באפך תוכיחני ואל־בחמתך תיסרני
3 חנני יהוה כי אמלל אני רפאני יהוה כי נבהלו עצמי
4 ונפשי נבהלה מאד ואת יהוה עד־מתי

After this symmetrically constructed first section the psalm continues with another complaint prayer formed according to the pattern of traditional prayer (vv. 5–8). Thoughts of confidence in Yahweh only appear in the final section which is addressed to »workers of evil« and refer to Yahweh in the third person (vv. 9–11).

In a few further examples the pattern of traditional prayer is found at the beginning of the psalm, whereas the end part is constructed in a different way. This is the case in Ps 69 and 102.

Ps 69 2 הושיעני אלהים כי באו מים עד־נפש
3 טבעתי ביון מצולה ואין מעמד
באתי במעמקי־מים ושבלת שטפתני
4 יגעתי בקראי נחר גרוני
כלו עיני מיחל לאלהי
5 רבו משערות ראשי שנאי חנם
עצמו מצמיתי איבי שקר
אשר לא־גזלתי אז אשיב

The first section of this long psalm contains a simple and very personal complaint prayer, which in its style resembles some of the examples above. The »deep waters« and »mire« are mentioned again in a further prayer (vv. 15–16), but otherwise the first prayer section has little in common with the problems dealt with later in the psalm. Even the length of the verse diverges clearly from the rest of the psalm. Even if the composition of the whole reveals features that speak for a conscious plan, the composer probably obtained most of his material from tradition, finding there smaller and larger units for use as building blocks.²⁹⁷

---

²⁹⁶ For this interpretation, see Beyerlin 1970, 125–129.
²⁹⁷ Kraus 1978, 641, has no doubts about the unity of Ps 69. Seybold 1973, 137, regards

A similar impression is given by Ps 102.

Ps 102

2 יהוה שמעה תפלתי ושועתי אליך תבוא
3 אל־תסתר פניך ממני ביום צר לי
   הטה־אלי אזנך ביום אקרא מהר ענני
4 כי־כלו בעשן ימי . ועצמותי כמו־קד נחרו
5 הוכה־כעשב ויבש לבי כי־שכחתי מאכל לחמי
6 מקול אנחתי דבקה עצמי לבשרי
7 דמיתי לקאת מדבר הייתי ככוס חרבות
8 שקדתי ואהיה כצפור בודד על־גג
9 כל־היום חרפוני אויבי מהוללי בי נשבעו
10 כי־אפר כלחם אכלתי ושקוי בבכי מסכתי
11 מפני־זעמך וקצפך כי נשאתני ותשליכני
12 ימי כצל נטוי ואני כעשב איבש

In this case the discrepancy between the beginning of the psalm and what follows is even greater. Vv. 2–12 contain a prayer consisting of several petitions and a complaint which arises from the narrow perspective of individual suffering, resembling the above examples from Ps 88, 38, 6, and 69. From v. 13 on, the psalm reveals completely different views, even theological reflection (vv. 13, 26–28). The background situation is without doubt the Exile, and the prayer concerns those who love »the stones of Zion« (v. 15) and are imprisoned (v. 21).[298] The beginning of the psalm which knows nothing of this situation can only be understood as an old complaint prayer – or part of one – which was used as a building block for a new larger complaint psalm in a new situation. Nothing speaks for the whole psalm having been composed at one time.[299]

The two last-mentioned psalms, Ps 69 and 102, are good examples of one of the greatest dilemmas in the exegesis of the psalms. Scholars

---

Ps 69 as »klar gegliedert« and suggests that the final form was acquired by writing. On the other hand, Becker 1966, 45–48, and 1975, 91–92, regards Ps 69 as an example of »collective reinterpretation«, i. e. an originally individual complaint psalm (vv. 2–30) which was later on used as a congregational one and adapted for this purpose by the addition of further verses.

[298] See e. g. Kraus 1978, 867–868; Becker 1966, 43, and 1975, 91.

[299] Seybold 1973, 142, and Kissane 1954, II 141, consider Ps 102 to be a unity. Duhm 1922, 368, on the other hand, is determined about the necessity to divide it between v. 12 and v. 13. Schmidt 1934, 184–185, sees in vv. 2–12, 24–25 an old complaint prayer that was used again in a later situation. Oesterley 1939, 433–434, agrees with Schmidt but regards the old prayer as post-exilic. Becker 1966, 43–45, also follows Schmidt but is more interested in the »reinterpreted« new whole. Kraus 1978, 864–866, is hesitant – »Denn wie soll man sich diesen Kompositionsvorgang vorstellen?« (p. 865) – and interprets all the different parts of Ps 102 as relating to the historical situation of the Exile. Veijola 1982, 115, seems to leave the question open.

who wish to explain complex psalms like these as unities – even if it causes great trouble – must also date them to one particular period. If one of the various parts provides clear grounds for a late dating, the whole psalm becomes post-exilic and late, as is the case with Ps 69 and 102.[300] On the other hand, if it is admitted that some parts were taken as such from tradition, the parts may be given a different dating. The occurrence of prayer sections composed according to the pattern of traditional prayer – a full prayer in itself – as part of Ps 69 and 102 clearly suggests that these psalms came about by a natural process of growth and the addition of further elements. The passages of traditional prayer may have been used as such, perhaps as part of a ritual, a long time before they became embedded into the psalms we know.

3.3 *The Origin and Relative Dating of the Traditional Prayer*

It is generally reckoned that psalms contain both older material and later expansions, additions and reworkings of the old material. Indeed, the late fixing of the text and collection of the OT Psalter renders it possible for each and every psalm to have gone through a redaction. Nevertheless, this possibility is not always taken into consideration in the exegesis and dating of long and complex psalms. It must be admitted that the dating of psalms is an uncertain business for which few reliable criteria exist. This should not, however, lead to the dating of long psalms according to their youngest elements. It is true, the possibility of »reinterpretation« is increasingly taken into account in the more recent exegesis of the psalms, and this trend even allows for a more differentiated view in questions of dating, but it is an exegesis which seems to be most interested in the final result, in the psalm as it appears in the Psalter.[301] On the other hand, elements that were used again in a new whole were not always »reinterpreted«. The »reinterpretation« only constitutes one aspect of the process whereby smaller and larger units could be utilized again in the composition of new psalms. It is in the interest of the form-critical research to discover such units.

One criterion for recognizing a relatively old element within an individual prayer psalm, as I see it, could be the simple form of traditional prayer with its conventional prayer imperatives. The traditional prayer,

---

[300] For Ps 69, see e.g. Oesterley 1939, 327; Kraus 1978, 642. For Ps 102, see e.g. Kissane 1954, II 141; Kraus 1978, 865; Veijola 1982, 55–57, 79–82, 88–91, discusses Ps 102 within a group of exilic complaint psalms which reveal similarities in language to Ps 89 and thus confirm its exilic origin. In Ps 102 the points of contact with Ps 89 are, however, found in the latter part of the psalm.

[301] See particularly Becker 1966 and 1975.

as described above, may be considered the form of prayer which the individual petitioner would have used at the time the psalm tradition was a living force, during the centuries before the Exile. One of the basic observations concerning the traditional prayer is that it is capable of functioning as an independent prayer. Even as a part of a longer psalm, it frequently retains its independence in the shape of different verse length, different vocabulary, or different subject matter in comparison with the rest of the psalm. A long psalm may consist of several fairly independent prayer sections and other elements which have been added to them more or less at random, without any conscious overall scheme. This type of »adding style« seems to be characteristic of most individual prayer psalms, particularly in the latter half of the psalm where even prayer sections often lose their pattern. On the other hand, prayer psalms with a conscious plan also exist. One example is Ps 22:2–22 which is often regarded as the prototype of an individual complaint psalm.[302] It consists of two sections of complaint, both culminating in imperative petitions (vv. 12, 20–22) of which the latter repeats the former and appears to be the climax of the whole in a way not paralleled by other individual prayer psalms. Other features that are not exactly common are the most effective opening with why-questions and the reference to Yahweh's earlier great deeds for Israel and for the individual petitioner.[303] On the other hand, the exception here, too, proves the rule: the petition in v. 12 follows the pattern of traditional prayer, although without the address. In contrast with a conscious, symmetrical arrangement, like that in Ps 22 or in the latter part of Ps 57, the appearance of sections of traditional prayer as principal elements in psalms that are characterized by the »adding style« gives an impression of spontaneity and greater originality.

For the sake of comparison, a few words should also be said about the form of the prayers in congregational complaint psalms. It was observed in our analysis of the prayer imperatives that some of the conventional prayer words were employed in congregational as well as in individual psalms, although differences were also found. The pattern of traditional prayer does not, however, appear to be central in the composition of congregational complaint psalms. The only congregational psalm beginning with a prayer and introducing a longer section of complaint by כי is Ps 83 (vv. 2–9). In some psalms a cluster of several prayer

---

[302] Recently Fuchs 1982, 39–40.
[303] See Westermann 1984, 64–65. The conscious overall scheme does not exclude the possibility that old material was also used in this psalm, as emphasized by Westermann. Becker 1966, 49–53, and 1975, 92–96, again interprets Ps 22 as an example of the »reinterpretation«: vv. 2–22 a complaint psalm, vv. 23–27 thanksgiving, vv. 28–32 interpretative verses.

imperatives occurs at the end of the psalm (Ps 44:24–27, 74:18–23, 90:13–17). Some others use the petitions to frame the main part (Ps 106:4,47 [304]) or as a refrain (Ps 80:4,8,20). Motivation clauses introduced by כי are not particularly common in congregational prayers (Ps 44:26, 74:20, 79:7, 8, 82:8). Instead, these psalms often refer to Yahweh's great deeds in Israel's past. Most of the congregational complaint psalms are clearly conditioned by the national catastrophe of the Exile and thus datable to exilic or post-exilic times.[305] Since, however, they apparently imply the existence of an earlier practice of individual prayer – and since even old individual prayers were »reinterpreted« in the new problematic situation posed by the Exile – it seems most natural to regard the traditional prayer in our relative dating as preceding the congregational complaints. The differences found in the employment of the various petitions rather speak for this than the reverse order of precedence. Accordingly, the most clearly datable petition »remember« (see Section 1.11) which appears in congregational psalms, in the two acrostics Ps 25 and 119, and in Neh is nowhere found in the genre of individual complaint proper.

Furthermore, several details in the traditional prayer suggest that its original source antedates not only the congregational complaint psalms but also the Exile. As regards the petitions, the most frequent type of petition »save«, »deliver« (see Section 1.1) represents vocabulary which finds early attestation in personal names and in the earliest sources of the Pentateuch, but on the other hand, soon becomes archaic and is supplanted by »help« (עזר), which, however, occupies a rather marginal position among the psalms petitions. To take another example, the petition »teach me«, frequent in the acrostic psalms and clearly connected with post-exilic Torah religiosity, is found only once in individual complaints, in Ps 143 which is also otherwise clearly datable to post-exilic times (see Section 3.4 below). The absence of »help me«, »teach me«, and »remember« from individual complaints proper cannot be attributable to their unsuitability in this context, since they do occur both in the two acrostics, Ps 25 and 119, which also represent individual prayer, and in clearly post-exilic prose prayers. Also bearing in mind the above discussion on features which speak for an oral background, on the structural affinity with normal everyday requests in Hebrew, and on the lack of hymnic epithets in the address, one ends up with an accumulation of criteria for a relatively speaking early dating and with hardly any reverse arguments. Actually, nothing speaks against the pre-exilic origin of the pattern of traditional prayer and of the conventional language of prayer used in it. It seems more probable that these most

---

[304] For the problematic character of Ps 106, see Kraus 1978, 899–901.
[305] See e.g. Kraus 1978, 53; Veijola 1982, 176–210.

personal prayers which arise from situations of individual peril – illness, persecution, and desertion – were preserved as the heritage of the preexilic religious life rather than created as new forms of prayer in the situation of the Exile. It is quite possible that some of these original prayers even survived till the final form of the Psalter.

The original »Sitz-im-Leben« of the traditional prayer may well be thought of along the lines sketched by Gerstenberger, i.e. the smaller forms of cultic life assigned for individuals with their primary group in the critical situations of life.[306] What, apart from this prayer, belonged to the rite is completely outside the scope of this study. That we do not have the means for discovering much about this ritual life should be clear to anyone. A collection of 150 psalms which did not receive a fixed form until perhaps the third century B.C. – when the rites were no longer in use – is but a fragment when considered against the centuries of living psalm tradition before the Exile. Nevertheless, it is possible to distinguish in the Psalter passages of traditional prayer which pertain to different troubles and different attitudes of the supplicant – or rather, which could be used as models of prayer by various supplicants – whether in deep distress and suffering or in more confident spirits, wishing to express both requests and thanks and to confess to Yahweh.[307] Most of the various situations of life cannot be found in the psalms – and should not be expected to be found. That a large number of prayers concerning the enemy were preserved to us may reflect the situation that pertained during the fixing of the collection, a time of suffering and of many enemies for the people of Israel. On the other hand, the users of the OT Psalter have always been able to »reinterpret« the psalms prayers in the light of their own personal situation.

As for the performance of the rite, Gerstenberger postulates a ritual expert as having taken a leading position in it.[308] We should perhaps see this person – at least as far as the more ancient times are concerned

---

[306] Gerstenberger 1980, 147–160.

[307] Beyerlin 1970, 154–155, makes a sharp distinction between prayer psalms (»Bittgebetgattung«) and complaint psalms (»Klageliedgattung«), of which only the latter are characterized by poignant complaint, a distinction which surprisingly also agrees with the distinction between psalms with or without an institutional background (in the former case »institutionsbezogen«). It is difficult to agree with Beyerlin regarding this dichotomy. Firstly, one can hardly say that his prayer psalms would be absolutely free from complaint. E.g. Ps 5 and 17 clearly complain about enemies in describing them. Secondly, Beyerlin seems not only to introduce a new division of the genres but also a new definition of genre (»Gattung«), in that he regards the various genres as building blocks which can be combined into different wholes without being bound to one particular function or one particular »Sitz-im-Leben«. If »Gattung« and »Sitz-im-Leben« do not correspond to each other, we are no longer dealing with Gunkel's terminology.

[308] Gerstenberger 1980, 134–137, 168–169.

– as resembling an oral poet who is expert in the conventional forms of prayer and the formulaic phrases used in them and is capable of producing new combinations of the traditional material for the needs of the various situations of life where prayers were needed.[309] The fixing of these traditional prayers into a written form should not be assigned to a date too early in a society in which most people were illiterate.[310] To judge from the fact that so little is known about ritual life before the Exile, the process of recording these traditions was obviously seriously interrupted by the beginning of the Exile.

3.4 The Developed Form of the Traditional Prayer

Our analysis of the imperative prayer and its context resulted in the recognition of a characteristic pattern of prayer frequently found in individual complaint psalms, the traditional prayer consisting of address, petitions, and expressions of complaint or confidence or the like introduced by כי. The more extensive examples of this pattern could be identified as tradition blocks with a possibly independent existence before becoming part of a longer psalm. However, a good deal of our material, the less extensive cases – where the whole pattern is found, for instance, within a line – do not fit into this picture. Since the pattern of traditional prayer was found to be the normal pattern of making a request in Hebrew, it is natural that it was applied in prayer texts quite unconsciously. Nevertheless, these texts also reveal a thread of development, leading from the simple individual prayer to skilful and even artificial forms of prayer language using repetition of the same pattern.

The pattern of traditional prayer could probably be employed also in the more simple and spontaneous forms of prayer not only once but twice or even several times, so that the whole consisted of strophes of prayer. In the later development of psalms in the hands of professional singers or sacerdotal psalm specialists after the Exile, the traditional prayer imperatives and the traditional pattern of prayer were molded into a new whole. In the OT Psalter we even come across a psalm type with multiple employment of single prayer imperatives and short כי clauses or other completing expressions, each pair usually occupying no more space than one line.

---

[309] For a description of the activity of an oral poet using formulaic techniques, see Culley 1967, 5–9.

[310] It is hardly probable that prayer texts were offered for the use of worshipers – like hymn books nowadays – in temples and holy places. Cf. Gerstenberger 1980, 137, who assumes that the »ritual expert« had texts at his disposal. Fuchs 1982, 298, 312–313, supposes that prayer texts could be used by every one in the temple, a clear anachronism.

The two clearest examples of the developed form of the traditional prayer are found in Ps 86 and 143. The petitions and other phrases used in these psalms are for the most part highly traditional.³¹¹ They have been composed most probably on the basis of a study of older psalms, although at the same time they reveal new features. The skilfulness of the composition seems to imply the written form as the original.³¹²

Ps 86

הטה־יהוה אזנך ענני כי־עני ואביון אני
2 שמרה נפשי כי־חסיד אני
הושע עבדך אתה אלהי הבוטח אליך
3 חנני אדני כי אליך אקרא כל־היום
4 שמח נפש עבדך כי אליך אדני נפשי אשא
5 כי־אתה אדני טוב וסלח ורב־חסד לכל־קראיך
6 האזינה יהוה תפלתי והקשיבה בקול תחנונותי
7 ביום צרתי אקראך כי תענני

One of the petitions שמח (v. 4) occurs nowhere else in individual prayer psalms and only once in a congregational psalm in Ps 90:15. Another possibly late feature is the employment of עבדך instead of the first person singular (vv. 2, 4; see above p. 49). The middle part of the psalm is a combination of theological reflection, praise, and complaint.³¹³ Further petitions occur in vv. 11 and 16–17, however, in less traditional form and vocabulary.

In Ps 143, the first half of the psalm follows the more extensive pattern.

Ps 143

יהוה שמע תפלתי האזינה אל־תחנוני
באמנתך ענני בצדקתך
2 ואל־תבוא במשפט את־עבדך כי לא־יצדק לפניך כל־חי
3 כי רדף אויב נפשי דכא לארץ חיתי הושיבני במחשכים
כמתי עולם – – – – – –

---

³¹¹ For Ps 86, see Duhm 1922, 329: »eine Sammlung von Zitaten«; Kissane 1954, II 76: »largely made up of quotations«. For Ps 143, see Duhm 1922, 469: »eine Blumenlese aus allen möglichen Klageliedern«. If not taken as degradation, these statements describe the psalms in question rather well. For the later post-exilic and Jewish practice of composing psalms on the basis of traditional elements and quotations, not because of inability to compose totally new poetry but in order to stay within the ancient psalmodic tradition, see Holm-Nielsen *StTh* XIV (1960), 1–53.

³¹² Beyerlin 1970, 30, regards Ps 86 as a unity, whereas Gunkel 1926, 376, divides it in two between verses 13 and 14.

³¹³ According to Perlitt 1969, 213–214, the formula dealing with Yahweh's mercy Ps 86: 15 (cf. v. 5), which also occurs in Ex 34:6, Joel 2:13, Jon 4:2, Ps 103:8, and Neh 9:17, must be regarded as post-deuteronomistic.

The rest of the psalm consists of the rapid succession of prayer imperatives and completing motivations with or without כי.

Ps 143

7 מהר ענני יהוה כלתה רוחי
אל־תסתר פניך ממני ונמשלתי עם־ירדי בור
8 השמיעני בבקר חסדך כי־בך בטחתי
הודיעני דרך־זו אלך כי־אליך נשאתי נפשי
9 הצילני מאיבי יהוה אליך כסתי
10 למדני לעשות רצונך כי־אתה אלוהי
רוחך טובה תנחני בארץ מישור
11 למען־שמך יהוה תחיני בצדקתך תוציא מצרה נפשי
12 ובחסדך תצמית איבי והאבדת כל־צררי נפשי
כי אני עבדך

N.B. the use of עבדך also in this psalm (vv. 2, 12). The petition למדני (v. 10) is otherwise found only in the acrostic psalms Ps 25 and 119. Another link to Ps 119 may be seen in the subjunctive תחיני (v. 11), which corresponds to the petition חיני frequently found in Ps 119 but not elsewhere (see above Section 1.10). The frequent employment of prepositional phrases referring to Yahweh's divine attributes has been discussed above (p. 64; for other features, see also pp. 65, 73). Furthermore, the plea that Yahweh would not »enter into judgement« with the petitioner (v. 2) sounds extraordinary in comparison with the frequent prayers which ask for justice.[314] This petition and its motivation clause, »for no man living is righteous before thee«, can only be understood against the background of the post-exilic theological reflection over Israel's guilt.[315] It may also be observed that the כי clauses in our last two examples no longer perform their old function as an expression of the theme of the prayer, but have become less meaningful, containing a description of prayer or general remarks that have less relevance to the situation of the eventual supplicant. This phenomenon could be seen as an example of the process of spiritualization.[316] The pleas are urgent, but misery no longer shows its face.

To a lesser degree, the same development in the form of the imperative prayer may be discerned in Ps 142:7–8.

Ps 142

7 הקשיבה אל־רנתי כי־דלותי מאד
הצילני מרדפי כי אמצו ממני
8 הוציאה ממסגר נפשי להודות את־שמך
בי יכתרו צדיקים כי תגמל עלי

---

[314] Kraus 1978, 1117, regards it as a »Fremdkörper«.
[315] Cf. the prayers in Ezra 9, Neh 9, and Dan 9. See also Westermann 1977, 158–159; v. Rad 1966, I 394–395.
[316] See Becker 1966, 31–32; Holm-Nielsen *StTh* XIV (1960), 10. Westermann 1977, 143, interprets Ps 143 as an expression of spiritual suffering. Cf. Duhm 1922, 469: »es wird dem Leser schwer, solche Klagen ernst zu nehmen«.

In Ps 69:14–19 the use of the pattern is less regular and variety is produced by the employment of prepositional motivations.

Ps 69

14 ואני תפלתי־לך יהוה עת רצון
אלהים ברב־חסדך ענני באמת ישעך
15 הצילני מטיט ואל־אטבעה אנצלה משנאי וממעמקי־מים
16 אל־תשטפני שבלת מים ואל־תבלעני מצולה
ואל־תאטר־עלי באר פיה
17 ענני יהוה כי־טוב חסדך כרב רחמיך פנה אלי
18 ואל־תסתר פניך מעבדך כי־צר־לי מהר ענני
19 קרבה אל־נפשי גאלה למען איבי פדני

It should be noted that two verses do not conform to the pattern, viz. vv. 15–16, which function as a link with the beginning of the psalm, even here an indication of the composite character of the psalm.

When the pattern of traditional prayer is used in this short, repetitive form, the motivations which attach themselves to the petitions – whether כי clauses or prepositional phrases – actually seem to justify the title »motivations for divine intervention«. Furthermore, it was particularly the more theological type of »motivation for divine intervention« that continued its existence in later prayer language, in both Hebrew and Greek (cf. e.g. Dan 9:18–19, Prayer of Manasseh 13, Ode 14:25, Mt 6:13 K L W Δ Θ Π etc.).[317] That is, the formal element, which in the more ancient pattern of prayer contained the theme of the prayer, describing the petitioner's distress or expressing his confidence in Yahweh, in the later form acquires more theological content, whereas ever less and less room is left for complaint.[318]

3.5 Prayer Literature in the Psalter

The acrostic psalms, Ps 25 and 119, which have not been dealt with so far, also contain a good deal of traditional material, but represent a late artificial form in its utilization. Some of the psalms with a more skilful structure, discussed above, supposedly acquired their final form in writing, but nevertheless obviously shared the contemporary cultic use of the more ancient pieces. The two acrostic psalms again could be called prayer literature in a special sense, since the literary form seems to play a primary role in their composition.[319]

---

[317] For further discussion on the Greek form, which contains ὅτι in place of כי, see Aejmelaeus, »OTI causale in Septuagintal Greek«, in La Septuaginta en la investigacion contemporanea, pp. 115–132.

[318] See also Westermann 1977, 157.

[319] For the term »prayer literature«, see Ruppert ZAW 84 (1972), 576–582; Kraus 1978, 59. The literary character and origin of certain psalms should perhaps not be taken

In our analysis of the imperative petitions, the two acrostic psalms 25 and 119 were discovered to contain several occurrences of the conventional prayer words of the individual complaints. On the other hand, they reveal a number of recurring petitions which do not occur – or occur most rarely – in the individual complaint proper, such as למדני »teach me«, זכר »remember«, הבינני »give me understanding«, חיני »give me life« (see above Sections 1.10 and 1.11). The total number of petitions is very high in these two psalms, in fact the highest among the psalms of the Psalter, Ps 25 containing 16 cases (of which 1 negated) and Ps 119 as many as 62 cases (of which 7 negated). The next is Ps 86 with a total of 15 imperative petitions.

The appearance of the imperative petitions in Ps 25 and 119 does not seem to follow any discernible pattern. They cannot be said to constitute a compositional factor. The priority of the acrostic principle is most clearly seen in the appearance of hifʿil imperatives in the ה section. The petitions are scattered throughout the psalms and in most cases occur without the address. Motivating כי clauses have been attached to imperative petitions in the following cases: Ps 25:5,6,11,16, 19, 119:22,35,39,43,66,94,153,176. All of the motivation clauses are short and they reveal a somewhat peculiar character. Complaint is rarely found in them: Ps 25:11,16,19. As theological motivations we find the following: Ps 25:5 כי־אתה אלהי ישעי »for you are the God of my salvation«, 25:6 כי מעולם המה »(remember your mercy and your steadfast love) for they have been from of old«, 119:39 כי משפטיך טובים »for your ordinances are good«. All other motivations in Ps 119 contain the perfect of the first person singular, e.g. v. 22 כי עדתיך נצרתי »for I have kept your testimonies«, v. 43 כי למשפטך יחלתי »for my hope is in your ordinances«, v. 153 כי־תורתך לא שכחתי »for I have not forgotten your law«. The outward appearance of certain lines thus resembles the pattern of prayer as observed in such psalms as Ps 86 and 143. The contents of these motivations, however, have no parallels in other psalms. On the other hand, Ps 119 also frequently employs prepositional phrases, in particular, ones referring to Yahweh's »word« or »ordinances«, not paralleled by other psalms, either (see above Section 2.2.2). The characteristic motivations of Ps 119 can only be understood as part of Torah religiosity,[320] whereas in Ps 25 one may discern closer

---

offhand as an implication of detachment from the cult. Holm-Nielsen *StTh* XIV (1960), 8–10, emphasizes that in the changed circumstances after the Exile even the concept of cult was changed and the so-called non-cultic psalms could probably have their place in the new cultic forms of later times.

[320] See Kraus 1978, 997. Cf. the doom of Duhm 1922, 428: »eine solche Ahnungslosigkeit gegenüber allem, was außerhalb der eigenen dunklen Zelle existiert, eine solche Abwesenheit höheren Wahrheitsdranges findet sich nicht etwa im jüdischen Gesetztum« (Ps 119).

affinity with the traditional complaint prayer language, though combined with characteristics of this later type of religiosity.[321] It is only with serious reservations that these psalms – particularly Ps 119 – could be considered as representative even partly of the genre of individual complaint. They reveal only a slight formal resemblance to this genre and do not share the main ideas or the »Sitz-im-Leben«.[322]

---

[321] For Ps 25, see Kraus 1978, 351–352; Ruppert *ZAW* 84 (1972), 576–582. Holm-Nielsen *StTh* XIV (1960), 45–48, sees the background of Ps 25 in wisdom literature. Schmidt 1934, 46, wonders at the expressivity of the prayer in spite of the artificiality of the form.

[322] E.g. Kraus 1978, 351, 997, wants to find characteristics of the old genres in these psalms. See also v. Rad, *Gesammelte Studien,* 230. Holm-Nielsen *StTh* XIV (1960), 24–35, does not find a place for Ps 119 even in the changed later forms of the cult. He regards it as part of wisdom literature, deliberately written in imitation of the ancient psalmodic traditions.

4. Conclusions and Methodological Considerations

It remains to gather together the main strands of the above study and to make a few comments on the results and on the methodological consequences they suggest with regard to the form-critical study of the OT Psalter in general.

4.1 The formal analysis, which aimed at a characterization of what may be called the most essential element in a prayer psalm, the imperative prayer and its closest context, revealed a frequently employed pattern of prayer – address to Yahweh, imperative petitions, expressions of complaint or confidence in Yahweh or the like introduced by כי – a pattern which springs from the natural way of expressing a request or a prayer within the resources of the Hebrew language. This pattern was called the traditional prayer.

4.2 The traditional prayer may be called traditional for several reasons. Firstly, it employs traditional language, conventional prayer words and formulaic expressions, even to a higher degree than other elements in the psalms. This speaks for a long oral tradition behind the written form of the prayers that have been preserved to us in the Book of Psalms. Secondly, the traditional prayer reveals a form of prayer which without doubt was used by private petitioners since ancient times, constituting as such a unit capable of functioning as an independent complete prayer. Thirdly, comparison with congregational complaints and the late acrostic psalms and prose prayers revealed features of form as well as of vocabulary – particularly in the petitions used – which speak for an early, probably pre-exilic origin of the pattern of traditional prayer and the conventional language used in it. It is possible that this simple, spontaneous form of prayer had its origin in the private prayer and was taken up, elaborated on, and fixed into normative models of prayer in the organized cult.

4.3 The pattern of traditional prayer was discovered to constitute a frequently employed compositional factor within the structure of individual complaint psalms. In a few psalms the pattern was found to occur only once, in others twice or several times. Furthermore, sections of the traditional prayer were found to occur as building blocks in large complex psalms. This discovery suggested the possibility of parts of long and complex psalms being older than the whole composition and having perhaps existed as independent psalms. As for the dating of such psalms, the possible criteria for a late dating only concern the final composition. As for the exegesis, it becomes more important than ever to give full consideration to the divergent background situations of the parts and of the whole psalm. There is no one »case history« to be discovered behind a compound psalm.

4.4 A probably later development in the composition of psalms was discovered in the employment of the pattern of traditional prayer in skilful repetition of single lines with a short petition and a short motivation. A clear detachment from the original function of the pattern was seen in prayer literature.

4.5. As for the formal characterization of complaint psalms by Gunkel, a few adjustments were found to be necessary. Since the majority of imperative prayers in the individual complaint psalms were found to follow the pattern of traditional prayer, it became obvious that the imperative petitions in their normal position do not follow – as is often explained – but precede the element of complaint or the expression of confidence, being most frequently even syntactically connected with the following context. The so-called »initial plea« in most cases consists of the frequently recurring conventional prayer imperatives – petitions for hearing as well as petitions for help – and should be regarded as the first full prayer of the psalm, by no means simply preparation for a further prayer. The »motivations for divine intervention« introduced by כי were discovered to be above all expressions of the theme of the prayer – whether complaint or confidence in Yahweh – expressions by which the supplicant could give life and meaning to the often most unspecific conventional petitions. Actual motivations, which are used to strengthen the prayer, were found to appear in a short form and with various contents mainly in the later, developed form of the traditional prayer and in the prayer literature employing traditional as well as new material. Prepositional phrases attached to the petitions for motivation were found to be infrequent and relatively late.

4.6 As for the genre of the psalms discussed in the present study, our results suggest that the old group of complaint psalms – with a few exceptions – should be retained as one of the main genres. But, the title »prayer psalms of the individual« would be the most natural one to be used of this group. This group of psalms obviously satisfies the requirements of a genre. From the limited viewpoint of the prayer element we may consider the following characteristics.

The common language of these psalms includes the conventional language of prayer, with frequently recurring imperative petitions and more extensive formulaic phrases fixed already in oral tradition. Later psalms of the group employ this language through imitation or literary dependence. A common form element, recurring in various developments in most of these psalms may be seen in the pattern of traditional prayer.

The common theme of the genre is simply a request by an individual petitioner to Yahweh. The appearance of complaint, expressions of confidence, or other such elements along with the request is conditioned by the situations of life for which the psalms were intended and in which they could be used.

The »Sitz-im-Leben« of the prayer psalms certainly underwent changes through the various periods of Israel's history. The traditional prayer probably had its place in the smaller forms of the pre-exilic cultic life. This is obviously the original »Sitz-im-Leben« of the genre. One should not postulate complex and fixed written prayer psalms – at least not the psalms of the Psalter as such – in this period, but see it rather as the flowering time of the living oral tradition of prayer psalms and only the beginning of its fixing. In the post-exilic period the increasingly fixed traditions had their place in the changed and changing forms of cultic life and eventually also in individual devotion. As regards the prayer psalms of the individual, the role of the oral tradition and its fixing, however, obviously has a widely different significance to the final result than is the case with the other genres.

Abbreviations

AASF	Annales Academiae Scientiarum Fennicae.
ATD	Das Alte Testament Deutsch.
BHS	*Biblia Hebraica Stuttgartensia.*
BKAT	Biblischer Kommentar. Altes Testament.
BWANT	Beiträge zur Wissenschaft vom Alten und Neuen Testament.
BZAW	Beihefte zur Zeitschrift für die alttestamentliche Wissenschaft.
FRLANT	Forschungen zur Religion und Literatur des Alten und Neuen Testamentes.
HUCA	*Hebrew Union College Annual.*
LSJ	Liddell-Scott-Jones *Greek-English Lexicon.*
RGG	Die Religion in Geschichte und Gegenwart.
RSV	The Revised Standard Version.
SBS	Stuttgarter Bibelstudien.
StTh	*Studia Theologica.*
ThB	Theologische Bücherei.
THAT	Theologisches Handwörterbuch zum Alten Testament.
ThWNT	Theologisches Wörterbuch zum Neuen Testament.
TWAT	Theologisches Wörterbuch zum Alten Testament.
VT	*Vetus Testamentum.*
VT Suppl	*Vetus Testamentum Supplement Volume.*
WMANT	Wissenschaftliche Monographien zum Alten und Neuen Testament.
ZAW	*Zeitschrift für die alttestamentliche Wissenschaft.*
ZThK	*Zeitschrift für Theologie und Kirche.*

Bibliography

1. Text Editions, Dictionaries, and Concordances

Biblia Hebraica Stuttgartensia, ediderunt K. Elliger et W. Rudolph. Stuttgart 1969–1976.
Duden, *Das große Wörterbuch der deutschen Sprache I–VI.* Herausgegeben unter Leitung von Günther Drosdowski. Mannheim–Wien–Zürich 1976.
Gesenius, Wilhelm, *Hebräisches und Aramäisches Handwörterbuch über das Alte Testament.* Bearbeitet von F. Buhl. Unveränderter Neudruck der 1915 erschienenen 17. Auflage. Berlin–Göttingen–Heidelberg 1962.
The Greek New Testament, edited by Kurt Aland, Matthew Black, Carlo M. Martini, Bruce M. Metzger, and Allen Wikgren. Second Edition. Stuttgart 1968.
Hatch, Edwin – Redpath, Henry A., *A Concordance to the Septuagint and the other Greek Versions of the Old Testament.* Oxford 1897–1906.
Koehler, Ludwig – Baumgartner, Walter, *Lexicon in Veteris Testamenti libros.* Leiden 1953.
– *Hebräisches und aramäisches Lexicon zum Alten Testament.* Dritte Auflage, neubearbeitet von Walter Baumgartner. Lieferungen: I א-מבח Leiden 1967, II נבמ-מבח Leiden 1974, III נבמ-ראה Leiden 1983.
Liddell, Henry George – Scott, Robert, *A Greek-English Lexicon.* Revised and augmented throughout by Henry Stuart Jones. Ninth edition, reprinted. Oxford 1968.
Mandelkern, Solomon, *Veteris Testamenti concordantiae Hebraicae atque Chaldaicae.* Lipsiae 1896.
Septuaginta, Vetus Testamentum Graecum, Auctoritate Academiae Scientiarum Gottingensis editum:
    III, 1 Numeri, edidit John William Wevers. Göttingen 1982.
    VIII, 3 Esther, edidit Robert Hanhart. Göttingen 1966.
    IX, 3 Maccabaeorum liber III, edidit Robert Hanhart. Göttingen 1960.
    X Psalmi cum Odis, edidit Alfred Rahlfs. 2., durchgesehene Auflage. Göttingen 1967.

2. Works Consulted

Ackroyd, Peter R., *I & II Chronicles, Ezra, Nehemiah: Introduction and Commentary.* Torch Bible Commentaries. London 1973.
Aejmelaeus, Anneli, *Parataxis in the Septuagint: A Study of the Renderings of the Hebrew Coordinate Clauses in the Greek Pentateuch.* AASF, B Diss 31. Helsinki 1982.
– »OTI *causale* in Septuagintal Greek.« A paper read at the V Congress of the International Organization for Septuagint and Cognate Studies 1983 in Salamanca, Spain; *La Septuaginta en la investigacion contemporanea,* ed. N. Fernández Marcos, Textos y Estudios Cardenal Cisneros 34, Madrid 1985, pp. 115–132.

– »Function and Interpretation of כי in Biblical Hebrew.« A paper read at the International Meeting of Society of Biblical Literature 1984 in Strasbourg, France. Manuscript (to be published in *Journal of Biblical Literature*).

Alt, Albrecht, *Gott der Väter*. BWANT, III. Folge, Heft 12. Stuttgart 1929. (= Kleine Schriften I, München 1953, pp. 1–78.)

Amsler, S., »קום.« THAT II, cols. 635–641.

Bartelmus, Rüdiger, *HYH: Bedeutung und Funktion eines hebräischen »Allerweltswortes« – zugleich ein Beitrag zur Frage des hebräischen Tempussystems*. Münchener Universitätsschriften. Arbeiten zu Text und Sprache im Alten Testament. 17. Band. München 1982.

Barth, Ch., »חלק.« TWAT I, cols. 1003–1008.

Bauer, H. – Leander, P., *Historische Grammatik der hebräischen Sprache des Alten Testamentes*. Halle 1922. Nachdruck Hildesheim 1965.

Becker, Joachim, *Israel deutet seine Psalmen*. SBS 18. Stuttgart 1966.

– *Wege der Psalmenexegese*. SBS 78. Stuttgart 1975.

Begrich, Joachim, »Die Vertrauensäußerungen im israelitischen Klagelied des Einzelnen und in seinem babylonischen Gegenstück.« *ZAW* 46 (1928), pp. 221–260 (= *Gesammelte Studien zum Alten Testament*. ThB 21. München 1964. Pp. 168–216).

– »Das priesterliche Heilsorakel.« *ZAW* 52 (1934), pp. 81–92 (= *Gesammelte Studien zum Alten Testament*. ThB 21. München 1964. Pp. 217–231).

Bergmann, U., »נצל.« THAT II, cols. 96–99.

– »עזר.« THAT II, cols. 256–259.

Bergsträsser, G., *Hebräische Grammatik mit Benutzung der von E. Kautzsch bearbeiteten 28. Auflage von Wilhelm Gesenius' hebräischer Grammatik*. I. Teil. Leipzig 1918. II. Teil. Leipzig 1929. Nachdruck Hildesheim 1962.

Beyerlin, Walter, *Die Rettung der Bedrängten in den Feindpsalmen der Einzelnen auf institutionelle Zusammenhänge untersucht*. FRLANT 99. Göttingen 1970.

– »Innerbiblische Aktualisierungsversuche: Schichten im 44. Psalm.« *ZThK* 73 (1976), pp. 446–460.

Beyse, K.-M., »חוש.« TWAT II, cols. 820–822.

Crüsemann, Frank, *Studien zur Formgeschichte von Hymnus und Danklied in Israel*. WMANT 32. Neukirchen-Vluyn 1969.

Culley, Robert C., *Oral Formulaic Language in the Biblical Psalms*. Near and Middle East Series 4. Toronto 1967.

Dahood, Mitchell, *Psalms I-III*. The Anchor Bible. New York 1966–1970.

Delekat, L., *Asylie und Schutzorakel am Zionheiligtum: Eine Untersuchung zu den privaten Feindpsalmen*. Leiden 1967.

Dik, Simon C., *Coordination: Its implications for the theory of general linguistics*. Diss. 1968. Amsterdam 1968.

Duhm, Bernh., *Die Psalmen*. Kurzer Hand-Kommentar zum Alten Testament. Abteilung XIV. Zweite, vermehrte und verbesserte Auflage. Tübingen 1922.

Eissfeldt, Otto, *Hexateuch-Synopse*. Leipzig 1922. Nachdruck Darmstadt 1983.

Freedman, D. N. – Lundbom, J., »חנן.« TWAT III, cols. 23–40.

Freedman, D. N. – O'Connor, P., »יהוה.« TWAT III, cols. 533–554.

Fuchs, Ottmar, *Die Klage als Gebet: Eine theologische Besinnung am Beispiel des Psalms 22*. München 1982.

Gamper, Arnold, *Gott als Richter in Mesopotamien und im Alten Testament: Zum Verständnis einer Gebetsbitte*. Innsbruck 1966.

Gemser, B., »The Importance of the Motive Clause in Old Testament Law.« *VT Suppl* I (1953), pp. 50–66.
- »The *rîb-* or Controversy-Pattern in Hebrew Mentality.« *VT Suppl* III (1960), pp. 120–137.

Gerstenberger, Erhard, »Der klagende Mensch.« *Probleme biblischer Theologie. Gerhard von Rad zum 70. Geburtstag.* Herausgegeben von H. W. Wolff. München 1971. Pp. 64–72.
- »Psalms«. *Old Testament Form Criticism.* Edited by J. H. Hayes. Second printing. San Antonio 1977. Pp. 179–224.
- *Der bittende Mensch: Bittritual und Klagelied des Einzelnen im Alten Testament.* WMANT 51. Neukirchen-Vluyn 1980.

Gesenius, Wilhelm – Kautzsch, E., *Hebräische Grammatik.* 28. Auflage. Leipzig 1909.

Gray, John, *I & II Kings: A Commentary.* Second, Fully Revised, Edition. The Old Testament Library. London 1970.

Gunkel, Hermann, *Reden und Aufsätze.* Göttingen 1913.
- *Ausgewählte Psalmen.* 4. Auflage. Göttingen 1917.
- *Die Psalmen.* Göttinger Handkommentar zum Alten Testament. II. Abteilung. 2. Band. 4. Auflage. Göttingen 1926.
- »Psalmen.« RGG IV. 2. Auflage. Tübingen 1930. Cols. 1609–1627.
- *Einleitung in die Psalmen: Die Gattungen der religiösen Lyrik Israels.* Zu Ende geführt von Joachim Begrich. Göttingen 1933.

Holladay, William L., *The Root šûbh in the Old Testament.* Leiden 1958.

Holm-Nielsen, Svend, »The Importance of Late Jewish Psalmody for the Understanding of OT Psalmodic Tradition.« *StTh* XIV (1960), pp. 1–53.

Jenni, E., »למד.« THAT I, cols. 872–875.

Jeremias, Jörg, *Theophanie: Die Geschichte einer alttestamentlichen Gattung.* WMANT 10. Neukirchen-Vluyn 1965.
- »Lade und Zion.« *Probleme biblischer Theologie. Gerhard von Rad zum 70. Geburtstag.* Herausgegeben von H. W. Wolff. München 1971. Pp. 183–198.

Johnson, Norman B., *Prayer in the Apocrypha and Pseudepigrapha: A Study of the Jewish Concept of God.* Journal of Biblical Literature. Monograph Series. Volume II. Philadelphia, Penn. 1948.

Kissane, Edward J., *The Book of Psalms: Translated from a Critically Revised Hebrew Text: With a Commentary.* Vol. I (Ps 1–72). Dublin 1953. Vol. II (Ps 73–150). Dublin 1954.

Kraus, Hans-Joachim, *Psalmen I–II.* BKAT XV. 3., unveränderte Auflage. Neukirchen,Vluyn 1966. 5., grundlegend überarbeitete und veränderte Auflage. Neukirchen-Vluyn 1978.

König Friedrich Eduard, *Historisch-kritisches Lehrgebäude der hebräischen Sprache.* Band III. Zweite Hälfte. 2. Teil. Leipzig 1897. Nachdruck Hildesheim – New York 1979.

Labuschagne, C. J., »ענה.« THAT II, cols. 335–341.

van der Lugt, Pieter, *Strofische structuren in de bijbels-hebreeuwse poëzie.* Theologische Academie uitgaande van de Johannes Calvijnstichting te Kampen. Diss. Kampen 1980.

Mayer, Werner, *Untersuchungen zur Formensprache der Babylonischen »Gebetsbeschwörungen«.* Studia Pohl. Series Maior 5. Rome 1976.

Mowinckel, Sigmund, *Psalmenstudien I.* Oslo 1921.
- *The Psalms in Israel's Worship I–II.* Translated by D. R. Ap-Thomas. Oxford 1962.

Muilenburg, James, »The Linguistic and Rhetorical Usages of the Particle כי in the Old Testament.« *HUCA* XXXII (1961), pp. 135–160.

Müller, Hans-Peter, »Gott und die Götter in den Anfängen der biblischen Religion: Zur Vorgeschichte des Monotheismus.« *Monotheismus im Alten Testament und seiner Umwelt.* Herausgeber O. Keel. Fribourg 1980. Pp. 99–142.

Noth, Martin, *Die israelitischen Personennamen im Rahmen der gemeinsemitischen Namengebung.* BWANT, III. Folge, Heft 10. Stuttgart 1928.

- *Das vierte Buch Mose: Numeri: übersetzt und erklärt.* ATD 7. Göttingen 1966.
- »Tendenzen theologischer Forschung in Deutschland.« *Gesammelte Studien zum Alten Testament II.* ThB 39. München 1969. Pp. 113–132.

Oesterley, W. O. E., *The Psalms: Translated with Text-Critical and Exegetical Notes.* First published in 1939 London, reprinted. London 1962.

Perlitt, Lothar, *Bundestheologie im Alten Testament.* WMANT 36. Neukirchen-Vluyn 1969.

Plöger, Otto, »Reden und Gebete im deuteronomistischen und chronistischen Geschichtswerk.« *Festschrift für Günter Dehn.* Hrsg. von W. Schneemelcher. Neukirchen 1957. Pp. 35–49.

von Rad, Gerhard, *Das erste Buch Mose: Genesis: übersetzt und erklärt.* ATD 2/4. Göttingen 1952–1953.

- »Zelt und Lade.« *Gesammelte Studien zum Alten Testament.* ThB 8. München 1958. Pp. 109–129 (= *Neue Kirchliche Zeitschrift* 42 (1931), pp. 476–498).
- »›Gerechtigkeit‹ und ›Leben‹ in der Kultsprache der Psalmen.« *Gesammelte Studien zum Alten Testament.* ThB 8. München 1958, Pp. 225–247 (= *Festschrift für Alfred Bertholet.* Tübingen 1950. Pp. 418–437).
- *Theologie des Alten Testaments I: Die Theologie der geschichtlichen Überlieferungen Israels.* Fünfte, durchgesehene Auflage. München 1966.

Ringgren, H., »גאל.« TWAT I, cols. 884–890.

Rose, Martin, *Jahwe: Zum Streit um den alttestamentlichen Gottesnamen.* Theologische Studien 122. Zürich 1978.

Ruppert, L., »Psalm 25 und die Grenze der kultorientierten Psalmenexegese.« *ZAW* 84 (1972), pp. 576–582.

Sauer, G., »שמר.« THAT II, cols. 982–987.

Sawyer, J. F., »ישע.« TWAT III, cols. 1035–1059.

Scharbert, J., »ברך.« TWAT I, cols. 808–841.

Schmidt, Hans, *Das Gebet der Angeklagten im Alten Testament.* BZAW 49, pp. 1–46. Gießen 1928.

- *Die Psalmen.* Handbuch zum Alten Testament. Erste Reihe 15. Tübingen 1934.

Schnutenhaus, F., »Das Kommen und Erscheinen Gottes im Alten Testament.« *ZAW* 76 (1964), pp. 1–22.

Schottroff, Willy, *Der altisraelitische Fluchspruch.* WMANT 30. Neukirchen-Vluyn 1969.

Schult, H., »שמע.« THAT II, cols. 974–982.

Schüpphaus, J., »בלע.« TWAT I, cols. 658–661.

Seeligmann, I. L., »Zur Terminologie für das Gerichtsverfahren im Wortschatz des biblischen Hebräisch.« *Festschrift zum 80. Geburtstag von Walter Baumgartner.* VT Suppl XVI. Leiden 1967. Pp. 251–278.

Seybold, Klaus, *Das Gebet des Kranken im Alten Testament: Untersuchungen zur Bestimmung und Zuordnung der Krankheits- und Heilungspsalmen.* BWANT, V. Folge, Heft 19. Stuttgart–Berlin–Köln–Mainz 1973.

Smend, Rudolf, *Jahwekrieg und Stämmebund: Erwägungen zur ältesten Geschichte Israels.* FRLANT 84. Zweite, durchgesehene und ergänzte Auflage. Göttingen 1966.
- *Die Entstehung des Alten Testaments.* Theologische Wissenschaft. Band 1. Zweite, durchgesehene und ergänzte Auflage. Stuttgart–Berlin–Köln–Mainz 1981.

Soggin, J. Alberto, *Judges: A Commentary.* Translated by John Bowden from the Italian original. The Old Testament Library. London 1981.
- »שוב.« THAT II, cols. 884–891.

Sonsino, Rifat, *Motive Clauses in Hebrew Law: Biblical Forms and Near Eastern Parallels.* Society of Biblical Literature. Diss. Series 45. Ann Arbor, Michigan 1980.

Stähli, H.-P., »רום.« THAT II, cols. 753–761.

Stamm, J. J., »פדה.« THAT II, cols. 389–406.

Stolz, F., »ישע.« THAT I, cols. 785–790.

Veijola, Timo, *Das Königtum in der Beurteilung der deuteronomistischen Historiographie: Eine redaktionsgeschichtliche Untersuchung.* AASF, B 198. Helsinki 1977.
- *Verheißung in der Krise: Studien zur Literatur und Theologie der Exilszeit anhand des 89. Psalms.* AASF, B 220. Helsinki 1982.

Vriezen, Th. C., »Einige Notizen zur Übersetzung des Bindewortes *kī*.« *Von Ugarit nach Qumran. Festschrift für Otto Eissfeldt.* BZAW 77, pp. 266–273. Berlin 1958.

Wagner, S., »דרש.« TWAT I, cols. 313–329.

Watters, William R., *Formula Criticism and Poetry of the Old Testament.* BZAW 138. Berlin–New York 1976.

Weiser, Artur, *Die Psalmen.* ATD 14/15. 6. Auflage. Göttingen 1963.

Wendel, Adolf, *Das freie Laiengebet im vorexilischen Israel.* Leipzig 1931.

Westermann, Claus, *Lob und Klage in den Psalmen.* 5., erweiterte Auflage von *Das Loben Gottes in den Psalmen.* Göttingen 1977.
- *Genesis.* BKAT I. Neukirchen-Vluyn 1981.
- *Ausgewählte Psalmen.* Göttingen 1984.

de Wette, W. M. L., *Commentar über die Psalmen.* Fünfte Auflage. Heidelberg 1856.

Wevers, John Wm., »A Study in the Form Criticism of Individual Complaint Psalms.« *VT* VI (1956), pp. 80–96.

Widengren, Geo, *The Accadian and Hebrew Psalms of Lamentation as Religious Documents: A Comparative Study.* Uppsala 1937.

Zimmerli, Walther, »חנן und Derivate.« ThWNT IX, pp. 366–372.
- »חסד.« ThWNT IX, pp. 372–377.

Please find
    Index of Biblical Passages
on pp. 301 ff.

Ludwig Schmidt

Literarische Studien
zur Josephsgeschichte

Inhaltsverzeichnis

Vorwort 125

I. Literarische Probleme der Josephsgeschichte und ihre Lösung – ein kritischer Überblick 127

II. Analyse von Gen 37,1–35; 42,14–47,31; 49,1a.28b–33; 50,1–22 142
   a) Gen 37,1–35 142
   b) Gen 42,14–38 151
   c) Gen 43,1–34 158
   d) Gen 44,1–34 162
   e) Gen 45,1–28 166
   f) Gen 46,1–34 181
   g) Gen 47,1–12 193
   h) Gen 47,13–31 201
   i) Gen 49,1a.28b–33; 50,1–22 207

III. Analyse von Gen 37,36; 39,1–42,13; 48,1–22 218
   a) Gen 37,36; 39,1–23 218
   b) Gen 40,1–23 227
   c) Gen 41,1–57 232
   d) Gen 42,1–13 247
   e) Gen 48,1–22 253

IV. Zusammenfassung und Weiterführung 272
   a) Die Josephsgeschichte des Jahwisten 272
   b) Die Josephsgeschichte des Elohisten 281
   c) Die Josephsgeschichte in der Priesterschrift . 287
   d) Die Josephsgeschichte des Jehowisten 289
   e) Endredaktion und Zusätze 293
   f) Konsequenzen für die Pentateuchforschung 295

Literaturverzeichnis 296

Stellenregister 307

Vorwort

Die literarischen Probleme der Josephsgeschichte beschäftigen mich, seit ich im Sommersemester 1977 erstmals ein Seminar über dieses Thema gehalten habe. Erste Ergebnisse habe ich im Sommersemester 1981 in meiner Erlanger Antrittsvorlesung „Überlegungen zur Josephsgeschichte" vorgetragen, die nicht publiziert wurde. Inzwischen konnte ich die damals gewonnenen Einsichten zu der vorliegenden Arbeit vertiefen und weiterführen.

Mein Dank gilt meinem Assistenten Herrn Dr. Dr. Matthias Augustin, der mich bei den Korrekturen tatkräftig unterstützt und das Stellenregister angefertigt hat, und Frau Isolde Weinicke, die das Manuskript mit großer Sorgfalt geschrieben hat. Besonders danken möchte ich ferner Herrn Professor Dr. Otto Kaiser und dem Verlag Walter de Gruyter für die Aufnahme der Studie in die Reihe „Beihefte zur Zeitschrift für die alttestamentliche Wissenschaft".

Erlangen, im November 1985   Ludwig Schmidt

I. Literarische Probleme der Josephsgeschichte und ihre Lösung – ein kritischer Überblick

Die literarischen Probleme des Pentateuch werden gegenwärtig in der Forschung wieder eingehend diskutiert. War bis vor wenigen Jahren die neuere Urkundenhypothese, nach der mit den drei weithin parallel laufenden Quellenschriften des Jahwisten, des Elohisten und der Priesterschrift zu rechnen ist, eine weitgehend anerkannte Basis, so hat sich das Bild vor allem durch die Arbeiten von R. Rendtorff und H. H. Schmid grundlegend verändert[1]. Es mehren sich die Zweifel, ob eine Urkundenhypothese tatsächlich geeignet ist, den Befund zureichend zu erklären[2]. In dieser Diskussion kommt der Josephsgeschichte von Gen 37–50 eine besondere Bedeutung zu, da sie auch von einigen Vertretern der neueren Urkundenhypothese – abgesehen von späteren Erweiterungen und wenigen Fragmenten aus P – als literarisch einheitlich angesehen wird[3]. Läßt sich demgegenüber zeigen, daß die Josephsgeschichte neben P aus zwei literarisch selbständigen Erzählfäden zusammengesetzt ist, so ist das für die neuere Urkundenhypothese eine wichtige Stütze. Sie würde sich auch an einem schwierigen Komplex bewähren.

Dabei können für die Untersuchung zwei Stücke unberücksichtigt bleiben. Die Juda-Tamar-Erzählung von Gen 38 unterbricht eindeutig die Josephsgeschichte. Dasselbe gilt für die Stammessprüche in Gen 49,2–27. Sie sind nachträglich in die priesterschriftliche Darstellung vom Tode Jakobs, zu der v. 1a.28bα (ab »da segnete er sie«) – 33aα.b gehört[4], eingefügt worden und wurden dabei durch v. 1b.

---

[1] R. Rendtorff, Das überlieferungsgeschichtliche Problem des Pentateuch, BZAW 147, 1977; H. H. Schmid, Der sogenannte Jahwist, Zürich 1976.

[2] Vgl. die Überblicke über die neuere Forschung bei A. H. J. Gunneweg, Anmerkungen und Anfragen zur neueren Pentateuchforschung, ThR NF 48 (1983) 227–253; E. Otto, Stehen wir vor einem Umbruch in der Pentateuchkritik?, VF 22 (1977) 82–97; E. Zenger, Wo steht die Pentateuchforschung heute?, BZ 24 (1980) 101–116; ders., Auf der Suche nach einem Weg aus der Pentateuchkrise, ThRv 78 (1982) 353–362.

[3] Vgl. z. B. O. H. Steck, Die Paradieserzählung. Eine Auslegung von Genesis 2,4b–3,24, 1970 = ders., Wahrnehmungen Gottes im Alten Testament, 1982, 9–116; H. Donner, Die literarische Gestalt der alttestamentlichen Josephsgeschichte, 1976; E. Otto, Die »synthetische Lebensauffassung« in der frühköniglichen Novellistik Israels, ZThK 74 (1977) 371–400; F. Crüsemann, Der Widerstand gegen das Königtum, 1978, 143–155.

[4] Zu v. 33aβ vgl. II i.

28 a.bα* mit dem Kontext verbunden. Aus dieser Verklammerung mit P geht hervor, daß diese Sammlung von Stammessprüchen erst sehr spät in die Pentateuchüberlieferung eingefügt wurde. Dem entspricht, daß der Mosesegen von Dtn 33, der ebenfalls Stammessprüche enthält, nicht zum Grundbestand des deuteronomistischen Werkes gehört, sondern auch erst spät in Dtn eingegliedert wurde[5].

Abgesehen von P ist die literarische Analyse der Josephsgeschichte sehr umstritten. Es fällt auf, daß der Vater die Namen Israel und Jakob trägt, und daß sowohl Juda als auch Ruben als Sprecher der Brüder auftreten. Man hat deshalb oft angenommen, daß es eine jahwistische Fassung gab, zu der Israel und Juda gehören, und eine elohistische Darstellung, für die Jakob und Ruben charakteristisch sind. In den Einzelheiten weichen allerdings die Zuweisungen beträchtlich voneinander ab. So gehören z. B. die Träume Josephs in Gen 37,5 ff. nach H. Gunkel zu E, während sie O. Eißfeldt und M. Noth zu J rechnen[6].

Demgegenüber wurde von W. Rudolph bestritten, daß sich die Josephsgeschichte auf zwei Erzählfäden aufteilen lasse. Sie sei eine im wesentlichen einheitliche Erzählung, die ursprünglich selbständig war und von J in sein Werk aufgenommen wurde[7]. Mit dieser Auffassung konnte sich W. Rudolph zunächst nicht durchsetzen. Erst der Einschnitt, den die Arbeiten von G. v. Rad[8] für die Interpretation der Erzählung bedeuten, führte dazu, daß seine These – wenn auch teilweise mit Modifikationen – zunehmend aufgegriffen wird. G. v. Rad betonte mit Recht, daß die Josephsgeschichte im Unterschied zu den Erzväterüberlieferungen nicht aus Einzelsagen oder Sagenkränzen besteht. »Die Josephsgeschichte ist durch und durch novellistisch«[9]. Sie stamme

---

[5] Zu Dtn 33 vgl. z. B. M. Noth, Überlieferungsgeschichtliche Studien, 1943, 40. Wegen dieser Analogie und ihrer Verknüpfung mit P kann man diese Stammessprüche nicht zu J rechnen, wie H. Seebaß, Geschichtliche Zeit und theonome Tradition in der Joseph-Erzählung, 1978, 69 f., annimmt. Daß sie erst spät eingefügt wurden, spricht auch dagegen, daß zumindest die Jakobsgeschichte auf den Jakobsegen in Gen 49 zu erzählt sei, wie Ina Willi-Plein, Historiographische Aspekte der Josefsgeschichte, Henoch 1 (1979) 305–331, meint. Nach I. Willi-Plein sind diese Stammessprüche die Grundlage für den Gesamtentwurf der Vätergeschichte (325).

[6] H. Gunkel 402; M. Noth, Überlieferungsgeschichte des Pentateuch, 1948, 31; O. Eißfeldt, Hexateuch-Synopse, 1922, 76*. Vgl. auch die Aufstellung über die unterschiedliche Aufteilung von Gen 45 bei H. Donner, Gestalt, 22.

[7] W. Rudolph, Die Josefsgeschichte, in: P. Volz/W. Rudolph, Der Elohist als Erzähler – ein Irrweg der Pentateuchkritik?, BZAW 63, 1933, 143–184. Nach W. Rudolph stammen Gen 46,1aβ–5a und 48,15f. von einem Bearbeiter, der auch Gen 20; 21,8–32; 31,2.4–16; 35,1–4.7 eingefügt hat (177–179).

[8] G. v. Rad, Josephsgeschichte und ältere Chokma (1953), in: ders., Gesammelte Studien zum Alten Testament, ³1965, 272–280; ders., Die Josephsgeschichte, 1954 = ders., Gottes Wirken in Israel, 1974, 22–41; ders., Das erste Buch Mose. Genesis, ⁹1972.

[9] G. v. Rad, Josephsgeschichte, 272. Damit wandte sich G. v. Rad gegen H. Gunkel 396,

als ursprünglich selbständige Erzählung aus der älteren Weisheit. Bei seinen Belegen differenzierte G. v. Rad aber nicht zwischen J und E, obwohl er an der Quellenscheidung in der Josephsgeschichte festhielt. Damit war das Problem gestellt, ob sich eine Aufteilung auf J und E vertreten läßt, wenn hier beide in Theologie und sonstigen Anschauungen völlig übereinstimmen. H. Donner hat diese Frage prägnant formuliert: »Man kann nicht beides haben: die Josephsgeschichte als Novelle *und* als Bestandteil der Pentateuchquellen J und E. Entweder ist sie doch ein Sagenkranz nach Art der Abraham-, mehr noch der Jakobüberlieferungen, dann ist sie in einer jahwistischen und in einer elohistischen Fassung denkbar und zu erwarten. Oder sie ist in der Tat eine Novelle im Sinne G. v. Rads, dann gehört sie weder zu J noch zu E, sondern ist als eine literarische Größe für sich anzusehen.«[10] Da sich die Josephsgeschichte aber deutlich von den Abraham- und Jakobüberlieferungen abhebt, wird sie heute weithin als im wesentlichen literarisch einheitlich verstanden. Allerdings gehen die Auffassungen über ihre Datierung und die Zeit ihrer Eingliederung in die Pentateuchüberlieferung weit auseinander.

Wie schon W. Rudolph so nehmen auch O. H. Steck, T. N. D. Mettinger, E. Otto und F. Crüsemann an, daß die Josephsgeschichte als selbständige Novelle in der davidisch-salomonischen Zeit entstanden ist und von dem Jahwisten in sein Werk aufgenommen wurde[11]. Auch H. Donner setzt sie in der Zeit Salomos oder bald danach an. Er ist aber der Auffassung, daß sie erst von dem Jehowisten in die Pentateucherzählung eingefügt wurde[12]. Das nimmt auch P. Weimar an, nach dem die Josephsgeschichte jedoch erst um 700 entstanden ist[13]. Für noch

---

der die Josephsgeschichte als Sagenkranz bezeichnete. H. Gunkel erkannte zwar die enge Verzahnung der einzelnen Stücke, meinte aber: »Hieraus sieht man also, daß *die einzelnen Sagen,* aus denen auch die Josephgeschichte bestehen muß, gegenwärtig sehr *stark miteinander verwoben sind.*« Da nach H. Gunkel die Genesis eine Sammlung von Sagen ist, mußte für ihn auch die Josephsgeschichte auf einzelne Sagen zurückgehen, vgl. auch H. Greßmann, Ursprung und Entwicklung der Joseph-Sage, in: H. Schmidt (Hg.), Eucharisterion 1 (FS H. Gunkel), 1923, 1–55.

[10] H. Donner, Gestalt, 14. Vgl. schon R. N. Whybray, The Joseph Story and Pentateuchal Criticism, VT 18 (1968) 522–528.

[11] O. H. Steck, Wahrnehmungen, 107–111 Anm. 291; T. N. D. Mettinger, Solomonic State Officials, Lund 1971, 152–154; E. Otto, Lebensauffassung, 387 f., der Gen 37, 28 a. 29 f. 36; 41, 50–52; 46, 1 b–5 a; 48, 1 f. 8–14 (15 f.). 17–21; 50, 23–25 als spätere Zusätze ansieht; F. Crüsemann, Widerstand, 143–145.

[12] H. Donner, Gestalt, 24–27. Nach H. Donner stammen dagegen Gen 41, 50–52; 46, 1 aβ–5 a; der vorpriesterschriftliche Bestand in Gen 48 und 50, 23–25 aus J oder E.

[13] P. Weimar, Untersuchungen zur Redaktionsgeschichte des Pentateuch, BZAW 146, 1977, 24–26.

wesentlich jünger hält sie A. Meinhold, der in ihr eine Diasporanovelle sieht[14].

Eine Sonderstellung nehmen G. W. Coats, C. Westermann und Ina Willi-Plein ein. Nach G. W. Coats bestand die Josephsgeschichte ursprünglich aus Gen 37, 1–47, 27 a; außer Gen 38 und 47, 13–26 enthalte sie nur wenige Erweiterungen. Sie stamme aus der Zeit Salomos; es lasse sich aber nicht entscheiden, ob sie von J übernommen oder geschaffen wurde[15]. Die Besonderheit bei G. W. Coats besteht darin, daß er teilweise auch Stellen wie 37, 1 f., die im allgemeinen P zugewiesen werden, für den Grundbestand in Anspruch nimmt und mit wesentlich weniger Erweiterungen rechnet als z. B. H. Donner und E. Otto. In seinem Kommentar unterscheidet C. Westermann zwischen einer Josephsgeschichte im engeren Sinn, zu der Gen 37; 39–45 und partiell 46–50 gehören, und dem Abschluß der Jakobsgeschichte in Gen 37 und Teilen von 46–50. Der Verfasser der eigentlichen Josephsgeschichte habe vermutlich in der davidisch-salomonischen Zeit die ihm vorgegebene Jakobsgeschichte als Exposition benutzt und seine Erzählung in die Jakobsgeschichte eingefügt. Es könne sich bei ihm nicht um den Jahwisten handeln, da J sein Werk aus Überlieferungen komponiert habe, während in die Josephsgeschichte keine mündlich tradierten Erzählungen aufgenommen worden seien[16]. Ähnlich wie C. Westermann unterscheidet auch I. Willi-Plein zwischen Josephs- und Vätergeschichte. Sie hält aber daran fest, daß die Josephsgeschichte als eigenes literarisches Werk entstanden ist, das zunächst unabhängig von der Vätergeschichte tradiert wurde[17]. Der Verfasser, der zur Zeit Jerobeams I. im Nordreich anzusetzen sei, wolle die beiden Fragen beantworten: »a) Wie kamen die Söhne Israels nach Ägypten? und b) Wie verhalten sich die Größen Josef-Ephraim-Manasse-Israel zueinander?«[18].

Die Verfechter der literarischen Einheitlichkeit der vorpriesterlichen Josephsgeschichte stimmen somit lediglich darin überein, daß sich die Erzählung nicht auf zwei parallele Fäden aufteilen läßt. Dabei wird verschiedentlich J. Wellhausen vorgeworfen, daß er die Einheitlichkeit nur bestritten habe, um die neuere Urkundenhypothese durchhalten zu können[19]. J. Wellhausen schreibt: »Die Hauptquelle ist auch für diesen letzten Abschnitt der Genesis JE. Es ist zu vermuten, dass dies Werk

---

[14] A. Meinhold, Die Gattung der Josephsgeschichte und des Estherbuches: Diasporanovelle I, ZAW 87 (1975) 306–324; II, ZAW 88 (1976) 72–93.
[15] G. W. Coats, From Canaan to Egypt, Washington 1976, 79.
[16] C. Westermann 8–12.16.
[17] Nach I. Willi-Plein, Aspekte, 311, gehören zur Josephsgeschichte: »Gen. 37, 2*–36 a; 39–45, 28 + 46, 4*; 46, 5 b. 28–34; 47 (außer v. 28); 48; 49, 33 aβ; 50, 1–11. 14–22 a. 26.«
[18] I. Willi-Plein, Aspekte, 322 f.
[19] W. Rudolph, BZAW 63, 146; H. Donner, Gestalt, 7 f.; F. Crüsemann, Widerstand, 143 Anm. 11; C. Westermann 8.

hier wie sonst aus J und E zusammengesetzt sei; unsere früheren Ergebnisse drängen auf diese Annahme und würden erschüttert werden, wäre sie nicht erweisbar. Ich halte das Beginnen, ›diese fliessende Erzählung von Joseph nach Quellen zerstückeln zu wollen‹, nicht für verfehlt, sondern für so notwendig, wie überhaupt die Dekomposition der Genesis. Vgl. de Wette Beiträge II 146ss.«[20] Hier macht J. Wellhausen zunächst auf ein Problem aufmerksam, das sich stellen würde, wenn die Josephsgeschichte – abgesehen von P – literarisch einheitlich wäre. Es würde dann für J oder für E zwischen der Vätergeschichte und dem Exodus eine Brücke fehlen. Dadurch würde aber eine Aufteilung der Vätergeschichte auf J und E, deren Notwendigkeit für J. Wellhausen evident war, fraglich. Damit wendet sich J. Wellhausen gegen jene Forscher, die zu seiner Zeit an der literarischen Einheitlichkeit der Josephsgeschichte festhielten. Schon aus dem Hinweis auf W. M. L. de Wette geht aber hervor, daß die Doppelsträngigkeit der Josephsgeschichte für J. Wellhausen nicht zweifelhaft war und von ihm keineswegs nur um der neueren Urkundenhypothese willen behauptet wurde. W. M. L. de Wette hatte in seiner Behandlung von Gen 37–50 gegen die damaligen Vertreter der Einheitlichkeit zeigen wollen, daß die Erzählung markante Doppelungen enthält, die nur mit der Annahme zweier Rezensionen zu erklären sind[21]. J. Wellhausen begründet dann zunächst an 37,25–36; 39,1, warum man tatsächlich mit J und E rechnen muß. Für J. Wellhausen ergab sich somit aus der Josephsgeschichte selbst, daß sie aus zwei Darstellungen besteht, auch wenn er sah, daß die Aufteilung im einzelnen erhebliche Schwierigkeiten bereitet.

Wie grundlegend sich aber in den letzten Jahren die Forschungssituation gewandelt hat, geht daraus hervor, daß gegenwärtig nur noch vereinzelt[22] und dann teilweise mit beträchtlichen Modifikationen in der Josephsgeschichte zwischen J und E unterschieden wird. Das wird bei L. Ruppert besonders deutlich. Nachdem er sich 1965 weitgehend

---

[20] J. Wellhausen, Die Composition des Hexateuchs und der historischen Bücher des Alten Testaments, ³1899.

[21] W. M. L. de Wette, Beiträge zur Einleitung in das Alte Testament II, 1807 (Nachdruck 1971), 142–168. W. M. L. de Wette schließt sich hier ausdrücklich K. D. Ilgen an, freilich kritisiert er, daß K. D. Ilgen zu weit gehe und willkürlich werde. Er habe aber in den wichtigsten Punkten die Doppelheit der Erzählungen erkannt (142).

[22] So hält z. B. K. R. Melchin, Literary Sources in the Joseph Story, ScEs 31 (1979) 93–101, in einer stilistischen Analyse von Gen 37; 39,1–6a und 44,18–45,15 in Auseinandersetzung mit G. W. Coats an der Aufteilung auf J und E fest, wobei er im wesentlichen den Zuweisungen von M. Noth, Pentateuch, 31 und 38, folgt. Stärker an H. Gunkel orientiert sind O. Keel-M. Küchler, Synoptische Texte aus der Genesis, I Die Texte; II Der Kommentar, Fribourgh 1971, und K. Jaroš, Die Stellung des Elohisten zur kanaanäischen Religion, ²1982, 15.

der Literarkritik von H. Gunkel angeschlossen hatte[23], hat er diese Sicht jüngst erheblich modifiziert[24]. Er hält zwar nach wie vor daran fest, daß in der Josephsgeschichte J und E vertreten sind, meint aber nun, daß große Teile erst von dem Jehowisten geschaffen wurden[25]. Für J bleiben bei L. Ruppert weitgehend nur Fragmente. Das ist bei H. Seebaß anders, der allerdings in seinen Zuweisungen an J und E teilweise beträchtlich von früheren Quellenscheidungen abweicht[26]. Auch H. Seebaß rechnet aber mit einer umfangreichen späteren Bearbeitung der Josephsgeschichte, zu der nach ihm alle Stellen gehören, an denen Joseph zum zweiten Mann Ägyptens aufsteigt. Sie werde vor allem in Gen 39–41; 45; 47,13–26 greifbar. Im Unterschied zu L. Ruppert ist nach H. Seebaß diese Bearbeitung jedoch erst in nachexilischer Zeit vorgenommen worden. Freilich stellt sich bei diesen Analysen die Frage, ob die Annahme von jahwistischen und elohistischen Bestandteilen der Josephsgeschichte noch berechtigt ist, wenn für sie wie bei L. Ruppert und H. Seebaß die unterschiedlichen Bezeichnungen des Vaters, die für die früheren Quellenscheidungen einer der wichtigsten Ausgangspunkte waren, tatsächlich belanglos sein sollten.

Daneben gibt es freilich die Auffassung, daß es sich bei den unterschiedlichen Namen des Vaters und bei den verschiedenen Sprechern der Brüder doch um Spannungen handelt, die literarisch zu erklären sind. Die Urkundenhypothese wird aber durch eine Ergänzungshypothese ersetzt. Nach D. B. Redford ist eine Rubenversion mit Jakob als Vater, die zwischen 650 und 425 entstand, später durch eine Judaschicht mit Israel und dann noch durch den Herausgeber der Genesis ergänzt worden[27]. Demgegenüber bestand nach H.-C. Schmitt der Grundbestand aus einer Judaversion mit dem Vater Israel, die aus der frühen Königszeit stammt. Sie sei in exilischer oder nachexilischer Zeit durch eine umfangreiche Bearbeitung ergänzt worden, in der Ruben zum Sprecher der Brüder wurde, und der Vater den Namen Jakob trug; noch später sei Gen 39[28].

Gegenüber dieser Vielfalt von Meinungen ist aber auf einige Beobachtungen hinzuweisen, die längst bekannt sind. Aus ihnen geht m. E.

---

[23] L. Ruppert, Die Josephserzählung der Genesis, 1965.
[24] L. Ruppert, Das Buch Genesis II, 1984.
[25] L. Ruppert schreibt 467 Anm. 201: »So werden Motive wie Josef, der jüngste (!) Sohn Israels, das vornehme *Ärmel*kleid (37,3, vgl. 37,23*), die ehebrecherische Ägypterin (Gen 39*), Josef als der zweite Mann Ägyptens (in Gen 41 und Gen 45), Josefs Agrarpolitik (47,13–26), die große Juda-Rede (44,18–34) vermutlich erst durch den Jehowisten in die JE eingebracht worden sein, wohl auch Juda selbst in der Rolle des zweiten guten Bruders (neben Ruben).« Erst der Jehowist habe den Patriarchen Israel genannt.
[26] Vgl. die Auflistung bei H. Seebaß, Zeit, 90.
[27] D. B. Redford, A Study of the Biblical Story of Joseph, VT. S 20, 1970.
[28] H.-C. Schmitt, Die nichtpriesterliche Josephsgeschichte, BZAW 154, 1980.

eindeutig hervor, daß die Josephsgeschichte nach Abzug ihrer priesterschriftlichen Teile aus zwei Darstellungen besteht, die erst nachträglich miteinander verbunden wurden. Das soll zunächst an fünf Beispielen gezeigt werden: 1. Die Bezeichnungen Israel und Jakob für den Vater wechseln teilweise recht abrupt. So heißt es in 45,27b: »Da wurde der Geist Jakobs, ihres Vaters, lebendig.« Darauf folgt in v. 28: »Da sprach Israel ...« Dieser Wechsel kann bei Annahme eines Verfassers nicht zureichend erklärt werden. Gelegentlich hat man allerdings angenommen, daß er sachliche Gründe hat. G.W.Coats meint, daß der Vater Israel genannt werde, wenn es um den Weg nach Ägypten gehe[29]. Diese Deutung, die für 45,28 erwägenswert sein mag, läßt sich aber für andere Stellen nicht halten. So steht nach G.W.Coats in 37,3 Israel, weil das Gewand, das der Vater Joseph schenkt, den Verrat der Brüder motiviere, durch den Joseph nach Ägypten kommt. In 37,13 heiße der Vater Israel, weil durch seinen Auftrag Joseph schließlich nach Ägypten muß. Diese Interpretation wird jedoch von den Texten selbst nicht nahegelegt. Warum wird im Zusammenhang mit den Träumen in 37,10 einfach von »seinem Vater« gesprochen, obwohl diese Träume in 37,19f. für das Verhalten der Brüder ebenfalls von Bedeutung sind? In 42,36 und 43,6 reagiert der Vater jeweils auf die ihm mitgeteilte Forderung Josephs, Benjamin nach Ägypten zu bringen. Er heißt zwar in 43,6 Israel, in 42,36 jedoch Jakob. Schließlich wird der Vater in 46,2.5a Jakob genannt, obwohl er auf dem Weg nach Ägypten ist. In anderer Weise versucht I. Willi-Plein den Wechsel zu erklären. Der Vater heiße Jakob, wo es um die persönliche Geschichte Josephs und seiner Brüder gehe, er werde dagegen Israel genannt, wenn ein stammes- oder volksgeschichtlicher Aspekt hineinspiele[30]. Auch dadurch wird der Unterschied zwischen 42,36 und 43,6 nicht verständlich. Außerdem ist in 37,13 kein stammes- oder volksgeschichtlicher Aspekt zu erkennen. Es läßt sich überdies zeigen, daß Israel und Joseph eindeutig als individuelle Personen dargestellt werden[31]. Der Wechsel zwischen Israel und Jakob läßt sich somit nicht sachlich erklären.

Daß ein Verfasser beide Bezeichnungen »promiscue« gebraucht habe, oder daß der Grund für den Wechsel durch die weitere Textüberlieferung verdeckt worden sei[32], bleibt unbefriedigend. Dies gilt um so mehr, als in 42,29ff. und 43,1ff. die verschiedenen Bezeichnungen mit einem unterschiedlichen Sprecher der Brüder verbunden sind. In 42,29ff. heißt der Vater Jakob, Sprecher der Brüder ist Ruben, in 43,1ff. stehen dafür Israel und Juda[33].

---

[29] G.W.Coats, Canaan, 70f.   [30] I.Willi-Plein, Aspekte, 319f.   [31] Vgl. IVa.
[32] W.Rudolph, BZAW 63, 149–151; vgl. auch H.Donner, Gestalt, 39.
[33] Nach C.Westermann 129, geht aus den Formulierungen »ihr Vater« und »zu ihnen« in 43,2 hervor, daß Kap. 43 keine literarisch selbständige Einheit sei. Das ist von den

2. Dieses Argument gewinnt an Gewicht, weil sich 42,29 ff. und 43,1 ff. auch in einem anderen Punkt unterscheiden. Nach 42, 29 ff. hat Joseph bei der ersten Reise der Brüder Simeon als Geisel genommen; er soll nur freigelassen werden, wenn die Brüder mit Benjamin zurückkehren. In dem Gespräch zwischen dem Vater und den Brüdern vor der zweiten Reise in 43,1 ff. wird aber Simeon nicht erwähnt. Hier zwingt lediglich die andauernde Hungersnot die Brüder dazu, nochmals nach Ägypten zu ziehen. »Der Mann« hat aber angekündigt, daß sie ihn nicht wiedersehen dürfen, wenn sie nicht ihren jüngsten Bruder mitbringen (43,3.7). Weder für den Vater noch für die Brüder spielt hier eine Rolle, daß Simeon in Ägypten ist.

Er wird allerdings in 43,14 und 43,23 erwähnt. 43,14 ist jedoch ein Zusatz, da die Gottesbezeichnung El šadday in Gen – abgesehen von 49,25, wo der Text wohl entsprechend zu ändern ist [34] – nur bei P vorkommt. Außerdem schließt v. 15 nahtlos an v.13 an [35]. Nun hat C. Westermann für die Ursprünglichkeit von v.14 angeführt, daß die Erzählung an dieser Stelle ein Wort des Abschieds enthalten haben müsse [36]. Dieses Argument ist aber keineswegs zwingend. Die gleiche Überlegung, wie sie C. Westermann anstellt, hat offenbar einen Späteren dazu veranlaßt, v.14 einzufügen. Für ihn mußte der Vater vor der schwierigen zweiten Reise der Brüder einen Abschiedssegen gesprochen haben. In seinen Formulierungen greift der Verfasser von v.14 die beiden Darstellungen von 42,29 ff. und 43,1 ff. auf. Nach 42,29 ff. mußte die zweite Reise dem Zweck dienen, Simeon zu befreien. In v. 14b nimmt der Ergänzer 42,36 auf, für Joseph gebraucht er aber in v. 14a einen Ausdruck, der nicht aus 42,29 ff., sondern aus 43,1 ff. stammt. Interessanterweise besteht bei der Bezeichnung für Joseph zwischen 42, 29 ff. und 43,3 ff. ein kleiner, aber wichtiger Unterschied. In 42,30.33 wird Joseph als »der Mann, der Herr des Landes« bezeichnet, in 43,3 ff. aber durchgehend nur als »der Mann«. Ein Grund für diesen Wechsel läßt sich bei der Annahme eines Verfassers wieder nicht erken-

---

Vertretern einer Quellenscheidung auch nicht behauptet worden. Die Frage ist nur, ob 43,1 ff. tatsächlich 42,29 ff. voraussetzt. Die Erwägung von C. Westermann 128, daß Israel in 43,6.8.11 eine spätere Änderung sein könnte, »deren Motiv wir nicht kennen«, bedeutet letztlich den Verzicht auf eine Erklärung. Gegen seine weitere Vermutung, daß »der Name Israel an den wenigen Stellen auch nachträglich eingefügt sein kann«, spricht 43,6, wo der Name Israel nicht wie in v.8.11 durch eine Apposition erläutert wird. Tatsächlich bereitet der Wechsel Israel/Jakob der Quellenscheidung auch nur in 46,2 und in Kap. 48 Schwierigkeiten, die sich aber lösen lassen (vgl. IIf und IIIe).

[34] Vgl. z. B. C. Westermann z. St.
[35] H. Gunkel 449, rechnet v.14a zu E und v.14b zu J. Das scheitert aber daran, daß das »und ich« in v.14b deutlich dem *El šadday* von v.14a korrespondiert. In sich ist v.14 einheitlich.
[36] C. Westermann 132.

nen. Wegen der Gottesbezeichnung El šadday dürfte 43,14 jünger sein als P[37].

Ein Zusatz ist auch 43,23b, wo Simeon nochmals erwähnt wird. Dieser Halbvers unterbricht den Zusammenhang zwischen v. 23a und v. 24. In v. 24ff. begegnen alle Brüder Joseph in seinem Haus. V. 23b wurde somit notwendig, als die unterschiedlichen Darstellungen von 42,29ff. und 43,1ff. in einem Werk vereinigt wurden. V. 23b stammt von diesem Redaktor und ist somit älter als 43,14.

Wenn aber nach 43,1ff. Simeon auf der ersten Reise von Joseph nicht als Geisel zurückbehalten wurde, kann entgegen der Annahme von D. B. Redford die Judaschicht keine Ergänzung eines Grundbestandes mit Ruben sein. Ein späterer Bearbeiter hätte nicht völlig außer Acht lassen können, daß nach 42,29ff. Simeon in Ägypten festgehalten wird.

3. Auf eine Dublette stößt man auch bei dem Motiv, daß die Brüder das Geld wiederfinden, das sie Joseph auf der ersten Reise für das Getreide bezahlt haben. Nach 42,27f. finden sie ihr Geld, als sie auf der Rückreise in einer Herberge übernachten. So wird der Vorgang auch in 43,21 und 44,8 dargestellt, die beide zur Judaversion gehören[38]. Dagegen kommt in 42,35 das Geld erst an den Tag, als die Brüder zu Hause ihre Säcke vor dem Vater ausleeren. W. Rudolph wollte diese Spannung dadurch lösen, daß er v. 35 – ohne »sie« und »ihr Vater« – hinter v. 28a stellte[39]. Dabei hat er aber übersehen, daß das Geld in 42,27; 43,21 und 44,8 in den Säcken oben liegt, in 42,35 aber unten, denn aus diesem Grund kommt es erst zum Vorschein als die Säcke entleert werden. D. B. Redford, H. Donner, H.-C. Schmitt und C. Westermann nehmen an, daß es sich bei 42,35 um einen Zusatz handelt[40]. Ein Späterer habe den Hinweis vermißt, wie der Vater von dem wiedergefundenen Geld Kenntnis erhalten hatte (43,12). Da nach 42,29 die Brüder dem Vater alles berichtet hatten, was ihnen widerfahren war, habe er 42,35 eingefügt. Nun hat aber bereits J. Wellhausen darauf hingewiesen, daß 42,35 in der Rubenversion durch 42,25 vorbereitet wird[41]. Nach diesem Vers haben die Brüder in Ägypten außer Getreide auch Reiseproviant erhalten. Sie brauchten deshalb ihre Säcke unter-

---

[37] H.-C. Schmitt, BZAW 154, 45f., weist v. 14 seiner Rubenschicht zu, da sich in dem Vers der charakteristische Stil der Priesterschrift sonst nicht nachweisen lasse. Das ist jedoch nicht erforderlich, wenn es sich um einen Zusatz handelt. Gegen die Rubenschicht spricht, daß in ihr sonst nie *El šadday* vorkommt.

[38] In 42,27f. wird allerdings nur berichtet, daß ein Bruder sein Geld gefunden hat. Hier dürfte die Darstellung von dem Redaktor wegen 42,35 gekürzt worden sein (vgl. IIc).

[39] W. Rudolph, BZAW 63, 160f.

[40] D. B. Redford, VT. S 20, 150ff.; H. Donner, Gestalt, 46f.; H.-C. Schmitt, BZAW 154, 40f.; C. Westermann 120.

[41] J. Wellhausen, Composition, 57.

wegs nicht zu öffnen. Damit ist 42,35 aber in der Rubenversion fest verankert. Auch die unterschiedliche Darstellung, wie das Geld gefunden wird, ist ein deutlicher Hinweis, daß es sich bei der Juda- und der Rubenversion um zwei parallele Erzählungen handelt[42].

4. In Gen 45 wird zweimal geschildert, wie sich Joseph seinen Brüdern zu erkennen gab. In v. 3 sagt er: »Ich bin Joseph, lebt mein Vater noch?«, in v. 4: »Ich bin Joseph, euer Bruder, den ihr nach Ägypten verkauft habt«. Besondere Beachtung verdient die Frage in v. 3: »Lebt mein Vater noch?« Ob ihr Vater noch lebt, hatte Joseph die Brüder bei ihrer zweiten Reise schon in 43,27 gefragt, und sie hatten diese Frage in 43,28 bejaht. In der großen Rede Judas von 44,18–34 ist die Tatsache, daß der Verlust Benjamins dem Vater den Tod bringen würde, Dreh- und Angelpunkt seiner Argumentation. Unmittelbar danach kann Joseph nicht die Frage stellen: »Lebt mein Vater noch?« In 45,3 kommt somit eine Darstellung zu Wort, in der Gen 43 f. nicht enthalten war. Hier wird zugleich deutlich, daß es sich bei der Rubenversion gegen H.-C. Schmitt nicht um eine Bearbeitung der Judaerzählung, sondern um eine Parallelfassung handelt. Warum sollte ein Bearbeiter nach den vorangegangenen beiden Kapiteln Joseph jetzt noch diese Frage stellen lassen? Sie wird im weiteren Verlauf von Gen 45 nicht ausdrücklich beantwortet, und hat somit für die jetzige Darstellung eine untergeordnete Bedeutung.

Nun ist gegen die Verteilung von 45,3 f. auf zwei Fassungen verschiedentlich eingewandt worden, daß es sich um keine echten Dubletten handle. Der Verfasser verwende in der Josephsgeschichte auch sonst als künstlerisches Mittel die Verdoppelung einer Szene, wie z. B. aus den beiden Träumen Josephs in 37,5 ff. hervorgehe[43]. Bei dieser Argumentation wird aber ein wichtiger Unterschied übersehen. Die beiden Träume in 37,5 ff. widersprechen sich weder formal, noch sachlich, sondern der zweite bringt durch die Einbeziehung von Vater und Mutter eine Steigerung zu dem ersten Traum. 45,3 steht hingegen in klarem sachlichen Widerspruch zu Gen 43 f. Deshalb kann diese Doppelung nicht von einem Verfasser der Josephsgeschichte stammen, sondern *nur* von einem Redaktor, der hier zwei Fassungen miteinander verbunden hat. Dieser Redaktor nimmt in 45,3 die Frage Josephs auf, weil er von der Reaktion der Brüder berichten wollte. Dadurch konnte er 45,4 aus der anderen Darstellung als Steigerung anfügen. Mit 45,15, das aus je-

---

[42] Die Auffassung, daß es sich bei v. 35 um einen Zusatz handelt, wird auch damit begründet, daß der Vater erst in v. 36 auf den Bericht von v. 29–34 reagiert. Das ist richtig. Angesichts der festen Verankerung von 42,35 in der Rubenversion folgt daraus jedoch nur, daß für ihren Verfasser das gefundene Geld ein Nebenmotiv ist. Zu seiner Funktion vgl. IIb.

[43] Vgl. H. Donner, Gestalt, 22 f.; G. W. Coats, Canaan, 67; C. Westermann 156.

ner Fassung stammt, zu der auch 45,3 gehört[44], konnte er außerdem verdeutlichen, daß das Verhältnis zwischen den Brüdern und Joseph jetzt in Ordnung ist: Die Brüder können nun mit Joseph reden.

Diese Beobachtungen führen zu zwei grundsätzlichen Überlegungen. Einmal wird an 45,3f. deutlich, daß der Redaktor bemüht war, die verschiedenen Darstellungen möglichst weitgehend in sein Werk aufzunehmen. Zum anderen zeigen die Verse, daß für literarische Stilmittel zwischen zwei Ebenen zu unterscheiden ist. Sie können sowohl von einem Erzähler als auch von einem Redaktor gebraucht werden. In der Josephsgeschichte wird das Mittel der Doppelung von dem Verfasser der Rubenschicht *und* von dem Redaktor verwandt. Beide lassen sich jedoch eindeutig unterscheiden. Während die Doppelungen in der Rubenfassung keine formalen und sachlichen Widersprüche enthalten, ist das bei dem Redaktor anders, weil er die Doppelungen mit Hilfe ihm überlieferter Texte herstellt. Dadurch mußte er gewisse Spannungen in Kauf nehmen. Der Nachweis, daß ein Text nach einem bestimmten Prinzip gestaltet ist, ist somit kein Beweis für seine literarische Einheitlichkeit, wenn gegen sie andere formale oder sachliche Gründe sprechen. Dieser Gesichtspunkt, der m.E. gegenwärtig in der literarkritischen Diskussion vernachlässigt wird, läßt sich auch an weiteren Stellen der Josephsgeschichte aufweisen, auf die noch zurückzukommen sein wird. In Gen 45,3f. sind jedenfalls eindeutig zwei verschiedene Darstellungen nachträglich miteinander verbunden worden.

5. Zu dem gleichen Ergebnis führt die Analyse von 37,25-30. In v. 25-27 kommt Juda durch die vorüberziehende ismaelitische Karawane auf die Idee, Joseph an die Ismaeliter zu verkaufen. Die Brüder stimmen seinem Plan zu. Nach v. 28 aber ziehen midianitische Kaufleute Joseph aus der Zisterne und verkaufen ihn an die Ismaeliter. Ruben kehrt in v. 29f. zu der Zisterne zurück und stellt entsetzt fest, daß der Knabe nicht mehr da ist. Dieser Abschnitt enthält mehrere Spannungen. Wie kann Ruben Joseph in der Zisterne suchen, nachdem er dem Plan zu seinem Verkauf zugestimmt hatte? Außerdem müßten nach v. 27 die Brüder Joseph verkauft haben. Auffällig ist auch, daß in v. 28 Midianiter und Ismaeliter genannt werden. Trotz dieser Probleme hielt W. Rudolph daran fest, daß der Abschnitt einheitlich ist. Ruben habe dem Plan zum Verkauf nur scheinbar zugestimmt. Die Midianiter aber seien den Brüdern zuvorgekommen und hätten Joseph an die Ismaeliter verkauft[45]. Nun mag sich zwar der Redaktor die Ereignisse so vorgestellt haben. Die Schwierigkeiten des Textes sind damit jedoch nicht gelöst. V. 28aß ist deutlich die Fortsetzung von v. 27. Wie kann außerdem Ruben dem Plan zum Verkauf auch nur scheinbar zustimmen, wenn er

---

[44] Vgl. IIe.
[45] W. Rudolph, BZAW 63, 153f.; ähnlich I. Willi-Plein, Aspekte, 313.

doch Joseph zum Vater zurückbringen wollte? (v. 22). Das ist ein nicht lösbarer Widerspruch. In v. 29 f. wird auch durch nichts angedeutet, daß Ruben von dem Verkaufsplan etwas wußte. Deshalb genügt es nicht, lediglich v. 28 aα als Glosse auszuscheiden, wie z. B. H. Donner und G. W. Coats vorgeschlagen haben[46]. Man müßte dann weiter annehmen, daß Ruben von dem Verkaufsplan nichts wußte. Das scheitert aber an v. 25–27 und 29. In v. 25–27 sind die Brüder zusammen; daß Ruben fehlt, müßte schon gesagt werden, und in v. 29 geht Ruben offenbar von den Brüdern aus zu der Zisterne und kehrt in v. 30 zu ihnen zurück.

Diese Beobachtungen sprechen auch dagegen, daß es sich bei der Rubenschicht um eine Erweiterung der Judafassung handelt. Wollte ein Ergänzer wirklich Ruben als Kontrastfigur Juda zur Seite stellen, wie H.-C. Schmitt meint[47], so hätte er Ruben für v. 25–27 ausschalten müssen. Das wäre im Anschluß an v. 24, der ebenfalls zur Rubenschicht gehört, leicht möglich gewesen[48]. Erst recht kann hier die Judaschicht keine Ergänzung eines Grundbestandes mit Ruben sein, wie D. B. Redford will. Warum sollte ein Bearbeiter den Verkaufsplan einfügen, wenn dann doch die Midianiter und nicht die Brüder Joseph an die Ismaeliter verkaufen? So wird der Wortlaut von v. 25–30 nur verständlich, wenn hier zwei Darstellungen zusammengearbeitet sind. Nach der Judafassung hat Juda den Brüdern vorgeschlagen, Joseph an die Ismaeliter zu verkaufen, und sie haben zugestimmt und Joseph verkauft (v. 25–27.28 aß). Nach der Rubenversion haben hingegen Midianiter Joseph gestohlen und nach Ägypten gebracht. Ruben kehrt zu der Zisterne zurück und muß feststellen, daß Joseph nicht mehr da ist (v. 28 aα.b. 29 f.)[49]. Damit ist sein Plan von v. 22 gescheitert, ihn zum Vater zurückzubringen.

Die Dubletten in v. 25–30 werden auch von C. Westermann anerkannt, der v. 25 (ab »da hoben sie ihre Augen auf«). 26 f. 28 aß.b als Variante zur Rubenfassung betrachtet: »Deutlicher kann eine Variante wohl kaum als solche gekennzeichnet werden. Es ist offenbar Absicht des Erzählers der Josephgeschichte, der seinen Hörern zu erkennen

---

[46] H. Donner, Gestalt, 44 f.; G. W. Coats, Canaan, 61.
[47] H.-C. Schmitt, BZAW 154, 19 f.; vgl. auch H. Donner, Gestalt, 37–39.
[48] E. Otto, Lebensauffassung, 388, sieht in v. 28 aα. 29 f. einen Zusatz, der die Ahnherrn davon entlasten solle, Joseph verkauft zu haben. Aber Ruben kommt auch an anderen Stellen, die E. Otto zum Grundbestand rechnet, eine wichtige Funktion zu, und ihr Bild von Ruben stimmt mit 37, 29 f. überein.
[49] Schwierig ist nur die Zuweisung von v. 28 b. Mit J. Wellhausen, Composition, 53; H. Gunkel 403; L. Ruppert, Josephserzählung, 30; u. a.; wird man diesen Halbvers zur Rubenfassung rechnen müssen, da in ihr sonst der Übergang nach Ägypten fehlt. Er ist in der Judafassung dadurch gegeben, daß nach v. 25 die Ismaeliter auf dem Weg nach Ägypten sind.

gibt, daß ihm zwei Versionen vorgegeben sind, wie Joseph nach Ägypten kam, und daß er beide zu Wort kommen lassen will.«[50] Das dürfte freilich schwerlich die Absicht des ›Erzählers‹ gewesen sein, denn v. 28 stellt deutlich den Versuch dar, die verschiedenen Fassungen miteinander auszugleichen. Vor allem aber lassen sich die beiden Varianten nicht von der übrigen Josephsgeschichte trennen. Wenn hier Ruben und Juda zu verschiedenen Fassungen gehören, dann ist es zumindest naheliegend, daß das auch für die sonstigen Stellen gilt, an denen diese Brüder als Sprecher auftreten. Tatsächlich wird sich bei den Einzelanalysen zeigen, daß das unterschiedliche Bild, das hier von Ruben und Juda gezeichnet wird, ihrer Charakterisierung an anderen Stellen entspricht. Damit bestätigt auch 37,25–30, daß die vorpriesterschriftliche Josephsgeschichte auf zwei Fassungen zurückgeht.

Bereits aus den genannten Beispielen, die sich vermehren ließen, geht hervor, daß die vorpriesterschriftliche Josephsgeschichte literarisch nicht einheitlich ist. Sie läßt sich auch nicht durch eine Ergänzungshypothese erklären. Vielmehr besteht sie aus zwei verschiedenen literarischen Darstellungen, die später miteinander verbunden wurden. Daß sie sich in Thematik und Linienführung deutlich unterscheiden, wird in den folgenden Kapiteln gezeigt werden.

Nun ist schwer vorstellbar, daß beide Fassungen für sich überliefert wurden, ehe man sie später in die Pentateucherzählung eingliederte. Sie waren also Bestandteil verschiedener, die Josephsgeschichte übergreifender Darstellungen. Damit kommt der Josephsgeschichte für die gegenwärtige Diskussion über die Entstehung des Pentateuch eine wesentliche Bedeutung zu. An diesem schwierigen Komplex wird deutlich, daß die neuere Urkundenhypothese beibehalten werden muß. Das ergibt sich, wie nochmals zu betonen ist, aus längst bekannten Beobachtungen. Keines der für die Josephsgeschichte angeführten Beispiele ist neu. Von da aus stellt sich m. E. die Frage, ob die gegenwärtige Pentateuchkrise nicht zum Teil darauf beruht, daß heute wohl begründete Ergebnisse der Vergangenheit mit Argumenten bestritten werden, die einer genaueren Prüfung nicht standhalten. Natürlich müssen diese Ergebnisse weitergeführt und gegebenenfalls auch modifiziert werden. Grundsätzlich ist aber, wie selbst aus der Josephsgeschichte hervorgeht, die neuere Urkundenhypothese immer noch die geeignete Basis, um die Entstehung des Pentateuch zu erklären. Es ist somit weiterhin mit den Quellenschriften J, E und P zu rechnen.

Dann lassen sich bereits aufgrund des unterschiedlichen Namens des Vaters die beiden Fassungen der vorpriesterschriftlichen Josephsgeschichte jeweils einer Quellenschrift zuweisen. Der Jahwist erzählt in Gen 32,23–32, daß der Erzvater Jakob den neuen Namen Israel erhal-

---

[50] C. Westermann 32.

ten hat. Dagegen berichtet der Elohist nichts von einer Umbenennung Jakobs. Deshalb gehört die Version mit Israel/Juda zu J und die andere mit Jakob/Ruben zu E.

Die Übereinstimmungen zwischen diesen beiden Fassungen bedürfen freilich der Erklärung. M. Noth und G. Fohrer haben angenommen, daß J und E auf eine gemeinsame Grundlage zurückgehen, die sie unabhängig voneinander weitergebildet haben[51]. Dagegen sprechen aber in der Josephsgeschichte zwei Beobachtungen, auf die bereits Hannelis Schulte hingewiesen hat[52]:

1. Sowohl bei J (43,9) als auch bei E (42,37) übernimmt vor der zweiten Reise der Sprecher der Brüder gegenüber dem Vater für Benjamin eine Bürgschaft. Während aber bei J Juda tatsächlich vor Joseph für Benjamin eintreten muß (44,18ff.), ringt bei E Ruben mit seiner Bürgschaft lediglich dem Vater die Zusage ab, daß Benjamin mitziehen darf. »Doch hat der Elohist bereits den als Geisel im Gefängnis schmachtenden Simeon als Druckmittel, brauchte also dieses Motiv gar nicht. Er bringt es nur, weil es ihm vorgegeben war.«[53] Damit wird bei E ein Element, das bei J für den Fortgang der Handlung konstitutiv ist, auf eine einzelne Situation beschränkt und damit zum Nebenmotiv. Das läßt sich nur so erklären, daß der bürgende Bruder von E aus der jahwistischen Fassung übernommen wurde. Für H.-C. Schmitt ist die Bürgschaft Rubens allerdings ein wichtiges Argument dafür, daß es sich bei der Rubenschicht um eine Bearbeitung der Judafassung handelt. Sie werde nur verständlich, wenn mit ihr Juda ein ›idealer‹ Bruder zur Seite gestellt werden solle[54]. Dagegen sprechen aber die Beispiele, die oben für die Doppelsträngigkeit der Josephsgeschichte gegeben wurden. Tatsächlich ist dieses Motiv in einer eigenen elohistischen Darstellung

---

[51] M. Noth, Pentateuch, 40ff.; G. Fohrer, Einleitung in das Alte Testament, [12]1979, 141ff.

[52] Hannelis Schulte, Die Entstehung der Geschichtsschreibung im Alten Israel, BZAW 128, 1972, 15–17. In ihrer Analyse der Josephsgeschichte, 9–35, rechnet H. Schulte mit einem komplizierten Wachstumsprozeß. Sie unterscheidet zwischen einer »Ägyptergeschichte«, die vom Aufstieg Josephs in Ägypten und seinen Maßnahmen gegen die Hungersnot berichtete und zu der 39,20ff.; (40); 41; 47,13–26 gehörten, und einem ursprünglich anonymen »Brüdermärchen«, das in der mündlichen Tradition auf Jakob und seine fünf Söhne übertragen wurde. Es sei dann noch um Benjamin und die zweite Reise erweitert worden. Aus diesen Überlieferungen habe der Jahwist seine Josephsgeschichte geschaffen. Der Elohist kenne aber noch das Brüdermärchen von Jakob und seinen Söhnen und habe es seiner Darstellung zugrundegelegt, in die er freilich Elemente aus der jahwistischen Fassung eingearbeitet habe (vgl. die Zusammenfassung 27f.). Gegen diese Rekonstruktion gelten aber die gleichen Einwände, die G. v. Rad gegen die Lösungen von H. Gunkel und H. Greßmann geltend gemacht hat (Vgl. oben Anm. 9).

[53] H. Schulte, BZAW 128, 16.

[54] H.-C. Schmitt, BZAW 154, 18f.

durchaus sinnvoll, auch wenn es in ihr lediglich ein Nebenmotiv ist. So wie Ruben einst Joseph zum Vater zurückbringen wollte (37,22), setzt er nun alles dafür ein, daß Simeon wieder freikommt. Mit 42,37 unterstreicht also der Elohist das Bild, das er in Kap. 37 von Ruben gezeichnet hat.

2. Bei J läßt Joseph auf der zweiten Reise seinen Becher in den Sack Benjamins legen (44,1f.*). Das ist eine Steigerung zu dem Geld, das die Brüder auf der ersten Reise in ihren Säcken wiederfinden[55]. Damit wird zugleich die Handlung vorangetrieben. Bei E fehlt hingegen der Becher. Deshalb ist es hier für den Fortgang der Handlung eigentlich nicht erforderlich, daß die Brüder ihr Geld wiederfinden. Auch 42,35 ist bei E ein Nebenmotiv, das ohne Folgen bleibt. Das wird ebenfalls nur verständlich, wenn E das Geldmotiv aus der jahwistischen Version übernommen und entsprechend seiner anderen Linienführung abgewandelt hat.

Schon diese beiden Beispiele zeigen, daß in der Josephsgeschichte E die jahwistische Fassung als Vorlage benutzt und sie bewußt umgestaltet hat. Kennt der Elohist aber hier das jahwistische Werk, dann ist es auch sonst seine Grundlage. Die Gemeinsamkeiten zwischen J und E beruhen also nicht auf einer gemeinsamen Vorlage, sondern der Elohist hat J für seine eigene Geschichtsdarstellung benutzt.

---

[55] H. Gunkel 452f.

II. Analyse von Gen 37,1–35; 42,14–47,31; 49,1 a.28 b–33; 50,1–22

Auch wenn in der vorpriesterschriftlichen Josephsgeschichte deutlich eine jahwistische und eine elohistische Fassung zusammengearbeitet sind, bleibt die Frage, wie weit sich die beiden Erzählungen noch voneinander abheben lassen. Die unterschiedlichen Lösungen, die dafür in der Forschung vertreten wurden, zeigen, daß eine literarische Aufteilung hier erhebliche Schwierigkeiten bereitet. Deshalb sollen im folgenden zunächst jene Stücke untersucht werden, bei denen sich m. E. die Zuweisung an J oder E gut begründen läßt. An ihnen wird auch die unterschiedliche Linienführung bei J und E sehr schön deutlich. Außerdem ist zu fragen, ob an einigen Stellen, die bisher nur mit erheblichen Schwierigkeiten zugeordnet werden konnten, nicht die Priesterschrift zu Wort kommt, die dann in der Josephsgeschichte freilich stärker vertreten wäre, als in der Regel angenommen wird.

a) Gen 37,1–35

V. 1 f. stammt aus P, wie schon aus der Formulierung »in dem Land der Fremdlingsschaft seines Vaters« in v. 1 und der Toledotformel und der Angabe über das Alter Josephs in v. 2 hervorgeht. Zudem läßt sich v. 2 mit der Darstellung in v. 3 ff. nicht vereinbaren. Nach v. 2 hütet Joseph das Vieh gemeinsam mit den Söhnen der Bilha und der Silpa, während er sich nach v. 12 ff. bei dem Vater aufhält und von diesem einmal zu seinen Brüdern gesandt wurde, um sich nach ihrem Wohlergehen zu erkundigen. Nach v. 2 b trug Joseph dem Vater zu, was man diesen Söhnen Böses nachsagte. Diese Schilderung wird nur verständlich, wenn sie die Ursache für den Konflikt zwischen Joseph und den Brüdern angibt, der aber in v. 3 ff. anders begründet wird. Die Einleitung in v. 1 f. hebt sich somit klar von der Fortsetzung in v. 3 ff. ab. Darauf ist in der Forschung immer wieder hingewiesen worden[56].

Das hat nun allerdings G. W. Coats bestritten. Nach ihm sind die Verse – vielleicht mit Ausnahme der Toledotformel – in der Josephsgeschichte fest verankert[57]. Der Anfang in v. 1 entspreche strukturell dem

---

[56] Vgl. z. B. H. Gunkel 492. Deshalb kann v. 2 aβ.b gegen H. Seebaß, Zeit, 76 f., keinesfalls zu E gerechnet werden.

[57] Vgl. zum folgenden G. W. Coats, Canaan, 8–12.

Abschluß in 47,27a. Aber dagegen spricht schon, daß der Vater an beiden Stellen verschieden bezeichnet wird. Es wurde oben gezeigt, daß sich der Wechsel zwischen Jakob und Israel nicht in der Weise von G. W. Coats erklären läßt. G. W. Coats meint weiter, daß die Tätigkeit Josephs als Hirte keinen Widerspruch zum Folgenden darstelle. Joseph sei in v. 12 ff. nicht deshalb beim Vater, weil er kein Hirte sei, sondern er werde vom Vater dadurch bevorzugt, daß er ihn von der Arbeit freigestellt habe. Davon findet sich aber im Text nicht einmal eine Andeutung. Freilich stellt R. Rendtorff aufgrund von 37,2 und 41,46a fest, »daß für den Exegeten, der nicht *vorher* davon überzeugt ist, daß es eine P-Josephgeschichte geben muß, eine solche nicht existiert«[58]. Natürlich ist P nicht aufgrund von 37,2 als eigene Quellenschrift nachweisbar. Aus v. 2 ergibt sich nur, daß dieser Vers zum Folgenden in einer erheblichen Spannung steht. Wenn sich aber anderwärts die herkömmlich P zugewiesenen Stücke als Bestandteile eines eigenen Werkes erweisen lassen – und das ist in der Tat möglich[59] –, und wenn v. 1 f. Elemente enthält, die sonst für die Priesterschrift charakteristisch sind, muß man diese Verse zu P rechnen.

Das wird hier zusätzlich dadurch gestützt, daß v. 2 eine Bemerkung enthält, aus der hervorgeht, daß die beiden Verse ursprünglich nicht mit v. 3 ff. literarisch verbunden waren. Die Feststellung in v. 2 aβ »und er war ein Knabe« hat den Exegeten schon immer Schwierigkeiten bereitet, weil nicht zu erkennen ist, welche Funktion sie nach der Angabe über das Alter Josephs in v. 2a haben sollte. Deshalb haben H. Gunkel und O. Procksch hier den Text geändert[60]. Nach C. Westermann ist *nʿr* »im Sinn von Bursche, Gehilfe oder Hütejunge wie in Ex 33,11 zu verstehen«[61]. Diese Interpretation ist aber ebenso problematisch wie eine Änderung des Textes. Kann man wirklich annehmen, daß der Verfasser von v. 2 Joseph den Söhnen der Nebenfrauen Jakobs untergeordnet hat? Zudem wird durch »und er war ein Knabe« deutlich der Zusammenhang unterbrochen. Die folgenden Worte »mit den Söhnen der Bilha ...« sollen erläutern, was »mit seinen Brüdern« in v. 2aα gemeint ist. Dann sind die fraglichen Worte ein Zusatz, der im Blick auf die Darstellung in v. 3 ff. eingefügt wurde. Hier ist Joseph für den Vater »Sohn des Alters« (v. 3) und damit erheblich jünger als die anderen Brüder. Das ist er auch in v. 30, wo Ruben von ihm als *yld* spricht. Mit »und er war ein Knabe« in v. 2aβ soll also die Spannung ausgeglichen werden, daß nach P Joseph bereits 17 Jahre alt war, als es zum

---

[58] R. Rendtorff, BZAW 147, 115.
[59] Vgl. z. B. L. Schmidt, Pentateuch, in: H. J. Boecker u. a., Altes Testament, 1983, 80–101.
[60] H. Gunkel 492, ändert die Punktation von *nʿr* und übersetzt »er empörte sich über«; O. Procksch 554, schlägt vor *nrʿ* zu lesen = »er war schlecht behandelt«.
[61] C. Westermann 61; vgl. auch G. v. Rad 286.

Konflikt mit den Söhnen der Bilha und der Silpa kam, daß er aber im Folgenden deutlich ein Kind ist, das wesentlich jünger ist als die Brüder.

Damit geht aus dieser Bemerkung hervor, daß der Rest von v. 1 f. zunächst nicht durch v. 3 ff. fortgesetzt wurde. Sie stammt von dem Endredaktor des Pentateuch oder einem Späteren, der die Spannung zwischen v. 2 und v. 3 ff. empfunden hat. Da der Endredaktor den Aufriß der Priesterschrift zugrundelegte, mußte er v. 1 f.* aus P der jehowistischen Darstellung in v. 3 ff. voranstellen. Er erreichte dadurch zugleich eine inhaltliche Steigerung. Zunächst ist das Verhältnis zwischen Joseph und einigen Brüdern gespannt, dann sind alle Brüder Joseph feindlich gesinnt.

Auch inhaltlich paßt v. 2 zur Priesterschrift. Ihr Verfasser bemüht sich, von der Väterzeit ein friedliches Bild zu zeichnen. Offenbar mußte er aber den Weg Josephs nach Ägypten doch mit einem Konflikt zwischen Joseph und seinen Brüdern begründen, da er anders nicht erklären konnte, wie Joseph nach Ägypten kam. Er hat aber durch die Beschränkung auf die Söhne der Nebenfrauen Jakobs die Auseinandersetzung bewußt abgemildert. Wie sie zu dem Ergebnis führte, daß Joseph nach Ägypten mußte, läßt sich nicht mehr sagen, da die Fortsetzung von v. 2 bei P von dem Endredaktor nicht aufgenommen wurde. Er entschied sich für die anscheinend ausführlichere Darstellung des jehowistischen Werkes, mit der er hier offenbar P nicht verbinden konnte.

Für die Analyse von v. 3 ff. ist wichtig, daß oben gezeigt werden konnte, daß in v. 25–30 J und E zu Wort kommen. Dem entspricht, daß in v. 3–11 eine doppelte Exposition gegeben wird. Nach v. 3 liebt Israel Joseph mehr als seine Brüder, weil er für ihn »Sohn des Alters« ist. Diese Liebe findet darin ihren sichtbaren Ausdruck, daß Israel für ihn ein besonderes Gewand anfertigt[62]. Sie ist nach v. 4 der Grund dafür, daß die Brüder Joseph hassen. Dagegen hat sich nach v. 5–11 der Konflikt an den beiden Träumen Josephs entzündet. Durch sie wurden die Brüder auf Joseph eifersüchtig (v. 11)[63]. Das ist eine in sich jeweils schlüssige Motivation für das folgende Geschehen. Die beiden Einleitungen sind zwar jetzt durch v. 5b und 8b miteinander verzahnt. Aber v. 5b, der in LXX fehlt, unterbricht eindeutig den Zusammenhang zwischen v. 5a und 6. Daß auch v. 8b sekundär ist, ergibt sich daraus, daß hier von »seinen Träumen« die Rede ist, obwohl bisher nur von einem Traum erzählt worden war. Außerdem werden hier »seine Worte« er-

---

[62] Gegen M. Noth, Pentateuch, 31.38, und H. Seebaß, Zeit, 76, dürfen deshalb v. 3a und 3b nicht verschiedenen Quellenschriften zugeteilt werden.

[63] Gegen H. Seebaß, Zeit, 76 ff., lassen sich die beiden Träume nicht auf J und E verteilen. Der zweite Traum ist eine Steigerung des ersten, die Doppelung der Träume also ein Stilmittel.

wähnt. Das kann sich nur auf v. 2 beziehen. In v. 8 b ist somit P vorausgesetzt. Die beiden Expositionen stehen also ursprünglich unverbunden nebeneinander. Sie unterscheiden sich auch dadurch, daß für das Verhalten der Brüder in v. 4 *śn'* = »hassen«, in v. 11 jedoch *qn'* = »eifersüchtig sein« gebraucht wird. Da in v. 3 der Vater Israel heißt, gehört v. 3 f. zu J. Dann muß der Grundbestand von v. 5–11 aus E stammen. Zu ihm gehören auch nicht die ersten Worte von v. 10 »da erzählte er (ihn) seinem Vater und seinen Brüdern«, da bereits in v. 9 gesagt wird, daß Joseph seinen Brüdern diesen Traum mitteilte. Ein Späterer stellte die Frage, woher der Vater von dem Traum wußte, und fügte deshalb v. 10 aα¹ ein[64]. Zu E gehören somit v. 5 a. 6–8 a. 9. 10 aα².β.b. 11.

Daß es sich bei den beiden Einleitungen tatsächlich um Dubletten handelt, wird durch 42,7–9 bestätigt. Hier wird zweimal berichtet, daß Joseph seine Brüder bei dem ersten Zusammentreffen in Ägypten erkannt hat. In v. 7 wird diese Feststellung so weitergeführt, daß sich Joseph gegen die Brüder fremd stellt und sie fragt, woher sie gekommen sind. Darauf antworten die Brüder. In v. 8 aber heißt es nochmals: »Da erkannte Joseph seine Brüder«. Darauf folgt: »Sie aber erkannten ihn nicht«. In v. 9 erinnert sich Joseph zunächst an die Träume und sagt dann: »Ihr seid Kundschafter...« Diese Darstellung läßt sich mit v. 7 nicht vereinbaren. Nachdem Joseph das Gespräch mit den Brüdern begonnen hat, kann nicht nochmals berichtet werden, daß er sie erkannte. Auch der Vorschlag, v. 8 als Glosse auszuscheiden[65], führt nicht weiter. Dann würde immer noch v. 9 a das Gespräch unterbrechen. Er müßte nach v. 7 a stehen[66]. Bei v. 7 und v. 8 f. handelt es sich somit eindeutig um Dubletten. Die Fassung, zu der 42,7 gehört, kannte die Träume nicht, während sich für die Version von 42,8 f. diese Träume jetzt erfüllt haben. Damit kann es als gesichert gelten, daß die beiden Expositionen in Gen 37 tatsächlich auf J und E zu verteilen sind.

Die Verse 12–17 gehören wegen Israel in v. 13 a überwiegend zu J und schließen direkt an v. 4 an. Das gilt allerdings nicht für v. 13 b. 14 a. Die Worte Josephs in v. 13 b »Hier bin ich« passen nicht als Antwort auf den Auftrag, den er in v. 13 a erhält, sondern setzen eine Anrede des Vaters voraus, wie bereits J. Wellhausen erkannt hat[67]. Das wird zwar in

---

[64] Daß diese Worte sich mit v. 9 stoßen, hat bereits LXX erkannt und sie deshalb ausgelassen. Da der Vater aber von dem Traum erfahren mußte, hat LXX in v. 9 nach »und er erzählte ihn« »seinem Vater und« eingefügt. Sie setzt somit den MT von v. 10 voraus und glättet ihn.

[65] D. B. Redford, VT. S 20, 31; H.-C. Schmitt, BZAW 154, 41 Anm. 163.

[66] Dieser Einwand gilt auch gegen C. Westermann 112 f., der v. 8–9 a als Parenthese versteht. Offen bleiben kann hier zunächst, ob v. 9 bβ abzutrennen ist (vgl. dazu IIId).

[67] J. Wellhausen, Composition, 53, unter Verweis auf Gen 22, 2. 7. 11; 27, 1; 31, 11. Zusätzlich wären noch 46, 2; Ex 3, 4 und I Sam 3, 4 ff. zu nennen. Auch in Jes 6, 8 steht »Hier

der neueren Forschung nahezu durchgehend bestritten. Bisher wurde aber kein Beleg genannt, daß »Hier bin ich« als Reaktion auf einen Auftrag stehen kann. Da v. 14b[68] nahtlos an v. 13a anschließt, ist deshalb v. 13b.14a E zuzuweisen. Die Gründe, warum der Redaktor hier den J-Faden durch E erweitert hat, dürften darin zu suchen sein, daß er v. 14a als Präzisierung des Auftrags aufnehmen wollte. Er erreicht damit zugleich einen wirkungsvollen Kontrast: Der Sohn, der ausgesandt wird, um sich nach dem šālôm seiner Brüder und des Viehs zu erkundigen, erleidet im Folgenden Unheil.

Auffällig ist, daß bei J Joseph nicht sofort auf die Brüder trifft, sondern in v. 15–17 zunächst einem Mann begegnet, der ihm mitteilt, daß die Brüder nach Dothan weitergezogen sind. Das ist im Ablauf deutlich ein retardierendes Element. Der Leser, der von v. 4 her gespannt ist, was sich bei der Begegnung mit den Brüdern ereignen wird, muß sich einen Augenblick gedulden. Dadurch wird seine Spannung gesteigert[69].

Für die Analyse von v. 18–24 ist zu beachten, daß in v. 21f. eine Dublette vorliegt. Das geht schon daraus hervor, daß v. 22 eine ausführliche neue Einleitung hat. Daß sie in einem Teil der LXX-Überlieferung fehlt, zeigt, daß sie teilweise schon früh als problematisch empfunden wurde. Gerade deswegen darf man sie aber nicht streichen[70]. Zu diesem wichtigen formalen Argument kommen sachliche Gründe hinzu. Der Aufforderung in v. 22: »Vergießt nicht Blut« entspricht sachlich in v. 21b: »Wir wollen ihn nicht ums Leben bringen«. Dadurch ist sie eigentlich überflüssig. Schließlich heißt es in v. 21a: »Da rettete er ihn aus ihrer Hand«, in v. 22b aber: »um ihn aus ihrer Hand zu retten, um ihn zu seinem Vater zurückzubringen«. Damit wird in v. 21a und v. 22b ein verschiedener Akzent gesetzt. Nach v. 21 besteht die Rettung darin, daß Joseph nicht getötet wird, nach v. 22 aber darin, daß er zu seinem Vater zurückgebracht wird. Da v. 29f. v. 22 voraussetzt, gehört dieser Vers zu E. Dann müßte v. 21 aus J stammen[71]. Dazu paßt

---

bin ich« nicht nach einem Auftrag. Voraus geht hier die Frage: »Wen soll ich senden, und wer will für uns gehen?«

[68] Hier ist »aus dem Tal Hebrons« eine Glosse zum Ausgleich mit P, wo sich Jakob nach 35,27 in Hebron aufhält. Eine Textänderung, wie sie H. Seebaß, Zeit, 77f., vorschlägt, ist überflüssig.

[69] Solche retardierenden Elemente sind, wie sich im folgenden zeigen wird, gerade für die jahwistische Darstellung charakteristisch. Das spricht gegen die Zuweisung von v. 15–17 an E durch L. Ruppert, Josephserzählung, 30. Gründe, warum hier E vorliegen sollte, sind m. E. nicht zu erkennen.

[70] Gegen C. Westermann 32, und O. Procksch 385.

[71] H.-C. Schmitt, BZAW 154, 23f. Anm. 76, sieht in v. 21 einen Zusatz, um »Ruben in ein noch besseres Licht zu stellen, indem er ihn die in v. 22b genannte Absicht auch seinen Brüdern gegenüber äußern läßt«. Das steht aber nicht in v. 21.

freilich nicht, daß Ruben der Sprecher ist. Hier muß bei J Juda gestanden haben, das vom Redaktor in Ruben abgeändert wurde. Gegen diese Lösung, die schon J. Wellhausen erwogen hat[72], ist verschiedentlich eingewandt worden, daß sie durch keinen Textzeugen gestützt werde[73]. Damit werden aber die textkritische und die redaktionsgeschichtliche Ebene miteinander verwechselt. Die Lesart »Juda« könnte nur in einem Text bezeugt sein, der J vor seiner Verbindung mit E bietet. Daß ein solcher Text gefunden wird, ist kaum zu erwarten. Tatsächlich konnte der Redaktor in v. 21 f. nicht Juda *und* Ruben auftreten lassen. Mit v. 22 wird jetzt v. 21 präzisiert und weitergeführt. Deshalb mußte in beiden Versen derselbe Bruder sprechen. Wegen v. 29 f. war aber v. 22 nur im Munde Rubens möglich. Aus diesem Grund hat der Redaktor in v. 21 das »Juda« seiner Vorlage in »Ruben« geändert. Dadurch erreichte er in v. 21 f. eine sinnvolle Abfolge der Aussagen. Aus den Spannungen, die aber trotzdem zwischen beiden Versen bestehen, geht jedoch hervor, daß sie erst von dem Redaktor miteinander verbunden wurden.

Die Art, wie er hier J und E miteinander verknüpft hat, bietet auch den Schlüssel für v. 18–20. In v. 18 planen die Brüder, Joseph zu töten. Das wird durch v. 19 f. begründet und weitergeführt. Da in v. 19 f. die Träume und Zisternen erwähnt werden, gehören diese Verse zu E. Nun setzt v. 21 voraus, daß auch bei J die Brüder Joseph töten wollten. Deshalb ist zu fragen, ob nicht die entsprechende Aussage in v. 18 aus J stammt. Tatsächlich ist dieser Vers eigenartig formuliert. In v. 18a heißt es: »da sahen sie ihn von ferne«. Darauf folgt: »und bevor er sich ihnen genaht hatte«. Es ist nicht zu erkennen, welche Funktion diese Worte nach v. 18a haben sollen. Schon aus v. 18a geht hervor, daß Joseph noch nicht bei den Brüdern ist, als diese planen, ihn zu töten. Dagegen würde sich v. 18b gut an v. 17 anschließen, da Joseph in v. 17b und v. 18bα das Subjekt ist. Durch den Anfang von v. 18b »und bevor« wird die Darstellung gegliedert. Auch in v. 23 dient eine zeitliche Bestimmung der Gliederung des Geschehens und beide Angaben sind deutlich aufeinander bezogen. V. 23 a.bα[74] gehört jedoch klar zu J, da hier der Rock Josephs erwähnt wird. Dann stammt auch v. 18b von J und wurde dort durch v. 21.23 a.bα fortgesetzt. Da in v. 24 der Vorschlag ausgeführt wird, den Ruben in v. 22 gemacht hat, ist dieser Vers zu E zu rechnen. Zu J gehören somit v. 18b.21 (mit Juda). 23a.bα, zu E v. 18a. 19f.22.24. Beide Darstellungen bilden jeweils einen in sich geschlossenen Zusammenhang.

Gegen eine solche Aufteilung hat W. Rudolph eingewandt, daß dann bei J »zu dem negativen Vorschlag, Josef nicht zu töten, ein positi-

---

[72] J. Wellhausen, Composition, 54.
[73] D. B. Redford, VT. S 20, 142; H. Donner, Gestalt, 38 Anm. 74.
[74] V. 23 bβ ist eine Glosse, vgl. z. B. C. Westermann 24.

ver Gegenvorschlag, ohne den die Brüder bei ihrem großen Haß niemals bereit gewesen wären, auf die Tötung zu verzichten« fehle[75]. Damit übersieht aber W. Rudolph eine Eigentümlichkeit der jahwistischen Darstellung. Ähnlich wie J mit v. 15–17 durch ein retardierendes Element die Spannung steigert, führt er in v. 18b.21.23 a.bα das Geschehen nur allmählich dem Höhepunkt entgegen, der in dem Verkauf Josephs besteht. Die Brüder planen, Joseph zu töten (v. 18b). Der Grund ist nach v. 4 klar und braucht nicht mehr wiederholt zu werden. Diesen Plan verhindert Juda (v. 21). Wie aber werden die Brüder dann mit Joseph umgehen? Sie ziehen ihm zunächst den Rock aus, der die Liebe des Vaters zu ihm sichtbar macht (v. 23*). Das kann aber nicht alles sein. Doch erst die ismaelitische Karawane läßt Juda jene Lösung finden, die verhindert, daß die Brüder doch noch Joseph töten und die trotzdem das Objekt des Hasses aus ihrer Mitte entfernt (v. 25–27.28 aß). Demgegenüber ist bei E der Ablauf wesentlich einfacher, weil Ruben in v. 22 sofort jenen Vorschlag unterbreitet, dem die Brüder folgen (v. 24). Nur das unerwartete Auftreten der Midianiter verhindert, daß der geheime Plan Rubens gelingt (v. 28 aα.b.29 f.). Dadurch wird zugleich das Bild des Bruders einfacher. Ruben weiß sich für Joseph verantwortlich. Juda hingegen will nur keinen Mord. Er haßt aber, wie an v. 25 ff. deutlich wird, Joseph in gleicher Weise wie die übrigen Brüder.

V. 31–33 gehören wegen der Rolle, die hier der Rock Josephs spielt, überwiegend zu J. Ob daneben noch Bruchstücke aus E enthalten sind[76], mag hier offenbleiben. Dagegen stößt man in v. 34f. wieder auf eine Dublette. Nachdem in v. 34b.35a berichtet wurde, daß der Vater lange um Joseph trauerte und sich nicht trösten ließ, kommt v. 35b »da beweinte ihn sein Vater« eindeutig zu spät. V. 35b als abschließende Zusammenfassung zu verstehen[77], ist eine Notlösung, die das Problem verdeckt. Außerdem spricht der Vater in v. 35a davon, daß er in die שׁאל hinabsteigen wird. Daß er in die שׁאל hinabsteigt oder hinabgebracht wird, wird in der Josephsgeschichte noch in 42,38; 44,29.31 erwähnt. Wie noch zu zeigen sein wird, gehören diese Stellen alle zu J. Nun muß v. 34a aus E stammen, da hier der Vater Jakob heißt. Daran schließt sich v. 35b nahtlos an. Dann sind v. 34b.35a zu J zu rechnen. Der Redaktor hat v. 34a aus E aufgenommen, weil hier die Trauerriten geschildert werden, die der Vater vollzog, während J nur davon spricht, daß der Vater trauerte. Wieder präzisiert also der Redaktor die jahwistische Darstellung aus E. V. 35b aber wurde von ihm aufgenommen, weil darauf schon bei E v. 36 folgte[78], und durch v. 35b.36 ein wirkungsvoller Abschluß von Kap. 37 erreicht wird.

---

[75] W. Rudolph, BZAW 63, 153.   [76] So z. B. H. Gunkel 403.
[77] So z. B. W. Rudolph, BZAW 63, 155; C. Westermann 37.   [78] Vgl. IIIa.

In 37,3–35 sind also J und E vertreten. Zu J gehören: V.3.4.12. 13a.14b*.15–17.18b.21 (mit Juda) .23a.bα.25–27.28aβ.31–33*.34b. 35a, zu E: V.5a.6–8a.9.10*.11...13b.14a...18a.19f.22.24.28aα.b.29f. ..34a.35b.

Diese Aufteilung ist bereits von H. Gunkel vorgeschlagen worden[79]. Die Untersuchung hat gezeigt, daß seine Argumente nach wie vor stichhaltig sind. Die Eckpfeiler einer Analyse müssen v.3–11 und 25–30 sein, da sich hier eindeutige Dubletten finden. Auch aus der Tatsache, daß die Träume erst nachträglich durch v.8b und noch später durch v.5b mit v.3f. verknüpft wurden, geht hervor, daß sie nicht organisch mit v.3f. verbunden sind. Das haben Spätere empfunden. Von da aus lassen sich dann auch die sonstigen Spannungen in v.3–35 lösen. Soweit die Einwände gegen die Analyse von H. Gunkel auf der Struktur der Erzählung beruhen, hat sich gezeigt, daß diese Struktur erst von dem Redaktor geschaffen wurde. Nur so läßt sich verstehen, daß Spannungen bleiben. Auch stilistisch besteht zwischen J und E ein Unterschied. Bei J enthält die Darstellung retardierende Elemente, sie fehlen bei E. Dagegen hat E mit den beiden Träumen eine Doppelung, zu der es bei J keine Analogie gibt. Der Redaktor hat sich bemüht, die jahwistische und die elohistische Fassung möglichst weitgehend in sein Werk aufzunehmen. Nur so läßt es sich erklären, daß er v.18a an passender Stelle in den J-Faden von v.15–17.18b einfügte. Gelegentlich konnte er aber anscheinend J und E nicht miteinander verknüpfen, sondern mußte sich für eine Version entscheiden. In der Darstellung, wie der Vater von dem Verlust Josephs erfuhr (v.31–33), ist E höchstens mit Fragmenten vertreten. Auch in der Schilderung, wie der Vater Joseph zu den Brüdern sandte, ist E mit v.13b.14a nur lückenhaft erhalten. Aufs Ganze gesehen hat der Redaktor in v.3–35 J zugrundegelegt und Stücke aus E jeweils als Weiterführungen eingefügt. Dadurch ist J im Unterschied zu E vollständig erhalten.

Allerdings legen es zwei Einzelheiten in der jahwistischen Darstellung nahe, daß sie nicht von J geschaffen wurde. Nach v.3 ist Joseph für Israel »Sohn des Alters«. Das läßt sich mit der Darstellung der Geburt der Söhne Jakobs in Gen 29,31–30,24 nicht vereinbaren. Außerdem versuchen in v.35a »alle seine Söhne und alle seine Töchter«, den Vater zu trösten. Nach der sonstigen Überlieferung hat aber Jakob nur die Tochter Dina[80]. Das sind deutliche Hinweise, daß J mit seiner Josephsgeschichte eine ursprünglich selbständige Novelle in sein Werk aufgenommen hat. Tatsächlich läßt sich v.3 als der Anfang einer solchen Novelle vorstellen. Hier erhält der Leser die wesentlichen Infor-

---

[79] H. Gunkel 401–404.
[80] Auf beide Punkte hat W. Rudolph, BZAW 63, 181f., mit Recht hingewiesen.

mationen. Daß er weiß, wer Israel, Joseph und die Brüder sind, kann der Verfasser wohl voraussetzen. C. Westermann ist allerdings der Auffassung, daß v. 3 keine hinreichende Exposition sei, weil der Vers sofort mit einer Handlung einsetze[81]. Aber damit ist die Inversion nicht beachtet. Sie zeigt an, daß mit v. 3 etwas Neues beginnt. Daß die jahwistische Josephsgeschichte tatsächlich ursprünglich selbständig war, wird sich durch Beobachtungen an anderen Stellen bestätigen.

Aus den literarkritischen Ergebnissen zu 37,3–35 folgt, daß die Thematik der Josephsgeschichte bei J und E trotz aller Verwandtschaft verschieden ist. Bei J wird der Ablauf der Ereignisse ausschließlich von der menschlichen Ebene her entwickelt. Die Liebe des Vaters zu Joseph weckt den Haß der Brüder. Damit ist die besondere Beziehung zwischen dem Vater und Joseph der Ausgangspunkt des Geschehens. Der Vater, der von diesem Haß nichts weiß, schickt Joseph zu den Brüdern, und ahnungslos folgt Joseph seinem Befehl. Dadurch können die Brüder jetzt ihrem Haß freien Lauf lassen, auch wenn Juda die Tötung Josephs verhindert. Sie verkaufen Joseph an Ismaeliter, die nach Ägypten ziehen, ohne zu ahnen, daß sie ihm dort wieder begegnen werden. Beim Vater aber erwecken sie den Eindruck, daß Joseph von einem wilden Tier zerrissen wurde. So muß Israel um Joseph trauern. In seiner Trauer aber wird nochmals die Liebe sichtbar, die er zu diesem Sohn empfand. Auch nach langer Zeit gelingt es den Söhnen und Töchtern nicht, ihn aus seiner Trauer herauszureißen. Er wird als Trauernder in die š'l hinabsteigen. Damit ist hier das Verhältnis des Vaters zu Joseph der Leitfaden der Darstellung. Der Konflikt ist ausschließlich von menschlichen Gefühlen bestimmt, vom Vater ohne Absicht ausgelöst und auf die Spitze getrieben. Das Handeln der Brüder führt zunächst dazu, daß der Vater in tiefer Trauer zurückbleibt.

Bei E hingegen entsteht der Konflikt an den beiden Träumen, in denen Joseph angekündigt wird, daß er mächtiger werden soll als die Brüder. Die Brüder wollen verhindern, daß diese Träume in Erfüllung gehen. Damit lautet das Thema hier: Joseph und die Brüder. Der Vater ist zu einer Nebenfigur geworden. Daß er Joseph wegen seines zweiten Traums schilt, unterstreicht nur, wie unwahrscheinlich es ihm erscheint, daß sich diese Träume erfüllen (v. 10*). Er führt mit seinen Worten den Einwand weiter, den die Brüder gegen den ersten Traum erhoben haben (v. 8a): Sollte ausgerechnet Joseph zu einer Herrschaftsstellung über sie aufsteigen? Trotzdem bewahrt der Vater das Wort (v. 11). Er weiß, daß ein solcher Traum nicht ohne Bedeutung ist. Die Gestalt des Vaters dient also nur dazu, die Besonderheit der Träume Josephs zu unterstreichen. Diese Beobachtungen werden dadurch bestätigt, daß E nur an einer Stelle ausdrücklich auf diese Träume zurückkommt. In

---

[81] C. Westermann 9f.

42,9 erinnert sich Joseph an seine Träume. Obwohl ihm in dem zweiten Traum eine Vorrangstellung auch gegenüber dem Vater angekündigt wird, vermeidet es E, im Blick auf den Vater davon zu sprechen, daß sich die Träume realisiert haben. Daran wird nochmals deutlich, daß es E eben um Joseph und die Brüder geht. Tatsächlich bleibt der Vater im weiteren Verlauf von Gen 37 eine – notwendige – Nebenfigur, wie aus v. 34 a. 35 b hervorgeht. Hier vollzieht Jakob für Joseph die Trauerriten. Durch nichts wird aber angedeutet, daß Joseph für ihn ein besonderer Sohn war. Er trauert um ihn so, wie ein Vater eben um einen verstorbenen Sohn trauert.

Nun steht für E hinter den Träumen Gott. Mit ihnen kündigt also Gott Joseph eine Vorrangstellung gegenüber den Brüdern an. Dadurch nimmt hier das Geschehen nicht vom Vater sondern von Gott seinen Ausgang. Diese Träume lösen bei den Brüdern jene Eifersucht aus, die den Fortgang der Handlung bestimmt. Die Brüder wollen verhindern, daß die Träume in Erfüllung gehen und fördern damit – wie der weitere Verlauf zeigt – gerade ihre Realisierung. Wenn der edle Ruben mit seinem Bemühen scheitert, Joseph zum Vater zurückzubringen, so stellt sich von den Träumen her für den Leser die Frage: Was hat Gott damit vor? Im Unterschied zu J steht bei E Gott am Anfang, und der Leser erwartet von vornherein eine Antwort auf die Frage, was Gott mit diesen Ereignissen erreichen will. Beide Fassungen stimmen zwar darin überein, daß sich das Geschehen anders entwickelt, als es die beteiligten Menschen planen, aber E setzt mit den Träumen von vornherein einen markanten theologischen Akzent. Außerdem macht er deutlich, daß sein Thema lautet: Joseph und die Brüder. Auch diese inhaltlichen Beobachtungen zu 37,3–35 werden sich durch die Untersuchung weiterer Stücke bestätigen.

b) Gen 42,14–38

Der Anfang des Berichts von der ersten Reise der Brüder nach Ägypten in 42,1–13 bereitet literarkritisch erhebliche Schwierigkeiten. Deshalb soll er erst später untersucht werden[82]. Dagegen bilden 42,14–26 weitgehend einen geschlossenen Zusammenhang. Da hier Ruben der Sprecher der Brüder ist, und Simeon von Joseph als Geisel genommen wird, stammt dieser Abschnitt aus E. Das gilt allerdings nicht für v. 20b »da taten sie so«. Diese Bemerkung unterbricht die Abfolge zwischen v. 20 a und 21 und ist deshalb ein Zusatz. Ein Späterer vermißte, daß die Brüder den Aufforderungen Josephs von v. 18–20 a nachgekommen waren, die in v. 18 mit »das tut« eingeleitet werden, und

---

[82] Vgl. IIId.

fügte deshalb v. 20 b ein. Für den Elohisten war selbstverständlich, daß die Brüder so handelten, wie es Joseph geboten hatte, da es für sie keine Alternative gab. Eine nachträgliche Ergänzung ist auch in v. 25 a vorgenommen worden. Hier ist die Konstruktion schwierig, weil einem finiten Verb ein Infinitiv nebengeordnet ist. Sie ist, wie H. Gunkel erkannt hat[83], dadurch entstanden, daß ein Späterer den Satz »daß man ihre Säcke (Gefäße) mit Getreide fülle und« eingefügt hat. Er vermißte den Hinweis, daß die Brüder das Getreide erhalten haben und schob deshalb diese Bemerkung ein. Für E verstand sich auch das von selbst. Deshalb schilderte der Elohist in v. 25 nur, welche weiteren Gaben Joseph den Brüdern zukommen ließ.

Die elohistische Darstellung ist in v. 14–26 wieder von dem Thema Joseph und die Brüder bestimmt. Dabei verwendet E in v. 14–20 a das Mittel der Doppelung, um das Gewicht der Szene zu unterstreichen. Das Verhalten Josephs in v. 18–20 ist eine Steigerung zu v. 14–17. Zwar klingt sein Befehl in v. 18–20 a zunächst wie eine Abmilderung von v. 14–17, da jetzt nur ein Bruder in Ägypten bleiben muß. Tatsächlich werden aber erst durch ihn die Brüder vor ihre eigentliche Bewährungsprobe gestellt. Sie müssen einen Bruder in Ägypten zurücklassen, der nur freikommen wird, wenn sie mit Benjamin zurückkehren. Einst haben sie Joseph verlassen, werden sie nun auch Simeon im Stich lassen? Gerade weil ihnen Joseph das Getreide mitgibt, das sie zum Überleben benötigen, ist die Frage gestellt, wie sie sich diesem Bruder gegenüber verhalten. Nicht der Hunger soll sie zu einer zweiten Reise nach Ägypten zwingen. Wenn sie mit Benjamin zurückkehren, dann geschieht das ausschließlich um des gefangenen Bruders willen. Die Reaktion der Brüder in v. 21 f. bezieht sich auf die beiden Szenen in v. 14–20. In v. 21 gestehen sie zunächst die Schuld ein, die sie einst gegenüber Joseph auf sich geladen haben. Dabei sehen sie eine Entsprechung. Weil sie damals das Flehen Josephs nicht erhört haben, ist diese Not über sie gekommen. Damals haben sie Joseph nicht gehört, jetzt wurde ihre Beteuerung nicht gehört, daß sie redlich sind, sondern sie wurden in den Gewahrsam gelegt. Darauf erinnert Ruben in v. 22 die Brüder daran, daß er sie vergeblich davor gewarnt hatte, sich an Joseph zu verfehlen. Jetzt wird sein Blut gefordert. Das bezieht sich darauf, daß ein Bruder in Ägypten zurückbleiben muß. Ihm droht das Geschick, das nach der Meinung Rubens einst Joseph erlitten hat. Für Ruben ist Joseph tot. Dieses Geständnis der Schuld bringt Joseph zum Weinen. Trotzdem hält er aber an seinem Plan fest. Er muß ihn weiterverfolgen, weil die Brüder nur durch die Tat beweisen können, daß sie inzwischen zu anderen Menschen geworden sind und einen Bruder nicht im Stich lassen (v. 23 f.).

---

[83] H. Gunkel 445.

Und doch hat ihr Geständnis positive Folgen. Joseph läßt ihnen ihr Geld in ihre Säcke legen und Reiseproviant für den Weg geben (v. 25*). Dadurch wird den Brüdern seine Fürsorge zuteil. Diese Deutung von v. 25, die u. a. G. v. Rad vertreten hat [84], ist freilich umstritten. Nach H. Gunkel schafft sich Joseph damit die Möglichkeit, die Brüder später des Gelddiebstahls zu beschuldigen [85], während nach C. Westermann der Erzähler hier »das gleiche unlösliche Ineinander von Härte und dem Willen zur Versöhnung« darstellt, das Josephs Verhalten gegenüber den Brüdern bei der ersten Reise bestimme [86]. Nun ist aber zu beachten, daß die Frage des Geldes bei E von Joseph anscheinend nicht mehr aufgegriffen wird. Da Geld und Reiseproviant in v. 25 nebeneinanderstehen, dürften beide Gaben auch den gleichen Sinn haben. Daß den Brüdern die Wegzehrung offen übergeben, das Geld aber heimlich in ihre Säcke getan wird, ergibt sich aus der Situation. Das Geld kann den Brüdern nicht offen zurückgegeben werden, weil sie sonst nach dem Grund dieser Bevorzugung fragen müßten. Da sich Joseph den Brüdern jedoch nicht zu erkennen geben will, weil sonst sein Plan verhindert würde, kann er ihnen in diesem Punkt seine Fürsorge nur heimlich zuteil werden lassen.

Die elohistische Darstellung in v. 14-26 erweist sich damit als eine durchdachte Komposition, die ganz an dem Thema Joseph und seine Brüder orientiert ist. Die Forderung Josephs, Benjamin nach Ägypten zu bringen, dient hier nur dem Ziel, festzustellen, ob die Brüder Simeon im Stich lassen oder nicht. Sie beruht aber – und das ist, wie sich im folgenden zeigen wird, ein markanter Unterschied zu J – nicht darauf, daß zwischen Joseph und Benjamin eine besonders enge Beziehung besteht. Daran wird die Ausrichtung bei E auf alle Brüder nochmals besonders deutlich.

Durch die klare Gedankenfolge in v. 14-26 wird es außerdem unmöglich, aus diesem Abschnitt ein älteres überlieferungsgeschichtliches Stadium der Josephsgeschichte zu erschließen, in dem die zweite Reise mit Benjamin fehlte. Nach H. Schulte kannte noch der Elohist eine Fassung, in der sich Joseph den Brüdern nach ihrem Aufenthalt im Gefängnis zu erkennen gab [87]. Aber wie oben gezeigt wurde, ist gegen H. Schulte der Gefängnisaufenthalt der Brüder durch die Forderung, Benjamin zu holen, nicht sinnlos geworden, sondern hat in der elohistischen Darstellung eine wichtige Funktion. Auch das Weinen Josephs weist nicht darauf hin, daß sich Joseph danach einmal den Brüdern zu erkennen gegeben hätte. Es ist lediglich Reaktion auf das Geständnis

---

[84] G. v. Rad 314.
[85] H. Gunkel 445.
[86] C. Westermann 118.
[87] H. Schulte, BZAW 128, 14f.; vgl. schon H. Gunkel 441.

der Brüder. Hier ist kein Stoff nachträglich zerdehnt worden[88], sondern es handelt sich um eine bewußte literarische Gestaltung.

Sie wird durch v. 29–37 fortgesetzt, wie schon Jakob, Ruben und die Bezugnahme auf v. 14–26 zeigen. Die Brüder berichten nach der Heimkehr dem Vater, was ihnen widerfahren ist (v. 29–34). Daß sie ihren Aufenthalt im Gefängnis nicht erwähnen, beruht darauf, daß sie den entscheidenden Punkt unterstreichen wollen: Benjamin muß mit nach Ägypten. Darauf leeren sie ihre Säcke aus, und dabei kommt das Geld zum Vorschein. Das versetzt sie und ihren Vater in Furcht (v. 35). Was von Joseph ein Akt der Fürsorge war, wird für die Brüder und den Vater ein Anlaß zur Furcht, weil sie die Zusammenhänge nicht durchschauen. Wie unter I dargestellt wurde, stammt dieses Motiv aus J und ist hier bei E zu einem Nebenmotiv geworden. Es hat bei E die Funktion, zu unterstreichen, wie rätselhaft für die Brüder die Ereignisse sein mußten. Sie haben einen Bruder verloren und ihr Geld gewonnen. Durch v. 35 wird zugleich der Vater in dieses Rätsel einbezogen. Auch ihn versetzt der Fund des Geldes in Furcht, weil er ihn nicht zu deuten vermag und so mit einer unerklärlichen Begebenheit konfrontiert ist.

Auf den Bericht der Brüder reagiert Jakob in v. 36 zunächst mit der Feststellung: »Mich macht ihr kinderlos«. In der Folge fällt auf, daß für ihn Joseph und Simeon offenbar auf einer Ebene stehen. Durch nichts wird angedeutet, daß er Joseph besonders geliebt hat. Hier wird der Unterschied zwischen J und E wieder deutlich greifbar. In v. 36 fürchtet der Vater, Benjamin ebenso zu verlieren wie Joseph und Simeon. Er hat also Simeon bereits aufgegeben. Nicht so Ruben. Er will in v. 37 durch seine Bürgschaft Jakob dazu bewegen, Benjamin nach Ägypten mitziehen zu lassen. Diese Bürgschaft ist in Entsprechung zu v. 36 gestaltet. Hatte Jakob dort geklagt: »Mich macht ihr kinderlos«, so will in v. 37 Ruben ohne Söhne sein, wenn er Benjamin nicht wieder zurückbringt. In dieser Bürgschaft Rubens findet die Wandlung der Brüder ihren markanten Ausdruck. Sie zeigt nicht, daß sich ihre Einstellung zum Vater geändert hat[89], sondern sie ist von der Notlage Simeons bestimmt. Weil die Brüder im Unterschied zum Vater Simeon nicht aufgeben wollen, tut Ruben alles, damit der Vater Benjamin doch noch mitziehen läßt.

Um so mehr muß es überraschen, daß der Vater in v. 38 diese Bürgschaft ablehnt. Damit nimmt er den Brüdern die Chance, den Wandel ihrer Gesinnung vor Joseph unter Beweis zu stellen. Bereits das zeigt, daß v. 38 nicht zu E gehört. Der Elohist kann seine Darstellung nicht auf die Frage zuspitzen, ob die Brüder Simeon im Stich lassen, und ihnen dann durch den Vater die Möglichkeit nehmen, ihren Bruder

---

[88] So H. Gunkel 441.
[89] So C. Westermann 121.

aus Ägypten zu befreien. Dieser Widerspruch ist wieder ein klarer Beweis dafür, daß die Josephsgeschichte nicht literarisch einheitlich ist. Wenn H. Donner die Bürgschaft Rubens als »etwas rasch und voreilig« beurteilt[90], so ist damit die Linienführung in 42,14 ff. verkannt. Außerdem weicht v. 38 in einem Punkt von v. 36 ab. In v. 36 stehen für den Vater Joseph, Simeon und Benjamin auf einer Ebene. In v. 38 hat er dagegen zu Joseph und Benjamin ein besonderes Verhältnis: Der Bruder Benjamins ist tot, und dieser ist allein übriggeblieben. Deshalb wäre sein Tod besonders schmerzlich[91]. Das entspricht der Rede Judas in 44,18 ff. Auch in der Formulierung stimmt v. 38 mit 44,29 weitgehend überein. V. 38 stammt somit aus J. Bei E kann die Bürgschaft Rubens nur die Folge gehabt haben, daß Jakob zustimmte, daß Benjamin mitzog. Darauf machten sich hier die Brüder sofort auf den Weg nach Ägypten.

Damit ist bei E 42,14 ff. das Gegenbild zu der elohistischen Darstellung in Kap. 37. Die Brüder werden von Joseph auf die Probe gestellt, ob sie nochmals einen Bruder preisgeben. Sie gestehen nicht nur ihre Schuld an Joseph ein, sondern sie bestehen auch die Probe. Ihre Gesinnung hat sich grundlegend gewandelt.

Wie schon in I dargestellt wurde, stammen v. 27 f. aus J. Freilich geben diese beiden Verse einige Probleme auf. In v. 28 b rufen die Brüder aus: »Was hat uns Elohim da getan!« Hier fällt die Gottesbezeichnung Elohim auf. Da die Brüder unter sich sind, läßt sie sich nicht damit erklären, daß ein Nichtisraelit von Gott redet oder Gesprächspartner ist, wie man es für Elohim in 43,23 und 44,16 erwägen könnte. Deshalb wird dieser Ausruf häufig zu E gerechnet. So stellt etwa M. Noth fest: »Der Redaktor hat in v. 28 b ein Element der E-Erzählung etwas willkürlich vorweggenommen, weil er es im Anschluß an den J-Passus v. 27.28 a gut brauchen konnte.«[92] Wie aus Kap. 43 f. hervorgeht, wird damit jedoch ein wichtiges Strukturelement der jahwistischen Darstellung übersehen. In ihr ist der Becher, der in dem Sack Benjamins gefunden wird, eine Steigerung zu dem Geld, das die Brüder in ihren Säcken entdeckt haben. In 44,16 sagt aber Juda zu Joseph: »Gott hat den Frevel deiner Knechte gefunden«. Wie Geld und Becher einander entsprechen, so korrespondieren auch die beiden Aussagen über Gott in 42,28 und 44,16. Diese Beziehung wird nicht nur über die Brüder hergestellt. In 43,23 erhalten sie von dem Hausverwalter Josephs eine Deutung für das gefundene Geld. Es ist ein Schatz, den ihnen ihr Gott und der Gott ihres Vaters zukommen ließ. Auch hier steht Elohim. In Gen 45 wird

---

[90] H. Donner, Gestalt, 38.
[91] Diesen Unterschied hat C. Westermann 121, erkannt, ohne freilich daraus die literarischen Konsequenzen zu ziehen.
[92] M. Noth, Pentateuch, 38 Anm. 135; vgl. u. a. auch H. Gunkel 442; O. Procksch 408.

den Brüdern dann von Joseph das Geschehen mit dem Becher interpretiert. Damit stößt man auf eine sorgfältig durchdachte Struktur: Den Fund des Geldes führen die Brüder auf Elohim zurück, er wird ihnen durch den Hausverwalter als Gabe Elohims gedeutet. Bei dem Becher war für die Brüder ebenfalls Elohim wirksam, die Interpretation erfolgt hier – das ist eine beabsichtigte Steigerung – durch Joseph selbst. Auf die literarkritischen Konsequenzen, die sich aus dieser Beobachtung für Gen 45 ergeben, wird noch einzugehen sein.

Vorläufig bleibt festzuhalten, daß v. 28b zu J gehört. C. Westermann meint zwar, daß dieser Ausruf der Brüder nur nach ihrem Eingeständnis der Schuld in v. 21 verständlich sei: »Es ist Gott, der in dem Zusammenhang von Schuld und Strafe am Werk ist.«[93] Aber damit wird v. 28b überinterpretiert, die Aussage ist einfacher. Der Fund des Geldes ist für die Brüder unerklärlich und ruft bei ihnen deshalb Entsetzen hervor. Aus diesem Grund führen sie ihn auf Gott zurück. Gott muß hier am Werk gewesen sein, ohne daß die Brüder seine Absicht erkennen können. Mehr besagt v. 28b nicht.

Damit ist die Gottesbezeichnung Elohim in der Josephsgeschichte allein kein Kriterium für die Zuweisung an J oder E. Daß in ihr auch von J Elohim gebraucht wird, läßt sich freilich nur so erklären, daß sie J bereits vorlag. Was schon die jahwistische Darstellung in Gen 37 nahelegte, wird durch die Verwendung von Elohim zu einer gesicherten These. Mit seiner Josephsgeschichte hat der Jahwist eine Vorlage übernommen und sie in der Gottesbezeichnung nicht an seinen Sprachgebrauch angeglichen. Dafür gibt es eine Parallele. Zu J gehört auch die Erzählung von dem Kampf Jakobs am Jabbok in Gen 32,23 ff., in der in v. 31 Elohim steht. Hier hat J eine ihm tradierte Einzelerzählung mit Elohim in sein Werk integriert, obwohl er selbst Jahwe gebraucht. J konnte also Elohim beibehalten, wenn diese Gottesbezeichnung in seiner Vorlage stand.

Schwierigkeiten bereitet in 42,28 auch, daß nach diesem Vers nur ein Bruder sein Geld gefunden hat. In 43,12.18 ff. und 44,8 haben dagegen alle Brüder ihr Geld wiederbekommen. C. Westermann sieht darin allerdings keinen Widerspruch: »Für den Erzähler und für seine Hörer aber ist klar, daß damit die Entdeckung des Geldes durch alle Brüder erzählerisch dargestellt ist ... Bei der hohen Kunst des Erzählens, die die Josephgeschichte bestimmt, konnte der Erzähler von seinen Hörern auch ein hohes Maß an Mitdenken erwarten.«[94] Aber v. 28 besagt für sich genommen eindeutig, daß nur ein Bruder sein Geld gefunden hat. Wer die späteren Stellen nicht kennt, kann nicht auf den Gedanken kommen, daß alle ihr Geld entdeckt haben sollen. Zu beachten

---

[93] C. Westermann 119.
[94] C. Westermann 119.

ist außerdem, daß v. 27.28 a in 44,11 f. eine Entsprechung hat. Dort öffnen alle Brüder ihre Säcke, und der Becher wird schließlich bei Benjamin gefunden. Nach v. 27 öffnet zunächst ein Bruder seinen Sack und findet das Geld. Hier muß ursprünglich folgen, daß es danach alle entdeckt haben. Die Kunst des Erzählers besteht darin, daß er die Reihenfolge bei dem Becher umkehrt.

Dann hat der Redaktor in 42,28 ausgelassen, wie alle Brüder das Geld entdecken, weil er aus E v. 35 aufnehmen wollte. Er konnte aber nicht zweimal berichten, daß alle Brüder das Geld finden. Für ihn entsteht durch v. 35 eine Steigerung zu v. 28. Zunächst fand ein Bruder das Geld, und das versetzte die Brüder in Furcht. In v. 35 aber entdeckten alle bei dem Vater das Geld, und sie und ihr Vater fürchteten sich. Eben die Einbeziehung des Vaters ist die von dem Redaktor beabsichtigte Steigerung, um derentwillen er v. 35 aus E aufnahm. Auch bei diesem Motiv hat der Redaktor eine bewußte Komposition hergestellt. Die Spannungen zeigen aber, daß sie erst von dem Redaktor stammt. Hieß es freilich in v. 28 ursprünglich, daß alle Brüder ihr Geld gefunden haben, so ist das im Blick auf 42,35 wieder ein eindeutiges Kennzeichen, daß die Josephsgeschichte aus zwei literarischen Fassungen besteht.

Eigenartig ist allerdings, daß in v. 27 für Sack sowohl $śq$ als auch $'mtḥt$ gebraucht werden. Die jahwistische Darstellung hat sonst immer den Begriff $'mtḥt$, der im Alten Testament nur in der Josephsgeschichte vorkommt[95]. Das legt es nahe, daß $'t\ śqw$ von dem Redaktor in v. 27 eingefügt wurde, der damit jenes Wort aufnahm, das in v. 25 von E für Sack gebraucht wurde. Der Einwand von H.-C. Schmitt, daß das Objekt bei »öffnen« notwendig genannt werden müßte[96], gilt nur für den jetzigen Zusammenhang, der jedoch redaktionell ist. Wie Ex 2,6 zeigt, muß das Objekt nicht stehen, wenn es sich eindeutig aus dem Vorhergehenden ergibt. Was bei J unmittelbar vor v. 27 stand, wissen wir nicht. Aus der Bezeichnung »der eine« in v. 27 geht aber hervor, daß unmittelbar zuvor von den Brüdern die Rede war. Es ist gut möglich, daß dabei auch ihre Säcke erwähnt wurden.

Von den verschiedenen sprachlichen Differenzen, die von Vertretern einer Quellenscheidung außer dem Namen des Vaters für J und E angenommen wurden, hat sich damit eine bestätigt. E gebraucht das im Alten Testament häufige $śq$, J das sonst nicht belegte $'mtḥt$. Das ist wie-

---

[95] Nach I. Willi-Plein, Aspekte, 311 Anm. 17, läßt sich die Differenz zwischen den beiden Begriffen keinesfalls literarkritisch auswerten, da mit $śq$ grundsätzlich der Sackstoff bezeichnet werde. Daß aber ein Erzähler, der – wie I. Willi-Plein annimmt – 42,35 als bewußte Doppelung zu 42,27 f. geschaffen hat, hier ein anderes Wort verwendet, ist damit nicht erklärt. Daß beide Begriffe nicht von demselben Verfasser gebraucht wurden, ergibt sich im übrigen aus den weiteren Beobachtungen (vgl. I), die zeigen, daß 42,35 von einem anderen Autor stammt als 42,27 f.
[96] H.-C. Schmitt, BZAW 154, 40.

der ein Anzeichen dafür, daß E von J abhängig ist. Das seltene Wort wurde von E durch das übliche ersetzt.

Mit v. 27 f. hat der Redaktor die elohistische Darstellung aus J ergänzt, weil nach 43,21 und 44,8 die Brüder ihr Geld in der Herberge gefunden haben. Deshalb sollte auch bei ihm wenigstens ein Bruder dort sein Geld entdeckt haben. Vor allem dürfte aber der Redaktor v. 27 f. aufgenommen haben, weil die Brüder hier das Geschehen auf Gott zurückführen. Dieser Hinweis war ihm wichtig. Außerdem wollte er, wie erwähnt, 42,35 aus E als Steigerung von v. 27 f. verstanden wissen. Es ist allerdings kaum zufällig, daß E in 42,35 Gott nicht erwähnt. Der Elohist hatte anscheinend Bedenken, den Vater und die Brüder das gefundene Geld mit Gott in Beziehung setzen zu lassen, weil es den Brüdern von Joseph geschenkt worden war. So unterstreicht er zwar durch 42,35 das Rätsel des Geschehens, vermeidet es aber, daß es die Brüder und der Vater mit Gott in Verbindung bringen. Es wird sich auch noch an anderen Stellen zeigen, daß der Elohist die unmittelbare Identifikation einer menschlichen Handlung mit dem Tun Gottes vermieden hat. Aus der Analyse geht hervor, daß der Abschnitt 42,14–38 überwiegend aus E stammt. J ist hier nur mit v. 27 f. und 38 vertreten. Wie bei J die Begegnung zwischen Joseph und den Brüdern auf der ersten Reise verlief, läßt sich aus diesen Fragmenten nicht entnehmen. Anhaltspunkte bieten aber Kap. 43; 44 und 42,1–13. Darauf wird bei der Analyse dieser Stücke zurückzukommen sein.

c) Gen 43, 1–34

Wie bereits unter I dargestellt wurde, geht daraus, daß der Vater Israel heißt, Juda der Sprecher der Brüder ist und Simeon, der in Ägypten gefangen ist, keine Rolle spielt, eindeutig hervor, daß der Abschnitt 43,1–13 zu J gehört. Tatsächlich läßt sich aus 43,7 entnehmen, daß hier das Gespräch zwischen Joseph und den Brüdern bei der ersten Reise schon am Anfang anders abgelaufen sein muß als bei E. Dort haben nach 42,32 (vgl. auch 42,13) die Brüder von sich aus die Familienverhältnisse offen gelegt, um den Vorwurf zu entkräften, sie seien Kundschafter. Nach 43,7 hat sie hingegen Joseph gefragt, ob ihr Vater noch lebt und ob sie noch einen Bruder haben. So wird der Vorgang auch in 44,19 dargestellt. C. Westermann sieht freilich darin keinen Widerspruch: »Der Erzähler hat hier durchaus mit Absicht und mit tiefer Einsicht in die Vorgänge variiert.«[97] Diese psychologische Erklärung ist aber durch den Wortlaut von 43,7 nicht gedeckt, und sie wird durch

---

[97] C. Westermann 130; vgl. auch W. Rudolph, BZAW 63, 162.

44,19 widerlegt, wo Juda den Vorgang gegenüber Joseph genauso schildert, wie er ihn in 43,7 dem Vater berichtet. 43,1 ff. weicht, wie schon in I erwähnt, auch darin von 42,29 ff. ab, daß Joseph »der Mann« und nicht »der Mann, der Herr des Landes« genannt wird. In der Bezeichnung »der Mann« stimmen also J und E überein, sie wird aber bei E durch »der Herr des Landes« präzisiert. Das legt es wiederum nahe, daß der Elohist J gekannt hat[98]. Er will mit seiner Erweiterung hervorheben, daß die hohe Stellung Josephs den Brüdern schon bei ihrer ersten Reise bekannt wurde.

Da für 42,38 bei J der Anschluß nach vorn fehlt, hat man verschiedentlich vermutet, daß der Redaktor in 43,1 ff. die ursprüngliche Abfolge leicht verändert hat. In Aufnahme einer Überlegung von J.Wellhausen, der sich auf 44,26 berief[99], nahm H.Gunkel an, daß die Brüder den Auftrag des Vaters, wieder nach Ägypten zu ziehen (v.2), mit der Forderung beantworteten, daß Benjamin mit muß. Sie hätte der Vater durch 42,38 zunächst abgelehnt und darauf sei sie von Juda mit 43,3 ff. begründet worden. »Diese Worte Judas setzen voraus, daß Israel von solcher Forderung des Joseph bisher noch nichts gehört hat.«[100]

Gegen diesen Vorschlag spricht schon, daß in v.2 ff. kein Bruch zu erkennen ist. Vor allem läßt sich die Rekonstruktion nicht mit 44,24 ff. vereinbaren. In 44,23 erinnert Juda Joseph daran, daß dieser bei der ersten Reise gesagt habe, die Brüder dürften ihn ohne Benjamin nicht wiedersehen. Darauf heißt es in 44,24: »Und es geschah, als wir zu deinem Knecht, meinem Vater, hinaufkamen, da taten wir ihm kund die Worte meines Herrn«. Danach haben die Brüder sofort nach ihrer Rückkehr dem Vater die Forderung Josephs mitgeteilt. Wie der Vater auf sie reagiert hat, bleibt in 44,24 offen. 44,26 setzt aber voraus, daß er sie ablehnte. Nur so läßt sich verstehen, daß nach 44,24 die Brüder ausdrücklich darauf hinweisen, daß sie ohne Benjamin nicht nach Ägypten können. In der Sache entsprechen ihre Worte den Ausführungen Judas in 43,3–5. Die Rede des Vaters stimmt in 44,24 und 43,2 wörtlich überein. Daß die Ablehnung des Vaters in 44,24 übergangen wird, ist dadurch bedingt, daß sie in der Rede Judas vor Joseph begründen sollte, warum Juda Benjamin keinesfalls in Ägypten zurücklassen kann. Deshalb steht sie hier erst in 44,27–29. In 44,30–34 stellt Juda dann die Konsequenzen dar, die sich für ihn aus diesen Worten des Vaters ergeben. Daraus folgt, daß 42,38 nicht umgestellt werden darf. Wie aus 44,24 hervorgeht, haben die Brüder auch bei J dem Vater nach ihrer Rückkehr von ihrer Reise berichtet. Da sie erst in 43,7 Einzelheiten ihrer Begegnung mit Joseph schildern, ging es dabei um die Forderung

---

[98] Darauf hat H.-C.Schmitt, BZAW 154, 47, mit Recht hingewiesen.
[99] J.Wellhausen, Composition, 57.
[100] H.Gunkel 448.

Josephs, ihren jüngsten Bruder mitzubringen. Sie wurde von dem Vater mit 42,38 abgelehnt. Vielleicht haben die Brüder den Vater auch über das gefundene Geld informiert, da in 43,12 der Vater davon weiß.

Sowohl E als auch J enthielten somit einen Bericht der Brüder. Der Redaktor nahm aber die elohistische Fassung auf, weil nur in ihr von Simeon die Rede war und nach 42,14–26 die Brüder dem Vater von der Geiselnahme Simeons berichten mußten. Er hat damit der ausführlicheren Fassung des Elohisten gegenüber der knappen Darstellung bei J den Vorzug gegeben. Es war für ihn einfach, am Schluß von Gen 42 E und J miteinander zu verzahnen. Er brauchte nur die Ablehnung der Forderung Josephs bei J auf das Bürgschaftsangebot Rubens bei E (42,37) zu beziehen. Eine Umstellung des Ablaufs bei J war für den Redaktor somit nicht erforderlich.

Tatsächlich ergibt 43,1 ff. nach 42,38 einen guten Sinn. Wegen der andauernden Hungersnot fordert der Vater die Brüder auf, nochmals nach Ägypten zu ziehen (v. 1 f.). Darauf wiederholt Juda die Forderung Josephs, die der Vater zunächst abgelehnt hatte, und zeigt die Konsequenzen auf, die sich aus ihr für die Brüder ergeben (v. 3–5). Israel stellt jetzt die Frage, woher Joseph erfahren hatte, daß die Brüder noch einen weiteren Bruder haben (v. 6). Er kann wegen der Hungersnot diese Forderung nicht mehr einfach ablehnen. So will er wenigstens wissen, wie es zu ihr gekommen ist. Darauf antworten die Brüder in v. 7, und Juda bietet sich in v. 8–10 als Bürge an. V. 10 bestätigt, daß J den Ablauf so dargestellt hat. Hier sagt Juda, daß sie längst zurückgekehrt wären, wenn sie nicht gezögert hätten. Dieses Zögern wird nur verständlich, wenn der Vater zunächst die Mitnahme Benjamins abgelehnt hatte.

Damit folgt aber aus 43,1 ff., daß J die zweite Reise der Brüder anders begründete als E. Sie ist bei J dadurch notwendig geworden, daß die Hungersnot anhält. Offenbar wußte jedoch Joseph, daß sie länger dauern würde. Seine Forderung, Benjamin bei einer zweiten Reise mitzubringen, setzt voraus, daß die Brüder nochmals nach Ägypten ziehen müssen. Nach J ist Joseph also bekannt, daß die Hungersnot längere Zeit dauern wird. Er hat darauf seinen Plan mit den Brüdern abgestellt.

Wie aus 43,7 hervorgeht, ist die Darstellung bei J an dem Vater und an Benjamin orientiert. Joseph erkundigt sich von sich aus, ob der Vater noch lebt, und ob es noch einen Bruder gibt. Damit greift J für den Vater seine Exposition in 37,3 auf, nach der zwischen dem Vater und Joseph ein besonders enges Verhältnis bestand. Neu ist, daß sich Joseph auch mit Benjamin eng verbunden weiß. Diese Beziehung zwischen Joseph und Benjamin ist bei J nur für die beiden Reisen nach Ägypten von Bedeutung, wie sich im folgenden zeigen wird.

Die Forderung Josephs, Benjamin mitzubringen, beherrscht die Darstellung in 43,1–13. Für die Brüder und den Vater ist es ein Rätsel, was »der Mann« mit ihr beabsichtigt. Trotzdem können sie sich ihr wegen der Hungersnot nicht entziehen. Nur so können sie überleben (v. 8). Deshalb versucht Juda, den Vater mit seiner Bürgschaft umzustimmen (v. 8–10), und Israel muß nachgeben. Der Vater will freilich durch seine Anweisungen in v. 11–13 verhindern, daß »der Mann« erzürnt werden könnte. Deshalb sollen die Brüder nicht nur Geld für Getreide und Benjamin mitnehmen, sondern auch Geschenke und das gefundene Geld. So unternimmt auch der Vater alles, damit Benjamin zurückkehren kann.

Dieses Bemühen scheint in der Fortsetzung v. 15–23 a [101]. 24–34 zunächst Erfolg zu haben. Allerdings ist gelegentlich bezweifelt worden, daß dieser Abschnitt einheitlich ist, da v. 17b wörtlich mit v. 24a übereinstimmt. Deshalb rechnet H.-C. Schmitt mit der Möglichkeit, daß es sich bei v. 18–24a um eine Erweiterung von dem Verfasser seiner Rubenschicht handelt [102]. Dann müßte man aber alle Stellen, an denen das Auffinden des Geldes erwähnt wird, J absprechen. Sie sind jedoch, wie unter b) gezeigt wurde, im Gegensatz zu der Auffassung von H.-C. Schmitt im Kontext fest verankert [103]. Die Wiederaufnahme von v. 17b in v. 24a kann somit nicht literarkritisch ausgewertet werden. Sie dient hier dazu, den Ablauf in verschiedene Szenen zu gliedern: Dialog mit dem Hausverwalter v. 17b–23a, Begegnung mit Joseph v. 24–34 [104].

Der Befehl Josephs an seinen Hausverwalter in v. 16 zeigt, daß er die Brüder freundlich bewirten will. Sie aber fürchten wegen des Geldes Schlimmes, wenn sie in das Haus Josephs gebracht werden. Deshalb wollen sie diese Angelegenheit regeln, bevor sie das Haus betreten. In v. 23a gibt ihnen der Hausverwalter die Deutung, daß ihnen ihr Gott und der Gott ihres Vaters mit dem Geld einen Schatz zukommen ließ. Damit ist für die Brüder die Angelegenheit erledigt, sie brauchen keine Angst mehr zu haben. Dem Leser freilich stellt sich die Frage, was Joseph mit dem Geld beabsichtigte. Sie wird auch durch v. 24–34 nicht beantwortet, sondern seine Spannung wird hier weiter gesteigert. Die

---

[101] Zu v. 23b vgl. I.
[102] H.-C. Schmitt, BZAW 154, 44 f. Anm. 173.
[103] H. Seebaß, Zeit, 90, weist 43, 14a. 18*–23 E und 43, 1–13. 14b–17. 24b–34 J zu. Das ist ein Beispiel, wie problematisch die von H. Seebaß vorgenommenen Zuweisungen häufig sind. 43, 12.18*, die den gleichen Begriff für »Sack« haben, werden auf J und E verteilt. 42, 35, wo ein anderes Wort für Sack steht, und wo die Lage des Geldes 43, 12 widerspricht, wird wie 43, 12 zu J gerechnet. Dagegen soll 42, 28 zu E gehören, obwohl hier – wie in 43, 12 – das Geld oben im Sack liegt. Hier wie auch sonst des öfteren hat H. Seebaß die Unterschiede zwischen J und E nicht erkannt. Deshalb werden von ihm Abschnitte wie die beiden Träume in Kap. 37 aufgeteilt, obwohl sie aus einer Quellenschrift stammen, und andere, die wie 42, 12–34 deutliche Spannungen enthalten, als einheitlich beurteilt.
[104] Vgl. u. a. C. Westermann 133.

Brüder bringen zunächst Joseph ehrfurchtsvoll ihr Geschenk dar und beantworten demütig seine Frage nach dem Vater (v. 26-28).

Darauf tritt Benjamin in den Mittelpunkt. Er wird von J durch die Bezeichnung »seinen Bruder, den Sohn seiner Mutter« deutlich von den übrigen Brüdern abgehoben. Ihn zeichnet Joseph mit den Worten »Gott möge dir gnädig sein mein Sohn« aus (v. 29), während er die Brüder insgesamt nur freundlich gegrüßt hatte (v. 27). H.-C. Schmitt hat zwar erwogen, ob diese Worte nicht eine Erweiterung sind, da in v. 29 die Rede Josephs zweimal mit »da sprach er« eingeleitet wird, ohne daß dazwischen eine Reaktion der Brüder geschildert wird[105]. Dagegen spricht aber, daß Benjamin auch in v. 30 eine Sonderstellung zukommt. Dann hat das zweite »da sprach er« in v. 29 gliedernde Funktion. Es soll anzeigen, daß Joseph nun nicht mehr die Brüder anredet, sondern sich an Benjamin wendet. Das geschieht, ohne daß die Brüder die Gelegenheit haben, die Frage Josephs zu beantworten. Daran soll deutlich werden, wie brennend Joseph an Benjamin interessiert ist. Dem entspricht, daß nach v. 30 Joseph wegen Benjamin in seine Kammer geht und weint. Das ist ein markanter Unterschied zu E. Bei E weinte in 42, 24 Joseph, weil sich die Brüder ihre Schuld eingestanden hatten. Bei J weint Joseph dagegen, weil er Benjamin wiedersehen darf. Das hat freilich keine Konsequenzen. Der Leser wird weiter auf die Folter gespannt. Es kommt zu dem Mahl mit Joseph und den Brüdern, bei dem sich für die Brüder Merkwürdiges ereignet, weil sie gemäß ihrem Alter angeordnet werden. Darüber staunen sie, aber auch das hat keine Folgen (v. 33). Das Mahl, bei dem Benjamin die fünffache Portion erhält, endet fröhlich (v. 34). So werden in v. 16-34 eine Reihe von merkwürdigen Begebenheiten geschildert. Es ereignet sich viel, und doch geschieht nichts. Die Hoffnung des Lesers, daß sich Joseph zu erkennen gibt, wird bewußt enttäuscht. Damit stellt dieser Abschnitt ein retardierendes Element dar, das die Spannung weiter steigern soll. Der Handlungsablauf wird also bewußt auf den Höhepunkt hin zerdehnt.

d) Gen 44, 1–34

Auf diesen Höhepunkt führt der Abschnitt 44, 1–17 hin, der nur am Anfang zwei kleinere literarische Erweiterungen enthält. Nach v. 1b und 2aß haben die Brüder bzw. Benjamin auch dieses Mal ihr Geld zurückerhalten. Das kann nicht ursprünglich sein, weil sonst die Brüder beim Öffnen der Säcke als Diebe entlarvt würden. Es kommt aber darauf an, daß nur Benjamin – und zwar ausschließlich wegen des bei ihm gefundenen Bechers – als Dieb erscheint[106]. Ein Späterer war der Auf-

---
[105] H.-C. Schmitt, BZAW 154, 44f. Anm. 173.
[106] Vgl. u. a. H. Gunkel 453.

fassung, daß Joseph, nachdem er bei der ersten Reise den Brüdern das Geld in die Säcke legen ließ, auch bei der zweiten so verfahren sein müßte. Damit hat er aber die Linienführung von J zerstört, in der der Becher im Sack Benjamins dem Geld entspricht, das die Brüder früher in ihren Säcken gefunden haben.

In dem Aufbau folgt die Darstellung weitgehend 43, 16–34. Am Anfang steht der Auftrag Josephs an den Hausverwalter. Daraus sind in 44, 1 f.*4–5 zwei Anweisungen geworden, weil die Abreise der Brüder für das Geschehen notwendig war. Darauf kommt es zu einer Begegnung zwischen den Brüdern und dem Hausverwalter (v. 6–13), und schließlich treffen die Brüder auf Joseph (v. 14–17)[107]. Aus diesem parallelen Aufbau hat C. Westermann geschlossen, daß hier wieder das literarische Mittel der Doppelung gebraucht werde[108]. Das ist für ihn ein weiteres Kennzeichen, daß die eigentliche Josephsgeschichte von einem Verfasser stammt. Dabei übersieht aber C. Westermann, daß die Gestaltung von den Doppelungen bei E grundlegend abweicht. Bei E haben die Doppelungen die Funktion, eine grundlegende Aussage zu wiederholen und dabei zugleich zu steigern. So wird durch die beiden Träume in 37, 5 ff. unterstrichen, daß Joseph eine Vormachtstellung über seine Brüder angekündigt ist. In 42, 14–20 wird deutlich, daß Joseph die Verteidigung der Brüder gegen den Vorwurf, sie seien Kundschafter, nicht hören will, sondern sie absichtlich in Bedrängnis bringt. Solche Doppelungen fehlen in der jahwistischen Darstellung, soweit sie bisher analysiert wurde. Für sie ist vielmehr charakteristisch, daß einzelne Szenen und Motive einander korrespondieren, wie an Geld und Becher besonders deutlich wird. Dadurch kann hier mit einem gleichen Aufbau eine inhaltlich unterschiedliche Darstellung verbunden sein. So nimmt das Geschehen für die Brüder in 43, 16 ff. einen guten Verlauf, in 44, 1 ff. aber einen schlechten. 43, 16 ff. stellt im Ablauf ein retardierendes Element dar. Das ist bei den Doppelungen in E so nie der Fall. Damit unterscheiden sich J und E in der Josephsgeschichte auch stilistisch erheblich voneinander. Bei E finden sich die Doppelungen, bei J hingegen Strukturanalogien. Deshalb kann J in 44, 8 die sich entsprechenden Motive von Geld und Becher miteinander verknüpfen: Da die Brüder das Geld, das sie in ihren Säcken gefunden haben, zurückbrachten, ist nach ihrer Meinung erwiesen, daß sie den Becher Josephs nicht gestohlen haben können.

In 44, 1–17 prüft Joseph, wie sich die Brüder gegenüber Benjamin verhalten. Es geht dabei nicht um die Frage, wie die Brüder überhaupt

---

[107] J. Wellhausen, Composition, 58, und H. Gunkel 445, lesen in v. 16 statt »da sprach Juda« »da sprachen sie«, da so zu der Rede Judas in v. 18 ff. eine Steigerung erreicht werde. Dagegen hat C. Westermann 145, mit Recht auf v. 14 verwiesen, durch den Juda als Sprecher der Brüder vorbereitet wird.

[108] C. Westermann 142.

zu einem der ihren stehen. So stellt zwar E in 42,14 ff. die Probe dar, die Joseph den Brüdern auferlegt hatte. Aber die Tatsache, daß bei J Joseph den Becher gezielt in dem Sack Benjamins verstecken läßt, zeigt, daß es hier um das Verhältnis der Brüder zu Benjamin geht. Das hat L. Ruppert bestritten. Nach ihm verfolgt Joseph lediglich den Zweck, Benjamin bei sich zu behalten[109]. Dagegen spricht aber schon das Interesse an dem Vater, das Joseph wiederholt bekundet hat.

Joseph stellt bewußt eine ähnliche Situation her, wie sie mit seinem Verkauf in Gen 37 entstand. Damals hatten die Brüder Joseph als Sklaven verkauft. Werden sie jetzt Benjamin als Sklaven zurücklassen? Der Hausverwalter gibt ihnen dazu die Möglichkeit. Schon bevor er den Becher findet, legt er fest: »Bei wem er gefunden wird, soll mir zum Sklaven sein, ihr aber sollt unschuldig sein« (v. 10 b). An Benjamin handeln die Brüder jedoch anders als einst an Joseph. Diesen Bruder geben sie nicht preis. Voll Trauer kehren sie zu Joseph zurück und fallen vor ihm nieder (v. 13 f.). Früher war ihnen Joseph ausgeliefert gewesen, jetzt stehen sie ohnmächtig vor ihm: Sie alle wollen das Geschick auf sich nehmen, das Benjamin bestimmt ist.

Das sagt Juda in v. 16. Hier findet sich auch der Satz: »Gott hat den Frevel deiner Knechte gefunden«. Er wird des öfteren auf die Schuld gedeutet, die die Brüder gegenüber Joseph auf sich geladen haben: »Juda ist natürlich nicht so naiv, den Benjamin für einen Dieb zu halten; wenn er von der ›Schuld deiner Knechte‹ spricht ..., kann er damit nur ihr Verbrechen an Joseph meinen, das nun seine Sühne zu finden scheint.«[110] Nach H. Gunkel hingegen sind die Brüder zwar der Meinung, daß ihr Unglück durch eine Sünde hervorgerufen wurde, sie denken aber nicht an eine bestimmte Schuld[111]. Beide Auffassungen werden aber dem Anfang von v. 16 nicht gerecht. Hier sagt Juda: »Was sollen wir meinem Herrn sagen, was sollen wir reden und womit sollen wir uns rechtfertigen?« Hier sieht Juda eindeutig keine Möglichkeit, sich gegen den Vorwurf des Diebstahls zu verteidigen. Weil der Becher in seinem Sack gefunden wurde, ist Benjamin objektiv als Dieb erwiesen. Freilich fährt Juda nicht fort: »Du hast den Frevel deiner Knechte gefunden«, obwohl der Hausverwalter den Becher entdeckt hat. Er spricht vielmehr von Gott. Daran wird deutlich, daß die Brüder dieses Geschehen nicht verstehen können. Sie sind keine Diebe, und doch wurde Benjamin des Diebstahls überführt. Das ist ein Rätsel, hinter dem für Juda nur Gott stehen kann. Das entspricht 42,28. Dort konnten sich die Brüder nicht erklären, wie sie wieder zu ihrem Geld gekom-

---

[109] L. Ruppert, Josephserzählung, 111 f.
[110] L. Ruppert, Josephserzählung, 110 f.; vgl. auch O. Procksch 257; H.-C. Schmitt, BZAW 154, 44 f. Anm. 173; C. Westermann 146.
[111] H. Gunkel 455.

men sind. Deshalb sahen sie darin Gott am Werk. Hier ist ihnen unverständlich, wie der Becher bei Benjamin gefunden werden konnte. Aus diesem Grund führen sie das Ereignis auf Gott zurück. Obwohl subjektiv unschuldig, sind sie von Gott des Frevels überführt worden. Was Gott damit beabsichtigt, ist den Brüdern verborgen.

Daran wird deutlich, daß 44,16 in der jahwistischen Josephsgeschichte nicht die letzte Aussage über Gott sein kann. Juda hat mit seinen Worten eine Frage über Gott aufgeworfen, die beantwortet werden muß. Zunächst bleibt sie freilich offen. Offen bleibt auch für Joseph, warum die Brüder nicht bereit sind, ohne Benjamin zurückzukehren, sondern zu seinen Sklaven werden wollen. Diesen Vorschlag lehnt er in v. 17 ab: Nur der Dieb soll sein Sklave sein, die anderen aber müssen zu ihrem Vater zurück.

Damit gibt Joseph Juda die Gelegenheit zu seiner großen Rede von 44,18–34, die bei J den Wendepunkt bildet. Die sachliche Exposition steht in v. 20. Danach haben die Brüder auf der ersten Reise zu Joseph gesagt: »Wir haben einen alten Vater und einen kleinen Knaben des Alters, und sein Bruder ist tot, und er ist allein von seiner Mutter übriggeblieben, und sein Vater liebt ihn.« Ihre Notlage ruft bei den Brüdern keineswegs die Erinnerung an jene Schuld hervor, die sie einst an Joseph auf sich geladen haben. Für sie ist Joseph tot. Das ist keine Notlüge[112]. Die Brüder haben einst durch das blutige Gewand bei dem Vater den Eindruck erweckt, daß Joseph tot ist. Was damals eine bewußte Lüge war, ist inzwischen auch für die Brüder zu einem Faktum geworden: Joseph ist tot. Dieser Meinung sind sie auch jetzt. Gerade dadurch, daß der Erzähler Juda keine vorsichtigere Formulierung in den Mund legt, sondern ihn ausdrücklich sagen läßt, daß Joseph tot ist, macht er deutlich, daß für die Brüder Joseph tatsächlich gestorben ist. Der Vater hat nur noch Benjamin.

Dieser Sohn wird ähnlich beschrieben wie Joseph in 37,3. Er ist »Knabe des Alters«, wie Joseph »Sohn des Alters« war. Hieß es von Joseph: »Israel liebte Joseph mehr als seine Söhne«, so wird von Benjamin gesagt: »und sein Vater liebt ihn«. Das hat aber bei Benjamin nicht zur Folge, daß die Brüder ihn hassen. Bei ihm akzeptieren sie, daß ihn der Vater liebt. Dieses andere Verhalten ist darin begründet, daß der Vater den Tod dieses Sohnes nicht überleben würde. Er hat Joseph noch nicht vergessen. Wenn ihm auch Benjamin genommen würde, würde er sterben. So hat der Vater nach v. 28 f. gesagt. Diese Worte nehmen die Brüder ernst. Sie haben an der langen Trauer des Vaters um Joseph gesehen (37,34b.35a), wie schwer er von dem Verlust dieses Sohnes getroffen wurde. Deshalb können sie nicht riskieren, daß er nun auch noch auf Benjamin verzichten muß. Die Brüder treten also für Benja-

---

[112] Gegen H. Gunkel 456.

min ein, weil sie nicht am Tod des Vaters schuldig werden wollen. Ihr Handeln ist von dem Verhältnis des Vaters zu *diesem* Sohn bestimmt. Begann die Josephsgeschichte bei J in 37,3 mit dem Vater und Joseph, so geht es an dem Wendepunkt in 44,18ff. um den Vater und Benjamin.

Der Grund, warum der Vater gerade zu diesen beiden Söhnen ein besonders inniges Verhältnis hat, wird in 44,27 genannt: »Seine Frau« hat ihm diese beiden Söhne geboren. Hier kommt weder die Mutter der übrigen Söhne noch ihre Kinder in den Blick. Nur die Mutter von Joseph und Benjamin ist für den Vater *seine Frau*. Deshalb sind ihm ihre Kinder besonders kostbar. Weil die Brüder das bei Benjamin gelten lassen, bietet Juda schließlich an, an Stelle Benjamins zum Sklaven Josephs zu werden. Er kann das Unheil nicht sehen, das über seinen Vater hereinbrechen würde, wenn die Brüder ohne Benjamin zurückkehren (v. 33f.). Juda ist bereit, um des Vaters willen ein schweres Geschick auf sich zu nehmen und damit die Bürgschaft einzulösen, die er für Benjamin eingegangen ist.

Das ist eine völlig andere Auffassung von der Wende als beim Elohisten in 42,14ff. Dort stehen die Brüder auf einer Ebene, und der Vater gibt Simeon auf, weil er nicht auch noch Benjamin verlieren will. Bei J wird hingegen zwischen den Brüdern differenziert, weil der Vater zu ihnen eine unterschiedliche Beziehung hat. Bei E und bei J sind zwar die Brüder andere geworden. Bei E geben aber die Brüder Simeon nicht preis, weil er ihr Bruder ist. Bei J halten dagegen die Brüder um des Vaters willen an Benjamin fest. Dieser Unterschied spiegelt sich darin, daß sich bei E die Brüder an ihre Schuld gegenüber Joseph erinnern, während sie bei J ihre Verfehlung längst vergessen haben.

e) Gen 45, 1–28

Gen 45 gibt erhebliche literarkritische Probleme auf. Für ihre Lösung sind zwei Ergebnisse der bisherigen Untersuchungen wichtig:

1. Die Gottesbezeichnung Elohim kann in der Josephsgeschichte nicht als Kriterium dienen, um J und E voneinander zu scheiden.

2. Joseph wußte bei J, daß die Hungersnot längere Zeit andauern würde.

Für die Analyse geht man am besten von zwei eindeutigen Dubletten aus. Wie in I bereits dargestellt wurde, gibt sich in v. 3 und v. 4 Joseph zweimal den Brüdern zu erkennen. Da er in v. 4 erwähnt, daß er von ihnen nach Ägypten verkauft wurde, stammt dieser Vers aus J. Nach 37,25 war die ismaelitische Karawane, an die die Brüder Joseph verkauften, auf dem Weg nach Ägypten. Die Brüder haben ihn also bei J tatsächlich nach Ägypten verkauft. Dann ist v. 3 E zuzuweisen.

Die zweite Dublette besteht zwischen v. 9 ff. und v. 16-18. In v. 9 ff. gibt Joseph den Brüdern die Botschaft an den Vater mit auf den Weg, daß er mit seiner Familie und seinem Besitz nach Ägypten kommen soll. In v. 16-18 erhält hingegen Joseph von dem Pharao den Befehl, seinen Brüdern zu sagen, daß sie sich mit ihrem Vater in Ägypten niederlassen sollen. Allerdings ist verschiedentlich bestritten worden, daß es sich hier um eine Dublette zu v. 9 ff. handelt. In v. 16 ff. bestätige der Pharao vielmehr die Einladung Josephs an den Vater[113]. Dagegen spricht freilich, daß sich der Pharao nicht auf diese Einladung bezieht und sie folglich nicht kennt. Auch das ist jedoch nach H. Donner kein Beweis, daß es sich um eine Dublette zu v. 9 ff. handelt: »Aber was ist einleuchtender und erfreut das Herz des Lesers mehr, als daß der Pharao tatsächlich – anscheinend ohne mit Joseph darüber gesprochen zu haben – genau das befiehlt, was Joseph seinen Brüdern längst aufgetragen hatte (v. 16-20)?«[114] Dagegen spricht aber die Darstellung in 46, 28-34. Hier kündigt Joseph den Brüdern an, daß er dem Pharao die Ankunft seiner Brüder und des Hauses seines Vaters melden will (46, 31). Der Pharao weiß somit noch nichts von dem Vater und den Brüdern Josephs. Dann kann er sie nicht nach Ägypten eingeladen haben. Auch das ist freilich bestritten worden. So schreibt W. Rudolph: »45, 16 ff. enthält die Einladung des Pharao an Jakob und seine Söhne, in 46, 31 ff. hören wir von Josefs Absicht, ihre *Ankunft,* die die Folge jener Einladung war, dem Pharao zu melden«[115]. Aber in 46, 31 ff. erwähnt Joseph die Einladung des Pharao nicht, wie es bei dieser Interpretation notwendig wäre. Wenn Joseph zudem nach 46, 31.32 aα dem Pharao sagen will: »Meine Brüder und das Haus meines Vaters, die im Lande Kanaan waren, sind zu mir gekommen, und die Männer sind Kleinviehhirten«, so geht daraus eindeutig hervor, daß der Pharao über die Brüder noch völlig uninformiert ist[116]. Er kennt nicht ihren Beruf, ja, er weiß nicht einmal, daß Joseph Brüder hat, die im Lande Kanaan wohnten. Das läßt sich mit 45, 17, wo die Brüder aufgefordert werden, nach Kanaan zu ziehen und von dort wieder nach Ägypten zu kommen, schlechterdings nicht vereinbaren. Es paßt aber zu 45, 9 ff., da hier Joseph ohne Wissen des Pharao den Vater zur Übersiedlung nach Ägypten auffordert. Damit wird durch 46, 28-34 bestätigt, daß es sich bei 45, 9 ff. und 45, 16-18 um Dubletten handelt. Da der Vater in 46, 28 ff. Israel heißt, und Juda erwähnt wird, gehört dieser Abschnitt zu J. Das gilt dann auch für 45, 9 ff., wobei noch zu untersuchen bleibt, was hier im einzelnen von J stammt. In 45, 16-18 kommt dagegen E zu Wort[117].

---

[113] W. Rudolph, BZAW 63, 163 f.; C. Westermann 162.   [114] H. Donner, Gestalt, 23.

[115] W. Rudolph, BZAW 63, 163; vgl. auch H. Donner, Gestalt, 23; C. Westermann 186.

[116] Vgl. auch H.-C. Schmitt, BZAW 154, 52 f. Anm. 207.

[117] H. Seebaß, Zeit, 53 ff., weist v. 16 ff. P zu. Das geht schon deshalb nicht, weil v. 2, den H. Seebaß a.a.O. 90, zu E rechnet, v. 16 vorbereitet.

Die Ergebnisse, die zu den Dubletten in v. 3/4 und v. 9 ff./16–18 erzielt wurden, bilden eine geeignete Basis für die weitere Untersuchung. V. 1 ist bei J die unmittelbare Fortsetzung von 44,34. Nach der Rede Judas gibt sich Joseph seinen Brüdern zu erkennen. Dabei legt er darauf Wert, daß kein Fremder anwesend ist. Hatte Joseph beim Anblick Benjamins zunächst noch »an sich gehalten« (43,31), so ist er dazu nach der Rede Judas nicht mehr imstande. In v. 2 wird berichtet, daß Joseph weinte, und daß das die Ägypter hörten[118]. Damit wird deutlich v. 16 vorbereitet, wonach die Kunde von der Ankunft der Brüder in das Haus des Pharao kam. V. 2 gehört deshalb zu E, an ihn schloß sich bei E v. 3 an, während bei J v. 4 direkt auf v. 1 folgte.

Von J stammt auch v. 9–14, da dieser Abschnitt in 46,28 ff. vorausgesetzt wird[119]. In 45,10 fordert Joseph den Vater auf, im Lande Gosen zu wohnen, in 46,28 kommt der Vater in das Land Gosen. Die Formulierung in 45,10b entspricht weitgehend 46,32b. Zudem läßt es sich mit der elohistischen Darstellung nicht vereinbaren, daß in 45,9 ff. die Brüder einen Auftrag für den Vater erhalten. Sie haben hier die Frage Josephs von v. 3: »Lebt mein Vater noch?« noch nicht beantwortet, wie an v. 15 deutlich wird, der – wie noch zu zeigen ist – zu E gehört.

Nun wird freilich verschiedentlich v. 9 E zugewiesen, da hier Elohim steht[120]. Das scheitert jedoch auch daran, daß für v. 10 eine Einleitung erforderlich ist, die nur v. 9 bietet. Nach H. Gunkel ist in v. 10a »du sollst mir nahe sein« eine Dublette zu »du sollst im Lande Gosen wohnen«, die aus E stamme[121]. Aber hier besteht ein glatter Zusammenhang. Die Worte besagen nicht, daß der Vater sich direkt bei Joseph aufhalten wird. Er ist im Lande Gosen Joseph nahe, weil Joseph hier im Unterschied zu seinem bisherigen Wohnort im Lande Kanaan mit ihm zusammentreffen kann (46,29f.).

Tatsächlich ist der Abschnitt v. 9–14 klar aufgebaut. Die Brüder sollen dem Vater rasch die Botschaft Josephs mitteilen. Sie beginnt mit der Feststellung, daß ihn Gott zum Herrn für ganz Ägypten gemacht hat. Sie bildet die Basis für die folgenden Anweisungen und ist deshalb unverzichtbar. Nur weil Joseph zum Herrn für Ägypten geworden ist, kann er den Vater auffordern, zu ihm zu kommen und ihm einen bestimmten Wohnort zusagen (v. 9f.). Ohne v. 9 aß bliebe dem Vater unverständlich, wie Joseph solche Versprechungen machen kann. In v. 11 sagt Joseph dann dem Vater zu, ihn dort zu versorgen, weil die Hun-

---

[118] V. 2 bβ: »und man hörte (es) im Haus des Pharao« ist wahrscheinlich eine Glosse. Sie wurde im Blick auf v. 16 eingefügt, wo von dem Haus des Pharao die Rede ist.
[119] So z. B. auch O. Eißfeldt, Hexateuch-Synopse, 93*.
[120] So z. B. H. Gunkel 457.
[121] H. Gunkel 457 f.

gersnot noch fünf Jahre währen wird. Damit unterstreicht Joseph, daß der Vater nach Ägypten übersiedeln muß. V. 11 fügt sich also gut in die Botschaft ein. Bereits zu Kap. 43 wurde gezeigt, daß Joseph mit einer längeren Dauer der Hungersnot rechnet. Es wäre deshalb eigenartig, wenn dieser Punkt hier bei J keine Rolle gespielt hätte. So ist v. 11 bei J fest verankert[122]. Dann weiß aber Joseph bei J, daß die Hungersnot noch fünf Jahre währen wird.

Durch die Botschaft Josephs an den Vater wird bei J die Übersiedlung nach Ägypten ausschließlich zu einer Entscheidung des Vaters. Mit ihr wird zugleich das besondere Verhältnis zwischen Joseph und dem Vater unterstrichen. Joseph will, daß ihm der Vater nahe ist (v. 10). Beides entspricht dem Befund, daß bei J der Vater eine zentrale Rolle hat. Dabei stellt J erneut eine Strukturanalogie her. In 43,29 hatte Joseph Benjamin mit dem Wunsch ausgezeichnet: »Gott möge dir gnädig sein, mein Sohn«. Seine Botschaft an den Vater beginnt er mit der Feststellung, was Gott an ihm getan hat. Auch diese Stellen mit Elohim korrespondieren einander. Zu Benjamin und dem Vater hat Joseph ein besonderes Verhältnis, zu beiden redet er von Elohim. Bleibt der Wunsch für Benjamin zunächst rätselhaft, so wird in den Worten an den Vater eindeutig von Gott gesprochen. Damit bietet 45,9 eine Steigerung.

Mit v. 12 f. kommen dann die Brüder ins Spiel. Dabei wird in v. 12 zwischen den übrigen Brüdern und Benjamin differenziert. Es sind »eure Augen und die Augen meines Bruders Benjamin«, die gesehen haben, daß Joseph zu ihnen geredet hat. Die Brüder und Benjamin können also dem Vater bestätigen, daß es sich wirklich um eine Botschaft Josephs handelt. Der Bekräftigung dieser Botschaft dient auch v. 13, der deshalb keine Dublette zu v. 9 ist[123]. Joseph läßt nach v. 9 aß dem Vater sagen: »Gott hat mich zum Herrn für ganz Ägypten gemacht«. Die Brüder aber sollen nach v. 13a dem Vater die Herrlichkeit Josephs erzählen. Damit bestätigen sie seine Worte. Die abschließende Aufforderung, daß sie eilen und den Vater herabbringen sollen, entspricht dem Befehl von v. 9 aα, daß die Brüder eilen und zum Vater hinaufziehen sollen. Diese Entsprechungen zwischen v. 9 und v. 13 zeigen, daß beide Verse von demselben Verfasser stammen. Den Abschluß der Szene bildet dann v. 14: Joseph fällt Benjamin weinend um den Hals, und Benjamin weint an seinem Hals. Damit wird 43,30 weitergeführt. Dort konnte Joseph seinen Gefühlen zu Benjamin nicht freien Lauf lassen,

---

[122] In 50,21 steht zwar *kwl* pilp. = versorgen bei E (vgl. IIi). Es ist jedoch eine Überbewertung der Wortstatistik, wenn H. Gunkel 457, u. a. daraus schließen, daß 45,11 aus E stammen müsse. Durch die literarische Abhängigkeit des Elohisten von J können seltene Begriffe bei J und bei E vorkommen.

[123] Gegen H. Gunkel 458; L. Ruppert, Josephserzählung, 115; H.-C. Schmitt, BZAW 154, 222.

weil er seine Identität noch nicht preisgeben wollte. Nachdem das aber geschehen ist, braucht er seine Tränen nicht mehr zurückzuhalten, und Benjamin erwidert die Gefühle Josephs. So findet das besondere Verhältnis zwischen Joseph und Benjamin seinen sichtbaren Ausdruck. Über die übrigen Brüder weint Joseph in der jahwistischen Darstellung nie.

Von einem Weinen Josephs an den Brüdern berichtet allerdings v. 15, aber dieser Vers stammt aus E. Das zeigt v. 15 b: »und danach redeten seine Brüder mit ihm«. Damit wird deutlich auf v. 3 b Bezug genommen[124]. Dort konnten die Brüder die Frage Josephs nach dem Vater nicht beantworten, weil sie entsetzt darüber waren, Joseph vor sich zu haben. Erst nachdem Joseph gezeigt hat, daß er mit ihnen Frieden geschlossen hat (v. 15 a), können sie mit ihm reden. Auch bei E ist das Weinen Josephs in v. 15 a die Weiterführung einer früheren Aussage. In 42,24 hatte Joseph heimlich geweint, nachdem sich die Brüder ihre Schuld an ihm eingestanden hatten. Jetzt weint er an ihnen. Damit ist deutlich, daß sich in 42,14-45,15 J und E in den Aussagen über das Weinen Josephs charakteristisch voneinander abheben. Es bezieht sich bei J immer auf Benjamin, bei E hingegen durchgehend auf alle Brüder. Auch in der Einladung des Pharao, nach Ägypten zu übersiedeln, kommt bei E in v. 16-18 den Brüdern das entscheidende Gewicht zu. Im Gegensatz zu J liegt hier die Entscheidung bei ihnen und nicht bei dem Vater. Er ist vielmehr eine Nebenfigur, die auf der gleichen Stufe wie die »Häuser« der Brüder steht. Das zeigt, daß die Rolle der Brüder hier nicht nur dadurch bedingt ist, daß sie und nicht der Vater durch Vermittlung Josephs von dem Pharao angesprochen werden. Hier findet vielmehr wieder die andere Linienführung bei E ihren Ausdruck.

In 45,1-18 gehören somit v.1.4.9-14 zu J, v.2a.bα.3.15-18 zu E. Nun wurde bereits zu 44,16 darauf hingewiesen, daß die Worte Judas über Elohim verlangen, daß Joseph den Brüdern das Geschehen im Blick auf Elohim interpretiert. Nur in diesem Fall entsprechen sich die Motive von Geld und Becher wirklich, da in 43,23 der Hausverwalter den Brüdern das gefundene Geld als Gabe Elohims gedeutet hat. Diese Interpretation müßte bei J Joseph zwischen v. 4 und v. 9 gegeben haben. Auch für E ist zu erwarten, daß Joseph nach v. 3 an die Brüder weitere Worte richtete, ehe er mit v. 15 der Versöhnung sichtbaren Ausdruck gab. Deshalb kann die Frage nur sein, ob J und E in v. 5-8 nachweisbar sind, oder ob eine der beiden Darstellungen von dem Redaktor übergangen wurde.

Die Analyse dieser Verse ist freilich außerordentlich schwierig, so daß die Zuweisungen weit auseinandergehen[125]. Deutlich ist aber, daß

---

[124] Vgl. z. B. H. Gunkel 460.
[125] Vgl. die Übersicht bei H. Donner, Gestalt, 22.

der Abschnitt klar überfüllt ist. Dreimal heißt es, daß Gott Joseph vor den Brüdern hergesandt bzw. ihn hierher gesandt hat (v. 5 b.7.8). Weiter fällt auf, daß sowohl v. 5 als auch v. 8 mit »und nun« beginnen. Damit wird in der Regel eine Folgerung eingeleitet, so daß dieses Stück zwei Folgerungen enthält. Vor allem befremdet jedoch, daß in v. 5 f. drei *ky*-Sätze unmittelbar nacheinander stehen. Diese Beobachtungen schließen es aus, daß v. 5–8 oder auch nur v. 5–7 literarisch einheitlich sind.

V. 5 aβ stammt mit Sicherheit aus J, da hier der Verkauf Josephs erwähnt wird. In v. 11 läßt Joseph bei J dem Vater mitteilen, daß die Hungersnot noch fünf Jahre andauern wird. Das sagt Joseph in v. 6 den Brüdern, so daß auch dieser Vers zu J zu rechnen ist. Dann stammt v. 5 b aus E, da durch diesen Satz die problematische Häufung von *ky*-Sätzen entsteht. V. 5 aβ.6 lassen sich ohne Schwierigkeit miteinander verbinden. Da v. 7 glatt an v. 6 anschließt, kommt auch hier J zu Wort. Auf die sachlichen Probleme dieses Verses wird zurückzukommen sein. V. 8 weicht in der Beschreibung der Stellung, die Joseph erlangt hat, geringfügig von v. 9 (J) ab. Hat Gott Joseph nach v. 9 zum Herrn für ganz Ägypten gemacht, so ist er nach v. 8 von Gott eingesetzt worden »zum Vater für den Pharao und zum Herrn für sein ganzes Haus und als Herrscher über das ganze Land Ägypten«. Das spricht dafür, daß v. 8 zu E gehört. In v. 16 wird bei E nochmals das Haus des Pharao erwähnt, in 42,29 ff. bot E mit »der Mann, der Herr des Landes« eine etwas ausführlichere Beschreibung der Stellung Josephs als J in 43,1 ff., wo Joseph nur als »der Mann« bezeichnet wird. Überdies läßt sich v. 8 glatt an v. 5 b anschließen. Erst dann kommt auch der Gegensatz, den v. 8 ausdrückt, voll zur Geltung. Joseph zieht hier aus der Tatsache, daß er von Gott zur Erhaltung des Lebens vor den Brüdern hergesandt wurde, den Schluß, daß ihn nicht die Brüder, sondern Gott nach Ägypten gesandt hat (v. 8 a). Dort hat ihm Gott eine besondere Stellung verliehen (v. 8 b). Die Probleme, die teilweise in der Abfolge von v. 7 und v. 8 gesehen werden[126], sind also dadurch bedingt, daß hier J und E miteinander verknüpft wurden. Nun bedarf v. 5 b bei E eines Vordersatzes, und das macht es wahrscheinlich, daß eine der beiden Aufforderungen Josephs in v. 5 aα aus E stammt. Mit v. 5 b hat der Redaktor E als Ergänzung in die jahwistische Darstellung eingearbeitet. Deshalb dürfte in v. 5 aα »Nicht entbrenne es in euren Augen« aus E stammen, während »und nun: Seid nicht bekümmert« zu J gehört und hier durch v. 5 aβ fortgesetzt wurde.

---

[126] Vgl. C. Westermann 157 f. Nach C. Westermann lautet die ursprüngliche Reihenfolge v. 7 aα. 8 b. 8 a. Später sei v. 7 aβ.b eingefügt und dabei in v. 8 eine Umstellung vorgenommen worden. Diese Erklärung ist zumindest nicht einfacher als die Verteilung auf zwei Quellen. Sie löst die Probleme auch nur teilweise. Außerdem ist schwer einzusehen, warum die Umstellung in v. 8 vorgenommen worden sein sollte.

In v. 5–8 sind somit J und E vollständig erhalten. Der Redaktor hat aus E nur »da sprach Joseph« ausgelassen, das nach v. 3 gestanden haben muß, weil in v. 4 und v. 5 a Joseph bei J bereits redete. Daß der Redaktor in v. 5–8 J und E aufnahm, beruht darauf, daß den Worten Josephs ein besonderes Gewicht zukommen sollte. Außerdem hat er mit v. 8 a eine prägnante theologische Formulierung in sein Werk integriert. Das Vorgehen des Redaktors läßt sich somit verständlich machen. Das stützt die vorgenommenen Zuweisungen.

Dem Abschnitt v. 5 aα¹.aβ.6 f. kommt in der jahwistischen Josephsgeschichte eine Schlüsselstellung zu, da hier Joseph seinen Brüdern das Geschehen deutet. Bisher blieb für sie und den Leser offen, welchen Sinn die breit geschilderten Ereignisse hatten. Nun wird er ihnen von Joseph enthüllt. Charakteristisch für J ist, daß Joseph, nachdem er sich den Brüdern zu erkennen gab, sofort sagt: »Und nun seid nicht betrübt, daß ihr mich hierher verkauft habt«. Eigentlich müßte sich jetzt die Frage stellen, was aus den Brüdern werden soll, die an Joseph schuldig wurden. Aber sie wird durch die Aufforderung Josephs sofort als Thema ausgeschaltet. Das entspricht der jahwistischen Darstellung in Gen 43 f., wo die Schuld der Brüder an Joseph ebenfalls keine Rolle spielte. Jetzt, wo sie eigentlich nicht mehr übergangen werden kann, darf sie nicht auftreten, weil Joseph erkennt, daß sein Weg sinnvoll war, und Gott mit diesem Weg eine besondere Absicht verfolgte. Das sagt er den Brüdern in v. 6 f. Die Hungersnot wird noch fünf Jahre währen. Im Blick auf sie hat Gott Joseph den Brüdern nach Ägypten vorausgesandt (v. 7 aα).

In v. 7 aβ.b wird dann erläutert, welches Ziel Gott damit intendierte. Diese Aussagen bereiten Schwierigkeiten, wenn man š'ryt als Rest versteht. So schreibt z. B. C. Westermann: »Es ist nicht verständlich, warum Jakobs Familie als ein ›Rest‹ bezeichnet wird. Ein Rest wovon?«[127] Da der Begriff im Pentateuch nur hier vorkommt und sonst überwiegend in der prophetischen Literatur begegnet, wird v. 7 immer wieder J abgesprochen[128]. Nach H.-C. Schmitt liegt hier eine Vorstellung vom Rest vor, die mit Stellen aus der späten Exilszeit verwandt ist, nach denen der dem Gericht entronnene Rest Träger des Heils ist[129]. Gegen eine Deutung aufgrund der späteren Vorstellungen vom Rest spricht aber – unabhängig von der Datierung –, daß die Brüder kein Rest sind. Der Begriff müßte hier völlig losgelöst von seiner eigentlichen Bedeutung gebraucht worden sein, und das ist recht unwahrscheinlich. Bereits O. Procksch hat auf II Sam 14,7 verwiesen, wo š'ryt

---

[127] C. Westermann 157.
[128] So z. B. L. Ruppert, Josephserzählung, 116.
[129] H.-C. Schmitt, BZAW 154, 167 f.; H. Seebaß, Zeit, 52 f., rechnet v. 6 f. zu seiner nachexilischen Bearbeitungsschicht.

eindeutig das Übrigbleibende im Sinne der Nachkommenschaft bedeutet[130]. Das ist mit dem Begriff auch in Gen 45,7 gemeint. Gott hat Joseph vor den Brüdern hergesandt, um für sie Nachkommenschaft im Lande zu bereiten.

Diese Interpretation wird durch die Fortsetzung bestätigt: »und für euch am Leben zu erhalten zu einem großen Entrinnen«. Verschiedentlich hat man hier zu dem Verb ein Objekt vermißt und nach LXX und Sam *l* vor »Entrinnen« gestrichen[131]. Der MT stellt aber eindeutig die lectio difficilior dar und ergibt einen Sinn. Das Objekt zu dem Verb ist wie in v. 7 aβ die Nachkommenschaft. Auch der Begriff »Entrinnen« kommt überwiegend an jüngeren Stellen vor, er ist aber in Gen 32,9 (J) und II Sam 15,14 bereits in alten Texten belegt. V. 7 ist somit zu übersetzen: »Da hat mich Gott vor euch hergesandt, um euch zu bereiten Nachkommenschaft im Land und für euch am Leben zu erhalten zu einem großen Entrinnen«. Damit kommen hier die Nachkommen der Brüder in den Blick. Das geschieht bei J nicht ganz unvorbereitet. In 43,8 will Juda mit Benjamin nach Ägypten, »daß wir leben und nicht sterben, sowohl wir, als auch du, als auch unsere Kinder«. Später heißt es in 45,10 in der Botschaft an den Vater: »und du sollst mir nahe sein, du und deine Söhne und die Söhne deiner Söhne«. Trotzdem mag es überraschen, daß in 45,7 das Ziel Gottes nicht in der Erhaltung des Vaters und der Brüder gesehen wird, sondern darin, daß den Brüdern Nachkommen gegeben und am Leben erhalten werden. Hierin kommt zum Ausdruck, daß für den Verfasser die Familie Israels eine Zukunft haben sollte. Um dieser Zukunft willen mußte Israel mit seiner Familie nach Ägypten übersiedeln, weil nur dadurch ein Überleben während der Hungersnot möglich war. Diese Zukunft ist zwar nicht das Thema des Verfassers, aber er signalisiert mit 45,7, daß er von einer solchen Zukunft weiß. Das wird sich bei 46,28–34 bestätigen.

E folgt mit seiner theologischen Interpretation in v. 5 aα².5 b.8 grundsätzlich der jahwistischen Vorlage. Hier führte die Bürgschaft Rubens (42,37) dazu, daß die Brüder mit Benjamin nach Ägypten ziehen konnten, um Simeon zu befreien. Als Joseph die Brüder mit Benjamin sah, gab er ihnen Simeon zurück. Auf diesen Abschnitt hat der Redaktor zugunsten der jahwistischen Darstellung verzichtet, weil diese wesentlich ausführlicher war. Der Ablauf läßt sich aber aus den Stellen, die er von E aufgenommen hat, erschließen. Danach weinte Joseph (v. 2 a.bα). Er weint bei E, weil die Brüder Simeon nicht preisgegeben und so die ihnen auferlegte Probe bestanden haben. Nachdem sich Joseph ihnen zu erkennen gibt, und sie bestürzt sind (v. 3), deutet ihnen Joseph

---

[130] O. Procksch 415.
[131] Vgl. z. B. BHS; H. Gunkel 459; L. Ruppert, Josephserzählung, 123.

sein Geschick. Sie sollen nicht über sich zornig werden[132], weil ihn Gott zur Erhaltung des Lebens – und das heißt zur Erhaltung ihres Lebens [133] –, vor ihnen hergesandt hat (v. 5 aα²·b).

Damit wird hier auch bei E die Frage nach der Schuld der Brüder abgewehrt. Das Geschehene war notwendig, weil es zur Erhaltung ihres Lebens geschehen mußte. Dabei setzt v. 5 b einen etwas anderen Akzent als J. Hier geht es bei dem Handeln Gottes tatsächlich um die Brüder selbst. In v. 8 a unterstreicht dann Joseph, daß wirklich Gott am Werk war und nicht die Brüder. Das entspricht der elohistischen Darstellung in Gen 37, in der nicht die Brüder Joseph nach Ägypten verkauft haben. Die Midianiter haben ihn vielmehr heimlich gestohlen. Eben dadurch ist für E erwiesen, daß der Weg Josephs tatsächlich von Gott nach Ägypten gelenkt wurde. Daß Gott Joseph dort eine bedeutende Stellung verschafft hat (v. 8 b), ermöglicht es Joseph, für die Erhaltung des Lebens der Brüder zu wirken. Seine Erkenntnis über die Absicht Gottes verwehrt es also Joseph, sich an den Brüdern zu rächen. Zum Zeichen, daß das Verhältnis in Ordnung ist, küßt Joseph die Brüder und weint an ihnen (v. 15). Die vergangene Schuld steht nicht mehr zwischen Joseph und den Brüdern.

Diese theologische Deutung, die Joseph den Brüdern gibt, ist knapper als bei J. Sie beschränkt sich auf die Herausarbeitung des entscheidenden Punktes, und sie setzt darin einen anderen Akzent, daß es nun um die Brüder selbst geht. Auffallend bleibt, daß die Frage nach der Schuld der Brüder zurückgedrängt wird, obwohl sie von E in 42,14 ff. thematisiert wurde. Das ist jedoch dadurch bedingt, daß E die Frage nach der Schuld der Brüder in 50,15 ff. theologisch beantworten wollte. Im Unterschied zu J ist die theologische Deutung, die Joseph in Gen 45 bei E den Brüdern gibt, eine vorläufige Interpretation. Sie ermöglichte es, entsprechend der jahwistischen Vorlage zur Übersiedlung nach Ägypten überzugehen, ohne daß für E damit alles gesagt ist, was im Blick auf die Schuld der Brüder theologisch zu sagen war.

Läßt sich für v. 1–18 eine eindeutige Aufteilung auf J und E vornehmen, so bereiten die folgenden Verse 19–21 aα erhebliche Schwierigkeiten. Sie wirken teilweise wie eine Dublette zu v. 16–18. Das läßt sich zwar noch als beabsichtigte Doppelung erklären[134]. Die eigenartige Einleitung von v. 19 »Dir aber ist geboten« ist jedoch ein klarer Hinweis darauf, daß v. 19 nicht von Haus aus die Fortsetzung von v. 18 war[135]. Allerdings wird hier der Text häufig in Anlehnung an LXX in

---

[132] Zu dieser Bedeutung von v. 5 aα² vgl. z. B. C. Westermann 159.
[133] C. Westermann 158, betont zwar, daß aus dem Fehlen eines Objekts hervorgehe, daß die Absicht Gottes nicht nur die Familie Jakobs betreffe. V. 5 b ist aber im Zusammenhang nur sinnvoll, wenn es hier um das Leben der Brüder geht.
[134] G. W. Coats, Canaan, 47.
[135] So mit Recht H. Seebaß, Zeit, 53 f.

»Gebiete ihnen« geändert[136]. Der MT stellt jedoch gegenüber LXX eindeutig die lectio difficilior dar und muß deshalb beibehalten werden. Dadurch besteht in v. 19 zwischen der Einleitung und der Fortsetzung eine Diskrepanz. Die Befehle waren ursprünglich direkt an die Brüder gerichtet. Durch den Anfang von v. 19 wird ein notdürftiger Ausgleich mit v. 16–18 hergestellt, wo Joseph vor dem Pharao steht und von ihm einen Auftrag für die Brüder erhält. Diese seltsame Verknüpfung ist ein Hinweis darauf, daß durch sie nachträglich ein vorgegebener Text an v. 18 angeschlossen wurde. Deshalb ist v. 19–21 aα weder als Ganzes ein sekundärer Einschub[137], noch kann v. 19 allein als Glosse ausgeschieden werden[138].

Woher stammt aber der Grundbestand von v. 19? Zur Beantwortung dieser Frage muß weiter ausgeholt werden. Verschiedentlich wird v. 19 ohne den Anfang zu J gerechnet[139]. Joseph habe hier den Brüdern die Mitnahme von Wagen aufgetragen. Dafür wird auf v. 27 verwiesen, wonach Joseph seinem Vater Wagen gesandt hat, um ihn zu tragen. Diese Aussage stamme ebenfalls aus J. Nun ist jedoch 45,19 eng verwandt mit 46,5b. An beiden Stellen haben die Wagen den Zweck, den Vater, die Kinder und die Frauen nach Ägypten zu bringen. In 46,5b heißt der Vater jedoch Jakob, und es wird ausdrücklich gesagt, daß der Pharao die Wagen gesandt hat. H. Gunkel streicht zwar hier »Jakob« und »Pharao« als spätere Auffüllungen[140]. Das ist jedoch bei »Pharao« nicht möglich. Es muß gesagt werden, wer die Wagen gesandt hat. Da Joseph nicht unmittelbar zuvor genannt wird, kann er hier auch nicht implizit das Subjekt gewesen sein. Dann dürfte in diesem Halbvers aber auch »Jakob« ursprünglich sein.

Spricht schon diese Beobachtung dagegen, daß 46,5b aus J stammt, so wird das durch weitere Überlegungen bestätigt. Bei J müßte dieser Halbvers auf 46,1aα »da brach Israel auf und alles, was ihm gehörte« folgen. Danach kommt 46,5b aber zu spät. Hier wird von Vorbereitungen unmittelbar vor dem Aufbruch berichtet. Außerdem schließt 46,28 – wie oben bereits erwähnt J – schlecht an v. 5b an. In 46,28 wird das Objekt »Juda« betont vorangestellt, während der Vater als Subjekt nicht ausdrücklich genannt wird. Das ist verständlich, wenn der Vers ursprünglich direkt auf 46,1aα folgte. Nur so ergibt sich auch ein lückenloser Zusammenhang. Wohl aus diesem Grund hat H. Gunkel angenommen, daß 46,5b ursprünglich vor 46,1aα stand[141]. Es ist

---
[136] Vgl. z.B. BHS; H. Gunkel und O. Procksch z. St.
[137] So z.B. O. Eißfeldt, Hexateuch-Synopse, 93*f.
[138] So H. Seebaß, Zeit, 54.
[139] So z.B. H. Gunkel 460; L. Ruppert, Josephserzählung, 116.
[140] H. Gunkel 463.
[141] H. Gunkel 461.

aber schwer zu begründen, warum später eine Umstellung vorgenommen worden sein sollte. Außerdem ist, wie unten gezeigt werden soll, die Voraussetzung von H. Gunkel nicht richtig, daß 45,27 aβ mit den Wagen zu J gehört. 46,5b stammt also mit Sicherheit nicht aus J. Das gilt dann auch für 45,19.

46,5b schließt aber auch nicht glatt an v. 5a aus E an[142]. Nach v. 5a »da machte sich Jakob auf von Beerseba« kommt v. 5b ebenfalls zu spät. Außerdem hat bei E Jakob bereits in v. 1aβ seinen Wohnort verlassen. Nun wird 46,6 mit Recht zu P gerechnet, wie die Ähnlichkeit der Formulierungen in v. 6 mit 12,4b. 5 und 36,6 zeigt. 46,6 setzt aber voraus, daß bei P zuvor von einem Subjekt im Plural die Rede war. Ein solches Subjekt enthält v. 5b. V. 5b-6 bilden einen geschlossenen Zusammenhang. Zunächst werden in v. 5b, wie in 12,5 und 36,6, die Personen und danach in v. 6 der Besitz erwähnt. Zwar weicht 46,5b darin von den anderen priesterschriftlichen Stellen ab, daß hier nicht der Ahnherr, sondern seine Söhne Subjekt sind. Aber das gilt auf jeden Fall auch für 46,6 und spricht deshalb nicht dagegen, daß auch v. 5b aus P stammt. Für P spricht positiv, daß in Ex 1,1a.2-4.5b die Söhne Jakobs aufgeführt werden, die nach Ägypten kamen[143]. Sie werden hier wie in 46,5b als *bny yśr'l* bezeichnet. Daraus ergibt sich für P folgender Sprachgebrauch: P erwähnt in 35,10, daß Jakob den Namen Israel von Gott erhalten hat. Diese Umbenennung spielt aber für den Erzvater selbst bei P keine Rolle, er heißt hier durchgehend Jakob. Seine Söhne werden jedoch als »die Söhne Israels/die Israeliten« bezeichnet, sobald es um die Übersiedlung nach Ägypten geht. Deshalb können in 46,5b »Jakob« und »die Söhne Israels/die Israeliten« nebeneinanderstehen. Mit *bny yśr'l* betont P bewußt, daß zwischen den Söhnen Jakobs und den Israeliten eine Kontinuität besteht. Sie stellen bereits das Volk Israel dar, sobald es um ihre Übersiedlung nach Ägypten geht.

Aus 46,5b folgt somit, daß 45,19 abgesehen von »dir ist geboten« aus P stammt. Daran schließen sich v. 20 und v. 21aα glatt an. Tatsächlich besteht auch zwischen v. 21aα und v. 21aβ eine Spannung. Nach v. 21aα »da taten so die Söhne Israels/die Israeliten« wurden die Anweisungen des Pharao ausgeführt. Danach kommt v. 21aβ »da gab ihnen Joseph Wagen nach dem Befehl des Pharao« zu spät. Hier kommt somit eine andere Darstellung zu Wort, nach der Joseph aus eigener Initiative den Brüdern Wagen mitgab. »Nach dem Befehl des Pharao« ist als redaktionelle Verknüpfung mit v. 19-21aα von dem Endredaktor des Pentateuch eingeschoben worden.

Dieser Redaktor hat auch am Anfang von v. 19 Joseph als Vermittler der folgenden Anweisungen eingefügt. Daraus geht hervor, daß sie

---

[142] Zu 46,5a vgl. IIf.
[143] Zur literarischen Analyse von Ex 1,1-5 vgl. W. H. Schmidt, Exodus, 1974ff., 9ff.

bei P von dem Pharao direkt an die Brüder gerichtet wurden. Dem entspricht, daß nach 46,5b Pharao die Wagen gesandt hat. Da bei E in v. 17f. aber nur Joseph vor dem Pharao steht, machte der Redaktor v. 19f. zu einem Auftrag an Joseph für die Brüder. Bei P standen somit die Brüder vor dem Pharao[144]. Er gebot ihnen, Wagen für ihre Frauen, Kinder und für den Vater mitzunehmen, und nach Ägypten zu übersiedeln. Seine Anweisungen unterstrich er mit v. 20. Die Brüder brauchen sich über die Hausgeräte, die sie in Kanaan zurücklassen, nicht grämen, weil ihnen das Beste des ganzen Landes Ägypten gehören soll. Zwar heißt es in 46,6, daß die Brüder ihren Besitz nach Ägypten mitgenommen haben. Aber das widerspricht insofern nicht v. 20, weil der Pharao mit seinen Worten unterstreichen will, daß die Brüder eine bevorzugte Behandlung erfahren sollen. Außerdem ist in 45,20 von den »Hausgeräten«, in 46,6 aber von dem in Kanaan erworbenen Besitz die Rede. Nach v. 21 aα haben die Brüder diese Anweisungen ausgeführt. 46,5b schließt glatt an 45,21 aα an und dürfte bei P auch direkt auf 45,21 aα gefolgt sein.

Mit 45,19–21 aα setzt P die elohistische Darstellung voraus und steigert sie. Die Brüder werden nicht mehr durch Vermittlung des Joseph, sondern vom Pharao direkt aufgefordert, nach Ägypten zu übersiedeln. Aus E stammen auch die Wagen. Während sie aber bei E Joseph aus eigenem Entschluß den Brüdern mitgab, hat sie nach P der Pharao gesandt. P ist somit hier die literarische Neugestaltung der elohistischen Darstellung, die der Verfasser aus dem jehowistischen Werk kannte. Er will betonen, daß die Übersiedlung nach Ägypten auf den Wunsch des Pharao hin erfolgte, der den Brüdern dafür auch seine besondere Fürsorge zuteil werden ließ, ja er hatte ihnen sogar zugesagt, daß es ihnen in Ägypten an nichts fehlen solle. Wie der Vater die Rückkehr der Brüder aufnahm, wird von P übergangen. In 46,5b–6 kommt es nur darauf an, daß Jakob tatsächlich mit seiner ganzen Familie nach Ägypten kam. So wird bei P einerseits die Fürsorge Pharaos ausgemalt, die Darstellung aber andererseits auf die Übersiedlung nach Ägypten konzentriert. Das war offenbar für P der wesentliche Punkt.

Für die Analyse von v. 21 aβ–28 geht man am besten von v. 25–28 aus. In v. 25 wird berichtet, daß die Brüder zu ihrem Vater zurückkehren. Er heißt hier Jakob, der Vers gehört somit zu E. Daran schließt sich v. 26 glatt an. Die Brüder teilen dem Vater mit, daß Joseph noch lebt und Herrscher über das ganze Land Ägypten ist. Die Aussage über seine führende Stellung ist nicht indirekte Rede, sondern *ky* wird hier

---

[144] Dem entspricht, daß in 47,7ff. bei P Jakob vor dem Pharao steht, vgl. IIg. Auch O. Procksch 553, der 45,17.18 a.bβ.19.21 aα zu P rechnet, und H. Seebaß, Zeit, 54, nach dem v. 16–18. 20. 21 aα zu P gehören, haben erkannt, daß P in Gen 45 vertreten ist. Ihre Zuweisungen lassen sich allerdings nicht halten.

als deiktische Partikel gebraucht: »Joseph lebt noch, ja er ist Herrscher über das ganze Land Ägypten«[145]. Diese Formulierung entspricht 45,8 (E). Der Vater aber glaubt den Brüdern nicht. Darauf teilen sie ihm in v. 27 aα zunächst die Worte Josephs mit. Das bezieht sich eindeutig auf v. 9–14, wo bei J Joseph den Brüdern eine Botschaft an den Vater mitgegeben hat. Tatsächlich wird im jetzigen Wortlaut von v. 27 der Vater auf doppelte Weise davon überzeugt, daß die Brüder die Wahrheit sagen: Einmal durch die Worte Josephs und zum anderen durch die Wagen, die Joseph gesandt hat. Wie die von E in v. 5 aα².b.8 berichteten Worte Josephs an die Brüder den Vater davon überzeugt haben sollten, daß Joseph wirklich lebt, müßte ein Rätsel bleiben. Die Begründung mit den Wagen ist auch völlig zureichend. V. 27 aα ist somit J, v. 27 aβ.b E. V. 28 gehört wegen Israel zu J und folgte hier direkt auf v. 27 aα. Der Vater erwähnt wie bei J in 46,30 seinen Tod.

Damit geht aus v. 27 hervor, daß das Motiv der Wagen aus E stammt. Es findet sich auch in v. 21 aβ*: »Da gab ihnen Joseph Wagen«. Das ist die notwendige Vorbereitung für v. 27 aβ.b, so daß auch v. 21 aβ zu E gehört. Verschiedentlich hat man zwar zwischen v. 17 und v. 21 aβ einen Widerspruch gesehen. Der Pharao rede in v. 17 nur von Lasttieren, und Joseph schenke in v. 23 dem Vater Esel und Eselinnen, aber keine Wagen[146]. Schon W. Rudolph hat jedoch mit Recht darauf hingewiesen, daß Esel und Wagen eine unterschiedliche Funktion haben[147]. Die Esel sind zum Transport des Getreides und der Geschenke bestimmt, die Wagen aber dazu, Jakob nach Ägypten zu bringen (v. 27 aβ). Deshalb besteht hier keine Spannung. Zu v. 21 aβ – ohne: »auf Befehl des Pharao« – ist v. 21 b–24 die Fortsetzung. V. 21 aβ und v. 21 b sind durch das gleiche Subjekt miteinander verbunden. Die Formulierung »von dem Besten Ägyptens« in v. 23 begegnet ähnlich in v. 18. Zwar wollen O. Procksch und L. Ruppert[148] v. 22–24 a wegen der Erwähnung der Geschenke zu J stellen. Aber v. 22 knüpft mit der Inversion deutlich an v. 21 b an. Zu E gehören somit: V. 21 aβ*.b–26.27 aβ.b, zu J v. 27 aα.28.

Am Schluß von Gen 45 läßt somit der Redaktor vor allem E zu Wort kommen. Das ist darin begründet, daß hier die jahwistische Darstellung wesentlich knapper gewesen sein dürfte. Bei J haben die Brüder bereits in 44,1 f.* so viel Getreide bekommen, wie sie tragen konnten. Joseph brauchte sich deshalb um den Proviant für ihre Reise nicht mehr zu kümmern, nachdem er sich ihnen zu erkennen gegeben hatte. Außerdem treibt bei J Joseph in 45,9.13 die Brüder zur Eile an. Das spricht

---

[145] Vgl. W. Rudolph, BZAW 63, 164 f.
[146] H. Gunkel 457.
[147] W. Rudolph, BZAW 63, 164.
[148] O. Procksch 262; L. Ruppert, Josephserzählung, 116.

dafür, daß nach v. 14 sofort ihre Rückkehr zum Vater geschildert wurde. Geschenke waren hier überflüssig, weil der Vater rasch nach Ägypten kommen sollte. Wegen v. 9–14 nahm aber der Redaktor v. 27 aα aus J auf. Ihm kam es darauf an, daß die Brüder die Botschaft Josephs tatsächlich ausgerichtet haben. V. 28 aus J ist jetzt eine gute Weiterführung von v. 27 b E, aus der hervorgeht, wie der Vater zu Joseph steht. Aus diesem Grund hat der Redaktor v. 28 an v. 27 b angeschlossen. Auch am Schluß von Gen 45 zeigt sich, daß der Redaktor jeweils der ausführlicheren Darstellung den Vorzug gegeben hat und sie durch Stücke aus der knapperen Fassung ergänzte, weil er eine möglichst vollständige Wiedergabe seiner Quellen erreichen wollte. Dabei konnte der Redaktor durch Aufnahme des E-Fadens eine abgerundete Komposition schaffen. V. 22 ist nun die Weiterführung von 43, 34. Hatte Joseph dort die Brüder unter Bevorzugung Benjamins mit einem gemeinsamen Mahl ausgezeichnet, so beschenkt er sie nun, wobei Benjamin eine besonders große Gabe erhält. Die Geschenke an den Vater in v. 23 korrespondieren dem Geschenk, das der Vater in Gen 43 Joseph überbringen ließ. Auf diese Beziehungen hat vor allem L. Ruppert hingewiesen[149]. Sie sind jedoch gegen L. Ruppert erst von dem Redaktor hergestellt worden.

Bei J steht in v. 27 aα.28 wieder das Verhältnis zwischen dem Vater und Joseph im Mittelpunkt. Für den Vater ist an der Botschaft Josephs nur wichtig, daß dieser Sohn noch lebt. Weder die hohe Stellung Josephs, noch seine Zusagen wegen der andauernden Hungersnot spielen für ihn eine Rolle. Es kommt dem Vater lediglich darauf an, daß er vor seinem Tod nochmals Joseph sehen kann. Deshalb will er sich auf den Weg machen.

Im Unterschied zu J werden bei E die Brüder vor ihrer Abreise von Joseph mit Proviant für den Weg versorgt (v. 21 b). Das entspricht 42, 25, wo die Brüder bei der ersten Reise außer Getreide auch Nahrung für den Weg erhalten haben. In v. 22 f. wird von den Geschenken Josephs für die Brüder und den Vater berichtet. Hier hat Joseph nun auch bei E zu Benjamin und dem Vater eine besonders enge Beziehung, da diese beiden größere Gaben erhalten als die Brüder. Das ist jedoch ein Nebenmotiv, aus dem nochmals hervorgeht, daß E von J literarisch abhängig ist. Aus der bisherigen Darstellung von E ergibt sich nicht, warum Joseph jetzt Benjamin bevorzugt. Noch in v. 15 behandelt Joseph alle Brüder gleich. Auch die Fortsetzung zeigt, daß die Verse bei E keine tragende Funktion haben. In v. 27 aβ.b wird der Vater nicht durch die Geschenke, sondern durch die Wagen davon überzeugt, daß die Brüder die Wahrheit gesagt haben. Das ist angesichts der reichen Ga-

---

[149] L. Ruppert, Josephserzählung, 116.

ben, die Joseph dem Vater sendet, erstaunlich. Gerade dadurch beweist aber diese Stelle, daß es sich bei v. 22 f. um ein Nebenmotiv handelt.

E greift hier Elemente der jahwistischen Darstellung auf und prägt sie um. Die Geschenke an die Brüder sind ein zusätzliches Zeichen jener Versöhnung, die Joseph bereits mit v. 15 gestiftet hatte. Die Quelle für E ist 43,34, wo bei J die Brüder Anteil am Essen erhalten hatten und Benjamin eine fünffache Portion bekam. Bei E erhält er nicht nur wie die Brüder ein Feierkleid sondern fünf. Während bei J aber 43,34 zu den retardierenden Elementen gehört, die die Spannung steigern, wird bei E daraus ein zusätzlicher und für die Handlung nicht notwendiger Gunsterweis Josephs. Daß Benjamin außer den Feierkleidern noch Geld erhält, dürfte dadurch bedingt sein, daß auch bei E die Brüder auf der ersten Reise ihr Geld zurückerhalten haben. Jetzt wird Benjamin von Joseph ebenfalls mit Geld beschenkt. Damit wandelt E zugleich das Motiv des silbernen Bechers ab, der bei J im Sack Benjamins versteckt wurde. Die Geschenke an den Vater in v. 23 sind eine Umkehrung der Gaben, die bei J der Vater nach 43,11 Joseph überbringen ließ. Gab dort der Vater den Brüdern etwas von den »besten Erzeugnissen des Landes« mit auf den Weg, so sendet bei E Joseph dem Vater »von dem Besten Ägyptens«. Wurden aber bei J die Geschenke von dem Vater mitgegeben, um »den Mann«, dessen Verhalten für ihn und die Brüder rätselhaft war, günstig zu stimmen, so sind die Gaben Josephs an den Vater bei E lediglich ein Zeichen für die hervorragende Stellung, die Joseph in Ägypten einnimmt. Wieder tritt ein Motiv, das bei J für den Ablauf der Handlung wichtig war, in seiner Umprägung bei E ganz an den Rand. Daß der Vater in v. 23 außerdem noch Nahrung für seinen Weg nach Ägypten erhält, entspricht dem Reiseproviant für die Brüder. Auch der Vater mußte für seinen Weg von Joseph versorgt werden. In v. 22 f. nimmt E also Motive aus J auf und prägt sie um. Dabei verlieren sie ihre Bedeutung für den Ablauf, den sie bei J hatten.

In v. 24 bringt E dann wieder sein Thema »Joseph und die Brüder« zur Geltung. Joseph gibt den Brüdern zum Abschied die Mahnung mit: »Ereifert euch nicht auf dem Weg«. Damit kümmert sich Joseph um das Verhältnis der Brüder zueinander[150]. Sie sollen, ohne daß es zu einem neuen Streit kommt, in die Heimat zurückkehren. Mit dem Schluß in v. 25.26.27 aß.b setzt E einen etwas anderen Akzent als J. Die Brüder betonen vor dem Vater die hohe Stellung, die Joseph in Ägypten erlangt hat. Sie ist es offenbar, die den Vater zur Übersiedlung nach Ägypten bewegen soll. Der Vater kann den Brüdern freilich zunächst nicht glauben. Das entspricht in gewisser Weise der Reaktion der Brüder, als sich Joseph ihnen zu erkennen gab. Sie konnten vor Bestürzung Joseph nicht antworten (v. 3). Dem Vater aber wird sein Herz kalt, weil er den

---

[150] Vgl. auch C. Westermann 163.

Brüdern nicht glauben kann. Erst die von Joseph mitgesandten Wagen, die die Worte der Brüder bestätigen, lassen seinen Geist wieder aufleben. Auch der Vater ist nun überzeugt, daß Joseph lebt und in Ägypten herrscht.

Selbst in Kap. 45, das allgemein als schwierig gilt, lassen sich somit J und E klar voneinander abheben. Zu J gehören: V. 1.4.5 aα¹.β.6.7. 9–14...27 aα.28; zu E: V. 2 a.bα.3...5 aα².b.8.15–18.21 aβ*.b.22–26. 27 aβ.b. Dabei hat sich bestätigt, daß J und E in der Josephsgeschichte thematisch verschieden ausgerichtet sind. Bei J liegt das Gewicht auf der besonderen Beziehung zwischen Joseph und dem Vater, bei E hingegen auf dem Verhältnis zwischen Joseph und den Brüdern. Das ist bei E nur in v. 22 f. anders, aber die besonderen Geschenke Josephs für Benjamin und den Vater gehören zu den Nebenmotiven, die sich verschiedentlich auch sonst bei E finden, und an denen besonders deutlich wird, daß E von J literarisch abhängig ist. Es konnte auch durchsichtig gemacht werden, wie der Redaktor vorgegangen ist. Er wollte seine Vorlagen möglichst vollständig aufnehmen. Dadurch kommt es vor allem in v. 3–8 zu Doppelungen, mit denen der Redaktor das Gewicht dieser Szene unterstreicht.

Außer J und E ist in Gen 45 auch P mit v. 19*–21 aα vertreten, wie aus der redaktionellen Verklammerung am Anfang von v. 19 hervorgeht. Außerdem stellt das Stück zu v. 16–18 eine Dublette dar. In der Priesterschrift wurden die Brüder Josephs von dem Pharao aufgefordert, mit ihren Familien und dem Vater nach Ägypten zu übersiedeln. Der Endredaktor hat diesen Abschnitt in die jehowistische Darstellung eingefügt, weil er 46,5 b.6, wo wieder P zu Wort kommt, vorbereitet. Wegen v. 16–18 konnte er aber nicht wie P den Pharao direkt zu den Brüdern reden lassen. Deshalb machte er mit »Dir aber ist geboten« am Anfang von v. 19 Joseph zum Übermittler. Er hat auch zum Ausgleich mit v. 19 in v. 21 aβ die Worte »nach dem Befehl des Pharao« eingefügt.

f) Gen 46, 1–34

Im vorangegangenen Abschnitt wurde bereits erwähnt, daß hier v. 1 aα.28–34 aus J stammen, da der Vater Israel genannt wird, und in v. 28 Juda vorkommt. In v. 1 aα.28–30 geht es darum, daß sich der Vater und Joseph begegnen. Hier hat der Begriff »sehen« die Funktion eines Leitwortes. Er steht schon in 45,28. Der Vater will sich auf den Weg machen, um Joseph zu sehen, bevor er stirbt. In v. 1 aα bricht Israel auf, er sendet in v. 28 Juda voraus zu Joseph, damit sich dieser vor ihm in Gosen ›sehen läßt‹. Nach MT wäre zwar in v. 28 aβ zu lesen »um Weisung zu geben (lᵉhôrot) vor ihm nach Gosen«, und I. Willi-Plein hat jüngst diese Lesart verteidigt. Sie sei so zu verstehen, »dass Josef ›Anweisung geben‹, d. h. sozusagen Passierscheine ausstellen soll, um im voraus einen problemlosen Grenzübertritt zu gewährleisten«[151]. Aber die Brüder konnten auf ihren Reisen ohne die Schwierigkeiten zu Joseph kommen, die nach I. Willi-Plein hier der Vater befürchtet. Zudem ist ihre Interpretation der Versuch, einer schwierigen Lesart eine Bedeutung abzugewinnen, die sich aus ihr selbst nicht gerade nahelegt. MT ergibt somit hier keinen Sinn. Wie J. Wellhausen erkannt hat, ist hier mit Sam »l^{e}herā'ōt = um sich sehen zu lassen« zu lesen[152]. Der Vater wartet nicht, bis er in Gosen angelangt ist, sondern er sendet schon bei seinem Aufbruch Juda zu Joseph. Damit unterstreicht der Verfasser, wie sehr es dem Vater darauf ankommt, Joseph zu sehen. Die besondere Beziehung zwischen dem Vater und Joseph führt dazu, daß der Vater es kaum erwarten kann, Joseph wiederzusehen. Ihr entspricht das Verhalten Josephs in v. 29. Joseph läßt sich bei dem Vater in Gosen sehen[153], fällt ihm um den Hals und weint lange. Das ist eine Steigerung zu 45,14. Dort war Joseph Benjamin aus Freude über das Wiedersehen weinend um den Hals gefallen. Jetzt weint er, weil er den Vater wiedersehen darf, und er weint lange, weil seine Verbindung mit dem Vater noch enger ist als mit Benjamin.

In dem Motiv, daß Joseph weinte, wird die Linienführung der jahwistischen Josephsgeschichte besonders deutlich. Es begegnet erstmals in 43,30. Dort kann Joseph seiner Freude, Benjamin zu sehen, noch nicht Ausdruck geben und weint in seiner Kammer. In 45,14 kann er endlich am Halse Benjamins weinen, und in 46,29 fällt er dem Vater um den Hals und weint lange. So drückt das Weinen Josephs seine besondere Verbindung mit dem Vater und mit Benjamin aus. Mit 46,29 ist ein vorläufiger Höhepunkt der Darstellung erreicht. Das kommt auch in den Worten des Vaters von v. 30 zum Ausdruck: Nachdem Israel gesehen hat, daß Joseph lebt, will er gerne sterben. Meinte er einst, daß er trauernd zu seinem Sohn in die š^e'l hinabsteigen müsse (37, 35 a),

---

[151] I. Willi-Plein, Aspekte, 308 Anm. 11.
[152] J. Wellhausen, Composition, 59; vgl. auch L. Ruppert, Josephserzählung, 140. Dagegen wollen O. Procksch 263, und C. Westermann 179, nach LXX »l^{e}hiqqārôt = um ihm zu begegnen« lesen. Dann läßt sich jedoch graphisch nicht erklären, wie MT entstanden ist. Außerdem wird dabei übersehen, daß r'h die Funktion eines Leitwortes hat.
[153] Das ni. von r'h steht mit 'l überwiegend bei Gotteserscheinungen (z. B. Gen 12,7; 18,1; 26,2). Es kommt aber in I Reg 18,1 f.15 für das Auftreten des Elia vor Ahab vor, das sich von einer Gotteserscheinung doch stärker abhebt, als L. Ruppert, Josephserzählung, 140, annimmt. Die Konjektur von C. Westermann 180, »und als er ihn sah« hat an der Textüberlieferung keinerlei Anhaltspunkt. Durch sie wird zudem die Entsprechung zwischen v. 28 und v. 29 zerstört, die C. Westermann nicht erkannt hat. Vielleicht soll durch die Wahl des ni. in v. 28 f. die hohe Stellung Josephs betont werden. Dafür könnte sprechen, daß in v. 29 ausdrücklich gesagt wird, daß er seinen Wagen anspannen läßt. Als hoher Beamter reist Joseph natürlich mit einem Wagen.

so kann er nun getrost sterben. Auch hier zeigt sich, daß das Verhältnis zwischen dem Vater und Joseph die jahwistische Darstellung bestimmt, und daß in sie die besondere Beziehung Josephs und des Vaters zu Benjamin eingebaut ist. Der Vater war über den Verlust Josephs untröstlich. Sollte aber auch Benjamin verloren gehen, so würde er mit »Kummer« bzw. »im Bösen« in die שאל hinabgebracht werden (42,38; 44,29.31). Er durfte aber Benjamin behalten und Joseph nochmals sehen. So bildet 46,30 auch im Blick auf den Vater eine erste Abrundung der jahwistischen Josephsgeschichte.

Da der Vater mit seinem Tod rechnet, ist in v. 31–34, wo Joseph die Brüder über seinen Plan mit dem Pharao informiert, von ihm nicht mehr die Rede. Der Text ist hier an zwei Stellen später erweitert worden. In v. 31a fehlt »und zu dem Hause seines Vaters« in LXX. Diese Worte sind im MT nachgetragen worden, weil in v. 31b außer den Brüdern auch das Haus des Vaters erwähnt wird[154]. V. 32aβ »denn Männer von Viehbesitz sind sie« unterbricht den Zusammenhang, der deutlich zwischen v. 32aα und 32b besteht[155]. Da in v. 34 die Brüder vor dem Pharao sagen sollten, daß sie »Männer von Viehbesitz« sind, war ein Späterer der Meinung, daß das schon Joseph dem Pharao sagen wollte und fügte deshalb v. 32aβ ein.

In dem Grundbestand von v. 31–34 teilt Joseph den Brüdern mit, daß er dem Pharao ihre Ankunft und das Kommen des Hauses seines Vaters melden will und gibt ihnen Anweisungen, wie sie sich verhalten sollen. Wie bereits unter e) ausgeführt wurde, geht aus diesem Abschnitt eindeutig hervor, daß hier die Übersiedlung nach Ägypten ohne Einladung des Pharao erfolgte. Joseph will dem Pharao sagen, daß seine Verwandten mit ihrem gesamten Besitz zu ihm gekommen sind. Es handelt sich also nicht um einen kurzen Besuch. Deshalb muß der Pharao eine Entscheidung über ihren Aufenthaltsort treffen. Joseph will mit seinen Worten bei dem Pharao und mit den Instruktionen für die Brüder erreichen, daß ihnen das Land Gosen zugewiesen wird, das Joseph bereits in seiner Botschaft von 45,9ff. für den Vater und seine Familie ausgewählt hatte.

Auffällig ist, daß Joseph hier großen Wert darauf legt, daß wirklich das Land Gosen zum Aufenthaltsort bestimmt wird. Daraus geht wieder hervor, daß die jahwistische Josephsgeschichte nicht von J ge-

---

[154] H. Gunkel 464; C. Westermann 185.
[155] H. Gunkel 464; W. Rudolph, BZAW 63, 165; C. Westermann 186f. H. Seebaß, Zeit, 82 Anm. 15 hält auch v. 33.34a für eine Erweiterung, »um neben dem Kleinvieh der Brüder ... auch Großviehbesitz nachzuweisen«. Das Großvieh wird aber auch in 45,10 und 46,32b genannt. Warum v. 34b nicht gut an v. 34a anschließt, wie H. Seebaß meint, ist m. E. nicht einsichtig. Ebensowenig läßt sich daraus, daß Joseph in 47,2 von sich aus fünf Brüder zum Pharao bringt, während er in 46,33 erwartet, daß der Pharao die Brüder rufen läßt, schließen, daß v. 33.34a sekundär ist.

schaffen wurde. Bei J wird außerhalb der Josephsgeschichte Gosen nie erwähnt[156]. Dann ist die Betonung von Gosen in der Josephsgeschichte ein deutliches Indiz dafür, daß J hier eine Vorlage in sein Werk aufgenommen hat. Ihrem Verfasser war es im Unterschied zu J wichtig, daß die Familie Israels in Gosen angesiedelt wurde. Daraus stellt sich die Frage, warum er in dieser Weise an Gosen interessiert war. Nach C. Westermann haben allerdings die Anweisungen an die Brüder in v. 33 f. einen anderen Sinn: »Der Pharao soll wissen, daß seine Brüder keinerlei Ambitionen haben, nun auch hoch hinaus zu wollen, protegiert von ihrem Bruder, Pharaos höchstem Minister.«[157] Aber diese Interpretation wird durch v. 34 eindeutig widerlegt. Danach sollen die Brüder nach den Anweisungen Josephs vor dem Pharao reden, »damit ihr im Lande Gosen bleiben dürft«. Daß der Plan Josephs in 47,1 ff. ohne Schwierigkeiten in Erfüllung geht, bestätigt nur, daß er ihn klug eingefädelt hat. Es kommt dem Verfasser somit tatsächlich auf Gosen als Aufenthaltsort an.

Das läßt sich mit H. Gunkel nur so erklären, daß Joseph die Möglichkeit schaffen will, daß die Nachkommen Israels später einmal Ägypten wieder verlassen. Aus diesem Grund will er sie in der Nähe der ägyptischen Grenze ansiedeln[158]. Dagegen hat H.-C. Schmitt eingewandt, daß die Juda-Schicht mit keinem Wort andeute, daß sie auf die Auszugsgeschichte vorausblicke[159]. Joseph wähle in 45,10 Gosen, damit der Vater in seiner Nähe wohne. »Offensichtlich denkt die Juda-Schicht hier an eine völlig problemlose Rückkehr der unter Joseph Eingewanderten.«[160] Damit wird aber einerseits 45,10 überinterpretiert. Die Stelle besagt nicht, daß Gosen nahe an dem Herrschaftssitz des Pharao liegt, wo sich Joseph aufhält, sondern der Vater ist Joseph nahe, wenn er in Ägypten ist. 46,29 erweckt durchaus nicht den Eindruck, daß sich Joseph in unmittelbarer Nähe von Gosen befindet. Zum anderen bleibt hier ungeklärt, warum Joseph alles unternimmt, damit seine Verwandten in Gosen wohnen dürfen.

Dieses Motiv setzt somit deutlich eine Überlieferung von dem Auszug voraus. Ihre konkrete Fassung läßt sich aus der jahwistischen Josephsgeschichte nicht erschließen, da es ihrem Verfasser nur darum geht, daß Joseph bereits bei der Übersiedlung nach Ägypten die Möglichkeit geschaffen hat, daß die Nachkommen Israels später Ägypten wieder verlassen. Man kann aber fragen, ob er nicht die bei E erhaltene

---

[156] Ex 8,18; 9,26 stammen m. E. nicht von J, sondern von dem Jehowisten. Die Argumente können hier nicht dargelegt werden.
[157] C. Westermann 187.
[158] H. Gunkel 463 f.; vgl. auch L. Ruppert, Josephserzählung, 145.
[159] H.-C. Schmitt, BZAW 154, 124 f. Anm. 145.
[160] H.-C. Schmitt, BZAW 154, 129.

Überlieferung voraussetzt, daß Israel aus Ägypten geflohen ist[161]. Dann würde es gut verständlich, warum es dem Verfasser darauf ankommt, daß die Familie Israels an der ägyptischen Grenze in Gosen angesiedelt wird. Daß für ihn die Rückkehr problemlos gewesen sein müsse, wie H.-C. Schmitt meint, läßt sich aus seiner Darstellung schon deshalb nicht entnehmen, weil diese Zukunft nicht sein Thema ist. Der Verfasser weist aber mit 46,31–34 und mit 45,7 über den Gegenstand seiner Darstellung hinaus. Was sich damals ereignet hat, war für die künftige Geschichte von Bedeutung. Die Übersiedlung nach Ägypten ermöglichte es, daß die Familie Israels weiterlebte, und ihre Ansiedlung im Lande Gosen war die Voraussetzung, daß die Nachkommen Israels später Ägypten wieder verlassen konnten.

Der Abschnitt v. 1 aβ-5 a bildet eine eigene Szene. Das geht schon daraus hervor, daß er durch v. 1 aβ: »da kam er nach Beerseba« und v. 5 a: »da brach Jakob auf von Beerseba« gerahmt ist. H. Gunkel, der das Stück E zuweist, hält zwar v. 1 aβ für eine redaktionelle Verknüpfung, weil Jakob bei E in Beerseba wohne[162], aber H.-C. Schmitt hat mit Recht betont, daß die Opfer Jakobs in v. 1 b als etwas Besonderes dargestellt werden, und Jakob deshalb hier nicht in Beerseba wohnen könne[163]. Daß v. 1 aβ-5 a aus E stammt, legen folgende Beobachtungen nahe: Mit Ausnahme von v. 2 aα heißt der Vater Jakob. In v. 2 b wird er von Gott mit seinem Namen angerufen[164]. Gott beginnt seine Rede in v. 3 mit »Ich bin der El«, wozu sich nur bei E in Gen 31,13 eine Parallele findet.

Freilich wird der Abschnitt häufig als ein spätes Stück angesehen. So ist er z. B. nach E. Blum, nach dem die Josephsgeschichte zu Anfang des 8. Jh.s im Nordreich entstanden ist, im Zusammenhang mit der exilischen Komposition der Vätergeschichte gebildet worden[165]. Tatsächlich entspricht er nicht dem Thema der elohistischen Josephsgeschichte. Geht es in ihr um Joseph und die Brüder, so steht hier eindeutig der Vater im Mittelpunkt. Auch inhaltlich bestehen erhebliche Unterschiede: »Die nächtliche Vision und Audition eines Erzvaters am Heiligen Ort, die Selbstoffenbarung des Gottes der Väter, die Nachkommenschaftsverheißung und die Beistandszusage sind der Atmosphäre der Josephnovelle ganz fremd.«[166] Außerdem bezieht sich nach L. Ruppert die

---

[161] Ex 14,5 a.
[162] H. Gunkel 461.
[163] H.-C. Schmitt, BZAW 154, 59.
[164] Vgl. IIa zu 37,13 b.
[165] E. Blum, Die Komposition der Vätergeschichte, 1984, 297 ff.; vgl. zu seiner Interpretation der Josephsgeschichte 229 ff. Zu 46,1 aβ-5 a vgl. u. a. auch W. Rudolph, BZAW 63, 149. 177 ff.; L. Ruppert, Josephserzählung, 130 ff.; D. B. Redford, VT. S 20, 18–20; H.-C. Schmitt, BZAW 154, 59–62; C. Westermann 169 ff.
[166] H. Donner, Gestalt, 29.

Aufforderung in v. 3: »Fürchte dich nicht, nach Ägypten hinabzuziehen« auf Gen 26,2, wo Jahwe Isaak gebietet: »Ziehe nicht hinab nach Ägypten«. »Derselbe Gott, der Gott seines Vaters, gestattet dies nun dem ›Jakob‹«[167]. D.B. Redford ist der Auffassung, daß 46,2b–4 so eng mit Gen 26,24 verwandt ist, daß man annehmen müsse, daß v. 1–4 zumindest nach 26,24 überarbeitet worden sei[168]. Weder 26,2 noch 26,24 gehören aber zu E. Schließlich fällt in v. 2 die Formulierung »in Gesichten der Nacht« auf, da sie im Alten Testament sonst nicht vorkommt. Für den Begriff »*mr'h* = Gesicht« gibt es höchstens in I Sam 3,15 einen Beleg vor dem 6. Jh. Das legt es nach L. Ruppert und C. Westermann ebenfalls nahe, daß der Abschnitt v. 1aβ–5a jung ist[169].

Bei einer Reihe von Forschern beruht diese Beurteilung allerdings teilweise darauf, daß entweder – wie von W. Rudolph und C. Westermann – die Existenz einer eigenen elohistischen Quellenschrift bestritten oder – wie von E. Blum – eine Urkundenhypothese überhaupt abgelehnt wird. Schon aufgrund der bisher angestellten Untersuchungen ist aber mit der selbständigen Quellenschrift E zu rechnen. Dann handelt es sich jedoch bei den genannten Beobachtungen, die für E als Verfasser von v. 1aβ–5a sprechen, um Elemente, die für den Elohisten so charakteristisch sind, daß es nicht angeht, den Abschnitt E abzusprechen. Sie finden sich sonst im Pentateuch weder bei J oder P, noch in Erweiterungen, sondern ausschließlich bei E.

Freilich läßt sich mit E nicht vereinbaren, daß der Vater in v. 2aα als Israel bezeichnet wird. In v. 2 fällt aber der harte Wechsel von Israel zu Jakob auf. Gott spricht zu Israel, er nennt ihn jedoch mit dem Namen Jakob. Auch in v. 5a heißt der Vater Jakob. Außerdem steht in v. 2a zweimal die Redeeinleitung »da sprach er«, die hier jedoch nicht die Funktion einer Gliederung hat. Beides spricht dafür, daß »zu Israel in Gesichten der Nacht« ein späterer Einschub ist. Durch v. 1b ist hinreichend klar, daß Gott zu dem Erzvater redet. Ein Späterer wollte aber das Objekt verdeutlichen und wählte dafür wegen v. 1aα Israel. Vor allem kam es ihm jedoch darauf an, daß Gott in »Gesichten der Nacht«[170] geredet hat. Eine gewisse Parallele ist dazu der späte Text Gen 15,1 ff., wo in v. 1 ebenfalls betont wird, daß das Wort Jahwes an

---

[167] L. Ruppert, Josephserzählung, 130 f.
[168] D. B. Redford, VT. S 20,20.
[169] L. Ruppert, Josephserzählung, 132; C. Westermann 171. Nach E. Blum, Komposition, 249, greift der Abschnitt in dreierlei Hinsicht auf Gen 26 zurück: Durch die Bezeichnung »Gott seines/deines Vaters« werde eine Beziehung zu der Verbindung Isaaks mit Beerseba in Gen 26 hergestellt. Jakob werde hier geboten, was Isaak verboten wurde, und die Opfer Jakobs könnten den von Isaak nach 26,25 in Beerseba errichteten Altar voraussetzen. Außerdem bestehe in der Mehrungsverheißung und dem Befehl zum Aufbruch eine Beziehung zu Gen 12,1–3.
[170] Möglicherweise ist der Singular zu lesen, vgl. z.B. H. Gunkel z. St.

Abraham »im Gesicht (*mḥzh*)« erging. An beiden Stellen werden Erzväter wesentlich stärker im Lichte der Prophetie gesehen, als es für Abraham schon bei dem Elohisten der Fall ist, der in Gen 20,7 Abraham als Prophet bezeichnet. Ursprünglich lautete v. 2a lediglich: »Da sprach Gott: Jakob, Jakob«. Da der Einschub in v. 2a sowohl v. 1aα aus J, als auch v. 1aβ–5a aus E voraussetzt, ist er frühestens bei der Vereinigung von J und E entstanden. Vermutlich ist er aber noch jünger.

Zwar redet nach dem Elohisten Gott sonst in Gen in der Nacht bzw. im Traum (z. B. 20,3; 31,11). Das ist auch bei den Gottesreden von 21,12 f. und 22,2 vorausgesetzt, da hier Abraham jeweils am frühen Morgen den Auftrag ausführt, den er von Gott empfangen hat. In 46,1 aβ ff. besteht aber eine andere Situation als bei den sonstigen Gottesreden. Hier sind die Worte Gottes die Antwort auf die Opfer Jakobs. Mit seinen Opfern will Jakob erreichen, daß ihm Gott seine Entscheidung über den weiteren Weg mitteilt, in der Gottesrede erfährt Jakob dann, was Gott beabsichtigt. Auch in der elohistischen Bileamperikope von Num 22 f.[171] bringt der Moabiterkönig Balak zunächst Opfer – hier allerdings Brandopfer – dar, ehe Bileam von Gott darüber informiert wird, daß er Israel nicht verwünschen darf (Num 23,1 f.* 14). Diese Opfer sind die Voraussetzung, daß Bileam erfährt, wie Gott zu dem Anliegen Balaks steht. Freilich muß sich Bileam dazu von dem Ort des Opfers entfernen. Das ist aber dadurch bedingt, daß nur Bileam Gott begegnen kann, und Balak dann von ihm die Entscheidung Gottes erfahren soll. Dagegen bedurfte Jakob keines Mittlers. Daß entgegen der sonstigen Darstellung des Elohisten in seiner Vätergeschichte Gott in Gen 46,1 aβ–5a nicht in der Nacht zu dem Erzvater spricht, ist also dadurch bedingt, daß die Gottesrede nur hier die Antwort auf das Opfer eines Erzvaters ist.

Freilich hat D. B. Redford richtig beobachtet, daß zwischen den Gottesreden in 46,2–4 und 26,24 eine Beziehung besteht. Ihr Aufbau stimmt auffällig überein. In 26,24 heißt es: »Ich bin der Gott Abrahams, deines Vaters«, das entspricht weitgehend 46,3a: »Ich bin der El, der Gott deines Vaters«. Darauf folgt jeweils: »Fürchte dich nicht«. Die Begründung ist in 26,24 im Unterschied zu 46,3 zwar nicht die Mehrung, sondern lautet »denn ich bin mit dir«. Aber die Zusage des Beistandes kommt in 46,4 vor, und in 26,24 wird Isaak nach dem Beistand Jahwes die Mehrung zugesagt. Diese zahlreichen Übereinstimmungen sind so markant, daß beide Texte nicht unabhängig voneinander entstanden sein können. Nun ist die Verheißung von 26,24 aber erst von dem Endredaktor des Pentateuch oder einem noch Späteren eingefügt wor-

---

[171] Zur literarischen Analyse vgl. L. Schmidt, Die alttestamentliche Bileamüberlieferung, BZ NF 23 (1979) 234–261.

den[172]. Daß in 26,24 Isaak von Jahwe nicht mit seinem Namen gerufen wird und in der Einleitung der Verheißung »der El« fehlt, zeigt, daß diese Verheißung nicht von dem Verfasser von 46,1aβff. stammt. Zwischen beiden Zusagen besteht zudem ein gewichtiger sachlicher Unterschied, aus dem hervorgeht, daß 26,24 erheblich jünger ist. In 26,24 erhält Isaak die Verheißung »um Abraham, meines Knechtes willen«. Wie in 22,15–18 und 26,3b–5 wird hier die Verheißung von Jahwe mit dem Gehorsam Abrahams begründet. Das fehlt in 46,3f. Diese Zusage ist nicht die Reaktion Gottes auf das Verhalten eines Erzvaters, sondern beruht ausschließlich auf dem Willen Gottes. Dann hat der Verfasser von 26,24 46,3f. als Vorlage benutzt. Da von ihm auch 26,25aα stammt, setzen die Opfer Jakobs in 46,1b nicht den dort berichteten Altarbau Isaaks voraus. Das zeitliche Verhältnis zwischen 46,2b–4 und 26,24 ist also umgekehrt als D.B. Redford annimmt.

Dagegen besteht zwischen dem Verbot in 26,2: »Ziehe nicht nach Ägypten hinab« und 46,3 keine Beziehung. In 26,2 ist »Ziehe nicht nach Ägypten hinab, wohne in dem Land, das ich dir sagen werde« eine literarisch sekundäre Erweiterung der Jahwerede, die ursprünglich nur aus v.2aα.3a bestand[173]. Von demselben Ergänzer stammt v.1aβ.γ: »außer der früheren Hungersnot, die in den Tagen Abrahams war«. Daraus geht hervor, welche Absicht er mit seinen Einschüben verfolgt. Ihm war aufgefallen, daß Abraham bei der Hungersnot von 12,10 nach Ägypten zog, Isaak aber nicht. Das erklärte er damit, daß Jahwe Isaak den Weg nach Ägypten verboten hatte. Es geht bei der Erweiterung in 26,2 also ausschließlich um den Kontrast zu 12,10. Während in 26,2 durch v.1aβ.γ der Bezug zu 12,10 eindeutig hergestellt wird, fehlt in 46,3 jeder Hinweis darauf, daß hier ein Gegensatz zu 26,2 ausgedrückt werden soll. Man mag zwar der jetzigen Komposition von Gen eine solche Beziehung entnehmen, sie hatte aber weder der Verfasser der Erweiterung in 26,2, noch der Autor von 46,3 im Blick. Schließlich muß sich die Formulierung »der Gott seines/deines Vaters« keineswegs auf Gen 26 beziehen, da Isaak auch bei E der Vater Jakobs ist. Aus den tatsächlichen oder vermeintlichen Beziehungen zwischen 46,2–4 und Kap. 26 ergibt sich somit nicht, daß 46,1aβ–5a nicht von E stammt.

Nun geht dieser Abschnitt auf keine mündliche Überlieferung zurück, sondern ist rein literarisch[174]. Er setzt durchgehend die Schilderung des Elohisten in Kap. 45 voraus. Nur aus ihr wird verständlich,

---

[172] Vgl. L. Schmidt, Pentateuch, 98 f.
[173] Vgl. L. Schmidt, Überlegungen zum Jahwisten, EvTh 37 (1977) 230–246, 232 Anm. 10.
[174] Er setzt gegen H. Gunkel 462, nicht voraus, daß bei E das Heiligtum in Beerseba durch Isaak gegründet wurde. Nach 21,33, wo »den Namen Jahwes« Zusatz ist, wurde es bei E von Abraham errichtet. Die Hinweise auf Isaak beziehen sich in 46,1aβff. ausschließlich darauf, daß Isaak der Vater Jakobs ist.

warum Jakob nach Beerseba zieht. Durch sie ist es auch bedingt, daß Gott in v. 3 Jakob nicht auffordert, nach Ägypten zu ziehen, sondern ihm für seinen Weg Mut zuspricht. Jakob ist bereits unterwegs nach Ägypten. Schon diese Beobachtungen sprechen gegen die Auffassung von H. Donner, daß zwar v. 1 aβ–5 a aus E stammt, die elohistische Darstellung von dem Aufenthalt Josephs in Ägypten aber ansonsten nicht mehr erhalten sei[175].

Gerade wenn das Stück von E gebildet wurde, wird die Frage um so dringlicher, warum der Elohist mit ihm sein Thema Joseph und die Brüder unterbrochen hat. Nun weist 46, 2 aβ–4 eine Verwandtschaft mit 31, 11.13 auf, auf die auch E. Blum aufmerksam macht[176]. In 31, 11 ruft der Bote Gottes ebenfalls Jakob mit seinem Namen an – hier freilich ohne Verdoppelung –, und dieser antwortet: »Hier bin ich«. In 31, 13 sagt er dann zu Jakob: »Ich bin der El von Bethel, wo du eine Mazzebe gesalbt, wo du mir ein Gelübde gelobt hast. Nun mache dich auf, ziehe aus diesem Land und kehre zurück in das Land deiner Verwandtschaft«. Das ist bei E ein Wendepunkt im Leben Jakobs. Er wird durch eine Gottesrede eingeleitet, in der Jakob – wie das »der El« zeigt –, feierlich an das erinnert wird, was einst in Bethel geschah. Aufgrund der Beziehung, die Gott dort gestiftet hat, erhält Jakob nun den Befehl, in die Heimat zurückzukehren. In 46, 3 ist Bethel durch »der Gott deines Vaters« ersetzt. Auch damit wird aber auf eine grundlegende Gottesbeziehung Jakobs hingewiesen. Er ruft mit seinen Opfern den Gott seines Vaters an, und dieser Gott sagt ihm u. a. seinen Beistand zu. Wie 31, 13 zeigt, handelt es sich auch hier um einen Wendepunkt im Leben Jakobs. Seine Bedeutung wird dadurch unterstrichen, daß jetzt der Gott seines Vaters zu Jakob redet. Im Unterschied zu J genügte es dem Elohisten nicht, daß der Vater nach Ägypten zog, weil er Joseph wiedersehen wollte. Für ihn war diese Übersiedlung ein so einschneidender Schritt, daß er einer theologischen Absicherung bedurfte.

Damit ist freilich die Absicht des Elohisten nicht voll erfaßt, weil sich so weder die Mehrungsverheißung in v. 3 erklären läßt, noch, warum Jakob in Beerseba und nicht in Bethel opfert. Beides wird erst aus seiner Darstellung der Väterzeit verständlich. Im Unterschied zu J und P erhalten die Erzväter bei E vor 46, 3 keine Mehrungsverheißung, in der ihnen Gott die Entstehung des Volkes Israel ankündigt[177]. Gott sagt in 21, 12 Abraham lediglich zu: »denn in Isaak soll dir Same genannt werden«. Es genügt, daß Abraham wissen darf, daß die Linie seines Geschlechts über Isaak weiterlaufen wird. Zwar heißt es dann in

---

[175] H. Donner, Gestalt, 28–30.
[176] E. Blum, Komposition, 247, der allerdings für 46, 1 aβ ff. eine literarische Abhängigkeit von 31, 11.13 postuliert.
[177] Vgl. dazu und zum folgenden L. Schmidt, Pentateuch, 96 f.

21,13: »und auch den Sohn der Magd will ich zum Volk machen«. Hier klingt an, daß auch die Nachkommenschaft von Isaak zahlreich sein wird. Der Akzent liegt aber auf der Zusage für den Sohn der Magd. Das zeigt, daß E den jahwistischen Abschnitt Gen 12, 1–3 kennt, nach dem Jahwe Abraham zu einem großen Volk machen will. Er selbst vermeidet es aber bewußt, Abraham diese Verheißung zuteil werden zu lassen[178]. Sie erhält erst Jakob in 46,3. Damit ergeht sie, als Jakob auf dem Weg nach Ägypten ist. In Ägypten wird die Geschichte der Erzväter zur Volksgeschichte werden. Mit seiner Übersiedlung nach Ägypten leitet Jakob diesen Übergang ein, und deshalb läßt ihm der Elohist auf seinem Weg die Mehrungsverheißung zuteil werden.

So erklärt es sich auch, daß Jakob in Beerseba dem Gott seines Vaters opfert und von diesem Gott die Zusagen von v. 3 f. erhält. In Beerseba haben nach E Abraham und Isaak gewohnt. Jakob aber steht im Begriff, das Land zu verlassen, in dem sie gelebt haben. Dadurch bildet seine Übersiedlung nach Ägypten einen tiefen Einschnitt. Deshalb erbittet Jakob mit seinen Opfern den Beistand des Gottes seines Vaters für diesen Weg. Jener Gott, den bereits sein Vater verehrt hat, soll sich auch in dem Neuen, das Jakob beginnt, als wirksam erweisen. Tatsächlich sagt ihm dieser Gott seinen Beistand zu. Er verheißt ihm aber mit der Mehrung zu einem großen Volk zugleich etwas Neues. So markiert der Elohist mit 46,1 aβ–5 a eine Wende in dem persönlichen Leben Jakobs *und* eine Wende gegenüber der bisherigen Geschichte der Väterzeit. Darin geht dieser Abschnitt über 31,13, in dem es allein um Jakob selbst ging, hinaus.

Diese Linie führt E mit der Berufung des Mose in Ex 3, 1 bβ.4 b*. 6.9–14*[179] weiter, die erneut einen Wendepunkt darstellt. Der Anfang der Gottesrede ist hier analog zu Gen 31,11.13; 46,2 aβ–4 gestaltet[180]. Gott ruft Mose mit seinem Namen an, und dieser antwortet: »Hier bin ich« (v. 4b). Darauf sagt Gott: »Ich bin der Gott deines Vaters, der Gott Abrahams, der Gott Isaaks und der Gott Jakobs« (v. 6a). Nur an diesen drei Stellen hat E für Gott eine Selbstvorstellungsformel. Schon daraus geht hervor, daß sie eng aufeinander bezogen sind. Zwar fehlt in Ex 3,6 a »der El«. Aber das ist dadurch bedingt, daß E diese Bezeichnung fast nur in der Väterzeit gebraucht. Erst in seinen Bileamsprüchen von Num 23 läßt er Bileam von El und auch von Jahwe sprechen, um diese Worte besonders feierlich zu gestalten. In Ex 3 ist die Beauftra-

---

[178] Auch Gen 15 scheidet als Beleg für eine Mehrungsverheißung bei E aus, da in diesem Kapitel m. E. der Elohist nicht vertreten ist.

[179] Zu dieser Analyse von Ex 3 vgl. L. Schmidt, Pentateuch, 90 f.

[180] Auf die Ähnlichkeiten zwischen Gen 46,2–4 und Ex 3,4 b.6 a hat schon P. Weimar, Die Berufung des Mose, 1980, 192, hingewiesen. Allerdings hat P. Weimar Gen 31,11.13 nicht berücksichtigt.

gung des Mose in v. 9 ff.* durch v. 6 b, wo berichtet wird, daß Mose sein Gesicht verhüllte, von der Selbstvorstellungsformel getrennt. Aber das beruht darauf, daß sich dieses Geschehen am Gottesberg abspielt. Deshalb muß Mose hier, nachdem er erfahren hat, wer mit ihm redet, sein Gesicht verhüllen. In Gen 31, 11.13 redet der Bote Gottes im Traum, und auch in 46, 1 aß ff. ist Jakob Gott nicht unmittelbar begegnet. Sachlich bilden jedoch die Selbstvorstellung Gottes und der Auftrag für Mose wie an den anderen Stellen eine Einheit. In der Selbstvorstellung geht es zunächst um die grundlegende Gottesbeziehung. Sie bildet die Basis für den folgenden Auftrag. Wenn sich Gott dem Mose hier als der Gott seines Vaters vorstellt und das mit den Worten »der Gott Abrahams, der Gott Isaaks und der Gott Jakobs« erläutert, so soll daran deutlich werden, daß in der Berufung des Mose jener Gott wirksam ist, der schon an diesen Vätern gehandelt hat und von ihnen verehrt wurde. Auf diese Weise verknüpft hier E die Väterzeit mit der Volksgeschichte.

Damit ergibt sich bei E folgende Linie: Durch Gen 31, 11.13 vollzieht sich bei Jakob eine Wende, die nur seine Person betrifft. Mit Gen 46, 1 aß–5 a schafft Gott eine Wende für Jakob selbst, durch die Verheißung des großen Volkes, zu dem Jakob werden soll, vollzieht Gott aber zugleich einen Einschnitt zur Väterzeit. Mit der Berufung des Mose in Ex 3 wendet Gott schließlich das Geschick jenes Volkes, das aufgrund seiner Zusage an Jakob entstanden ist. Daran wird erneut deutlich, daß man diese drei Stellen nicht verschiedenen Verfassern zuweisen kann, und daß auch bei E Väter- und Volksgeschichte miteinander verzahnt sind, wenn auch in charakteristisch anderer Weise als bei J oder bei P.

Der doppelte Aspekt, daß es sich um eine Wende im Leben Jakobs und einen Einschnitt zur Väterzeit handelt, bestimmt durchgehend die Zusagen Gottes in Gen 46,3 f. Nach v.3 soll sich Jakob nicht fürchten, nach Ägypten hinabzuziehen, weil ihn Gott dort zu einem großen Volk machen will. Durch diese Mehrungsverheißung wird die Reise Jakobs nach Ägypten zu einem notwendigen Weg. Deshalb sagt ihm Gott in v. 4 seinen Beistand zu. Er kündigt ihm aber außerdem an, daß er ihn wieder nach Palästina hinaufbringen wird. Das kann sich nicht nur darauf beziehen, daß der tote Jakob nach Kanaan zurückgebracht werden wird[181]. Die Betonung der Rückführung durch den inf. abs. läßt vielmehr erkennen, daß es bei ihr auch um das große Volk geht, das in Ägypten aus Jakob entstehen soll[182]. Diese Zusage ist dadurch bedingt, daß E im Unterschied zu J und P keine Landverheißung enthält. Aus

---

[181] So z. B. H. Gunkel 463.
[182] Vgl. u. a. L. Ruppert, Josephserzählung, 134; H.-C. Schmitt, BZAW 154, 59 Anm. 241; C. Westermann 172.

ihr wurde in diesen Quellenschriften deutlich, daß der Aufenthalt in Ägypten im Ablauf der Heilsgeschichte nur eine Zwischenstation sein sollte. Das war er aber auch für E. Deshalb darf hier Jakob erfahren, daß es eine Rückkehr geben wird. Sein Weg nach Ägypten ist um der Mehrung willen notwendig, aber er ist nicht das Ziel der Wege Gottes. Das wollte E an der für den Anfang der Volksgeschichte entscheidenden Stelle herausarbeiten.

Dabei macht E mit v. 4b deutlich, daß Jakob selbst in Ägypten sterben wird. Mit Recht weist C. Westermann darauf hin, daß der Verfasser hier das Motiv aus 45,28; 46,30 aufgreift, daß der Vater vor seinem Tod nochmals Joseph in Ägypten sehen wollte[183]. Es dient bei E aber dazu, Jakob seinen Tod in Ägypten anzukündigen. Die Darstellung der Ankunft Jakobs in Ägypten aus E ist nicht erhalten, da der Redaktor hierfür mit 46,28–34 J den Vorzug gab. Da er sonst jeweils die ausführlichere Darstellung zu Wort kommen läßt, ist zu vermuten, daß der Begegnung zwischen Joseph und dem Vater bei E nicht das gleiche Gewicht zukam wie bei J. Der Elohist hat also auch hier einem tragenden Element der jahwistischen Josephsgeschichte eine andere Funktion gegeben.

Die thematische und formale Sonderstellung von 46,1aß–5a bei E ist somit durch den Aufbau des elohistischen Werkes bedingt, mit dem sich E von J und P abhebt. Es ist für E charakteristisch, daß erst an dieser Stelle die Volksgeschichte in den Blick kommt. Mit der Übersiedlung nach Ägypten vollzieht sich im Leben Jakobs eine Wende, durch die sich zugleich der Übergang von der Väter- zur Volksgeschichte ereignet. Da bei E beide nur hier in Gen miteinander verknüpft werden, ist das Stück für E unverzichtbar. Seine Eigenart belegt somit nicht, daß es erst aus späterer Zeit stammt, sondern der Elohist mußte wegen der Gliederung, die er seinem Werk gegeben hat, mit diesem Abschnitt das Thema Joseph und die Brüder unterbrechen.

Damit verbleiben noch 46,5b–7. Wie bereits in IIe begründet wurde, gehört v. 5b.6 zu P. In der Regel wird auch v. 7 P zugeschrieben[184]. Dagegen spricht aber 47,5f.[185]. Deshalb wird man annehmen müssen, daß v. 7 als Überleitung zu der Liste in v. 8–27, die allgemein

---

[183] C. Westermann 173. Er sieht hier allerdings eine Verknüpfung der Väterverheißungen mit dem persönlichen Geschick des Ahnherrn wie in dem späten Text Gen 15,13–16. Der wesentliche Unterschied ist aber, daß dort Abraham Auskunft über die Zukunft erhält, damit er weiß, wann die Landverheißung von 15,7ff. in Erfüllung geht. Gerade sie spielt in 46,3f. keine Rolle. Auch die Einzelheiten des geschichtlichen Ablaufs werden im Gegensatz zu 15,13–16 nicht erwähnt. Das zeigt, daß 46,3f. älter ist.
[184] Vgl. z. B. H. Gunkel; O. Procksch und C. Westermann z. St.; M. Noth, Pentateuch, 18; L. Ruppert, Josephserzählung, 130; H.-C. Schmitt, BZAW 154, 52.
[185] Vgl. IIg.

als ein Nachtrag zu P angesehen wird, nachträglich in die Priesterschrift eingefügt wurde.

Das Ergebnis der Analyse von Kap. 46 lautet somit: V. 1 aα.28–31 a (ohne »und zu dem Haus seines Vaters«). 31 b.32 aα.b–34 stammen aus J. Mit v. 28–30 erreicht hier die Josephsgeschichte einen ersten Höhepunkt. Zu E gehören v. 1 aβ–5 a. Durch die Gottesrede vollzieht sich für E eine Wende für Jakob, und es erfolgt ein Einschnitt zur Väterzeit. V. 5 b.6 ist zu P zu rechnen, dagegen sind v. 7–27 ein Zusatz zu P.

g) Gen 47, 1–12

In v. 5 f. weicht die LXX erheblich vom MT ab. In ihr folgen auf v. 4 die Worte »da sprach Pharao zu Joseph«, dann kommt v. 6 b MT: »Sie mögen im Lande Gosen wohnen, und wenn du weißt, daß unter ihnen tüchtige Männer sind, so setze sie zu Obersten des Viehbesitzes über das, was mir gehört«. Darauf steht ein Stück, das im MT fehlt: »Da kamen nach Ägypten zu Joseph Jakob und seine Söhne, und es hörte Pharao, der König von Ägypten«, und erst jetzt kommt v. 5.6 a MT: »Da sprach Pharao zu Joseph folgendermaßen: Dein Vater und deine Brüder sind zu dir gekommen. Das Land Ägypten, vor dir ist es, in dem besten Teil des Landes laß deinen Vater und deine Brüder wohnen«. Durch diese Lesart der LXX entsteht zu v. 1–4 eine Dublette. Hier sind der Vater und die Brüder schon längst in Ägypten, und fünf der Brüder waren bereits von Joseph dem Pharao vorgestellt worden. Deshalb hat J. Wellhausen die LXX-Fassung als die lectio difficilior angesehen und darin viele Nachfolger gefunden[186]. In jüngster Zeit mehren sich jedoch die Stimmen, die im Anschluß an W. Rudolph den MT für ursprünglich halten[187]. Nach W. Rudolph läßt sich nicht erklären, wie aus der Lesart der LXX MT entstanden sein sollte, der durchaus sinnvoll sei. V. 5 b sei logisch v. 6 untergeordnet: »weil es sich bei den Ankömmlingen um deine nächsten Verwandten handelt, so gilt v. 6«[188]. Das habe der Übersetzer nicht verstanden und deshalb eine Einschaltung und Umstellung vorgenommen. C. Westermann sieht im MT die kunstvolle Verbindung zweier Audienzen zu einer. Die Szene mit den Brüdern vor Pharao in v. 2–4 sei in die Audienz des Joseph eingebaut. Der Pharao nehme die Mitteilung Josephs in v. 1 in seiner Antwort an Joseph mit v. 5 b nochmals auf, weil sie von v. 1 zu weit entfernt stehe. »Entscheidend spricht gegen G als den ursprünglichen Text, daß darin

---

[186] J. Wellhausen, Composition, 51 f.; vgl. z. B. H. Gunkel; O. Procksch z. St.; L. Ruppert, Josephserzählung, 142 f.; H. Seebaß, Zeit, 55 f.
[187] W. Rudolph, BZAW 63, 165 ff.; D. B. Redford, VT. S 20, 159 f.; H.-C. Schmitt, BZAW 154, 63 Anm. 260; C. Westermann 187 f.
[188] W. Rudolph, BZAW 63, 166.

der Aufbau der Audienz verkannt ist; die Einfügung von G unterbricht störend den Bericht der Audienz.«[189]

Bereits L. Ruppert hat aber mit Recht darauf hingewiesen, daß man damit »den Übersetzer die kleinere Schwierigkeit durch das Schaffen einer größeren – die grobe Zerreißung des Zusammenhanges, wie ihn die Septuaginta bietet! – beseitigen« lasse, weil er den Widerspruch zu v. 1 geschaffen hätte[190]. Tatsächlich bietet der MT auch, abgesehen von der Spannung zu v. 1, keinen glatten Zusammenhang. Nach v. 6a soll Joseph seinen Vater und seine Brüder im besten Teil des Landes wohnen lassen, nach v. 6b sollen sie im Lande Gosen wohnen. Beides steht unverbunden nebeneinander. Vor allem läßt sich aber v. 11 mit dem MT von v. 6 nur schwer vereinbaren. Hier heißt es: »Da ließ Joseph seinen Vater und seine Brüder wohnen und gab ihnen Besitz im Lande Ägypten, in dem besten Teil des Landes, im Lande Ramses, wie Pharao geboten hatte«. Hier wird deutlich auf v. 6a Bezug genommen, es fehlt aber das Land Gosen von v. 6b. W. Rudolph hat zwar unter Berufung auf griechische Minuskeln hinter »seine Brüder« die Worte »im Lande Gosen« einfügen wollen. »Das Land Ramses«, das diese Minuskeln auch bieten, sei als Randglosse in den MT gekommen[191]. Aber es bleibt unerklärbar, wie »im Lande Gosen« im MT ausgefallen sein sollte. Dagegen läßt sich aufgrund der Rolle, die das Land Gosen in 47,1ff. spielt, gut erklären, warum diese Worte in einem Teil der LXX-Überlieferung eingefügt wurden. Anders löst C. Westermann das Problem von v. 11. Er rechnet in v. 11 »da gab er ihnen Besitz im Lande Ägypten, im Lande Ramses« zu P. Der Rest gehöre zu der eigentlichen Josephsgeschichte. Wegen v. 6 müsse hier auf »im Besten des Landes« »im Lande Gosen« gefolgt sein[192]. Warum sollte aber ein Redaktor mit dem nur hier belegten Begriff »im Lande Ramses« aus P die Formulierung »im Lande Gosen« ersetzt haben, obwohl in 47,6b – aber verschiedentlich auch sonst in der Josephsgeschichte – gerade das Land Gosen als Aufenthaltsort für den Vater und die Brüder Josephs genannt wird? Schließlich findet sich in dem Plus der LXX die Formulierung »Pharao, der König von Ägypten«, während sonst einfach »Pharao« steht. Das spricht dafür, daß sie der Übersetzer in seiner hebräischen Vorlage vorfand. So führen verschiedene Überlegungen zu dem Ergebnis, daß die Lesart der LXX in v. 5f. eindeutig ursprünglich ist. Die dadurch gegebene Dublette zu v. 1ff. wurde anscheinend später als so hart empfunden, daß sie durch die Fassung des MT beseitigt wurde.

---

[189] C. Westermann 188.
[190] L. Ruppert, Josephserzählung, 143.
[191] W. Rudolph, BZAW 63, 166f.
[192] C. Westermann 191.

Aus dieser Dublette folgt, daß in v. 1–12 zwei unterschiedliche Darstellungen zu Wort kommen. V. 1–4 ist die unmittelbare Fortsetzung von 46, 31–34* und gehört deshalb zu J. Joseph führt aus, was er dort den Brüdern angekündigt hat, und die von ihm ausgewählten fünf Brüder reden vor dem Pharao entsprechend den Anweisungen, die sie von Joseph erhalten haben. Zwar hat man gelegentlich daran Anstoß genommen, daß v. 4 mit »da sprachen sie zu dem Pharao« eine neue Einleitung enthält, obwohl auch in v. 3b die Brüder sprechen. H. Gunkel und O. Procksch nehmen aus diesem Grund an, daß zwischen v. 3b und v. 4 eine Frage des Pharao ausgefallen sei[193], H.-C. Schmitt rechnet mit der Möglichkeit, daß v. 4 von dem Verfasser seiner Ruben-Schicht ergänzt wurde[194]. Bei beiden Vorschlägen wird jedoch die Funktion der doppelten Redeeinleitung verkannt. Sie dient wie in 43, 29 der Gliederung, wie C. Westermann mit Recht betont hat[195]. Mit v. 3b beantworten die Brüder die Frage des Pharao nach ihrem Beruf. Ihre Rede in v. 4 geht über diese Frage und über die Anweisungen Josephs hinaus. Sie schildern die Situation, die sie gezwungen hat, nach Ägypten zu kommen, und äußern die Bitte, im Lande Gosen wohnen zu dürfen. So tragen die Brüder zu ihrem Teil dazu bei, daß der Plan Josephs gelingen kann.

Danach wendet sich – entsprechend LXX ist »da sprach Pharao zu Joseph« einzufügen – der Pharao an Joseph und teilt ihm seine Entscheidung mit (v. 6b): Er entspricht der Bitte der Brüder; sie dürfen im Lande Gosen wohnen, ja Joseph erhält sogar den Auftrag, falls unter den Brüdern tüchtige Leute sind, sie zu Aufsehern über den Viehbesitz des Pharao zu machen. Dieses Motiv spielt im folgenden keine Rolle mehr. Mit ihm will der Verfasser zeigen, daß der Pharao Joseph überaus günstig gesonnen war. An v. 6b schließt sich v. 12 glatt an, der somit ebenfalls aus J stammt[196]. Dafür spricht auch, daß mit v. 12 jetzt die beiden wesentlichen Punkte geregelt sind, die Joseph in seiner Botschaft an den Vater in 45, 9–11 angesprochen hatte: Der Vater darf mit seiner Familie mit Zustimmung des Pharao im Lande Gosen wohnen (vgl. 45, 10), und er und seine Familie werden von Joseph versorgt (vgl. 45, 11). Es ist Joseph also gelungen, die Absicht zu realisieren, die er in der Botschaft an den Vater ausgesprochen hatte.

In die jahwistische Darstellung hat der Endredaktor einen Abschnitt aus P eingefügt. Daß zumindest der Grundbestand des nach Ab-

---

[193] H. Gunkel 465; O. Procksch 265.
[194] H.-C. Schmitt, BZAW 154, 63 Anm. 261.
[195] C. Westermann 188.
[196] Die Zuweisung von v. 12 an E, wie sie z. B. von H. Gunkel 461, vorgenommen wird, beruht darauf, daß dann 45, 11 zu E gerechnet wird. Ist das aber nicht richtig (vgl. IIe), dann gehört u. a. mit O. Eißfeldt, Hexateuch-Synopse, 97*; O. Procksch 266; H. Seebaß, Zeit, 90, auch 47, 12 zu J.

zug von J verbleibenden Textes aus P stammt, ergibt sich schon aus der Bezeichnung »Pharao, der König von Ägypten«. Sie begegnet weder bei J, noch bei E, kommt hingegen mehrmals bei P vor[197]. Freilich bereitet der Anfang Schwierigkeiten. Er lautet nach LXX: »Da kamen nach Ägypten zu Joseph Jakob und seine Söhne«. Das ist eine eindeutige Dublette zu 46,6aβ.b: »da kamen sie nach Ägypten, Jakob und all sein Same mit ihm«, die nicht ursprünglich sein kann. Sie ist dadurch entstanden, daß in P 46,8-27 eingefügt wurde. Dieser Einschub wurde mit dem Verfahren der Wiederaufnahme vorgenommen. Der Ergänzer wiederholte in 47,5b LXX mit einer leichten Abänderung 46,6aβ.b, um dadurch den Anschluß an den P-Faden wiederherzustellen, den er mit seinem Einschub unterbrochen hatte.

Daraus ergeben sich zwei Folgerungen. Zum einen geht aus der Verknüpfung der Liste in 46,8-27 mit dem Kontext von P eindeutig hervor, daß sie eingefügt wurde, als die Priesterschrift noch für sich überliefert wurde. Sie gehört also zu P^s. Zum anderen bezieht sich die Wiederaufnahme auf 46,6aβ.b, nicht aber auf 46,7. 46,7 stammt deshalb ebenfalls von dem Ergänzer und ist von ihm zur Vorbereitung von 46,8ff. eingeschoben worden. Bei P folgten die Worte aus 47,5b LXX: »und es hörte Pharao, der König von Ägypten« unmittelbar auf 46,6b. Sie wurden entsprechend der LXX durch 47,5.6a (MT) fortgesetzt. Daran schließt der Abschnitt v.7-11 glatt an. Daß auch er aus P stammt, zeigen verschiedene Formulierungen. In v.9 steht der Begriff »Fremdlingsschaft«, der im Pentateuch nur bei P belegt ist. Die Angabe über das Alter Jakobs entspricht hier 47,28 aus P. In v.8 kommt die Wendung »die Tage der Jahre deines Lebens« vor, die in v.9 leicht abgewandelt aufgenommen wird. Sie steht mit geringfügigen Variationen auch in Gen 23,1; 25,7; 47,28 bei P. Schließlich ist der Begriff 'ḥzh in v.11 in Gen nur bei P belegt[198].

Nun hat allerdings L. Ruppert v.8-10 P^s zugewiesen[199]. Die Altersangabe in v.9 sei aus 47,28 errechnet, und nur hier sei von den »Tagen der Jahre der Fremdlingsschaft« die Rede, während es bei P sonst immer »Land der Fremdlingsschaft« heiße. »Vor allem dürfte Jakobs Klage über die Kürze seines Lebens nicht von P stammen, da dieser in 47,28 durch die Zahlensymbolik gerade *dieses* Leben als ein höchst vollkommenes andeutet«[200]. Die Differenzen zu anderen P-Stellen sind aber nicht so gravierend, wie L. Ruppert annimmt. V.9 paßt insofern gut zu P, als dort Abraham mit 175 (25,7) und Isaak mit 180 Jahren

---

[197] Gen 41,46a; Ex 6,11; 14,8. Es ist deshalb nicht konsequent, wenn M. Noth, Pentateuch, 38, das Stück E zuweist, obwohl er sich für die Lesart der LXX entscheidet.
[198] Gen 17,8; 23,4.9.20; 36,43; 48,4; 49,30; 50,13.
[199] L. Ruppert, Josephserzählung, 149ff.
[200] L. Ruppert, Josephserzählung, 149.

(35,28) sterben, so daß das Lebensalter Jakobs tatsächlich noch nicht an das seiner Väter heranreicht. Bei dem Begriff »Fremdlingsschaft« ist zu beachten, daß er von P stets mit einem Suffix oder in einer constructus-Verbindung (37,1) gebraucht wird. Kanaan ist das Land der Fremdlingsschaft der Väter. Von da aus ist der Weg zu der Formulierung »meiner Fremdlingsschaft« in v. 9 nicht weit. Dieser Begriff legte sich zudem aus der Situation Jakobs nahe. Er ist in Ägypten und nicht in Kanaan. Jakob hatte auch schon lange in Paddan-Aram geweilt. Dadurch ist sein Leben tatsächlich ein Leben der Fremdlingsschaft. Im Unterschied zu Abraham und Isaak mußte er viel unterwegs sein. Weil Jakob aber von sich ausgeht, spricht er auch im Blick auf seine Väter von »den Tagen ihrer Fremdlingsschaft«.

Schließlich stellt sich die Frage, was P mit der Begegnung zwischen Jakob und Pharao ohne v. 8-10 beabsichtigt haben sollte. Die Priesterschrift hat die jehowistische Darstellung der Väterzeit außerordentlich stark gekürzt. Sie wird nur an den Punkten ausführlich, die ihr theologisch wichtig sind. Dazu gehören etwa Gen 17; 23; 28,1-9. Warum hat P dann die Szene mit Jakob und dem Pharao in 47,7 geschaffen? Das wird nur verständlich, wenn darauf schon bei P v. 8-10 folgten. In diesem Stück gibt Jakob eine Deutung der Väterzeit, und dadurch ist es bei P von sachlichem Gewicht. Ohne die Fortsetzung ist v. 7 bei P kaum vorstellbar. Es ist deshalb folgerichtig, wenn P. Weimar nicht nur v. 8-10, sondern auch v. 5.6 a.7.11 als einen späteren Zuwachs beurteilt[201]. Allerdings hält auch P. Weimar in v. 5f. den Text der LXX für ursprünglich. Das aber spricht entscheidend gegen seine Auffassung. Damit entsteht eine Dublette, die sich nicht auf einen späteren Ergänzer zurückführen läßt. Aus ihr geht vielmehr eindeutig hervor, daß hier zwei parallele Darstellungen nachträglich miteinander verbunden wurden. Warum – wie P. Weimar meint – 47,27b aus P nicht bruchlos an v. 11 anschließt, ist nicht einzusehen.

Freilich stimmt v. 7b wörtlich mit v. 10a überein. Nach E. Blum ist das »eine klassische redaktionelle Wiederaufnahme«, durch die sich v. 8f. als Einschub ausweise[202]. Nun ist jedoch eine Wiederaufnahme nicht immer ein Hinweis auf eine literarische Erweiterung. Schon bei J ist 43,24a eine Wiederaufnahme von 43,17b, die der Gliederung des Textes dient. In Gen 17 hat auch P eine Wiederaufnahme als Stilmittel gebraucht. Hier entspricht v. 3a: »Da fiel Abram auf sein Gesicht« weitgehend dem Anfang von v. 17a: »Da fiel Abraham auf sein Gesicht«. Nur der Name des Erzvaters ist wegen v. 5 verändert. P hat nach v. 3a nicht berichtet, daß der Erzvater wieder aufgestanden wäre, v. 3b-16

---

[201] P. Weimar, Aufbau und Struktur der priesterschriftlichen Jakobsgeschichte, ZAW 86 (1974) 174-203, 197 Anm. 99.
[202] E. Blum, Komposition, 252f. Anm. 56, vgl. auch 448 Anm. 8.

enthalten ausschließlich Reden Gottes. Die Wiederaufnahme von v. 3 a in v. 17 a kann dann nur verdeutlichen wollen, daß durch die Reden Gottes die Handlung nicht weitergeführt wird. Sie sind vielmehr eine Explikation der Zusage Gottes an den Ahnherrn in v. 2. Eine etwas andere Funktion hat die Wiederaufnahme in 47,7-10. Die Anweisung des Pharao, die er in v. 6 a erhält, führt Joseph erst in v. 11 aus. Durch v. 7-10 wird auch hier die Handlung nicht vorangetrieben. Die Begegnung Jakobs mit dem Pharao ist eine eigene, in sich gerundete Szene, die mit v. 7 a eine Einleitung und in v. 10 b einen Abschluß hat. Durch die Wiederaufnahme von v. 7 b in v. 10 a soll der Charakter von v. 7-10 als eigene Szene unterstrichen werden. Sie ist somit kein Hinweis auf eine literarische Erweiterung. In ähnlicher Weise hat E in Gen 22 die Wiederaufnahme als Stilmittel gebraucht. Hier wird v. 6 b in v. 8 b wieder aufgenommen, um das Gespräch zwischen Abraham und Isaak als eigene Szene zu kennzeichnen. Die Wiederaufnahme ist somit in der jahwistischen Josephsgeschichte, bei E und bei P als Stilmittel belegt. Sie ist also durch die Jahrhunderte hindurch angewandt worden. Daraus dürfte es zu erklären sein, daß vielfach auch literarische Erweiterungen mit Hilfe einer Wiederaufnahme mit dem vorgegebenen Text verbunden wurden. Auch die Wiederaufnahme von v. 7 b in v. 10 a spricht also nicht dagegen, daß der Abschnitt v. 7-10 zu P gehört. Aus den dargelegten Gründen ergibt sich positiv, daß »und es hörte Pharao, der König von Ägypten« aus LXX und v. 5.6 a.7-11 zu P zu rechnen ist.

Mit diesem Abschnitt hat P die jahwistische Darstellung von 47,1 ff. grundlegend umgestaltet[203]. Hier teilt nicht Joseph dem Pharao die Ankunft seiner Verwandten mit und versucht die Genehmigung zu erhalten, sie im Lande Gosen anzusiedeln. Vielmehr erfährt der Pharao, daß der Vater und die Brüder zu Joseph gekommen sind. Darauf läßt er Joseph rufen und gibt ihm den Auftrag, sie in dem besten Teil des Landes anzusiedeln. Es war also bei P allein der Wille des Pharao, daß die Familie Jakobs einen bevorzugten Wohnsitz erhielt. Damit führt P seine Darstellung von 45,19*-21 aα weiter. Dort hatte der Pharao die Brüder direkt aufgefordert, mit ihrem Vater nach Ägypten zu kommen, und er hatte ihnen als Ausdruck seiner besonderen Fürsorge Wagen mitgegeben. Außerdem sagte er ihnen zu, daß ihnen das Beste des ganzen Landes Ägypten gehören soll. Diese Zusage löst der Pharao nun dadurch ein, daß der Vater und die Brüder im besten Teil des Landes wohnen sollen. Joseph erhält dazu den Auftrag, weil es ihm durch seine Stellung zukommt, die Anweisung des Pharao auszuführen. Damit hat P in seiner Darstellung Motive aus J und E miteinander verbunden. Die Zusage, daß den Brüdern das Beste des ganzen Landes Ägypten gehören soll in 45,19*-21 aα, stammt aus dem elohistischen Abschnitt

---

[203] Vgl. zum folgenden vor allem L. Ruppert, Josephserzählung, 147 ff.

45,16–18. Bei E spielte aber der Ort der Ansiedlung keine Rolle. J hingegen war es wichtig, daß die Verwandten Josephs im Lande Gosen wohnten. Auch dieses Motiv greift P auf. Er verknüpft es so mit dem aus E stammenden Element, daß der Familie Jakobs der beste Teil Ägyptens als Wohnort zugewiesen werden soll. Damit wird hier deutlich, daß P sowohl J als auch E – und damit die jehowistische Darstellung – als Vorlage für seine literarische Neugestaltung benutzt hat.

Nach der Anweisung des Pharao an Joseph bringt dieser in v. 7 den Vater zum Pharao, und Jakob segnet den Pharao. Damit bedankt sich Jakob für die Gunst, die ihm der Pharao erweist. Die Tatsache, daß Jakob vor Pharao nicht huldigend niederfällt, zeigt, daß er von P hier als ein Mann gezeichnet wird, der dem Pharao überlegen ist. H. Gunkel stellt mit Recht fest: »wie ein Gottesmann tritt Jaqob mit einem Segensgruße vor den König und mit einem Segen entfernt er sich wieder«[204]. Allerdings darf man in diesen Segen auch nicht zuviel hineinlegen. Nach L. Ruppert kommt hier zum Ausdruck, daß die Verheißung an Abraham nicht nur bei J sondern auch bei P über Israel hinausreiche[205]. Damit wird jedoch v. 7b. 10a überinterpretiert. In Gen 17 wird bei P eindeutig die Heilsgeschichte auf Abraham und seine Nachkommen durch Isaak beschränkt. Segen kann es freilich auch außerhalb dieser Heilsgeschichte geben, wie die Zusage Gottes in 17,20 zeigt, daß er Ismael segnen will. Aber dieser Segen gibt keinen Anteil an der besonderen Stellung, die Israel vor Gott haben darf. Deshalb besagt der Segen, den Jakob dem Pharao erteilt, nicht mehr, als daß der Pharao von einem besonderen Mann gesegnet wird und dadurch eine Steigerung seiner Lebenskraft erfährt.

Eben dadurch wird verständlich, daß der Pharao in v. 8 mit der Frage nach dem Alter Jakobs reagiert. Vor ihm steht der greise Patriarch, dessen Lebenskraft durch das Alter, das er erreicht hat, dokumentiert wird. Deshalb will der Pharao wissen, wie alt Jakob genau ist. Seine Antwort in v. 9 soll den Pharao in Erstaunen setzen[206]. Obwohl Jakob mit 130 Jahren ein stattliches Alter erreicht hat, kommt es doch nicht an die Lebenszeit seiner Väter heran. In diesem Zusammenhang läßt P Jakob von den Tagen der Jahre seiner Fremdlingsschaft sprechen. Damit gibt Jakob eine Deutung seiner Existenz und des Lebens seiner Väter. Bei P hatte Gott den Vätern für sich und ihre Nachkommen das Land Kanaan verheißen[207]. Trotzdem blieb es für sie das Land ihrer Fremdlingsschaft, in dem ihnen nur die Grabhöhle von Machpela gehörte, die Abraham in Gen 23 gekauft hat. Jakob aber konnte durch

---

[204] H. Gunkel 495.
[205] L. Ruppert, Josephserzählung, 151; ähnlich C. Westermann 190f.
[206] Vgl. z.B. H. Gunkel 495.
[207] Gen 17,8; 28,4; 35,12.

seine Übersiedlung nach Ägypten nicht einmal mehr in diesem Land wohnen. Dadurch wird sein Leben tatsächlich zu einer Fremdlingsschaft. Während er es miterleben darf, daß die Mehrungsverheißung an Abraham in Gen 17 und an ihn selbst in 35,9–12 sich zu erfüllen beginnt (47,27b), wird die Landverheißung für ihn nicht realisiert werden.

Gerade von 47,9 her werden seine Worte in 48,3f., die allgemein zu P gerechnet werden, verständlich. Hier erzählt Jakob Joseph, was ihm Gott einst in Luz zugesagt hat. Bei der Landverheißung findet sich jedoch eine interessante Abweichung. Sie lautet in 35,12: »Das Land aber, das ich dem Abraham und dem Isaak gegeben habe, will ich dir geben, und deinem Samen nach dir will ich das Land geben«. Demgegenüber heißt es in 48,4b: »und ich will dieses Land deinem Samen nach dir als dauernden Besitz geben«. Hier ist nicht mehr davon die Rede, daß auch Jakob dieses Land erhalten soll. Diese Abweichung gegenüber 35,12 wird durch 47,9 vorbereitet. Daraus geht nochmals hervor, daß 47,7–10 von P stammt. Durch seine Übersiedlung nach Ägypten muß Jakob fern von dem verheißenen Land leben und dadurch ist sein Leben zu seiner Fremdlingsschaft geworden. Von ihm her wird aber auch das Leben seiner Väter zu ihrer Fremdlingsschaft. Wie das Geschick Jakobs zeigt, wird die Landverheißung in der Väterzeit nicht eingelöst. Der letzte Patriarch muß Kanaan verlassen, so daß zwischen dem Leben im verheißenen Land und dem Besitz dieses Landes keine kontinuierliche Linie verläuft. Die Landverheißung wird sich erst für die Nachkommen der Väter erfüllen, und dazu wird es angesichts der Übersiedlung Jakobs nach Ägypten eines neuen Eingreifens Gottes bedürfen.

Mit v.7–10 hat P eine Entsprechung zu der Szene von 45,19*–21aα geschaffen, in der die Brüder vor dem Pharao stehen. Jakob bedankt sich nun für die Fürsorge des Pharao, die einst in dessen Anweisungen an die Brüder sichtbar wurde, und die mit der Aufforderung an Joseph von v.6a ihren Höhepunkt erreicht hat. Obwohl der Pharao ihm und seiner Familie den besten Teil des Landes Ägypten zuweisen läßt, bleibt das Leben Jakobs aber eine Fremdlingsschaft, weil die Erfüllung der Landverheißung aussteht. Daran kann die Fürsorge des Pharao nichts ändern.

In v.11 führt Joseph die Anweisung des Pharao von v.6a aus. Auffällig ist, daß er dem Vater und seinen Brüdern im besten Teil des Landes Ägypten *Besitz* gibt. Das widerspricht der jahwistischen Darstellung, in der nach v.4 die Brüder lediglich als Fremdlinge in Ägypten weilen wollen, worauf C. Westermann mit Recht hinweist[208]. Aber mit dieser Aussage gibt P nochmals jener theologischen Intention Aus-

---

[208] C. Westermann 191.

druck, die schon in v. 9 zu erkennen war. Im verheißenen Land Kanaan konnten die Väter außer der Grabhöhle keinen Besitz erwerben. In Ägypten erhalten Jakob und die Brüder Eigentum in dem Land, das ihnen aber nicht verheißen ist. Daß P hier von dem »Lande Ramses« spricht, geht auf Ex 12,37 aus J zurück, wo die Israeliten beim Exodus aus Ramses aufbrechen. P hat die Bezeichnung »im Lande Ramses« gebildet, weil ihm bei J »das Land Gosen« vorgegeben war, es also um das Wohnen in einem Land als Teil Ägyptens ging. Da die Israeliten nach der P vorgegebenen Überlieferung später in Ramses gewesen waren, machte der Verfasser aus diesem Ortsnamen eine Landschaftsbezeichnung.

In 47,1–12 hat der Endredaktor die P-Darstellung auf J folgen lassen. Nur v. 12 aus J stellte er an den Schluß des Abschnittes, weil von der Versorgung des Vaters und seiner Familie natürlich erst die Rede sein konnte, nachdem ihnen ihr Wohnort angewiesen war. Für den Redaktor bot P eine Steigerung zu dem Bericht von J. Daß Jakob den Pharao segnete, ist nun auch der Dank des Patriarchen für die Gunst, die der Pharao bei J den Brüdern erwiesen hat. Offenbar war dem Endredaktor an der priesterschriftlichen Darstellung aber ebenfalls wichtig, daß Jakob und seine Familie ihren Wohnsitz im besten Teil des Landes Ägypten zugewiesen erhielten. Deshalb nahm er in Kauf, daß eine Dublette entstand. Sie wurde erst später im MT durch eine Kürzung und Umstellung des Textes beseitigt. Daraus geht hervor, daß man für den Endredaktor mit der Annahme vorsichtig sein muß, daß er Umstellungen vorgenommen hat. Zumindest in der Regel nahm er eher eine Dublette in Kauf, als daß er den Ablauf, wie er ihm in der Priesterschrift und dem jehowistischen Werk vorgegeben war, veränderte[209].

h) Gen 47,13–31

Bei diesem Abschnitt besteht über die Aufteilung von v. 27–31 weitgehend Übereinstimmung. V. 27b gehört zu P, wie schon daraus hervorgeht, daß mit dem Verb 'ḥz der Begriff 'ḥzh aus v. 11 aufgenommen wird. V. 27b folgte bei P unmittelbar auf v. 11. Der Vater und die Brüder werden in dem ihnen zugewiesenen Land ansässig und mehren sich sehr. Jetzt beginnt bei P also die Zeit der Erfüllung der Mehrungsverheißung an die Väter. Die für diese Zusage charakteristischen Verben prh und rbh[210] kommen hier bei P für die Väterzeit erstmals in einem berichtenden Stück vor. Aus P stammen auch die chronologischen

---

[209] Nur bei Gen 19,29 hat der Endredaktor ein Stück aus P umgestellt. Das hat hier aber besondere Gründe, vgl. M. Noth, Pentateuch, 13.
[210] Gen 17,2.6; 28,3; 35,11; vgl. auch 48,4.

Angaben in v. 28, mit denen die Notiz über das Alter Jakobs in v. 9 weitergeführt wird.

Dagegen gehören v. 27a.29-31 zu J, da hier der Vater durchgehend Israel heißt. Nachdem in 46,31-47,5a LXX. 12 bei J das Gewicht auf den Brüdern lag, weil der Vater mit seinem baldigen Tod rechnete (46,30), stehen nun wieder der Vater und Joseph im Zentrum. V. 27a bildet nicht den Abschluß zu der Entscheidung über den Wohnort und die Versorgung der Familie Israels, wie häufig angenommen wird[211], sondern dient als Einleitung zu v. 29-31. Das geht schon daraus hervor, daß hier die Brüder nicht genannt werden. In v. 29-31 läßt Israel Joseph schwören, daß er ihn nicht in Ägypten, sondern in seinem Grab[212] bestatten wird. Damit bereiten die Verse die Schilderung von der Überführung des toten Vaters nach Kanaan in Gen 50 vor. Der Verfasser gibt ihnen dadurch ein besonderes Gewicht, daß er die Szene etwas zerdehnt. Bereits in v. 29 fordert Israel Joseph auf, ihm zu schwören. In v. 30b aber sagt Joseph zunächst nur zu, daß er nach dem Wort des Vaters handeln wird. Es bedarf einer nochmaligen Aufforderung, ehe Joseph schwört. Der Wunsch des Vaters läßt sich wohl nur so erklären, daß der Verfasser eine Überlieferung kannte, nach der Israel in Kanaan begraben wurde. Sie machte es für ihn erforderlich, daß der Vater trotz seiner Übersiedlung nach Ägypten in seiner Heimat bestattet wurde. Nach L. Ruppert[213] geht zwar dieser Wunsch des Vaters auf die Landverheißung zurück, um derentwillen er in dem verheißenen Land begraben werden möchte. Da die Landverheißung in der jahwistischen Josephsgeschichte jedoch sonst nirgends eine Rolle spielt, ist diese Annahme jedenfalls für die Vorlage von J kaum zu halten. Daß der Vater die Verantwortung für sein Begräbnis in die Hände Josephs legt, unterstreicht in ihr nochmals die besonders enge Beziehung zwischen dem Vater und Joseph.

Erhebliche Schwierigkeiten bereitet der Abschnitt v. 13-26, in dem von Reformen berichtet wird, die Joseph während der Hungersnot in Ägypten durchführte. In dem Stück kommen weder der Vater noch die Brüder vor. Dadurch hebt es sich von der Darstellung bei J und E von 42,14ff. an ab. Es scheint auch den Zusammenhang zwischen 47,12 und 47,27a zu unterbrechen, worauf bereits J. Wellhausen hingewiesen hat[214]. Verschiedentlich wollte man das Problem durch eine Umstel-

---

[211] So z. B. H. Gunkel 465; C. Westermann 191.
[212] MT hat in v. 30 allerdings »in ihrem Grab«. Wie bereits J. Wellhausen, Composition, 60, unter Verweis auf 50,5 hervorgehoben hat, ist im MT das Suffix nachträglich an die priesterschriftliche Vorstellung angeglichen worden, daß die Erzväter in demselben Grab bestattet wurden. Zu lesen ist »in meinem Grab«.
[213] L. Ruppert, Josephserzählung, 167.
[214] J. Wellhausen, Composition, 59.

lung lösen. Ursprünglich sei 47,13-26 auf Kap. 41 gefolgt, die Erwähnungen des Landes Kanaan seien in v. 13-15 erst nachträglich eingefügt worden[215]. Die Umstellung sei erfolgt, weil v. 18 von dem zweiten Jahr der Hungersnot handle, während sich die Begebenheiten von Kap. 42 bereits im ersten Jahr ereignen. Dagegen hat aber L. Ruppert mit Recht darauf hingewiesen, daß das Stück durch den Begriff »Brot« stichwortartig mit v. 12 verknüpft ist[216]. Schon aus der Voranstellung dieses Wortes in v. 13 geht hervor, daß hier v. 12 vorausgesetzt wird. Dann sind aber auch die Nennungen des Landes Kanaan in v. 13-15 keine Zusätze.

Wegen seiner Sonderstellung wird der Abschnitt des öfteren für eine spätere Erweiterung gehalten[217]. In ihm wird nach D. B. Redford für die Steuerfreiheit der Priester die Situation reflektiert, die unter den Saiten und später bestand[218]. Auch nach H. Seebaß ist das Stück nachexilisch, da es die Sesostris-Legende voraussetze, die erst im 5. Jh. belegt sei[219]. Bereits H.-C. Schmitt hat aber gegen D. B. Redford darauf hingewiesen, daß nicht klar ist, ob der Verfasser wirklich an Steuerfreiheit denke, da es um den Landbesitz der Priester gehe. Im übrigen gebe es für die Steuerfreiheit an den Tempeln auch schon alte Belege[220]. H. Seebaß stützt sich auf eine Konjektur des MT. Er ist in v. 21a nicht in Ordnung, wo es heißt: »das Volk aber ließ er zu den Städten hinüberziehen«. Hier muß wegen v. 19 und v. 25 ursprünglich berichtet worden sein, daß Joseph das Volk zu Sklaven machte. Tatsächlich lautet der Text in LXX und Sam: »das Volk aber machte er zu Sklaven«, und diese Lesart wird meist für ursprünglich gehalten[221]. H. Seebaß ändert hingegen lediglich das Verb nach LXX und Sam und will lesen: »und er machte es (das Volk) städteweise zu Sklaven«. Er führt dazu aus: »Eine solche städteweise Dienstbarmachung dürfte jedoch der Reflex der Neueinteilung Ägyptens in 36 Gaue mit abgabenpflichtiger Landzuweisung nach der Sesostris-Legende sein«[222]. Diese Beziehung ist äußerst hypothetisch. Vor allem läßt sich aber die zugrundeliegende textkritische Entscheidung nicht halten, da unerklärbar bleibt, warum LXX und Sam aus den Städten Sklaven gemacht haben sollten. Damit

---

[215] So z.B. H. Gunkel 465f.
[216] L. Ruppert, Josephserzählung, 143f., mit weiteren Argumenten gegen eine Umstellung.
[217] So u.a. H.-C. Schmitt, BZAW 154, 64ff.; C. Westermann 192ff.
[218] D. B. Redford, VT. S 20, 236-239.
[219] H. Seebaß, Zeit, 56ff.
[220] H.-C. Schmitt, BZAW 154, 140-142 Anm. 253.
[221] Vgl. BHS und die Kommentare. Nach L. Ruppert, Josephserzählung, 159, sollte durch die Lesart des MT später die Aussage vermieden werden, daß Joseph die Ägypter zu Sklaven gemacht hat.
[222] H. Seebaß, Zeit, 59.

gibt es aber keine inhaltlichen Kriterien für die Datierung des Abschnittes. Hinter der Erzählung dürften »allgemein israelitische Vorstellungen über die ägyptischen Verhältnisse stehen, so daß in ihr kaum mit Detailkenntnissen über bestimmte historische Gegebenheiten zu rechnen ist«[223].

Diese ägyptischen Verhältnisse werden durch die Erzählung auf das Wirken Josephs zurückgeführt. Daß bei dem Geld auch von dem Lande Kanaan die Rede ist, beruht auf dem Kontext. Die Brüder Josephs waren aus Kanaan zum Getreidekauf nach Ägypten gekommen, und das ließ erwarten, daß auch andere aus Kanaan diesen Weg gegangen waren. Nur wenn auch im Lande Kanaan das Geld ausgegangen war, war dann aber verständlich, daß in dem reicheren Ägypten die Leute nicht mehr über Geld verfügten. Deshalb wird in v. 13–15 auch das Land Kanaan erwähnt, obwohl es um die Begründung ägyptischer Verhältnisse geht. Diese Beobachtung spricht dagegen, daß es sich bei dem Stück um eine ursprünglich für sich tradierte Einzelerzählung handelt[224]. Auch die Formulierung von v. 14 setzt voraus, daß früher schon berichtet wurde, daß Joseph Getreide verkaufte, und außerdem wird – wie erwähnt – mit dem Anfang von v. 13 gezielt an v. 12 angeknüpft. Daß Joseph in v. 16 den Ägyptern für ihr Vieh Brot gibt, ist nur sinnvoll, wenn die Ägypter kein Geld mehr haben, so daß v. 13–15 a notwendig vorangehen müssen. V. 15 aβ ist somit gegen L. Ruppert nicht der Anfang einer selbständigen Erzählung. Als Exposition würden hier außerdem zu viele Fragen offen bleiben.

47, 13–26 ist also eine literarische Bildung und schloß an 47, 12 aus J an. Sachlich besteht zu J kein Widerspruch. Man hat zwar »das zweite Jahr« in v. 18 verschiedentlich auf das zweite Jahr der Hungersnot gedeutet[225], und daraus geschlossen, daß der Abschnitt nur mit einer zweijährigen Dauer der Hungersnot rechne[226]. Aber das wird dem Text schwerlich gerecht. Die Angabe in v. 18 bezieht sich deutlich auf die Aussage von v. 17, daß Joseph um den Preis ihres Viehbesitzes die Ägypter »in diesem Jahr« fürsorglich geleitet hat. V. 17 kann aber nicht das erste Jahr der Hungersnot im Blick haben, da nach v. 13–15 Joseph zunächst das Geld des Landes Ägypten in den Besitz des Pharao gebracht hat. Es wäre auch überraschend, wenn die Ägypter sofort beim Eintreten der Hungersnot ihr Vieh an Joseph verkaufen müßten. So läßt sich v. 18 durchaus mit der siebenjährigen Hungersnot bei J vereinbaren.

---

[223] H.-C. Schmitt, BZAW 154, 140–142 Anm. 253.
[224] Gegen L. Ruppert, Josephserzählung, 154f., der in v. 15 aβ–26 eine Einzelerzählung sieht; H.-C. Schmitt, BZAW 154, 140–142 Anm. 253, und C. Westermann 192ff., die auf die Frage der Abgrenzung im einzelnen nicht eingehen.
[225] Vgl. z. B. H. Gunkel 468.
[226] Vgl. G. v. Rad 336; H.-C. Schmitt, BZAW 154, 65 Anm. 267.

Auch formal zerreißt der Abschnitt nicht die jahwistische Darstellung, da – wie oben gezeigt – v. 27a die Einleitung zu v. 29–31 bildet und nicht unmittelbar v. 12 fortsetzt. Durch v. 13–26 wird die Zeit zwischen der Versorgung Israels und seiner Familie in v. 12 und dem nahen Ende des Vaters in v. 27a.29–31 ausgefüllt. Insofern läßt sich das Stück durchaus als ein retardierendes Element verstehen, wie es bei J schon häufiger zu beobachten war. Hier finden sich auch an zwei anderen Stellen Hinweise auf ägyptische Verhältnisse. Nach 46,34 sind alle Schafhirten[227] den Ägyptern ein Greuel. Damit begründet Joseph, warum die Brüder dem Pharao als Beruf angeben sollen, daß sie Schafhirten sind. Dadurch hat die Bemerkung in der Erzählung eine Funktion. Anders steht es dagegen mit 43,32. Daß die Ägypter nicht zusammen mit den Hebräern essen dürfen, weil das für sie ein Greuel ist, ist für den Ablauf belanglos. Der Verfasser nimmt hier die Gelegenheit wahr, seine Leser über eine ägyptische Sitte zu informieren, die ihm eigenartig erschien[228]. Von da aus ist es denkbar, daß er in 47,13–26 ägyptische Verhältnisse im Blick auf Landbesitz und Abgaben zur Sprache bringen wollte, die von den israelitischen abwichen.

Tatsächlich entspricht die Darstellung in 47,13–15 in einem Punkt der Botschaft, die Joseph in 45,9–11 den Brüdern für den Vater aufgetragen hat. Joseph sagt dort in v. 11 dem Vater zu, daß er ihn im Lande Gosen versorgen will, weil die Hungersnot noch fünf Jahre andauern wird, »damit du nicht verarmst, du und dein Haus und alles, was dir gehört«. Joseph geht hier davon aus, daß der Vater, wenn er in Kanaan bleibt, in Ägypten Getreide kaufen muß. Das würde aber wegen der langen Dauer der Hungersnot zu seiner Verarmung führen. Deshalb ist es möglich, daß schon bei J das ganze Geld des Landes Kanaan zum Pharao kam. Außerdem wird in 41,56bα von J berichtet, daß Joseph den Ägyptern Getreide verkauft hat[229].

Schließlich sagen die Ägypter in 47,19 zu Joseph: »Gib Samen, daß wir leben und nicht sterben«. In 43,8 hatte bei J Juda zu dem Vater gesagt: »Sende den Knaben mit mir, und wir wollen uns aufmachen und gehen, daß wir leben und nicht sterben«. So weist der Abschnitt 47,13–26 verschiedene Beziehungen zur jahwistischen Josephsgeschichte auf. Sie machen es wahrscheinlich, daß er bereits in ihr als ein retardierendes Element, das die Leser über auffällige ägyptische Verhältnisse informieren sollte, enthalten war. Dafür spricht vor allem auch, daß nach E Joseph in den Jahren der Fülle von den Ägyptern den

---

[227] Hier und in 47,3 ist der Plural zu lesen, vgl. BHS.
[228] Vgl. z. B. H. Gunkel 452; C. Westermann 136.
[229] Zur Zuweisung von 41,56bα vgl. IIIc. Diese Stelle übersieht C. Westermann 194f., der zu v. 14 lediglich auf 41,57 verweist und meint, daß in der Josephserzählung »das Kaufen nur von den von auswärts Kommenden berichtet wird«.

Fünften erhoben hat (41,34b)[230]. Die beiden Aussagen über die Abgabe des Fünften in 41,34b und 47,13ff. können nicht unabhängig voneinander entstanden sein. Dabei setzt 47,13ff. aber 41,34b nicht voraus. Hier hat Joseph die Abgabe des Fünften erstmals während der Hungersnot eingeführt und zu einer ständigen Ordnung gemacht. Dann hat der Elohist den Fünften aus 47,13ff. entnommen und ihn zu einer Steuer in den fetten Jahren umgebildet. Damit setzt E 47,13-26 als Bestandteil des jahwistischen Werkes voraus.

Merkwürdig ist freilich, daß nach v.16f. die Ägypter ihren gesamten Viehbesitz zu Joseph gebracht haben. Wegen v.17a »da brachten sie ihren Viehbesitz zu Joseph« kann nicht gemeint sein, daß die Ägypter ihr Vieh nur rechtlich Joseph bzw. dem Pharao übereigneten, sondern sie müssen es tatsächlich zu Joseph gebracht haben[231]. Diese Vorstellung ist unrealistisch. Aber das gilt unabhängig davon, ob der Abschnitt 47,13-26 von dem Verfasser der jahwistischen Josephsgeschichte oder einem Ergänzer stammt. Nun hat freilich C.Westermann die Auffassung vertreten, daß der Aufbau in v.18-26 unorganisch sei[232]. Da sich die Josephsgeschichte bei J bisher als eine sorgfältige Komposition erwies, müßte 47,13-26 dann ein Einschub sein. Nach C.Westermann antwortet Joseph mit v.23f. auf die Worte der Ägypter in v.18f. Diese Antwort komme nach v.20-22 zu spät, da hier schon das Ergebnis mitgeteilt werde. Aber v.23f. ist anders zu verstehen. In v.19 fordern die Ägypter Joseph auf, sie und ihr Land zu erwerben und ihnen Saatgut zu geben. In v.20f. kauft Joseph die Ägypter und ihr Land. Darauf wird in v.22 berichtet, warum Joseph das Land der Priester nicht erworben hat. Die Worte Josephs in v.23a: »Siehe ich habe heute euch und euer Ackerland für den Pharao gekauft« beziehen sich nicht auf v.18f., sondern auf v.20f. Danach gibt Joseph den Ägyptern das Saatgut, für das sie sich in v.18f. verkaufen wollten. Von ihm war in v.20f. noch nicht die Rede. Der Abschnitt ist somit durchaus sinnvoll aufgebaut[233]. Er kann auch aufgrund seiner Komposition nicht J abgesprochen werden.

Der Verfasser will mit 47,13-26 ägyptische Verhältnisse, so wie sie ihm bekannt sind, auf das Wirken Josephs zurückführen. Er verfolgt also ausschließlich eine ätiologische Absicht. Nach F.Crüsemann spiegeln sich freilich in dem Stück, das er für einen Anhang zur Josephsgeschichte hält, die Diskussionen um das Königtum in der frühen Königszeit[234]. Das nimmt auch H.-C.Schmitt an: »Es scheint sich bei den Tra-

---

[230] Vgl. IIIc.
[231] Vgl. G. v. Rad 336; C.Westermann 195.
[232] C.Westermann 193ff.
[233] Vgl. auch H.Gunkel 468f.; G. v. Rad 336.
[234] F.Crüsemann, Widerstand, 149-151.

denten von Gen 47,13 ff. also um Kreise zu handeln, die die in Ägypten herrschenden Verhältnisse einer alle Macht und allen Besitz in der Hand des Königs vereinigenden Staatsform für Israel als Vorbild propagieren wollen, indem sie Joseph zu ihrem Schöpfer machen.«[235] F. Crüsemann und H.-C. Schmitt verweisen darauf, daß in I Sam 8,11–17 eben das als negative Folge des Königtums dargestellt werde, was in 47,13–26 als positive Maßnahme Josephs für die Ägypter geschildert sei, weil es der Erhaltung ihres Lebens diene. In beiden Texten gehe es somit bei verschiedener Wertung um dieselben Phänomene. Nun stammt aber I Sam 8,11 ff. m. E. erst von Dtr. Dabei ist I Sam 8,17 mit seiner Ankündigung, daß die Israeliten zu Sklaven des Königs werden sollen, sogar ein Zusatz[236]. Es läßt sich somit nicht belegen, daß der Verfasser mit 47,13–26 politische Absichten im Blick auf das israelitische Königtum verfolgt hätte. Wenn er ägyptische Verhältnisse mit dem Handeln Josephs begründet, so bewirkt Joseph die Lebensrettung der Ägypter (v. 25) auf eine Weise, daß der Pharao aus ihr großen Nutzen zieht. Damit dankt Joseph dem Pharao dafür, daß er seiner Absicht, die Familie Israels im Lande Gosen wohnen zu lassen, gefolgt ist.

Das Ergebnis zu 47,13–31 lautet somit: Zu J gehören v. 13–26. 27 a. 29–31. In v. 13–26 führt der Verfasser ägyptische Verhältnisse auf das Wirken Josephs zurück und schafft damit für seine Josephsgeschichte wieder ein retardierendes Element. In v. 27 a. 29–31 läßt Israel Joseph schwören, ihn im Lande Kanaan zu begraben. Damit wird die Überführung des toten Ahnherrn in Gen 50 vorbereitet. Dagegen stammen v. 27 b. 28 aus P, wo sie unmittelbar auf v. 11 folgten.

i) Gen 49,1 a.28 b–33; 50,1–22

Wie schon in I dargestellt wurde, sind die Stammessprüche in 49,2–27 erst spät in die Pentateuchüberlieferung aufgenommen worden. Sie wurden dabei durch v. 1 b und durch v. 28 a und den Anfang von v. 28 b »und dies ist es, was zu ihnen ihr Vater geredet hatte« mit dem Kontext verklammert. Daß der Rest von Kap. 49 weitgehend aus P stammt, ergibt sich bereits daraus, daß hier Jakob von seinen Söhnen in der Höhle Machpela begraben werden will, die – wie P in Gen 23 berichtet – einst Abraham als Begräbnisstätte gekauft hatte. Bei 49,33 aβ »und er versammelte seine Füße zu dem Bett« dürfte es sich freilich um ein Fragment aus J handeln. Bei J wird das Bett des Vaters in 47,31 erwähnt. Von ihm ist nochmals in 48,2 b die Rede, wo der Vater wieder

---

[235] H.-C. Schmitt, BZAW 154, 140–142 Anm. 253.
[236] L. Schmidt, Deuteronomistisches Geschichtswerk, in: H. J. Boecker u. a., Altes Testament, 1983, 101–114, 106.

Israel heißt. Die Frage, was J zwischen 47,31 und 49,33 aβ berichtet hat, wird später zu erörtern sein[237]. Vorläufig ist nur festzuhalten, daß 49,33 aβ vermutlich aus J stammt. Darauf muß J erzählt haben, daß der Vater starb. Diese Bemerkung hat der Endredaktor durch 49,33 b aus P ersetzt[238].

In dem Abschnitt 49,1a.28b*.29–33aα.33b wird nochmals die Absicht deutlich erkennbar, die P bei seiner Darstellung der Väterzeit verfolgt hat. Nur die Stätte ihres Begräbnisses gehört in dem verheißenen Land den Vätern. Deshalb werden sie und ihre Frauen mit Ausnahme der Rahel dort bestattet. Daß Jakob seinen Söhnen befehlen muß, ihn in Machpela zu begraben, beruht darauf, daß nach P die Patriarchen von ihren Söhnen bestattet wurden. So wie einst Isaak und Ismael den Abraham und Esau zusammen mit Jakob den Isaak begraben haben (Gen 25,9f.; 35,29), so will Jakob nun, daß ihn seine Söhne gemeinsam bestatten. Die Ausführung seines Befehls wird in 50,12f. berichtet, so daß auch diese beiden Verse zu P gehören. 50,12 schließt unmittelbar an 49,33 b an.

Der Rest von 50,1–14 stammt überwiegend aus J. In v.2b heißt der Vater Israel. Mit v.4aβ–6 wird 47,29–31 aufgenommen, wo der Vater Joseph schwören ließ, ihn im Lande Kanaan zu begraben, und in v.8b wird das Land Gosen erwähnt. Freilich ist der Text deutlich überfüllt. V.10 enthält eine Dublette, da in v.10a und v.10b jeweils von der Totenklage über den Vater erzählt wird. Für sie steht in v.10a *mspd*, in v.10b hingegen *'bl*. Außerdem wechselt das Subjekt. Dabei fällt auf, daß Joseph in v.10b nicht mit seinem Namen genannt wird. Deshalb kann v.10b nicht einem Bearbeiter zugewiesen werden[239]. In diesem Fall wäre doch wohl Joseph ausdrücklich genannt worden. Mit v.10b ist v.11 durch den Begriff *'bl* untrennbar verbunden. V.10a und v.10b.11 gehen also auf zwei verschiedene Darstellungen zurück. Sie wurden redaktionell dadurch miteinander ausgeglichen, daß später in v.11 die Ortsangabe »in Goren-Atad« eingefügt wurde[240]. Nun wird in v.10b im Unterschied zu v.10a Joseph bei der Totenklage besonders hervor-

---

[237] Vgl. IIIe.
[238] Vgl. z.B. H.Gunkel 475; C.Westermann 224.
[239] Gegen H.-C.Schmitt, BZAW 154, 74.
[240] So z.B. H.Gunkel 489; O.Procksch 287; L.Ruppert, Josephserzählung, 189f.; H.Seebaß, Zeit, 89; C.Westermann 227f. Die Totenklage setzt voraus, daß der Vater in unmittelbarer Nähe dieses Ortes begraben wurde. Nach dem jetzigen Text lag das Grab in beiden Fassungen im Ostjordanland. Das hält M.Noth, Pentateuch, 96, für ursprünglich. Andere sind hingegen der Auffassung, daß nur eine Darstellung das Ostjordanland erwähnte, und es in der anderen nachgetragen wurde. Nach H.Gunkel 489; O.Procksch 287f.; L.Ruppert, Josephserzählung, 189, gehört die Lokalisierung im Ostjordanland zu v.10b.11. Es läßt sich aber m.E. nicht ausschließen, daß sie ursprünglich nur in v.10a stand.

gehoben. Das entspricht der engen Beziehung zwischen Joseph und dem Vater bei J, so daß v. 10 b.11 aus J und v. 10 a aus E stammen dürften.

Eigenartig ist der Ablauf in v. 2–4 aα. Nachdem in v. 2–3 a berichtet wird, daß der Vater einbalsamiert wurde, und die Einbalsamierung 40 Tage dauerte, ist in v. 3 b–4 aα von einer 70-tägigen Trauer der Ägypter die Rede. Beide Angaben konkurrieren doch etwas miteinander, zumal in Ägypten in der Regel »die Zeit der Trauer zwischen Tod und Beerdigung siebzig Tage beträgt«, worin die für die Einbalsamierung benötigte Zeit eingeschlossen ist [241]. Außerdem dauert nach v. 10 b die Totenklage sieben Tage, während v. 10 a interessanterweise keine Zeitangabe enthält. V. 4 aβ läßt sich auch ohne Schwierigkeiten an v. 3 a anschließen. Das legt es nahe, daß v. 1–3 a.4 aβ–6 zu J gehören, und v. 3 b–4 aα zu E. Bei E ist die Trauer der Ägypter gut verständlich, da der Pharao den Brüdern – und damit auch dem Vater – in 45, 16–18 durch Joseph eine bevorzugte Stellung in Ägypten zusagen ließ. Der Redaktor hat hier also die jahwistische Fassung durch E ergänzt, weil es auch ihm darauf ankam, daß der Vater von den Ägyptern hoch geachtet worden war.

In den Einzelheiten schwierig zu beurteilen ist der Abschnitt v. 7–9. Wegen der Erwähnung des Landes Gosen gehört v. 8 eindeutig zu J, aber schon H. Gunkel wies mit Recht darauf hin, daß v. 7 und v. 8 überfüllt zu sein scheinen [242]. Nun setzt v. 14 a v. 8 voraus, da an beiden Stellen die Brüder genannt werden. Aus v. 14 a ergibt sich jedoch, daß aus v. 7 »da zog hinauf Joseph, um seinen Vater zu begraben, und es zogen mit ihm« ebenfalls zu J gehört, da diese Aussagen in v. 14 a aufgenommen werden. Eigenartig ist aber, daß in v. 7 b außer allen Knechten des Pharao auch »die Ältesten seines Hauses und alle Ältesten des Landes Ägypten« genannt werden. Nur an dieser Stelle ist im Pentateuch für Ägypten von Ältesten die Rede. Deshalb könnte es sich bei der Erwähnung der Ältesten um einen Zusatz handeln, der im Blick auf 45, 8 eingefügt wurde, wo für die Stellung Josephs ebenfalls zwischen dem Haus des Pharao und dem Land Ägypten differenziert wird [243].

Offen bleiben muß, ob schon bei J »alle Knechte des Pharao« an dem Trauerzug teilnahmen. In v. 14 a kehren Joseph »und seine Brüder und alle, die mit ihm hinaufgezogen waren« nach Ägypten zurück. Diese Formulierung schließt zwar nicht aus, daß auch Ägypter beteiligt waren [244], sie läßt sich aber auch verstehen, wenn hier nur der in v. 8 ge-

---

[241] C. Westermann 225.
[242] H. Gunkel 488.
[243] Auf die Entsprechung zwischen 45, 8 und 50, 7 b hat C. Westermann 226, aufmerksam gemacht.
[244] Gegen H.-C. Schmitt, BZAW 154, 75.

nannte Personenkreis – »das ganze Haus Josephs, seine Brüder und das Haus seines Vaters« – vorausgesetzt wird. Daß in v. 11 die Bewohner des Landes den Ortsnamen Abel-Mizraim darauf zurückführen, daß hier eine Totenklage der Ägypter stattfand, setzt die Erwähnung der Knechte des Pharao in v. 7 nicht zwingend voraus. Da Joseph und seine Verwandten aus Ägypten kommen, werden sie für den Erzähler von den Einheimischen für Ägypter gehalten worden sein. Wegen v. 11 könnte ein Späterer die Knechte des Pharao in v. 7 eingefügt haben. Man muß somit mit der Möglichkeit rechnen, daß bei J ursprünglich keine Ägypter an dem Trauerzug teilnahmen [245], ohne daß sich das freilich zwingend erweisen ließe.

Dagegen gehört v. 9 sicher mit v. 10a zusammen. Dem hier genannten »sehr gewichtigen« Lager entspricht die »sehr große und gewichtige« Totenklage in v. 10a. V. 9 unterscheidet sich von v. 7 und v. 14a auch dadurch, daß hier die Begleiter Josephs mit der Präposition ʿm und nicht mit ʾt eingeführt werden. V. 9.10a sind also aus E, während v. 7 in einem schwer zu bestimmenden Grundbestand und v. 8 zu J gehören, und dort durch v. 10b.11.14 [246] fortgesetzt wurden. An v. 14 schließt v. 22 unmittelbar an. Nachdem in v. 14 von der Rückkehr nach Ägypten die Rede war, wird hier festgestellt, daß Joseph in Ägypten blieb und 110 Jahre lebte [247]. Zwar hat R. Rendtorff darauf hingewiesen, daß bei den sonst J und E zugewiesenen Texten eine solche Angabe über das Lebensalter fehlt [248]. Aber sie hat hier eine besondere Funktion. 110 Jahre galten in Ägypten »als ideale Lebensdauer« [249]. So macht der Verfasser mit dieser Angabe deutlich, daß Joseph ein hohes Alter erreichte und somit ein erfülltes Leben hatte [250].

---

[245] So H. Seebaß, Zeit, 53, und für seine Juda-Schicht H.-C. Schmitt, BZAW 154, 75.

[246] V. 14b fehlt in LXX und wird deshalb verschiedentlich als Glosse angesehen, vgl. z. B. H. Gunkel 490; O. Procksch 286; L. Ruppert, Josephserzählung, 190. C. Westermann 228f., macht aber mit Recht darauf aufmerksam, daß mit diesem Halbvers bewußt das Ende jenes Teils der Josephsgeschichte markiert werden soll, der in 47,29 – nach der hier vorgelegten Untersuchung in 47,27a – beginnt. Der Übersetzer der LXX könnte den Halbvers aus stilistischen Gründen ausgelassen haben, da er etwas schwerfällig an v. 14a anschließt. Außerdem steht v. 14b in Spannung zu v. 13, wo alle Söhne den Vater begraben haben. Auch das könnte den Übersetzer dazu veranlaßt haben, v. 14b nicht wiederzugeben.

[247] So H. Gunkel 491; H.-C. Schmitt, BZAW 154, 78f.

[248] R. Rendtorff, BZAW 147, 136 Anm. 10.

[249] C. Westermann 235.

[250] C. Westermann 234ff., sieht in v. 22 einen Nachtrag. Dagegen spricht aber die enge Verbindung zwischen v. 14 und v. 22, die C. Westermann 235, erkannt hat, ohne daraus die Konsequenzen zu ziehen. Er ist hier von den Argumenten von R. Rendtorff beeinflußt, von dem aber die Funktion der Altersangabe nicht beachtet wird. Daß eine solche Angabe sonst bei J und E fehlt, zeigt nur erneut, daß J mit der Josephsgeschichte ein ihm tradiertes Werk aufgenommen hat.

Zu J gehören in 50,1–22 somit: V. 1–3 a.4 aβ–6.7*.8.10 b.11.14.22. Auch hier ist die Darstellung wieder ganz an der besonders engen Beziehung zwischen dem Vater und Joseph orientiert. Das zeigt bereits v. 1, wo Joseph nochmals weint. Die Aussage geht hier dadurch über 46,29 hinaus, daß Joseph nun den toten Vater auch küßt. So wird nochmals unterstrichen, wie sehr Joseph den Vater liebte. Er läßt dann die Leiche einbalsamieren (v. 2–3 a). Das geschieht, um sie nach Kanaan bringen zu können. Die Dauer von 40 Tagen ist sonst für die Einbalsamierung nicht belegt[251]. Daraus dürfte hervorgehen, daß der Verfasser über die ägyptischen Verhältnisse keine präzisen Kenntnisse hatte. Joseph kann allerdings Ägypten nicht ohne die Zustimmung des Pharao verlassen, die er in v. 4 aβ–6 einholt. Hier fällt auf, daß sich Joseph an »das Haus des Pharao« als Vermittler wendet. Daraus hat H.-C. Schmitt geschlossen, daß Joseph nicht als der zweite Mann im Staat gedacht ist, er sei vielmehr ein hoher Beamter unter anderen[252]. Sonst müsse er nicht den Hofstaat, der ihm untergeordnet sei, um Vermittlung bitten. In der Regel wird die Stelle freilich so erklärt, daß Joseph als Trauernder nicht vor dem Pharao erscheinen könne[253]. Dafür spricht, daß Joseph in 47,1 ff. freien Zugang zu dem Pharao hat. Es ist von diesem Abschnitt her nicht einzusehen, warum Joseph durch seine Stellung gehindert sein sollte, dem Pharao jetzt unmittelbar sein Anliegen vorzutragen. Hinzuweisen ist auch auf 45,9 »Gott hat mich zum Herrn für ganz Ägypten gemacht«. Damit wird Joseph klar als der zweite Mann in Ägypten beschrieben. Für den Verfasser war der Grund, warum sich Joseph an das Haus des Pharao wenden mußte, anscheinend so selbstverständlich, daß er auf eine explizite Begründung verzichtete. Für seinen Wunsch nennt Joseph in v. 5 den Eid, den er in 47,29–31 seinem Vater geschworen hat. Er weist aber außerdem ausdrücklich darauf hin, daß er nach dem Begräbnis zurückkehren will. Damit macht er deutlich, daß es ihm wirklich nur darum geht, dem Willen seines Vaters zu entsprechen. Wie in 47,1 ff. erfüllt der Pharao auch dieses Mal den Wunsch Josephs (v. 6).

Mit Joseph ziehen zumindest alle Familienmitglieder in das Land Kanaan hinauf, nur die Kinder und das Vieh bleiben im Lande Gosen zurück (v. 7*.8). Im Lande Kanaan aber veranstaltet Joseph eine siebentägige Trauerfeier, die für die Bewohner des Landes so eindrücklich ist, daß man nach ihr den Ort Abel Mizraim benennt (v. 10 b.11). Darauf kehren Joseph und seine Begleiter wieder nach Ägypten zurück (v. 14). Dabei wird die besondere Stellung Josephs betont. Es ist »sein Vater«, zu dessen Begräbnis man hinaufgezogen war, und die Rückkehr er-

---

[251] C. Westermann 225.
[252] H.-C. Schmitt, BZAW 154, 76 f.
[253] H. Gunkel 488 f.; L. Ruppert, Josephserzählung, 190 f.; C. Westermann 225.

folgt, »*nachdem er seinen Vater* begraben hatte«. Mit v. 22 wird kurz die Situation nach dem Begräbnis des Vaters in den Blick genommen. Joseph hatte die Ansiedlung der Brüder und des Hauses seines Vaters im Lande Gosen betrieben, weil sie dort auch über den Tod des Vaters hinaus eine gesicherte Existenz haben sollten (46,31-34*). Deshalb stellt der Verfasser nun fest, daß Joseph und das Haus seines Vaters in Ägypten blieben, und daß Joseph dort jenes hohe Alter erreichte, das sein Leben als eine gelungene Existenz heraushebt.

Aus dem Schluß der jahwistischen Josephsgeschichte in Gen 50[254] geht nochmals mit aller Deutlichkeit hervor, daß in ihr die Beziehung zwischen dem Vater und Joseph das beherrschende Thema ist. Sie beginnt in 37,3 mit den Worten: »Israel aber liebte Joseph mehr als alle seine Söhne«. Dieser Exposition entspricht der Schluß. Hier wird deutlich, wie sehr auch Joseph seinen Vater geliebt hat. Die Brüder sind Randfiguren. Sie sind zwar an dem Begräbnis beteiligt, aber die Initiative liegt bei allem, was geschieht, bei Joseph. So ist es tatsächlich »sein Vater«, der hier letztmals die liebende Fürsorge seines Sohnes erfährt. Daß Joseph aber nicht nur der liebende Sohn, sondern ein besonderer Mann war, macht der Verfasser mit v. 22b deutlich. Das hohe Alter, das Joseph erreichen durfte, entspricht der Auszeichnung, die ihm nach 45,9 Gott dadurch zuteil werden ließ, daß er ihn zum Herrn für ganz Ägypten machte. So sind in dem Schluß bei J zwei Linien miteinander verbunden, die bereits in dem bisher analysierten Bestand der jahwistischen Josephsgeschichte sichtbar wurden. Das besondere Gewicht liegt aber auf dem Verhältnis zwischen dem Vater und Joseph.

In v. 1-14 ist E nur mit Fragmenten vertreten. Hier wurde der Vater nach seinem Tod von den Ägyptern 70 Tage lang beweint (v. 3b.4aα). Darauf zog Joseph nach Kanaan hinauf, um den Vater zu begraben. Von dieser Darstellung ist mit v. 9 nur jener Teil erhalten, der berichtet, daß Joseph von Wagen und Reitern begleitet wurde. Daß Joseph auch bei E die Zustimmung des Pharao brauchte, um nach Kanaan zu ziehen, ist unwahrscheinlich, da v. 4aβ-6 ganz zu J gehört. Für E erlaubte es die hohe Stellung, die Joseph in Ägypten einnahm, daß er diese Entscheidung selbständig traf. In Kanaan hielten dann Joseph und seine Begleiter eine große Totenklage (v. 10a). Darauf kehrten sie nach Ägypten zurück. Auch dieses Element wurde von dem Redaktor zugunsten der jahwistischen Fassung ausgelassen.

Dagegen stammt der Abschnitt v. 15-21, zu dem eine Parallele bei J fehlt, aus E. Das zeigt bereits der Anfang von v. 15: »Da sahen die Brüder Josephs, daß ihr Vater gestorben war«. Diese Feststellung läßt

---

[254] Die Analyse von v. 23-26 ist außerordentlich schwierig und in der Forschung umstritten. Das Stück kann hier übergangen werden, weil es für die Analyse der Josephsgeschichte nicht von wesentlicher Bedeutung ist.

sich mit v. 8 und v. 14 nicht vereinbaren, da dort die Brüder an dem Begräbnis des Vaters teilgenommen haben. Sie können dann nicht erst nach der Rückkehr nach Ägypten den Tod des Vaters zur Kenntnis nehmen. Selbst wenn man die Aussage so verstehen wollte, daß den Brüdern erst jetzt zum Bewußtsein kam, welche Folgen der Tod des Vaters für sie haben könnte[255], bleibt die Spannung wegen des gemeinsamen langen Weges mit Joseph bestehen. Dazu kommt, daß v. 22 unmittelbar an v. 14 anschließt. Bei E haben also die Brüder nicht an dem Begräbnis des Vaters teilgenommen, sondern sich nach der Rückkehr Josephs an ihren Bruder gewandt.

Allerdings ist C. Westermann der Auffassung, daß der Abschnitt v. 15–21 von einem Bearbeiter stammt: »Die nochmalige Versöhnung Josephs mit seinen Brüdern hat für den Erzählverlauf der Josepherzählung keine notwendige Funktion.« Die Angst der Brüder werde hier nicht motiviert[256]. Nun wird in v. 15–21 aber die Schuld der Brüder thematisiert. Das war für die elohistische Darstellung in 42, 14ff. charakteristisch. Bei der Analyse von Gen 45 wurde bereits darauf hingewiesen, daß E hier auffälligerweise diese Frage übergeht, und daß sich das nur erklären läßt, wenn sie E am Schluß in 50, 15ff. ausführlich behandeln wollte[257]. Das Stück bietet also die notwendige Abrundung der elohistischen Darstellung. Für E spricht außerdem, daß Joseph weint, als die Brüder ihre Schuld bekennen lassen (v. 17). Wie in 42, 24 und 45, 15 weint Joseph also auch hier im Blick auf die Brüder. Schließlich enthält der Abschnitt eine bewußte Doppelung, wie sie E bei den beiden Träumen Josephs in 37, 5ff. und der Begegnung zwischen Joseph und den Brüdern in 42, 14–20 als Stilmittel gebrauchte.

Verschiedentlich ist diese Doppelung allerdings durch eine Aufteilung des Textes auf J und E beseitigt worden. Das Hauptargument ist, daß es sich bei v. 16f. und v. 18 um eine Dublette handle, von der v. 18 direkt an v. 14 anschließe. Eine Dublette liege auch in v. 19–21 vor, da Joseph in v. 19 und v. 21 die Brüder auffordert, sich nicht zu fürchten. Zu E werden dann nur v. 15–17.19f. gerechnet, während v. 18.21 aus J stammen sollen[258]. Gegen diese Aufteilung spricht jedoch, daß bei J v. 22 direkt an v. 14 anschließt. Außerdem ist v. 18 nur dann eine Dublette zu v. 16f., wenn man in v. 16 *wyṣww* mit der LXX in *wygśw* ändert. MT ist jedoch die lectio difficilior, und am Anfang von v. 18 »da gingen *auch* seine Brüder« ist v. 16f. vorausgesetzt. V. 21 aber ist keine

---

[255] C. Westermann 231.
[256] C. Westermann 230f.; vgl. auch D. B. Redford, VT. S 20, 163f., der den Abschnitt als Ergänzung ansieht und ihn seiner Juda-Schicht zuweist.
[257] Vgl. IIe.
[258] So z. B. O. Procksch 288.428; L. Ruppert, Josephserzählung, 189; O. Eißfeldt, Hexateuch-Synopse, 105*f., wobei O. Eißfeldt auch den Schluß von v. 20 bβ J zuweist.

Dublette zu v. 19, da Joseph hier die Folgerung aus seinen Ausführungen von v. 19 f. zieht, wie schon die Einleitung mit *wʿth* zeigt. Der Abschnitt v. 15—21 ist also literarisch einheitlich[259]. Er besteht aus den beiden Szenen v. 15—17 und v. 18—21.

In der ersten Szene befürchten die Brüder, daß ihnen Joseph jetzt, nachdem der Vater tot ist, das Böse vergelten könnte, das sie ihm einst angetan haben (v. 15). Für sie hatte sich Joseph also in 45,15 nur um des Vaters willen mit ihnen versöhnt. Deshalb wagen sie nicht, selbst zu Joseph zu kommen, sondern wenden sich an ihn durch Boten (v. 16). Hier klingt bei E die jahwistische Auffassung von dem engen Verhältnis zwischen Joseph und dem Vater an. Sie wird aber im Unterschied zu J auf die Schuld der Brüder angewandt. Eben diese besondere Beziehung gibt der Botschaft, die der Vater den Brüdern für Joseph aufgetragen hat, ihr Gewicht (v. 17 aα). Sie ist keine Erfindung der Brüder[260], obwohl E bisher von ihr nichts berichtet hatte. Der Elohist gebraucht hier das Stilmittel der Nachholung. Ein Tatbestand wird dabei erst an der Stelle erwähnt, an der er für den Fortgang der Handlung von Bedeutung ist. In gleicher Weise hat E in 42,21 f. nachholend berichtet, daß die Brüder das Flehen Josephs in der Zisterne nicht erhört und die Warnung Rubens vor einer Verfehlung an dem Knaben nicht beachtet haben. Diese Ereignisse sind erst wichtig, als sich die Brüder ihre Schuld eingestehen, weil ihre Einsicht für den weiteren Verlauf von Bedeutung ist. Ebenso kann für E die Botschaft des Vaters erst Interesse beanspruchen, als sie Joseph übermittelt wird, und Joseph reagieren muß.

Die Botschaft des Vaters in v. 17 aα besagt, daß er nicht will, daß Joseph an den Brüdern Rache nimmt, sondern ihnen vergibt. Damit kommt in ihr zum Ausdruck, daß bei E — wieder im Unterschied zu J — der Vater an seinen Söhnen in gleicher Weise interessiert ist. Er will für sie alle ein gesichertes Leben. Mit v. 17 aβ ziehen die Brüder aus den Worten des Vaters den Schluß: »und jetzt vergib doch die Missetat der Knechte des Gottes deines Vaters«. Sie sind sich anscheinend nicht sicher, daß der Wille des Vaters zureicht, um Joseph zur endgültigen Versöhnung zu bewegen. Deshalb appellieren sie zusätzlich an die religiöse Gemeinsamkeit, die zwischen ihnen und Joseph besteht. Gerade durch sie sind sie zu einer Familie verbunden, und dem möge Joseph mit seiner Vergebung Rechnung tragen. Als Joseph die Worte der Brüder hört, weint er (v. 17 b). Sie zeigen ihm, daß er von den Brüdern nicht verstanden wurde. Es war ihm eben nicht, wie sie vermuten, um den Vater, sondern um die Brüder selbst gegangen.

Die Begründung gibt Joseph in der zweiten Szene (v. 18—21), die dadurch eine Steigerung zu der ersten darstellt. In v. 18 kommen die

---

[259] So z. B. auch H. Gunkel 490 ff.; W. Rudolph, BZAW 63, 175; H.-C. Schmitt, BZAW 154, 78.
[260] So mit Recht z. B. H. Gunkel 490; G. v. Rad 355; C. Westermann 231.

Brüder selbst zu Joseph, fallen vor ihm nieder und sagen: »Siehe, wir sind deine Knechte«. Damit greift E 44,16 aus J auf. Dort hatte Juda Joseph angeboten, daß die Brüder seine Sklaven werden, weil der Becher in dem Sack Benjamins gefunden worden war. Der Elohist bezieht dieses Angebot auf ihre einstige Verfehlung an Joseph, weil das die einzige Schuld ist, die in seiner Josephsgeschichte eine Rolle spielt. Damit bringt der Elohist hier zugleich seine Exposition von 37,5ff. nochmals zur Geltung. Die Brüder waren auf Joseph eifersüchtig geworden, weil sie in seinen Träumen die Ankündigung sahen, daß Joseph über sie herrschen sollte (37,8a). Sie hatten verhindern wollen, daß Joseph eine solche Stellung erlangt. Jetzt aber müssen sie vor ihm niederfallen und zugeben, daß sie ihm völlig ausgeliefert sind. Was sie einst befürchtet haben, scheint sich nun zu erfüllen.

Joseph aber macht ihnen in v. 19–21 deutlich, daß er zwar die hohe Stellung einnimmt, die ihm in den Träumen angesagt wurde, daß diese aber zu anderen Folgen führt, als die Brüder vermuten. Mit den Worten »Fürchtet euch nicht« will er ihnen die Angst nehmen, und er nennt als Begründung: »denn bin ich an der Stelle Gottes?« Sie besagt nicht, wie L. Ruppert unter Verweis auf Gen 30,2 annimmt: »Joseph ist es von seiner *sittlichen* Einstellung her unmöglich, an den Brüdern Vergeltung zu üben, wie diese fürchten, da er als Mensch dazu kein Recht hat.« Damit wolle Joseph den Brüdern keine göttliche Vergeltung in Aussicht stellen, sondern ihnen zu verstehen geben, daß die Befürchtung, die ihrer Bitte zugrundeliege, eine Zumutung sei [261]. Dann bliebe das Problem der Schuld der Brüder aber immer noch ungelöst. Sie müßten zwar nicht die Rache Josephs fürchten. Es wäre jedoch durchaus möglich, daß Gott ihre Verfehlung an ihnen heimsucht. Was aus der Schuld der Brüder wird, kann aber bei E nicht offen bleiben. Der Abschnitt v. 15–21 hat vielmehr die Funktion, diese Frage abschließend zu beantworten. Joseph kann den Brüdern das Böse nicht vergelten, weil er sich damit gegen das Wirken Gottes stellen würde, wie er in v. 20 deutlich macht [262]. Hier expliziert Joseph, was er mit seiner Frage von v. 19b gemeint hat. Wie in 45,8 stellt E auch in v. 20 einen Kontrast her zwischen dem Handeln der Brüder und dem Wirken Gottes. Beschränkte sich E für die Brüder aber in 45,8 auf die Feststellung Josephs: »Nicht ihr habt mich hierher gesandt, sondern Gott«, so fixiert Joseph jetzt ihre Schuld: »Ihr aber gedachtet gegen mich Böses, Gott aber gedachte es zum Guten«. Die Schuld der Brüder darf nicht verniedlicht werden. Sie hatten wirklich Böses mit Joseph im Sinn. Aber Gott hat aus diesem Bösen etwas Gutes werden lassen.

Diese Aussage läßt sich nicht dahingehend verallgemeinern, als ob Gott jegliches Böse, das Menschen planen und tun, zu etwas Gutem

---

[261] L. Ruppert, Josephserzählung, 195.
[262] So mit Recht z.B. H. Gunkel 490; G. v. Rad 355.

machen würde. Sie ist streng auf die Ereignisse der Josephsgeschichte bezogen. An ihnen wird deutlich, daß Gott nicht an die menschlichen Absichten gebunden ist. Das Böse, das Menschen planen, kann nicht verhindern, daß Gott seinen Willen durchsetzt. G. v. Rad hat zu v. 20 darauf hingewiesen, daß nach Prov 16,8 und 20,24 Jahwe den Weg eines Menschen lenkt. »Der Leser muß sich aber bewußt bleiben, daß das Wort Josephs Kap. 50,20 durch sein geradezu schroffes Auseinanderhalten von göttlichem und menschlichem Tun etwas Extremes aussagt. Es verweist ja das Handeln Gottes in eine radikale Verborgenheit, Ferne und Unerkennbarkeit.«[263] Das dürfte jedoch nicht die Intention des Elohisten treffen. Gewiß ist Joseph – worauf G. v. Rad hinweist – bei E der charismatische Deuter. Aber seine Interpretation wird durch den Ablauf der Ereignisse als evident erwiesen. Sie muß die Brüder und den Leser überzeugen. Bei E beginnt die Josephsgeschichte mit den Träumen Josephs. Wenn sich die Brüder gegen Joseph stellen, so wenden sie sich damit gegen eine Absicht Gottes, die ihnen bekannt ist. Auch im weiteren Verlauf bleibt bei E das Handeln Gottes nicht verborgen. Der Elohist vermied es, die Brüder Joseph nach Ägypten verkaufen zu lassen. Das hat zumindest auch den Grund, zu verdeutlichen, daß tatsächlich Gott Joseph nach Ägypten gebracht hat (45,8). Im Rahmen der elohistischen Josephsgeschichte drückt deshalb v. 20 aus, daß das Böse der Menschen die Absicht Gottes nicht zu durchkreuzen vermag, sondern von Gott benutzt werden kann, um sein Ziel zu realisieren[264].

Von diesem Ziel spricht Joseph in v. 20bβ: »damit er tue, wie es jetzt ist, am Leben zu erhalten ein zahlreiches Volk«. Auch hier präzisiert Joseph den Brüdern, was er ihnen bereits in 45,5b gesagt hatte: »denn zur Erhaltung des Lebens hat mich Gott vor euch hergesandt«. Verschiedentlich wird das zahlreiche Volk so verstanden, daß Joseph hier sein lebenerhaltendes Wirken für die Ägypter und die Familie seines Vaters im Blick habe[265]. Das kann jedoch nach dem Zusammenhang kaum gemeint sein, da es in ihm um Joseph und die Brüder geht. Auch v. 21, in dem außer den Brüdern ihre Kinder erwähnt werden, legt es nahe, daß unter dem zahlreichen Volk lediglich die Brüder und ihre Kinder zu verstehen sind. In 46,3 hatte Gott Jakob verheißen, daß er ihn in Ägypten zu einem großen *gôy* machen will. Wenn Gott jetzt durch das Wirken Josephs ein zahlreiches Volk am Leben erhält, so will E damit deutlich machen, daß sich diese Verheißung zu erfüllen beginnt. Jakob ist zwar noch nicht zu einem großen *gôy*, wohl aber schon zu einem zahlreichen Volk geworden.

---

[263] G. v. Rad 361.
[264] Zur Kritik an G. v. Rad vgl. auch L. Ruppert, Josephserzählung, 195 ff.
[265] L. Ruppert, Josephserzählung, 197; C. Westermann 232.

In v. 20 greift also E in umgekehrter Reihenfolge die beiden Aussagen von 45,5b.8 auf. Er präzisiert sie dadurch, daß er nun die Schuld der Brüder und die Verheißung von 46,3 einbezieht. In v. 21a zieht Joseph aus dem Wirken Gottes, das er in v. 19f. den Brüdern gedeutet hat, für sich die Folgerung: Sie brauchen sich wirklich nicht zu fürchten, er will sie und ihre Kinder versorgen. Damit ist ihr Angebot von v. 18, seine Knechte zu sein, endgültig abgewiesen. Die Vorrangstellung Josephs führt zu einem anderen Ergebnis, als die Brüder dachten. Gerade durch sie kann Joseph sie und ihre Kinder am Leben erhalten, wie es der Absicht Gottes entspricht. Daß Joseph sie dann in v. 21b tröstet und zu ihrem Herzen redet, soll ihnen endgültig die Furcht nehmen. Damit besiegelt Joseph die in v. 15 von den Brüdern angezweifelte Versöhnung.

An dem Schluß in 50,15–21 wird die thematische Geschlossenheit der elohistischen Josephsgeschichte nochmals besonders deutlich. In ihr stehen Joseph und die Brüder am Anfang und am Ende, und am Beginn und am Schluß steht auch Gott, wobei die Schuld der Brüder das verbindende Element bildet. Gott hatte Joseph in den Träumen eine Sonderstellung angekündigt. Das weckte die Eifersucht der Brüder. Sie wollten verhindern, daß die Träume in Erfüllung gehen. Gott aber hat seinen Willen gegen die Brüder durchgesetzt und sie gerade dadurch mit ihren Kindern als zahlreiches Volk am Leben erhalten. Die Einsicht in diese Absicht, die Gott mit dem Weg Josephs verfolgte, führt zur endgültigen Versöhnung zwischen Joseph und den Brüdern.

Der Jehowist hat in 50,1–22 J und E so miteinander verbunden, daß wie in Gen 37 die Themen von J und E – Joseph und der Vater und Joseph und die Brüder – aufeinander folgen. Deshalb kommt in v. 1–14 – abgesehen von v. 12f. aus P – überwiegend J zu Wort. E ist hier lediglich mit Fragmenten vertreten. Aus ihnen geht hervor, daß der Redaktor J und E vollständig aufnehmen wollte, so weit ihm das möglich war. Ließ sich für v. 3b.4aα noch ein sachlicher Grund angeben, warum der Redaktor dieses Stück aus E bringt, so ist das bei v. 9.10a kaum möglich. Hier hat der Redaktor J aus E ergänzt, weil er die Darstellung des Elohisten mit J verbinden konnte.

Der Endredaktor hat dann v. 12f. aus P eingefügt. Aus dem Anfang von v. 13 »Da brachten ihn seine Söhne in das Land Kanaan« wird wieder deutlich, daß es sich bei P um keine Bearbeitungsschicht, sondern um ein eigenes Werk handelt. Diese Worte kommen zu spät, weil der Trauerzug mit dem toten Vater bereits in v. 10 in Kanaan angekommen ist. Die Stellung von v. 12f. erklärt sich daraus, daß der Endredaktor aus P das Begräbnis des Vaters in Machpela aufnehmen wollte. Dabei nahm er, wie schon in 47,5ff. eher eine Dublette, die durch v. 13aα entsteht, in Kauf, als daß er die P-Fassung kürzte. Auch der Endredaktor will somit seine Vorlagen möglichst weitgehend in sein Werk integrieren.

III. Analyse von Gen 37,36; 39,1–42,13; 48,1–22

Aufgrund der in II erzielten Ergebnisse soll im folgenden der Rest der Josephsgeschichte analysiert werden, der teilweise außerordentlich schwierige literarische Probleme enthält. Sie lassen sich aber weitgehend lösen, wenn man von den vorangegangenen Untersuchungen ausgeht.

a) Gen 37,36; 39,1–23

Gen 39 nimmt schon dadurch in der Josephsgeschichte eine Sonderstellung ein, weil nur hier der Gottesname Jahwe gebraucht wird. Nun hat bereits H. Greßmann geurteilt: »*Die Erzählung von dem ehebrecherischen Weib ist ein junges, der Joseph=Sage später aufgepfropftes Reis.*«[266] Er nennt dafür zwei Gründe: Einmal werde durch Gen 39 der geradlinige Ablauf zerstört. Bei E steige in Gen 40f. Joseph direkt vom Sklaven zum Minister auf, und diese Darstellung müsse ursprünglicher sein, als das Auf und Ab des Weges Josephs, das durch Gen 39 entstehe. Zum anderen verlange der Abschnitt über die Frau eigentlich, daß sie entlarvt und bestraft werde. Daraus gehe hervor, daß Gen 39 später in den Zusammenhang eingefügt wurde. Dabei sei der ursprüngliche Schluß weggebrochen worden. So erkläre es sich auch, daß dieses Kapitel im Kontext isoliert stehe[267].

Für H. Greßmann ist das allerdings ein überlieferungsgeschichtliches und kein literarisches Urteil. Literarisch gehört Gen 39 nach ihm zu J. In Aufnahme seiner Beobachtungen ist gelegentlich vermutet worden, daß Gen 39 von J in die ihm überlieferte Josephsgeschichte eingefügt oder zumindest stark überarbeitet wurde[268]. Demgegenüber sind D.B. Redford und H.-C. Schmitt der Auffassung, daß das Kapitel auch literarisch sekundär ist[269]. Als Argumente nennt H.-C. Schmitt: Es sei vom Kontext isoliert, nur in ihm sei Joseph Gefangener, auch durch den Gebrauch von Jahwe und im Stil hebe es sich markant von der Josephsgeschichte ab. Es stamme von dem späten Jahwisten, der die von

---

[266] H. Greßmann, Ursprung, 23f.
[267] H. Greßmann, Ursprung, 25.
[268] H. Schulte, BZAW 128, 17ff.; vgl. auch L. Ruppert, Josephserzählung, 55f.
[269] D.B. Redford, VT. S 20, 147.181f. u.ö.; H.-C. Schmitt, BZAW 154, 81ff.

einem elohistischen Bearbeiter geschaffene Pentateuchdarstellung erheblich erweitert habe[270].

Für die Analyse kommt m. E. 37,36 und 39,1 eine Schlüsselstellung zu. Bei diesen Versen handelt es sich um eine klare Dublette. Sie unterscheiden sich hauptsächlich dadurch voneinander, daß Joseph in 37,36 von den Midianitern[271], in 39,1 aber von den Ismaelitern verkauft wird. Gelegentlich wird angenommen, daß 37,36 aus 39,1 von jenem Mann gebildet wurde, der Gen 38 eingefügt hat[272]. Dagegen spricht jedoch, daß hier die Midianiter und nicht die Ismaeliter Joseph verkaufen. Es ist nicht einzusehen, warum der Ergänzer in diesem Punkt von 39,1 abgewichen sein sollte. In 37,36 ist klar die elohistische Darstellung von v. 28 aα vorausgesetzt, nach der midianitische Kaufleute Joseph aus der Zisterne gestohlen haben.

Nun ist 39,1 deutlich überfüllt. Nachdem Potiphar als »der Kämmerer des Pharao, der Oberste der Leibwache« charakterisiert wurde, fällt das nicht determinierte »ein ägyptischer Mann«, das auf diese Beschreibung folgt, auf[273]. Zudem ist von dem »Obersten der Leibwache« erst wieder in 40,3.4; 41,10.12 die Rede. Hier hält sich aber Joseph in dem Haus des »Obersten der Leibwache« auf. Nach 39,20 hat ihn jedoch sein ägyptischer Herr in das Gefängnis geworfen. Deshalb kann das Haus des Ägypters von 39,2 ff. nicht das Haus des Obersten der Leibwache sein. Aus diesen Beobachtungen ergibt sich eindeutig, daß in 39,1 »Potiphar, der Kämmerer des Pharao, der Oberste der Leibwache« ein Zusatz ist[274]. Diese Einfügung läßt sich nur erklären, wenn dem Ergänzer 37,36 vorgegeben war. Damit handelt es sich aber bei 37,36 und 39,1 um zwei Darstellungen, die erst nachträglich durch die Erweiterung in 39,1 aneinander angeglichen wurden. Von ihnen gehört 37,36 wegen der Erwähnung der Midianiter zu E. Der Vers bildet hier zusammen mit v. 35 b den Abschluß der Exposition: Der Vater beweint Joseph, hält ihn also für tot, während doch die Midianiter Joseph nach Ägypten an Potiphar verkauft haben. Der Grundbestand von 39,1 nennt hingegen die Ismaeliter und stammt deshalb aus J, da die Brüder

---

[270] H.-C. Schmitt, BZAW 154, 100–116.
[271] In 37,36 ist statt »Medaniter« »Midianiter« zu lesen. Medaniter ist gegen H.-C. Schmitt, BZAW 154, 23 Anm. 75, nicht die lectio difficilior, sondern sinnlos, da die Medaniter in Gen 37 sonst nicht erwähnt werden.
[272] D. B. Redford, VT. S 20, 136; H.-C. Schmitt, BZAW 154, 23 Anm. 75; C. Westermann 37. H. Donner, Gestalt, 45, hält den Vers für eine noch spätere Glosse. Dagegen sehen W. Rudolph, BZAW 63, 154, und H. Seebaß, Zeit, 73 Anm. 37, nur in v. 36 b einen Zusatz aufgrund von 39,1.
[273] So mit Recht z. B. M. Noth, Pentateuch, 26 Anm. 77.
[274] Vgl. z. B. H. Gunkel; O. Procksch; C. Westermann z. St. Die Formulierung in 39,1 läßt sich also nicht so erklären, daß »ein ägyptischer Mann« aufgrund von 39,2.5 nachgetragen wurde, wie H. Donner, Gestalt, 45, annimmt.

bei J Joseph an eine ismaelitische Karawane verkauft haben. Er folgte bei J unmittelbar auf 37,35 a.

Dann ergibt sich aus 37,36 und 39,1, daß J und E ihre Darstellung unterschiedlich gegliedert haben. In 39,1 zeigt die Inversion an, daß bei J damit etwas Neues beginnt. Bei J schloß die Exposition seiner Josephsgeschichte mit 37,35 a. Sie beginnt in v. 3 f. mit der besonderen Beziehung zwischen dem Vater und Joseph, und sie endet mit den Konsequenzen, die der Tod seines Lieblingssohnes für den Vater hat. Er ist untröstlich und wird trauernd zu seinem Sohn in die š'l hinabsteigen. Mit dem Grundbestand von 39,1 setzt J demgegenüber eine Zäsur. Es wird im folgenden nicht um Vater und Sohn, sondern um das Geschick Josephs in Ägypten gehen. Der Elohist hat hingegen seine Exposition an Joseph ausgerichtet. Deshalb verfolgt er in ihr den Weg Josephs bis zu seiner Existenz als Sklave in Ägypten. Den Einschnitt bildet hier 40,2[275]. 37,35b.36a ist durch die Inversion in v. 36 deutlich von 40,2 abgehoben. Bei E leitet also die Begegnung Josephs mit dem Obersten der Mundschenke und dem Obersten der Bäcker einen neuen Abschnitt ein.

Hat J in 39,1 aber berichtet, daß Joseph von einem Ägypter gekauft wurde, dann muß hier auch erzählt worden sein, was ihm bei diesem Mann widerfahren ist. So ergibt sich aus v. 1 zwingend, daß auch der Rest des Kapitels im wesentlichen aus J stammt. Ältere Versuche, Teile von Gen 39 E zuzuweisen, sind mit Recht aufgegeben worden[276]. Nur an zwei Stellen wurde die jahwistische Darstellung später erweitert. In v. 4 »da fand Joseph Gnade in seinen Augen, und er bediente ihn, und er setzte ihn als Aufseher über sein Haus ...« hat die Gunst, die Joseph bei seinem Herrn gewinnt, zwei verschiedene Folgen. Dabei fällt auf, daß das Subjekt wechselt, ohne daß in v. 4b der Ägypter ausdrücklich genannt wird. Zudem stellt L. Ruppert mit Recht fest: »Auch steht diese Aussage, daß Joseph seinen Herrn bedienen durfte ..., in starker Spannung zu der folgenden, daß dieser ihn über das ganze Haus setzte«[277]. Man wird deshalb mit L. Ruppert annehmen müssen, daß v. 4aβ von dem Redaktor 40,4 nachgebildet wurde. Dort wird Joseph den beiden Gefangenen zu ihrer persönlichen Bedienung beigegeben. Der Redaktor war anscheinend der Meinung, daß Joseph dann

---

[275] Zur Zuweisung von 40,2 vgl. IIIb.
[276] J. Wellhausen, Composition, 54, rechnet v. 6–19 zu E; O. Procksch 230 ff. 390 ff., teilte auch diesen Abschnitt auf J und E auf. Gegen J. Wellhausen spricht, daß dann nicht erhalten wäre, wie bei J Joseph in das Gefängnis kam. O. Procksch übersieht, daß v. 4b und v. 8b von dem gleichen Verfasser stammen müssen. Außerdem ist 40,2 bei E die unmittelbare Fortsetzung von 37,36 (vgl. IIIb). Deshalb lassen sich gegen H. Gunkel 421, auch nicht Teile von v. 2 und v. 4 E zuweisen. Vgl. im übrigen gegen die Aufteilung auf J und E L. Ruppert, Josephserzählung, 43 f.
[277] L. Ruppert, Josephserzählung, 44.

auch schon bei dem Ägypter eine solche Funktion ausgeübt haben müsse[278]. Außerdem dürfte der Schluß von v. 10 »um mit ihr zu sein«, der eine überflüssige Verdeutlichung enthält, später nachgetragen worden sein[279].

Ein Problem stellt m. E. v. 5 dar. Nach diesem Vers hat Jahwe das Haus des Ägypters um Josephs willen gesegnet, so daß der Segen Jahwes auf allem ruhte, was dem Ägypter im Haus und auf dem Feld gehörte. Das ist eine typische Anschauung des Jahwisten, die er bereits in seiner programmatischen Eröffnung der Vätergeschichte in Gen 12,1–3 zum Ausdruck bringt. Dort will Jahwe die Menschen segnen, die den Empfänger der Verheißung segnen und dadurch die Sonderstellung anerkennen, die Jahwe Abraham und seinen Nachkommen gegeben hat[280]. In 39,3f. setzt der Ägypter Joseph über seinen Besitz, weil er merkte, daß Jahwe mit Joseph war. Damit trägt er dem besonderen Verhältnis Rechnung, in dem Jahwe zu Joseph steht. Deshalb wird in v. 5 sein Haus von Jahwe gesegnet. Nun läßt aber nach v. 3 Jahwe alles gelingen, was Joseph tut. Von daher wäre zu erwarten, daß der Segen, den der Ägypter empfängt, auf das Wirken Josephs[281], und nicht unmittelbar auf Jahwe zurückgeführt wird. Zwischen v. 3f. und v. 5 besteht somit eine Spannung. Dazu kommt, daß das Thema Segen in v. 21–23 nicht vorkommt, obwohl dort sonst alle Aussagen über Jahwe von v. 2–6 wieder aufgenommen werden. Außerdem läßt sich v. 6 unmittelbar an v. 4 anschließen. Der Zusammenhang ist dann sogar erheblich glatter. Diese Beobachtungen sprechen dafür, daß v. 5 von J in seine Vorlage eingefügt wurde. Für den Jahwisten war das Verhalten des Ägypters ein Modell dafür, wie alle Sippen des Erdbodens in dem davidisch-salomonischen Großreich für sich den Segen Jahwes erwerben können. Seiner Vorlage ging es hingegen ausschließlich darum, daß

---

[278] Gegen v. 4aβ sprechen also stilistische und sachliche Gründe, nicht hingegen, daß šrt bei E, ʿbd aber bei J vorkomme, wie C. Westermann 59, annimmt. Deshalb läßt sich mit dem Argument von C. Westermann, daß nur šrt die Bedienung einer Person bedeuten könne, v. 4aβ nicht als ursprünglich erweisen.

[279] H. Gunkel 424; C. Westermann 63. Nach ihnen soll dadurch die anstößige Formulierung »um neben mir zu liegen« ersetzt werden. Warum sie anstößig gewesen sein sollte, ist jedoch nicht einsichtig. Deshalb wird man in dem Zusatz eine Verdeutlichung sehen müssen.

[280] Vgl. im einzelnen L. Schmidt, Israel ein Segen für die Völker?, ThViat 12 (1975) 135–151. Gegen H.-C. Schmitt, BZAW 154, 100–112, der diese Vorstellung seinem späten Jahwisten zuweist, ist m. E. daran festzuhalten, daß zwischen den Formulierungen mit brk ni. und hitp. ein sachlicher Unterschied besteht, und daß Gen 12,3; 28,14 von dem Jahwisten aus der Zeit Salomos stammt.

[281] So wird v. 5 zwar von H. W. Wolff, Das Kerygma des Jahwisten, in: ders., Gesammelte Studien zum Alten Testament, ²1964, 345–373, 366, gedeutet, vgl. dagegen aber meinen Aufsatz in ThViat 12, 139f.

Jahwe Joseph alles gelingen ließ, und dieser dadurch zum Hausverwalter des Ägypters aufstieg.

Nun ist allerdings H. Seebaß der Auffassung, daß J in Gen 39 wesentlich schwächer vertreten ist, und L. Ruppert ist ihm jüngst darin gefolgt[282]. H. Seebaß rechnet nur v. 1.20.21 aβ.b.22 a.23 aα zu J. Der Rest stamme aus nachexilischer Zeit. Nach H. Seebaß gehören somit in Gen 39 alle Stellen mit Jahwe zu einer späten Bearbeitung[283]. Dagegen spricht bereits, daß die von ihm postulierte Abfolge in v. 20.21 aβ nicht glatt ist. Danach hat sein ägyptischer Herr Joseph die Gunst des Obersten des Gefängnisses gewinnen lassen, er sei das Subjekt von v. 21 aβ.b. Dann würde aber zwischen v. 20b, wo Joseph das Subjekt ist, und v. 21 aβ ein Subjektwechsel vollzogen, der nicht markiert würde. Vor allem setzt aber diese Lösung voraus, daß Potiphar und seine hohe Stellung in 39,1 ursprünglich sind. Nur wenn ein hoher ägyptischer Beamter Joseph gekauft hat, kann er ihm die Gunst des Obersten des Gefängnisses verschaffen. Da Joseph jedoch, wie oben gezeigt wurde, bei J lediglich von einem Ägypter gekauft wurde, muß hier Jahwe das Subjekt von v. 21 aβ gewesen sein. V. 21 aβ setzt also v. 21 aα zwingend voraus. Dann lassen sich weder die Stellen mit Jahwe in Gen 39 J absprechen, noch die Erzählung von der ehebrecherischen Frau, da nur durch sie begründet wird, wie Joseph aus dem Haus seines ägyptischen Herrn in das Gefängnis kommt. Gen 39 ist somit – von den besprochenen Ausnahmen abgesehen – literarisch einheitlich und gehört zu J.

Wie schon erwähnt, beginnt bei J mit 39,1 der Abschnitt über den Aufstieg Josephs in Ägypten. Er wird bereits durch v. 2 a »Da war Jahwe mit Joseph, und er wurde ein Mann, der Gelingen hatte«, auf Jahwe zurückgeführt. V. 2 a hat für den Aufstieg Josephs die gleiche Funktion, die 37,3 f. bei J für das Ganze seiner Josephsgeschichte zukommt. In 37,3 f. setzt die Liebe des Vaters zu Joseph die Ereignisse in Gang. In

---

[282] H. Seebaß, Zeit, 79; L. Ruppert 230 ff.
[283] H. Seebaß nimmt an, daß Gen 39 in zwei Stufen erweitert wurde. Zunächst sei v. 2 aβ. 4 a.6 b–19 eingefügt worden. Dieser Einschub stehe in Verbindung mit der Tradition von Joseph als dem zweiten Mann Ägyptens. Von einem zweiten Bearbeiter stamme v. 2 aα.b. 3. 4 b–6 a. 21 aα. 23 aβ.b; er deute das Gelingen Josephs im Sinne von Ps 1,3 (Zeit, 79 Anm. 3). So sei es zu erklären, daß in v. 9 als Gottesbezeichnung Elohim, im Rahmen aber Jahwe stehe. Aus der Wiederholung von v. 4b in v. 6a gehe hervor, daß v. 4b–6a ein Nachtrag sei. Außerdem sei v. 3b eine spätere theologische Explikation von v. 2aβ. Für den Wechsel zwischen Jahwe und Elohim ist aber zu beachten, daß der Erzähler Jahwe verwendet, hingegen Joseph von Elohim sprechen läßt. Da v. 8 b v. 4 b voraussetzt, gehört v. 4 b–6 a zur gleichen Schicht wie v. 6 b ff. Mit v. 6 a wird v. 4 b bewußt wieder aufgenommen. Auch daß v. 3 b nicht von demselben Verfasser wie v. 2 aβ stammen könne, ist nicht zwingend. Deshalb rechnet L. Ruppert in Gen 39 nur mit einer Bearbeitung, die er dem Jehowisten zuschreibt, von dem auch v. 1 stamme.

39,2 ist es der Beistand Jahwes mit Joseph, der das Geschehen vorantreibt. In beiden Fällen handelt es sich darum, daß eine Person in einer besonderen Beziehung zu Joseph steht. Diese strukturelle Übereinstimmung spricht ebenfalls dafür, daß Gen 39 von J stammt. Freilich wird in Gen 37 bei J das Geschehen im Unterschied zu 39,2 rein von der menschlichen Ebene her entwickelt. Aber der Aufstieg Josephs in Ägypten war für den Verfasser offenbar nicht mehr ausschließlich innerweltlich darstellbar. Wenn aus dem jungen Mann, der als Sklave nach Ägypten verkauft wurde, der Herr über ganz Ägypten werden sollte, mußte Jahwe ins Spiel gebracht werden. Dabei genügte es anscheinend nicht, in der Rückschau auf Gott zu verweisen, wie es in Gen 45,9 geschieht, sondern für den Verfasser war es notwendig, Jahwe bereits am Anfang zu nennen. Nimmt bei E durch die Träume Josephs die gesamte Josephsgeschichte von Gott ihren Ausgang, so gilt das bei J zunächst für den Aufstieg Josephs.

Freilich hat H.-C. Schmitt in der Beistandsformel eine Stütze für seine Spätdatierung von Gen 39 gesehen. Mit ihr werde hier eine Verbindung zu der Erzväterüberlieferung hergestellt: »Joseph wird dargestellt als ein ›Israelit‹, der an der den Erzvätern zuteilgewordenen Beistandsverheißung partizipiert.«[284] Dabei übersieht aber H.-C. Schmitt, daß die Beistandsformel in Gen 39 anders gebraucht wird als in der Väterüberlieferung. Mit der Zusage, daß er mit Isaak oder Jakob sein will, verspricht Jahwe bei J in Gen 26,3; 28,15; 31,3 diesen Erzvätern, daß er sie beschützen will. In Gen 39 hat hingegen der Beistand Jahwes zur Folge, daß Joseph mit seinem Wirken Erfolg hat. Der Beistand Jahwes bewirkt also nicht nur den Schutz, sondern den Aufstieg Josephs. Das ist ein deutlicher Unterschied. Aus ihm geht hervor, daß die Beistandsformel hier nicht dazu dient, Joseph mit den Vätern zu verbinden. Das hat G.v. Rad erkannt. Er verweist für die Formel auf I Sam 16,18 und will ihren Gebrauch in Gen 39 von dem Bildungsideal weisheitlicher Kreise her verstehen. Dabei meint er: »Dieser Hinweis auf Jahwe hat hier aber nur mittelbar theologische Bedeutung.«[285] Dagegen spricht – wie L. Ruppert mit Recht hervorgehoben hat[286] –, daß in Gen 39 die Hinweise auf Jahwe zu häufig sind. Sie haben für das Geschehen eine konstitutive Bedeutung. Joseph steigt zum Hausverwalter auf, weil der Ägypter erkennt, daß Jahwe mit Joseph ist (v. 3f.). Joseph erhält später in dem Gefängnis eine besondere Stellung, weil Jahwe mit ihm ist und

---

[284] H.-C. Schmitt, BZAW 154, 113, der Gen 26,24; 28,15; 31,3 ebenfalls zu der späten jahwistischen Redaktion rechnet. Auch nach C. Westermann 58, soll durch die Beistandsformel eine Verbindung zwischen dem Wirken Jahwes für Joseph und für die Erzväter hergestellt werden.
[285] G. v. Rad 298.
[286] L. Ruppert, Josephserzählung, 46.

ihm Huld zuwendet, so daß er die Gunst des Obersten des Gefängnisses gewinnt (v. 21). Nur der Beistand Jahwes bewirkt somit, daß Joseph Erfolg hat. In diesem Sinn wird die Beistandsformel erstmals in der davidisch-salomonischen Zeit gebraucht. Mit ihr werden in I Sam 10,7 die Siege Sauls, die er nach seiner Begegnung mit dem Seher haben wird, begründet. Nach I Reg 1,37 hat der Beistand Jahwes David eine erfolgreiche Herrschaft ermöglicht[287]. Berücksichtigt man, daß nach Gen 45,9 Gott Joseph zum Herrn für ganz Ägypten gemacht hat, dann nimmt der Verfasser in Gen 39 offenbar diesen politischen Gebrauch der Beistandsformel auf.

In 39,2 hat der Beistand Jahwes, durch den Joseph zu einem Mann wird, der Gelingen hat, zunächst zur Folge, daß Joseph in dem Haus seines ägyptischen Herrn bleiben darf und nicht zur Feldarbeit herangezogen wird. Damit lebt er unter den Augen seines Herrn. Dadurch kann dieser erkennen, daß Jahwe mit Joseph ist und ihm alles gelingen läßt (v. 3). Man mag fragen, wie der Ägypter erkennen kann, daß gerade *Jahwe* mit Joseph ist. Aber der Verfasser hat hier kein Problem gesehen. Darin stimmt er mit J überein, denn in Gen 26,28 sagen Abimelech und Pichol zu Isaak: »Wir haben gewiß gesehen, daß Jahwe mit dir ist«. Obwohl weder sie noch der Ägypter Jahwe verehren, können sie für J und den Verfasser der jahwistischen Josephsgeschichte doch erkennen, daß Jahwe mit einem Menschen ist, und daraus die richtige Folgerung ableiten. Sie besteht für den Ägypter darin, daß er Joseph zum Hausverwalter macht und ihm seinen ganzen Besitz anvertraut (v. 4 aα.b). Welches hohe Maß an Vertrauen sein Herr Joseph entgegenbrachte, wird durch v. 6 a verdeutlicht. Er kümmerte sich nur noch um das Essen. So hat Joseph durch den Beistand Jahwes eine Vertrauensstellung erlangt.

Seinem Aufstieg bei dem Ägypter entspricht der Aufstieg Josephs im Gefängnis, von dem in v. 21–23 berichtet wird.[288] V. 21 »da war Jahwe mit Joseph und wandte ihm Huld zu[289] und gab ihm Gunst in den Augen des Obersten des Gefängnisses« ist analog zu v. 2a »da war Jahwe mit Joseph, und er war ein Mann, der Gelingen hatte«. In v. 22 setzt der Oberste des Gefängnisses Joseph über alle Gefangenen. Das

---

[287] Die Beistandsformel ist in der Aufstiegsgeschichte Davids besonders häufig (I Sam 16,18; 17,37; 18,12.14.28; 20,13; II Sam 5,10). Da aber ihre Datierung m. E. fraglich ist, sollen hier aus diesen Belegen keine Folgerungen gezogen werden.

[288] Vgl. zum Folgenden H. Gunkel 428.

[289] Die Formulierung »und wandte ihm Huld zu« in v. 21 aβ ist im AT singulär. Deshalb liest H. Gunkel 428, bei dem Verb statt qal hi.: »er ließ ihn Gunst gewinnen«. Damit würde die Stelle Esr 7,28; 9,9 entsprechen. Dort folgt aber im Unterschied zu Gen 39,21, vor wem die Huld gewonnen wurde. Deshalb ist m. E. in Gen 39,21 MT beizubehalten. Erst in v. 21b wird berichtet, welche Folgen das Wirken Jahwes für Joseph hatte.

entspricht v. 4, wo der Ägypter Joseph zum Hausverwalter macht. Nach v. 23 aα hat sich der Oberste, wie der Ägypter in v. 6 a, um nichts mehr gekümmert. Das geschah nach v. 23 aβ.b, weil Jahwe mit Joseph war, und was er tat, gelingen ließ. Dazu ist v. 3 zu vergleichen: »da sah sein Herr, daß Jahwe mit ihm war und alles, was er tat, ließ Jahwe in seiner Hand gelingen«. Die Feststellung über das erfolgreiche Wirken Josephs ist in v. 21-23 offenbar bewußt an den Schluß gestellt. Aus den Übereinstimmungen mit v. 2-4.6 geht aber hervor, daß es sich bei v. 21-23 um eine bewußte Analogie zu dem Aufstieg bei dem Ägypter mit einigen stilistischen Variationen handelt.

Dadurch wird der Aufstieg Josephs bei dem Ägypter zu einem retardierenden Element, das die Handlung nicht weiterführt. Solche retardierenden Elemente sind für die jahwistische Josephsgeschichte charakteristisch. Der Aufbau in 39,2-23 entspricht vor allem der Abfolge in 43,16-44,17[290]. Dort besteht zwischen der Darstellung in 43,16-34 und 44,1-17 eine enge Entsprechung. Während aber 43,16ff. die Handlung nicht weiterführt, wird durch 44,1-17 der Wendepunkt, der durch die Rede Judas in 44,18ff. eintritt, vorbereitet. Der Ablauf ist vor diesem Höhepunkt von dem Verfasser absichtlich zerdehnt worden. Das gleiche Stilmittel hat er auch in 39,2ff. angewandt. Das erfolgreiche Wirken Josephs im Gefängnis ist die Voraussetzung dafür, daß er von dem Pharao eine führende Position erhält. Der Verfasser stellt aber zunächst dar, daß Joseph bei einem Ägypter zum Hausverwalter aufstieg und scheiterte, um das Geschehen vor einem Höhepunkt zu zerdehnen. Aus dieser Übereinstimmung im Aufbau geht nochmals hervor, daß 39,2ff. von Anfang an zu der jahwistischen Josephsgeschichte gehörte. Interessanterweise hat E in beiden Fällen den Ablauf stark vereinfacht. Joseph gibt sich bei E, so ist hier der Ablauf zu rekonstruieren, den Brüdern bei ihrer zweiten Reise nach Ägypten sofort zu erkennen, und Joseph wird von den Midianitern direkt an den Obersten der Leibwache verkauft, bei dem Joseph auf den Obersten der Mundschenke und den Obersten der Bäcker trifft. In der Josephsgeschichte ist somit der einfache Ablauf, den E schildert, jünger als die jahwistische Darstellung mit ihren retardierenden Elementen.

In 39,7-20 führt die Begehrlichkeit der Frau des Ägypters dazu, daß Joseph von ihrem Mann in das Gefängnis geworfen wird. Dieser Abschnitt setzt den Kontext voraus. Das wird an v. 8 besonders deutlich, da hier Formulierungen aus v. 4b.6a aufgenommen werden. Tatsächlich ist die Argumentation Josephs in v. 8f., daß er mit einem Ehebruch das Vertrauen seines Herrn mißbrauchen würde, nur sinnvoll, wenn v. 2-4.6 vorhergehen. Es kann sich deshalb bei v. 7ff. gegen D. B. Redford um keine Einzelerzählung handeln, die nachträglich in den

---

[290] Vgl. II d.

Zusammenhang eingefügt wurde[291]. Das zeigt auch der Schluß in v. 19b.20. Daß Joseph nicht rehabilitiert und die Frau nicht bestraft wird, erklärt sich nur daraus, daß der Verfasser ausschließlich an dem Geschick Josephs interessiert ist. Es gibt keinerlei Anzeichen dafür, daß die Erzählung ursprünglich anders endete, und der Schluß weggebrochen wurde. Vielmehr kam es dem Verfasser lediglich darauf an, daß Joseph ins Gefängnis geworfen wurde, weil er von dort aus zum Herrn für ganz Ägypten werden sollte. Deshalb darf man aus der Strafe, die Joseph empfängt, nicht schließen, daß sein Herr von der Schuld Josephs nicht überzeugt gewesen wäre[292]. In Verbindung mit v. 20 läßt sich v. 19b nicht anders verstehen, als daß sich sein Zorn gegen Joseph richtete. Aber er konnte Joseph nicht härter bestrafen, wenn dieser noch zu einer führenden Stellung aufsteigen sollte.

Nun gibt es ein ägyptisches Märchen von den zwei Brüdern, in dem die Frau des älteren vergeblich versucht, den jüngeren zu verführen. Die Darstellung in 39,7 ff. weist zu diesem Märchen so zahlreiche Berührungspunkte auf, daß es dem Verfasser bekannt gewesen sein dürfte[293]. Er hat hier also eine ägyptische Erzählung für seine Josephsgeschichte aufgegriffen und abgewandelt. Zu den Veränderungen, die er vorgenommen hat, gehört, daß Joseph sein Kleid bei der Frau zurücklassen muß, das diese dann als Beweis für ihre Anschuldigungen benutzt (v. 12 ff.)[294]. Damit spielt hier wie in der jahwistischen Fassung von Gen 37 das Kleid Josephs eine wichtige Rolle: »Wieder ist Josephs Kleid das corpus delicti wie in 37,31–34, und wieder ist es das Mittel einer Täuschung«[295]. Um dieser Entsprechung willen hat der Verfasser das Motiv des Kleides in seine Überlieferung eingefügt. Auch sonst bestehen Beziehungen zu der jahwistischen Darstellung in Gen 37, die es verständlich machen, daß der Verfasser das ägyptische Märchen aufgriff. Bei J liebt der Vater Joseph mehr als seine anderen Söhne, weil er der Sohn des Alters ist. Das führt dazu, daß die Brüder Joseph hassen und ihn schließlich verkaufen. Nach 39,6b war Joseph von schöner Gestalt. Das ist anscheinend der Grund, warum die Frau Joseph begehrt. Hier wie dort hat die Person Josephs eine Besonderheit, die menschliche Gefühle weckt. Aus ihnen entspringen jeweils Handlungen, durch die Joseph erniedrigt wird, obwohl er unschuldig ist.

Freilich erfährt das Geschehen in 39,7 ff. dadurch eine Zuspitzung, daß der Verfasser in v. 2–4 nachdrücklich betont hat, daß Jahwe mit Jo-

---

[291] D.B. Redford, VT. S 20, 181 f.
[292] Gegen C. Westermann 64.
[293] Das hat H.-C. Schmitt, BZAW 154, 116 Anm. 105, nachgewiesen, vgl. auch C. Westermann 61.
[294] In dem Märchen fügt sich die Frau Wunden zu, die den Annäherungsversuch des jüngeren Bruders beweisen sollen, vgl. z. B. C. Westermann 61.
[295] C. Westermann 63.

seph war. Ihm kam es darauf an, herauszuarbeiten, daß der Aufstieg Josephs auf das Wirken Jahwes zurückgeht. Das unterstreicht er dadurch, daß Joseph in 39,7 ff. zunächst noch tiefer sinkt. Wenn Jahwe trotzdem im Gefängnis Joseph zu einem neuerlichen Aufstieg verhilft, ist klar, daß Jahwe mit Joseph etwas Besonderes vorhat. Aufgrund der Darstellung in Gen 39 kann Joseph in 45,9 mit Recht sagen, daß ihn Gott zum Herrn für ganz Ägypten gemacht hat. Weil ihm Gott diese Stellung in Ägypten verliehen hat, ist er tatsächlich von Gott vor den Brüdern hergesandt worden, wie Joseph in 45,7 den Brüdern sagt. Nur von Gen 39 her ist also die theologische Deutung des Geschehens verständlich, die Joseph in 45,7.9 den Brüdern und dem Vater gibt. Damit ist Gen 39 auch sachlich ein wesentlicher Bestandteil der jahwistischen Josephsgeschichte.

Warum der Verfasser hier Jahwe und nicht Elohim verwendet, wird sich kaum mehr klären lassen. 39,2-4.21-23 sind die einzigen Stellen in der Josephsgeschichte, an denen der Erzähler selbst von Gott spricht. Sonst hat er die Hinweise auf Gott immer den handelnden Personen in den Mund gelegt, und dabei gebraucht er durchgehend Elohim[296]. Das ist auch in 39,9 der Fall. Deshalb läßt sich mit der Gottesbezeichnung Jahwe nicht begründen, daß Gen 39 oder Teile dieses Kapitels noch nicht in der Josephsgeschichte standen, die J in sein Werk aufgenommen hat.

Als Ergebnis bleibt somit festzuhalten: Gen 39 ist in der jahwistischen Josephsgeschichte die Einleitung zu dem Aufstieg Josephs in Ägypten. Er wird hier darauf zurückgeführt, daß Jahwe mit Joseph war. In seine Vorlage hat der Jahwist v. 5 eingefügt, weil er in dem Handeln des Ägypters ein Modell sah, wie alle Sippen des Erdbodens für sich Segen erwerben können. Von dem Jehowisten stammen in v. 1 »Potiphar, der Kämmerer des Pharao, der Oberste der Leibwache« und v. 4 aβ. Durch beide Einschübe soll Gen 39 mit der elohistischen Darstellung verzahnt werden.

b) Gen 40, 1–23

Hier enthält der Anfang in v. 1–5 einige Unebenheiten. In v. 1 und v. 5 b werden der Mundschenk und der Bäcker des ägyptischen Königs genannt, nach v. 2 handelt es sich aber um den Obersten der Mundschenke und den Obersten der Bäcker. Auch der Ort, an dem sie mit Joseph zusammentreffen, wird unterschiedlich bezeichnet. Nach dem Anfang von v. 3 wurden sie von dem Pharao in das Haus des Obersten der Leibwache in Gewahrsam gelegt. Nach v. 3 aβ und v. 5 b handelt es sich

---

[296] Vgl. auch C. Westermann 58.

um das Gefängnis. Nun hat H. Donner bestritten, daß die Begriffe *mšmr* und *byt hshr* miteinander in Widerspruch stehen, wie man früher häufig angenommen hat[297]. Der Begriff *mšmr* bezeichne »einen Zustand, nämlich den des Gefangenseins, des Gewahrsams«[298]; innerhalb des Gefängnisses befinde man sich im Gewahrsam. Diese Beobachtung zu *mšmr* ist zwar richtig, trotzdem wird aber in 40,1-5 der Ort unterschiedlich bezeichnet. Nach v. 3 aα befindet sich das Gewahrsam im Haus des Obersten der Leibwache. Schon stilistisch wirkt die folgende Erwähnung des Gefängnisses in v. 3 aβ wie ein Nachtrag, und dieser Eindruck wird dadurch bestätigt, daß sonst in der Josephsgeschichte Gewahrsam und Gefängnis nie miteinander verbunden sind. Wichtig ist vor allem 41,10. Hier sagt der Oberste der Mundschenke, daß ihn Pharao in das Gewahrsam im Haus des Obersten der Leibwache gelegt hat. Das entspricht 40,3 aα, während ein Äquivalent zu v. 3 aβ fehlt. Die Begriffe »das Haus des Gefängnisses« und »das Haus des Obersten der Leibwache« stammen somit sicher nicht von der gleichen Hand[299].

Nun gehören v. 2.3 aα.4 schon wegen der Erwähnung des Obersten der Leibwache zu E. Sie folgten hier unmittelbar auf 37,36[300]. Tatsächlich unterscheidet sich die Stellung Josephs in 40,4 erheblich von der, die er in 39,21-23 erlangt hat. Nach 39,22 hat der Oberste des Gefängnisses Joseph über alle Gefangenen gesetzt. Mundschenk und Bäkker müßten ihm somit untergeordnet sein. In 40,4 aber wird er von dem Obersten der Leibwache dem Obermundschenken und Oberbäcker beigegeben, um sie zu bedienen[301]. Das wird von 37,36 her verständlich. Der Oberste der Leibwache hat Joseph von den Midianitern als Sklave erworben und stellt ihn nun seinen beiden prominenten Gefangenen zur persönlichen Dienstleistung zur Verfügung. In v. 3 aβ.b und v. 5 b wird hingegen 39,20-23 vorausgesetzt, wie aus dem Begriff Gefängnis und der Erwähnung der Gefangenschaft Josephs in v. 3 b hervorgeht. Freilich lassen sich diese Stücke nicht J zuweisen[302]. V. 3 aβ.b setzt eindeutig v. 3 aα, und v. 5 b v. 5 a voraus. V. 3 aβ.b und v. 5 b sind also hinzugefügt worden, um die elohistische Darstellung mit 39,21-23 auszugleichen. Sie stammen deshalb vermutlich von dem Jehowisten[303].

---

[297] So z. B. H. Gunkel 427.
[298] H. Donner, Gestalt, 40 f.; so auch C. Westermann 72 f.
[299] Die Auffassung von H. Donner setzt im übrigen voraus, daß die Nennung Potiphars in 39,1 ursprünglich ist, vgl. dazu aber III a.
[300] Den Namen Potiphar nennt E nur in 37,36.
[301] Auf diesen Unterschied wird mit Recht häufig hingewiesen, vgl. z. B. H. Gunkel 427; L. Ruppert, Josephserzählung, 62; G. v. Rad 302.
[302] Gegen J. Wellhausen, Composition, 55. H. Gunkel 427, rechnet v. 3 aβ.b zu J; O. Eißfeldt, Hexateuch-Synopse, 81*, hingegen v. 5 b.
[303] Vgl. M. Noth, Pentateuch, 38 Anm. 134; auch H.-C. Schmitt, BZAW 154,34, hält sie für Zusätze.

Nun stimmt v. 5 b in den Begriffen »Mundschenk«, »Bäcker« und »der König von Ägypten« mit v. 1 überein. Daraus haben W. Rudolph und H.-C. Schmitt geschlossen, daß es sich bei v. 1 aβ.b ebenfalls um einen Zusatz handelt[304]. Er ist nach W. Rudolph aufgrund von 41,9 entstanden, wo der Oberste der Mundschenke von seinen Verfehlungen spricht, um in 40,1–3 die gleiche Abfolge wie in 41,9f. herzustellen. Kann man schon zweifeln, ob 41,9f. für einen Späteren der Anlaß gewesen sein kann, um v. 1 aβ.b einzufügen, so wird diese These durch die oben gewonnenen Ergebnisse zu Gen 39 unmöglich. Der Aufstieg Josephs in dem Gefängnis zielt darauf ab, daß Joseph eine noch höhere Position erlangt. Von da aus ist es gut verständlich, daß er bei J dort mit dem königlichen Mundschenk und dem Bäcker zusammentraf. V. 1 ist die Einleitung zu dieser Begegnung. Das wird dadurch bestätigt, daß v. 1 aα »und es geschah nach diesen Begebenheiten« genau mit 39,7 aα übereinstimmt[305]. Wie der Aufstieg Josephs im Gefängnis (39,21–23) seinem Aufstieg bei dem Ägypter (39,2–4.6) entspricht, so folgt darauf bei J jeweils ein Stück, das mit »und es geschah nach diesen Begebenheiten« eingeleitet ist. Dabei stellte der Abschnitt, der mit 40,1 beginnt, das Gegenbild zu dem Fall Josephs in 39,7–20 dar. Der Redaktor hat in v. 5 b also die Terminologie der jahwistischen Fassung in v. 1 aufgegriffen.

Dagegen hat W. Rudolph eingewandt, daß v. 1 in der Luft hinge, weil im folgenden J nicht mehr zu Wort komme, »und was hätte der Redaktor für ein Interesse daran, diese nur stilistischen Abweichungen in seine Darstellung aufzunehmen?«[306] Damit hat W. Rudolph das Verfahren des Redaktors verkannt. E bot anscheinend im folgenden die ausführlichere Darstellung, und deshalb hat der Redaktor ihr den Vorzug gegeben. Ebenso hat er bei der ersten Reise der Brüder für ihre Begegnung mit Joseph nur in der Einleitung J berücksichtigt und sich ab 42,11b ganz an E gehalten[307]. Umgekehrt hat er bei der zweiten Reise zugunsten der breiten jahwistischen Darstellung E erst wieder aufgenommen, als die Brüder schon gemeinsam vor Joseph standen (45,2*). Deshalb läßt sich die Tatsache, daß die Fortsetzung von 40,1 aus J nicht erhalten ist, nicht gegen die Zuweisung dieses Verses an J verwenden. Daß der Redaktor diesen eigentlich überflüssigen Vers aufgenommen hat, zeigt, daß er seine Quellen möglichst vollständig zu Wort kommen lassen wollte. Das war hier möglich, weil er aus J und E eine

---

[304] W. Rudolph, BZAW 63, 157 f.; H.-C. Schmitt, BZAW 154, 34.
[305] Darauf hat G. W. Coats, Canaan, 22, hingewiesen. Durch die Zuweisung von v. 1 aα an E bei J. Wellhausen, Composition, 55, und H. Gunkel 427, wird dieser Aufbau von J zerstört.
[306] W. Rudolph, BZAW 63, 157.
[307] Vgl. III d.

sinnvolle Abfolge herstellen konnte: Mundschenk und Bäcker hatten sich gegen ihren Herrn verfehlt (v. 1). Deshalb wurde Pharao über seine beiden Beamten zornig und gab sie in den Gewahrsam im Haus des Obersten der Leibwache (v. 2.3 aα). Dieses Haus wird von dem Redaktor dann durch v. 3 aβ.b mit dem Gefängnis gleichgesetzt, in dem Joseph gefangen war. So wird an 40, 1–5 nochmals deutlich, wie der Jehowist bei seiner Redaktion vorgegangen ist. 40, 1 ist bei J die notwendige Fortsetzung von 39, 21–23 [308].

Was auf v. 1 bei J folgte, läßt sich nicht mehr rekonstruieren. V. 5 a.6–23 bilden weitgehend einen geschlossenen Zusammenhang, sie sind die elohistische Fortsetzung von v. 2.3 aα.4. Das geht schon daraus hervor, daß hier durchgehend von dem Obersten der Mundschenke und dem Obersten der Bäcker die Rede ist [309]. In v. 15 a verweist Joseph darauf, daß er aus »dem Land der Hebräer« gestohlen wurde. Das entspricht der elohistischen Darstellung in 37, 28 aα.b. Allerdings setzt die Fortsetzung in v. 15 b »und auch hier habe ich nichts getan, daß sie mich in die Grube geworfen haben« voraus, daß sich Joseph unschuldig im Gefängnis befindet. Hier wird somit auf 39, 7 ff. aus J angespielt. Da v. 15 b jedoch durch *wgm* mit v. 15 a verbunden ist, handelt es sich bei dem Halbvers nicht um ein Fragment aus J [310]. Er wurde vielmehr vom Jehowisten eingefügt, der dadurch das Geschick, das Joseph nach 39, 7 ff. in Ägypten erlitt, ebenfalls zur Geltung bringen wollte [311]. Ansonsten ist das Stück aber – abgesehen von der Glosse »von dir« in v. 19 a – literarisch einheitlich [312].

---

[308] H.-C. Schmitt, BZAW 154, 34, weist allerdings mit Recht darauf hin, daß die Juda-Schicht sonst nicht die Bezeichnung »der König von Ägypten«, sondern »Pharao« verwendet. Gegen H.-C. Schmitt läßt sich aber diese Beobachtung nicht literarkritisch auswerten. In 39, 20 werden »die Gefangenen des Königs« erwähnt. Das ist gegen G. v. Rad 303, kein Zusatz, sondern dadurch wird die Begegnung Josephs mit dem Mundschenk und dem Bäcker vorbereitet. J hat also in 39, 21–40, 1 »König« statt »Pharao«, übrigens wieder ein Indiz, daß in 39, 1 die Identifikation des Ägypters mit Potiphar nicht ursprünglich ist. Der Grund für den Wechsel zu Pharao ließe sich vielleicht erkennen, wenn erhalten wäre, wie bei J Joseph zum Pharao kam. Da das leider nicht der Fall ist, kann man den Wechsel nur konstatieren, aber nicht begründen.

[309] Nur in v. 13 steht »sein Mundschenk«. Das erklärt sich aber aus der Rede Josephs, vgl. schon J. Wellhausen, Composition, 55 Anm. 1.

[310] So z. B. H. Gunkel 427; O. Procksch 236. Daß sich v. 15 b nicht von v. 15 a isolieren läßt, hat W. Rudolph, BZAW 63, 157, mit Recht betont.

[311] Nach C. Westermann 76, sind beide Begründungen in v. 15 notwendig. Aber der Verweis darauf, daß er aus seiner Heimat gestohlen wurde, genügt völlig für die Bitte Josephs an den Obermundschenk, daß er ihn befreien möge. Auch M. Noth, Pentateuch, 38 Anm. 134, sieht in v. 15 b einen Zusatz.

[312] Daß es sich bei »von dir« in v. 19 a um eine Glosse handelt, geht aus v. 20 hervor. In v. 13–19.20 wird bewußt die gleiche Formulierung gebraucht, daß der Pharao das Haupt der beiden Männer erheben wird. Erst die Fortsetzung macht dann deutlich,

Für E beginnt mit 40,2-23* der Aufstieg Josephs in Ägypten. Dazu hat der Elohist aus seiner jahwistischen Vorlage die Personen des Mundschenks und des Bäckers aufgenommen, die er – wie schon Potiphar – als Oberste bezeichnet. Nicht aus seiner Vorlage dürften hingegen die Träume stammen. Wie schon in Gen 37 hat auch hier der Elohist die Träume selbst gebildet. Den Träumen kommt bei E für den Aufstieg Josephs die Funktion eines Leitmotivs zu. In Gen 37 kündigt Gott Joseph durch die beiden Träume an, daß er zu einer führenden Position aufsteigen wird. In Gen 40 erweist Joseph seine Fähigkeit zur Traumdeutung, die es ihm ermöglicht, in Gen 41 die Träume des Pharao zu deuten. Dadurch erlangt er in Ägypten eine besondere Stellung, die ihn über seine Brüder hinaushebt, so daß E in 42,9 konstatieren kann, daß die Träume von Gen 37 in Erfüllung gegangen sind. Mit 40,2-23* bereitet E somit die Deutung der Träume des Pharao durch Joseph vor.

Wie in Gen 37 und 41 handelt es sich um zwei Träume. Sie haben freilich eine gegensätzliche Bedeutung, weil sie auf zwei Personen verteilt werden. Die Zweizahl dient aber auch hier der Bestätigung und Steigerung. Es soll deutlich werden, daß Joseph tatsächlich Träume deuten kann, und aus der Tatsache, daß Joseph den Traum des Oberbäckers negativ interpretiert, geht hervor, daß er den Beamten nicht nach dem Mund geredet hat. Diese Fähigkeit Josephs erfährt in v. 8 eine für E wesentliche Interpretation, auf die u. a. H. Gunkel und E. L. Ehrlich hingewiesen haben [313]. Die beiden Beamten sagen in v. 8 a: »Wir haben einen Traum geträumt und haben niemand, der ihn deute«. Für sie ist Traumdeutung eine Wissenschaft, die man gelernt haben muß. Dieser Auffassung tritt Joseph in v. 8 b entgegen: »Traumdeutung steht bei Gott«. Sie hängt also lediglich davon ab, ob Gott einem Menschen die Fähigkeit verleiht, einen Traum zu deuten. Da Joseph die Träume richtig ausgelegt hat, wie E in v. 22 b feststellt, ist er von Gott inspiriert. Die Besonderheit des Sklaven Joseph besteht also darin, daß er von Gott inspiriert ist. Damit unterscheidet sich E von der Auffassung, die in Gen 39 zum Ausdruck kommt. Bei J hat Gott Joseph dadurch ausgezeichnet, daß er ihn erfolgreich wirken läßt. Bei E hat Joseph hingegen von Gott das Charisma der Traumdeutung erhalten. Dieses Charisma beschränkt sich jedoch nicht auf Träume. Wenn bei E Joseph den Brü-

---

daß ihr Geschick aber verschieden sein wird. Nach H. Gunkel 431, stammt v. 14 bβ »und führe mich aus diesem Haus heraus« aus J, weil hier Joseph um die Befreiung aus dem Gefängnis bitte. »Haus« bezieht sich aber auf das Haus des Obersten der Leibwache, bei dem Joseph Sklave ist. Nur aus v. 14 bβ wird deutlich, was der Obermundschenk für Joseph bei dem Pharao erreichen soll, deshalb gehört das Stück zu E. Ohne das Eingreifen des Pharao konnte hier Joseph nicht freikommen, weil es sich bei dem Obersten der Leibwache um einen hohen Beamten des Pharao handelt.

[313] H. Gunkel 429; E. L. Ehrlich, Der Traum im Alten Testament, BZAW 73, 1953, 65 ff.

dern in 45,5b.8 und 50,15–21 das Geschehen deutet, so deckt er damit auf, was den Brüdern verborgen war. Joseph hat also überhaupt von Gott die Fähigkeit erhalten, Geschehenes auszulegen. Sie bewährt sich zunächst an den Träumen und später an der Deutung seines Weges und des Geschicks der Brüder. Weil sich aber seine Interpretation der Träume als richtig erwiesen hatte, ist seine Deutung der Geschichte glaubwürdig. So besteht bei E zwischen der Traumdeutung und der Auslegung der Geschichte durch Joseph eine innere Beziehung.

Weil bei E 40,2–23* die Funktion hat, die Deutung der Träume des Pharao durch Joseph vorzubereiten, war es erforderlich, daß der Obermundschenk die Bitte Josephs von v.14.15a zunächst nicht erfüllte (v.23). Dadurch enthält hier auch die Darstellung des Elohisten ein retardierendes Element. Es hebt sich aber charakteristisch von der Art ab, in der verschiedentlich bei J der Ablauf zerdehnt wird. Bei E hat 40,2–23* eine wesentliche Funktion für die Handlung. Nur weil Joseph hier erwiesen hat, daß er fähig ist, Träume zu deuten, wird er in Gen 41 zum Pharao gebracht. Durch v.23 schafft E also die Voraussetzung für Gen 41. So wird auch hier deutlich, daß sich J und E im Stil erheblich voneinander unterscheiden[314].

c) Gen 41, 1–57

Da in 41,9–13 auf die elohistische Darstellung von Gen 40 Bezug genommen wird[315], gehört der Abschnitt v.1–32, in dem die beiden Träume des Pharao und ihre Deutung durch Joseph geschildert werden, ebenfalls zu E. Das geht auch daraus hervor, daß hier für die Möglichkeit der Traumdeutung die gleiche Auffassung vertreten wird wie in 40,8. Nach 40,8 kann man Traumdeutung nicht lernen, sie ist vielmehr eine Gabe Gottes. In 41,8 erweisen sich die ägyptischen Wahrsager und Weisen als unfähig, die Träume des Pharao zu deuten. Sie scheitern also mit ihrem erlernten Wissen. In 41,16 korrigiert Joseph die Meinung, die der Pharao in v.15 geäußert hat, daß Joseph ein besonders fähiger Traumdeuter ist. Er sagt: »Ich komme nicht in Betracht, Gott ist es, der dem Pharao Gutes antworten wird.« Wie in 40,8 steht auch hier die Deutung der Träume bei Gott. Joseph vermag sie nur aufzuschlüsseln, weil er von Gott inspiriert ist[316].

---

[314] D. B. Redford, VT. S 20, 205 f., hat die Erwähnung des Geburtstags des Pharao in v.20 für seine Spätdatierung der Josephsgeschichte in Anspruch genommen, vgl. dagegen aber H.-C. Schmitt, BZAW 154, 138 f.

[315] Vgl. im einzelnen H. Gunkel 432.

[316] Bereits an den inhaltlichen Beziehungen zu Gen 40 scheitert die Auffassung von H. Seebaß, Zeit, 48 f., daß in Gen 41 die Träume und ihre Deutung von einem nachexilischen Bearbeiter stammen.

Die breiten Ausführungen über die künftige Hungersnot in v. 30–32 sind allerdings verschiedentlich damit erklärt worden, daß hier auch J mit Fragmenten vertreten ist. Nach H. Gunkel und L. Ruppert ist v. 30 a »Und es werden kommen sieben Hungersjahre nach ihnen, und es wird die ganze Sättigung im Lande Ägypten vergessen werden« eine Dublette zu v. 30 b.31, wonach man von der Sättigung *b'rṣ* nichts mehr spüren wird. Hier bezeichne *'rṣ* die Erde. Bei E kündige Joseph mit v. 30 b.31 eine Hungersnot für die ganze Erde an, bei J in v. 30 a hingegen nur für Ägypten[317]. Nun setzt aber v. 30 a v. 29 voraus. »Nach ihnen« kann sich nur auf die sieben Jahre in v. 29 beziehen. V. 30 b aber hängt ohne v. 30 a in der Luft. Außerdem muß *'rṣ* in v. 30 b.31 auf Ägypten bezogen werden, da in v. 31 v. 29 aufgenommen wird und in diesem Vers ausdrücklich von der großen Sättigung in dem ganzen Lande Ägypten die Rede ist[318]. In den Träumen und ihrer Deutung geht es also nur um Ägypten. Die kommende Hungersnot wird in v. 30–32 ausführlich geschildert, weil auf dieser Ankündigung das Gewicht liegt.

Nicht von E stammt allerdings v. 14 aβ »da holte man ihn rasch aus der Grube«. Hier ist vorausgesetzt, daß sich Joseph im Gefängnis befindet. Wie 40,15 b stammt auch 41,14 aβ von dem Jehowisten, der dadurch nochmals die elohistische Darstellung mit dem Ablauf bei J verknüpft hat. Damit hat er zugleich eine bestimmte Linie hergestellt. Bei E haben die Brüder in Gen 37 den unschuldigen Joseph in die Grube geworfen. Das gleiche Geschick erleidet er in Ägypten, weil er unschuldig in das Gefängnis kommt. Der Jehowist stellt also eine bewußte Analogie her zwischen dem Geschick, das Joseph durch die Brüder und in Ägypten erfährt. Während aber der Diebstahl durch die Midianiter in Gen 37 für Joseph keine wirkliche Wende bringt, kommt er in Ägypten »aus der Grube« zu einer hohen Stellung.

Während der Abschnitt v. 1–32 mit Ausnahme von v. 14 aβ literarisch einheitlich ist, gibt es in v. 33–57 erhebliche Spannungen. Das gilt bereits für v. 33–36. In v. 33 schlägt Joseph vor, daß der Pharao einen klugen und verständigen Mann über Ägypten einsetzen soll. Nach v. 34 a aber soll der Pharao Aufseher über das Land bestellen. In v. 34 b ist dann im Singular davon die Rede, daß er – der Pharao oder der Mann von v. 33? – den Fünften erheben soll. In v. 35 wechselt das Subjekt, »sie sollen alle Speise dieser kommenden guten Jahre sammeln und Getreide unter der Hand des Pharao aufhäufen«. Eigenartig ist hier vor allem,

---

[317] H. Gunkel 432; L. Ruppert, Josephserzählung, 68 f.
[318] Daran scheitert der Vorschlag von O. Eißfeldt, Hexateuch-Synopse, 84*, v. 31 J zuzuweisen. Dagegen spricht außerdem, daß hier v. 21 aufgegriffen wird. H. Gunkel 432, sieht auch in v. 32 bβ eine Dublette zu v. 32 bα, da hier die Wiederholung des Traums nochmals gedeutet werde. Aber daß die Angelegenheit bei Gott feststeht *und* von ihm eilends ausgeführt wird, unterstreicht nur, daß der Pharao rasch handeln muß.

daß Joseph sowohl die Bestellung eines Mannes als auch mehrerer Aufseher vorschlägt, und daß der Numerus zwischen v. 34b und v. 35 wechselt. Nach H. Donner ist dieser Text freilich »einheitlich und einleuchtend«. Joseph schlage zunächst die Einsetzung eines Mannes vor. Bei wirtschaftspolitischen Maßnahmen von solcher Tragweite seien aber Aufsichtsbeamte nötig, die um der königlichen Autorität willen nicht dieser Mann, sondern der Pharao einsetzen soll. Der Plural in v. 35 sei unpersönlich zu verstehen. Mit ihm werde das Subjekt des Sammelns und Speicherns bewußt offen gelassen[319].

Diese Lösung scheitert aber an v. 34b, da in v. 35a nicht der Fünfte, sondern die gesamte Speise der guten Jahre gesammelt werden soll. Außerdem unterbricht v. 34b den Zusammenhang von v. 34a und v. 35a, da die Aufseher von v. 34a eindeutig das Subjekt von v. 35a sind. Zudem steht v. 34b in Widerspruch zu 47, 13–26, da dort nicht vorausgesetzt ist, daß der Fünfte schon früher erhoben wurde. Deshalb kann v. 34b nicht, wie H. Donner meint, als Vorbereitung dieses Abschnitts verstanden werden. Aufgrund solcher Überlegungen wird v. 34b verschiedentlich als Glosse beurteilt. Ihr Verfasser wolle die Maßnahmen, die Joseph in v. 33–35 vorschlägt, zu 47, 13 ff. in Beziehung setzen[320]. Damit sind aber die Probleme, die v. 34b aufgibt, nur teilweise gelöst. Es ist zwar denkbar, daß Joseph neben der Einsetzung eines Mannes die Bestellung von Aufsehern vorschlägt, die diesem untergeordnet sind[321]. V. 33 und v. 34a stehen aber unverbunden nebeneinander. Sowohl der Mann als auch die Aufseher sollen über das Land (Ägypten) eingesetzt werden, ohne daß über ihr Verhältnis eine Aussage gemacht wird. Daraus geht m. E. eindeutig hervor, daß v. 33 und v. 34a nicht von demselben Verfasser stammen. Dann ist v. 34b mit v. 33 zu verbinden. Subjekt von v. 34b ist ursprünglich der Mann, den nach v. 33 der Pharao bestellen soll. Erst dadurch, daß v. 34a in diesen Zusammenhang eingefügt wurde, ist der Pharao zum Subjekt von v. 34b geworden.

Eine Dublette findet sich auch in v. 35. Hier ist »und sie mögen Getreide aufhäufen ...« (v. 35bα) eine Parallele zu »und sie mögen sammeln alle Speise ...« (v. 35a). Das wird durch Überlegungen zum Text bestätigt. Die Konstruktion in v. 35b ist recht hart, man vermißt vor »Speise« ein Verb. Nun wird in v. 48 berichtet, daß Joseph alle Speise der sieben guten Jahre sammelte und in die Städte tat. Deshalb wird mit Recht vielfach in v. 35b vor »Speise« »*wytnw* = und sie mögen tun« eingefügt[322]. Der Ausfall des Verbs läßt sich aber nur so erklä-

---

[319] H. Donner, Gestalt, 42 f.; ähnlich schon D. B. Redford, VT. S 20, 165 f.
[320] W. Rudolph, BZAW 63, 158; H.-C. Schmitt, BZAW 154, 38; C. Westermann 95.
[321] So außer H. Donner z. B. auch W. Rudolph, BZAW 63, 158; H.-C. Schmitt, BZAW 154, 37; C. Westermann 95.
[322] Vgl. z. B. H. Gunkel 437; L. Ruppert, Josephserzählung, 69 Anm. 2; H. Donner, Gestalt, 41 Anm. 84; H.-C. Schmitt, BZAW 154, 36 Anm. 139.

ren, daß man schon früh v. 35 bα »und sie mögen Getreide aufhäufen« als Dublette zu v. 35 a empfunden hat. Sie sollte dadurch beseitigt werden, daß man das Verb vor »Speise« ausließ, so daß MT in v. 35 b jetzt lautet: »und sie mögen Getreide aufhäufen unter die Hand des Pharao als Speise in den Städten und verwahren«. Nach dem ursprünglichen Wortlaut führt hingegen Joseph in v. 48 genau das aus, was er in v. 35 a.bβ vorgeschlagen hat. Nach v. 49 aber hat Joseph das Getreide angehäuft, dessen Menge er nicht mehr zählen konnte. Damit entspricht v. 49 v. 35 bα. Warum ein Verfasser die Reihenfolge der Aussagen bei der Ausführung gegenüber dem Vorschlag Josephs abgeändert haben sollte, läßt sich ebensowenig erklären wie der Wechsel zwischen den Begriffen *'kl* und *br*. Zudem ist nach v. 48 die Aussage von v. 49 überflüssig, daß Joseph Getreide anhäufte. Von v. 48 f. aus läßt sich v. 35 auch nicht so erklären, daß hier vom Sammeln und Aufspeichern des Getreides so die Rede ist, daß das Aufspeichern das Sammeln voraussetze[323]. In v. 48 speichert Joseph das Getreide in den Städten, ohne daß v. 35 bα aufgenommen würde. Deshalb stammen v. 35 a.bβ.48 und v. 35 bα.49 von verschiedenen Verfassern.

Wie erwähnt ist v. 35 a die direkte Fortsetzung von v. 34 a, so daß v. 34 a.35 a.bβ zur gleichen Quellenschrift gehören. Sie werden durch v. 36 fortgesetzt, wie der Begriff *'kl* zeigt. V. 35 bα ist dann mit v. 33.34 b zu verbinden. Dazu paßt freilich nicht, daß das Verb im Plural steht. Für ihn ist aber der Redaktor verantwortlich, der dadurch v. 35 bα an v. 35 a anglich. Anders konnte er diese Stücke wohl kaum miteinander verbinden. Er hat in v. 33–36 die beiden Quellenschriften sehr geschickt miteinander verknüpft. Mit v. 33 und v. 34 a nahm er jeweils die Bestellung der Personen auf. Darauf schloß er in v. 34 b den Vorschlag zur Erhebung des Fünften an, der für ihn die Voraussetzung für das Sammeln und Anhäufen des Getreides ist, von dem J und E in v. 35 berichteten. An den Schluß des Stückes stellt er dann die Angabe des Zwecks dieser Maßnahmen in v. 36. Diese durchdachte literarische Komposition ist aber, wie die genannten Beobachtungen zeigen, nicht einheitlich. Daß der Redaktor v. 35 bα aufgenommen hat, beruht darauf, daß er später v. 49 bringen wollte, weil für ihn die hier erwähnte Fülle des Getreides über das hinausging, was in v. 48 berichtet wurde. V. 49 wurde aber bei E durch v. 35 bα vorbereitet, und diese Absicht verfolgte auch der Redaktor, als er v. 35 bα aus E aufnahm.

Schon der Widerspruch zwischen 47,13 ff. und v. 34 b legt es nahe, daß v. 33.34 b.35 bα zu E gehören. V. 33 schließt zudem glatt an v. 32 an. Außerdem fehlt der Begriff *br* in jenen Texten, die sicher J zuzuweisen sind. In 42,25 steht er in einem Zusatz, in 45,23 bei E, und außer in 41,35.49 noch in 42,3, wo ebenfalls E zu Wort kommt[324]. Dem-

---

[323] So W. Rudolph, BZAW 63, 158.   [324] Vgl. III d.

gegenüber ist für J das Wort ʼkl charakteristisch. In Gen 43f. fehlt br, während ʼkl wiederholt gebraucht wird³²⁵. Zwar ist in der Josephsgeschichte Vorsicht angebracht, aus unterschiedlichen Begriffen auf verschiedene Verfasser zu schließen. So verwenden J (43,2; 47,14) und E (42,19.26) für Getreide auch das Wort šbr. Bei ʼkl und br spricht aber die Streuung der Belege eindeutig dagegen, daß diese Begriffe von einem Verfasser promiscue gebraucht wurden³²⁶. Daß E ʼkl durch br ersetzt, läßt sich einfach erklären. Das Wort ʼkl bezeichnet allgemein die Nahrung, br hingegen das Getreide. E hat somit einen allgemeineren Begriff von J durch ein präzises Wort ersetzt. Neben den verschiedenen Begriffen für Sack unterscheiden sich also J und E tatsächlich auch darin, daß J ʼkl, E hingegen br verwendet. Schließlich wird die Analyse von v. 37 ff. bestätigen, daß v. 33.34b.35bα zu E gehört. Dann sind v. 34a.35a.bβ.36 J zuzuweisen³²⁷. Auch bei J weiß somit Joseph, daß Jahre des Überflusses – nach v. 48 handelt es sich um sieben Jahre – und sieben Jahre der Hungersnot kommen werden. Woher Joseph bei J diese Erkenntnis hat, läßt sich leider nicht mehr ermitteln. Schon oben wurde aber festgestellt, daß die Forderung Josephs an die Brüder, Benjamin auf einer zweiten Reise mitzubringen, voraussetzt, daß er mit einer langen Dauer der Hungersnot rechnet³²⁸. Sie wird nach 45,6.11 auch bei J sieben Jahre währen. Damit ist der jahwistische Bestand von v. 33–36 im ganzen dieses Werkes gut verankert.

Die elohistische Fassung ist auch hier deutlich eine Umgestaltung von J. Hatte Joseph bei J vorgeschlagen, mehrere Aufseher zu bestellen, so rät er nach E, einen Mann einzusetzen. Damit wird bei E ein Überraschungsmoment in der jahwistischen Darstellung beseitigt. Es besteht

---

³²⁵ 43,2.4.20.22; 44,1.25.
³²⁶ Gegen H. Donner, Gestalt, 46; H.-C. Schmitt, BZAW 154, 37f.
³²⁷ So im wesentlichen auch H. Gunkel 433; L. Ruppert, Josephserzählung, 69, die allerdings v. 36b zu E rechnen. Es besteht aber m. E. kein Grund, v. 36 aufzuteilen. Für v. 33–36 sind zwar die verschiedensten Zuweisungen vorgeschlagen worden, wie schon aus dem knappen Überblick bei H. Donner, Gestalt, 42, hervorgeht. Dabei sind aber Spannungen und Zusammenhänge nicht zureichend beachtet worden. Wenn M. Noth, Pentateuch, 31.38, v. 34a.35b J und v. 34b.35a E zuweist, so wird damit der Zusammenhang zwischen v. 35a und v. 35bβ zerstört, wie v. 48 bestätigt. Außerdem wird der Plural in v. 35a unverständlich. O. Eißfeldt, Hexateuch-Synopse, 84*, rechnet v. 34.35bα zu E und v. 33.35a (mit Singular). bβ* zu J. Dann ist der Plural in v. 35bα nicht zu erklären. Außerdem wird der Zusammenhang zwischen v. 32, den auch O. Eißfeldt zu E rechnet, und v. 33 zerrissen, und es wird auch die deutliche Spannung in v. 34 nicht beachtet. Gegen O. Procksch 235 ff., der in v. 34b das Verb mit LXX in den Plural setzt und den ganzen Vers J zuweist, spricht, daß LXX eindeutig eine Glättung des MT bietet. Trotz der unterschiedlichen Aufteilungen von v. 33–36 in der Forschung läßt sich somit auch hier ein klares Ergebnis gewinnen.
³²⁸ Vgl. IIc.

darin, daß bei J der Pharao im Unterschied zu dem Vorschlag Josephs diesen allein mit der Aufgabe betraut, das Getreide zu sammeln, und ihm dazu eine besonders hohe Stellung verleiht. Bei E kommt Joseph hingegen zu seiner Position, weil er durch die Deutung der Träume als jener kluge und weise Mann erwiesen ist, der nach seinem Rat die Vorkehrungen für die Hungersnot treffen sollte (v. 37 ff.).

Die Abgabe des Fünften hat der Elohist aus 47, 13 ff. Er nahm dieses Motiv auf, um seine Vorlage zu präzisieren. Wenn nach J alle Speise der guten Jahre gesammelt werden sollte, so war damit natürlich nur das gemeint, was nach der Versorgung der Bevölkerung übrigblieb. Wenn E die Abgabe auf den Fünften beschränkt, so wird die Darstellung dadurch klarer. Außerdem konnte bei E nach v. 49 Joseph eine ungeheure Menge an Getreide anhäufen. Damit, daß der Fünfte eine solche Fülle erbringt, unterstreicht E den reichen Ertrag, den Ägypten in den sieben fetten Jahren einbringen konnte. Im übrigen dürfte es für E problematisch gewesen sein, Joseph für eine Steuer, die in Ägypten dauernd erhoben wurde, verantwortlich zu machen. Deshalb griff der Elohist zwar das Motiv des Fünften aus 47, 13 ff. auf, gab ihm jedoch eine andere Funktion. Außerdem beseitigt E hier wieder Nebenzüge der jahwistischen Darstellung. Nach J soll das Getreide in den Städten aufbewahrt werden (v. 35 bβ), nach v. 48 hat Joseph den Ertrag aus dem Gebiet einer Stadt in dieser Stadt aufbewahrt. Dieses Element wird im folgenden nicht mehr aufgenommen. Es ist deshalb auch von E übergangen worden. Dem Elohisten genügte es, daß das Getreide in die Verfügungsgewalt des Pharao kommen sollte (v. 35 bα). So bestätigt sich an der elohistischen Fassung in v. 33–36, daß E J zur Vorlage hatte und Nebenelemente der jahwistischen Darstellung zugunsten der Hauptlinie tilgte.

In v. 37–40 schildert der Elohist, wie der Pharao Joseph zum zweiten Mann in Ägypten bestellte. H. Gunkel und L. Ruppert sehen zwar in v. 38 und v. 39 eine Dublette, weil der Pharao hier zweimal die einzigartige Weisheit Josephs anerkenne [329]. Beide Aussagen sind aber nebeneinander sinnvoll, weil sich der Pharao in v. 38 an seine Diener, in v. 39 jedoch an Joseph wendet. Daß der Abschnitt aus E stammt, geht schon daraus hervor, daß Joseph in v. 40 über das Haus und über das Volk des Pharao gesetzt wird [330]. Diese Differenzierung entspricht 45, 8 aus E, wonach Joseph von Gott zum Herrn für das ganze Haus des Pharao und als Herrscher über das ganze Land Ägypten eingesetzt wurde. Sie fehlt bei J. Hier hat nach 45, 9 Gott einfach Joseph zum Herrn für ganz Ägypten gemacht. V. 37 entspricht in seiner Formulierung weitgehend

---

[329] H. Gunkel 433; L. Ruppert, Josephserzählung, 69.
[330] In v. 40a ist die Bedeutung von *yšq* unklar, vgl. D. B. Redford, VT. S 20, 166 Anm. 4; C. Westermann 97.

45,16b bei E. Bevor Pharao Joseph zum führenden Mann in Ägypten macht, und bevor er die Brüder zur Übersiedlung nach Ägypten auffordert, stellt E jeweils fest, daß »die Sache (es) gut war in den Augen Pharaos und in den Augen (aller) seiner Knechte«. Damit will E unterstreichen, daß die Entscheidungen Pharaos dem Willen seines Hofes entsprechen. Es kam E anscheinend darauf an, daß diese wesentlichen Beschlüsse vom Hof mitgetragen werden.

Wichtig ist aber vor allem, daß in v. 37–40 aufgegriffen wird, was E in Gen 40f. über die Möglichkeit der Traumdeutung ausgeführt hat. Wenn der Pharao in v. 39 zu Joseph sagt: »Nachdem dir Gott all das kundgetan hat«, so akzeptiert er damit, daß die von Joseph gegebene Deutung der Träume von Gott stammt. Weil Gott Joseph diese Fähigkeit verliehen hat, ist er ein Mann, in dem der Geist Gottes ist (v. 38). Dadurch ist niemand klüger und weiser als er (v. 39b). C. Westermann bestreitet zwar, daß der Pharao hier von einer Inspiration Josephs spricht: »Er meint nicht eine ›Inspiration‹ Josephs..., sondern eine herausragende politisch-wirtschaftliche, eine staatsmännische Begabung«.[331] Damit kommt aber v. 39 nicht zu seinem Recht. Hier begründet der Pharao die besondere Weisheit Josephs ausdrücklich damit, daß ihm Gott die Bedeutung der Träume kundgetan hat. Weil Joseph von Gott inspiriert wurde, steht zu erwarten, daß er auch eine schwierige politische Situation gut bewältigen wird. Der Geist Gottes ermöglicht somit Joseph die Deutung der Träume *und* das kluge politische Handeln. So erklärt es sich auch, daß E den Aufstieg Josephs mit der Deutung der Träume der beiden Beamten beginnen läßt und nicht – wie J – mit einem erfolgreichen Wirken Josephs. An die Stelle des Beistandes Jahwes bei J tritt somit bei E die Inspiration Josephs durch den Geist Gottes.

Literarisch uneinheitlich sind auch v. 41–44. In diesem Stück gibt es außerdem Dubletten zu v. 40. In v. 41 befremdet die neue Einleitung »Da sprach Pharao zu Joseph«, da der Pharao schon in v. 39f. zu Joseph geredet hat. Außerdem wird hier nochmals die Einsetzung Josephs über Ägypten berichtet. H. Gunkel will zwar v. 40 und 41 so miteinander verbinden, daß v. 40 von dem Entschluß des Pharao und v. 41 von seiner Durchführung handle[332]. Aber v. 41 bringt gegenüber v. 40 nichts Neues, schon in v. 40 erhält Joseph seine hohe Stellung[333]. Außerdem

---

[331] C. Westermann 96f.
[332] H. Gunkel 438; ähnlich z. B. W. Rudolph, BZAW 63, 159; L. Ruppert, Josephserzählung, 69; C. Westermann 97.
[333] Nach D. B. Redford, VT. S 20, 167, setzen der Imperativ »siehe« und das Perfekt »ich habe gesetzt« v. 40 voraus. Aber das Perfekt bezeichnet hier, wie z. B. in Jer 1,10 den Akt der Einsetzung, und »siehe« entspricht in seiner Funktion hnh. Beides weist somit nicht auf v. 40 zurück.

wird in v. 41 nicht wie in v. 40 und 45,8 zwischen dem Haus des Pharao und Ägypten bzw. dem Volk unterschieden. Zusammen mit der neuen Einleitung geht daraus hervor, daß v. 41 nicht die ursprüngliche Fortsetzung von v. 40 ist.

Diese Beobachtung wird durch v. 44 bestätigt. Dieser Vers kommt nach v. 43 eindeutig zu spät. Nachdem dort der Pharao Joseph auf seinem zweiten Wagen fahren ließ und ihm das Volk huldigte[334], kann keine Rede Pharaos zu Joseph folgen, die seine Stellung genauer definiert. C. Westermann sieht zwar in v. 44 den Abschluß der Einsetzung Josephs, die durch v. 41 und v. 44 gerahmt werde[335]. Dazu paßt aber nicht v. 43 b: »So setzte er ihn über das ganze Land Ägypten«. Mit dieser Feststellung ist die Einsetzung Josephs abgeschlossen. Nach W. Rudolph stand v. 44 ursprünglich vor v. 46 b[336], aber es läßt sich kaum begründen, warum der Vers nachträglich umgestellt worden sein sollte. Außerdem enthält v. 44 eine klare Dublette zu v. 40. Mit »ich bin Pharao« macht der Pharao deutlich, daß Joseph ihm untergeordnet bleiben soll. Das aber hat er bereits in v. 40 mit den Worten festgestellt: »Nur um den Thron will ich größer sein als du«. Durch v. 41 und v. 44 entsteht also eine Dublette zu v. 40. H.-C. Schmitt sieht in ihnen freilich nachträgliche Erläuterungen zu der Stellung Josephs: »Schon die inhaltliche Ähnlichkeit von v. 41 und v. 44 macht eine ursprüngliche Zusammengehörigkeit in einem Parallelbericht nicht gerade wahrscheinlich.«[337] Aber zumindest in v. 41 wird die Stellung Josephs nicht über das hinaus präzisiert, was schon in v. 40 gesagt wurde, und v. 44 ist deutlich eine Interpretation von v. 41. Nach v. 41 hat der Pharao Joseph über das ganze Land Ägypten eingesetzt. Mit v. 44 erläutert er, daß davon seine eigene Stellung nicht berührt wird, wohl aber soll ohne die Zustimmung Josephs niemand sonst in Ägypten handeln können. H.-C. Schmitt hat die Probleme erkannt, die v. 41 und v. 44 im Kontext bereiten. Seine These, daß die Josephsgeschichte nicht aus parallelen Darstellungen besteht, hindert ihn aber daran, aus diesem Befund die notwendigen Konsequenzen zu ziehen. V. 41 und v. 44 lassen sich nur verstehen, wenn sie aus J stammen. Nun setzt die Einleitung »da sprach Pharao zu Joseph« in v. 44 voraus, daß dieser Vers bei J nicht unmittelbar auf v. 41 folgte. Da v. 43 zu v. 44 nicht paßt, ist v. 42 zu J zu rechnen[338] und v. 43 zu E. Bei J und E machte also der Pharao Joseph durch

---

[334] Die Bedeutung von 'brk ist umstritten, vgl. die Kommentare und H.-C. Schmitt, BZAW 154, 148 f.

[335] C. Westermann 99.

[336] W. Rudolph, BZAW 63, 159.

[337] H.-C. Schmitt, BZAW 154, 39.

[338] Allerdings sind D. B. Redford, VT. S 20, 208–226, und H.-C. Schmitt, BZAW 154, 146 f., der Auffassung, daß v. 42 von neuassyrischen Vorstellungen beeinflußt ist. Aber die Frage, in welcher Zeit in Ägypten jene Verhältnisse bestanden, die J und E

ein Wort *und* eine Handlung zu dem zweiten Mann in Ägypten.

Auf v. 44 folgte bei J v. 45 a. Der Name des Priesters von On Potiphera entspricht Potiphar, dem Namen des Obersten der Leibwache bei E (37,36). Daß »der Ruben-Schicht die Identität beider Namen im Ägyptischen angesichts der verschiedenen Schreibweise im Hebräischen wohl gar nicht bekannt war«, wie H.-C. Schmitt meint[339], ist recht problematisch. Man wird vielmehr anzunehmen haben, daß E den Namen des Priesters bei J auf den Obersten der Leibwache übertragen hat. Der ägyptische Name, den Pharao in v. 45 a dem Joseph verleiht, kommt im folgenden nicht mehr vor. Der Verfasser bringt damit wieder Kenntnisse zur Geltung, die er über Ägypten hat. Dort erhielten verschiedentlich semitische Sklaven ägyptische Namen[340]. Daß der Verfasser freilich nicht schon den Ägypter von 39,1 oder den Obersten des Gefängnisses, sondern erst den Pharao Joseph einen solchen Namen beilegen läßt, zeigt, daß er mit dieser Benennung eine besondere Absicht verbindet. Mit seinem Namen und durch die Verheiratung mit der Tochter eines Priesters macht Pharao den Joseph zu einem Glied der ägyptischen Oberschicht. In ihr soll Joseph als der zweite Mann in Ägypten nach dem Willen des Pharao verankert werden.

In v. 37-45 a gehören somit v. 37-40.43 zu E, v. 41.42.44.45 a zu J. Der Jehowist hat hier wohl J und E vollständig aufgenommen. Bei J dürfte v. 41 unmittelbar auf v. 36 gefolgt sein. Der Pharao reagierte auf den Vorschlag Josephs überraschenderweise damit, daß er nicht viele Aufseher einsetzte, sondern Joseph zum zweiten Mann in Ägypten machte. Da E für die Erhöhung Josephs eine ausführlichere Begründung bot, hat der Jehowist zunächst v. 37-40 aus E aufgenommen und daran v. 41 aus J angeschlossen. Die Reihenfolge für die Handlungen in v. 42 f. ergab sich von selbst. Die Fahrt auf dem zweiten Wagen und die Huldigung in v. 43 aus E konnten nur auf v. 42 folgen. Durch v. 43 hat der Jehowist allerdings den Zusammenhang zwischen v. 41 f. und v. 44 zerstört. Aber das war unvermeidlich, wenn er hier J und E aufnehmen wollte. Weil der Jehowist in diesem Abschnitt beide Quellenschriften zu Wort kommen läßt, wird die Einsetzung Josephs bei ihm doppelt berichtet. Diese Doppelung ist beabsichtigt. Durch sie erhält die Erhöhung Josephs ein besonderes Gewicht. Der Jehowist hat hier somit wieder die Doppelung als stilistisches Mittel eingesetzt. Auch bei diesem Abschnitt geht jedoch aus den Spannungen hervor, daß diese Doppelung erst durch die Verbindung zweier unterschiedlicher Darstellungen entstanden ist.

---

    voraussetzen, ist in der Forschung derart kontrovers, daß die verschiedenen Thesen nicht für die Literarkritik verwertet werden können; vgl. schon F. Crüsemann, Widerstand, 145 Anm. 26.

[339] H.-C. Schmitt, BZAW 154, 39 Anm. 151.

[340] Vgl. z. B. S. Herrmann, Israels Aufenthalt in Ägypten, 1970, 67.

V. 45 b entspricht sachlich v. 46 b und kann weder zu J noch zu E gerechnet werden. Ob es sich um eine Variante zu v. 46 b handelt, die versehentlich in den Text kam [341], oder ob v. 45 b als Prolepse von v. 46 b eingefügt wurde, als man v. 46 a eingeschoben hat, wie E. Blum will [342], braucht hier nicht entschieden zu werden. Jedenfalls stammt v. 46 a aus P. Dafür spricht außer der Altersangabe für Joseph die Formulierung »Pharao, der König von Ägypten«, die bei J und E fehlt. Mit v. 46 a kommt somit in der Josephsgeschichte nach 37,1 f. erstmals wieder P zu Wort. Wie hier Joseph zu dem Pharao kam und von diesem eine besondere Stellung erhielt, ist nicht mehr erhalten. P. Weimar ist der Auffassung, daß P darüber nichts enthielt. Nach ihm lautet der Text von P zwischen 37,1 f. und 41,46 a, den der Endredaktor übergangen hat, etwa: Da verkauften seine Brüder Joseph nach Ägypten. Da stand Joseph vor Pharao, dem König von Ägypten [343]. Aber auch P muß berichtet haben, welche Bedeutung seine Begegnung mit dem Pharao für Joseph hatte. Von dieser Schilderung ist aber mit v. 46 a nur noch der Schluß erhalten. Was P zwischen 37,2 und 41,46 a enthielt, läßt sich nicht mehr rekonstruieren. Der Endredaktor hat der Darstellung des Jehowisten den Vorzug gegeben, weil sie anscheinend ausführlicher war. Mit ihr konnte er offenbar die Fassung von P nicht verknüpfen. Deshalb nahm er aus P lediglich v. 46 a auf, da er das chronologische Gerüst der Priesterschrift zur Basis seines Werkes machte.

Von v. 46 b–52 gehören nach den Ergebnissen zu v. 33–36 v. 48 [344] zu J und v. 49 zu E. Als Einleitung zu v. 48 stammt auch v. 46 b aus J, während v. 47, der diesen Zusammenhang unterbricht, zu E zu rechnen ist [345]. H. Gunkel sieht in v. 46 b allerdings die direkte Fortsetzung von v. 43 und ordnet den Halbvers deshalb E zu. Joseph stelle sich mit einer feierlichen Ausfahrt dem Land als sein neuer Herr vor [346]. Dann würde v. 46 b noch zur Einsetzung Josephs gehören. So will in der Tat der Jehowist v. 46 b verstanden wissen. Eine Zäsur entsteht bei ihm erst durch v. 47, wo berichtet wird, daß das Land einen reichen Ertrag brachte. Der Endredaktor teilt diese Auffassung, wenn er v. 46 a aus P vor v. 46 b einordnet. Trotzdem dürfte erst der Jehowist v. 46 b so interpretiert haben. Bei E ist die Einsetzung Josephs mit v. 43 b abgeschlossen. Nach

---

[341] Vgl. die Kommentare.
[342] E. Blum, Komposition, 232. Für ihn ist das ein Zeichen, daß die in der Regel P zugewiesenen Stücke einer Bearbeitungsschicht angehören. Das scheitert aber schon an jenen Stellen, die in den Analysen bisher P zugewiesen werden mußten.
[343] P. Weimar, Aufbau, 195 Anm. 86.
[344] In v. 48 ist wohl mit Sam und LXX zu lesen: »alle Speise der sieben Jahre, in denen ›Überfluß‹ war im Lande Ägypten«, vgl. die Kommentare.
[345] So z. B. auch O. Eißfeldt, Hexateuch-Synopse, 85*.
[346] H. Gunkel 439; vgl. auch L. Ruppert, Josephserzählung, 69.

der in v. 43 erwähnten Huldigung Josephs hat v. 46 b keine Funktion. Dagegen ist der Halbvers für die Darstellung des Jahwisten notwendig. V. 48 ist mit v. 47 nur locker verbunden. Da das Subjekt gegenüber v. 47 wechselt, müßte hier Joseph eigentlich als Subjekt ausdrücklich genannt werden. Ging aber v. 46 b v. 48 voraus, dann wird verständlich, warum der Name Joseph in v. 48 nicht fällt. Auch sachlich paßt v. 46 b gut zu v. 48. Joseph verläßt den Pharao und durchzieht das ganze Land Ägypten (v. 46 b). Er sammelt die gesamte Speise der sieben Jahre des Überflusses und lagert sie in den Städten und zwar so, daß er die Speise des Gefildes einer Stadt in dieser Stadt aufbewahrt (v. 48). In v. 48 ist also vorausgesetzt, daß Joseph Ägypten durchzogen hat, und das wird in v. 46 b berichtet. Bei E wird hingegen in v. 49 Joseph ausdrücklich genannt. Das spricht dafür, daß hier v. 49 unmittelbar auf v. 47 folgte.

Die elohistische Darstellung weist somit in v. 37 ff. eine klare Gliederung auf. V. 37–40.43 handeln von der Einsetzung Josephs, den Abschluß bildet v. 43 b. In v. 47 wird durch das Subjekt Land eine Zäsur angezeigt. In v. 47.49 geht es um die Tätigkeit Josephs. So hat E die Einsetzung und die Tätigkeit Josephs klar voneinander abgesetzt. Bei J bilden hingegen v. 41.42.44.45 a.46 b.48 einen durchlaufenden Zusammenhang, der unter dem Thema des Aufstiegs Josephs steht. Zu seinem Aufstieg gehört auch sein Wirken in den sieben Jahren des Überflusses. Der Jehowist hat hingegen die Gliederung von E aufgegriffen. Bei ihm gehören v. 37–45 a.46 b zu der Einsetzung Josephs, von der seine Tätigkeit in den fetten Jahren (v. 47–49) durch v. 47 abgehoben wird.

In v. 50–52 wird erzählt, daß Joseph zwei Söhne geboren wurden, bevor die Hungersnot begann. Da er für die Erklärung ihrer Namen in v. 51 f. als Gottesbezeichnung Elohim gebraucht, werden die Verse in der Regel E zugewiesen[347]. Nun hat sich aber gezeigt, daß in der Josephsgeschichte Elohim kein literarkritisches Kriterium sein kann. Dann sprechen mehrere Beobachtungen dafür, daß v. 50–52 nicht aus E stammt. Hier wird die Notiz über die Heirat Josephs in v. 45 a aus J vorausgesetzt. Zwar ist v. 50 b, wo die Frau Josephs ausdrücklich genannt wird, ein Zusatz. Hier wird nur wiederholt, was aus v. 45 a bereits bekannt ist, und außerdem unterbricht v. 50 b den Zusammenhang von v. 50 a und v. 51[348]. Aber auch ohne v. 50 b besteht eine Verbindung zu v.

---

[347] So z. B. H. Gunkel 433; O. Procksch 404 f.; O. Eißfeldt, Hexateuch-Synopse, 85*; L. Ruppert, Josephserzählung, 86 f.; H. Seebaß, Zeit, 90. V. 50 b, der auf v. 45 a Bezug nimmt, wird dann entweder als redaktioneller Ausgleich mit J (so H. Gunkel) oder als Fragment aus J (so O. Eißfeldt) angesehen. H. Gunkel und O. Eißfeldt rechnen auch v. 51 bβ »und das ganze Haus meines Vaters« zu J, da in v. 51 der Name Manasse doppelt erklärt werde. Diese Worte hängen aber ohne den Rest von v. 51 in der Luft.

[348] Vgl. H. Gunkel 433; L. Ruppert, Josephserzählung, 86; H.-C. Schmitt, BZAW 154, 39 Anm. 151.

45 a. Daß Joseph seine beiden Söhne geboren wurden, bevor die Hungersnot begann, läßt sich am besten verstehen, wenn er geheiratet hat, als er zum zweiten Mann Ägyptens aufgestiegen ist. Das aber wird in v. 45 a berichtet. Außerdem hat H. Donner mit Recht darauf hingewiesen, daß durch v. 50–52 der Zusammenhang zwischen v. 49 und v. 53 unterbrochen wird[349]. Schließlich fügt sich v. 51 nicht nahtlos in die elohistische Darstellung ein, weil Joseph dann auch seine Träume vergessen haben müßte, an die er sich in 42,9 durchaus erinnert. V. 50 a. 51 f. gehört somit zu J[350].

Wie schon aus der Inversion in v. 50 a hervorgeht, bildet dieses Stück bei J den Abschluß des Aufstiegs Josephs. Hier besteht somit die Wende, die Joseph erfahren darf, darin, daß er in dem Land, in dem er in das Gefängnis geworfen wurde, zu einer führenden Stellung aufsteigt und eine eigene Familie erhält. Erst dadurch ist sein Glück vollkommen. Das drückt Joseph in der Deutung der Namen seiner Söhne aus. In v. 51 begründet er den Namen Manasse damit, daß ihn Gott all seine Mühsal und das ganze Haus seines Vaters vergessen ließ. Mit der Erwähnung des Hauses seines Vaters ist schwerlich nur gemeint, »daß ich meinem Vaterhaus fern bin«, wie C. Westermann annimmt[351]. Das Haus des Vaters war der Ort, wo ihm durch die Liebe des Vaters eine bevorzugte Stellung zukam. Daran muß sich Joseph nun nicht mehr voll Sehnsucht erinnern, weil seine Position in Ägypten weit über das hinausgeht, was ihm der Vater geben konnte. Daß für Joseph das Haus des Vaters dann keine Rolle mehr spielt, wird daran deutlich, daß es bei der Deutung des Namens Ephraim in v. 52 nicht mehr erwähnt wird. Hier geht es allein um den Kontrast, daß ihn Gott gerade in dem Land seines Elends fruchtbar gemacht hat. Die Namen beider Söhne begründet also Joseph mit der Wende, die Gott seinem Leben gegeben hat. Dadurch erfährt die Darstellung des Aufstiegs Josephs bei J ihre Abrundung. An ihrem Beginn hatte der Erzähler in Gen 39 wiederholt betont, daß Jahwe mit Joseph war. Jetzt, wo deutlich ist, welche Folgen der Beistand Jahwes für Joseph hatte, spricht Joseph selbst aus, daß er seinen Aufstieg Gott verdankt. Damit bereitet der Verfasser die Worte Josephs von 45,9 vor, daß ihn Gott zum Herrn für ganz Ägypten gemacht hat. Während bei E der Leser nach dem Aufstieg Josephs noch immer vor der Frage steht, wie seine Träume von Gen 37 in Erfüllung gehen werden, kann er bei J nach v. 51 f. eigentlich nicht damit rechnen, daß Joseph nochmals mit den Brüdern zusammentrifft. Ihre Begegnung ist hier eine von Joseph und dem Leser unerwartete neue Wende.

---

[349] H. Donner, Gestalt, 27.
[350] Nach H. Donner, Gestalt, 27, sprechen auch »Formulierungsweise und Sprachgebrauch eher für den Jahwisten«.
[351] C. Westermann 101.

Auch in v. 53–57 bestehen erhebliche Spannungen. Das gilt zunächst für v. 54 b und v. 55. In v. 54 bβ heißt es: »aber im ganzen Land Ägypten war Brot«, v. 55 beginnt: »da hungerte das ganze Land Ägypten«. W. Rudolph hat zwar mit Recht darauf hingewiesen, daß man aus v. 54 b nicht schließen darf, daß Ägypten von der weltweiten Hungersnot nicht betroffen war. V. 54 bβ beziehe sich »auf das Brot in den Speichern Josefs«[352]. Diese Deutung wird dadurch gestützt, daß Joseph nach v. 56 bα und 42,6[353] den Ägyptern Getreide verkauft hat. In diesem Punkt stimmen J und E überein. Aber auch wenn v. 54 b sachlich mit v. 55 vereinbar ist, stoßen die Formulierungen doch zu hart aufeinander. Auf v. 54 b kann nicht folgen, wie der Hunger in Ägypten bewältigt wurde, da das nach v. 54 b zunächst kein Thema sein kann. Deshalb sieht C. Westermann in v. 54 b einen Zusatz[354]. Nun ließe sich zwar verstehen, daß ein Späterer sofort verdeutlichen wollte, daß die Hungersnot alle Länder betraf. Es bleibt aber rätselhaft, warum er mit v. 54 bβ die Spannung zu v. 55 geschaffen haben sollte. Das spricht dafür, daß auch diese Spannung darauf zurückgeht, daß der Jehowist hier J und E miteinander verbunden hat.

V. 53 knüpft unmittelbar an v. 49 an und gehört deshalb zu E. Dazu ist v. 54 die Fortsetzung[355]. Der Elohist schildert in v. 49 zunächst, daß Joseph eine ungeheure Menge Getreide angehäuft hat. Darauf stellt E in v. 53 f. fest, daß die fetten Jahre aufhörten und die Jahre der Hungersnot anfingen, wie Joseph vorhergesagt hatte. Diese Hungersnot erstreckte sich über alle Länder, aber in Ägypten gab es Brot. E kommt es hier nur auf den Gegensatz zwischen der in allen Ländern herrschenden Hungersnot und Ägypten an. Daß Joseph den Ägyptern Getreide verkaufte, ist für ihn hier nicht von Interesse. Genau das aber hatte J geschildert, und das erklärt, warum der Jehowist hier an v. 54 ein Stück aus J anschloß. V. 55 hat seine unmittelbare Fortsetzung in v. 56 bα[356], so daß v. 55.56 bα aus J stammt. Bei J dürfte dieses Stück

---

[352] W. Rudolph, BZAW 63, 159; so auch H.-C. Schmitt, BZAW 154, 37.
[353] Vgl. zu 42,6 III d.
[354] C. Westermann 102.
[355] V. 54 b läßt sich gegen H. Gunkel 433, und L. Ruppert, Josephserzählung, 68 f., von v. 53.54 a nicht trennen.
[356] In v. 56 bα ist der Text gestört. Bei dem Verb *šbr* ist hi. zu lesen. Der vorangehende Relativsatz ergibt keinen Sinn. Vielleicht ist hier das Nomen *šbr* einzufügen, das dann durch eine Haplographie zu dem folgenden Verb ausgefallen ist. Sam ergänzt *br*. Dagegen spricht nicht nur, daß das die einzige Stelle in der jahwistischen Josephsgeschichte mit *br* wäre, sondern auch, daß der Ausfall dieses Wortes graphisch schwer zu erklären ist. Aus der in Anlehnung an die LXX vorgenommenen Konjektur »da öffnete Joseph alle ›Speicher von Getreide‹« (so z. B. C. Westermann z. St.) läßt sich die Entstehung des MT jedenfalls kaum verständlich machen.

unmittelbar auf v. 52 gefolgt sein. Hier wird mit v. 50 a. 51 f. der Aufstieg Josephs abgeschlossen. Damit enden bei J zugleich die sieben Jahre der Sättigung. Das geht einerseits daraus hervor, daß J in v. 48 ausdrücklich sagt, daß Joseph während der sieben Jahre der Sättigung alle Speise sammelte, und es wird zum anderen aus der Bemerkung in v. 50 a deutlich, daß Joseph seine beiden Söhne geboren wurden, bevor das Jahr der Hungersnot kam. So beginnt bei J mit v. 55 ein neuer Abschnitt. Auch in Gen 12, 10–13, 1 wird durch die Inversion in 12, 16 der Abschluß einer Szene markiert, die hier v. 14–16 umfaßt, und in v. 17 mit einem impf. cons. ein neuer Abschnitt eingeleitet.

Schwierig zu beurteilen sind v. 56 a. bβ und v. 57. V. 56 a »und die Hungersnot war über die ganze Erde hin« trennt die Aufforderung Pharaos an das Volk in v. 55 von den Maßnahmen Josephs, die in v. 56 bα berichtet werden. Welche Funktion die Aussage von v. 56 bβ haben soll »da war die Hungersnot groß im Lande Ägypten«, ist nicht recht zu erkennen[357]. Interessanterweise fehlt sie in LXX. Sie entspricht aber der Feststellung in v. 57 b »denn die Hungersnot war groß auf der ganzen Erde«. Das zeigt, daß v. 56 bβ und v. 57 von dem gleichen Verfasser stammen[358]. Für eine Lösung der Probleme ist deshalb von v. 57 auszugehen. Dieser Vers wird vielfach zu J gerechnet[359]. Das scheitert aber an 42, 5. Hier wird in v. 5 a »da kamen die Söhne Israels, um Getreide zu kaufen mitten unter denen, die kamen« 41, 57 a aufgenommen: »und alle Welt kam nach Ägypten zu Joseph, um Getreide zu kaufen«. 42, 5 und 41, 57 stammen somit von dem gleichen Verfasser. Nun steht aber 42, 5 in seinem Kontext recht isoliert. C. Westermann stellt mit Recht fest: »V. 5 a wiederholt eher V. 3, als daß er ihn weiterführt ... Über V. 3 hinaus hat V. 5 nur ›inmitten der Kommenden‹, was keinen rechten Sinn ergibt.«[360] W. Rudolph meint zwar, daß v. 3 den Aufbruch der Brüder und v. 5 ihre Ankunft in Ägypten berichte[361]. Aber es müßte doch ausdrücklich gesagt werden, daß sie zu Joseph kamen. Weil diese Angabe fehlt, läßt sich v. 5 nicht einfach mit v. 3 f. verbinden[362]. Dagegen wird die Konstruktion in v. 5 verständlich, wenn dieser

---

[357] C. Westermann 85, verbindet v. 56 bβ als Temporalsatz mit v. 56 bα und übersetzt: »als der Hunger drückend wurde im Lande Ägypten«. Das läßt sich grammatisch kaum rechtfertigen. Außerdem wäre v. 56 bβ eine überflüssige Wiederholung von v. 55 aα.

[358] V. 56 bβ und v. 57 können deshalb gegen O. Eißfeldt, Hexateuch-Synopse, 86*, nicht auf J und E verteilt werden.

[359] So z. B. H. Gunkel 432 f.; M. Noth, Pentateuch, 31; L. Ruppert, Josephserzählung, 68. Dagegen weisen O. Eißfeldt, Hexateuch-Synopse, 86*, und O. Procksch 405, v. 57 E zu.

[360] C. Westermann 110.

[361] W. Rudolph, BZAW 63, 160.

[362] V. 5 steht auch in Spannung zu v. 6 b »da kamen die Brüder Josephs und fielen vor ihm mit dem Angesicht zur Erde nieder«, da v. 6 bα eine Dublette zu v. 5 a ist.

Vers ursprünglich direkt auf 41,57 folgte, wie C. Westermann erkannt hat[363]. Er nimmt allerdings an, daß der Vers nachträglich umgestellt wurde. Das läßt sich nur schwer begründen. Nun werden in 42,5 die Brüder Josephs als »die Söhne Israels« bezeichnet. Dieser Ausdruck kommt in 37,3–50,22 weder bei J noch bei E vor. Er steht dagegen in 45,21 aα und 46,5 b bei P[364]. Daraus geht hervor, daß auch 42,5 aus P stammt[365]. Das gilt dann auch für 41,56 bβ.57. In 41,56 bβ.57; 42,5, wozu als Einleitung vielleicht auch noch 41,56 a[366] gehört, liegt somit die priesterschriftliche Einleitung zu der Begegnung der Brüder mit Joseph vor.

Tatsächlich unterscheidet sich 41,57 auch geringfügig von der Auffassung, die J und E über die Tätigkeit Josephs vertreten. Nach 42,6 hat Joseph bei E nur an die Bevölkerung Ägyptens Getreide verkauft. Bei J bringt in 47,13 ff. Joseph das Geld des Landes Ägypten und des Landes Kanaan in das Haus des Pharao. Das spricht dafür, daß er hier nur an die Bevölkerung Ägyptens und Kanaans und nicht wie in 41,57 an alle Welt Getreide verkaufte. P hat mit 41,57 also den Kreis der Käufer über die jehowistische Vorlage hinaus erweitert. Auf der anderen Seite hat P diese Vorlage in einem wichtigen Punkt gekürzt. P berichtet nicht, daß der Vater die Brüder zu ihrer Reise aufgefordert hätte. Es kommt der Priesterschrift also nur darauf an, daß die Hungersnot die Brüder zu dem Weg nach Ägypten zwang. Das entspricht 45,21 aα; 46,5 b, denn hier fällen nach P die Brüder die Entscheidung zur Übersiedlung nach Ägypten.

Der Endredaktor hat v. 56 a.bβ.57 an den Schluß von Gen 41 gestellt, weil v. 57 die Reise der Brüder, von der in 42,1 ff. berichtet wird, vorbereitet. Die unglückliche Stellung von v. 56 a erklärt sich wohl daraus, daß dieser Redaktor den Zusammenhang von v. 56 bβ und v. 57 bei P nicht zerreißen wollte, da sich v. 56 bβ und 57 b entsprechen. Dadurch konnte er v. 56 bα aus J nicht, wie es sachgemäßer gewesen wäre, nach v. 56 bβ einordnen. Wenn er auf 42,5 nicht verzichten wollte, konnte er diesen Vers nur an seiner jetzigen Stelle einfügen. So läßt sich auch bei diesem Stück das Vorgehen der Redaktion verständlich machen.

---

[363] C. Westermann 110 f.

[364] Vgl. II e. »Die Söhne Israels« werden in der Josephsgeschichte sonst nur noch in 46,8 und 50,25 erwähnt. 46,8 gehört zu P^s (vgl. II g). Die Zuweisung von 50,25 muß hier offen bleiben.

[365] So auch O. Procksch 555; D. B. Redford, VT. S 20, 135 Anm. 1. 168. D. B. Redford sieht in P allerdings keine eigene Quellenschrift, sondern eine Bearbeitungsschicht. P sei der »Genesis Editor«.

[366] V. 56 a wird verschiedentlich als Zusatz angesehen, der v. 57 vorbereiten soll (so z. B. H. Gunkel 440; H.-C. Schmitt, BZAW 154, 37 Anm. 142). Es läßt sich aber schwer begründen, warum eine solche Ergänzung vorgenommen worden sein sollte. Das spricht dafür, daß auch v. 56 a aus P stammt.

Der Komplex 41,33–57 gehört literarisch zu den schwierigsten Stücken der Josephsgeschichte. Man kann verstehen, daß angesichts der unterschiedlichen Zuweisungen, die für die einzelnen Bestandteile vorgenommen wurden, gegenwärtig die Tendenz besteht, ihn – vielleicht mit Ausnahme einzelner Zusätze – als einheitlich zu verstehen. Das scheitert aber an den deutlichen Spannungen, die sich nicht harmonisieren lassen. Tatsächlich kann man auch hier J und E noch deutlich voneinander abheben, wobei in v. 46a und v. 56a.bβ.57 außerdem noch P zu Wort kommt. Zu J gehören: V. 34a.35a.bβ (mit Textänderung) .36. 41.42.44.45a.46b.48.50a.51.52.55.56bα; aus E stammen: V. 33.34b. 35bα (mit Singular). 37–40.43.47.49.53f. Spätere Zusätze sind v. 45b und v. 50b.

d) Gen 42,1–13

Nach v. 1a hat Jakob erkannt, daß es in Ägypten Getreide gibt. Da der Vater hier »Jakob« heißt, gehört v. 1a zu E. Er folgte bei E direkt auf 41,54. Wenn nach 41,54 in allen Ländern Hungersnot herrschte, so war davon auch das Land Kanaan betroffen, in dem Jakob mit seinen Söhnen lebte. Außerdem erkennt Jakob in v. 1a, was E in 41,54 mit den Worten konstatiert hatte »aber in dem ganzen Land Ägypten war Brot«. So schließt v. 1a bei E nahtlos an 41,54 an.

Schwierigkeiten bereitet dagegen die Abfolge von v. 1 und v. 2. Hier befremdet vor allem, daß nach v. 1b in v. 2 für die Rede des Vaters mit »da sprach er« nochmals eine Einleitung steht. Sie ist übrigens von LXX ausgelassen und somit schon dort als problematisch empfunden worden. Das legt es nahe, daß v. 1 und v. 2 von verschiedenen Verfassern stammen. Dann wäre v. 2 aus J[367]. M. Noth weist zwar v. 1a und v. 2 E zu[368], aber dann würde bei E fehlen, wen Jakob in v. 2 anredet. Zudem kann v. 1b nicht, wie M. Noth annimmt, aus J stammen, da hier der Vater Jakob heißt. M. Noth vermutet zwar, daß in v. 1b ursprünglich Israel stand, das später wegen v. 1a in Jakob geändert wurde[369]. Aber für eine solche Änderung bei der Bezeichnung des Vaters fand sich in den bisher analysierten Stücken kein weiterer Beleg. H.-C. Schmitt sieht in v. 1b einen Zusatz: »Intention der Glosse scheint es zu sein, auf die – wohl im schlechten Gewissen begründete – Furcht der Brüder vor der Reise nach Ägypten hinzuweisen«[370]. Dann fehlt aber

---

[367] So z. B. H. Gunkel 441; L. Ruppert, Josephserzählung, 88.
[368] M. Noth, Pentateuch, 38. Dagegen rechnet O. Eißfeldt, Hexateuch-Synopse, 86*, v. 1 a. 2 zu J. Aber das »Jakob« in v. 1a läßt sich gegen O. Eißfeldt, a.a.O. 267*, nicht als redaktioneller Ersatz für »Israel« erklären.
[369] M. Noth, Pentateuch, 31 Anm. 101.
[370] H.-C. Schmitt, BZAW 154, 41 Anm. 163; vgl. C. Westermann 109.

für die Rede des Vaters in v. 2 ebenfalls der Adressat. Dieses Problem ließe sich allerdings dadurch lösen, daß man v. 1 bα »da sprach Jakob zu seinen Söhnen« als ursprüngliche Einleitung seiner Worte in v. 2 ansieht, die nach der Einfügung von v. 1 bβ mit »da sprach er« wieder aufgenommen worden wäre. Zwar ist die erneute Nennung Jakobs in v. 1 bα unnötig, sie fehlt deshalb in LXX. Aber literarkritische Folgerungen können daraus nicht abgeleitet werden. Trotzdem bestehen erhebliche Bedenken, v. 1 bβ als Zusatz abzutrennen. Die Intention des Ergänzers, die H.-C. Schmitt erschließt, wird in v. 1 bβ keineswegs eindeutig ausgedrückt. Sie wäre aber von einem Späteren doch wohl klarer formuliert worden. Deshalb muß es dabei bleiben, daß v. 1 zu E gehört. Hier wies der Vater mit v. 1 b auf die Ratlosigkeit seiner Söhne angesichts der Hungersnot hin.

Daß v. 2 aus J stammt, wird auch dadurch nahegelegt, daß die Begründung, die der Vater hier für die Reise nach Ägypten gibt, in 43,8 im Munde Judas vorkommt. Sie lautet an beiden Stellen: »daß wir leben und nicht sterben«. Bei E wäre sie schwer verständlich. Hier behält Joseph in 42,14ff. Simeon zurück, um die Brüder auf die Probe zu stellen, ob sie diesen Bruder ebenfalls preisgeben. Das setzt aber voraus, daß die Brüder nicht wegen der Hungersnot gezwungen sind, wieder nach Ägypten zu kommen. Zwar erstreckt sich nach 41,54 bei E die Hungersnot über alle Länder, sie ist aber anscheinend doch nicht so schwer, daß die Brüder ohne den Weg nach Ägypten nicht überleben können. Das ist bei J anders. Hier beruht die Forderung Josephs, Benjamin mitzubringen, falls ihn die Brüder nochmals sehen wollen, auf seinem Wissen, daß sie wegen der Hungersnot wieder nach Ägypten reisen müssen. V. 2 ist also bei J gut verankert, während der Vers bei E nicht ganz konsequent wäre. Freilich muß auch bei E der Vater nach v. 1 b seine Söhne aufgefordert haben, nach Ägypten zu ziehen. Das ist anscheinend vom Jehowisten zugunsten von v. 2 aus J ausgelassen worden. Der Grund dürfte sein, daß der Jehowist wegen der Begründung, die der Vater hier gibt, nicht auf v. 2 verzichten wollte. Umgekehrt müßte J vor v. 2 berichtet haben, daß die Hungersnot auch im Lande Kanaan herrschte und der Vater davon erfuhr, daß es in Ägypten Getreide gab. Außerdem müßten seine Söhne eingeführt worden sein. Darauf hätte der Jehowist zugunsten von E verzichtet. An dieser Überlegung wird deutlich, daß die Zuweisung von v. 2 an J nicht unproblematisch ist.

Sicher ist hingegen, daß v. 3 und v. 4 zu E gehören. In v. 4 a wird der Vater Jakob genannt. Dieser Halbvers läßt sich von v. 3 nicht trennen, da er erläutert, warum nach v. 3 nur zehn Brüder hinabzogen, um von Ägypten Getreide (*br*) zu kaufen. V. 4 b gehört als Begründung von v. 4 a ebenfalls zu E. Daß der Vater hier fürchtet, Benjamin könne ein

Unheil begegnen, entspricht allerdings 42,38 und 44,29 bei J. Deshalb hat man verschiedentlich v. 4 oder wenigstens v. 4b J zugewiesen[371]. Aber v. 4b setzt klar v. 4a voraus, und v. 4a gehört wegen »Jakob« eindeutig zu E[372]. Daß der Elohist in v. 4b eine Formulierung aufgreift, die sonst bei J vorkommt, zeigt nur, daß er die jahwistische Darstellung gekannt hat[373]. Sachlich ist v. 3f. bei E gut verankert. Nach 37,9 träumte Joseph, daß sich vor ihm Sonne, Mond und elf Sterne verneigen. Der Elohist hat somit bei den Brüdern von vornherein Benjamin mit im Blick.

Dem entspricht, daß in 50,15ff. alle Brüder sich vor Joseph fürchten. Anscheinend ist bei E auch Benjamin schuldig geworden. Demgegenüber war bei J Benjamin an dem Verkauf Josephs nicht beteiligt. In Gen 37 hat bei J der Leser den Eindruck, daß Joseph der jüngste Sohn Israels ist. Zu seiner Überraschung erfährt er erstmals bei dem Gespräch zwischen Joseph und den Brüdern auf der ersten Reise von einem weiteren Bruder. Benjamin war zur Zeit von Gen 37 bei J anscheinend noch so klein, daß er keine Rolle spielen konnte. In Gen 43,29 ist er offenbar erheblich jünger als Joseph. Da der Elohist aber mit 37,9 elf Brüder erwähnt, mußte er in 42,3 f. feststellen, daß nur zehn die Reise nach Ägypten antraten, und er mußte auch begründen, warum Benjamin nicht mitzog. Dafür griff er jene Begründung auf, mit der bei J in 42,38 der Vater den Brüdern zunächst nicht gestattete, der von Joseph auf der ersten Reise erhobenen Forderung nachzukommen.

Da 42,5 aus P stammt[374], ist v. 6 – ohne »er war der Machthaber über das Land«[375] – die elohistische Fortsetzung von v. 3f. Die betonte Feststellung in v. 6a, daß Joseph dem Volk des Landes Getreide verkaufte, wäre bei J nach 41,56bα nicht sinnvoll, da sie nur Bekanntes wiederholen würde. Hier wird von E eine Information nachgeholt, weil sie begründet, warum die Brüder auf Joseph treffen, als sie von Ägypten Getreide kaufen wollen. Da Joseph den Ägyptern Getreide verkaufte, gab es im ganzen Lande Ägypten Brot, wie E in 41,54 festgestellt hatte. Aber E berichtet von diesem Verkauf nicht in 41,54, sondern erst an

---

[371] So rechnet z. B. M. Noth, Pentateuch, 31, v. 4 zu J; H. Gunkel 441, v. 4b.
[372] M. Noth, Pentateuch, 31 Anm. 101, nimmt zwar an, daß in v. 4a der Name des Vaters ursprünglich gefehlt haben könne, aber damit wird der Zusammenhang von v. 3 und v. 4 übersehen. Das gilt auch gegen D. B. Redford, VT. S 20, 168, der v. 4 seinem »Genesis Editor« zuweist.
[373] Das hat H.-C. Schmitt, BZAW 154, 43 Anm. 170, für seine Ruben-Schicht mit Recht betont. Es dürfte dann aber auch für die mit v. 2a weitgehend übereinstimmende Formulierung von v. 1a bei E gelten.
[374] Vgl. III c.
[375] Hier handelt es sich, wie die lockere Verknüpfung mit dem Kontext zeigt, um einen Zusatz, vgl. z. B. C. Westermann 111.

der Stelle, an der er für den Fortgang der Handlung wichtig ist. Solche Nachholungen waren bei E auch in 42,21f. und 50,16f. zu beobachten. Bei ihrer Begegnung mit Joseph fallen die Brüder demütig vor ihm nieder (v.6b). Damit gehen die Träume Josephs, die in Gen 37 geschildert wurden, in Erfüllung. In v.9a erinnert sich Joseph an seine Träume. Daß v.8.9a.bα zu E gehören, wurde bereits in IIa gezeigt. Dort wurde auch begründet, warum v.7 zu J zu rechnen ist.

Allerdings ist H. Gunkel der Auffassung, daß die Worte »da redete er hart mit ihnen« aus E stammen und dort nach v.9a standen[376]. Das ergibt sich für H. Gunkel aus 42,30, da die Söhne dort Jakob berichten, daß »der Mann, der Herr des Landes« hart mit ihnen geredet habe. Dann hätte der Redaktor diese Worte aus v.9 nach v.7 vorgezogen. Es läßt sich aber nicht begründen, warum sie der Redaktor nicht an ihrer ursprünglichen Stelle belassen hat. Sie wären als Einleitung zu dem Vorwurf, die Brüder seien Kundschafter, auch bei ihm sehr gut geeignet. Tatsächlich sind sie bei J in v.7 durchaus sinnvoll. Mit der Frage, woher sie gekommen sind, stellt Joseph den Brüdern keine neutrale Frage. Sie enthält schon einen Vorwurf oder drückt zumindest ein Mißtrauen aus. Das zeigt die Reaktion der Brüder. Sie beantworten nicht nur die Frage nach ihrer Herkunft, sondern geben außerdem sofort als Zweck ihrer Reise an, daß sie gekommen sind »um Speise zu kaufen«. Sie spüren also, daß in der Frage ein Mißtrauen zum Ausdruck kommt, das sie mit der Angabe über den Zweck ihrer Reise ausräumen wollen. Joseph hat somit bei J schon mit der Frage nach ihrer Herkunft, hart mit ihnen geredet. So wird an v.7 erneut deutlich, daß man in der Josephsgeschichte nicht damit zu rechnen hat, daß der Redaktor an der Schilderung von J und E Umstellungen vorgenommen hat. Er behielt vielmehr den jeweiligen Ablauf bei und beschränkte sich darauf, die beiden Darstellungen so weit möglich zu Wort kommen zu lassen und sie miteinander zu verknüpfen.

Wie fest v.7 bei J verankert ist, geht aus den Bezeichnungen für die Brüder in Kap. 43f. hervor. Sie werden dort im Blick auf Joseph nie als »seine/meine Brüder« bezeichnet[377], sondern sind »die Männer«. Diese Formulierung ist zwar dort notwendig, wo Joseph zu seinem Hausverwalter von den Brüdern spricht (43,16; 44,1.4). Sie läßt sich aber etwa in 43,15.33 und 44,3 nicht damit erklären, daß noch nicht bekannt werden darf, daß es sich bei diesen Männern um die Brüder Josephs handelt. Daß die Brüder in Kap. 43f. lediglich als die Söhne des Vaters oder als die Männer bezeichnet werden, wird nur durch 42,7 verständlich. Hier wird berichtet, daß sich Joseph fremd gegen sie stellte. Deshalb sind sie im folgenden nicht mehr seine Brüder, nur Benjamin wird

---

[376] H. Gunkel 442.
[377] Den Ausdruck »die Brüder Josephs« hat nur E in 42,3.6; 45,16; 50,15.

in 43,29f. »sein Bruder« genannt. Das ändert sich mit 45,1, »als sich Joseph seinen Brüdern zu erkennen gab«. Von nun an sind die Brüder wieder »seine/meine Brüder« (vgl. z. B. 45,4; 46,31). So macht der Erzähler mit seinen Formulierungen deutlich, wie sich Joseph jeweils zu den Brüdern stellt.

Aus der Analyse von v. 7–9 bα folgt, daß auch in v. 10–13 J und E vertreten sind. In v. 10 sagen die Brüder: »deine Knechte sind gekommen, um Speise zu kaufen«. Damit wiederholen sie, was sie bereits in v. 7 als den Zweck ihrer Reise genannt haben[378]. V. 10 gehört somit zu J. Nun hat nach 43,7 und 44,19 Joseph die Brüder auf der ersten Reise gefragt, ob ihr Vater noch lebt und ob sie noch einen Bruder haben. Das macht es wahrscheinlich, daß auch v. 11a aus J stammt. In v. 7 hat sich Joseph gegenüber den Brüdern fremd gestellt. Er tat so, als wisse er nicht einmal, aus welchem Land sie gekommen sind. Deshalb können die Brüder nicht davon ausgehen, daß er gemerkt hat, daß sie Brüder sind. Sie antworten in v. 7 mit der Angabe ihrer Herkunft und des Zwecks ihrer Reise. Darauf erhob Joseph gegen sie einen Vorwurf, den sie mit v. 10.11a abweisen. Sie sind tatsächlich gekommen, um Speise zu kaufen, und sie sind alle Söhne eines Mannes. Damit ist nun die Voraussetzung geschaffen, daß sich Joseph danach erkundigt, ob ihr Vater noch lebt und ob sie noch einen Bruder haben. Aus v. 10.11a geht hervor, daß Joseph auch bei J den Brüdern den Vorwurf gemacht hat, Kundschafter zu sein. Nur so wird verständlich, daß sie den Zweck ihrer Reise wiederholen. Vor allem aber wird dann erklärbar, warum sie in v. 11a sagen, daß sie Söhne eines Mannes sind. Wenn sie Brüder sind, haben sie sich nicht in feindlicher Absicht zusammengeschlossen[379], so daß durch v. 11a der Vorwurf Josephs tatsächlich widerlegt ist.

Dieser Vorwurf wird allerdings in 43,3–7 und 44,19ff. nicht erwähnt. Daraus hat J. Wellhausen geschlossen, daß er in der jahwistischen Darstellung nicht enthalten war, und H.-C. Schmitt ist J. Wellhausen darin für seine Juda-Schicht gefolgt[380]. Nach J. Wellhausen hat sich Joseph sofort, nachdem die Brüder erwähnt hatten, daß sie aus dem Lande Kanaan kommen, danach erkundigt, ob ihr Vater noch lebt, und sie noch einen Bruder haben. Sie hätten diese Frage beantwortet, und darauf habe Joseph gefordert, daß sie Benjamin mitbringen, wenn sie ihn nochmals sehen wollen. Diese Lösung scheitert aber daran, daß 42,10 wegen 42,7 zu J gehören muß. Damit hat Joseph auch hier den

---

[378] *šbr 'kl* steht in 42,7.10; 43,2.4.20.22; 44,25. Die Wendung hat bei J geradezu die Funktion eines Leitwortes. Von daher fällt *šbr br* in 42,3 eindeutig aus dem jahwistischen Zusammenhang heraus. Warum der Verfasser hier von seinem sonstigen Sprachgebrauch abgewichen sein sollte, ist unverständlich.
[379] Vgl. z. B. H. Gunkel 443; C. Westermann 113f.
[380] J. Wellhausen, Composition, 56f.; H.-C. Schmitt, BZAW 154, 42 Anm. 167. 43f. 48f.

Brüdern vorgeworfen, sie seien Kundschafter. Daß dieser Vorwurf in 43,3-7 und 44,19ff. nicht wiederholt wird, erklärt sich daraus, daß es an beiden Stellen nur darauf ankommt, daß Joseph die Mitnahme Benjamins gefordert hat. Deshalb kann in 43,7 und 44,19 auch die Frage Josephs nach ihrer Herkunft und die Antwort der Brüder übergangen werden. Es geht dem Verfasser hier eben nicht um einen vollständigen Bericht von der ersten Begegnung der Brüder mit Joseph. Bei J hat die Forderung Josephs, Benjamin mitzubringen, keine Beziehung zu dem Kundschaftervorwurf. Deshalb ist sie in 43,3ff. dem Vater und den Brüdern völlig unverständlich[381]. Den Vorwurf Josephs haben die Brüder bei J mit v.11a erschöpfend widerlegt. Sonst könnte sie übrigens Joseph auch nicht mit Getreide beladen nach Kanaan zurückkehren lassen.

Aus dem Bericht, den die Brüder in v.30ff. dem Vater geben, folgt, daß v.11b und v.13 zu E gehören. Sie werden in v.31 f. mit geringfügigen Variationen referiert. Danach haben übrigens die Brüder erst nach der Beteuerung, daß sie redlich sind, ihre Familienverhältnisse offengelegt. Das stützt die Zuweisung von v.11a an J. Ein Problem bildet v.12, der häufig zu J gerechnet wird. Das wird damit begründet, daß die Formulierung »Die Blöße des Landes seid ihr gekommen zu sehen« eine Dublette zu dem Vorwurf Josephs bei E »Ihr seid Kundschafter« (v. 9bα.14) bilde. Da sie auch in v.9bβ vorkommt, würde dann auch v.9bβ zu J gehören[382]. Für v.12 entsteht dadurch aber für den Ablauf bei J eine Schwierigkeit, die sich nicht lösen läßt. Es ist nicht zu sehen, wie die Brüder hier auf den erneuten Vorwurf von v.12 geantwortet haben sollen. Die Frage Josephs nach Vater und Bruder muß bei J vielmehr unmittelbar auf v.11a gefolgt sein. Deshalb ist v.12 zu E zu rechnen. Dann ist fraglich, ob v.9bβ aus J stammt. Möglicherweise hat der Jehowist den Vorwurf Josephs bei J zugunsten von E ausgelassen. Andererseits würde sich v.9bβ gut in die jahwistische Darstellung einfügen. In ihr steht der Begriff »kommen« auch in v.7 und v.10. In v.7 fragt Joseph die Brüder: »Woher seid ihr gekommen?«, in v.10 wehren sie sich gegen einen Vorwurf mit den Worten: »Nein mein Herr, deine Knechte sind gekommen, um Speise zu kaufen«. Das würde gut zu v.9bβ passen: »um die Blöße des Landes zu sehen, seid ihr gekommen«. So bleibt die Zuweisung von v.9bβ unsicher, auch wenn einiges dafür spricht, daß dieses Stück aus J stammt. In diesem Fall hat E in v.12 die Formulierung von v.9bβ aus J aufgegriffen, um den Vorwurf Josephs sprachlich zu variieren.

---

[381] Damit entfällt das Argument von H.-C. Schmitt, der Kundschaftervorwurf sei sekundär, weil er »kaum durch das Mitbringen eines Bruders überzeugend entkräftet werden« könne (BZAW 154,42 Anm. 167).

[382] So z.B. H. Gunkel 441; O. Eißfeldt, Hexateuch-Synopse, 86*; M. Noth, Pentateuch, 31; L. Ruppert, Josephserzählung, 88.

Jedenfalls beginnt bei E das Gespräch Josephs mit den Brüdern in v. 9 bα.11 b.12 f. mit einem doppelten Redegang. Das entspricht der Szenendoppelung in v. 14–20. Sie wird also formal durch den Eingang des Gesprächs vorbereitet. Auch er enthält eine Steigerung. Zunächst wehren sich die Brüder gegen den Vorwurf Josephs nur mit der Feststellung, daß sie redliche Leute und keine Kundschafter sind (v. 11b). Nachdem aber Joseph seinen Vorwurf in v. 12 wiederholt hat, decken sie ihre Familienverhältnisse auf (v. 13). Das gibt Joseph in v. 14 ff. die Gelegenheit, sie auf die Probe zu stellen. Dadurch hat der Elohist zwischen dem Vorwurf Josephs und seiner Forderung, Benjamin mitzubringen, eine Beziehung hergestellt. Bringen die Brüder Benjamin zu Joseph, so ist damit erwiesen, daß sie die Wahrheit gesagt haben und keine Kundschafter sind. Im Unterschied zu J ist somit die Forderung Josephs bei E gut begründet. Der Elohist hat das Rätsel beseitigt, das die jahwistische Darstellung absichtlich enthielt.

Nun ist gegen die Aufteilung von v. 9–13 auf J und E verschiedentlich eingewandt worden, daß dadurch die Dramatik des Gesprächs zerstört werde[383]. In der Tat ergibt sich hier ein guter Zusammenhang. H.-C. Schmitt stellt zu v. 9b mit Recht fest: »Wer nicht bereits weiß, daß in 42,1 ff. zwei Quellen vorliegen müssen, wird nie auf den Gedanken kommen, in dem Nebeneinander dieser beiden Formulierungen eine Dublette zu sehen«[384]. Auch die Aussagen der Brüder über ihre Familienverhältnisse in v. 11a und v. 13 passen gut zusammen. Sie teilen Joseph zunächst mit, daß sie alle Söhne eines Mannes sind (v. 11a), und erst als das nicht genügt, legen sie in v. 13 ihre Familienverhältnisse genauer dar. Daß der Abschnitt aber trotzdem nicht einheitlich ist, ergibt sich zwingend aus v. 7–9 a. An diesem Stück scheitern alle Versuche, v. 7–13 unter Ausscheidung einzelner Zusätze einem Verfasser zuzuweisen. Es ist somit dem Jehowisten gelungen, in v. 9–13 aus J und E einen geschlossenen Ablauf herzustellen.

In 42,1–13 bleibt damit lediglich die Zuweisung von v. 2 und v. 9 bβ an J unsicher. Deutlich ist hingegen, daß v. 7.10.11 a aus J, v. 1 ... 3 f.6*. 8.9 a.bα.11 b–13 aus E und v. 5 aus P stammen.

e) Gen 48, 1–22

In Gen 48 stammt der Abschnitt v. 3–6 aus P, da Jakob in v. 3 f. sich auf die Erscheinung des *El-šadday* in Luz und die Verheißung bezieht, von denen P in Gen 35,9 ff. berichtet hat. Zwar weicht der Wortlaut in

---

[383] So z.B. W. Rudolph, BZAW 63, 160; D. B. Redford, VT. S 20, 168 f.; C. Westermann 109.
[384] H.-C. Schmitt, BZAW 154, 42.

Einzelheiten von 35,11f. ab. So soll Jakob nach v.4 zu einer »Versammlung von ʿammim« werden, nach 35,11 aber zu einer »Versammlung von gôyim«. Das zeigt jedoch nur, daß bei P gôy und ʿam die gleiche Bedeutung haben. Der Verfasser will mit v.3-6 begründen, warum Ephraim und Manasse in Israel als Ahnherrn von Stämmen gelten, obwohl diese Funktion eigentlich nur den Söhnen Jakobs zukommt. Deshalb läßt P hier Jakob vor seinem Tod erklären, daß ihm Ephraim und Manasse wie Ruben und Simeon – und damit wie seine Söhne – sind. Jakob macht hier somit die beiden Kinder Josephs zu seinen eigenen Söhnen. Daß sie damit unter den Kindern dieser Söhne eine Sonderstellung haben, unterstreicht P durch v.6. Weder P noch die sonstige alttestamentliche Überlieferung kennt weitere Söhne Josephs. Es geht hier hypothetisch um die Möglichkeit, daß Joseph noch weitere Söhne bekommen könnte[385]. Sie sollen im Unterschied zu Ephraim und Manasse aber nicht zu Stammvätern werden.

V.7 schließt an v.6 nur locker an. Eine sachliche Beziehung zwischen der Erwähnung von Tod und Begräbnis der Rahel in v.7 und v.3-6 ist nicht zu erkennen. Das sieht allerdings E. Blum anders. Nach ihm besteht der inhaltliche Zusammenhang zwischen v.3f. und v.5f. darin, »daß die Einsetzung der beiden Enkel zu vollwertigen Söhnen ... als Mehrung Israels/Jakobs im Sinne des in v.4 zitierten Segens zu verstehen ist«. Diese Thematik sei auch der Anknüpfungspunkt für v.7: »Mit dem Hinweis auf Rahels Tod in Kanaan deutet Jakob an, daß er selbst ... mit der Mutter Josephs keine leiblichen Kinder mehr zeugen konnte und *deshalb* – gleichsam als Ersatz – die Söhne Josephs ›adoptiert‹.«[386] Diese Interpretation ist aber bedenklich. Daß die Einsetzung der Enkel als Mehrung im Sinne von v.4 verstanden werden soll, ist durch nichts angezeigt. P verweist in 47,27b ausdrücklich darauf, daß der Vater und die Brüder in Ägypten sehr zahlreich wurden. Damit beginnt sich die Mehrungsverheißung zu erfüllen. Hier – und nicht in der Einsetzung der Enkel – liegt eine Beziehung zur Mehrungsverheißung vor. Jakob verweist in v.3f. nur deshalb auf die Zusagen der Mehrung und des Landes, weil diese Verheißungen sein Interesse an seinen beiden Enkeln begründen.

Sie sollen in gleicher Weise wie seine Söhne an der Erfüllung dieser Verheißungen beteiligt sein. Es geht P also ausschließlich um eine Ätiologie für Ephraim und Manasse als Stammväter. Die Beziehung, die E. Blum zwischen v.3-6 und v.7 herstellt, ist konstruiert und ohne Anhaltspunkt am Text. Gegen sie spricht überdies die priesterschriftliche Aufzählung der Söhne Jakobs in Gen 35,23-26. Nach ihr wurden alle zwölf Söhne Jakobs in Paddan Aram geboren. Weshalb braucht er

---

[385] Vgl. z.B. C. Westermann 208.
[386] E. Blum, Komposition, 252.

dann einen Ersatz für die Söhne, die ihm Rahel durch ihren Tod im Lande Kanaan nicht mehr gebären konnte? Daß in v. 7 mit »was mich betrifft« Jakob betont zu sich selbst überleitet, ist dadurch bedingt, daß er in v. 7 von sich erzählt, nachdem es in v. 6 um die Nachkommenschaft Josephs gegangen war.

Schon aufgrund der fehlenden sachlichen Beziehungen zu v. 3–6 gehört v. 7 nicht zu P[387]. Dafür spricht auch, daß im Alten Testament nur in v. 7 Mesopotamien als Paddan bezeichnet wird, wofür bei P Paddan Aram steht[388]. Dieses »Paddan« macht es auch unwahrscheinlich, daß v. 7 aus E stammt und dort den Wunsch Jakobs einleitete, im Grab der Rahel begraben zu werden[389], oder daß v. 7 ursprünglich hinter v. 11 aα stand, wie W. Rudolph annimmt[390]. Nach W. Rudolph hat ein Späterer v. 7 umgestellt, weil in Gen 35 nach der Verheißung an Jakob in v. 16–20 von Tod und Begräbnis der Rahel berichtet wird, und er in Gen 48 die gleiche Abfolge erreichen wollte. In der Tat erklärt sich aus Gen 35, warum v. 7 auf v. 3–6 folgt, ohne daß es freilich der Annahme bedarf, daß v. 7 ursprünglich an anderer Stelle stand. Nach H.-C. Schmitt wurde v. 7 nachgetragen, weil ein Ergänzer »v. 3–6 offensichtlich als Rekapitulation von Gen 35 verstand und darin den Tod Rahels vermißte«[391]. Freilich stellt sich die Frage, warum er auf den Tod Rahels solchen Wert legte. Das erklärt sich aus 49,31. Hier erwähnt Jakob bei P, daß er Lea in der Höhle Machpela begraben hat, von Rahel ist nicht die Rede[392]. Das wurde später anscheinend als Lücke empfunden. Deshalb ließ ein Ergänzer Jakob bereits in 48,7 dem Joseph in Anlehnung an 35,16 ff. mitteilen, wo er Rahel begraben hat. Daran wird wieder deutlich, daß sich P nicht als Bearbeitungsschicht verstehen läßt. Wenn bei P Jakob seine Söhne nach 35,26 in Paddan Aram geboren wurden, so widerspricht das 35,16–20, wonach Benjamin in Kanaan zur Welt kam und Rahel bei seiner Geburt starb. Erst der Ergänzer von 48,7 hat diese Darstellung mit dem priesterschriftlichen Abschnitt 48,3–6 verbunden.

Der Rest von Gen 48 bereitet erhebliche Schwierigkeiten. Umstritten ist, ob auf 47,29–31 nicht sofort die Schilderung des Todes des Ahnherrn folgen müßte. Schon J. Wellhausen war der Auffassung, daß

---

[387] Gegen J. Wellhausen, Composition, 52, der allerdings feststellt, daß man über die Zuweisung von 48,7 Zweifel hegen könne.
[388] So mit Recht H.-C. Schmitt, BZAW 154, 67 Anm. 274.
[389] So z. B. H. Gunkel 471.
[390] W. Rudolph, BZAW 63, 169 f.; ähnlich L. Ruppert, Josephserzählung, 170, der allerdings v. 7 E zuweist.
[391] H.-C. Schmitt, BZAW 154, 67 Anm. 274; vgl. auch C. Westermann 209.
[392] Daß P in 49,31 Rahel nicht erwähnt, zeigt, daß der Verfasser eine Überlieferung von dem Rahelgrab kennt, nach der Rahel nicht in Machpela bestattet wurde.

die Darstellung dieses Todes mit 47,28; 47,29 und 48,1 dreimal eingeleitet wird, und J deshalb in Gen 48 nicht vertreten sein könne[393]. E. Blum hat jüngst die Gründe für die These, daß 47,29-31 mit 48,1 ff. unvereinbar sei, zusammengestellt. Mit der Formel »und es geschah nach diesen Begebenheiten« werde ein Neueinsatz markiert. Es werde außerdem die Szene von 47,29 ff., daß Joseph am Sterbebett des Vaters stehe, noch einmal eingeführt. Schließlich könne 47,31 b »da neigte sich Israel zum Kopfende des Bettes hin« nur bedeuten, daß sich der Vater sterbend zurücklege. Zu 47,29 ff. sei 50,1 ff. die Fortsetzung, die durch Gen 48 f. aufgesprengt werde. Nur die Notiz vom Tode des Vaters sei ausgefallen[394]. Aufgrund solcher Überlegungen wird dann der ohne v. 3-7 verbleibende Bestand in Gen 48 entweder, wie bei J. Wellhausen und M. Noth, zu E gerechnet[395], oder er wird, wie jetzt von E. Blum, als Erweiterung angesehen[396]. Allerdings sind diese Argumente nicht zwingend. Zu 47,31 b ist bereits oft auf I Reg 1,47 hingewiesen worden[397]. Dort verneigt sich der alte David auf seinem Lager und spricht ein Dankgebet. In gleicher Weise könnte mit 47,31 b gemeint sein, daß Israel Gott dafür dankt, daß ihm Joseph geschworen hat, seine Leiche nach Kanaan zu überführen. Daß dieses Gebet in 47,31 b nicht mitgeteilt wird, ist gegen E. Blum kein Gegenargument. In I Reg 1,47 wird das Gebet von dem Sich-Verneigen Davids abgehoben[398]. Dann fordert 47,31 b aber nicht, daß danach unmittelbar der Tod Israels berichtet wird. Auf die anderen Argumente wird später zurückzukommen sein.

Nun enthält Gen 48 auch ohne v. 3-7 erhebliche Spannungen. Das wird an v. 8-20 besonders deutlich. Die Segensworte Jakobs in v. 15 f. unterbrechen den Zusammenhang zwischen v. 14 und v. 17. Außerdem sind v. 10 bα und v. 13 b nahezu identisch. Warum muß Joseph seine Söhne zweimal zum Vater heranbringen, bis er sie segnet, nachdem der Vater bereits in v. 9 b angekündigt hat, daß er die Söhne segnen will?

---

[393] J. Wellhausen, Composition, 59.

[394] E. Blum, Komposition, 250 f.

[395] J. Wellhausen, Composition, 59 f.; M. Noth, Pentateuch, 38. Eine Sonderstellung nehmen W. Rudolph und H. Donner ein. Nach W. Rudolph, BZAW 63,170, nimmt der Erzähler in Gen 48 eine andere Tradition auf als in dem Rest der Josephsgeschichte. H. Donner, Gestalt, 30-34, folgt im wesentlichen der Aufteilung von H. Gunkel in J und E. Der Jehowist habe durch v. 2 b ihre Darstellungen mit der Josephsgeschichte verbunden.

[396] E. Blum, Komposition, 250 ff.

[397] Vgl. z. B. H. Gunkel 471; O. Procksch 268; L. Ruppert, Josephserzählung, 168.

[398] E. Blum, Komposition, 250 Anm. 38, sieht in dem Sich-verneigen einen ›würdigen‹ Ausdruck oder eine sprachliche Remineszenz an den Traum Josephs in 37,9 f. Letzteres scheidet aus, da 47,29-31 zu J gehört. Ein würdiger Ausdruck aber muß ebenfalls eine Bedeutung haben. Es gelingt E. Blum m. E. nicht, positiv aufzuzeigen, was 47,31 bedeuten soll.

W. Rudolph erklärt das damit, daß der Vater zunächst von seinem Gefühl übermannt wurde. Deshalb habe Joseph die Knaben von seinen Knien nehmen und für den Segen richtig aufstellen müssen[399]. Diese Deutung wirkt recht gekünstelt. Gegen sie spricht zudem, daß durch v. 12b der von W. Rudolph postulierte Zusammenhang unterbrochen wird. Ähnliche Einwände bestehen gegen E. Blum. Nach ihm gibt Joseph in v. 10b seine Söhne dem Vater zum Liebkosen auf den Schoß. Er nehme sie danach herunter (v. 12a), werfe sich vor dem Vater nieder (v. 12b) und plaziere die Söhne zu beiden Seiten Jakobs für den Segen (v. 13). Dies sei »ein völlig konsistenter Verlauf«[400]. Aber warum gibt Joseph zunächst die Söhne dem Vater auf den Schoß, wenn der Vater sie doch segnen wollte? Diese Spannung läßt sich nicht harmonisieren. Dann stammen aber v. 10b und v. 13b von verschiedenen Verfassern[401].

Aufgrund dieser und anderer Beobachtungen werden v. 8–20 von den meisten Vertretern einer Quellenscheidung aufgeteilt. Nach H. Gunkel gehören zu J: V. 9b.10a.13.14a.bα.17–20aα; zu E: V. 8.9a. 10b–12.15f. 20aβ.b[402]. Seine Aufteilung hat weithin Anerkennung gefunden[403]. Unterschiedlich wird vor allem v. 15f. beurteilt. L. Ruppert schreibt v. 15b. 16 einem E² zu, während H. Donner vermutet, daß v. 15f. aus P stammt und dort auf v. 6 folgte[404]. Auch H.-C. Schmitt hat sich mit einzelnen Modifikationen diesen Aufteilungen angeschlossen. Er rechnet v. 8a. 9b. 10a. 13f.*17–20aα* zur Juda-Schicht und v. 8b. 9a.10b.12 zur Rubenversion. Spätere Wucherungen seien v. 11 und v. 15f.[405].

Gegen diese Zuweisungen bestehen aber m. E. erhebliche Bedenken. In v. 8a und v. 11, die in der Regel zu E gerechnet werden, heißt der Vater Israel, obwohl ihn E in der Josephsgeschichte sonst durchgehend Jakob nennt. Das wird meist so erklärt, daß »Israel« hier ein später eingefügtes »falsches Explicitum« sei[406]. Zumindest für v. 11 läßt sich jedoch nicht verständlich machen, warum hier nachträglich »Is-

---

[399] W. Rudolph, BZAW 63, 171. Nach W. Rudolph ist lediglich v. 15 f. später nachgetragen worden.
[400] E. Blum, Komposition, 251 Anm. 44.
[401] Auch M. Noth, Pentateuch, 38, hält v. 8–20 mit Ausnahme von v. 15 f. für literarisch einheitlich. Daß der Vater hier auch bei E Israel heißt, beruhe darauf, daß E hier »eine Sonderüberlieferung *stammes*geschichtlichen Inhalts« aufgenommen habe (38 f. Anm. 136). Das scheitert aber schon an dem Nebeneinander von v. 10b und v. 13b.
[402] H. Gunkel 469.
[403] Vgl. z. B. O. Eißfeldt, Hexateuch-Synopse, 100f.*; L. Ruppert, Josephserzählung, 163; H. Donner, Gestalt, 31 f.
[404] L. Ruppert, Josephserzählung, 173 ff.; H. Donner, Gestalt, 32–34.
[405] H.-C. Schmitt, BZAW 154, 72.
[406] H. Gunkel 469; vgl. auch O. Eißfeldt, Hexateuch-Synopse, 100*.

rael« als Subjekt eingefügt worden sein sollte, da sich aus dem Schluß von v. 10b eindeutig ergibt, daß hier der Vater redet. Deshalb sieht H.-C. Schmitt in v. 11 einen Nachtrag[407]. Aber gerade dieser Vers ist, wie noch zu zeigen sein wird, in der Josephsgeschichte fest verankert. Das »Israel« in v. 11 läßt sich also mit der Zuweisung dieses Verses an E nicht vereinbaren.

Vor allem aber kann v. 19 nicht aus der frühen Königszeit und damit von J stammen. Hier sagt der Vater zu Joseph: »Ich weiß mein Sohn, ich weiß; auch er wird zu einem ʿam werden, und auch er wird groß werden. Aber sein kleinerer Bruder wird größer werden als er, und sein Same wird sein die Menge der gôyim«. C. Westermann stellt dazu mit Recht fest: »Der Ältere soll zu einem Volk werden und er soll groß werden; der Jüngere jedoch soll größer werden als der Ältere, und sein Same zu einer Schar von Völkern.« Er fährt dann aber fort: »Alle diese Wendungen sind aus bekannten Formulierungen der Mehrungsverheißung übernommen, nur daß dem einen, dem Jüngeren, mehr in Aussicht gestellt wird als dem anderen, dem Älteren.«[408] Die Formulierungen in v. 19 entsprechen jedoch keineswegs den Mehrungsverheißungen bei J und E. Der Ausdruck »die Menge (mlʾ) der gôyim« ist sonst nicht belegt. Auffällig ist besonders der Plural gôyim. Bei J wird Abraham in 12,2 verheißen, daß ihn Jahwe zu einem großen gôy machen will. Das spätere Israel bildet somit für J ein gôy. Dann kann der Jahwist nicht von dem Ahnherrn eines Stammes sagen, daß er zu »der Menge der gôyim« werden soll. Das gleiche gilt für den Elohisten, bei dem Gott Jakob in 46,3 zusagt, daß er ihn in Ägypten zu einem großen gôy machen will. Auch für E ist somit Israel lediglich ein gôy. Es fehlt jeglicher Beleg dafür, daß in vorexilischer Zeit für Israel jemals der Plural gôyim gebraucht worden wäre. Er findet sich erstmals in der Priesterschrift. Nach Gen 17,5 soll Abraham zum Vater einer Menge von gôyim werden. Das bezieht sich auf das spätere Israel, da nach 17,16 auch Sara zu gôyim werden soll. Es geht hier also um Abraham und Sara als den Ahnen Israels. Das wird dadurch bestätigt, daß nach 35,11 bei P aus Jakob eine »Versammlung von gôyim« entstehen soll. Für P besteht also Israel aus mehreren gôyim. Vermutlich ist P der Auffassung, daß die einzelnen Stämme jeweils ein gôy bilden. Das legt 48,4 nahe. Jakob berichtet Joseph hier von der Mehrungsverheißung von 35,11, weil Ephraim und Manasse zu Ahnherrn von Stämmen werden sollen. Ihre Nachkommen sind somit jeweils ein ʿam – der Begriff ist bei P, wie oben erwähnt, identisch mit gôy –, der zusammen mit den übrigen Stämmen »eine Versammlung von ʿammim« und damit Israel bildet.

---

[407] H.-C. Schmitt, BZAW 154,72.
[408] C. Westermann 215.

Selbst von dieser Auffassung weicht aber 48,19 dadurch ab, daß hier der Stamm Ephraim als »die Menge der *gôyim*« bezeichnet wird. Er ist im Unterschied zu P nicht mehr ein *gôy*, sondern besteht aus mehreren *gôyim*. Das hat schon A. Dillmann erkannt: *gôyim* »35,11 von den Stämmen Israels ... gebraucht, ist also hier im Grunde von noch kleinern Volksabtheilungen gesagt«[409]. Freilich hat A. Dillmann nicht gesehen, daß dieser Sprachgebrauch auf eine späte Zeit weist. Zu seiner Erklärung wird man zwei Stellen aus dem chronistischen Werk heranziehen müssen. In I Chr 13,2 ist von »allen Ländern Israels« die Rede, in II Chr 11,23 von »allen Ländern Judas und Benjamins«. Hier haben sowohl Israel als auch die Stämme Juda und Benjamin mehrere Länder. Diese Auffassung hat dann auch in der späten Verheißung von Gen 26,3b–5[410] ihren Niederschlag gefunden, in der Isaak »alle diese Länder« (v. 3b–4) zugesagt werden. Noch bei P steht in der Landverheißung durchgehend der Singular. War man jedoch der Auffassung, daß der einzelne Stamm über mehrere Länder verfügte, so konnte er auch als eine Vereinigung von *gôyim* verstanden werden. V.19 stammt also mit Sicherheit nicht aus vorexilischer Zeit und dürfte sogar jünger sein als P.

Nun läßt sich v. 19 nicht aus der Darstellung herauslösen, daß der Vater Ephraim und Manasse gesegnet hat. Da P bereits in v. 5 Ephraim vor Manasse genannt hat, gehört sie auch abgesehen von den Beobachtungen, die für eine noch spätere Ansetzung sprechen, nicht zu P. Folglich stammt sie aus keiner Quellenschrift. Da v. 10b in v. 13b aufgenommen wird, ist sie vielmehr eine späte Erweiterung zu dem Grundbestand von v. 8–12[411]. Zu ihr gehören v. 13.14[412].17–20. Zwar ist verschiedentlich bestritten worden, daß v. 20 einheitlich ist. So hält z. B. H. Gunkel v. 20 aβ.b nach v. 17–19 für überflüssig[413], und H.-C. Schmitt sieht hier »eine zweite Begründung für die Vorordnung Ephraims vor Manasse ..., die wesentlich gekünstelter als die der Juda-Schicht wirkt und von daher kaum ursprünglich mit ihr zusammengehört haben kann«[414].

---

[409] A. Dillmann 430. Demgegenüber will O. Procksch 269, *gôyim* auf die »Heiden« beziehen, die in Mittelpalästina von Josua unterworfen wurden. Da aber bei Manasse die Mehrung im Blick ist, kann sich die Aussage über Ephraim nicht auf die Eingliederung nichtisraelitischer Völker beziehen. Zwischen ʿam und *gôy* besteht in v. 19 kein Unterschied.

[410] Vgl. dazu L. Schmidt, Pentateuch, 98f.

[411] Das hat C. Westermann 215f., richtig erkannt. Er setzt das Stück allerdings in vorexilischer Zeit an.

[412] Ob v. 14bβ, der in LXX fehlt, eine Glosse ist (so z. B. H. Gunkel 472; H.-C. Schmitt, BZAW 154,68 Anm. 279), kann hier offenbleiben.

[413] H. Gunkel 469f.

[414] H.-C. Schmitt, BZAW 154,70 Anm. 292.

Aber inhaltlich läßt sich v. 20 durchaus mit v. 19 vereinbaren. Dort weiß der Vater, daß auch Manasse groß werden wird, Ephraim wird jedoch größer sein. Eben deshalb werden in dem Wort, mit dem Israel segnen wird, sowohl Ephraim als auch Manasse genannt, aber Ephraim an erste Stelle gesetzt. Nur in v. 20 bezeichnet Israel in der Josephsgeschichte ausschließlich das spätere Volk. Das ist ein weiteres Indiz dafür, daß dieses Stück spät ist[415]. Weil der Vater Ephraim und Manasse gesegnet hat, wird später Israel unter Berufung auf diese beiden segnen[416], und weil er Ephraim durch Handlung und Wort vor Manasse gestellt hat, wird in diesem Segen Ephraim vor Manasse genannt werden. Handlung und Wort gehören zusammen. In v. 13 f. 17–20 geht es also durchgehend darum, daß Ephraim den Vorzug vor Manasse hat, obwohl dieser der Erstgeborene war.

Diese Darstellung wird durch v. 10 a vorbereitet, so daß auch dieser Halbvers zu der Erweiterung gehört. Der Streit, ob in v. 10 a gemeint ist, daß der Vater blind ist, wodurch ein Widerspruch zu v. 8 a, wo er die Söhne Josephs sieht, entstehen würde[417], oder ob mit v. 10 a nur gesagt werden soll, daß der Vater nicht mehr richtig sehen kann[418], ist müßig. Die Bemerkung von v. 10 a hat nur einen Sinn für die Segnung der Knaben. Sie erklärt, warum Joseph meinen konnte, sein Vater habe irrtümlich seine Rechte auf den Kopf Ephraims gelegt (v. 17 f.). Auch v. 9 b gehört zu der Erweiterung. In v. 10 b–12 wird nicht gesagt, daß der Vater die Kinder gesegnet hat. Seiner Aufforderung in v. 9 b: »Bring sie doch zu mir, daß ich sie segne« entspricht Joseph erst in v. 13: »Da nahm Joseph die beiden ...«. V. 10 b läßt sich zudem ohne Schwierigkeiten an v. 9 a anschließen.

Zu der Erweiterung gehören somit: V. 9 b. 10 a. 13 f. 17–20. Der blinde – oder jedenfalls nahezu blinde – Vater (v. 10 a) segnet die beiden Söhne Josephs und gibt dabei dem jüngeren Ephraim den Vorzug vor Manasse. Damit sind hier zwei Motive miteinander verbunden, die sonst nur noch in einer alttestamentlichen Erzählung zusammen auftreten. In Gen 27, 1–45 erschleicht sich Jakob den Segen des blinden Isaak, den dieser seinem Erstgeborenen Esau zugedacht hat. Diese Übereinstimmung ist schwerlich ein Zufall. Gewiß besteht darin ein wesentlicher Unterschied zu 27, 1 ff., daß in der Erweiterung die Vorrangstellung Ephraims vom Vater gewollt ist, und daß beide Söhne von ihm gesegnet werden. Die Übereinstimmungen lassen sich jedoch nur so ver-

---

[415] Auch bei der Segnung durch Handauflegung handelt es sich nach C. Westermann 212, wahrscheinlich um »eine spätere Form«.
[416] Das »unter Berufung auf dich« bezieht sich auf jeden der beiden Söhne, vgl. H.-C. Schmitt, BZAW 154, 69 Anm. 290, und die dort genannte Literatur.
[417] So häufig, vgl. H. Gunkel 469.
[418] So z. B. W. Rudolph, BZAW 63, 171; H.-C. Schmitt, BZAW 154, 68.

stehen, daß der Verfasser 27,1 ff. als Vorlage benutzte und abwandelte[419]. Wie einst Isaak vor seinem Tod Jakob segnete und ihn Esau voranstellte, so hat Israel, bevor er starb, Ephraim Manasse vorgeordnet. Daß er trotzdem beide Söhne Josephs segnete, beruht darauf, daß sie anders als Esau beide zu Ahnherrn von Stämmen des Volkes Israel werden sollten. Es handelt sich bei der Erweiterung somit um eine bewußte Aufnahme und Abwandlung von Gen 27, 1–45, durch die erst in nachexilischer Zeit der Grundbestand in v. 8. 9 a. 10 b–12 weitergeführt wurde.

Dieser Grundbestand kann dann aber nicht mehr, wie üblich, zu E gerechnet werden. Als Hauptargument für diese Zuweisung gilt, daß die Segnung der Söhne Josephs eine Dublette zu diesem Stück sei[420]. Bei ihm handelt es sich aber, wie gezeigt, nicht um eine Variante aus einer anderen Quellenschrift, sondern um eine Erweiterung. Auch die Gottesbezeichnung Elohim in v. 11 ist hier wie an anderen Stellen der Josephsgeschichte kein Indiz für E, da der Verfasser der von J aufgenommenen Josephsgeschichte in allen Reden Elohim verwendet. Das Stück setzt zwar die Notiz über die Geburt der Söhne Josephs in 41,51f. voraus. Aber entgegen der herrschenden Auffassung stammen diese beiden Verse aus J[421]. Bereits das spricht dafür, daß auch der Grundbestand von 48, 8–12 zu J gehört. Das wird dadurch gestützt, daß hier der Vater Israel heißt. Zudem ist v. 11 bei J fest verankert. Israel sagt zu Joseph: »Zu sehen dein Angesicht habe ich nicht vermutet, und siehe, Gott hat mich auch deinen Samen sehen lassen«. Hier steht der Begriff »sehen«, dem bei J in 45, 28; 46, 1 aα. 28–30 geradezu die Funktion eines Leitwortes zukam[422]. Er drückt auch in v. 11 die besonders enge Beziehung des Vaters zu Joseph aus, die die jahwistische Josephsgeschichte charakteristisch von E und P unterscheidet.

Nun setzt die Frage Israels in v. 8 b: »Wer sind diese?« voraus, daß er die Söhne Josephs vorher nicht gesehen hat. Verschiedentlich hat man daraus geschlossen, daß der Vater dann erst kurz zuvor nach Ägypten gekommen ist. Er sei in dieser Fassung bald nach seiner Übersiedlung gestorben[423]. Das ließe sich allerdings mit J nur schwer vereinbaren. Zwar hat hier der Vater kaum wie bei P noch 17 Jahre in Ägypten gelebt (47,28). Aber aus 47,12 und 47,13–26 geht hervor, daß auch bei J der Vater vor seinem Tod einige Zeit in Ägypten verbracht hat. D. B. Redford nimmt an, daß v. 8 ff. ursprünglich auf 46,30 folgten, da sie unmittelbar hinter die Ankunft des Vaters in Ägypten gehörten[424].

---

[419] Darauf hat E. Blum, Komposition, 253, mit Recht hingewiesen. Allerdings hat er nicht erkannt, daß es sich dabei um eine Erweiterung handelt.
[420] Vgl. z. B. H. Gunkel 469.   [421] Vgl. III c.
[422] Vgl. II f.   [423] So z. B. G. v. Rad 340; C. Westermann 209.
[424] D. B. Redford, VT. S 20, 24.

In 46,29 kommt jedoch nur Joseph zu seinem Vater nach Gosen, seine Söhne werden nicht erwähnt. Bereits das spricht gegen eine Umstellung von 48,8ff. Da der Vater bei J nicht bei Joseph, sondern in Gosen wohnt, ist es hier durchaus möglich, daß er die Söhne Josephs noch nicht gesehen hat, obwohl er schon längere Zeit in Ägypten ist.

Dann muß der Erzähler freilich eine besondere Absicht verfolgen, wenn er den Vater erst kurz vor seinem Tod mit den Söhnen Josephs zusammentreffen läßt. Tatsächlich läßt sie sich aus dem Aufbau seines Schlußteils, der mit 47,27a beginnt, und den Formulierungen in 48,8ff. deutlich erkennen. Bei J kommt der Vater vor seinem Tod zweimal mit Joseph zusammen. Zunächst läßt er Joseph schwören, daß er ihn nicht in Ägypten begraben wird (47,29–31). Darauf kommt Joseph mit seinen beiden Söhnen zu dem sterbenden Vater (48,8ff.). Während der Verfasser sonst mit seinen Hinweisen auf Gott recht sparsam ist, wird in diesen Versen zweimal sehr betont Gott erwähnt. Joseph stellt dem Vater die Kinder mit den Worten vor: »Meine Söhne sind sie, die mir Gott hier gegeben hat« (v. 9a), und in v. 11 sagt der Vater »und siehe, Gott hat mich auch deinen Samen sehen lassen«. Durch diese Hinweise auf Gott stellt die Szene eine Steigerung zu 47,29–31 dar. Das Geschick Josephs und des Vaters wird nochmals theologisch gedeutet. Wie in 41,51f. erwähnt Joseph auch hier Gott im Zusammenhang mit seinen Söhnen. Diese Söhne zeigen, daß ihm Gott in Ägypten ein erfülltes Leben geschenkt hat. Darauf spricht in der jahwistischen Josephsgeschichte erstmals auch der Vater von Gott. Er hatte nicht hoffen können, Joseph nochmals zu sehen, aber Gott hat ihn sogar die Kinder Josephs sehen lassen. Damit hat Gott sein Leben, auf das zunächst durch den Verlust Josephs ein tiefer Schatten gefallen war, zu einem guten Ende gebracht [425].

Daß der Vater diese Deutung angesichts der Söhne Josephs ausspricht, unterstreicht wieder, daß in der jahwistischen Josephsgeschichte die Beziehung zwischen dem Vater und Joseph das zentrale Thema ist. Dabei steht zwar für den Verfasser die menschliche Seite dieses Verhältnisses eindeutig im Vordergrund seines Interesses. Er weiß aber, daß hinter den manchmal undurchschaubaren Ereignissen letztlich doch Gott steht. Deshalb läßt er den Vater in seinem letzten Wort diese theologische Deutung geben. Zugleich stellt er durch die Szene in 48,8ff.* eine Beziehung zu dem Aufstieg Josephs in Ägypten her. Dort schloß seine Darstellung mit einer Notiz über die Geburt der beiden Söhne und der theologischen Deutung ihrer Namen durch Joseph [426]. In der letzten Begegnung zwischen Joseph und dem Vater treten nun diese Söhne wieder auf. Sie geben dem Vater die Gelegenheit, seinen Weg theologisch zu deuten. Weil der Verfasser hier eine Korre-

---

[425] Vgl. dazu auch H. Gunkel 472. [426] Vgl. III c.

spondenz herstellen wollte, ließ er den Vater die Söhne Josephs erst unmittelbar vor seinem Tod sehen. Er hat damit den Aufstieg Josephs mit seinem Thema Joseph und der Vater verknüpft.

Den Abschluß der Szene in v. 8.9 a. 10 b. 11 bildet v. 12. Hier nimmt Joseph zunächst seine Söhne von den Knien des Vaters (v. 12 a). Man hat häufig vermutet, daß der Vater durch den Ritus der Kniesetzung die beiden Söhne Josephs adoptiert hat[427]. Dagegen spricht aber, daß er in v. 11 die Söhne ausdrücklich als »deinen Samen« bezeichnet. Sie bleiben somit bei J Nachkommen Josephs, die auf – oder an – den Knien des Vaters waren, damit er sie küssen und umarmen konnte[428]. In v. 12 b verneigt sich Joseph dann mit dem Angesicht zur Erde hin. Damit entspricht dieser Halbvers 47,31 b. Dort hatte sich Israel auf dem Bett verneigt, nachdem ihm Joseph geschworen hatte. Jetzt verneigt sich Joseph zur Erde hin, nachdem der Vater seine Söhne freundlich aufgenommen und seinen eigenen Weg theologisch gedeutet hat. An v. 12 b wird deutlich, daß die übliche Zuweisung von 47,29–31 an J und 48,8. 9 a. 10 b. 11 f. an E einen Zusammenhang zerreißt, der von dem Verfasser der jahwistischen Josephsgeschichte bewußt gestaltet wurde. Aus v. 12 b geht außerdem hervor, daß die Begegnung des Vaters mit den Söhnen Josephs damit abgeschlossen ist. So wie mit 47,31 b die Szene endet, in der der Vater Joseph schwören ließ, wird mit 48,12 b die Begegnung des Vaters mit den Söhnen Josephs abgeschlossen. Bei J folgte darauf sofort der Bericht von dem Tod des Vaters, von dem in 49,33 aß nur noch ein Fragment erhalten ist.

Der Jahwist hat also in 48,8 ff. weder erzählt, daß der Vater die Söhne Josephs gesegnet hat[429], noch daß er sie adoptierte. Ihm kam es ausschließlich auf die theologische Deutung durch den Vater in v. 11 an. Freilich ist die Szene später als Adoption verstanden worden, wozu die Formulierung von v. 12 a wesentlich beigetragen haben dürfte. Das zeigt die priesterschriftliche Darstellung in v. 3–6, mit der P 48,8 ff.* aufnimmt und umgestaltet. Daß die Vorlage für P hier tatsächlich 48,8 ff.* war, legt sich dadurch nahe, daß sich zu 47,29–31 ebenfalls eine Parallele bei P findet. Der Befehl Jakobs an seine Söhne, ihn in Machpela zu begraben in 49,1 a. 28 b–32 ist eine Abwandlung von 47,29–31. Da, wie schon erwähnt, P großes Gewicht darauf legt, daß

---

[427] So z. B. H. Gunkel 472; O. Procksch 424; G. v. Rad 341; H.-C. Schmitt, BZAW 154, 71 Anm. 300.
[428] So auch L. Ruppert, Josephserzählung, 170 ff.
[429] C. Westermann 210, meint zwar: »In beiden Sätzen von V. 12 ist dabei vorausgesetzt, daß Jakob die beiden Söhne Josephs gesegnet hat.« Aber das läßt sich aus v. 12 nicht entnehmen. Gegen C. Westermann 211, ist dann zwischen v. 11 und v. 12 auch kein Segenswort ausgefallen. C. Westermann kommt zu dieser These, weil er übersieht, daß auch v. 9 b von dem Ergänzer stammt, der in der Erweiterung zu Wort kommt.

ein Patriarch von allen seinen Söhnen begraben wird, mußte der Verfasser die Reihenfolge in seiner jahwistischen Vorlage umkehren. Deshalb redet bei P Jakob zunächst zu Joseph und adoptiert dessen Söhne (48,3-6). Danach ruft er seine Söhne und gibt ihnen den Befehl, ihn in Machpela zu bestatten. Durch diese Umstellung hat P zugleich gegenüber J einen anderen Akzent gesetzt. Mit seinen letzten Worten redet Jakob hier von dem Ort seines Begräbnisses. Damit steht bei P implizit die Frage des Landes am Schluß und trägt das Gewicht. Jakob will in dem verheißenen Land, in dem den Vätern nur die Stätte ihres Grabes gehörte, begraben werden. Wie schon mit 48,3-6, so weist auch mit diesem Schluß die Josephsgeschichte bei P über sich hinaus auf die Zeit, in der Israel das verheißene Land erhalten wird, während sich J in 48,8ff.* streng auf das Thema seiner Josephsgeschichte beschränkt hat.

Bei J folgte 48,8 auf v.2b. In v.2b heißt der Vater Israel. Außerdem wird hier wieder das Bett erwähnt, das schon in 47,31 vorkam. V.8 schließt unmittelbar an v.2b an. Dagegen können v.1-2a in ihrer jetzigen Fassung nicht aus J stammen. Der Vater trägt in v.2a den Namen Jakob. In v.1a wird Joseph mitgeteilt, daß sein Vater krank ist. Das überrascht nach 47,29-31, da der Vater bereits hier mit seinem Tod rechnet. Deshalb wird v.1-2a in der Regel E zugewiesen[430]. Allerdings hat die bisherige Analyse ergeben, daß entgegen der üblichen Quellenscheidung in Gen 48 E sonst nicht mehr zu Wort kommt. Man müßte somit annehmen, daß die elohistische Fortsetzung zugunsten von P und J durch die Redaktionen weggebrochen wurde. Da auch J berichtet haben muß, daß Joseph seine beiden Söhne zum Vater brachte, stellt sich die Frage, warum ein Redaktor dann dieses Fragment aus E aufnahm.

Nun beruht die Zuweisung von v.1 an E teilweise auf der Auffassung, daß in v.1 mit »und es geschah nach diesen Begebenheiten« ein neuer Einsatz vorliege. Dieses Argument ist jedoch m.E. problematisch. Die Formulierung »und es geschah nach diesen Begebenheiten« (v.1aα) steht auch in 39,7 und 40,1[431]. Sie hat hier bei J jeweils die Funktion, einen Abschnitt in zwei Szenen zu gliedern. Dabei wird mit ihr der zweite Teil eingeleitet, der das Geschehen weiterführt. In 39,1-20 ist Joseph in dem Haus des Ägypters. Dort steigt er zum Hausverwalter auf (v.1-6). Durch die in 39,7ff. geschilderten Ereignisse kommt Joseph in das Gefängnis, und das ist die Voraussetzung für seinen Aufstieg zum Herrscher über Ägypten. Mit 39,21 beginnt ein neuer Abschnitt. In 39,21-23 erhält Joseph durch den Beistand Jahwes eine Sonderstellung. Der zweite Teil wird durch 40,1 eingeleitet. Die Begegnung mit dem Mundschenk und dem Bäcker läßt Joseph schließlich mit

---

[430] Vgl. z.B. H. Gunkel 469.
[431] Darauf hat I. Willi-Plein, Aspekte, 308, hingewiesen.

dem Pharao zusammentreffen – die Darstellung von J ist hier nicht mehr erhalten –, und er wird von dem Pharao zu dem zweiten Mann in Ägypten gemacht. Die gleiche Funktion hat 48,1aα nach 47,29–31. Bei J beginnt der Schlußabschnitt seiner Josephsgeschichte mit 47,27a. Von den Begebenheiten, die sich unmittelbar vor dem Tod des Vaters abgespielt haben, erzählt J wieder in zwei Szenen: 47,29–31 und 48,2b. 8–12*. Nach der zweiten stirbt der Vater. Von daher würde 48,1aα als Einleitung der zweiten Szene bei J gut passen[432].

V.1aβ und v.2a können freilich, wie erwähnt, nicht zu J gerechnet werden. Zu erwägen bleibt m.E., ob hier teilweise nicht die Einleitung von P zu v.3–6 vorliegt. Im allgemeinen wird 47,27b.28; 48,3–6 als geschlossenes Stück aus P angesehen. Hier ist aber der Übergang von 47,28 zu 48,3 recht hart. Daß Jakob in 48,3–6 die Söhne Josephs adoptiert, würde besser verständlich, wenn Joseph zu dem Vater gekommen ist, weil er von seiner Krankheit erfahren hat (v.1aβ.2a). In 49,29 leitet Jakob seinen Befehl über den Ort seines Begräbnisses mit den Worten ein: »Ich werde zu meinen ›Stammesgenossen‹[433] versammelt«. Damit wird dieser Befehl ausdrücklich in der Situation Jakobs verankert. Weil Jakob jetzt sterben wird, regelt er die Frage seines Begräbnisses. Auch von daher stellt sich die Frage, ob ähnliches nicht für die Adoption der Söhne Josephs gilt. Dann würde Jakob seine Enkel zu diesem Zeitpunkt adoptieren, weil er krank ist und fühlt, daß sein Ende naht.

Nicht zu P gehört dagegen v.1b, da die Söhne Josephs hier in der Reihenfolge Manasse-Ephraim aufgeführt werden, während P in v.5 Ephraim voranstellt. Tatsächlich setzt P in v.3ff. nicht voraus, daß die Söhne anwesend sind. V.1b müßte dann aus J stammen, wobei der Endredaktor zwischen v.1aα und v.1b zugunsten von P aus J einen Satz ausgelassen hätte, der hier auf v.1aα folgte. V.1b setzt voraus, daß bei J Joseph zuvor genannt wurde. Bei v.1–2a fällt überhaupt auf, daß nicht ausdrücklich gesagt wird, daß Joseph zu dem Vater ging. Die

---

[432] Diesen Aufbau hat I.Willi-Plein, Aspekte, 316f., nicht erkannt. Nach ihr hat die Wendung »und es geschah nach diesen Begebenheiten« in 39,7 eine andere Funktion als in 40,1 und 48,1. Nur in 40,1 und 48,1 deute sie eine große Zäsur an. Von daher unterscheidet I.Willi-Plein in der Josephsgeschichte drei Teile: 1) In Kap. 37 und 39 werde Joseph als Jüngling geschildert, 2) in Kap. 40–47 werde der Mann Joseph dargestellt und 3) in Kap. 48–50 gehe es um Joseph als Ahnherr. Damit übersieht sie jedoch wichtige Einschnitte bei J. Hier beginnt mit 39,1 ein neuer Teil, und ebenso stellt 47,27a einen Neuansatz dar. Damit entfällt die m.E. nicht zu begründende These, daß die Formel »und es geschah nach diesen Begebenheiten« in der Josephsgeschichte eine unterschiedliche Funktion habe. Wie die Analysen gezeigt haben, lassen sich auch die inhaltlichen Feststellungen von I.Willi-Plein, die auf ihrer Gliederung aufbauen, nicht halten.

[433] Hier ist gegen MT der Plural zu lesen, vgl. die Kommentare z.St.

LXX hat deshalb nach v. 1 »er kam zu Jakob«. Diese Lesart wird gelegentlich für ursprünglich gehalten[434]. Es läßt sich aber schwer erklären, warum der Satz im MT ausgefallen sein sollte. So ist m. E. zu erwägen, ob die Fassung von v. 1 nicht dadurch entstanden ist, daß der Endredaktor hier J und P ungeschickt miteinander verbunden hat, und die LXX den Text glättete. Diese Überlegungen zu v. 1–2a bleiben notwendig hypothetisch. Es sollte aber deutlich werden, daß die Zuweisung an E keineswegs gesichert ist.

Sie läßt sich für v. 15 f., die – wie erwähnt – häufig zu E gerechnet werden, eindeutig ausschließen. Bei ihr ist vorausgesetzt, daß auch v. 8. 9a. 10b. 11 f. aus E stammen. Außerdem haben L. Ruppert, H. Donner und C. Westermann gezeigt, daß dieses Stück nicht in vorexilischer Zeit entstanden sein kann[435]. Das ergibt sich schon aus dem Aufbau. Die dreifache Nennung Gottes in einem Segenswort entspricht dem aaronitischen Segen in Num 6, 24–26. Außerdem »verweisen die hymnischen Prädikationen Gottes auf eine Vorstellungswelt, die im Alten Testament überwiegend exilisch und nachexilisch bezeugt ist«[436]. Deshalb hat H. Donner vermutet, daß v. 15 f. zu P gehört und dort auf v. 3–6 folgte. Dagegen sprechen aber gewichtige Gründe. In v. 15 wäre statt »da segnete er Joseph« mit LXX zu lesen »da segnete er sie«, da der Vater Joseph nicht in seinen Söhnen segnen kann, nachdem er diese in v. 5 adoptiert hat. Die Lesart der LXX erklärt sich aber daraus, daß der Vater in v. 14 den Söhnen die Hände auflegt. Sie ist also eine Glättung des MT, der als lectio difficilior nicht geändert werden darf. Dann kann v. 15 f. nicht zu P gehören. Gegen P spricht auch, wie H. Donner selbst einräumt[437], die Erwähnung des *ml'k*. Deshalb muß es sich bei v. 15 f. um einen Zusatz handeln[438].

Dann stellt sich die Frage, in welchem Verhältnis er zu der Erweiterung in v. 13 f. 17–20 steht. Da v. 15 f. den Zusammenhang zwischen v. 14 und v. 17 unterbricht, stammen die Verse nicht von dem gleichen Verfasser. Nach allgemeiner Auffassung ist v. 15 f. jünger als v. 13 f. 17–20. Sie bereitet aber erhebliche Schwierigkeiten. Wie soll man erklären, daß nach v. 13 f. später das Segenswort in v. 15 f. als Segen, den Joseph erhält, eingefügt wurde? Die Lesart der LXX in v. 15 zeigt, daß man das schon früh als Problem empfunden hat. Als Segen für Joseph

---

[434] So z. B. H. Gunkel 471; C. Westermann 206.
[435] L. Ruppert, Josephserzählung, 173–176, der allerdings schon den Untergang des Nordreichs als terminus a quo ansieht; H. Donner, Gestalt, 33 f.; C. Westermann 212–214.
[436] H. Donner, Gestalt, 33; für die Nachweise im einzelnen vgl. die in Anm. 435 genannten Arbeiten.
[437] H. Donner, Gestalt, 34.
[438] So auch H.-C. Schmitt, BZAW 154, 70 f.; C. Westermann 214.

wird v. 15 f. nur verständlich, wenn diese beiden Verse ursprünglich direkt auf v. 12 folgten. Tatsächlich schließt v. 15 gut an v. 12 an. Nach v. 12 b hat sich Joseph zur Erde hin verneigt. Darauf segnet der Vater Joseph mit v. 15 f. Die jahwistische Darstellung in dem Grundbestand von v. 8–12 wurde also zunächst in exilisch-nachexilischer Zeit um v. 15 f. erweitert. Dabei greift der Ergänzer das besondere Verhältnis auf, das bei J zwischen dem Vater und Joseph besteht. Es ist für ihn der Grund, daß der Vater Joseph in seinen beiden Söhnen segnet. Zugleich führt er mit seinen Aussagen über Gott v. 11 weiter. Ihm geht es nicht mehr nur um das Handeln Gottes in der Beziehung zwischen Israel und Joseph, sondern um das Wirken Gottes im ganzen Leben dieses Erzvaters. Ihn hat Gott in seinem gesamten Leben geweidet, und der *ml'k,* der hier doch wohl mit Gott identisch ist, hat ihn aus aller Not erlöst. Dem Ergänzer liegt aber zugleich daran, daß dieser Gott der Gott der Väter ist. Deshalb heißt es am Anfang des Segens in v. 15 b: »Der Gott, vor dem meine Väter gewandelt sind, Abraham und Isaak«. In seinen Aussagen über Gott erwähnt somit der sterbende Israel die gesamte Väterzeit, die – das dürfte die Intention des Ergänzers sein – mit ihm zu ihrem Abschluß kommt.

Mit seinem Segenswunsch für die Söhne Josephs nimmt der Vater dann die Zukunft in den Blick. Mit Recht stellt G. v. Rad fest: »Daß Jakob und seiner Väter Name ›in ihnen‹ genannt werden möge, soll wohl heißen, daß diese in Ägypten und von einer fremdländischen Mutter geborenen Knaben doch als vollbürtige Nachkommen der Erzväter gelten sollen«[439]. Wie die Erwähnung von Abraham und Isaak zeigt, ist hier nicht an eine Adoption der Kinder gedacht. Sonst könnte auch Joseph nicht in ihnen gesegnet werden. Als Nachkommen der Erzväter aber sollen sich die Knaben mehren. Sie erhalten also mit dem Segenswunsch Anteil an der Mehrungsverheißung, die den Patriarchen zuteil wurde.

Der Zusatz v. 15 f. war bereits vorhanden, als der Text um v. 9 b. 10 a. 13. 17–20 erweitert wurde. Der Verfasser dieser Ergänzung verstand die Segnung Josephs anscheinend so, daß der Vater dessen Söhne gesegnet hat. Das ist ein naheliegendes Mißverständnis, da v. 16 nur einen Segenswunsch für die Söhne enthält. Der Verfasser hat aber den ihm überlieferten Text in v. 15 a nicht entsprechend geändert, so daß nun die Spannung entsteht, daß der Vater schon in v. 9 b die Söhne segnen will, in v. 15 a aber Joseph segnet. Sie ist erst von der LXX beseitigt worden. Da es diesem Verfasser darauf ankam, daß Israel Ephraim Manasse vorgezogen hat, berichtete er, nachdem er mit v. 9 b. 10 a. 13 diese Szene vorbereitet hatte, in v. 14 zunächst, daß der Vater seine rechte Hand auf Ephraim und die linke auf Manasse legte. Darauf ließ

---

[439] G. v. Rad 343.

er das ihm vorgegebene Segenswort in v. 15 f. folgen. Da in ihm nichts über die Rangfolge der Söhne gesagt wird, konnte er Joseph in v. 17 f. den Versuch unternehmen lassen, die Handauflegung des Vaters zu korrigieren. Erst durch die Worte des Vaters in v. 19 und sein Segenswort von v. 20 steht fest, daß Ephraim den Vorrang gegenüber Manasse hat. Dabei rechnet der Vater in v. 19 mit der Mehrung beider Knaben, wenn auch Ephraim zahlreicher werden soll, und in dem Segenswort von v. 20 wird nach Ephraim auch Manasse erwähnt. Beides wird verständlich, wenn v. 16 vorausgesetzt ist, wo in dem Segenswunsch für die Söhne von ihrer Mehrung die Rede ist. Da aber schon v. 15 f. erst aus exilisch-nachexilischer Zeit stammt, wird durch diese Beobachtungen bestätigt, daß es sich bei v. 9 b. 10 a. 13 f. 17–20 um eine Erweiterung handelt, die in später nachexilischer Zeit entstanden ist.

Es bleiben noch v. 21 und v. 22. Auch hier heißt der Vater Israel (v. 21). Schon aus diesem Grund können die Verse nicht, wie vielfach angenommen wird[440], aus E stammen. Nun ist die Ankündigung des Vaters in v. 21 »Siehe ich sterbe, und es wird Gott mit euch sein und euch in das Land eurer Väter zurückbringen« etwas eigenartig formuliert. Vor allem fällt das Suffix »euch« auf. Nach allem, was in Gen 48 vorher erzählt wird, kann es sich nur auf Joseph und seine Söhne beziehen. Gemeint ist aber doch, daß Gott alle Söhne des Vaters zurückbringen wird. Das wird durch v. 22 bestätigt, da Joseph hier »eine Schulter« über seine Brüder hinaus in Palästina erhält. Danach kehren auch seine Brüder zurück.

Nun entspricht der Anfang der Rede Israels in v. 21 fast wörtlich 50, 24, wo Joseph zu seinen Brüdern redet. Dort kündigt ihnen Joseph dann an, daß sie Gott heimsuchen und aus diesem Land heraufführen wird. Auch hier steht das Suffix »euch«. Es ist aber fest verankert, da sich Joseph an seine Brüder wendet. Diese Übereinstimmungen machen es wahrscheinlich, daß v. 21 in Anlehnung an 50, 24 von einem Ergänzer eingefügt wurde[441]. Ihm ging es darum, daß nicht erst Joseph, sondern bereits der Vater vor seinem Tod die Rückkehr aus Ägypten als Plan Gottes angekündigt hatte. Dabei wählte er in v. 21 bβ eine Formulierung, die sonst nirgends im Pentateuch für die Aussage gebraucht wird, daß Gott die Israeliten aus Ägypten nach Palästina brachte. Nur hier steht dafür šwb hi. Damit will der Ergänzer verdeutlichen, daß es sich bei diesem Weg um eine Heimkehr in das Land der Väter handelt. Er hat außerdem die Formulierung von 50, 24 »aber Gott wird euch gewiß heimsuchen« durch »und es wird Gott mit euch sein« ersetzt. Damit

---

[440] So z.B. H. Gunkel 469 f.; O. Eißfeldt, Hexateuch-Synopse, 101*; O. Procksch 421; M. Noth, Pentateuch, 38; H. Seebaß, Zeit, 90.
[441] L. Ruppert, Josephserzählung, 164; C. Westermann 217; vgl. auch H.-C. Schmitt, BZAW 154, 72.

spielt er auf die Verheißung an Jakob in 46,4 an. Dort hatte Gott Jakob zugesagt, daß er mit ihm nach Ägypten hinabziehen und ihn heraufführen wird. Die Grundlage für v. 21 ist somit 50,24. Der Ergänzer spielt aber auch auf 46,4 an und setzt mit der Formulierung in v. 21 bβ einen eigenen Akzent.

Von v. 21 läßt sich v. 22 nicht trennen, da das einleitende »ich aber« in v. 22 voraussetzt, daß Israel schon geredet hat. Verschiedentlich sieht man in diesem Vers einen noch späteren Zusatz. So schreibt H.-C. Schmitt: »Der Vers fällt schon insofern aus dem Kontext heraus, als er in keinerlei sachlicher Beziehung zur Herausführung Israels durch Gott steht, sondern von einer Landverteilung durch Jakob spricht«[442]. Damit wird aber der Zusammenhang, der doch zwischen v. 21 und v. 22 besteht, verkannt. Weil der Vater weiß, daß Gott Joseph und seine Brüder in das Land ihrer Väter zurückbringen wird (v. 21) – wobei an ihre Nachkommen gedacht ist –, übereignet Israel dem Joseph einen besonderen Anteil an diesem Land (v. 22). Das ist die Folge davon, daß er zu Joseph eine besonders enge Beziehung hat. V. 21 und v. 22 sind somit sachlich gut miteinander verbunden.

Das ist freilich immer wieder bestritten worden. Nach H. Gunkel setzt v. 22 voraus, daß der Vater das Land an alle seine Söhne verteilt und dabei Joseph ein besonderes Stück gibt. Eine solche Erbteilung sei aber nur in Kanaan denkbar. Folglich handle es sich bei v. 22 um das Fragment einer alten Überlieferung, in der der Vater nicht nach Ägypten zog, sondern in Kanaan starb und dort vor seinem Tod an seine Söhne das Land verteilte[443]. Nun erhält Joseph in v. 22 »eine Schulter«, die der Vater mit seinem Schwert und seinem Bogen eingenommen hat. Mit »Schulter« wird auf Sichem angespielt. Der Vater hat also nach v. 22 Sichem erobert. Davon weiß das Alte Testament sonst nichts. Nach Gen 33,19 hat Jakob vielmehr ein Stück Land bei Sichem gekauft. Auf ihm wurden nach Jos 24,32 die Gebeine Josephs bestattet. Nun meint H. Gunkel, daß in Jos 24,32 Gen 33,19 und 48,22 »unorganisch« miteinander verwoben worden seien[444]. Aber Jos 24,32 setzt nicht voraus, daß Jakob dieses Stück Land dem Joseph übereignet hat. Von ihm heißt es in v. 32b: »und ›das‹[445] den Josephiten als Erbbesitz zuteil geworden war«. Damit wird lediglich festgestellt, daß den Josephiten dieses Land als Erbbesitz gehörte. Da in v. 32a ausdrücklich gesagt wird, daß es Jakob käuflich erworben hatte, kann sich v. 32b nicht auf

---

[442] H.-C. Schmitt, BZAW 154,71 Anm. 302; vgl. auch C. Westermann 217. H. Gunkel 474, und H. Donner, Gestalt, 32, die v. 21 zu E rechnen, halten v. 22 für einen Nachtrag.
[443] H. Gunkel 474f.; ähnlich H. Greßmann, Ursprung, 7–9; M. Noth, Pentateuch, 91f.; H.-C. Schmitt, BZAW 154,71f. Anm. 302; C. Westermann 217.
[444] H. Gunkel 475.
[445] Zum Text vgl. BHS.

Gen 48,22 beziehen. In Gen 34 wird zwar Sichem von Simeon und Levi erobert, aber die Stadt wird dadurch nicht zum Besitz Jakobs oder seiner Söhne. So ist die Angabe über Sichem in Gen 48,22 im Alten Testament singulär. Schon das läßt es fraglich erscheinen, daß hier auf eine alte Überlieferung angespielt wird, die nur sonst nicht mehr erhalten ist. Zudem wird in Gen nur noch in dem späten Stück Gen 14 von dem Kriegszug eines Patriarchen erzählt. Mit den sonstigen Jakobüberlieferungen läßt sich Gen 48,22 ebenfalls nicht verbinden. Das spricht dafür, daß hier keine alte Überlieferung im Hintergrund steht. Wie der Verfasser zu seiner Auffassung kam, läßt sich nicht mehr ermitteln. Vielleicht hat er den Erwerb eines Stückes Land durch Jakob in Gen 33,19 mit Gen 34 kombiniert.

Jedenfalls ist aber Gen 48,22 erst spät entstanden. Hier dürfte die Überlieferung vorausgesetzt sein, daß die Gebeine Josephs in dem Gebiet von Sichem bestattet wurden. Das wollte der Verfasser von v.21f. damit begründen, daß bereits Josephs Vater ihm Sichem übereignet hatte. Damit findet Joseph in einem Gebiet seine letzte Ruhe, das ihm rechtmäßig gehörte. Das erinnert an die Anschauung der Priesterschrift von dem Grab der Patriarchen. Sie werden bei P in jener Grabhöhle begraben, die einst Abraham erworben hatte (Gen 23). Hier wird auch Jakob bestattet, obwohl er in Ägypten gestorben ist. In Ägypten stirbt auch Joseph. Durch 48,22 werden aber seine Gebeine in der Heimat an einem Ort begraben, der sein Eigentum war.

Ist diese Überlegung richtig, dann wird hier die Auffassung der Priesterschrift, daß die Patriarchen in ihrem Eigentum bestattet wurden, auf Joseph übertragen. Dann wäre Gen 48,21f. freilich ein sehr später Zusatz. Diese Ansetzung wird dadurch gestützt, daß die Formulierung »das Land eurer Väter« in v.21 doch wohl die Erwähnung Abrahams und Isaaks in v.15 bereits voraussetzt. Daß die früheren Landesbewohner in v.22 als »Amoriter« bezeichnet werden, läßt sich mit einer solchen Datierung vereinbaren. In dem Abschnitt Gen 15,13–16, der aus nachexilischer Zeit stammt[446], werden sie ebenfalls »Amoriter« genannt. In welchem Verhältnis der Zusatz in v.21f. zu der Erweiterung in v.9b.10a.13f.17–20 steht, muß offenbleiben. Es ist nicht auszuschließen, daß beide Ergänzungen von dem gleichen Verfasser vorgenommen wurden.

Damit läßt sich die Entstehung von Gen 48 im wesentlichen noch nachzeichnen, auch wenn einzelne Fragen nicht geklärt werden konnten. Zu J gehören v.2b.8.9a.10b.11f., zu P v.3–6. Die Zuweisung von v.1–2a bleibt unsicher, der Text stammt entweder aus E oder ist aus J und P zusammengesetzt. Alles andere sind Zusätze. V.15f. wurde in

---

[446] Diese Datierung von Gen 15,13–16 kann hier nicht weiter begründet werden.

exilisch-nachexilischer Zeit eingefügt. Noch später sind v. 7, v. 9 b. 10 a.
13 f. 17–20 und v. 21 f., die erst nach P entstanden sind.

Dieses Ergebnis hat für die stammesgeschichtliche Interpretation
von Gen 48 erhebliche Konsequenzen. Nur die jahwistische Darstellung stammt aus vorexilischer Zeit. Sie enthält jedoch keine Aussage
über die Stämme Manasse und Ephraim. Die beiden Söhne Josephs
kommen ausschließlich als Individuen in den Blick. Sie sind die Kinder,
die Joseph in Ägypten geboren wurden, und dessen Vater Israel freut
sich, daß er sie sehen darf. Dagegen sind die Erweiterungen an den
Söhnen Josephs nur als Ahnherren der betreffenden Stämme interessiert. Durch v. 15 f. werden sie von Josephs Vater als legitime Nachkommen der Erzväter anerkannt. Damit gehören ihre Nachkommen notwendig zu Israel. Diesen Gesichtspunkt unterstreicht P in v. 3–6 dadurch, daß hier die beiden Söhne von Jakob adoptiert werden. In der
späten Erweiterung v. 9 b. 10 a. 13 f. 17–20 geht es in den Söhnen um das
Verhältnis zwischen den Stämmen Ephraim und Manasse. Auch v. 21 f.
hat neben der Funktion zu begründen, warum Joseph in dem Gebiet
von Sichem begraben wurde, stammesgeschichtliche Bedeutung. Hat
der Vater Sichem Joseph übereignet, dann gehört damit die Stadt
selbstverständlich zum Stammesgebiet seiner Nachkommen. In exilisch-nachexilischer Zeit ist somit die jahwistische Darstellung stammesgeschichtlich interpretiert und weitergeführt worden.

IV. Zusammenfassung und Weiterführung

Wie in den Analysen gezeigt wurde, lassen sich in der Josephsgeschichte J, E und P deutlich voneinander abheben, obwohl ihre Darstellungen später so geschickt miteinander verbunden wurden, daß die Josephsgeschichte heute weithin als einheitlich gilt. Bei näherer Betrachtung wird aber deutlich, daß nicht nur literarisch zwischen J, E und P zu unterscheiden ist, sondern daß die Verfasser auch jeweils ein anderes Thema behandeln. Nur für wenige Stellen blieb die Zuweisung fraglich. Das ist nicht überraschend, da alle drei Fassungen in wichtigen Punkten übereinstimmen. So ist z.B. jeweils eine Hungersnot der Anlaß, daß die Brüder Josephs nach Ägypten reisen. Da zudem E von J und P von dem jehowistischen Werk literarisch abhängig ist, bestehen zwischen den Darstellungen Berührungspunkte, die ihre Trennung erschweren. Es ist deshalb eher erstaunlich, wie weitgehend noch eine Aufteilung möglich ist. Im folgenden sollen nun die Ergebnisse der Analysen zusammengefaßt und weitergeführt werden.

a) Die Josephsgeschichte des Jahwisten

Zu J gehören abgesehen von unbedeutenden Glossen: 37,3.4.12. 13a.14b*.15–17.18b.21 (mit Juda). 23a.bα.25–27.28aβ.31–33*.34b. 35a; 39,1 (ohne »Potiphar, der Kämmerer des Pharao, der Oberste der Leibwache«). 2–4aα.b.5–23; 40,1 ...; 41,34a.35a.bβ (mit Textänderung). 36.41.42.44.45a.46b.48.50a.51.52.55.56bα ...; 42,2 (?) ... 7.9bβ (?). 10.11a ... 27*.28 ... 38; 43,1–13. 15–23a. 24–34; 44,1a.2aα.b. 3–34; 45,1.4.5aα^1.aβ.6.7.9–14 ... 27aα.28; 46,1aα.28 (mit Textänderung) –31*.32aα.b–34; 47,1–4 + »da sprach Pharao zu Joseph« (nach LXX). 6b.12.13–26.27a.29–31; 48,1aα (?) ... b (?). 2b.8.9a.10b.11f. ...; 49,33aβ ...; 50,1–3a. 4aβ–6.7*.8. 10b.11.14.22.

Diese Josephsgeschichte ist als selbständige literarische Erzählung entstanden. Das zeigen jene Stellen, die sachlich oder sprachlich von J abweichen. So steht für Gott in den Reden durchgehend Elohim. Entgegen Gen 29,1–30, 24 (J/E) ist Joseph für den Vater der »Sohn des Alters«, außerdem hat der Vater hier mehrere Töchter (37,35a). Auch die Bedeutung, die der Ansiedlung des Vaters und der Brüder in dem Land Gosen zukommt, hat bei J sonst keinen Anhaltspunkt. Die Josephsgeschichte ist dann von dem Jahwisten in sein Werk aufgenommen worden. Von ihm stammt aber nur 39,5. Das Verhalten des Ägypters zu Joseph war für J ein Modell, wie die Sippen des Erdbodens zur Zeit des davidisch-salomonischen Großreichs von Jahwe Segen erlangen konnten (Gen 12,3; 28,14). Deshalb hat der Jahwist hier seine Vorlage entsprechend erweitert. Ansonsten hat er sie jedoch ohne Änderung übernommen.

Entstanden ist die Josephsgeschichte in der davidisch-salomonischen Zeit. Die Rolle Judas als Sprecher der Brüder ist nicht denkbar, bevor der Judäer David auch zum König über die mittel- und nordpalästinensischen Stämme geworden war (II Sam 5,3). Außerdem ist der Verfasser an ägyptischen Verhältnissen interessiert. Das zeigt schon die Aufnahme eines ägyptischen Märchens in 39,7ff. Es wird erst recht deutlich an seinen Hinweisen, daß die Ägypter nicht mit den Hebräern essen dürfen (43,32) und daß Schafhirten für die Ägypter ein Greuel sind (46,34). Auch aus der Darstellung, daß Joseph die Abgabe des Fünften in Ägypten eingeführt hat (47,13–26), die zu seinem eigentlichen Thema ohne Beziehung ist, geht hervor, daß der Verfasser seine Leser auf ägyptische Verhältnisse hinweisen will, die von den israelitischen abwichen. Das wird am besten aus der davidisch-salomonischen Zeit verständlich, in der der kulturelle Einfluß Ägyptens erheblich war. Schließlich setzt die Josephsgeschichte auch voraus, daß die Überlieferungen von Jakob und von dem Exodus bereits gesamtisraelitisch verstanden wurden. Der Ahnherr heißt Israel, weil von ihm das spätere Volk Israel abstammt. Er übersiedelt mit seinen Söhnen nach Ägypten, weil ihre Nachkommen später dieses Land wieder verlassen haben. Da m.E. der Jahwist in der Zeit Salomos geschrieben hat[447], ist die Josephsgeschichte vermutlich in der ersten Hälfte seiner Regierung entstanden[448]. Sie wurde also rasch zu einem Bestandteil des umfassenden jahwistischen Geschichtswerkes.

Unterschiedlich wird in der Forschung die Frage beantwortet, ob die Josephsgeschichte auf ältere mündliche Überlieferungen zurückgeht, die der Verfasser ausgestaltet hat. Sie ist von M. Noth nachdrücklich verneint worden. Er betont gegen H. Greßmann und H. Gunkel, daß die Josephsgeschichte »unter Verwendung allgemeiner Erzählungsmotive« entstanden ist, daß ihr jedoch keine älteren Erzählungen über Joseph zugrundeliegen[449]. Dem hat H.-C. Schmitt unter Verweis auf 37,3 widersprochen, wo Joseph als »Sohn des Alters« bezeichnet wird. Hier sei Joseph der jüngste Bruder. Es habe deshalb »eine innerjosephitische Traditionsstufe« gegeben, in der Benjamin und Juda fehlten.

---

[447] L. Schmidt, Pentateuch, 94f.
[448] Mit ähnlichen Argumenten setzt auch H.-C. Schmitt, BZAW 154, 150–163, seine Juda-Schicht in der Zeit Salomos an.
[449] M. Noth, Pentateuch, 228.

Hier sei nur von einer Reise der Brüder erzählt worden, da die zweite lediglich dazu diene, auch Benjamin nach Ägypten zu bringen[450]. Gegen diese Auffassung bestehen m. E. erhebliche Bedenken. Bricht man die zweite Reise aus der Josephsgeschichte heraus, so fehlt ihr ein wesentliches Stück, das sachlich und stilistisch eng mit dem Kontext verbunden ist. So lassen sich z. B. der Vorwurf Josephs, die Brüder seien Kundschafter, sie hätten Geld gestohlen – wovon übrigens in der Josephsgeschichte nie die Rede ist –, und sie hätten den Becher entwendet, gegen H. Schulte nicht als drei Varianten des Motivs verstehen, daß Joseph die Brüder fälschlich beschuldigte[451].

Vielmehr sind das Geld, das die Brüder finden, und der Becher, den Joseph in den Sack Benjamins legen läßt, zwei Motive, die in ihrer Gestaltung von vornherein aufeinander angelegt sind. Rätselhaft bleibt zudem, wie in der postulierten Vorlage die erste Begegnung Josephs mit den Brüdern verlaufen sein soll. H. Schulte nimmt an, daß Joseph die Brüder zunächst in das Gefängnis warf und sich ihnen danach zu erkennen gab[452]. Aber das »Gefängnis« stammt aus E und kann schon wegen der literarischen Abhängigkeit des Elohisten von J, die H. Schulte erkannt hat, nicht für die ursprüngliche Fassung in Anspruch genommen werden. Man wird es deshalb als ein literarisches Stilmittel ansehen müssen, daß Benjamin erstmals in dem Gespräch Josephs mit den Brüdern auf der ersten Reise eingeführt wird. Überlieferungsgeschichtliche Konsequenzen dürfen somit daraus nicht gezogen werden.

Nun lokalisieren die westjordanischen Jakobüberlieferungen diesen Erzvater in Sichem und Bethel, die zum Gebiet des Hauses Joseph gehören. Daraus konnte leicht die Auffassung entstehen, daß zwischen Jakob und dem Ahnherrn des Hauses Joseph eine besondere Beziehung bestand. Auch 37,12.13 a.14 b*, wonach die Brüder das Vieh in Sichem weiden, setzt einen mittelpalästinensischen Wohnsitz des Vaters voraus. Daß das Erzählmotiv von dem jüngsten Sohn, der zu einer führenden Stellung aufsteigt, mit Joseph verbunden wurde, läßt sich dann erklären.

Auch in Gen 30,22–24 ist Joseph abgesehen von Benjamin der jüngste Sohn, wenn er auch hier im Unterschied zur Josephsgeschichte nicht für den Vater »der Sohn des Alters« ist. Beide Überlieferungen stimmen aber darin überein, daß außer Benjamin die übrigen Söhne bereits geboren waren, als Joseph zur Welt kam. Joseph war relativ jung

---

[450] H.-C. Schmitt, BZAW 154, 153; ähnlich schon H. Gunkel, Komposition, 69; H. Schulte, BZAW 128, 25 f. Nach H.-C. Schmitt handelt es sich um eine manassitische Überlieferung, die »wahrscheinlich auf eine noch ältere machiritische Tradition« zurückgehe (a.a.O. 153 Anm. 329).

[451] H. Schulte, BZAW 128, 27.

[452] H. Schulte, BZAW 128, 27.

und im Blick auf die Lokalisierung der westjordanischen Jakobüberlieferungen mit diesem Erzvater besonders verbunden. Deshalb konnte das Motiv von dem Aufstieg des Jüngsten mit ihm verknüpft werden, auch wenn er nicht der Jüngste war. Dann mußte freilich Benjamin zunächst außer Betracht bleiben. Aber Benjamin war ja durch die gemeinsame Mutter mit Joseph besonders verbunden und konnte deshalb für den Verfasser Joseph nicht gehaßt haben. Er durfte somit bei den Ereignissen, die in Gen 37 beschrieben werden, keine Rolle spielen. Das war dadurch möglich, daß für den Verfasser Benjamin anscheinend noch ein Kind war, als die anderen Brüder Joseph verkauften. Dafür spricht 43,29. Hier stellt Joseph den Brüdern, als er Benjamin sieht, die Frage: »Ist das euer jüngster Bruder?« Sie setzt voraus, daß er Benjamin nicht wiedererkannt hat, sondern aus dem Auftreten eines weiteren Bruders schließt, daß es sich um Benjamin handelt[453]. Es gibt also keine zureichenden Gründe für die Annahme, daß die Josephsgeschichte auf eine mündliche Überlieferung zurückgeht. Dagegen läßt sich die Sonderstellung Benjamins bei dem Verfasser verständlich machen.

Dann stellt sich aber m. E. die Frage, ob es in der mündlichen Überlieferung bereits eine Verbindung zwischen Jakob- und Exodusüberlieferung gegeben hat, als die Josephsgeschichte entstand. Ihr Verfasser kennt eine Tradition, nach der dieser Ahnherr in Palästina begraben wurde. Deshalb läßt Israel Joseph schwören, ihn nicht in Ägypten zu begraben, und Joseph bestattet dann den toten Vater in Palästina (47,29-31; 50,1ff.*). In diesen Stücken gestaltet der Verfasser sein Thema »Joseph und der Vater«, sie sind somit erst von ihm gebildet worden. Dann ist aber zweifelhaft, daß Jakob schon in der Überlieferung nach Ägypten übersiedelte. Wie konnte der Vater nach Ägypten ziehen, wo dann auch seine Nachkommen wohnten, wenn er doch in Palästina bestattet wurde? Diese Frage stellen, heißt sie beantworten. Anscheinend bestand noch zu der Zeit des Verfassers der Josephsgeschichte eine Lücke zwischen der gesamtisraelitisch verstandenen Überlieferung von Jakob, in der Jakob als der Ahnherr der Israeliten galt, und einer auf Israel ausgeweiteten Exodustradition. Man war zwar überzeugt, daß es die Nachkommen Jakobs waren, die Ägypten verlassen hatten, es fehlte aber eine Überlieferung, wie sie dorthin gekommen waren. Nach M. Noth war zwar bereits dem Verfasser der Josephsgeschichte vorgegeben, daß Jakob und seine Söhne nach Ägypten hinabzogen[454]. Aber die Credoformulierungen, auf die sich M. Noth stützt,

---

[453] So z. B. auch H. Gunkel 451.
[454] M. Noth, Pentateuch, 228. So auch G. v. Rad, Das formgeschichtliche Problem des Hexateuch (1938), in: ders., Gesammelte Studien zum Alten Testament, ³1965, 9-86, 63f.

sind jünger als die Josephsgeschichte und setzen damit ihre Existenz voraus[455]. Gerade daß hier in der Überlieferung eine Lücke bestand, ermöglichte die Entstehung der Josephsgeschichte.

Ob man aus der Rolle, die in ihr Joseph zukommt, schließen darf, daß sie in Mittelpalästina entstanden ist[456], ist allerdings fraglich. Tatsächlich würde sich so zwar am besten erklären, warum in ihr »Joseph und der Vater« das beherrschende Thema ist. Andererseits lassen die Bekanntschaft mit einem ägyptischen Märchen und die – wenn auch vagen[457] – Kenntnisse der ägyptischen Verhältnisse eher an den Umkreis des Königshofes denken. Dafür spricht auch, daß der Jahwist, der doch wohl in Juda geschrieben hat, die Josephsgeschichte schon bald nach ihrer Entstehung in sein Werk aufnehmen konnte. Außerdem stellt sich die Frage, ob die hohe künstlerische Gestaltung, die in der Josephsgeschichte sichtbar wird, nicht ein Hinweis darauf ist, daß sie in gebildeten Kreisen am königlichen Hof[458] oder in seiner Umgebung entstanden ist. Dann bleibt allerdings vorläufig offen, warum hier gerade Joseph zu einer tragenden Figur dieser Erzählung wurde.

Für den Stil der alten Josephsgeschichte ist charakteristisch, daß ihr Verfasser mit retardierenden Elementen arbeitet, durch die er den Ablauf der Handlung bewußt verzögert. So trifft Joseph in Gen 37 nicht sofort auf die Brüder, sondern er kann sie zunächst nicht finden. Erst nachdem ihm ein Mann mitgeteilt hat, daß sie nach Dothan gezogen sind, kommt er mit ihnen zusammen. Auch bei dieser Begegnung wird die Handlung zerdehnt. Zunächst ziehen ihm die Brüder nur jenes Gewand aus, an dem seine Bevorzugung durch den Vater sichtbar wird (37,23 a.bα). Später sehen sie eine ismaelitische Karawane, und Juda schlägt vor, den verhaßten Bruder zu verkaufen (37,25 ff.). In Ägypten endet der Aufstieg Josephs zum Hausverwalter eines Ägypters mit seinem tiefen Fall. Er wird in das Gefängnis geworfen (39,1*–20). Erst von dort aus steigt er zu dem zweiten Mann in Ägypten auf (39,21 ff.). Bei der zweiten Reise der Brüder wird zunächst breit geschildert, wie sie mit dem Hausverwalter und danach mit Joseph zusammen sind, ohne daß die Handlung voranschreitet (43,15–23 a.24–34). Sie wird erst mit dem Befehl Josephs an den Hausverwalter, seinen Becher in dem Sack Benjamins zu verstecken(44,1 f.*), weitergeführt. In 47,13–26 werden weder der Vater noch die Brüder erwähnt. Damit unterbricht

---

[455] Das gilt auch für das »kleine geschichtliche Credo« in Dtn 26,5–10, vgl. dazu z.B. L. Schmidt, »De Deo«, BZAW 143, 1976, 138 Anm. 33, und die dort genannte Literatur.

[456] So z.B. M. Noth, Pentateuch, 229 f.

[457] So gibt es z.B. keinen ägyptischen Beleg für 46,34, daß Schafhirten den Ägyptern ein Greuel waren, vgl. C. Westermann 187. Auch daß die Einbalsamierung 40 Tage dauerte (50,3a), ist dort nicht bezeugt.

[458] So z.B. H. Donner, Gestalt, 12 f.

das Stück den Zusammenhang zwischen 47,12 und 47,27a. Erst mit 47,27a kehrt der Verfasser zu seinem Thema zurück. Da der Vater in 47,29–31 die Frage seines Begräbnisses regelt, erwartet man, daß er danach stirbt und von Joseph in Palästina bestattet wird. Das wird jedoch erst in 49,33aβ; 50,1ff.* berichtet. Zuvor darf der Vater noch die beiden Söhne Josephs sehen (48,2b.8.9a.10b.11f.). Es läßt sich somit durchgehend beobachten, daß der Verfasser den Ablauf der Handlung mit retardierenden Elementen gestaltet hat.

Er füllt durch die Josephsgeschichte die Lücke, die in der Überlieferung zwischen Jakob als dem Ahnherrn Israels und dem Exodus bestand. Deshalb ist ihm wichtig, daß Joseph den Vater und die Brüder in Gosen wohnen ließ. Er kennt anscheinend eine Überlieferung, nach der ihre Nachkommen von dort nach Palästina gekommen sind. Nach 45,7 hat sogar Gott Joseph vor seinen Brüdern hergesandt, um ihnen Nachkommen zu geben und am Leben zu erhalten. Die Familie des Vaters mußte also nach Ägypten übersiedeln, weil sie nur dort eine Zukunft haben konnte. Die Möglichkeit, durch die Josephsgeschichte eine Lücke der Überlieferung zu schließen, ist freilich eher die Voraussetzung des Verfassers als sein Ziel. Das zeigt sich daran, unter welchen Aspekten der Vater und seine Söhne betrachtet werden. Der Verfasser setzt dabei zwar die politischen und stammesgeschichtlichen Verhältnisse seiner Tage voraus. Das wird besonders daran deutlich, daß Juda der Sprecher der Brüder ist, obwohl diese Funktion eigentlich dem ältesten Sohn zufallen müßte, der Juda in keiner Überlieferung ist. Vorausgesetzt wird aber auch, daß die Ahnherrn der Stämme als Söhne von Jakob/Israel gelten und Manasse und Ephraim von Joseph abstammen. Aber diese politischen und stammesgeschichtlichen Beziehungen sind nicht das Thema des Verfassers. Der Vater und seine Söhne werden vielmehr ausschließlich als Individuen gezeichnet. Mit Recht stellt H. Donner fest: »Jakob und seine zwölf Söhne repräsentieren in der Josephsgeschichte nicht Israel und seine zwölf Stämme, sondern gewissermaßen nur sich selbst.«[459] So läßt sich z.B. der Haß der Brüder auf Joseph in 37,4 nicht stammesgeschichtlich deuten. Hier geht es nicht um die Beziehung zwischen Stämmen, sondern um den Konflikt in einer Familie, in der der Vater einen Sohn begünstigt. Selbst die Begegnung zwischen dem Vater und den Söhnen Josephs in 48,8.9a.10b.11f. hat, wie bei der Analyse gezeigt wurde, keine stammesgeschichtlichen Implikationen. Hier soll vielmehr dargestellt werden, daß der sterbende Vater noch die Kinder seines Lieblingssohnes sehen durfte. Es geht also in der Josephsgeschichte durchgehend um die Beziehung zwischen Personen.

---

[459] H. Donner, Gestalt, 11.

Das Thema des Verfassers ist dabei »Joseph und der Vater«. Damit beginnt die jahwistische Josephsgeschichte in Gen 37,3 und damit endet sie in 50,1 ff.*. Dieses Thema bestimmt die Gliederung und die Darstellung im einzelnen. Die Exposition in den jahwistischen Bestandteilen von 37,3–35a ist an der besonderen Beziehung zwischen dem Vater und Joseph orientiert. Die Liebe des Vaters zu diesem Sohn weckt den Haß der Brüder. Aus diesem Grund verkaufen sie Joseph an Ismaeliter, die auf dem Weg nach Ägypten sind. Bei dem Vater aber erwecken sie den Eindruck, daß Joseph von einem wilden Tier zerrissen wurde. Er ist über den Verlust dieses Sohnes untröstlich.

Mit der Inversion in 39,1* macht der Verfasser deutlich, daß hier ein neuer Abschnitt beginnt. Er endet mit 41,50a.51f., wo von der Geburt der beiden Söhne Josephs, den Namen und ihrer Begründung durch Joseph berichtet wird. Dieser Teil handelt von dem Aufstieg Josephs in Ägypten. Dieser Aufstieg beruht darauf, daß Jahwe mit Joseph ist, wie der Verfasser in Gen 39 mehrfach betont. In der Deutung der Namen seiner Söhne bekennt dann Joseph selbst, daß ihm Gott nach allem Elend ein glückliches Leben geschenkt hat. Daß Joseph in Ägypten zum zweiten Mann aufgestiegen ist, ist die Voraussetzung dafür, daß ihn der Vater nochmals sehen kann.

Diese Begegnung mit dem Vater ist in 46,29f. der Höhepunkt des folgenden Abschnittes, der aus dem jahwistischen Faden in 41,55–47,26 besteht. Er beginnt damit, daß Joseph den hungernden Ägyptern Getreide verkaufte (41,55.56bα) und endet mit der Schilderung, daß er die Ägypter und ihr Land für den Pharao erwarb und den Ägyptern den Fünften auferlegte (47,13–26). So bildet das Wirken Josephs für die Ägypter in der Zeit der Hungersnot den Rahmen für die beiden Reisen der Brüder und für die Übersiedlung des Vaters mit seiner Familie nach Ägypten. Diese Beobachtung spricht nochmals dafür, daß 47,13–26 bereits bei J enthalten war. Der Getreideverkauf Josephs an die Ägypter ist der Anlaß, daß der Vater seine Söhne nach Ägypten schickt. Ihre beiden Reisen sind letztlich an dem Vater orientiert, obwohl hier die Brüder und Benjamin im Mittelpunkt stehen. Joseph stellt auf der zweiten Reise die Brüder auf die Probe, ob sie Benjamin preisgeben, so wie sie einst ihn den Ismaelitern ausgeliefert haben. Dabei geht es aber, wie die große Rede Judas in 44,18 ff. zeigt, nicht darum, wie sich die Brüder zu einem Bruder verhalten, sondern um ihre Stellung zu dem Vater. Anders als einst bei Joseph akzeptieren die Brüder bei Benjamin, daß ihn der Vater liebt. Sie lassen Benjamin nicht in Ägypten zurück, weil sie verhindern wollen, daß der Vater wegen des Verlustes dieses Sohnes mit Gram in die שׁאל hinabsteigt. Deshalb gibt sich Joseph ihnen nun in 45,1.4 zu erkennen, während er sich bisher von der ersten Begegnung an (42,7) fremd gegen sie gestellt hatte. Sie sind jetzt wieder »seine

Brüder«, nachdem sie der Verfasser in Gen 43f. nur als die Söhne des Vaters oder als »die Männer« bezeichnet hatte.

In 45,5 aα[1]. aβ. 6f. deutet Joseph den Brüdern seinen Weg. Daß die Hungersnot sie gezwungen hatte, nach Ägypten zu kommen, zeigt Joseph, daß er von Gott vor den Brüdern hergesandt wurde, damit ihnen Gott trotz der Hungersnot Nachkommenschaft gebe und am Leben erhalte. Hatte Joseph in 41,51f. seinen Aufstieg auf das Wirken Gottes zurückgeführt, so macht er hier deutlich, welche Absicht Gott mit ihm für die Brüder verfolgte. Damit werden zugleich die Hinweise auf Gott in 42,28; 43,23 und 44,16 zu ihrem Ziel geführt. Jetzt löst sich das Rätsel, warum Benjamin objektiv als Dieb entlarvt werden konnte, obwohl er unschuldig war (44,16). Die Brüder mußten nochmals mit Joseph zusammentreffen. Da die Hungersnot noch fünf Jahre währen wird, läßt Joseph in 45,9–13 den Vater auffordern, mit seiner Familie nach Ägypten zu übersiedeln. Mit seinem Hinweis, daß ihn Gott zum Herrn für ganz Ägypten gemacht hat, greift Joseph in 45,9 gegenüber dem Vater die theologische Deutung seines Weges auf, die er in 41,51f. gegeben hat. Es kommt dann zu dem Wiedersehen zwischen dem Vater und Joseph, und der Vater wird mit seiner Familie in Gosen angesiedelt und von Joseph versorgt (46,1 aα. 28–34; 47,1–12*).

Der Schlußteil beginnt mit 47,27 a. Hier steht die besondere Beziehung zwischen dem Vater und Joseph ganz im Mittelpunkt. Der Vater läßt zunächst Joseph schwören, daß er ihn nicht in Ägypten, sondern in seinem Grab bestatten wird (47,29–31). Danach bringt Joseph seine Söhne zu dem sterbenden Vater (48,2b. 8. 9a. 10b. 11f.). Als er sie sieht, gibt nun auch der Vater eine theologische Deutung seines Weges. Er meinte, Joseph nicht mehr zu sehen, aber Gott hat ihn sogar die Nachkommen Josephs sehen lassen. Wie einst Joseph bei der Namensgebung seiner Söhne seinen Weg auf das Wirken Gottes zurückgeführt hatte, so spricht nun der Vater aus, daß das Geschehen mit Joseph, das ihm einst großen Kummer bereitete, doch seinen guten Sinn hatte (48,11). Danach stirbt der Vater, und Joseph begräbt ihn gemeinsam mit seinen Verwandten im Lande Kanaan. Sie kehren danach nach Ägypten zurück und wohnen dort. Die jahwistische Josephsgeschichte schließt damit, daß Joseph 110 Jahre lebte und somit ein erfülltes Leben hatte (50,22 b).

Schon an der Beziehung, die zwischen 41,51f. und 48,11 besteht, wird deutlich, wie kunstvoll der Verfasser sein Thema »Joseph und der Vater« durchgeführt hat. In den Analysen wurde gezeigt, daß seine Linienführung auch an den verschiedenen Aussagen über den Kummer des Vaters angesichts des Verlustes von Joseph, über das Weinen Josephs, an dem Motiv des »Sehens« und an der Entsprechung zwischen Geld und Becher deutlich wird. Das soll hier nicht wiederholt werden. Nimmt man die verschiedenen Beobachtungen zusammen, so geht aus ihnen hervor, daß es sich bei der jahwistischen Josephsgeschichte um ein sorgfältig komponiertes Werk handelt.

Ihr Verfasser ist besonders an den Menschen mit ihren Gefühlen und ihrem Tun interessiert. Das zeigt bereits die Exposition in Gen 37. Weil Israel Joseph mehr liebt als seine Söhne, hassen die Brüder Joseph. Sie sehen in dem Verkauf an die Ismaeliter die Chance, ihn loszuwerden, ohne Blutschuld auf sich zu laden. Weil Joseph schön ist, begehrt ihn die Frau seines ägyptischen Herrn. Als er sie nicht erhört, verleumdet sie ihn und bringt ihn dadurch in das Gefängnis (39,6 ff.). Auch in der großen Rede Judas von 44,18–34 steht mit dem Verhältnis des Vaters zu Benjamin eine menschliche Beziehung im Mittelpunkt. Weil Juda nicht mitansehen könnte, wie der Vater voll Kummer stirbt, bietet er sich Joseph als Sklave an der Stelle Benjamins an. Die konstitutive Bedeutung, die für ihn die zwischenmenschlichen Beziehungen haben, macht der Erzähler auch an jenen Stellen deutlich, an denen er Joseph weinen läßt (43,30; 45,14; 46,29; 50,1). Sie beherrschen auch die Begegnung des Vaters mit den Söhnen Josephs in 48,8 ff. So haben in dieser Josephsgeschichte die menschlichen Gefühle und die Handlungen, die aus ihnen entspringen, wesentliche Bedeutung. Dazu gehört auch, daß Menschen hier verschiedentlich Geschehnisse widerfahren, die ihnen zunächst rätselhaft sind. Den Brüdern und dem Vater ist unverständlich, warum Joseph fordert, daß die Brüder Benjamin mitbringen müssen, wenn sie ihn wiedersehen wollen. Rätselhaft ist den Brüdern, wie sie ihr Geld wiederfinden konnten; unerklärbar, daß der Hausverwalter den Becher in dem Sack Benjamins entdeckte. Damit bestätigt sich für die jahwistische Josephsgeschichte, was G. v. Rad als Merkmal der salomonischen Zeit angesehen hat, wenn er schreibt: »Eine dieser neu ins Blickfeld getretenen Dimensionen, die uns aus der Literatur dieser Epoche besonders entgegentritt, ist das, was wir das Anthropologische nennen würden, d. h. eine Konzentration auf das Phänomen des Humanum im weitesten Sinne, auf seine Möglichkeiten und seine Grenzen, seine psychologische Kompliziertheit und seine Abgründigkeit.«[460]

Freilich redet der Erzähler auch von Gott. In den Analysen wurde gezeigt, daß das an wesentlich mehr Stellen geschieht, als von den Vertretern einer Quellenscheidung sonst angenommen wird. Vordergründig betrachtet handeln zwar Menschen, die dabei ihre eigenen Absichten verfolgen, und doch wirkt eben darin Gott. So haben zwar die Brüder Joseph an Ismaeliter, die auf dem Weg nach Ägypten waren, verkauft, aber Gott hat Joseph vor den Brüdern hergesandt (45,7). Der Pharao macht Joseph zum zweiten Mann in Ägypten (41,41 f.44), aber Joseph läßt dem Vater mitteilen: »Gott hat mich zum Herrn für ganz

---

[460] G. v. Rad, Josephsgeschichte, 273.

Ägypten gemacht« (45,9). Dadurch ist das Rätselhafte, das Menschen begegnet, letztlich umgriffen von Gott. In dieser Josephsgeschichte stehen verschiedentlich Menschen vor einem Rätsel, das schließlich von Gott her seine Lösung erfährt. Es dürfte diese Überzeugung sein, die dem Verfasser die Freiheit gegeben hat, sein besonderes Interesse den menschlichen Gefühlen und Taten zuzuwenden. Sie können nicht zu einem Chaos führen, weil Gott doch die Fäden in der Hand hält.

Der Jahwist hat diese Josephsgeschichte in sein Werk aufgenommen. Sie war für ihn die Brücke, die es ihm ermöglichte, die bisher getrennten Überlieferungen von den Erzvätern und dem Exodus in einer durchlaufenden Darstellung zu verbinden. E und P sind später in diesem Punkt dem Aufriß gefolgt, den J geschaffen hatte. Damit kommt dem Jahwisten für die literarischen Darstellungen im Pentateuch eine zentrale Bedeutung zu.

b) Die Josephsgeschichte des Elohisten

Zu E gehören abgesehen von unbedeutenden Glossen: 37,5 a. 6–8 a. 9. 10*. 11 ... 13 b. 14 a ... 18 a. 19. 20. 22. 24. 28 aα. b. 29. 30 ... 34 a. 35 b. 36; 40,2. 3 aα. 4. 5 a. 6–15 a. 16–23; 41,1–14 aα. b. 15–33. 34 b. 35 bα. 37–40. 43. 47. 49. 53. 54; 42,1 ... 3. 4. 6*. 8. 9 a. bα. (bβ?). 11 b. 12–25*. 26. 29–37 ...; 45,2 a. bα. 3 ... 5 aα². b. 8. 15–18. 21 aβ–26. 27 aβ. b ... 46,1 aβ–5 a ... (48,1–2 a?) ... 50,3 b. 4 aα ... 9. 10 a ... 15–21.

Der Elohist hat für seine Josephsgeschichte die jahwistische Darstellung als literarische Vorlage benutzt. Bereits in I wurde festgestellt, daß die Motive des Bruders, der für Benjamin bürgt, und des Geldes, das die Brüder wieder finden, aus J stammen. Diese Beobachtung wurde durch die Analysen gestützt. So erhält Benjamin bei E in 45,22 größere Geschenke als seine Brüder. Diese Bevorzugung ist hier jedoch nicht begründet, da bei E alle Brüder auf einer Stufe stehen, wie sich u. a. daran zeigt, daß Joseph in 45,15 über allen Brüdern – und nicht nur wie bei J in 45,14 am Halse Benjamins – weint. Dieses Motiv stammt somit aus 43,34 J, wonach Benjamin beim Mahl das Fünffache seiner Brüder erhalten hat. Es wird in 45,22 von E aufgenommen und umgestaltet. In 42,4 begründet bei E Jakob das Fehlen Benjamins auf der ersten Reise mit demselben Argument, mit dem der Vater bei J in 42,38 und 44,29 es zunächst ablehnt, daß Benjamin auf einer zweiten Reise mitzieht. Schließlich nennen die Brüder in ihrem Bericht, den sie in 42,29 ff. dem Vater von der ersten Reise geben, Joseph »den Mann, den Herrn des Landes« (42,30.33). Diese doppelte Beschreibung wird nur aus 43,3 ff. verständlich, wo bei J der Vater und die Brüder Joseph als »den Mann« bezeichnen. Bei J haben hier der Vater und die Brüder noch nicht den Rang erkannt, den Joseph in Ägypten erlangt hat. Erst

Joseph läßt dem Vater in 45,9 mitteilen, daß ihn Gott zum Herrn für ganz Ägypten gemacht hat. E nimmt in 42,30.33 die Bezeichnung »der Mann« aus J auf, läßt sie aber von den Brüdern erläutern. Sie wissen bei E bereits, daß Joseph zum eigentlichen Herrn Ägyptens geworden ist. Damit setzt E einen eigenen Akzent. So läßt sich immer wieder zeigen, daß E die jahwistische Josephsgeschichte gekannt und umgestaltet hat.

Von ihr weicht aber der Elohist im Stil erheblich ab. Er hat die retardierenden Elemente beseitigt. Schon die Begegnung der Brüder mit Joseph in Gen 37 wird von E straffer erzählt als bei J. Sie endet hier sofort damit, daß die Brüder Joseph in eine Zisterne werfen, womit er aus ihrem Kreis ausscheidet. Nach 37,36 haben Midianiter Joseph an den Obersten der Leibwache verkauft. Damit kommt Joseph hier ohne das Zwischenspiel bei J zu jenem Mann, bei dem er mit dem Obermundschenk und Oberbäcker zusammentrifft (40,2ff.*). Wie bei E die zweite Reise der Brüder verlief, bevor sich Joseph zu erkennen gab, ist zwar nicht mehr erhalten. Es gibt aber keinerlei Anzeichen dafür, daß sie so ausführlich und mit retardierenden Elementen dargestellt worden wäre als bei J. E hat auch 47,13ff. übergangen, obwohl aus dem Vorschlag Josephs in 41,34b, man möge den Fünften des Ertrags der guten Jahre einsammeln, hervorgeht, daß er diesen Abschnitt kennt.

Ein retardierendes Element bildet bei E nur 46,1aβ–5a. Dieser Abschnitt ist mit seinem Thema »Joseph und die Brüder« nur sehr locker verbunden. Er geht aber darauf zurück, daß für E mit der Übersiedlung Jakobs nach Ägypten die Heilsgeschichte beginnt. Deshalb wird dem Ahnherrn auf dem Weg nach Ägypten die Verheißung Gottes für sich und seine Nachkommen zuteil. Dagegen ist 40,2ff.* bei E im Ablauf fest verankert. Zwar vergißt der Obermundschenk Joseph, so daß dessen gelungene Traumdeutung zunächst ohne Folgen bleibt. Aber das geschieht, damit E die beiden Träume des Pharao erzählen kann. Joseph wird von dem Pharao geholt, weil er sich als erfolgreicher Deuter von Träumen erwiesen hat. So bildet 40,2ff.* die unabdingbare Voraussetzung für den Aufstieg Josephs. Abgesehen von 46,1aβ–5a und vereinzelten Nebenmotiven wie 42,35 und 45,22f. fehlen bei E retardierende Elemente.

Für diese Darstellung sind vielmehr die Doppelungen charakteristisch, in denen die zweite Aussage die erste steigert. Schon in der Exposition hat Joseph zwei Träume. Er deutet dann die beiden Träume des Obermundschenken und des Oberbäckers und zwei Träume des Pharao. In 42,14–20 wird der entscheidende Punkt der Begegnung Josephs mit den Brüdern durch zwei Szenen herausgearbeitet, nachdem schon der Anfang ihres Gesprächs aus einem doppelten Redegang bestand (42,9bα.11b.12f.). Auch der Schluß, in dem Joseph den Brüdern das Geschehen deutet, wird von zwei Szenen gebildet (50,15–21). Er stellt als Ganzes zugleich eine Doppelung zu der vorläufigen Deutung in 45,5 aα².b.8 dar. So ist die elohistische Josephsgeschichte durchgehend von Doppelungen bestimmt. Darin unterscheidet sie sich signifikant von der jahwistischen, in der es keine Doppelungen gibt.

Auch in der Gliederung weicht E von J ab. Sie läßt sich allerdings nur teilweise verfolgen, weil E nach der ersten Reise der Brüder nur noch fragmentarisch erhalten ist. Die Exposition besteht hier aus dem elohistischen Faden in 37,5–36, da die Inversion in v. 36 einen Abschluß markiert. E verfolgt zunächst den Weg Josephs von seinen Träumen bis zu seiner Existenz als Sklave in Ägypten. Mit 40,2 beginnt ein neuer Abschnitt, der bis 41,54 reicht. Mit der Feststellung, daß die sieben Jahre der Hungersnot kamen und in allen Ländern Hungersnot herrschte, es aber in Ägypten Brot gab (41,54), wird bei E die Schilderung des Aufstiegs Josephs und seines Wirkens in den guten Jahren abgeschlossen. In 42,1, wo der Vater erkennt, daß es in Ägypten Getreide gibt, fängt ein neuer Teil an, in dem die Brüder im Mittelpunkt stehen. Im Unterschied zu J berichtet E zunächst nicht, daß Joseph den Ägyptern Getreide verkaufte. Das wird bei E in 42,6 nachgeholt. Wenn E mit 42,1 einen neuen Abschnitt beginnen läßt, so soll damit deutlich werden, daß jetzt das Thema »Joseph und die Brüder« wieder aufgenommen wird.

Mit diesem Thema hebt sich E klar von J ab. Schon in der Exposition in Gen 37 geht es bei E darum, daß Joseph in seinen Träumen angekündigt wird, daß er einen höheren Rang bekleiden soll als seine Brüder. Weil er ihnen die Träume erzählt, werden sie auf ihn eifersüchtig. Die Wende besteht darin, daß die Brüder Simeon – anders als einst Joseph – als ihren Bruder nicht im Stich lassen, und am Schluß in Gen 50,15 ff. deutet Joseph den Brüdern die Ereignisse. Unter diesem Gesichtspunkt steht auch der Aufstieg Josephs. Er ist zwar bei E ebenfalls die Voraussetzung dafür, daß Joseph nochmals mit dem Vater zusammenkommt. Wichtiger ist hier jedoch, daß sich mit seinem Aufstieg seine Träume erfüllen. So gedenkt Joseph in 42,9 a, als die Brüder wegen seiner Stellung vor ihm niederfallen, an diese Träume.

In diesem Thema dürfte es begründet sein, daß bei E Ruben und nicht Juda der Sprecher der Brüder ist. Das mag zwar mit dadurch bedingt sein, daß der Elohist im Nordreich schreibt[461], und deshalb an einer Hervorhebung Judas kein Interesse haben konnte. Aber Ruben mußte vor allem als der erstgeborene Sohn Jakobs zum Sprecher werden, wenn sich das Gewicht von dem Vater auf die Brüder verlagerte. Dadurch mußte außerdem Benjamin eine andere Stellung einnehmen als bei J. Er ist bei E von Anfang an beteiligt. Nach 37,9 haben sich 11 Sterne und damit auch Benjamin vor Joseph verneigt. Wenn die Brüder auf Joseph eifersüchtig werden (37,11), gilt das dann bei E auch für

---

[461] Vgl. dazu L. Schmidt, Pentateuch, 97.

Benjamin. Da er danach in Gen 37 von E nicht ausgeschaltet wird, war er an jener Begegnung mit Joseph, die für diesen so schlimm endete, ebenfalls beteiligt. Dem entspricht, daß in 50,15 ff. sich »die Brüder Josephs«, also auch Benjamin, an Joseph wenden. Benjamin hat somit bei E Anteil an der Schuld der Brüder. Weil aber Benjamin bei E an den Ereignissen von Gen 37 beteiligt ist, mußte der Elohist mit 42,3 f. begründen, warum er auf der ersten Reise fehlte. Er durfte als der jüngste nicht mit. Mit keinem Wort deutet jedoch E hier oder sonst an, daß Benjamin ein Liebling des Vaters war. Für den Vater stehen vielmehr alle Söhne auf der gleichen Stufe, wie an seinen klagenden Worten von 42,36 besonders deutlich wird. Benjamin durfte also bei E lediglich deshalb nicht nach Ägypten, weil für ihn der Weg wegen seiner Jugend besonders gefährlich gewesen wäre. Abgesehen von 45,22 wird Benjamin bei E auch von Joseph nicht bevorzugt. So stehen sich hier Joseph und die Brüder gegenüber.

Von daher ist es unwahrscheinlich, daß E zwischen 46,5a und 50,3b sehr viel erzählt hat. Er muß zwar wegen 46,4 berichtet haben, daß Joseph seine Hand auf die Augen Jakobs legte. Aber die Darstellung war hier anscheinend so knapp, daß sie der Jehowist zugunsten der ausführlichen Fassung bei J übergangen hat. Auch aus diesem Grund ist fraglich, ob man 48,1-2a zu E rechnen darf. In dem erhaltenen Bestand von E war von den Söhnen Josephs vorher nicht die Rede. Es gibt kein Anzeichen dafür, daß die Redaktion eine entsprechende Notiz ausgelassen hätte. In Gen 41 ist kein Ort zu erkennen, an dem E von der Geburt der Söhne berichtet haben könnte. Unklar ist auch, welche Funktion bei E die Söhne in der letzten Begegnung zwischen Joseph und dem Vater gehabt haben sollten. Jedenfalls hat E nur knapp erzählt, wie der Vater Joseph wiedersah, in Ägypten lebte und starb.

Das Thema »Joseph und die Brüder« hat zur Folge, daß der Frage nach der Schuld der Brüder bei E zentrale Bedeutung zukommt. Das geht aus 42,21-24 und 50,15 ff. hervor. Sie wird in der jahwistischen Fassung nicht behandelt. Nun gibt es ein weiteres Beispiel dafür, daß den Elohisten das Problem der Schuld eines Menschen beschäftigt hat, obwohl es in seinen Überlieferungen keine Rolle spielte. Das ist die Erzählung von der Gefährdung der Ahnfrau (Gen 20,1b-17), in der E die beiden jahwistischen Fassungen von Gen 12,10-13,1 und 26,1 ff.* aufgreift und umgestaltet[462]. In Gen 26 wird die Schuldfrage von Abimelech kurz angesprochen. Er wirft Isaak vor, daß er Schuld über die Bevölkerung von Gerar gebracht hätte, falls sich jemand zu seiner Frau gelegt hätte, weil er meinte, sie sei die Schwester Isaaks (26,10). Da es aber nicht zu einem Ehebruch gekommen ist, handelt es sich lediglich

---

[462] Gen 20,1b-17 ist m.E. eine literarische Gestaltung des Elohisten. Das kann hier nicht begründet werden.

um eine Möglichkeit, die Abimelech mit seinem Befehl von 26,11 für die Zukunft ausschließt. Zum Ehebruch und damit zur Schuld kommt es aber in 12,10 ff. Obwohl der Pharao in dem guten Glauben handelt, Sara sei die Schwester Abrahams, wird er von Jahwe bestraft (12,17). Diese Darstellung war offenbar der Grund, daß der Elohist in 20,3 ff. das Problem von subjektiver Unschuld und objektiver Schuld behandelt. Er löst es so, daß es Gott verhinderte, daß sich Abimelech der Sara nahte und dadurch eine objektive Schuld beging (20,6). Offenbar stellte sich für E auch durch die jahwistische Josephsgeschichte die Frage nach der Schuld der Brüder. In seiner Antwort kommt wieder Gott die entscheidende Rolle zu. Weil Gott den bösen Plan der Brüder mit Joseph zum Guten wandte und ihn seinem Ziel dienstbar machte, ist die Schuld der Brüder aufgehoben (50,19 f.). Mit der Schuld der Brüder behandelt E somit ein Problem, das sich ihm aufgrund seiner Vorlage stellte.

Das gilt auch sonst für die elohistische Josephsgeschichte. Für E war es anscheinend unerträglich, daß der Vater einfach nach Ägypten zog, weil er Joseph noch einmal sehen wollte. Vielmehr hat Gott dieser Reise ausdrücklich zugestimmt, ja Jakob verheißen, daß er ihn in Ägypten zu einem großen Volk machen will (46,1 aβ–5 a). Auch an dem Bild Josephs in der jahwistischen Fassung hat E Veränderungen vorgenommen. Bei J profitiert zwar der Pharao von Joseph. Joseph weiß, wie man der kommenden Hungersnot begegnen kann (41,34 a.35*), und als sie eingetreten ist, macht er den Pharao reich; schließlich werden die Ägypter sogar zu Sklaven des Pharao (47,13–26). Aber für seine Familie verfolgt Joseph seine eigenen Pläne. Klug bringt er den Pharao dazu, daß der Vater mit seiner Familie in Gosen wohnen darf (47,1 ff.*). Dagegen hat bei E Joseph nicht die Absicht, seine Angehörigen nach Ägypten übersiedeln zu lassen. Nach 45,16–18 ist es der Pharao, der den Brüdern durch Joseph den Wunsch übermitteln läßt, daß sie mit ihrem Vater nach Ägypten kommen. Die Übersiedlung nach Ägypten geht also bei E auf den Pharao und auf Gott zurück.

Auch in seinem Verhalten zu den Brüdern unterscheidet sich bei E Joseph von J. Dort bleibt den Brüdern, dem Vater, aber auch dem Leser zunächst verborgen, warum Joseph fordert, daß Benjamin mit nach Ägypten kommt. Seine Maßnahme, durch den versteckten Becher zu prüfen, wie die Brüder bei Benjamin zu dem Vater stehen, stieß anscheinend beim Elohisten auf Bedenken. Deshalb hat er den Ablauf der beiden Reisen grundlegend verändert. Bei E will Joseph sofort die Brüder prüfen (42,15). Das bezieht sich auf ihr Argument, sie seien keine Kundschafter. Der Leser spürt aber, daß es eigentlich darum geht, wie die Brüder jetzt zueinander stehen. Das wird dadurch unterstrichen, daß sie sich angesichts des Verhaltens Josephs an ihre vergangene Schuld erinnern (42,21 ff.). Wenn Joseph betont, daß er Gott fürchtet

(42,18), ist klar, daß er keine bösen Absichten verfolgt. So ist das Handeln Josephs hier für den Leser sofort einsichtig.

Bei E kommt Joseph eine Sonderstellung zu, weil er von Gott mit einem besonderen Wissen begabt wird. Das zeigen bereits die Träume in Gen 37. Durch sie entsteht der Konflikt nicht mehr wie bei J durch rein innermenschliche Verhältnisse, sondern durch eine Erkenntnis, die Gott Joseph zukommen ließ. Sein Aufstieg gründet darin, daß Gott Joseph wissen läßt, was den anderen Menschen verborgen blieb. Er kann im Unterschied zu den Wahrsagepriestern und Weisen Ägyptens die Träume des Pharao deuten. Schon bei den Träumen des Obermundschenken und des Oberbäckers weist Joseph nachdrücklich darauf hin, daß Traumdeutung eine Sache Gottes ist (40,8), und er unterstreicht das vor dem Pharao (41,16). Das wird von dem Pharao in 41,39 ausdrücklich anerkannt, wenn er sagt »nachdem Gott dir all das kundgetan hat«. Dadurch steigt Joseph bei E zu einer führenden Stellung in Ägypten auf, weil ihn Gott eindeutig als einen besonderen Mann ausgewiesen hat. In 41,33 schlägt Joseph vor, einen klugen und weisen Mann über das Land Ägypten zu setzen. Nach 41,38 f. ist in Joseph der Geist Gottes, und es ist keiner klüger und weiser als er, weil ihm Gott die kommenden Ereignisse kundgetan hat. Mit der Einsetzung Josephs folgt also der Pharao nur dem Weg, den ihm Gott vorgezeichnet hat. So kann Joseph in 45,8 den Brüdern sagen, daß ihm Gott seine führende Stellung verliehen hat. Während bei J die Aussage, daß ihn der Pharao über das ganze Land Ägypten setzte (41,41) und daß ihn Gott zum Herrn für ganz Ägypten gemacht hat (45,9), nebeneinanderstehen, sind die Worte Josephs bei E in 45,8 die zwingende Konsequenz aus der Art, wie es zu seiner Einsetzung gekommen ist. Der Elohist vermißte anscheinend in seiner Vorlage jene theologische Eindeutigkeit, die er in seiner Darstellung geschaffen hat.

Das gilt auch für einen anderen Punkt. In 45,8 betont Joseph, daß ihn nicht die Brüder sondern Gott nach Ägypten gesandt hat. Das klingt zunächst wie eine Präzisierung der Aussage von J, daß Gott Joseph vor den Brüdern hergesandt hat (45,7), ist jedoch mehr. Bei E haben die Brüder tatsächlich Joseph nicht nach Ägypten gesandt. Sie haben ihn in eine Zisterne geworfen, aus der er ohne ihr Wissen von Midianitern gestohlen und nach Ägypten gebracht wurde. Da ihn Gott in Ägypten zum Herrn machte, muß Gott auch hinter dem Weg Josephs nach Ägypten gestanden sein. Auch hier gestaltet somit der Elohist den Ablauf so, daß er theologisch eindeutig wird. Dazu gehört ebenfalls, daß Joseph den Brüdern die Ereignisse deutet. Wenn in ihm der Geist Gottes ist, und er von Gott ein besonderes Wissen erhalten hat, ist klar, daß Joseph das Geschehen richtig interpretieren kann. Dem Elohisten geht es somit darum, die Gestalt Josephs und den Ablauf der Ereignisse durchsichtiger zu machen, als sie für ihn in seiner Vorlage waren. Deshalb hat er das Rätselhafte, ja Abgründige, das die jahwistische Darstellung vor allem bei der Schilderung der beiden Reisen enthält, beseitigt. E will also gerade unter theologischem Aspekt eine Eindeutigkeit des Geschehens herausarbeiten.

c) Die Josephsgeschichte in der Priesterschrift

Zu P gehören: 37,1.2 (ohne »und er war ein Knabe«) ...; 41,46a ... 56a(?).bβ.57; 42,5 ...; 45,19*–21aα; 46,5b.6; 47,5 (am Anfang ist nach LXX zu ergänzen »und es hörte Pharao, der König von Ägypten«). 6a.7–11.27b.28; (48,1aβ.2a?).3–6; 49,1a.28b*–33aα.b; 50, 12.13.

P ist somit in der Josephsgeschichte etwas stärker vertreten, als meist angenommen wird. Allerdings fehlt in den hier zusätzlich zu P gerechneten Stücken – abgesehen von 47,7–10 – die für die Priesterschrift charakteristische Begrifflichkeit. Sie darf man aber von dem Inhalt her nicht erwarten, da es hier nicht um die für P typischen theologischen Anschauungen geht. Nun hat E. Blum im Anschluß an R. Rendtorff nachzuweisen versucht, daß die P-Stücke in der Vätergeschichte – so weit sie nach seiner Auffassung mit Recht ausgegrenzt werden – nicht aus einer eigenen Quellenschrift stammen, sondern durch eine priesterliche Bearbeitung entstanden sind[463]. Seine Hauptargumente sind, daß P in der Vätergeschichte zu lückenhaft vertreten sei, um als eigene Quellenschrift gelten zu können, und daß die entsprechenden Texte Uminterpretationen anderer Stellen sind.

Es ist in diesem Zusammenhang nicht möglich, die Auffassung von E. Blum eingehend zu kritisieren. Es soll aber wenigstens darauf hingewiesen werden, daß selbst der priesterschriftliche Bestand in der Josephsgeschichte gegen seine These spricht. Hier handelt es sich z.B. bei 37,1f.; 45,19–21aα und 47,5 (mit Ergänzung). 6a.7–11 um eindeutige Dubletten zum Kontext. Sie werden mit ihm in 37,2 durch »und er war ein Knabe« und in 45,19 mit »Dir ist geboten« verklammert. Diese Verknüpfungen sind aber klar sekundär. Dann kann der Rest nicht als Bearbeitung verstanden werden, sondern er ist Bestandteil einer eigenen Darstellung. Das Gleiche ergibt sich aus 47,5 mit der Ergänzung der LXX. Daß hier hinter den Stand der Ereignisse zurückgegangen wird, der bereits in 47,1ff. erreicht ist, läßt sich für keinen Bearbeiter verständlich machen. Zudem geht aus der Wiederaufnahme von 46,6 in dem nach LXX zu rekonstruierenden ursprünglichen Text von 47,5 hervor, daß 46,7–27 in einen Zusammenhang eingefügt wurde, der die jahwistische Darstellung von 46,28ff. nicht enthielt. Auch die Tatsache,

---

[463] E. Blum, Komposition, 263 ff. und 420 ff.

daß 42,5 unmittelbar an 41,57 anschließt, während der Vers in seinem jetzigen Kontext Schwierigkeiten bereitet, läßt sich nicht erklären, wenn man ihn zu einer Bearbeitungsschicht rechnet. Da E. Blum für P von einem schmaleren Bestand ausgeht, ist er mit diesen Problemen nicht konfrontiert, die sich aber m. E. gerade hier stellen.

Gewiß werden damit die literarischen Spannungen statt einem Bearbeiter einem Redaktor zugeschrieben, wie E. Blum im Blick auf die Stellung von 35,9 ff. kritisch anmerkt[464]. Aber ein Bearbeiter und ein Redaktor stehen vor einer verschiedenen Situation. Ein Bearbeiter ergänzt einen ihm vorgegebenen Text, ein Redaktor aber verknüpft verschiedene Vorlagen miteinander. Dadurch können bei ihm Schwierigkeiten entstehen, die sich von den Spannungen aufgrund einer Bearbeitung deutlich unterscheiden. Deshalb muß zwischen Spannungen, die bei einem Bearbeiter denkbar sind, und Unausgeglichenheiten, die aufgrund der Verklammerung verschiedener Darstellungen entstehen, unterschieden werden. In der Josephsgeschichte sind, wie in den Analysen gezeigt wurde, die priesterschriftlichen Stücke deutlich Bestandteile einer eigenen Darstellung.

Freilich ist sie aus Gründen, auf die noch zurückzukommen sein wird[465], nur fragmentarisch erhalten. Erst ab 45,19* gibt es einen durchlaufenden P-Faden. Deshalb läßt sich nicht mehr sagen, wie bei P Joseph nach Ägypten kam und dort zu einer führenden Stellung aufstieg, und wie die Begegnung zwischen Joseph und den Brüdern ablief. Deutlich ist aber, daß der Verfasser das jehowistische Werk als literarische Vorlage benutzt hat. Die Anweisung des Pharao an die Brüder in 45,19f. ist eine Abwandlung des Auftrags, den Joseph in 45,16–18 bei E für die Brüder erhalten hat. Mit dem Befehl des Pharao an Joseph, den Vater und die Brüder im besten Teil des Landes wohnen zu lassen (47,5.6a) greift P 47,1ff. aus J auf, wo Joseph bei dem Pharao die Ansiedlung von Vater und Brüdern im Lande Gosen erreicht. Daß bei P Stücke aus J *und* E vorausgesetzt werden, zeigt, daß der Priesterschrift die jehowistische Darstellung zugrundeliegt.

Freilich wird bei P diese Vorlage wesentlich vereinfacht. In P folgen 41,57 und 42,5 direkt aufeinander. Auch hier ist somit die Hungersnot der Anlaß für die Reise der Brüder. Im Unterschied zu J und E spielt dabei aber der Vater keine Rolle. Die Initiative liegt, wie auch bei der Übersiedlung nach Ägypten in 46,5b.6, ausschließlich bei seinen Söhnen. Aus der Abfolge 41,57; 42,5 ergibt sich zum anderen, daß bei P Benjamin schon auf der ersten Reise dabei war. Er gehört zu den »Israeliten«, die »mitten unter denen, die gekommen waren« kamen. Dann aber kann P nur von einer Reise der Brüder berichtet haben. Eine

---

[464] E. Blum, Komposition, 267.
[465] Vgl. IV e.

zweite ist nur sinnvoll, wenn Benjamin bei der ersten fehlte, und dann auf einer zweiten ebenfalls zu Joseph kommt. P erzählte somit nur von einer Reise aller Brüder.

Sie wird unter dem Gesichtspunkt geschildert, daß sie der Anlaß war, daß die Brüder mit ihrem Vater nach Ägypten übersiedelten. Deshalb bezeichnet P in 42,5 die Brüder als »die Israeliten«. In Ägypten ist für P das Volk Israel entstanden (47,27b; Ex 1,7). Deshalb repräsentieren die Söhne Jakobs von dem Zeitpunkt an Israel, als sie sich erstmals nach Ägypten auf den Weg machen. Dort werden sie von dem Pharao aufgefordert, mit dem Vater und ihren Familien nach Ägypten zu kommen (45,19f.). Wie schon dem Elohisten so liegt auch P daran, daß die Übersiedlung nach Ägypten auf den Willen des Pharao zurückgeht. Über E hinaus unterstreicht das die Priesterschrift dadurch, daß der Pharao den Brüdern diesen Wunsch direkt mitteilt und ihnen durch die Wagen, die sie nach seinem Befehl aus Ägypten mitnehmen sollen, seine besondere Fürsorge für die Übersiedlung zuteil werden läßt. Auf dieser Linie liegt es auch, daß der Pharao in 47,5.6a nach der Ankunft des Vaters und der Brüder Joseph den Befehl erteilt, sie in dem besten Teil des Landes wohnen zu lassen. Allein der Pharao ist somit bei P dafür verantwortlich, daß die Israeliten zeitweise in Ägypten wohnten.

Stehen bei P ab 42,5 zunächst die Brüder im Zentrum, so in 47,7-10 und den priesterschriftlichen Stücken von Kap. 48-50 der Vater. Jakob deutet in 47,7-10 die Existenz der Erzväter als ein Leben ihrer Fremdlingsschaft. Er ist aber überzeugt, daß die Verheißungen Gottes in Erfüllung gehen werden. Deshalb begründet er in 48,3-6 die Adoption von Ephraim und Manasse mit den Zusagen, die er von Gott erhalten hat. Schließlich will er von seinen Söhnen in der Grabhöhle bestattet werden, die einst Abraham erworben hat, und in der die anderen Patriarchen mit ihren Frauen und auch Lea begraben sind (49,1a. 28b*-33aα). Jakob stirbt und wird von seinen Söhnen in dieser Höhle bestattet (49,33b; 50,12f.).

Die priesterschriftliche Darstellung hebt sich in der Josephsgeschichte klar von J und E ab. In ihr geht es mit der Übersiedlung nach Ägypten einerseits um die Zukunft. Deshalb stehen hier die Brüder als »die Israeliten« im Zentrum. Andererseits bildet sie den Abschluß der Väterzeit. Das macht P an jenen Stellen deutlich, in denen Jakob als der letzte der Patriarchen den Mittelpunkt darstellt.

d) Die Josephsgeschichte des Jehowisten

Vom Jehowisten stammen:
In 39,1 »Potiphar, der Kämmerer des Pharao, der Oberste der Leibwache«; 39,4aβ; 40,3aβ.b.5b.15b; 41,14aβ; 43,23b.

Der Jehowist hat sich in der Josephsgeschichte weitgehend darauf beschränkt, die Darstellungen von Jahwist und Elohist zusammenzuarbeiten. Von ihm selbst stammen lediglich einige Verklammerungen. Dabei hat er die Abfolge in J und E auch im einzelnen beibehalten. Es ließ sich nicht nachweisen, daß er Umstellungen vorgenommen hat, wie es vor allem für 42,28b und 42,38 häufig vertreten wird. Vielmehr stehen die Aussagen durchgehend in der Reihenfolge, die sie schon bei J und E hatten. Damit fehlt in der Josephsgeschichte jeder Anhaltspunkt, daß hier – wie z.B. auch W. Rudolph und C. Westermann als Vertreter der literarischen Einheitlichkeit der vorpriesterschriftlichen Josephsgeschichte annehmen – Texte nachträglich umgestellt wurden. Das dürfte für die Pentateuchforschung von grundsätzlicher Bedeutung sein.

Der Jehowist ist auch in den verschiedenen Bezeichnungen des Vaters Israel und Jakob seinen Vorlagen gefolgt. Weder er noch ein Späterer hat Israel durch Jakob ersetzt oder umgekehrt. Dadurch ergibt sich gelegentlich wie in 45,27f. ein harter Wechsel bei dem Namen des Vaters. Das war aber für den Jehowisten und die spätere Überlieferung kein Problem, weil eindeutig die gleiche Person gemeint war. Deshalb konnte auch ein Ergänzer in 46,2 »zu Israel« einfügen und damit 46,1aα aufnehmen, obwohl Gott dann in v.2aβ den Erzvater als »Jakob« anredet. Nur in 37,21 hat der Jehowist Juda als Sprecher der Brüder durch Ruben ersetzt. In 37,21f. konnte aber nur einer der Brüder für Joseph eintreten. Der Jehowist mußte sich deshalb zwischen Juda bei J (37,21) und Ruben bei E (37,22) entscheiden. Wegen 37,29f. und 42,22 machte er in 37,21 Ruben zum Sprecher. Das ist der einzige Fall, in dem der Jehowist den Wortlaut seiner Vorlage wesentlich verändert hat, und hier mußte er tatsächlich in den Text eingreifen. Dagegen ist die Änderung, die der Jehowist in 41,35bα vorgenommen hat, geringfügig. Hier setzte er nur das Verb in den Plural, um dieses Stück aus E an 41,35a aus J anschließen zu können.

Ansonsten bemühte sich der Jehowist darum, seine Quellen möglichst vollständig aufzunehmen. Er konnte allerdings nicht vermeiden, J und E teilweise zu übergehen, wenn sie sich nicht verbinden ließen. So mußte er nach 42,28a aus J auslassen, daß auch die anderen Brüder ihr Geld gefunden hatten, wenn er später 42,35 aus E bringen wollte. Was hier einsichtig ist, wird man auch für die anderen Stücke anzunehmen haben, die jetzt aus J oder E nicht mehr erhalten sind. Der Jehowist brachte jeweils die ausführlichere Darstellung und ergänzte sie, wenn möglich, aus der anderen. Man kann deshalb nicht feststellen, daß er hier eine bestimmte Quellenschrift zur Grundlage genommen hätte. Daß er in 37,3ff. E auf J folgen läßt, beruht einfach darauf, daß von den Träumen Josephs sinnvollerweise erst nach seiner Bevorzugung durch den Vater erzählt werden konnte.

Insofern bestätigt sich an der Josephsgeschichte nicht die These von M. Noth, daß J für den Jehowisten die Basis bildete[466]. M. Noth sieht zwar, daß der Redaktor in 40,2-41,32 die jahwistische Schilderung durch E ersetzt hat, hält das jedoch für einen Sonderfall, der insofern aber wahrscheinlich keine Ausnahme von der Regel bilde, als die Träume vermutlich Sondergut des Elohisten seien. Da der Redaktor hier E bevorzuge, »hat er dann auch in der zweiten Hälfte von Kap. 41 und in Kap. 42 E – gemischt mit J – verhältnismäßig stark zu Worte kommen lassen, um dann allerdings in Kap. 43 und Kap. 44 sich wieder ausschließlich an J zu halten«[467]. Hier zeigt sich, daß M. Noth letztlich nicht erklären kann, warum der Jehowist bei der Schilderung der ersten Reise der Brüder ab 42,11b weitgehend der elohistischen Darstellung gefolgt ist. Das wird nur verständlich, wenn er jeweils der ausführlicheren Fassung den Vorzug gab und sie aus der knapperen ergänzte.

Daß er in Kap. 43 f. J aufgenommen hat, ergab sich daraus, daß bei E sich nach 42,37 die Brüder mit Benjamin auf den Weg machten, um Simeon zu befreien. Hier war somit die Darstellung von J wesentlich breiter, während für die erste Reise E die umfangreichere Schilderung bot. Ähnliche Beobachtungen lassen sich auch sonst machen. So wird z. B. auch die Rückkehr der Brüder von ihrer zweiten Reise in 45,21 aß –28 weitgehend nach E geschildert, während J mit 45,27 aα. 28 nur fragmentarisch erhalten ist. Das übersieht M. Noth, weil er 45,16–28 zu J rechnet[468]. In der Josephsgeschichte ist somit J nur dann die Grundlage, wenn seine Darstellung ausführlicher war als die des Elohisten. Von da aus stellt sich die Frage, ob diese Beobachtung nicht für die jehowistische Redaktion insgesamt gilt.

Durch die Verbindung von J und E enthält die Josephsgeschichte des Jehowisten zahlreiche Doppelungen. Zwar hat schon der Elohist Doppelungen als Stilmittel benutzt. Zwischen diesen Doppelungen und denen, die auf den Jehowisten zurückgehen, besteht aber ein deutlicher Unterschied. Bei E fügen sie sich in die Darstellung nahtlos ein. Dagegen entstehen durch die Doppelungen, die der Jehowist geschaffen hat, Widersprüche zum Kontext. Daran wird deutlich, daß die Strukturanalyse eines Textes ihre Grenzen hat. Wie in den Analysen dargestellt wurde, wird in der neueren Forschung oft aufgrund der elohistischen Doppelungen bestritten, daß die sonstigen Doppelungen eine literarische Schichtung anzeigen. Wie aus der Josephsgeschichte hervorgeht, beweist jedoch der Befund, daß ein Text in bestimmter Weise strukturiert ist, noch nicht seine Einheitlichkeit. Er zeigt nur an, daß ein Text einmal diese Struktur erhalten hat. Man wird zwar – zumindest in der

---

[466] M. Noth, Pentateuch, 25 ff.
[467] M. Noth, Pentateuch, 27 f.
[468] M. Noth, Pentateuch, 31.

Regel – davon ausgehen können, daß ein in bestimmter Weise strukturierter Text einheitlich ist, wenn er weder in sich noch zu seinem Kontext Spannungen enthält. Bestehen hier aber Widersprüche, dann ist diese Struktur nicht ursprünglich, sondern sie ist dem Text erst später gegeben worden. Auch dieser Beobachtung in der Josephsgeschichte kommt m. E. für die gegenwärtige Pentateuchforschung grundsätzliche Bedeutung zu. Allein mit dem Stil läßt sich die literarische Einheitlichkeit eines Textes nicht begründen.

Der Jehowist unterstreicht mit den Doppelungen ähnlich wie schon E das Gewicht der betreffenden Szenen. Auch für ihn enthalten sie eine Steigerung. So sind die Worte Josephs in 45, 4 (J) »Ich bin Joseph, euer Bruder, den ihr nach Ägypten verkauft habt« jetzt eine Weiterführung seiner Feststellung von v. 3 (E) »Ich bin Joseph«. 41, 41 (J), wo der Pharao zu Joseph sagt: »Siehe, ich setze dich über das ganze Land Ägypten«, folgt auf 41, 40 (E), wo er Joseph mitteilt, daß Joseph über sein Haus und sein Volk sein soll, und der Pharao nur um den Thron größer sein will als Joseph. Beim Jehowisten – aber auch erst hier – teilt der Pharao in 41, 40 Joseph seinen Entschluß mit, danach setzt er mit 41, 41 Joseph formell in seine Stellung ein.

Diese Beispiele – für weitere sei auf die Analysen verwiesen – zeigen bereits, daß sich für den Jehowisten trotz aller Spannungen aus der Verbindung seiner Quellen ein sinnvoller Ablauf ergab. Mit seiner Redaktion setzte er zugleich Akzente. Deshalb hat er z. B. 37, 13b.14a aus E aufgenommen, obwohl er in 37, 12–17 sonst J gefolgt ist. Daß er dieses Fragment aus E bringt, läßt sich nur sachlich verstehen. Dem Jehowisten ging es um den Kontrast, daß Joseph von dem Vater gesandt wird, um nach dem šālôm der Brüder zu sehen, von ihnen jedoch Unheil erfährt. Auch sonst hat der Jehowist durch die Verbindung von J und E eine bestimmte Linienführung hergestellt. So korrespondieren die Geschenke Josephs in 45, 22f. (E) bei ihm den Gaben, die der Vater den Brüdern auf der zweiten Reise für Joseph mitgibt (43, 11 J). Dienten sie dazu, Joseph gnädig zu stimmen, so werden nun als Zeichen der Versöhnung mit den Brüdern sie und ihr Vater von Joseph reich beschenkt. Dem Ziel, Linien deutlich zu machen, dienen schließlich auch die Zusätze des Jehowisten in 40, 15b; 41, 14aβ. Durch sie wird nicht nur die jahwistische Darstellung, nach der sich Joseph im Gefängnis befand, mit der elohistischen verbunden, in der er als Sklave bei dem Obersten der Leibwache ist[469]. Der Jehowist setzt hier zugleich die Existenz Josephs im Gefängnis in Beziehung zu seinem Aufenthalt in der

---

[469] Der Jehowist setzte den Ägypter, der bei J Joseph erwarb, mit Potiphar gleich und ergänzte 39, 1 entsprechend. Dadurch ist bei ihm der Oberste des Gefängnisses dem Obersten der Leibwache untergeordnet. Deshalb kann er in 40, 4 aus E berichten, daß der Oberste der Leibwache Joseph zum Diener der beiden Beamten bestimmt hat.

Zisterne. Jetzt wird ihm durch den Pharao jene Befreiung zuteil, die ihm einst die Midianiter nicht verschafft hatten. So ist die Josephsgeschichte des Jehowisten mehr als die Addition zweier Vorlagen. Sie bildet vielmehr ein eigenes Ganzes.

Aus der Tatsache, daß in der Josephsgeschichte nur wenige Stellen von dem Jehowisten stammen, wird man allerdings nicht schließen dürfen, daß er sich auch sonst weitgehend auf die Wiedergabe seiner Vorlagen beschränkte. Er sah in diesem Komplex anscheinend keine Notwendigkeit, durch umfangreiche Zusätze dem Geschehen eine eigene Deutung zu geben. Für andere Abschnitte des Pentateuch besteht durchaus die Möglichkeit, daß der Jehowist seine Vorlagen erheblich erweitert hat[470].

e) Endredaktion und Zusätze

Von dem Endredaktor stammen vermutlich jene Stücke, durch die die jehowistische Josephsgeschichte mit P verknüpft wird. Das sind in 37,2 »und er war ein Knabe«; 37,8b und in 37,14b »aus dem Tal von Hebron«, wodurch die jehowistische Darstellung, nach der der Vater in der Nähe Sichems wohnte, an P angeglichen wird, da sich bei P Jakob in Hebron befand.

Auch der Endredaktor hat sich bemüht, seine Quellen möglichst vollständig zu Wort kommen zu lassen. Das wird an dem ursprünglichen Text von 47,5f., der in LXX erhalten ist, besonders deutlich. Hier hat er Jehowist und P so hart miteinander verbunden, daß der Text nachträglich in die Fassung des MT geändert wurde. Für den Endredaktor gilt ebenfalls, daß er jeweils der ausführlicheren Darstellung seiner Quellen den Vorzug gegeben hat. Bot sie der Jehowist und ließ sich P damit nicht verknüpfen, so hat der Endredaktor auf die entsprechenden Stücke aus P verzichtet, obwohl er seinem Werk die Priesterschrift zugrundelegte, wie schon aus 37,1f. hervorgeht. So erklärt es sich, daß bis 45,19 P nur noch fragmentarisch erhalten ist. Wenn z. B., wie in IVc dargelegt wurde, P nur von einer Reise der Brüder berichtet hat, und diese Darstellung relativ knapp war, so ließ sie sich kaum mit der umfangreichen Fassung des Jehowisten verbinden. Deshalb fehlt die Begegnung der Brüder mit Joseph aus P.

Für das Verfahren des Endredaktors der Josephsgeschichte gibt es Analogien. So stammen z. B. in dem Bericht über die Geburt Esaus und Jakobs in Gen 25,19–26 v. 19f. 26b aus P, v. 21–26a aus J[471]. V. 26b

---

[470] In der Plagenerzählung von Ex 7,14ff. hat z. B. der Jehowist seine jahwistische Vorlage erheblich erweitert. Das kann hier aber nicht im einzelnen dargestellt werden.
[471] Über diese Aufteilung besteht heute weitgehende Übereinstimmung, vgl. z. B. M. Noth, Pentateuch, 17.30.

setzt aber voraus, daß auch P erwähnt hat, daß Esau und Jakob geboren wurden. Das ließ sich anscheinend nicht mit der Darstellung des Jehowisten verknüpfen. Da sie ausführlicher war, hat der Endredaktor hier auf P verzichtet. Bereits M. Noth hat darauf hingewiesen, daß dieses Verfahren aber nicht dagegen spricht, daß der Endredaktor P als Grundlage gewählt hat[472]. Die Stellen, an denen die priesterschriftliche Darstellung fehlt, lassen sich somit erklären. Sie berühren nicht die Folgerung, die M. Noth aus dem Verfahren des Endredaktors gezogen hat, daß nur für die P-Erzählung »im allgemeinen das vollständige Erhaltensein des ursprünglichen Bestandes und daher ein lückenloser Zusammenhang der ausgeschiedenen Elemente untereinander zu erwarten ist«[473], wie R. Rendtorff meint[474]. Allerdings wird man stärker als M. Noth betonen müssen, daß dem Endredaktor daran lag, daß die jeweils ausführlichere Darstellung erhalten blieb. Deshalb ist in der Josephsgeschichte P bis 45,19 nur mit Fragmenten vertreten.

Die Aufnahme des in seinem Kontext recht isoliert stehenden Verses 42,5 wird sich freilich kaum nur damit erklären lassen, daß der Endredaktor P möglichst vollständig aufnehmen wollte. Ihm lag anscheinend daran, daß mit den Söhnen Jakobs »die Israeliten« nach Ägypten kamen. Damit folgt er der Auffassung von P, die in 46,8 auch von P^s vertreten wird. Daran wird deutlich, daß für den Endredaktor teilweise auch sachliche Gründe eine Rolle spielten.

Bei einigen Zusätzen ist offen, wann sie entstanden sind. So stammt z. B. 48,15 f. sicher nicht aus vorexilischer Zeit, fraglich ist aber, ob die Verse jünger oder älter sind als P. Eindeutig jünger sind hingegen 43,14; 48,7.9b.10a.13.14.17–22. Abgesehen von 48,7 werden mit diesen Zusätzen jahwistische Stücke weitergeführt. Deshalb stammen sie frühestens von dem Endredaktor, vielleicht sind sie aber auch noch jünger. Die Erweiterung 48,9b.10a.13.14.17–22 steht, wie in der Analyse gezeigt wurde[475], durch die Aussage, daß Manasse zu einer *ml'* der *gôyim* werden soll (v. 19), sachlich dem chronistischen Werk nahe, das vermutlich bereits eine Endredaktion des Pentateuch voraussetzt[476]. Einige Glossen, wie etwa 37,5b, fehlen noch in LXX. Daraus und aus der Textänderung in 47,5f. geht hervor, daß an dem Text der Josephsgeschichte noch lange gearbeitet wurde.

---

[472] Vgl. M. Noth, Pentateuch, 12ff.
[473] M. Noth, Pentateuch, 17.
[474] R. Rendtorff, BZAW 147,113. R. Rendtorff zitiert dort M. Noth, läßt allerdings seine wichtige Einschränkung »im allgemeinen« aus. Freilich bemüht sich R. Rendtorff, a.a.O. 113ff., um den Nachweis, daß es keine priesterschriftliche Vätergeschichte gegeben haben kann. Das läßt sich aber, wie in den Analysen gezeigt wurde, selbst für die Josephsgeschichte nicht halten.
[475] Vgl. III e.
[476] Vgl. R. Smend, Die Entstehung des Alten Testaments, ²1981, 35.

f) Konsequenzen für die Pentateuchforschung

Im folgenden sollen die Folgerungen, die sich aus dieser Untersuchung der Josephsgeschichte für die Pentateuchforschung ergeben, kurz zusammengefaßt werden:

1. Die neuere Urkundenhypothese bewährt sich an der Josephsgeschichte. Nur für wenige Stellen bleibt die Zuweisung unsicher. Dabei lassen sich J, E und P nicht nur literarisch voneinander abheben, sondern sie haben auch thematisch eine jeweils verschiedene Prägung. Gilt die neuere Urkundenhypothese aber für den schwierigen Komplex der Josephsgeschichte, dann ist an ihr für den Pentateuch festzuhalten.

2. Der Jahwist hat mit der Josephsgeschichte, die ihm als eigenes Werk überliefert wurde, erstmals eine zusammenhängende Darstellung geschaffen, in der Erzväter- und Exodusüberlieferung miteinander verbunden waren. Von da aus stellt sich die Frage, inwieweit nicht auch sonst der Aufriß der Darstellung im Pentateuch erst auf den Jahwisten zurückgeht. Insbesondere wäre m. E. zu prüfen, ob nicht die Überlieferungen von den verschiedenen Erzvätern erst von J miteinander in einer Darstellung verbunden wurden.

3. Der Elohist hat in der Josephsgeschichte J als literarische Vorlage benutzt, die Priesterschrift das jehowistische Werk. Dann kennt E auch sonst J und P den Jehowisten.

4. Es gibt kein Anzeichen dafür, daß in der Josephsgeschichte später Umstellungen vorgenommen wurden. Jehowist und Endredaktor folgen auch im einzelnen der Abfolge in ihren Quellen. Dann muß man auch sonst mit der Annahme von nachträglichen Umstellungen äußerst vorsichtig sein.

5. Der Nachweis, daß ein Text in bestimmter Weise strukturiert ist, beweist für sich genommen noch nicht, daß er literarisch einheitlich ist. Eine solche Struktur kann auch von einem Redaktor geschaffen werden. Das zeigen jene Doppelungen in der Josephsgeschichte, die auf den Jehowisten zurückgehen.

6. Jehowist und Endredaktor sind bemüht, ihre Vorlagen möglichst weitgehend aufzunehmen. Nur wenn sich die knappere Fassung nicht mit der ausführlichen verbinden ließ, haben sie sich auf die breitere Darstellung beschränkt. Daraus erklärt sich, daß bis 45,19 P in der Josephsgeschichte nur fragmentarisch erhalten ist. Dieses Prinzip dürfte dann aber auch außerhalb der Josephsgeschichte gelten.

7. In der Josephsgeschichte bildet J für den Jehowisten nicht die Grundlage, die er aus E ergänzt hätte. Vielmehr hat er jeweils die ausführlichere Darstellung zugrundegelegt, unabhängig davon, ob sie bei J oder E stand. Es ist deshalb zu vermuten, daß der Jehowist auch sonst so vorgegangen ist.

Literaturverzeichnis

Im folgenden werden nur Titel aufgeführt, auf die in der Arbeit Bezug genommen wird. Für eine Bibliographie zur Josephsgeschichte sei auf den Kommentar von C. Westermann verwiesen. Kommentare zur Genesis werden in den Anmerkungen nur mit Verfasser und Seitenzahl angegeben.

E. Blum, Die Komposition der Vätergeschichte, WMANT 57, 1984.
G. W. Coats, From Canaan to Egypt, CBQ.MS 4, 1976.
F. Crüsemann, Der Widerstand gegen das Königtum, WMANT 49, 1978.
A. Dillmann, Die Genesis, KeH 11, ^{6}1892.
H. Donner, Die literarische Gestalt der alttestamentlichen Josephsgeschichte, SHAW.PH 2, 1976.
E. L. Ehrlich, Der Traum im Alten Testament, BZAW 73, 1953.
O. Eißfeldt, Hexateuch-Synopse, Leipzig 1922.
K. Elliger/W. Rudolph (Hg.), Biblia Hebraica Stuttgartensia, Stuttgart 1967/77.
G. Fohrer, Einleitung in das Alte Testament, Heidelberg ^{12}1979.
H. Greßmann, Ursprung und Entwicklung der Joseph-Sage, in: H. Schmidt (Hg.), Eucharisterion 1 (FS H. Gunkel), FRLANT 36, 1923, 1–55.
H. Gunkel, Genesis, Göttingen ^{9}1977.
ders., Die Komposition der Joseph-Geschichten, ZDMG 76 (1922) 55–71.
A. H. J. Gunneweg, Anmerkungen und Anfragen zur neueren Pentateuchforschung, ThR NF 48 (1983) 227–253.
S. Herrmann, Israels Aufenthalt in Ägypten, SBS 40, 1970.
K. Jaroš, Die Stellung des Elohisten zur kanaanäischen Religion, OBO 4, ^{2}1982.
O. Keel-M. Küchler, Synoptische Texte aus der Genesis. I Die Texte; II Der Kommentar, BiBe 8,1.2, 1971.
A. Meinhold, Die Gattung der Josephsgeschichte und des Estherbuches: Diasporanovelle I, ZAW 87 (1975) 306–324; II, ZAW 88 (1976) 72–93.
K. R. Melchin, Literary Sources in the Joseph Story, ScEs 31 (1979) 93–101.
T. N. D. Mettinger, Solomonic State Officials, CB.OT 5, 1971.
M. Noth, Überlieferungsgeschichtliche Studien I, VSKG.G 18,2, 1943.
ders., Überlieferungsgeschichte des Pentateuch, Stuttgart 1948.
E. Otto, Die »synthetische Lebensauffassung« in der frühköniglichen Novellistik Israels, ZThK 74 (1977) 371–400.
ders., Stehen wir vor einem Umbruch in der Pentateuchkritik?, VF 22 (1977) 82–97.
O. Procksch, Die Genesis, KAT I, $^{2.3}$1924.
G. v. Rad, Das erste Buch Mose. Genesis, ATD 2/4, ^{9}1972.
ders., Das formgeschichtliche Problem des Hexateuch (1938), in: ders., Gesammelte Studien zum Alten Testament, ThB 8, ^{3}1965, 9–86.
ders., Josephsgeschichte und ältere Chokma (1953), ebd., 272–280.
ders., Die Josephsgeschichte (1954), in: ders., Gottes Wirken in Israel, Neukirchen-Vluyn 1974, 22–41.

Indices

Index of Biblical Passages

(A. Aejmelaeus, The Traditional Prayer in the Psalms)

Gen
11 44
24:10 32
25:30 89
26:24 48
28:15 . . . . 24, 25, 48
28:20 . . . . 24, 25, 48
29:21 89
32:8 90
32:10–13 . . . . 58, 89
32:12 . . . . 20, 90
32:23 32
43:15 32

Ex
3:14 . . . . 57, 58
32:1 89
32:12 36
32:13 42
34 58
34:6 . . . . 73, 104

Num
6:24–26 . . . 23, 24, 25, 26
10:31 89
10:35 . . . 32, 33, 34, 50, 51
10:36 . . . . 32, 34, 35
14:9 48

Deut
9:12 . . . . 40, 41
9:16 41
9:27 42
13:18 36
26:15 24
32:40–42 35
33:7 28
33:11 24

Josh
7:26 36

Judg
3:1,4 67
10:15 21
16:28 42

I Sam
12:10 21
23:2–4 31
23:11–12 31

II Sam
7:29 24
24:10 90

I Kings
3:9 90
8:25 24
8:44–45 38
18:24 31
18:26 31
18:37 31
19:4 90

II Kings
18:19–35 19
19:16 29
19:19 21
20:3 42
23:26 36

Is
33:2 23
37:17 29
37:20 21
38:3 42
44:17 . . . . 21, 90
63:15 29
63:17 36

Jer
2:27 . . . . 19, 21, 33
14:21 42
15:15 42
17:12–18 58
17:14 20
18:19 28
18:20 42

Hos
10:14 90

Joel
2:13 . . . . 73, 104

Jon
3:9 36
4:2 . . . . 73, 104

Ps
3 51
3:2 32
3:5 29
3:8 . . 16, 31, 33, 55, 76, 86
3:8–9 73
4 . . . . 51, 86
4:2 . . 21, 26, 27, 28, 29, 30, 49, 55, 83
4:2–6 81
4:4 28
5 . . . . 51, 86, 96, 102
5:2 26
5:2–3 . . . . 27, 73
5:2–11 75
5:3 . . . . 26, 55
5:4 28
5:8 61
5:9 . . . . 40, 41, 61, 62, 64
5:9–10 . . . . 71, 86
5:11 . . . 43, 44, 55, 74, 86
5:12 44
6 . . . . . 51, 53, 86, 97, 98
6:2 . . . . 36, 46, 53, 92

Ps

Reference	Pages
6:2–3	22, 51, 54
6:2–4	69, 70, 71
6:2–8	75
6:3	21, 48
6:5	16, 18, 35, 36, 61, 62
6:5–8	70, 86
6:6	59
6:8	96
6:9–10	28
7	33, 35, 37, 38, 51, 86
7:2	16, 17, 54, 55, 83
7:3	67
7:4–6	37
7:7	31, 33, 55
7:7–8	34
7:7–9	51
7:7–11	82
7:8	35, 36
7:8–10	44
7:9	37, 61
7:12–13	34, 35
7:13	35, 36
7:13–14	35
7:15	35
7:16–17	35
9	11, 51
9:2–15	53
9:14	21, 26, 28
9:20	31, 44, 46
9:21	44, 48
10	11, 51
10:1	46
10:12	31
10:15	43, 44
10:17	28
11	50
11:6	12
12	51, 86, 88
12:2	16
12:2–3	71
12:8	24
13	51
13:4	26, 28, 29, 30, 54
13:4–5	21, 67
13:5	64
16	51, 86, 88, 93, 94
16:1	24, 25, 55, 75
16:1–6	72, 75
16:7	72
17	51, 86, 88, 102
17:1	26, 27, 30, 37
17:1–5	80
17:3–5	37
17:6	26, 27, 29, 55, 83
17:6–8	67
17:7	56, 57
17:7–12	86
17:8	24, 25
17:8–9	66
17:9	24
17:10–12	67
17:13	16, 17, 18, 31, 43, 51
17:13–14	81
18:1	56
18:7	28
18:15	35
18:38	35
18:47	33
19	11
19:13	23
19:14	25, 44, 46, 49
20	49
20:10	16, 18, 29
21:10	44
21:14	31
22	51, 81, 100
22:2	47
22:12	46, 56, 86
22:12–19	71
22:20	39, 46, 52, 54, 56, 87
22:20–22	39, 51, 71
22:20–23	80
22:21	16
22:21–22	17
22:22	16
22:23–24	81
22:25	28
23	50, 51
23:3	61
23:4	48
25	11, 51, 101, 105, 106, 107, 108
25:2	46, 49
25:4	40, 41
25:5	40, 41, 61, 107
25:6	42, 107
25:7	42, 61
25:11	61, 107
25:16	21, 40, 75, 107
25:17	17
25:18	23, 26, 28
25:19	26, 28, 107
25:20	16, 24, 46, 49, 75
25:22	16, 17, 18
26	38, 51, 86
26:1	37, 74
26:1–2	51
26:1–8	75
26:2	39
26:2–8	74
26:9	46, 86
26:9–10	66, 67
26:9–11	56
26:11	16, 21
27	22, 51
27:5	96
27:7	21, 26, 29, 30
27:7–10	73, 86, 97
27:7–12	75
27:7–14	53
27:8–9	83
27:9	46, 49, 55
27:11	40, 41, 64
27:11–12	69, 71, 86, 96
27:14	97
28	51, 86
28:1	46, 65, 67, 83
28:2	26, 27, 28, 49, 83
28:3	46
28:4	37, 43, 47
28:5	74
28:6	28
28:9	16, 18, 24, 56, 82, 86
29:11	24
30	51
30:8	61
30:11	17, 21, 23, 26, 27, 28, 82, 86
31	51, 53, 75, 86, 95, 96
31:2	16, 27, 46, 49, 61, 62, 83
31:2–3	17
31:2–4	53, 96

Ps

Reference	Pages
31:2–6	72, 75
31:2–9	72
31:3	16, 26, 39, 49
31:4	61
31:8	28
31:10	21, 96
31:10–11	69
31:10–14	70, 72, 75, 86
31:11–14	70
31:15	83
31:15–16	87
31:16	16, 17
31:16–18	73, 86
31:17	16, 25, 49, 61, 62
31:18	46, 49
31:18–19	44
31:21	96
31:23	28
34:5	29, 30
34:7	28
34:18	28
35	33, 37, 38, 45, 47, 51, 86
35:1	37, 43
35:1–3	51
35:1–6	81
35:2	31, 33
35:2–3	35
35:4	53
35:4–6	44
35:11–14	37
35:17	55
35:17–18	80, 81
35:19	44
35:22	46, 55, 83
35:22–24	51
35:22–28	81
35:23	31, 55
35:24	37, 54, 55, 61, 62
35:24–25	44, 46
35:26	44
35:27	44
36:12	44, 46
37:2	40
38	22, 51, 86, 92, 98
38:2	46, 53, 97
38:2–4	69
38:2–15	70, 75
38:14	65
38:16	29
38:16–21	70
38:22	46, 55
38:22–23	52, 70, 82, 86
38:23	39, 56
39	51
39:5	40, 41, 80
39:8	83
39:8–12	79
39:9	16, 17, 46
39:9–11	56
39:9–12	86
39:13	26, 27, 28, 46, 71
39:13–14	86
39:14	65, 71
40	51
40:2	28
40:5–11	23
40:13–18	53
40:14	17, 39, 49, 54
40:14–15	96
40:14–18	53, 81
40:15–16	44
40:17	44, 82
40:18	39, 46, 55, 82, 86
41	22, 51, 92
41:2–4	70
41:3	24
41:5	21, 23, 48, 97
41:5–10	70, 86
41:5–11	91
41:11	21, 54, 65, 82, 86
41:12–14	70
42	75, 83
42:10	47
43	38, 51, 75, 83
43:1	17, 37, 55
43:1–2	72, 86
43:2	47
44	33
44:24	31, 46
44:24–27	101
44:25	47
44:27	16, 31, 61
51	51, 64, 86
51:3	21, 22, 23, 55, 61, 62
51:3–5	51
51:3–8	70, 75
51:4	23
51:9	23
51:11	23
51:11–15	80
51:12	55
51:13	46
51:15	18, 81
51:16	16, 17, 18, 55
51:16–19	74, 86
51:20	61, 63
51:20–21	82, 86
52	50
52:11	50
54	51, 53, 86, 88
54:3	16, 38, 55, 61, 62
54:3–4	28
54:3–5	69, 71
54:4	26, 27, 30, 55
54:5	32
54:7	43, 44, 61, 63
55	51, 86, 88
55:2	26, 27, 46
55:2–3	28, 51
55:2–4	80
55:2–6	79
55:2–9	70
55:3	26, 27, 29
55:10	43, 44, 55
55:10–15	70, 86
55:18	28
56	51, 86, 88, 94
56:2	21, 55, 76
56:2–3	71
56:8	43, 55, 63
56:8–10	80, 86
57	51, 86, 93, 94, 100
57:2	21
57:2–4	72
57:6	31, 82, 86
57:12	31, 82, 86
58:7	43
58:8–9	44
59	51, 86, 94
59:2	16, 17, 25, 55
59:2–4	69, 71
59:3	16, 17
59:5	26, 28, 31

Ps
59:5–6 . . . . . . 51, 82, 86
59:6 . . . 31, 44, 47, 54, 55
59:12 . . . . . 43, 47, 55, 67
59:12–14 44
59:14 . . . . 43, 63
59:17 75
60:4 48
60:7 . . . 16, 18, 19, 29, 67
60:13 . . . . 17, 66
61 . . . . . 51, 86, 88, 93, 94
61:2 . . . . 26, 27
61:2–6 72
61:3 . . . . 41, 83
61:4 75
61:7–8 72
61:9 72
62 50
62:13 50
63 50
63:4 75
63:8 75
63:10 12
64 . . . . 51, 86, 88
64:2 . . . . 26, 27, 49
64:2–3 . . . . . . 25, 28, 51
64:2–4 66
64:5–7 66
64:8–11 66
65:3 28
65:4 23
65:6 . . . . 29, 31
66:19 28
67 . . . . 24, 26
67:2 . . . . 24, 25
67:7 24
67:8 24
68 32
68:1 75
68:2 32
68:14 63
68:19 35
69 . 51, 64, 86, 88, 97, 98, 99
69:2 16
69:2–5 . . . . 70, 75
69:14 . 29, 61, 62, 63, 83, 87
69:14–19 . . 71, 75, 86, 106
69:15 . . . . 16, 17, 49

69:16 46
69:17 . 29, 40, 61, 63, 74, 75
69:17–19 51
69:18 . . . 29, 39, 46, 52, 71
69:19 . . . . . 16, 17, 40, 64
69:23 44
69:23–29 . . . . 45, 72
69:24 44
69:25 . . . . 43, 44, 56
69:25–27 86
69:26 44
69:27 72
69:28 . . . . 43, 44, 47
69:29 44
69:30 25
69:34 28
70 . . . . 51, 86
70:2 39
70:2–3 96
70:2–5 81
70:2–6 53
70:3–4 44
70:5 . . . . 44, 82
70:6 . . . . . 39, 46, 82, 86
71 . . . 51, 53, 75, 86, 95, 96
71:1 . . . . 46, 49, 83
71:1–3 . . . . 53, 96
71:1–8 72
71:2 . 16, 17, 26, 27, 61, 62
71:3 49
71:4 . . . . 16, 17, 55
71:9 . . . . 46, 56, 96
71:9–11 . . . . 71, 86
71:12 . . . . . 39, 46, 52, 55
71:12–13 . . . 53, 81, 82, 96
71:13 44
71:18 . . . . . 46, 81, 87, 96
71:20 41
72:1 47
73 . . . . 50, 51
73:18 12
73:24 12
73:27 12
74:1 47
74:2 42
74:18 42
74:18–23 101
74:19 46

74:20 26
74:22 . . . . . 31, 37, 38, 42
74:23 46
75 . . . . 50, 51
77 . . . . 50, 51
79:6 43
79:7–8 101
79:8 40
79:9 . . . 16, 17, 23, 55, 61
79:9–10 59
79:12 . . . . 37, 43
80 58
80:2 . . . . . . 26, 27, 31, 56
80:3 . . . . 31, 40
80:4 . . . . 25, 37, 101
80:5 . . . . 36, 55
80:8 . . . . 25, 37, 55, 101
80:15 . 26, 27, 28, 29, 35, 36,
                                55
80:18 18
80:19 41
80:20 . . . . 25, 37, 55, 101
82:8 . . . . 31, 37, 38, 101
83:2 46
83:2–9 100
83:10 . . . . 44, 48
83:12 . . . . 44, 48
83:14 . . . . 44, 48
83:16 44
83:17 44
83:18–19 44
84 28
84:9 . . . . 26, 55
84:9–10 27
84:10 . . . . 26, 56
85:5 . . . . 35, 37, 55
85:5–6 36
86 . . . . 51, 53, 86, 104, 107
86:1 . . . 26, 27, 29, 69, 71
86:1–5 75
86:1–6 51
86:1–7 71
86:2 . 16, 18, 19, 24, 49, 74
86:2–3 21
86:3 . . . . . . 21, 55, 73, 76
86:4–5 73
86:6 . . . . 26, 27, 28
86:7 29

Ps		
86:11 . . . . 40, 41	102:25–28 82	119:22 107
86:11–13 80	103 51	119:25 . . . . 41, 61
86:14 32	103:8 . . . . 73, 104	119:26 . . . . 29, 40
86:14–17 80	103:8–12 23	119:27 . . . . 40, 41
86:15 73	106 101	119:28 61
86:16 . 16, 18, 19, 21, 40, 48	106:1 79	119:29 21
86:16–17 . . . . 82, 86	106:4 . . . . . 42, 61, 101	119:31 46
86:17 . . . . 48, 65	106:5 67	119:33 . . . . 40, 41
88 . . . . 22, 28, 51, 75, 86,	106:8 61	119:33–40 51
88, 91, 92, 98	106:47 . . . 16, 55, 67, 101	119:34 40
88:2 . . . . 55, 83	107:1 79	119:35 . . . . . 40, 41, 107
88:2–19 . . . . 70, 75	108 94	119:37 41
88:3 . . . . . 26, 27, 49, 51	108:6 31	119:39 107
88:5 56	108:7 . . . 16, 18, 19, 29, 67	119:40 . . . . 41, 61
88:15 47	108:13 . . . . 17, 66	119:41 61
89 . . . . 58, 99	109 . . . . 51, 86, 88	119:42 30
89:18 61	109:1 . . . . 46, 55	119:43 . . . . 47, 107
89:48 42	109:1–5 . . . . 71, 75	119:44 25
89:51 42	109:6 . . . . 43, 56	119:49 42
90 58	109:6–15 . . . . . 44, 45, 82	119:58 . . . . 21, 61
90:7–9 36	109:6–20 . . . . 63, 71	119:64 40
90:11 36	109:12 44	119:65 61
90:12 . . . . 40, 41	109:14 44	119:66 . . . . 40, 107
90:13 . . . . 35, 36	109:21 . . 16, 48, 54, 55, 61,	119:68 40
90:13–17 101	63, 74, 75, 87	119:73 40
90:15 104	109:21–22 75	119:86 17
91:11 24	109:21–25 . . . . . . 71, 86	119:88 . . . . . . 25, 41, 61
94 45	109:22 75	119:94 . . . . . . 16, 19, 107
94:1 . . . . 31, 56	109:25–31 71	119:107 . . . . 41, 61
94:2 . . . 31, 33, 37, 43, 56	109:26 . . 16, 17, 54, 61, 62	119:108 . . . . 40, 41
94:9 28	109:26–27 65	119:116 . . . . 46, 61
96 53	109:27 63	119:121 46
97 53	109:29 17	119:122 . . . . . 44, 46, 49
98 53	113:4 33	119:124 . 40, 41, 48, 49, 61
98:1 18	115:1 48	119:125 . . . . 40, 49
99:2 33	115:12 24	119:132 . . . . . 21, 22, 40
102 . . . . 51, 86, 97, 98, 99	115:13 24	119:133 61
102:2 . . . . 26, 27, 49	116:1 28	119:134 . . . . . . 16, 17, 25
102:2–3 28	116:4 . . . . 17, 18	119:135 . . . . 25, 40
102:2–4 69	118:1 79	119:145 29
102:2–12 . . . . 70, 75	118:5 29	119:146 . . . . . . 16, 19, 25
102:3 . 26, 27, 29, 30, 39, 46	118:21 29	119:149 . . . 26, 27, 41, 61
102:3–4 52	118:25 . . . . . . 16, 18, 19	119:153 . . . 16, 26, 28, 107
102:4–12 70	119 . 11, 15, 18, 51, 64, 101,	119:154 . . . 17, 37, 41, 61
102:5 46	105, 106, 107, 108	119:156 . . . . 41, 61
102:11 92	119:8 46	119:159 . . . 26, 28, 41, 61
102:25 55	119:12 40	119:169 . . . . 40, 61
	119:17 . . . . 25, 49	119:170 . . . . 16, 61

Ps

119:176	49, 107
120	51, 86, 88
120:1	29, 83
120:1–4	81
120:2	16, 17, 18
121	25, 49, 50, 51
121:3–5	24
121:7	24
121:8	24
123:3	21
126	37
126:4	36, 37
128:5	24
130	28, 51, 86, 88
130:1	83
130:2	26, 27, 49, 51, 55
130:2–4	80
132	33
132:1	42
132:8	31, 32, 33
134:3	24
136:1	79
137:7	42
138:3	30
138:6	28, 33
138:8	47
139	11, 38
139:23	39
139:24	26, 28, 40
140	51, 86
140:2	16, 17, 25
140:2–3	66
140:4	66
140:5	24, 25, 66
140:6	66
140:7	26, 27, 28, 83
140:7–11	82
140:9	44, 47
140:10–11	44
141	51, 86
141:1	26, 27, 39, 83
141:1–6	82
141:3	48
141:8	46
141:9	24
141:10	44
142	51, 53
142:1	63
142:5	26, 65
142:5–8	72–86
142:6	83
142:7	16, 17, 26, 27, 28, 72, 75
142:7–8	105
142:8	17, 67
143	51, 53, 64, 65, 86, 101, 104, 105, 107
143:1	26, 27, 29, 30, 61, 62
143:1–6	71
143:2	46, 49
143:7	29, 39, 46, 52, 65
143:7–12	86
143:8	40, 41, 75
143:8–10	73, 75
143:9	16, 17
143:10	40, 41
143:11	17, 41, 61, 62, 63
143:12	44, 61, 63, 74
144	20
144:7	16, 17
144:11	16, 17
145:19	28

Job

7:7	42
10:9	42

Lam

1:9	29
1:11	29
1:20	29
2:8	44
2:20	29
3:19	42
5:1	29, 42

Dan

3:26–45	58
9	105
9:4–19	58
9:16–19	64
9:17	25
9:17–19	29
9:18–19	106
9:19	90

Ezra

9	105

Neh

1:5–11	58
1:8	42
3:36	29
5:19	42
6:14	42
9	105
9:5–37	58
9:17	104
13:14	42
13:22	42
13:29	42
13:31	42

I Chr

29:18	24

II Chr

14:10	21, 90
20:6–12	58

Esth

C 2–10	58

III Macc

6:2–15	58

Odes

7	58
12	58
12:13	106
14:25	106

PsSal

12:4	45

Mt

6:13	106

Stellenregister (in Auswahl)

(L. Schmidt, Literarische Studien zur Josephsgeschichte)

Genesis

12,1–3 . . . . . 190. 221	25,9f. 208	36,43 196
12,2 258	25,19–26 293	37 . . . 131. 141. 155. 161.
12,3 273	26,1ff. 284	164. 174. 217. 223. 226.
12,4f. 176	26,1 188	231. 233. 243. 249f. 265.
12,7 182	26,2 . . . . 182. 186. 188	275f. 280. 282–284. 286
12,10–13,1 . . . 245. 284f.	26,3–5 . . . . . 188. 259	37,1–35 142–151
12,10 188	26,3 223	37,1f. . 130. 142–144. 241.
12,17 285	26,11 285	287. 293
15,1ff. 186	26,24 . . . . 186–188. 223	37,1 197
15,7ff. 192	26,28 224	37,2 293
15,13–16 . . . . . 192. 270	27,1–45 . . . . 260f.	37,3–35 278
17 . . . . 197. 199f.	27,1 145	37,3ff. 290
17,2 201	28,1–9 197	37,3–11 . . . . 144f.
17,5 258	28,3 201	37,3f. 222
17,6 201	28,4 199	37,3 . 133. 160. 165f. 212.
17,8 . . . . 196. 199	28,14 . . . . 221. 273	272f. 278
17,16 258	28,15 223	37,4 . . . . 272. 277
17,20 199	29,31–30,24 . . . 149. 272	37,5–36 283
18,1 182	30,2 215	37,5ff. . 128. 136. 163. 213.
19,29 201	30,22–24 274	215. 281
20,1–17 284	31,3 223	37,5 294
20,3ff. 285	31,11 . . 145. 187. 189–191	37,8 . . . . 215. 293
20,3 187	31,13 189–191	37,9 . . . . 249. 283
20,6 285	32,9 173	37,10 133
20,7 187	32,23–32 . . . . . 139. 156	37,11 283
21,12f. . . . . . 187. 189f.	33,19 . . . . 269f.	37,12–17 . . 145f. 272. 292
21,33 188	34 270	37,12–14 274
22 198	35 255	37,13 . . . . . 133. 272. 292
22,2 . . . . 145. 187	35,9ff. 253. 288	37,14 . . . . 292f.
22,7 145	35,9–12 200	37,18–24 146–148
22,11 145	35,10 176	37,18 272
22,15–18 188	35,11f. 254	37,19f. 133
23 . . . . 197. 199. 207. 270	35,11 . . . . 201. 254. 258f.	37,21 . . . . 272. 290
23,1 196	35,12 . . . . 199f.	37,22 . . . . . 138. 141. 290
23,4 196	35,23–26 254	37,23 . . . . 272. 276
23,9 196	35,27 146	37,24 138
23,20 196	35,28 197	37,25–36 131
25,7 196	35,29 208	37,25ff. 276
	36,6 176	37,25–30 . . . 137–139. 148

Genesis

37,25–27 272	41,14 .... 289. 292	42,21 f. 214. 250
37,25 166	41,16 286	42,22 290
37,28 .. 129. 219. 230. 272	41,33–57 ... 233–247. 272	42,24 ..... 162. 170. 213
37,29 f. 129. 290	41,33 286	42,25 ..... 135. 179. 235
37,31–34 226	41,34 ...... 206. 282. 285	42,26 236
37,31–33 ..... 148. 272	41,35 .... 285. 290	42,27 f. . 135. 155–158. 272
37,34 f. 148. 165. 272	41,37–40 281	42,27 135
37,35 .... 182. 219 f. 272	41,38 f. 286	42,28 .. 135. 161. 164. 279.
37,36 .. 129. 148. 218–220.	41,40 292	290
228. 240. 282	41,41 f. 280	42,29 ff. ... 133–135. 159.
38 .... 127. 130	41,41 .... 286. 292	171. 281
39–41 132	41,43 281	42,29–37 154
39,1–23 .. 132. 218–227. 229.	41,44 280	42,29 135
231. 243. 265. 272. 278	41,46 ..... 143. 196. 287	42,30 .... 134. 250. 281 f.
39,1–20 ..... 264. 276	41,47.49 281	42,32 158
39,1–6 131	41,50–52 ..... 129. 278	42,33 .... 134. 281 f.
39,1 .. 131. 240. 278. 289.	41,51 f. 261. 262. 279	42,35 .. 135. 136. 141. 282.
292	41,53 281	290
39,2–4.6 229	41,54 .. 247–249. 281. 283	42,36 .. 133. 134. 136. 284
39,4 289	41,55 278	42,37 .. 140. 141. 160. 173.
39,5 273	41,56 .. 205. 249. 278. 287	291
39,6 ff. 280	41,57 ...... 205. 287 f.	42,38 . 154 f. 159. 160. 183.
39,7 ff. 230. 273	42,1 ff. 246. 281. 291	249. 272. 281. 290
39,7–20 229	42,1–13 ... 151. 247–253	43 f. .. 136. 155. 172. 236.
39,7 .... 229. 264	42,1 283	250. 279. 291
39,20 ff. 140. 230	42,2 272	43,1–34 .. 158–162. 169.
39,20–23 228	42,3 f. 284	179. 272
39,21 ff. 276	42,3 235	43,1 ff. 133–135. 171
39,21–23 .. 228 f. 230. 264	42,4 281	43,2 ..... 133. 236. 251
40 f. 218. 231. 238	42,5 . 245 f. 287–289. 294	43,3 ff. 134. 252. 281
40,1–23 ... 227–232. 281	42,6 ..... 244. 246. 283	43,3–7 .... 251 f.
40,1 .... 264 f. 272	42,7–9 145	43,3 134
40,2–41,32 291	42,7 .... 272. 278	43,4 251
40,2 ff. 282	42,9–11 272	43,6 .... 133 f.
40,2 .... 220. 283	42,9 . 151. 231. 243. 282 f.	43,7 ...... 134. 251 f.
40,3 .... 219. 289	42,11 ..... 229. 282. 291	43,8 ...... 173. 205. 248
40,4 .... 219 f. 292	42,12–34 161	43,9 140
40,5 289	42,12 f. 282	43,11 .... 180. 292
40,8 .... 232. 285	42,14 ff. .. 164. 174. 202.	43,12 .... 135. 156
40,15 ..... 233. 289. 292	213. 248	43,14 ..... 134. 135. 294
41,1–57 .. 140. 203. 232–	42,14–38 151–158	43,15–34 276
247. 284. 291	42,14–26 ... 151–154. 160	43,15 250
41,1–35 281	42,14–20 ... 163. 213. 252	43,16–44,17 225
41,1–32 .... 232 f.	42,15 285	43,16–34 .... 163. 225
41,9 f. 229	42,18 286	43,16 250
41,10 ...... 219. 228	42,19 236	43,17 197
41,12 219	42,21 ff. 285	43,18 ff. 156
	42,21–24 284	43,20 251

Genesis

43,21	135. 158
43,22	251
43,23	134. 135. 155. 170. 279. 289
43,24	135. 197
43,27	136
43,28	136
43,29f.	251
43,29	169. 195. 249. 275
43,30	169. 280
43,31	168
43,32	205. 273
43,33	250
43,34	179f. 281
44,1–34	162–166. 272
44,1–17	162–165. 225
44,1f.	141. 178
44,1	250. 276
44,3	250
44,4	250
44,8	135. 156. 158
44,11f.	157
44,16	155. 170. 215. 279
44,18–45,15	131
44,18ff.	140. 155. 225
44,18–34	136. 165f. 280
44,19ff.	251f.
44,19	158f. 251f.
44,23	159
44,24ff.	159
44,24	159
44,25	251
44,26	159
44,27–29	159
44,29	155. 183. 249. 281
44,30–34	159
44,31	183
44,34	168
45,1–28	128. 132. 136. 155f. 166–181. 188. 213
45,1–18	166–174
45,1	251. 272. 278
45,2	229. 281
45,3	136. 137. 281. 292
45,4	136. 251. 272. 278. 292
45,5	217. 232. 272. 279. 281. 283. 288
45,6	236. 272. 279. 288
45,7	185. 227. 272. 277. 279f. 286
45,8	209. 215–217. 232. 237. 239. 281. 283. 286
45,9ff.	183
45,9–14	272
45,9–13	279
45,9–11	195. 205
45,9	211f. 223f. 227. 237. 243. 279. 281f. 286
45,10	183f.
45,11	236
45,14	182. 280f.
45,15	136. 213f. 281
45,16–28	291
45,16–18	199. 209. 281. 285. 288
45,16	238. 250
45,19–21	174–177. 198. 200. 287
45,19f.	288f.
45,19	293–295
45,21–28	177–181. 291
45,21–27	281
45,21	246. 291
45,22f.	282. 292
45,22	281. 284
45,23	235
45,27f.	290f.
45,27	133. 272
45,28	133. 181. 192. 261. 272
46,1–34	181–193
46,1–5	128. 129. 185–192. 281f. 285
46,1.28–34	272. 279
46,1.28–30	181–183. 261
46,1	175. 290
46,2	133. 145. 290
46,3	216f. 258
46,4	269. 284
46,5f.	176f. 181. 192. 287
46,5	133. 175–177. 246. 284
46,6	176f. 196
46,7–27	193. 287
46,7	192f. 196
46,8–27	196
46,8	246. 294
46,28ff.	287
46,28–34	167. 168. 173
46,28	168. 175
46,29f.	168. 278
46,29	211. 262. 280
46,30	178. 202. 261
46,31–47,5.12	202
46,31–34	183–185.195.212
46,31	167. 251
46,32	168
46,34	205. 273. 276
47,1ff.	184. 211. 285. 287f.
47,1–12	193–201. 279
47,1–4.6	272
47,2	183
47,3	205
47,5ff.	217. 287
47,5f.	289. 293f.
47,7ff.	177
47,7–10	287. 289
47,11	201
47,12	202. 204. 261. 272. 277
47,13ff.	234f. 237. 282
47,13–31	201–207
47,13–26	130.132.140. 202–207. 234. 261. 272f. 276. 278. 285
47,14	236
47,27–31	201f.
47,27	143. 197. 200. 210. 254. 262. 265. 272. 277. 279. 287. 289
47,28	196. 256. 261. 265. 287
47,29–31	211. 255f. 262–265. 272. 275. 277. 279
47,29	256
47,31	207f. 256. 263f.
48,1–22	253–271
48,1–6	287
48,1f.	129. 264–266. 272. 281. 284
48,2	207. 277. 279
48,3–7	253–255
48,3–6	289

Genesis

48,3f.	200
48,4	196. 200f. 258
48,7	294
48,8ff.	280
48,8–20.	256–264. 266–268
48,8–14	129
48,8–12	272. 277. 279
48,9f.	294
48,11	279
48,13f.	294
48,15f.	128. 294
48,17–22	294
48,17–21	129
48,19	259
48,21f.	268–270
49	127f.
49,1.28–33.	207f. 263. 287. 289
49,2–27	127. 207
49,25	134
49,29	265
49,30	196
49,31	255
49,33	272. 277. 289
50	202. 207. 256
50,1ff.	275. 277f.
50,1–22	207–217
50,1–8. 10f. 14. 22	272
50,1	280
50,3	276. 284
50,3f.	281
50,5	202
50,9f.	281
50,12f.	289
50,12	287
50,13	196. 287
50,15ff.	174. 249. 283f.
50,15–21	232. 281f.
50,15	250
50,16f.	250
50,19f.	285
50,21	169
50,22	279
50,23–26	212
50,24	268f.
50,25	246

Exodus

1,1–5	176
1,7	289
2,6	157
3	190f.
3,4	145
6,11	196
7,14ff.	293
8,18	184
9,26	184
12,37	201
14,5	185
14,8	196
33,11	143

Numeri

6,24–26	266
22f.	187
23	190

Deuteronomium

26,5–10	276
33	128

Josua

24,32	269

I Samuel

3,4ff.	145
3,15	186
8,11–17	207
10,7	224
16,18	223f.
17,37	224
18,12	224
18,14	224
18,28	224
20,13	224

II Samuel

5,3	273
5,10	224
14,7	172
15,14	173

I Regum

1,47	256
18,1f. 15	182

Jesaja

6,8	145

Jeremia

1,10	238

Psalmen

1,3	222

Proverbia

16,8	216
20,24	216

Esra

7,28	224
9,9	224

I Chronik

13,2	259

II Chronik

11,23	259

JULIUS WELLHAUSEN

Abriß der Geschichte Israels und Judas
Lieder der Hudhailiten

Nachdruck der 1. Auflage 1984. Oktav. IV, 175 Seiten deutscher Text, 129 Seiten arabischer Text. 1985. Ganzleinen DM 134,- ISBN 3 11 009765 6
(Skizzen und Vorarbeiten, 1. Heft)

Die Composition des Hexateuchs und der historischen Bücher des Alten Testaments

4., unveränderte Auflage. Groß-Oktav. VI, 374 Seiten. 1963. Ganzleinen DM 60,-
ISBN 3 11 001265 0

Israelitische und jüdische Geschichte

Nachdruck der 9. Auflage 1958. Oktav. VIII, 371 Seiten. 1981. Ganzleinen DM 68,-
ISBN 3 11 001181 7

MARTIN NOTH
Die Welt des Alten Testaments
Einführung in die Grenzgebiete der Alttestamentlichen Wissenschaft

4., neubearbeitete Auflage. Groß-Oktav. XVI, 355 Seiten, 10 Textabbildungen, 1 Zeittafel. 1962. Ganzleinen DM 42,- ISBN 3 11 005244 X (Sammlung Töpelmann 2, 3)

RUDOLF MACUCH
Grammatik des samaritanischen Aramäisch

Groß-Oktav. LXXII, 427 Seiten. 1982. Granzleinen DM 290,- ISBN 3 11 008376 0
(Studia Samaritana, Band 4)

Preisänderungen vorbehalten

Walter de Gruyter  Berlin · New York

Hebräisches und aramäisches Wörterbuch zum Alten Testament

Herausgegeben von Georg Fohrer in Gemeinschaft mit Hans Werner Hoffmann, Friedrich Huber, Jochen Vollmer, Gunther Wanke

Oktav. X, 331 Seiten. 1971. Ganzleinen DM 36,- ISBN 3 11 001804 7

Hebrew and Aramaic Dictionary of the Old Testament

Edited by Georg Foher in cooperation with Hans Werner Hoffmann, Friedrich Huber, Jochen Vollmer, Gunther Wanke

English version by W. Johnstone
Octavo. XVI, 332 pages. 1973. Cloth DM 32,-
ISBN 3 11 004572 9

GEORG FOHRER

Theologische Grundstrukturen des Alten Testaments

Oktav. X, 276 Seiten. 1972. Kartoniert DM 58, - ISBN 3 11 003874 9
(Theologische Bibliothek Töpelmann, Band 24)

Altorientalische Texte zum Alten Testament

In Verbindung mit Erich Ebeling, Hermann Ranke, Nikolaus Rhodokanakis, herausgegeben von Hugo Gressmann

2., völlig neugestaltete und stark vermehrte Auflage. Groß-Oktav. 478 Seiten. 1926. Nachdruck 1970. Gebunden DM 79,- ISBN 3 11 002675 9

Preisänderungen vorbehalten

Walter de Gruyter  **Berlin · New York**